New York City

© Scott Barrow

"New York is not all bricks and steel. ... It is the place
where all the aspirations of the Western World meet
to form one vast master aspiration, as powerful
as the suction of a steam dredge."

H.L. Mencken, *Prejudices*, 1928

Executive Editorial Director	David Brabis
Chief Editor	Cynthia Clayton Ochterbeck
The Green Guide New York City	
Senior Editor	M. Linda Lee
Contributing Writers	Erich Strom, Tania Grossinger
Production Coordinator	Allison Michelle Simpson
Cartography	Peter Wrenn
Photo Editor	Brigitta L. House
Proofreader	Margaret Browning
Layout & Design	Marie-Pierre Renier, Michel Moulin
Cover Design	Agence Carré Noir
Production	Pierre Ballochard, Renaud Leblanc
Contact US:	The Green Guide Michelin Travel Publications One Parkway South Greenville, SC 29615 USA ☎ 1-800-423-0485 www.michelin-us.com TheGreenGuide-us@us.michelin.com

Special Sales:
For information regarding bulk sales, customized editions and premium sales, please contact our Customer Service Departments:
USA 1-800-423-0485   **UK** (01923) 205 240   **Canada** 1-800-361-8236

THE GREEN GUIDE:
The Spirit of Discovery

Leisure time spent with The Green Guide is also a time for refreshing your spirit, enjoying yourself, and taking advantage of our selection of restaurants, hotels and other places for relaxing. Immerse yourself in the local culture, discover new horizons, experience the local lifestyle–The Green Guide opens the door for you. Each year our writers go touring: visiting the sights, devising the driving tours, identifying the highlights, selecting the hotels and restaurants, checking the routes for our maps and plans.

Each title is compiled with great care, giving you the benefit of regular revisions and Michelin's first-hand knowledge. The Green Guide responds to changing circumstances and takes account of its readers' suggestions; all comments are welcome.

Come share our enthusiasm for travel, which has led us to discover more than 60 destinations around the world. Let yourself be guided by the best motive for travel—the spirit of discovery.

Contents

Flatiron Building

© Walter Bibikow

Bethesda Fountain, Central Park

Caffé Reggio, Greenwich Village

© Scott Barrow

Statue of Liberty, detail

© Patti McConville/DPA

Maps and Plans

COMPANION PUBLICATIONS

North America Road Atlas

A geographically organized atlas with extensive detailed coverage of the USA, Canada and Mexico. Includes 246 city maps, distance chart, state and provincial driving requirements and a climate chart.
– Comprehensive city and town index
– Easy-to-follow "Go-to" pointers

Map 583 Northeastern USA/ Eastern Canada

Large-format map providing detailed road systems and including driving distances, interstate rest stops, border crossings and interchanges.
– Comprehensive city and town index
– Scale 1:2,400,000 (1 inch = approx. 38 miles)

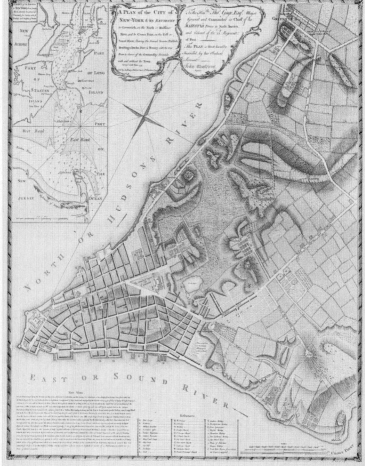

New York (1775) by John Montressor

Historic Urban Plans

Regional Road Atlas

Measuring a slim 4.5 x 10", and only fractions of an inch thick, Michelin's regional road atlases can actually fit in your glove box, your purse, or anywhere you need them. They are a convenient alternative to large, cumbersome road maps and you'll never have to worry about folding them up.
– Clear, colorful and easy-to-read cartography
– Detailed city maps are indexed alphabetically in the back of the book.
New York City is included in the following Regional Road Atlas titles:
 • New England Regional Road Atlas
 • Northeast Regional Road Atlas

Regional Road Atlas + Travel Guide

For the traveler who wants to know more of what to do along the way, without sacrificing portability, Michelin's Road Atlas + Travel Guide series is the perfect solution. You get the same great Michelin mapping from the road atlases, paired with charming hotel & restaurant selections, scenic tours, fabulous color photos and much, much more!
New York City is included in the following Regional Road Atlas titles:
 • Mid-Atlantic Regional Road Atlas + Travel Guide
 • Northeast corridor Regional Road Atlas + Travel Guide

LIST OF MAPS

MUSEUM PLANS

Using this guide

The Sights section of this guide is divided into eight areas: New York City's Midtown, Downtown, Uptown, The Bronx, Brooklyn, Queens, Staten Island and Excursions from the city. Within these sections, each **Entry Heading** is followed, where applicable, by public-transportation information and a map reference.

In the text, useful information such as sight location or street address, opening hours, admission charges, telephone number and Web address appears in *italics*. In addition, symbols indicate the nearest rapid-transit or bus stop **MTA**; wheelchair access &; on-site eating facilities ✗; camping facilities ⚠; on-site parking **P**; sights of interest to children **Kids**; and long lines ‖‖‖‖.

Throughout the guide you will find digressions—entertaining breaks from sightseeing that are marked by a purple bar and indicated on maps by a black dot ❶ with the corresponding map-reference number.

At the front of the guide, the **Address Book** section, edged with a marbleized band, features detailed information about hotels, restaurants, entertainment, shopping, sightseeing, kids activities, sports and recreational opportunities. In the description of hotels, the presence of a hotel swimming pool is indicated by the symbol ⌇; the presence of a full-service spa is indicated by the symbol **Spa**.

At the back of the guide, the section of blue pages offers **Practical Information** on planning your trip, getting there and getting around, basic facts, and tips for international visitors.

Addresses, phone numbers, opening hours and prices published in this guide are accurate at press time. We welcome corrections and suggestions that may assist us in preparing the next edition. Please send your comments to:

> Michelin Travel Publications
> Editorial Department
> P. O. Box 19001
> Greenville, SC 29602-9001
> Email: TheGreenGuide-us@us.michelin.com
> Web site: www.michelin-us.com

© Scott Barrow

Legend

*** **Highly recommended**
** **Recommended**
* **Interesting**

Sight symbols

➡ ▬▬▬ Walking tour with departure point and direction

Church, chapel	▓	Building described
Synagogue	▒	Other building
Letter locating a sight	▪	Small building
Other points of interest	⚓	Lighthouse
Statue, monument	▓▒	Park described – Other
Fountain	▓▒	Wooded park described – Other
Panorama – View	▓▒	Cemetery described – Other

All maps are oriented north, unless otherwise indicated by a directional arrow.

Other symbols

🛡 Interstate Highway   🛡 US Highway   Ⓢ Other Route

Highway, interchange	🛈	Visitor information
Toll road, bridge	⊞	Hospital
Tunnel with ramp	🎁	Gift shop
One way street	🚻	Restrooms
Pedestrian street – Steps	🛗	Elevator
Airport – Subway station	P ✉	Parking – Post Office
Train station – Bus station	—□—	Railroad passenger station
Ferry: cars and passengers	—‡—	Gate
Ferry: passengers only	⊂⊃	Stadium
Harbor cruise	❶	Digressions *(see text opposite)*

9

Map of Manhattan's
Principal Walks

And Selected Sights

1 **★★★ FIFTH AVENUE** Number and name of walk

★★★ Highly recommended

★★ Recommended

★ Interesting

For **Principal Sights** in the Bronx, Brooklyn, Queens and on Staten Island consult the appropriate borough map.

23 ★★★ **THE CLOISTERS**

22 ★ **HARLEM**

★ General Grant National Memorial

★ Hamilton Grange NM

★ Abyssinian Baptist

★ Schomburg Center for Research in Black Culture

2 Strivers' Row

3

HAMILTON HEIGHTS

City College of NY

1

Apollo Theatre

Harlem USA

★ Studio Museum in Harlem

Harlem Tourist Center & Harlem Gift Shop

Morningside Park

★★ Columbia University

★★ Cathedral of St. John the Divine

★ Riverside Park

Mount Morris Park

EL BARRIO

Jefferson Park

★ El Museo del Barrio

■ Museum of the City of New York ★★

THE BRONX

Major Deegan

Bruckner Blvd.

FDR Drive

HARLEM RIVER

RIVER

NEW JERSEY

1/2 mi   1 km

0   0

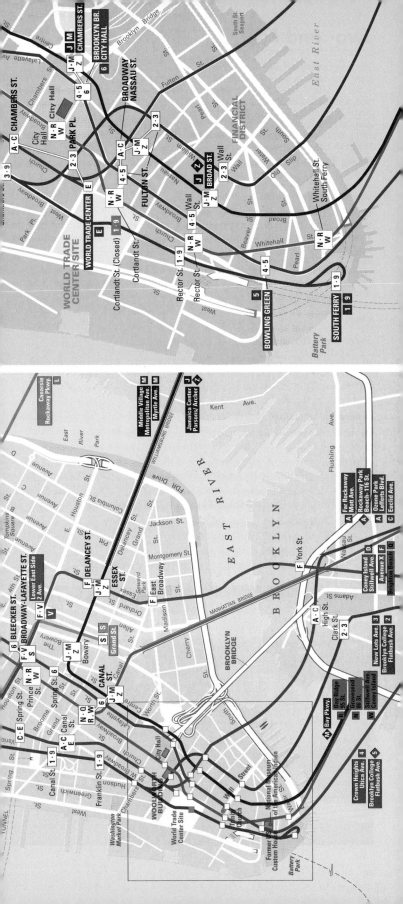

Two- and Four-Day Itineraries

The suggested itineraries below cover "must-see" attractions for visitors pressed for time. The two-day overview acquaints the visitor with Manhattan, while the four-day schedule offers more in-depth coverage. Consult the sight descriptions for historical and practical information on the various sights and museums. For visitors with additional time, or for those who wish to substitute certain sights on the suggested itineraries, we recommend consulting the museum section or the chapters on New York City's other four boroughs. See "New York Quintessentials" below for a list of fun things to do while in New York City.

Guided Tours – Discover New York by bus, boat or from the air with the numerous tours offered by various companies in the Big Apple. In addition to these orientation and thematic tours, the city also abounds in specialized walking tours *(for additional information about tours, see p 74)*.

Dining Out – On-site eating facilities are indicated under the individual sight description by means of the ℵ symbol. To experience the ambience of the city, you can savor a hearty meal in a neighborhood bistro, enjoy a freshly baked bagel with cream cheese—a New York institution—in one of the numerous coffeeshops lining the avenues, or pick up a salty pretzel slathered with mustard from a street vendor. A variety of delis and pizzerias offer casual dining; some are open 24hrs/day. Throughout this guide, colored boxes marked by a purple bar point out **digressions** from your itinerary (including world-class restaurants, cozy pastry shops and elegant bars). *For additional restaurant information, see the Address Book (p 53) or consult the Official NYC Guide (p 73).*

Two-Day Itinerary

First Day   Getting Acquainted with New York

Morning	Double-decker bus or trolley tour of Manhattan
Lunch	In Midtown
Afternoon	Metropolitan Museum of Art★★★
Evening	Broadway – Times Square★★ or Lincoln Center★★

Second Day   The Best of Manhattan

Morning	Rockefeller Center Area★★★, Fifth Avenue★★★, Financial District★★★
Lunch	In lower Manhattan
Afternoon	Ferry to Statue of Liberty★★★ and Ellis Island★★
Evening	SoHo★★ or Greenwich Village★★

Tour bus, Times Square

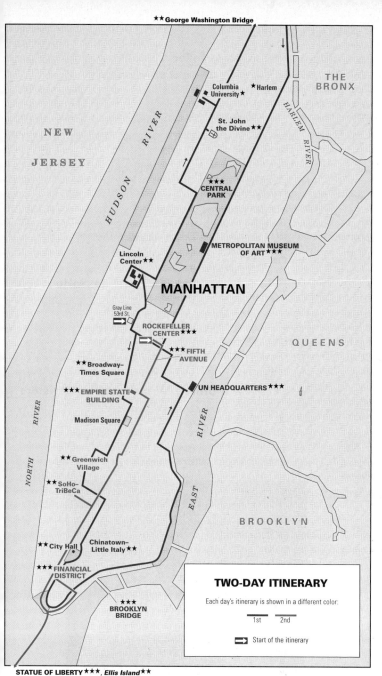

★★ George Washington Bridge

THE BRONX

NEW JERSEY

Columbia University ★   ★ Harlem

St. John the Divine ★★

HUDSON RIVER

HARLEM RIVER

★★★ CENTRAL PARK

Lincoln Center ★★

METROPOLITAN MUSEUM OF ART ★★★

MANHATTAN

Gray Line 53rd St.

ROCKEFELLER CENTER ★★★

QUEENS

★★★ FIFTH AVENUE

★★ Broadway–Times Square

UN HEADQUARTERS ★★★

★★★ EMPIRE STATE BUILDING

NORTH RIVER

Madison Square

EAST RIVER

★★ Greenwich Village

★★ SoHo–TriBeCa

BROOKLYN

★★ City Hall

Chinatown–Little Italy ★★

★★★ FINANCIAL DISTRICT

TWO-DAY ITINERARY

Each day's itinerary is shown in a different color:

1st   2nd

Start of the itinerary

★★★ BROOKLYN BRIDGE

STATUE OF LIBERTY ★★★, *Ellis Island* ★★

New York Quintessentials:

■ Sunday brunch at Tavern on the Green or lunch at Carnegie Deli
■ Dancing at the Rainbow Room
■ Soul food at Sylvia's in Harlem
■ Carriage tour of Central Park
■ Cocktails at the Oak Bar at the Plaza Hotel
■ Sunday bargain hunting on Orchard Street
■ Food shopping at Dean & Deluca or at Zabar's
■ Ice-skating at Rockefeller Center in winter
■ Shopping for fresh produce at the Union Square Greenmarket
■ Gallery hopping in SoHo on Saturday afternoon
■ Riding the Staten Island ferry at dusk

Four-Day Itinerary

First Day — From Rockefeller Center to Broadway

Morning	Rockefeller Center★★★, Museum of Modern Art★★★
Lunch	In Midtown
Afternoon	Circle Line Boat Tour
Evening	Broadway – Times Square★★

Second Day — From the Empire State Building to Lincoln Center

Morning	Empire State Building★★★, stroll along Fifth Avenue★★★ and 57th Street★ Central Park★★★
Lunch	Picnic in Central Park *(numerous delis are located around Columbus Circle)*
Afternoon	Metropolitan Museum of Art★★★ or Solomon R. Guggenheim Museum★★, Upper East Side★★
Evening	Lincoln Center★★

Third Day — From the Statue of Liberty to SoHo and Greenwich Village

Morning	Statue of Liberty★★★ and Ellis Island★★
Lunch	Ellis Island
Afternoon	Financial District★★★ Civic Center – Brooklyn Bridge★★, Chinatown – Little Italy★★
Evening	SoHo★★, TriBeCa★ or Greenwich Village★★

Fourth Day — From the United Nations to the Cloisters

Morning	UN Headquarters★★★, stroll along East 42nd Street★★, Grand Central Terminal★★, stroll along Park Avenue★★
Lunch	In Midtown
Afternoon	The Cloisters★★★, Fort Tryon Park★★
Evening	Dine in one of the elegant hotels surrounding Grand Army Plaza

New York City Marathon

© Scott Barrow

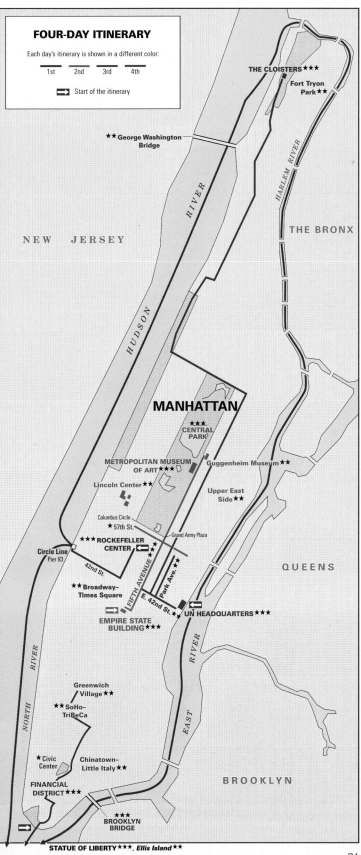

FOUR-DAY ITINERARY

Each day's itinerary is shown in a different color:

1st   2nd   3rd   4th

➡ Start of the itinerary

THE CLOISTERS ★★★

Fort Tryon Park ★★

★★ George Washington Bridge

HARLEM RIVER

THE BRONX

NEW JERSEY

HUDSON RIVER

MANHATTAN

★★★ CENTRAL PARK

METROPOLITAN MUSEUM OF ART ★★★

Guggenheim Museum ★★

Lincoln Center ★★

Upper East Side ★★

Columbus Circle

★ 57th St.

Grand Army Plaza

★★★ ROCKEFELLER CENTER

Circle Line Pier 83

42nd St.

★★ Broadway–Times Square

QUEENS

Park Ave. ★★

FIFTH AVENUE

E. 42nd St. ★★

UN HEADQUARTERS ★★★

EMPIRE STATE BUILDING ★★★

Greenwich Village ★★

★★ SoHo–TriBeCa

NORTH RIVER

EAST RIVER

★ Civic Center

Chinatown–Little Italy ★★

FINANCIAL DISTRICT ★★★

BROOKLYN

★★★ BROOKLYN BRIDGE

STATUE OF LIBERTY ★★★, *Ellis Island* ★★

View of Midtown from Roosevelt Island

Introduction
to New York City

The City of New York

By far the most populous city in the US, New York is a world unto itself by virtue of its size, the density and diversity of its population, its dynamic economic activity and its vibrant cultural life.

Location – Situated on the East Coast of the US at 40° north latitude and 74° west longitude, New York City is bordered by the Hudson River, Long Island Sound and the Atlantic Ocean. The city occupies the western end of Long Island, all of two smaller islands (Manhattan and Staten Island) and a piece of the mainland to the north, adjacent to the Hudson River. The islands provide protection for one of the largest and safest harbors in the world, ideal for oceangoing vessels. Access to the ocean is through the Narrows, a passage between Staten Island and Long Island. More than 578mi of coastline, including some 14mi of beaches, rims the city.

In addition to its major islands, New York City also encompasses several small islands, notably Liberty Island, home of the Statue of Liberty; Ellis Island, once the nation's leading immigration center; Riker's Island (located north of LaGuardia Airport), site of a large municipal prison; Governor's Island, a former US Coast Guard site; and Roosevelt Island, once home to public health institutions and now a middle-income residential location.

The total area of the five boroughs *(below)* that make up New York City is about 320sq mi; the longest distance between its boundaries, from the northeast to the southwest, is about 35mi. New York City's height above sea level varies from 5ft (Battery Park at the southern tip of Manhattan) to 400ft (Washington Heights in northern Manhattan). Its climate is continental *(for information about seasonal climates, see Practical Information section)*.

The Five Boroughs – New York City as it exists today was created in 1898 when, under state charter, the city was expanded from its original confines of Manhattan to incorporate Brooklyn (Kings County), Queens (Queens County), the Bronx (Bronx County) and Staten Island (Richmond County). The counties correspond to the original colonial administrative divisions, and the names still designate judicial districts. The five boroughs are not developed to the same extent: A few open spaces exist on the fringes of Brooklyn and Queens, and despite the construction of many new dwellings in the last decades, Staten Island is still somewhat countrified.

Brooklyn, situated on the southwest tip of Long Island, is today the most populous of the five boroughs. Queens, to the northeast of Brooklyn, is the largest and fastest growing. The heavily developed Bronx, the only borough that is part of the mainland, forms the gateway from the city to the affluent suburbs to the north. Although it remains the least populated borough, Staten Island has been growing since the

NEW YORK AND ADJACENT STATES

completion of the Verrazano-Narrows Bridge from Brooklyn in 1964. Manhattan, the smallest of the boroughs with an area of 22.7sq mi, constitutes the heart of the city. With a population of 1,537,195, it is the most densely populated county in the US. This tongue-shaped island is the center for much of New York's cultural, financial and retail activity. Although the consolidation of the five boroughs took place nearly a century ago, residents of the so-called outer boroughs traveling to Manhattan still say they are "going to the city."

Metropolitan Area – The city's vast metropolitan area, home to about 11,685,650 residents, encompasses 22 counties and planning regions extending more than 7,000sq mi. Seven of these counties are in New York State, nine in New Jersey and six in Connecticut. In addition to New York City, the area includes Newark, New Jersey (pop. 273,546) and 10 other cities with more than 100,000 people. Among the organizations responsible for the operation and expansion of regional transportation facilities are the Port Authority of New York and New Jersey, which oversees the 17-county area in those two states, and the Triborough Bridge and Tunnel Authority.

The State of New York – The city gave its name to the state (the 11th of the original 13 states of the Union), which by virtue of its economic expansion and political influence became known as the "Empire State." New York State extends from east of the Hudson River to the Great Lakes and Niagara Falls, and borders Canada on the north. The state is divided into counties, and its capital is Albany (New York City was the capital from 1784 to 1797).

ACCESS ROADS

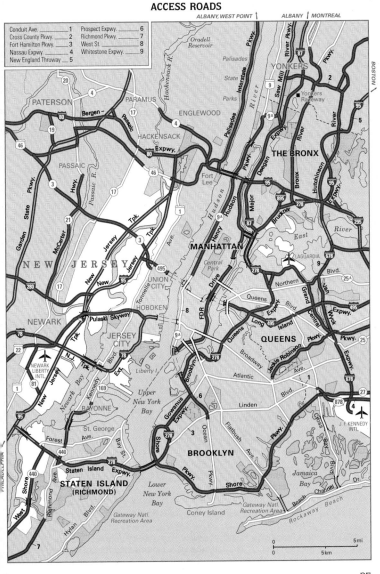

Conduit Ave.	1	Prospect Expwy.	6
Cross County Pkwy.	2	Richmond Pkwy.	7
Fort Hamilton Pkwy.	3	West St.	8
Nassau Expwy.	4	Whitestone Expwy.	9
New England Thruway	5		

Time Line

From Nieuw Amsterdam to New York

Before the arrival of Europeans, Algonquian- and Iroquoian-speaking Indians inhabited the island of Manhattan. The Algonquian tribe is credited for naming the island *Manhattan*, meaning "island of the hills." Following Henry Hudson's exploratory journey, the Dutch East India Company founded the colony of New Netherland on the site of present-day New York City in 1614. In 1625 the company established the trading post Nieuw Amsterdam. Unlike other American colonies, New York was not founded by a religious group, but for purely commercial purposes, and it became the private property of the Dutch West India Company. This fact, combined with the difficulty of attracting immigrants from a generally content Dutch populace, gave New York a cosmopolitan makeup from the very start, attracting French Huguenots and non-Dutch immigrants from Holland. A fort and roundout batteries were constructed at the southern tip of Manhattan Island, controlling the entrance to the Hudson River. A city grew up to the south of a defensive wall, while farms and estates, called *bouweries*, were established farther north on Manhattan Island, as well as in Brooklyn, Queens, Staten Island and the Bronx. Initially ruled by a director-general, the town attained some form of self-government in 1653. The British, already established in New England to the north, took control of the colony in the late 17C, accepting the surrender of Director-General Peter Stuyvesant in 1664.

1524	**Giovanni da Verrazano**, an Italian explorer in the service of the French king François I, is the first European to land on Manhattan.
1609	**Henry Hudson** sails up the river (now bearing his name) in his ship, the *Half Moon*, while on a voyage for the Dutch East India Company.
1614	The name New Netherland, given to the newly founded Dutch colony, designates the area around present-day New York City. The territory north of New York is called New England.
1625	The first permanent European settlement is established on Manhattan. The trading post is named **Nieuw Amsterdam** and includes a fort and 30 houses.
1626	**Peter Minuit** of the Dutch West India Company buys Manhattan from the Algonquin Indians in exchange for trinkets valued at 60 guilders, the equivalent of $24.
1647	**Peter Stuyvesant** is appointed Director-General of New Netherland, serving until 1664.
1653	The city of Nieuw Amsterdam receives a charter and municipal rule. Stuyvesant erects a protective wall along present-day Wall Street.
1660	The city grows from 120 houses to more than 300 in only four years.
1664	As a repercussion of the English and Dutch trading rivalries in Europe, the English take Nieuw Amsterdam without a struggle and rename it **New York** after the Duke of York, brother of the English king Charles II.

British Rule

New York blossomed as an important trading post in the colonies of North America, second only to Boston in the trade of furs and farm products. By 1700 the tip of Manhattan claimed some 4,000 residents and grew north beyond the Dutch palisade fortifications at Wall Street. Columbia University and the city's first library were founded, and at the same time, the city began its passionate embrace of journalism with the creation of several newspapers. Dutch language and culture began to wane in the century following Stuyvesant's surrender, although numerous Dutch families remained important in local society, government and business. New York's pivotal role as a commercial port for the American colonies placed the city in the center of the taxation controversies leading up to the American Revolution. The city was one of the first targets of the British Army, which occupied New York throughout the War for Independence.

1667	The Treaty of Breda, ending the second Anglo-Dutch war, confirms English control over the province of New Netherland. The city of New York passes under the English system of municipal government, and English replaces Dutch as the official language.
1673	The Dutch retake New York without a fight and rename it New Orange. By the Treaty of Westminster in 1674, the province of New Netherland becomes permanently English.
1720	With 7,000 inhabitants, New York is the third-largest city in the colonies.
1725	The city's first newspaper, the *New-York Gazette*, is founded by William Bradford.
1733-34	**John Peter Zenger** founds the *New York Weekly Journal*, in which he attacks the governor. A year later Zenger is imprisoned for slander. His acquittal marks the beginning of a free press.

1754	The city's first college, **King's College**, now Columbia University, opens. The New York Society Library is founded.
1763	Marking the end of the French and Indian War, or **Seven Years' War** (1756-63), the Treaty of Paris confirms English control of the North American continent.
1765	Meeting of the Stamp Act Congress in New York, where representatives from nine colonies denounce the English colonial policy of taxation without representation.
1766	Repeal of the Stamp Act. A statue is erected to **William Pitt**, the British statesman who did most to obtain the repeal.
1767	Parliament passes the Townshend Acts, a series of four acts that increases taxation and threatens the already established traditions of colonial self-government. The repeal three years later coincides with the Boston Massacre.
1776	The **Declaration of Independence** (July 4) is adopted and New Yorkers pull down the statue of George III at Bowling Green. On November 17, Fort Washington *(p 206)* in northern Manhattan falls and the British occupy all of present-day New York City until 1783.
1783	The **Treaty of Paris** (September 3) ends the American Revolution and England recognizes the independence of the 13 colonies. The last British troops evacuate New York, and George Washington returns to the city in triumph before bidding farewell to his troops at Fraunces Tavern on December 4.

Empire City

After briefly serving as US capital, New York established the commercial links and financial institutions that led the new nation into the Industrial Age. As the population of New York exploded beyond all predictions—despite outbreaks of yellow fever and cholera—the island of Manhattan grew northward along the gridiron plan established in the early 19C. Broadway, a poplar-lined residential boulevard by 1820, became a commercial thoroughfare by 1820. Following the opening of the Erie Canal in 1825, the city handled more trade than all other US ports combined and became a leading shipbuilding center. The population doubled in the 1820s as immigrants arrived by the thousands from Germany, Ireland and Scandinavia.

1784	New York City becomes the capital of New York State and a year later is named US capital under the Articles of Confederation.
1789	**George Washington**, elected first president, takes the oath of office at Federal Hall.
1790	The first official census counts 33,000 people in Manhattan. The federal capital moves to Philadelphia.
1792	Founding of the forerunner to the New York Stock Exchange.
1804	Vice President Aaron Burr mortally wounds political rival Alexander Hamilton in a duel on the Hudson River.
1812	**War of 1812**: the US declares war on Britain and the Port of New York suffers from the ensuing blockade until the war ends in 1814. Present City Hall opens.
1820	New York is the most populous city in the nation with 123,705 inhabitants. Growth also brings disease, including a severe yellow fever epidemic in 1822.
1825	Opening of the **Erie Canal**. New York becomes the gateway to the Great Lakes and the West as 500 new mercantile businesses open.

View of New York (c.1850)

1828	The South Street Seaport becomes the center of New York's port activities, handling more trade than all other US ports combined, including over half of the national import and a third of the export trade.
1832	Cholera epidemic kills 4,000 citizens.
1835	The Great Fire destroys an extensive area in the business district.
1845	Another fire levels 300 buildings in lower Manhattan. The first telegraph line connects the city to Philadelphia. The first baseball club, the New York Knickerbockers, is organized.

Growth and Greening

Large waves of immigration from Europe and the Americas spurred commercial and industrial growth which led to a doubling of the city's population every 20 years, exceeding a million people by 1875. Shantytowns developed on vacant land to the north of the growing city, while aging neighborhoods became slums, including the infamous "Five Points" district north of City Hall. The massive immigrant population fed a political machine based at Tammany Hall that established new heights of public graft and corruption in the 1860s and 70s by bilking taxpayers of tens of millions of dollars—more than $9 million during construction of the "Tweed Courthouse" alone. The adjacent city of Brooklyn blossomed with residences and factories. Following the success of America's first World's Fair here in 1853, New York established itself as the cultural capital of America with the creation of Central Park, the American Museum of Natural History and the Metropolitan Museum of Art.

1849	Astor Place Riot: 31 die and 150 are wounded in a theater riot protesting British actor William Macready.
1851	The *New York Times* is published for the first time.
1853	The World's Fair opens at the Crystal Palace. Modeled on London's Great Exhibition of 1851, the fair is an early showplace for iron and glass architecture and the technological advances of the Industrial Revolution.
1857	Construction of Central Park begins in the wake of a depression brought on by financial panic; the park is officially completed in 1876.
1860	New York City counts 813,660 inhabitants, as immigration from Ireland, Germany and other European countries continues. Brooklyn counts 279,000 residents, double the number it had 10 years earlier.
1863	The city is rocked by the Draft Riots. Opposition by the poor to the rich man's practice of hiring a substitute to fight the Civil War spreads to encompass general discontent and racism, leaving 1,200 dead and 8,000 injured.
1865	The Civil War ends. After President Abraham Lincoln is assassinated, his body lies in state at New York's City Hall.
1868	Opening of the El, the first elevated railway in lower Manhattan.
1869	On September 24, financier Jay Gould, who had tried to corner the gold market with his associate James Fisk, sells out and brings about the financial panic known as "Black Friday" *(p 125)*. The American Museum of Natural History is founded in Central Park's Arsenal.
1871	The *New York Times* finally exposes Boss Tweed's Tammany Hall ring of corrupt city officials. Tweed goes to prison, where he dies in 1878.
1872	The Metropolitan Museum of Art opens, moving to its present location in 1880.

A City of Immigrants

Wall Street became the center of banking, finance and insurance in the US, and by the second decade of the 20C it began occupying its key position in the world economy. Immigration not only continued but increased dramatically as the 19C waned, bringing new groups from Southern and Eastern Europe. New York became home to the largest Jewish community in the world as millions fled Russian persecution. Italian immigrants created Little Italy next to Chinatown, established in the 1870s but stunted by the Chinese Exclusion Act of 1882. Beginning in the late 1880s, Jacob Riis took his camera to New York's dark streets to expose the social ills of the tenement districts, ushering in the Progressive Era. Tammany Hall is again exposed by an 1894 investigation of police corruption led by New York native Theodore Roosevelt, launching a political career that would take him to the presidency. William Randolph Hearst's purchase of the *New York Journal* in 1895 and subsequent circulation battle with Joseph Pulitzer's *New York World* instigated the era of yellow journalism—largely responsible for the Spanish-American War.

1880-84	Some two million people arrive in New York City during a period of rapid immigration. Tenements and sweatshops proliferate, exploiting the new residents.
1882	Electricity is first offered for general use by Thomas Edison's plant in lower Manhattan.

1886	Inauguration of the Statue of Liberty.
1889	The first telephone exchange opens on Nassau Street two years after Alexander Graham Bell demonstrated his invention in New York.
1891	Carnegie Hall opens with Tchaikovsky's American conducting debut.
1892	The ongoing rush of immigration leads to the completion of the Ellis Island facility—more than 12 million persons will be processed here by the mid-1920s.
1898	**Greater New York City** is created, comprising five boroughs: Manhattan, the Bronx, Brooklyn, Queens and Staten Island. With a population of more than three million, New York is the world's largest city.
1900	The nation's first automobile show is held at Madison Square Garden.
1902	One of the city's first skyscrapers, the Flatiron Building, is completed.
1904	The first underground subway line opens.

Culture and Crash

New York served as the major US transshipment point for Allied matériel during World War I. Immigration began to slow following exclusionary legislation in the 1920s, but the city's population still increased from 4.8 million in 1910 to almost 7 million in 1930. Prohibition began in 1920, doubling the number of illegal liquor outlets in the city to 32,000 and providing the backdrop for bootlegging gangs and underworld influence in politics and government. Greenwich Village became an intellectual and artistic bohemia and the Algonquin Hotel's Round Table hosted the likes of the witty writers of the new *New Yorker* magazine. The Harlem Renaissance in African-American arts and letters introduced writers like Zora Neale Hurston and Langston Hughes, and jazz legends like Duke Ellington and Cab Calloway. A host of new theaters along 42nd Street perfected the Broadway musical with tunes written in Tin Pan Alley. The Armory Show and the Ashcan school promoted modern art in America in the 1910s, and the following decades saw the founding of the Museum of Modern Art, the Whitney Museum of American Art and the Solomon R. Guggenheim Museum. The gaiety of the Roaring 20s came to an end with the Wall Street stock market crash on Black Thursday, October 24, 1929, signaling the onset of the Great Depression.

1908	First celebration of New Year's Eve at Times Square.
1911	The Triangle Shirtwaist Company fire kills 145 sweatshop employees.
1913	The **Armory Show** introduces modern art to America.
1919	Formation of the Radio Corporation of America, followed shortly by the creation of the first broadcasting companies, NBC and CBS.
1920	**Black Thursday** bombing on Wall Street takes 35 lives.
1925	The *New Yorker* magazine is founded. Alain Locke's anthology *The New Negro: An Interpretation* marks the heyday of the Harlem Renaissance.
1929	Stock market crash (financial panic of October) signals the start of the Great Depression.
1931	The Empire State Building is completed after almost two years of work.
1932	Mayor Jimmy Walker resigns from office in another Tammany Hall scandal.

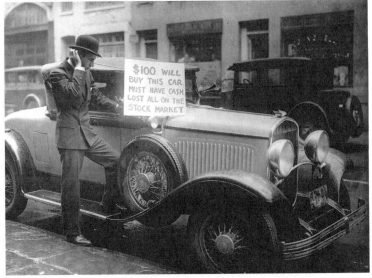

Hard times during the Depression

Standing Tall

The Great Depression prompted the closing of manufacturing plants in the city—thousands of homeless people slept in subway tunnels and waited in bread lines. Construction of the Rockefeller Center and two World's Fairs buoyed New York as reform mayor Fiorello La Guardia—"the Little Flower"—led the city through the trials of the Depression, arresting gangsters like "Lucky" Luciano and supervising huge public works projects. The first US public housing project—First Houses—was built in 1935 and followed by a dozen more in the next decade.

World War II made New York the busiest port in the world and solidified its international position in industry, commerce and finance. The United Nations established its headquarters in Manhattan following the war as the city began building again. The 1950s brought new immigrants, with large numbers arriving from Puerto Rico and Asia. A haven for refugee intelligentsia from Europe, New York made its bid for international cultural capital in the 1950s and 60s, welcoming painters Piet Mondrian, Jacques Lipchitz, Fernand Léger and others, while fostering a new generation of avant-garde artists such as Jackson Pollock, Willem de Kooning, Louise Nevelson and Andy Warhol. Off Broadway theaters enlivened the cultural scene and New York became a center for film and television.

Racial and labor tensions beset the city in the 1960s, and in 1975 the city government defaulted into bankruptcy. The setbacks only stimulated New Yorker pluck, and by 1981, the city's budget was balanced. Despite the 1987 stock market crash, by the late 1980s an upswing in the world economy led to a massive expansion on Wall Street that continued straight through the Bull Market of the late 1990s. Following the attack on the World Trade Center on September 11, 2001, which signaled the end of the stock market boom, New York continues to rebuild as it faces a fiscal crunch that rivals that of the 1970s. City residents, however, seem to have embraced the challenge with a spirit of sacrifice and cooperation.

1934	**Fiorello H. La Guardia** becomes mayor of New York City, serving until 1945.
1935	Harlem Riot exposes the effects of the Depression on African Americans.
1939-40	World's Fair at Flushing Meadow attracts more than 44 million visitors to preview postwar advances in domestic technology.
1945	**United Nations** charter is drafted in San Francisco, and the organization announces it will locate in New York City.
1959	Construction of Lincoln Center begins.
1964	The longest suspension bridge in the US, the Verrazano-Narrows Bridge, opens between Brooklyn and Staten Island. The **Harlem Uprising** is the first major manifestation of Northern black unrest in the Civil Rights era.
1964-65	**World's Fair** held on the same site as the 1939-40 fair features the modern concrete architecture of the New York State Pavilion and Hall of Science, and the 140ft-tall Unisphere model of the earth.
1965	Assassination of Malcolm X at the Audubon Ballroom in Harlem. November power blackout affects entire Northeast.
1968	Mayor John Lindsay walks the slums of New York, helping diffuse racial tensions during a summer of urban unrest.
1973	The World Trade Center opens in Manhattan.
1977	Ed Koch becomes mayor.
1980	John Lennon is assassinated in front of his New York City residence, the Dakota.
1989	New York City's first African-American mayor, David Dinkins, is elected.
1993	Terrorist bomb rocks the World Trade Center, injuring hundreds. Republican Rudy Giuliani is elected mayor.
1996	New York endures its worst blizzard in a century.
1997	New York City records its highest visitor count on record: 33 million domestic and international travelers.
1999	Some two million people fill Times Square for a 24-hour-long New Year's Eve celebration to welcome the new millennium.
2000	Former First Lady Hillary Clinton makes a historic run for a US Senate seat; Big Apple voters embrace her at the polls by a 3-to-1 ratio.
2001	On the morning of September 11th, in the worst terrorist attack in US history, hijackers crashed two passenger planes into the Twin Towers, destroying the entire World Trade Center and resulting in the loss of some 2,800 lives.
2002	Billionaire financial-data baron Mike Bloomberg is sworn in as mayor of a city in recovery. Residents return downtown and workers complete the clean-up of the World Trade Center.
2003	A cascading power outage leaves New York City in the dark for 29 hours beginning at 4pm on Thursday, August 14. The city estimates that the blackout cost $1 billion in lost revenue. In November, the Port Authority reopens the World Trade Center PATH station.

Economy

New York's $400 billion economy would rank 15th among the nations of the world. After two decades of growth, though, the city faces uncertain times. The attack on September 11 caused tremendous physical damage and briefly brought economic life to a standstill. At the same time, the city is coping with the end of the 18-year Wall Street bull market that filled its tax coffers. More than 120,000 jobs were lost between the summers of 2001 and 2002, and the city, which had been running surpluses and increasing services, faced a $5 billion deficit in 2003. Nevertheless, New York City boasts a powerful line-up of economic assets.

First is its sheer size: the New York area has the largest concentration of people, income, finance, industry and transportation of any urban area in the US. Some 8 million people live in New York City, twice as many as in any other American city. The economy provides more than 3.6 million jobs, most in an agglomeration of some 200,000 businesses notable for their diversity, and the city is home to 39 Fortune 500 companies.

New York streets have long been synonymous with some of the city's key industries: Wall Street with finance, Broadway with entertainment, Madison Avenue with advertising and Seventh Avenue with fashion.

The Port – New York's sheltered, ice-free harbor, and 750mi of shoreline easily accessible to the Atlantic yet safe from its buffeting, contributed to the city's early ascendancy. Ships anchored in safety, and as berths proliferated in lower Manhattan along the East and Hudson rivers, the city became a center of young America's trade with the world.

The port is the nation's third largest, although the advent of containership technology has forced most active piers from crowded Manhattan to roomier sites in Brooklyn, Staten Island and New Jersey, where the world's largest container terminal is at Port Newark/Elizabeth. More than 60 shipping lines serve the port. In 2001 the harbor handled $76 billion worth of cargo.

The **Port Authority of New York and New Jersey** manages the harbor's general cargo and containership terminals; six tunnels and bridges connecting the city with New Jersey; the region's major bus terminal on West 42nd Street; the Port Authority TransHudson (PATH) rapid-transit rail system; three major airports; and a heliport. The Port Authority built and owned the World Trade Center; it retains ownership of the site and will play an important role in determining its future.

Finance – New York's eminence as a seaport led to its dominant role in banking. The city is home to two of the country's three largest commercial banks, owned by financial services titans Citigroup and J.P. Morgan Chase, which have combined commercial banking assets of one trillion dollars. The liberalization of banking laws and a subsequent tidal wave of mergers and acquisitions have been reshaping the city's (and the country's) financial industry over the past few years. Before combining with J.P. Morgan in 2000, Chase had merged with competitor Chemical Bank, which had just finished its merger with Manufacturer Hanover's Trust. Citigroup comprises Citibank, insurance giant Travelers and brokerage house Salomon Smith Barney. All major financial institutions, domestic and foreign, maintain a presence in New York; among them are 219 foreign banks, including 20 of the top 25 foreign branches of

Inside the New York Stock Exchange

international banks. Banking accounts for 90,000 of the city's jobs. Much of the industry is crowded into the downtown Financial District, but it has expanded onto major Midtown avenues, including Park, Madison and Fifth, and its operations are now spreading to Queens and Brooklyn.

New York is also the place where the nation buys and sells its stock. More than 85 percent of US-based stock trades are conducted here, notably on Wall Street's New York Stock Exchange and the American Stock Exchange. The NYSE trades $42 billion worth of stocks every day; it has $12.3 trillion in stock available.

Closely related to New York finance are such large service industries as accounting, insurance and law. Three of the four biggest accounting firms, more than 900 insurance companies and 6,400 law firms, including many of the nation's top 25, are located in New York.

Transportation and Communication – New York is the only US city accessible by three major airports (John F. Kennedy, LaGuardia and Newark Liberty), which annually handle more than 77 million passengers (more than 55 million domestic and 22 million international). Travelers also arrive via a rail and bus network that brings in a million people daily, mostly commuters. The streets of New York are served by 12,000 taxicabs and 235 bus routes. But when New Yorkers need to get from here to there, day or night, they go underground. The subway system, stretching from Coney Island to the North Bronx, with some 468 stations and 656 miles of track, serves 4.6 million passengers a day. A continuing $34 billion capital-investment program, begun in 1982, has rehabilitated this once-neglected jewel in New York's transportation crown.

New York also reaches out to the world through communications. The city is home to four major television networks (ABC, NBC, CBS and Fox) and numerous cable channels (MTV, HBO, Biography). Film production in New York has increased 33 percent since 1993. The TV, film, and commercial industries employ 70,000 New Yorkers. The city is also the nation's print capital. Home to Time/Life and Condé Nast among other Midtown magazine empires, New York churns out some 350 consumer magazines. Major publishing houses McGraw-Hill, Bantam and Random House also have headquarters in the area. Printing and publishing account for some 71,000 jobs in the city, which is home to 15 daily newspapers and the Associated Press wire service.

New York is a world leader in advertising and public relations. The city's 900 ad agencies employ some 32,000 people. Madison Avenue is still the hub, but several agencies are moving to Greenwich Village. Public relations employs 10,000 people. With its more than 90 two- and four-year colleges and universities, the city is renowned as an outstanding center for higher learning and scientific research.

Computer Technology – New York City has more computer power than any other city in the nation. Its personal computers, microcomputers and mainframes are especially vital to the publishing, finance and medical industries. As a result, such service industries as electronic information, computer software, computer consulting and data processing have been growing at double-digit rates in the 1990s. New York City now claims 1,800 data-processing firms. Many are located in Manhattan, but the New York Stock Exchange, among others, has shifted its huge data-processing load to the city's large, new Metrotech Center in Brooklyn. Atop the city's expanding "old" high-tech industry, a thousand "new media" firms have blossomed, totaling out at about 8,500 firms. The city's new media industry, creating Web sites and digital content and enabling e-commerce, employed more than 100,000 in 1999 (just 18,000 four years earlier), dwarfing the size of old media industries such as broadcasting and publishing. More than half of those employees work in Silicon Alley, which stretches from the southern tip of Manhattan to 41st Street, with its heart in the Flatiron District. A number of these firms disappeared as quickly as they arrived (in the hangover days after the tech-stock bubble burst, the words "Silicon Alley" themselves became taboo). But the rise of AOL Time Warner's new headquarters in Columbus Circle indicates that New York's rank as a new-media power is secure.

Manufacturing – Manufacturing's share of the economy has long been declining—from 900,000 jobs in 1950 to 218,000 today. Still, New York's highly diverse manufacturing base comprises 10,400 companies, many relying on a reservoir of specialized labor skills. Today's **garment industry** has emerged from the city's 19C clothing workshops, embracing sophisticated Midtown high-fashion designers and tiny factories in Chinatown. Though the industry's presence, pressed by foreign competition, has been shrinking for decades, 56,700 New Yorkers still work in the various garment-making trades. One quarter of these workers are on Seventh Avenue, where designers and showrooms are centered and hand trucks clatter through the streets. Some high-end manufacturing remains in this traditional Garment Center, but most has been moved to Chinatown, Sunset Park in Brooklyn and the town of Flushing in Queens. About 90 percent of the nation's diamond imports come through New York. The traditional centers are Canal Street and West 47th Street ("Diamond and Jewelry Way"), between Fifth Avenue and the Avenue of the Americas. Overall the **diamond and jewelry industry** employs 34,000 New Yorkers, many with unique skills.

The city's important emerging industries, such as semiconductors, health-care equipment and computer equipment, also bank on high-skill workers.

Tourism – Visitors to New York are drawn by the city's glamour, fine dining and shopping, and an array of tourist meccas and cultural attractions. A remarkable range of retail shops attracts customers from around the world. Such names as Tiffany & Co. and Saks

Fifth Avenue evoke images of luxury shopping, and Macy's has long claimed the title of "the world's largest store."

In 2001, New York welcomed some 35 million visitors, who spent about $15 billion. Attendance at the city's 39 Broadway theaters reached 10.9 million during the 2001-2002 season. The city's more than 300 theaters range from Off-Off Broadway avant-garde houses to such large and famous showplaces as Radio City Music Hall, Carnegie Hall, Lincoln Center, and the Apollo. The city's tourism industry was gravely injured by the events of September 11; in the weeks and months following the attack, hotel vacancy rates soared and Broadway box-office sales plummeted. Tourism rebounded in 2002, but the city estimates 20,000 jobs in related industries have disappeared.

Fine art in New York is both an attraction to visitors and an industry in itself. Working artists have transformed entire Manhattan neighborhoods, including SoHo, TriBeCa and parts of Chelsea; now younger artists are reclaiming industrial space in Long Island City, Queens and in Brooklyn's Williamsburg and DUMBO (District Under the Manhattan Bridge Overpass) neighborhoods. The city boasts more than 500 art galleries, and its 160 museums include such world-class art attractions as the Metropolitan Museum of Art, the Museum of Modern Art and the Solomon R. Guggenheim Museum, as well as museums in such fields as photography, crafts, television and radio, and Jewish, African, American Indian and Latino culture. The estimated total economic impact of tourism on the New York economy in 2001 amounted to $22 billion.

Corina Lecca/Polo Ralph Lauren

Ralph Lauren runway show, Spring 2001

Population

New York City is the most populous city in the US. During the 1990's the city experienced considerable growth due to immigration at a pace not seen for nearly a century. Population expanded from 7,071,639 in 1980 to 8,008,278 people in 2000. Foreign-born residents accounted for 25 percent of the population in 1980, 28 percent in 1990, and 36 percent in 2000.

The surge in immigration continues a pattern begun in the mid-19C. New York has long been known for its diversity, traceable to the successive waves of immigration that arrived through the major port of entry into the New World. It has often been described as the "largest Irish city" or the "largest Jewish community" or the "second-largest Italian community" in the world. The influx of immigrants, which slowed following the restrictive immigration laws of the early 1920s, began again in the 1960s, with new arrivals coming from Latin America, Asia and the Middle East. It is a tribute to the city that New Yorkers have come to share a common outlook and way of life while retaining their ethnic identity and the pride of their cultural heritage. The influx of newcomers during the 1980s and 1990s transformed many neighborhoods in New York City. Expanding population in Manhattan's Chinatown, for example, has dislodged residents of Little Italy to the north. Similar developments have occurred in Brighton Beach in Brooklyn, where Russian immigration has been heavy, and in Washington Heights in northern Manhattan, where immigrants from the Dominican Republic have settled in large numbers.

Population from 1626 to 2001

1626	200	The first boatload of settlers brought by the Dutch to Nieuw Amsterdam consists primarily of French Huguenots.
1656	1,000	The first immigrants are followed by English, Scots, Germans and Scandinavians.
1756	16,000	
1790	33,000	

1800	60,000	Half of New York's population is of English origin.
1850s	630,000	Germans, Irish and Scandinavians arrive in large numbers.
1880	1,911,700	Eastern Europeans and Southern Italians immigrate in great waves; this influx continues until 1924.
1900	3,437,200	This figure includes residents of the five boroughs, which were incorporated in 1898.
1920	5,620,000	After World War I, black migration increases both from the American South and from the West Indies.
1924		Immigration laws limit foreign immigration.
1930	6,930,500	Decline in growth rate.
1950	7,892,000	After World War II many Puerto Ricans settle in New York.
1960	7,782,000	From 1950 to 1960, the city loses more than 100,000 inhabitants as many New Yorkers move to the suburbs.
1970	7,896,000	Out-migration of New York's population from the city to the suburbs continues, mirroring the overall trend of cities in the Northeast.
1980	7,071,639	
1990	7,322,600	New York's foreign-born population of two million persons reflects the great influx of immigrants from Asia, Latin America and the Caribbean since 1965.
1995	7,312,000	Population declines slightly.
1999	7,428,162	Newcomers arrive at a rate of 100,000 a year in the 1990s, offsetting other population losses.
2000	8,008,278	
2001	8,019,033	

A Cosmopolitan Mix

In the 19C and at the beginning of the 20C, recent immigrants, referred to as "hyphenated citizens" (Irish-Americans, Italian-Americans, German-Americans and so on), were often denied social status by the "aristocracy" of British and Dutch origin. However, the pyramid of New York society was unable to withstand the forces of change, and today these multicultural strands, together with the more recent waves of immigrants, make up the very fabric of New York's population.

The Irish – More than half a million New Yorkers are of Irish descent. It was the outbreak of the Irish potato famine in 1846 that touched off the mass exodus from Ireland. In 1890 one-fourth of all New Yorkers were Irish. From the beginning the Irish were drawn to public affairs and city government. Carrying on the religious tradition of their homeland, they have contributed significantly to the influence of the Roman Catholic Church in the US. Still quite a homogeneous group, Irish-Americans are famous for their exuberant celebration of St. Patrick's Day, March 17, to honor their patron saint.

Italian Family en Route to Ellis Island (c.1905) by Lewis W. Hine

Lewis W. Hine Collection, New York Public Library

Italians – Large-scale immigration, mainly of laborers and peasants from southern Italy and Sicily, started only after 1870. Some returned to the old country with their first savings, but the vast majority brought their families to settle in America. Many Italian immigrants started out in the building industry where they worked under the heavy hands of "padroni" (construction bosses); however, over the years, hard work and enterprise often combined to establish small family businesses, especially in the restaurant, contracting and trucking trades. After generations of economic and social rewards in the New World, the city's 700,000 Italian-Americans remain deeply attached to family traditions and community life. The colorful atmosphere of their homeland is still reflected in Little Italy.

Germans and Austrians – This group was probably the most rapidly assimilated, and one of the largest. Composed of conservatives and liberals, craftspeople, laborers, entrepreneurs and intellectuals, German-speaking immigrants no longer form a very unified group. Leaving behind them in most cases the language of the "old country," they still share a few national traditions. Germans arrived in great numbers during the 19C, particularly after the failed 1848-49 revolution in Germany. They settled mostly around Tompkins Square, later moving farther uptown. Some German atmosphere can still be found in Yorkville.

Chinese – Coming to the US in the mid-19C to work on railway lines and in mines, Chinese immigrants hailed mainly from Canton. The most recent newcomers, primarily from Hong Kong, Shanghai and Taiwan, have swelled their numbers to more than 360,000, with the greatest concentration living in steadily expanding Chinatown. Many second-generation Chinese make their home in boroughs other than Manhattan, particularly in Queens. The overall Asian population in the city increased by more than 50 percent during the 1990s, to its current count of 787,000.

Eastern Europeans – Before World War I, the massive waves of immigrants from the old Russian empire were not made up of Russians, but mostly of members of various minority nationalities—Ukrainians, Poles, Lithuanians and others. Like most newly arrived immigrants, they tended to congregate in the same neighborhoods as their countrymen. The 1917 Revolution brought only a trickle of so-called White Russians to New York as compared to the large numbers who immigrated to European capitals. Many Ukrainians and Russians, however, were among the displaced persons who settled in New York in the wake of World War II. During the 1980s and 90s, the number of immigrants from Russia sharply increased. The former Soviet Union has become New York's number-one source of new immigrants; their numbers have increased from 81,000 in 1990 to some 230,000 in 1999.

Jews – Sephardic Jews, originally from Spain and Portugal, had come to New York in the 17C, mostly via Holland and Latin America. Today, however, the majority of the New York Jews are of Eastern and Central European descent (Ashkenazi). Manhattan's Lower East Side was the first home for 1.5 million Jews who entered America between 1880 and 1910; a great number also settled in Brooklyn communities. The New York Jewish population has actively participated in economic and cultural endeavors, and the names of many Jewish individuals and institutions are woven into the history of New York.

African Americans – Although there were blacks among the early inhabitants of New York, it was only in the 20C that blacks migrated to the city in large numbers. Today, African Americans number about 2.1 million or roughly one-fourth of the New York population. Initial black migration came from the American South. In the past two decades, migration from the Caribbean has resulted in a new Caribbean community in upper Manhattan and Brooklyn.

The black community has richly contributed to the character of the city. It has produced distinguished writers, playwrights and performers, and the influence of "rhythm and blues" and jazz has greatly impacted the American musical scene. During recent decades many blacks have availed themselves of the great educational and economic opportunities offered in New York, thus increasing their numbers in the professions as well as in politics, government and private business. Particularly notable was the 1989 election of David Dinkins, the first African American to serve as mayor of New York City. Yet, despite the progress of some, many more black New Yorkers have yet to escape a heritage that includes centuries of slavery and discrimination. Numerous African-American neighborhoods in the city, including parts of Harlem in Manhattan, Bedford-Stuyvesant in Brooklyn and South Jamaica in Queens, show the effects of poverty—abandoned buildings, trash-strewn lots, shuttered stores. On many of the city's indices—unemployment, homelessness, infant mortality, school dropout ratio—African Americans continue to suffer disproportionately.

Latinos – The rapid growth of the Puerto Rican population has brought their number from less than a thousand in 1910 to almost 900,000 in 1990, with a decline in the past decade to 789,000. Puerto Ricans are American citizens, and as such are free to travel between Puerto Rico and the continental US without a visa or regard to quotas. The size of the city's Dominican community continues to surge, reaching 406,000. The Latino population, which includes Puerto Ricans and Dominicans together with the latest newcomers from the south (Mexicans, Cubans, Colombians, Ecuadorians and other Latin Americans), now forms more than one-fourth of the city's population, numbering more than 2.1 million in 2000 and representing its largest foreign-language group. The major concentration of the Puerto Rican population in the city is in the Bronx, but the heart of New York's Puerto Rican community is East Harlem, better known as El Barrio. Parts of the Upper West Side, the Bronx, Brooklyn and Queens are also host to significant numbers of Latin Americans. Mindful of their culture, Latinos have emerged as a vital community, lending a distinctive flavor to the city.

Additional Ethnic Groups – An influx of newcomers from the Asian subcontinent—India, Bangladesh and Pakistan—has created a thriving "little India" in Jackson Heights, and a sizable Greek community lives in Astoria *(p 278)*, both in Queens; a number of Armenians have settled in the Bronx. The liberalization of immigration regulations has brought an influx of such diverse ethnic groups as Koreans, Ecuadoreans, Vietnamese, Haitians, Arabs and Senegalese, making New York City home to more than 150 different nationalities.

Literature

In the rich literary life of contemporary America, New York is no doubt the most vital force. Indeed, the Naked City is home to many notable figures in fiction and journalism, from Walt Whitman to Norman Mailer, each celebrating the city's enduring vibrancy.

Early Literati – Two kinds of writers have left an indelible mark on New York's literary scene: those who were born here and those who flocked here as to a cultural mecca, adopting the city as their own with an almost religious fervor. The first of the latter group was probably "Common Sense" author and patriot Thomas Paine, who spent his last years in Greenwich Village at the dawn of the 19C. New York City typified the confidence and spunk of the young Republic at the time, although literary themes remained pastoral rather than urban. One of America's first literary giants was New York City-born **Washington Irving** (1783-1859). In his 1807 satirical essay collection *Salmagundi*, he referred to New York City as Gotham—the 13C English village where the inhabitants acted like madmen to prevent King John from residing there. Irving also wrote the parodic *A History of New York from the Beginning of the World to the End of the Dutch Dynasty* (1809) under the name Diedrich Knickerbocker, translated as "baker of marbles." He achieved lasting fame in America with *Rip Van Winkle* (1819) and *The Legend of Sleepy Hollow* (1820). Best known for his work *The Last of the Mohicans*, contemporary **James Fenimore Cooper** (1789-1851) lived in the city in the 1820s and wrote *The Pioneers* and *The Pilot* here, finding adventure not in the city but at sea and in the wilds of the frontier.

Herman Melville (1819-91) was born and lived most of his life in New York, writing his great seafaring saga *Moby Dick* here and continuing the literary tradition of the early 19C that focused on wilderness and adventure. Melville also set pieces in and around the city, including "Bartleby the Scrivener," an early perspective on the commercial metropolis. **Clement Clarke Moore** (1779-1863) resided south of 23rd Street in Chelsea, where he wrote the famous poem "A Visit from St. Nicholas," that defined the modern image of Santa Claus.

> *"There is no place like [New York], no place with an atom of its glory, pride, and exultancy. It lays its hand upon a man's bowels; he grows drunk with ecstasy; he grows young and full of glory, he feels that he can never die."*
> Thomas Wolfe, *From Death to Morning* (1935)

Late 19th-Century New York – By the mid-1800s, Americans had grown aware of their distinct national character, defined in part by the frontier but also by the energy generated through booming economic and technological growth. The Industrial Revolution brought about a transformation in the circumstances of life, changing forever the importance of the city, culture and morality. The new morality of the modern world was epitomized by one of America's greatest poets, **Walt Whitman** (1819-92). Born in New York City, Whitman worked as reporter and editor for the *Brooklyn Eagle* in the 1840s, developing his forceful physical style and pathbreaking sensuality in the bustling metropolis. Shortly after the first edition of *Leaves of Grass* in 1855, he served as editor for the *Brooklyn Times* and continued to capture the lusty spirit of his city in works like the classic *Crossing Brooklyn Ferry*.

Henry James (1843-1916) reversed the traditional role of writers coming to New York seeking fame. Born in the city, he set several novels and stories in New York, including *Washington Square* (1880), but spent most of his literary career as an expatriate in London, where he published his most famous work, *The Turn of the Screw*, in 1898. He returned to write *The American Scene* in 1907 but died a British subject in 1916. New York native **Edith Wharton** (1862-1937) berated and celebrated the Gilded Age of her hometown in novels like *The Age of Innocence*, which won the Pulitzer prize. The great romantic Gothicist **Edgar Allan Poe** (1809-49) lived in the Bronx in the 1840s as well as in Greenwich Village and wrote several of his poems and stories here, including "The Raven," first published in the *New York Evening Mirror* in 1845. **Stephen Crane** (1871-1900), a former *New York Tribune* reporter, helped bring the American novel into the big city with *New York City Sketches* and *Maggie: A Girl of the Streets* (1893), gaining his greatest fame with *The Red Badge of Courage* (1894). **Mark Twain** (Samuel Clemens, 1835-1910) reported on the city for several Western newspapers, residing in the Village during his sojourns here. **William Dean Howells** (1837-1920), the "dean of American letters," came to New York in 1889 to serve as a *Harper's* magazine editor. By the late 19C, the city had become the literary capital of the US, surpassing Boston and Philadelphia. The lure was so strong that English poet laureate John Masefield scrubbed floors in a saloon to support his New York address in the 1890s.

Bohemian Enclave – By the 1910s, Greenwich Village had become the country's bohemia, attracting avant-garde writers, artists and thespians, including playwright **Eugene O'Neill** (1888-1953), poet **Edna St. Vincent Millay** (1892-1950), author **Theodore Dreiser** (1871-1945) and poet **Edwin Arlington Robinson** (1869-1935). O'Neill based *The Iceman Cometh* and his 1921 Pulitzer prize-winning *Anna Christie* on his 1916 forays in the Village, while Millay used the neighborhood as the setting for *Second April* and

Renascence. The radical aspects of Village life included the socialist magazines *Seven Arts* and *The Masses*, the latter involving revolutionaries Max Eastman, Art Young, John Reed and Floyd Dell. Poet **Marianne Moore** (1887-1972) arrived in the city in 1921, becoming editor of the *Dial* in 1925 and living out her life in Brooklyn. She was followed in 1923 by North Carolina transplant **Thomas Wolfe** (1900-38), who wrote *Look Homeward, Angel* in 1929 and *You Can't Go Home Again* (published 1940). **F. Scott Fitzgerald** (1896-1940) brought his party to town on more than one occasion as the city cemented its cultural position in the late 1920s.

As the Village continued its ferment, the midtown Algonquin Hotel became host to the Thanatopsis, Literary Inside Straight and **Round Table** clubs. The latter group became an institution, led by drama critic and raconteur Alexander Woolcott, columnist Franklin P. Adams, and three figures associated with *The New Yorker* magazine: editor Harold Ross, author Dorothy Parker and humorist Robert Benchley. **The New Yorker**, established in 1925, elevated the standard of American discourse to a new, articulate and sophisticated level. For three generations its writing and criticism have attracted a nationwide audience, and its list of contributors includes many of the greatest 20C American writers, including essayists E.B. White and Edmund Wilson; novelists J.D. Salinger, Saul Bellow, John O'Hara and John Updike; film critic Pauline Kael; humorists James Thurber and Calvin Trillin; and musicologist Whitney Baillett.

African-American Letters – The concentration of African Americans in Manhattan's Harlem neighborhood after the turn of the century created an atmosphere of independence and cultural pride that fostered the 1920s awakening known as the Harlem Renaissance. Even earlier, pioneering poet and author **Paul Laurence Dunbar** (1872-1906), living in the African-American bohemia of the Tenderloin, had celebrated the black spirit in his 1902 *Sport of the Gods*. **W.E.B. DuBois'** *The Souls of Black Folk* (1903) brought recognition to the problem of the "color line"; he formed the NAACP in New York with poet James Weldon Johnson and others in 1909.

But it was the rapid growth and sometime prosperity of Harlem after 1910 that nurtured the greatest flowering of African-American arts and literature in the 1920s. **Alain Locke**'s 1925 *The New Negro: An Interpretation* summarized the attitude and expectations of a community that found, in New York City, the support and freedom to express itself. **Langston Hughes** (1902-67) captured the streets of Harlem in *The Weary Blues* (1926) and recognized that Harlem was no longer simply a place but a symbol of African-American identity. Other important poets included Countee Cullen (1903-46), with *One Way to Heaven* (1932), and James Weldon Johnson (1871-1938), who released *The Book of American Negro Poetry* in 1922. Novelists included Jean Toomer (1894-1967), author of *Cane* (1923); West Indian native Claude McKay (1890-1948), who wrote *Home to Harlem* (1928); and **Zora Neale Hurston** (1891-60), whose landmark *Their Eyes Were Watching God* was published in 1937, when the stark realities of the Great Depression and racism had eclipsed the optimism of the Harlem Renaissance.

Coming Out of the Depression – The Great Depression marked a respite in New York's literary history as the city's urban atmosphere provided the backdrop for Ellery Queen mysteries and for sophisticated sleuths Nick and Nora Charles in Dashiell Hammett's *The Thin Man*. New York-born **Henry Miller** (1891-1980) went bumming around Paris in the 1930s, where he wrote the pathbreaking *Tropic of Cancer* before returning to the city in 1940 and then relocating to the West Coast. New Yorker **John Dos Passos** (1896-1970) served up his critique of the nation in the novels *USA* and *Manhattan Transfer*. *Day of the Locust* author **Nathanael West** (1903-40) was born Nathan Weinstein in New York City before moving on to Hollywood. Others continued to make the pilgrimage to New York, including Spanish poet and playwright Federico García Lorca *(Poet in New York)* and Russian poet Vladimir Mayakovsky *(Brooklyn Bridge).*

Postwar Penmanship – New York emerged from World War II more powerful, attractive and determined than ever

Arthur Miller (1967)

Hutton Archive/Getty Images

as it sought to become the world's cultural capital. **Norman Mailer**'s hard-bitten, macho New York style rocked the world in 1948 with his sensational novel *The Naked and the Dead*. He continues to serve as a literary native son for the increasingly cosmopolitan metropolis. Playwright **Arthur Miller** wrote the epochal *Death of a Salesman* in 1949. The 1950s saw the great Welsh poet **Dylan Thomas** (1914-53) succumb to the lure of New York City and an excess of drink at the White Horse Tavern.

In the 1950s and 60s, New York evolved into the cultural capital of the Jet Age, as writers, artists and aesthetes gathered in Greenwich Village's Cedar Tavern, fostering the spontaneity and experimentation of New York school poets like Frank O'Hara and Barbara Guest and beats like **Allen Ginsberg** (1926-97), Jack Kerouac and Gregory Corso. The period marked a resurgence of African-American literature in New York, with poet **Amiri Baraka** (LeRoi Jones) and author **James Baldwin**, whose important novels *Go Tell It on the Mountain* (1952) and *Another Country* (1962) are set in the city. Langston Hughes achieved new levels of poetry and commentary with *Shakespeare in Harlem* (1942) and *Montage of a Dream Deferred* (1951), while **Ralph Ellison** (1914-94) fired an early civil rights salvo in 1952's *Invisible Man*.

A Living Tradition – During a 1963 newspaper strike, editors Robert E. Silver and Barbara Epstein founded one of the most important literary publications of the 20C, the *New York Review of Books*, now a biweekly that is indispensable to the serious and amateur critic alike. New York City is often the centerpiece for American comedies and slice-of-life dramas, as exemplified by comic playwrights **Neil Simon** and **Wendy Wasserstein**, and film directors **Woody Allen** and **Spike Lee**. The Black Arts movement of the 1960s brought **Nikki Giovanni**, **Maya Angelou** and **Gil Scott-Heron** to a growing audience that had become national in scope by the 1980s. **E.L. Doctorow** captured modern Gotham in a series of tragic and violent novels, including *Ragtime* (1978) and *Billy Bathgate* (1989). The moral vacuity of the 1980s provided the setting for **Tom Wolfe**'s searing *Bonfire of the Vanities* (1987), while Oscar Hijuelos' Pulitzer prize-winning *The Mambo Kings Play Songs of Love* (1989) captured the rhythms of the city's Cuban community. In *Underworld* (1997), Don DeLillo weaves the Bronx of the 1950s and 1990s into a complex tapestry of the postwar era. Other leading New York authors include Susan Sontag, Gore Vidal, and Paul Auster. The Nuyorican Poets Café in Alphabet City, propelled by its weekly poetry slams, has in recent years become a mecca for an exuberant, multicultural spoken-word movement. The city continues to draw literary pilgrims from across America and the globe, seeking critical approval, publishing opportunities and the manifold inspiration presented by the city's ongoing human drama.

Visual Arts

Preoccupied with settling their new nation, colonial New Yorkers had little time to spend painting or sculpting for other than the most practical reasons. The art of portraiture, though popular, was more a craft, practiced by itinerants and painters who made other livings. In the decorative and household arts, ethnic custom and functionality reigned. Because of such practicality, New York became a center of cabinet- and silver making long before its fairly recent ascent as a hub of the visual arts. Silversmith Cornelius Kierstede and furniture maker Duncan Phyfe stand out among early New York's finest artisans.

Hudson River School – The painters of the first distinctly American school of painting (1825-75) took their main inspiration from the dramatic scenery of the Hudson River Valley north of New York City. Artists **Thomas Cole** (1801-48), Asher B. Durand, Albert Bierstadt and Frederic E. Church embraced a romantic vision of nature and art, and imbued epic portrayals of America's grandiose landscapes with moral and transcendental meaning. These painters were among the many artists who swelled the ranks of the new art academies established in the city during the period, including the National Academy of Design (1825) and the Art Students League (1875).

Emergence of Modern Art – Founded in 1908, the artistic group "The Eight" sought to rebel against the conservatism of the New York academic establishment. Dubbed the Ashcan school in derisive reference to its bald urban realism, "The Eight" (particularly its most prominent members Robert Henri, George Luks and John Sloan) produced vivid, sympathetic portrayals of the rough edges of urban life, which inspired a rich tradition of 20C American Realism (George Bellows and Edward Hopper) and found parallels in Jacob Riis' and Lewis W. Hine's documentary photographs of the growing immigrant population.

Photographer Alfred Stieglitz exhibited avant-garde European art in his Little Galleries of the Photo Secession from 1905 to 1917. Also known as "291," the gallery served as a laboratory and launching pad for New York's first Modernist painters Arthur Dove, John Marin and Georgia O'Keeffe.

The watershed event in the history of modern art in America was New York's 1913 **Armory Show**, or International Exhibition of Modern Art, which displayed more than 1,300 objects—including works by European post-Impressionists, Fauvists and Cubists—and introduced the most recent European art to a largely unprepared and

Catskill Creek (1845) by Thomas Cole

bewildered American public. Marcel Duchamp's Cubist-inspired *Nude Descending a Staircase* provoked particular controversy. Despite the hostile public response, the exhibit attracted important collectors and can be credited with encouraging the tradition of patronage, which culminated in the founding of the Museum of Modern Art in 1929, the Whitney Museum of American Art in 1931 and the Guggenheim Foundation *(p 253)* in 1937.

After World War I, aspects of abstraction were explored by Stuart Davis, Patrick Henry Bruce and Charles Sheeler. The Great Depression brought an insular mood and public programs that fostered the social realism of Reginald Marsh and the mural painting of Thomas Hart Benton.

The Balance Shifts – Prior to the 1930s many American artists traveled abroad to study and observe the latest developments in experimental art. However, as war fermented and the Great Depression lingered in Europe, foreign artists fled to New York. The arrival of Frenchmen Fernand Léger and André Masson, Spaniard Joan Miró, and Germans Josef Albers and Max Ernst brought an unprecedented opportunity for direct contact with Surrealist and Abstract Art. In the decade after World War II, a true American avant-garde flowered, and New York emerged as a cultural mecca and world leader in the production and promotion of modern art. This period of fertile artistic activity culminated in the first radical American artistic movement, **Abstract Expressionism** (1946–late 1950s). Also known as the New York school, the Abstract Expressionists were divided among Action or Gesture painters (Jackson Pollock, Willem de Kooning, Franz Kline, Robert Motherwell and Clyfford Still), who emphasized the use of thick, sweeping brush strokes or dripped paint in the spontaneous, intuitive act of painting; and Color Field painters (Mark Rothko, Barnett Newman), who employed equally large but color-saturated canvases to envelop the spectator in meditative calm. As the Abstract Expressionists received international recognition, postwar American affluence prompted collecting and gallery activity. New York gradually came to the fore, replacing Paris as the epicenter of the art world. The late 1950s saw new artistic developments inspired by Abstract Expressionists: the brilliantly colored canvases of Stain Painting (Helen Frankenthaler), the simplified color fields of Hard Edge Painting (Al Held, Kenneth Noland) and the dramatic, shaped canvases of Frank Stella. In the 1960s, artists Roy Lichtenstein, Robert Rauschenberg, Andy Warhol and Claes Oldenburg debunked the high-art notions of Abstract Expressionism and irreverently employed comic-strip subjects and billboard painting techniques in the production of **Pop Art**. Also emerging in reaction to Abstract Expressionism, 1960s **Minimalist** sculptors (Donald Judd, Carl Andre) used nonreferential, geometric industrial forms to produce works of immediate and bold impact. The 1970s witnessed **Conceptual art**, whose adherents—environmental sculptors and performance artists—proposed ideas rather than the collectible object as the essence of art, and the revival of Realism (Philip Pearlstein, Chuck Close, Alex Katz and George Segal).

A Changing Scene – The richly pluralistic artistic atmosphere of the 1980s and 90s embraced the post-Modern movements of neo-Expressionism (Julian Schnabel, David Salle), Graffiti Art (Keith Haring, Jean-Michel Basquiat) and neo-Conceptualism (Barbara Kruger, Jenny Holzer), along with long-standing traditions of representation and painterly abstraction. In recent years, subjects anatomical, political and environmental have inspired artists on the leading edge—among them Damien Hirst and the

Artist Elizabeth Murray in her SoHo studio

"young British artists" who invaded New York in Brooklyn Museum's "Sensation" show, which reignited the simmering culture wars with a depiction of the Virgin Mary some considered sacrilegious. The ensuing contretemps—at one point the mayor threatened to evict the museum—and subsequent publicity piqued the public's curiosity. From the bohemian heart of SoHo and the Village, galleries and "alternative spaces" for viewing contemporary art radiate outward into adjacent neighborhoods such as West Chelsea and TriBeCa. Mainstream commercial galleries line 57th Street and upper Madison Avenue (from 70th to 90th streets). And, of course, New York's many museums (including the Whitney, which devotes a large Biennial Exhibit to recent American art) explore the restless world of contemporary art in more formal settings.

20C Outdoor Sculpture in Manhattan

New York's plazas and open spaces have long been used as showcases for the city's monumental sculpture. A selection of 20C outdoor sculpture is listed below.

Downtown

The Red Cube (1967)	Isamu Noguchi	*Plaza in front of Marine Midland Bank*
Group of Four Trees (1972)	Jean Dubuffet	*Plaza in front of Chase Manhattan Bank*
Untitled (1973)	Yu Yu Yang	*Plaza in front of Wall Street Plaza*
American Merchant Mariner Memorial (1991)	Marisol	*Battery Park*
Shadows and Flags (1977)	Louise Nevelson	*Louise Nevelson Plaza, intersection of Maiden Lane, William & Liberty Sts.*
Gay Liberation (1980)	George Segal	*Christopher Park, at Christopher St. & Sheridan Square*
Alamo (1967)	Bernard Rosenthal	*Astor Place, Lafayette & W. 8th Sts.*
NYC Manhole Cover	Lawrence Wiener	*W. 11th & Hudson Sts. (northeast corner)*

Midtown

Eye of Fashion (1976)	Robert M. Cronbach	*Fashion Institute of Technology Plaza, at W. 27th St. & Seventh Ave.*
Marriage of Real Estate and Money (2000)	Tom Otterness	*East side of Roosevelt Island, just south of Octagon Park*
The Garment Worker (1984)	Judith Weller	*Plaza at 555 Seventh Ave., at W. 39th St.*
Prometheus (1934)	Paul Manship	*Lower Plaza, Rockefeller Center*
Atlas (1937)	Lee Lawrie	*In front of International Building, Rockefeller Center*

News (1940)	Isamu Noguchi	*Associated Press Building, Rockefeller Center*
Lapstrake (1987)	Jésus Bautista Moroles	*Plaza in front of 31 W. 52nd St.*
Looking Toward the Avenue (1989)	Jim Dine	*Crédit Lyonnias Building plaza, Sixth Ave. between 52nd & 53rd Sts.*
Peace Form One (1980)	Daniel Larue Johnson	*Ralph J. Bunche Park, United Nations*
Single Form (1964)	Barbara Hepworth	*Pool in front of Secretariat Building, United Nations*
No. 9 (1974)	Ivan Chermayeff	*9 W. 57th St.*
Moonbird	Joan Miró	*58th St. plaza of 9 W. 57th St.*

Uptown

Reclining Figure (1965)	Henry Moore	*Plaza Pool, Lincoln Center*
Romeo and Juliet (1977)	Milton Hebald	*Central Park, near entrance to Delacorte Theater at W. 81st St.*
Night Presence IV (1972)	Louise Nevelson	*Park Ave. & 92nd St.*
Three-Way Piece:) Points (1967	Henry Moore	*On overpass at W.117th St. & Amsterdam Ave., Columbia University*
Bellerophon Taming Pegasus (1967)	Jacques Lipchitz	*Over entrance of Law Building (W. 116th St.), Columbia University*

© Brigitta L. House/MICHELIN

Prometheus (Paul Manship, 1934) presides over the ice-skating rink at Rockefeller Center

Architecture and City Planning

A stunning showcase for contemporary architecture, New York is first and foremost a city of skyscrapers. Yet beyond the skyline's perennially changing profile of steel and glass lies an architectural landscape remarkably rich in history and variety; indeed, the city leads the nation in preservation, encompassing thousands of buildings and historic districts that illustrate its development. From the elegant and elemental New York City brownstone to the dramatic ziggurat towers of the Roaring 20s, architecture is both stage and player in the drama of New York City.

From Commercial Colony to Democratic Republic – Engineer Cryn Fredericksz laid out the fort and town of Nieuw Amsterdam in 1625. The earliest views of the colony depict narrow, irregular streets (still seen in lower Manhattan) and quaint homes sporting sloping gambrel roofs and columned porches *(see illustration below)*. The English takeover of Manhattan in 1664 brought the Georgian style, whose symmetrical, solid facades typified the next phase of development, pushing north of Wall Street by 1700. Building in New York City halted during the British occupation, but renewed as the

young Republic came into its own from 1790 to 1820, adopting a modified Roman Classical architecture known as the Federal style. The style defined not only grand public edifices and mansions, but also commercial warehouses and shops that were fast replacing their Dutch antecedents (as seen at South Street Seaport).

In the 1830s Americans turned to ancient Greek architecture as a symbol of the new nation. Public buildings and homes across the nation displayed Greek

Dutch Colonial House

temple entrances in a new, confident show of democracy. Upper-class residential communities north of Houston Street saw the erection of "the Row" at Washington Square North (1831, Town & Davis) and Colonnade Row on Lafayette Street (1831, Seth Greer), wherein dwelt Delanos, Astors, and Vanderbilts. The Federal Hall National Memorial, with its Doric temple facade of Westchester County marble, is a landmark example of the style.

Manhattan Marches North – As New York rebounded from the Revolutionary War and grew in prosperity, it expanded to the north. City Engineer John Randel released the **Randel Plan** in 1811, which laid out a grid of streets from Houston Street all the way north to 155th Street and divided the city into narrow east-west blocks with 100ft-deep lots. The plan was criticized for ignoring the island's topography and extending so far north. The scale would prove prescient, but Manhattan's hills and outcroppings were methodically flattened over time.

Throughout the 19C, new residential areas were erected and then replaced with shops, hotels, restaurants and offices 10 or 20 years later. A serious fire in 1835 leveled 700 buildings in lower Manhattan, and another in 1845 consumed 300 structures, accelerating the process of building and rebuilding. New development reached Houston Street in 1820, 14th Street by 1840, 23rd Street by 1850 and 42nd Street by 1860. The improvement of public transportation from horse-drawn omnibuses in the 1830s to street railroads in the 1850s helped make the growth possible. Slums grew along with the city, as "rear buildings" and tenements proliferated in the 1840s and 50s and shantytowns filled the vacant lands in Central Park and upper Manhattan. Broadway became the barometer of Manhattan's urban and architectural development. By the 1830s hotels on Broadway had pushed residential uses into Washington Square and Greenwich Village. Union Square became a fashionable address by mid-century. In 1862 George William Curtis lamented Broadway's changes in *Harper's* magazine: "It was a street of three-story redbrick houses. Now it is a highway of stone and iron, and marble buildings." The Randel Plan had not provided for open space, and existing private parks like the Elgin Botanic Garden and St. John's soon became lucrative building sites. The development of Central Park in mid-century created much-needed open space and enhanced the prospect of real estate development around it.

Mid-Century Eclecticism – Gothic Revival architecture, inspired by John Ruskin in England and suited especially to churches, was popular in the US from 1840 on. Richard Upjohn's landmark Trinity Church, built in 1846, epitomized the style and the Romantic movement that fostered it, with its dark, dramatic central spire and atmospheric cemetery. Withers and Vaux used the style for the Jefferson Market Library in 1874 and the first Metropolitan Museum of Art building in 1880. Peter B. Wight's National Academy of Design (1865, demolished) at East 23rd Street and Park Avenue was an important example of "Ruskinian" Gothic, as is the surviving National Arts Club (1884, Calvert Vaux) at 15 Gramercy Park South.

By mid-century the vertical, rectangular facades of the Italianate style proved ideal for the narrow lots of the booming city. Easily adapted to row houses, storefronts or warehouses, this decorative style first appeared with the 1846 A.T. Stewart's department store (280 Broadway). Italianate became the preferred style for row houses, as witnessed in the brownstones of Brooklyn Heights, Gramercy Park and Harlem. Anglo-Italianate row houses, with lower entrance stairs and narrow facades, filled the streets of Chelsea.

The Italianate style was the basis for cast-iron commercial loft buildings constructed throughout lower Manhattan in the 1850s.

Haughwout Building

The new "fireproof" material was easily detailed with ornamental flourishes, and the rhythm of round-arched window arcades separated by attached columns could be repeated on multiple floors as buildings grew taller in an era of skyrocketing land values. The facades were often marbleized or painted like stone to reassure a public distrustful of the new glass-and-iron architecture. By 1872 there were almost three miles of cast-iron facades in lower Manhattan, including the elegant **E.V. Haughwout Building**.

Baron Haussmann's redesign of Paris in the 1850s and 1860s spawned a brief but intense affection for Parisian Second Empire architecture. Distinguished by the double-pitched mansard roof, the style befitted the extravagance of the Gilded Age and coincided with the 1870s development of the "Ladies Mile" along Fifth Avenue and Broadway from 10th Street to Madison Square. Former row houses sprouted mansard roofs punctuated by elaborate dormer windows as they were converted to retail uses, while new shops and department stores were designed in the style.

Badlands and Beyond: Manhattan Fills Up – By 1875 New York counted a million residents, and its neighboring boroughs were growing as well. The new elevated railroads built after 1868 connected downtown with once-distant areas around Central Park, leading to their rapid development. The Sixth Avenue El began operating in 1877, followed by the Third Avenue El in 1878, offering service all the way to 129th Street. Within two years elevated lines opened on Second and Ninth avenues. The year 1883 saw the completion of the Brooklyn Bridge, a dazzling display of structural supremacy that ushered in the era of skyscrapers. Elevated railways transformed the city's streetscapes, as did telegraph, telephone and electric lines, causing the city to require that such lines be buried after 1884.

As immigration expanded in the late 19C, slums grew as well, presenting new challenges for architecture and city planning. New York passed its first tenement law in 1867, with a much stricter version following in 1879. In 1880 the Improved Dwellings Assn. built a model tenement on First Avenue north of 71st Street designed by Vaux and Radford, but design did not solve social ills. Urban reform efforts in the 1890s demolished some slums to make way for Columbus and Seward parks.

Brownstones

In *A Backward Glance*, Edith Wharton, who was born in a brownstone in 1862, decried "this little low-studded rectangular New York, cursed with its universal chocolate-colored coating of the most hideous stone ever quarried." Despite such claims, the brownstone has become the quintessential symbol of the New York neighborhood, a legacy of various speculative booms of the 19C, when row after rhythmic row of identical town houses appeared along the city's long residential blocks. Characterized by high stoops, elegant cornices and large plate-glass windows, the four- and five-story buildings adopted many popular architectural stylings; initially the Italianate style (with heavy cornice and brackets) predominated, giving way to Renaissance Revival, Romanesque and Queen Anne designs. Builders first used cheap brown sandstone in the 1820s and 1830s as a substitute for limestone or marble. Over time, the term "brownstone" came to refer to the entire category of 19C town houses—be they faced with stone or brick.

Originally built to house a single family in grand style, the edifices were subdivided into apartments as neighborhoods declined, and rapidly came to symbolize inner-city decay. In recent years, however, brownstones have become fashionable as preservation enthusiasts reconvert many into single-family homes, restoring their original function and cachet. Found in Greenwich Village, Murray Hill, Gramercy Park, Harlem, and the Upper East and West sides of Manhattan, brownstones are also the dominant architectural feature in many parts of Brooklyn, including Park Slope and Brooklyn Heights.

R. Corbel/MICHELIN

The continuing growth of Manhattan led to the first apartment buildings, beginning with Richard Morris Hunt's 1869 Stuyvesant (demolished) on East 18th Street. Old Fifth Avenue mansions were razed for retail landmarks such as Tiffany & Co., and the entertainment district at Union Square was replaced in the 1880s by the "Rialto" along Broadway from Madison Square to 42nd Street. The Upper West Side grew less rapidly than the Upper East Side, even though Riverside Drive had been laid out in 1865. Upper-class apartment housing designed for Singer sewing-machine magnate Edward S. Clark was derided for being so far uptown it might as well be in the Dakotas. The assessment proved flawed, as buildings sprouted up along the Ninth Avenue El line, but the name stuck to Clark's Dakota Apartments (1884, Henry J. Hardenbergh), a triumph of Victorian eclecticism. By the end of the century, the last farms and fields in northern Manhattan had been developed.

Architecture for an Industrial Age – Homes erected in the 1880s sported late Victorian styles, including the Queen Anne, with its picturesque, asymmetrical compositions; the Romanesque Revival, with its rusticated sense of repose and strength; and the Beaux-Arts, with its connotations of continental sophistication and elegance. West End Avenue and Park Slope in Brooklyn included elegant examples of Queen Anne town houses and mansions, as did several apartment buildings on Gramercy Square. Romanesque Revival architecture came into national vogue with the career of **Henry Hobson Richardson**, who lived on Staten Island. The semicircular arches and heavy masonry of the style defined the City of Brooklyn Fire Headquarters (1892, Frank Freeman) and religious buildings such as the Eldridge Street Synagogue (1887, Herter Bros.), with its Moorish and Gothic elements. The Richardsonian Romanesque style found robust expression in the DeVinne Press Building (1885, Babb, Cook & Willard) at 399 Lafayette Street. The success of the Chicago World's Columbian Exposition of 1893 created a rage for Neoclassical architecture, and the New York firm of **McKim, Mead and White** was among its best practitioners, designing grand public edifices as embodied in the US Custom House (1907) at Bowling Green, and retail establishments like the original Tiffany's (1906) at 409 Fifth Avenue. The architects' work at Columbia University and New York University in the 1890s epitomized Beaux-Arts planning and design, and their incomparable Pennsylvania Railroad Station (demolished) of 1910 was modeled on the ancient Baths of Caracalla in Rome.

Richard Morris Hunt designed the Neoclassical facade of the Metropolitan Museum of Art between 1895 and 1902. Several apartment buildings on Broadway, such as the richly encrusted Ansonia Hotel (1904) and the Apthorp (1908), adopted elegant Beaux-Arts ornaments. The style was well suited to a mercantile capital like New York City and characterized the new residential areas on the Upper East and West sides. Grand Central Terminal (1913, Warren & Wetmore) and the New York Public Library (1911, Carrère and Hastings) are considered the height of Beaux-Arts design in New York City. The early 20C was a period of historical revival in architecture, as the Beaux-Arts style was joined by Dutch Colonial, Georgian, Tudor and Gothic Revival. A wealth of terra-cotta ornament made the various mimicries all the more effective. Eclectic revivals reached their height in vaudeville movie palaces like the Apollo (1914, George Keister) and the many theaters on Broadway.

R. Corbel/MICHELIN

Woolworth Building

Skyscrapers and Setbacks – Rapid growth in Manhattan helped pave the way for the skyscraper. James Bogardus erected the first cast-iron building at Washington and Murray streets (reconstructed) in 1848, and Elisha Graves Otis installed the first safety elevator in E.V. Haughwout's building in 1857, an innovation that made taller buildings practical. Iron beams—a predecessor to the skeletal steel frames of skyscrapers—were used for the Cooper Union of 1859. The first true skyscraper—supported entirely by a steel frame—appeared in Chicago in 1884. Chicago school architect Louis Sullivan designed the Bayard-Condict Building in 1894, but New York preferred a more eclectic design approach, from the 1899 Neoclassical Park Row Building by R.H. Robertson to Daniel H. Burnham's epochal Flatiron Building of 1902. The tradition of enveloping new architecture in historical forms reached its literal height in Cass Gilbert's stunning Gothic Revival Woolworth Building of 1913, which at 792ft remained the world's tallest building for a generation.

n 1916 New York City passed the nation's first zoning law to ensure adequate light and air into the canyonlike streets of the metropolis. Zoning required buildings to set their facades back from the street as they grew higher, and soon towers shaped like ancient ziggurats dotted the Manhattan skyline. This form, combined with new technologies and the streamlined aesthetics of modern art, led to the Art Deco skyscraper, which achieved its greatest expressions in New York. By the late 1920s vertical stone panels with expressionistic ornament and recessed windows marked the emergence of Art Deco architecture in landmarks like the Chrysler Building, with its zigzag steel conical crown, and the expressive General Electric Building, with its complex brick and terra-cotta skin. The Empire State Building is a muscular example of Art Deco refinement; it was the tallest building on earth for more than 40 years.

Planning for the Future – By the 1930s development could no longer march north in Manhattan to vacant land—areas had to be found where structures could be demolished and rebuilt, or built higher. The Financial District at the southern end of the island and Fifth Avenue near 42nd Street became high-rise office districts, and high-rise residential buildings appeared near Central Park. Park Commissioner and City Construction Coordinator Robert Moses began a rapid park expansion program under Mayor Fiorello La Guardia in 1934, increasing park space by a third in two years and planning the 1939 World's Fair at Flushing Meadow. La Guardia and Moses brought New York City into the automobile age with the construction of the Triborough Bridge; they approved the submergence of the last of the old elevated railways and oversaw construction of Laguardia Airport, the largest Works Progress Administration project in the country.
The Great Depression put a halt to most development for 20 years, but Rockefeller Center was built throughout the 1930s, proving that New York would continue to be the commercial capital of the world.

Postwar Prosperity and Preservation – Real estate awoke from its Depression-induced slumber in the late 1940s and New York began to build skyscrapers in the new International style, which eschewed ornament and setbacks for a boxlike slab set in an open plaza. Appropriately, one of these skyscrapers was the United Nations Headquarters, designed in 1947 by an international committee. The 1952 Lever House by **Skidmore, Owings & Merrill** introduced both the slab-plaza form and the new technology of the glass curtain wall, which soon achieved its clearest expression in the 1956 Seagram Building by **Ludwig Mies van der Rohe**. The style defined 1960s prosperity in buildings like the Marine Midland Bank (1967, Skidmore, Owings & Merrill).
Fulfilling its growing role as a world cultural mecca, Manhattan played host to innovative designs like Frank Lloyd Wright's spiraling study in white concrete, the Solomon R. Guggenheim Museum, a landmark of Modernism. The Whitney Museum of American Art (1966, Marcel Breuer) employed concrete in the very different vocabulary of a menacing Brutalist overhang, while the sensuous curves of Eero Saarinen's 1962 TWA Terminal at John F. Kennedy Airport were an international sensation.
Robert Moses continued to rebuild the

R. Corbel/MICHELIN

Lever House

city under a succession of mayors, creating a ring of expressways around the city, demolishing "slum" areas in urban renewal efforts and constructing tunnels and bridges that were later blamed for inducing blight. The continued rebuilding finally provoked public outcry against the demolition of Penn Station in 1962. Although the station was destroyed, the city passed one of the nation's strongest landmarks laws in 1965, extending protection over the next 30 years to some 19,000 buildings. Grand Central Terminal's attempt to demolish its landmark building led to the 1978 Supreme Court case upholding landmarks laws throughout the US.
Modernism reached its Manhattan apogee with the twin towers of the World Trade Center, encompassing an unprecedented 10 million square feet of office space. Post-Modernism arrived with the dramatic roofline of the 1978 Citicorp Center (Hugh Stubbins & Assocs.) and **Philip Johnson**'s 1982 AT&T Headquarters, with its famous Chippendale top. Other notable post-Modern building features include the mirror-glass facades of the Jacob Javits Convention Center (1986, I.M. Pei & Partners) and the varied roof designs of Cesar Pelli's several World Financial Center buildings (1985-88). The late 1990s have ushered in an era of Entertainment Architecture, an eclectic post-Modernism that revels in layered facades, dramatic lighting, and signage that seems to explode from the traditional wall plane. Not surprisingly, Times Square, where lights and signs are the rule, features numerous examples of this architectural playfulness. Office buildings in the area have been growing more playful, too, as seen in the collage of styles and geometries that make up the Fox and Fowle's Condé Nast

Building (1999) and the Reuters Building (2001) on opposite sides of Times Square. The new Westin Hotel (Arquitectonica, 2002) explodes in color: its tower, cleft in two from top to bottom, sets blue glass against vivid orange-pink.

Major civic showpieces befitting the city's renaissance include James Polshek's eye-catching sphere-in-a-glass-cube design for the Museum of Natural History's Rose Center for Space and Earth (2000) and the development of a "new" Penn Station, using the neighboring Beaux-Arts General Post Office building designed by McKim, Mead, and White. Renzo Piano's entry won the *New York Times'* competition for the newspaper's new headquarters—to be built, of course, in the Times Square area.

Undoubtedly, the project foremost in the city's mind is the rebuilding of the 16-acre World Trade Center site. In February 2003 Daniel Libeskind, a Polish-born architect who grew up in the Bronx, was chosen to be the lead architect for the complex of buildings that will replace the World Trade Center. Libeskind's design features a tower that soars to 1,776ft, representing the year that America gained her independence.

Architectural Glossary

Dutch Colonial (1620–1700) – Colonial architectural styles were imitations of their European contemporaries, modified slightly in deference to materials and climate, where applicable. Dutch architecture during the 17C and 18C was characterized by tall, narrow buildings with stepped-gable rooflines, familiar from the streets and *grachten* (canals) of Amsterdam and other port cities, where homes were taxed on their frontage. Farm *(bouwerie)* estates took their cues from the Dutch countryside, with sloping gambrel roofs and columned porches, as seen in the surviving Dyckman House in Manhattan and Wyckoff House in Brooklyn.

Georgian (1720–1790) – English Colonial architecture adopted the Renaissance interpretations of Classical architecture popular in the England of George I and George II, which emphasized symmetry and decorum. Frame, brick and stone houses featured hipped or sloping roofs with the gable end on the side, symmetrical window openings and a prominent central entrance, often ornamented with sidelights and a transom. The Van Cortlandt House is a good example. In larger public buildings, the style adopted more of the columns and pediments of its Classical ancestors, as seen in St. Paul's Chapel.

Federal (1780–1830) – Federal is the term used to describe the more robust and Roman interpretation of Georgian architecture adopted by the newly freed colonies at the end of the 18C. These buildings saw a more liberal use of Classical columns and pediments, especially on entrance doorways, which often sported fanlights, and an occasional balustrade rimming the roofline. New York's City Hall of 1811 represents a lovely example of the style.

Greek Revival (1820–1850) – The dramatic expansion of American democracy across the continent led to an architecture based on the pedimented, symmetrical orders of Classical Greek temples. Large public buildings often sported a lantern or cupola, with a two-story colonnaded facade. Vernacular versions included a low attic story; shallow roof; Doric, Ionic or Corinthian columns; and a pediment over the entrance. The Federal Hall National Memorial on Wall Street is a textbook Greek temple.

Gothic Revival (1840–1880) – Popular in England from the beginning of the 19C, the picturesque, asymmetrical forms of Gothic Revival facades often included towers, battlements and pointed-arch windows and gables. Linked to the Romantic movement, the style laid the basis for later picturesque movements like the Queen Anne. Smaller homes had intricately detailed bargeboards at the eaves and vertical siding, while larger homes and commercial buildings might include battlements, spires and gargoyles. Derived principally from medieval European cathedrals, the style was used for churches to great effect, as seen in Richard Upjohn's Trinity Church.

Italianate (1840–1880) – By mid-century, the Italianate style—with its heavy cornices and large brackets, decorated window lintels and convenient, rectangular massing—became the American standard for homes and commercial buildings. Based on more ornamental Renaissance forms than its staid Georgian cousin, the style featured tall, narrow windows with rounded arches often including incised or relief ornament, and high-stooped entrances accentuating the vertical rhythm of the style. Lower stoops typified the Anglo-Italianate style, adapted to Manhattan's narrow building lots. Executed in frame, brick and stone, the style is the basis for both New York brownstones and the typical cast-iron commercial facades, seen clearly in the E.V. Haughwout Building in lower Manhattan. More elaborate homes adopted the Italian-villa variant, with a Classical cupola, rusticated corner quoins, pediments and paired or arcaded windows.

Second Empire (1860–1880) – Inspired by Baron Haussmann's redesign of Paris in the 1850s, this grandiose style is characterized by a short, steeply-pitched mansard roof pierced by dormer windows. Generally symmetrical facades include quoined corners, projecting bays, windows flanked by pilasters, balustrades and an abundance of

Classical decoration. Often mansard roofs were added to Italianate buildings in a close approximation of the style. Good examples include the former Arnold Constable and Lord & Taylor stores on Broadway.

Romanesque Revival (1860–1900) – Suggestive of medieval castles, the round arches, deeply inset window and door openings, and rough stone finishes of the Romanesque style inspired architects attempting to create a sense of permanence in the rapidly changing landscape of industrial America. The style was refined by Boston architect H.H. Richardson and helped define American architecture. The original City of Brooklyn Firehouse on Jay Street and the American Museum of Natural History are excellent examples of the style.

Queen Anne (1880–1905) – This style is the one most commonly identified as "Victorian," with its asymmetrical composition, exuberant ornamentation and picturesque design marked by conical towers, projecting bays and elaborately decorated dormers and gables. The style is seen primarily in residential architecture like the Henderson Place Historic District.

Chicago School (1885–1905) – The new structural technology of the steel frame allowed for the development of the first skyscrapers in Chicago in the 1880s. The design of these buildings celebrated their engineering and purpose, summed up by Louis Sullivan's phrase "Form follows function" and expressed in a gridlike facade of brick or terra-cotta, pierced by large panes of glass. The earliest skyscrapers adopted elements of Queen Anne and Romanesque design and by the late 1890s incorporated the Beaux-Arts as well. Sullivan's 12-story Bayard-Condict Building (1899) on Bleecker Street bears the architect's characteristic foliate ornamentation.

Neoclassical or Beaux-Arts (1890–1920) – As architecture became an established profession in the 19C, a study of Classical orders at Paris' famous École des Beaux-Arts became de rigueur. At the same time, the success of Chicago's 1893 World's Columbian Exposition popularized the monumental forms of the Roman republic. Unlike the simpler Greek Revival style, Beaux-Arts architecture is more ornamental and sumptuous. Arched and arcaded windows, balustrades at every level, grand staircases, applied columns, decorative swags, garlands and even statuary embellish the edifices. The New York Public Library (1911), Grand Central Terminal (1913) and US Custom House (1907) at Bowling Green are premier examples of the style. Daniel Burnham's 1902 Flatiron Building made the style popular for skyscrapers.

Eclectic Revivals (1900–1925) – The plasticity of terra-cotta and the search for appropriate forms to herald the dawn of the American empire made a wide range of historical styles achievable and popular in the first three decades of the 20C. The Beaux-Arts evolved into Georgian Revival and Renaissance Revival styles used for clubs, town houses, hotels and apartment buildings. Gothic Revival distinguished schools like Hunter College and came to be called Collegiate Gothic. Colonial Revival was the preferred suburban house style, and Moorish, Tudor, Egyptian and Chinese designs encrusted numerous buildings, especially theaters. The increasing eclecticism of skyscraper design literally reached a new height with Cass Gilbert's Gothic-inspired Woolworth Building.

Art Deco/Moderne (1925–1940) – Rejecting the historical ornament applied to commercial buildings in the 1910s, Art Deco first appeared as a style of decoration during the 1925 "Exposition Internationale des Arts Décoratifs et Industriels Modernes" in Paris. New York's 1916 zoning law, which called for skyscrapers to "step back" to provide light and air to the street, helped define the architectural aspects of Art Deco, which utilized setbacks, recessed windows and spandrels, and continuous piers to emphasize verticality. Designed in smooth stone or shiny terra-cotta surfaces, edifices featured highly stylized decorative and sculptural elements in low relief with a pronounced muscularity and abstraction. The Chrysler Building, Empire State Building and Rockefeller Center are landmark examples.

International Style (1930–1970) – Applied ornament was abandoned altogether for sleek, sculptural lines in buildings, furniture and other designed objects, summarized by Mies van der Rohe's dictum "Less is more." Concrete, glass and steel were celebrated in buildings with box-like massing set in open plazas. Exterior walls of glass and steel derived their design from proportion and materials alone, allowing the structures to express their function. Lever House by Skidmore, Owings & Merrill and the Seagram Building by Mies van der Rohe are famous early International-style high rises.

Post-Modern (1975–present) – This style is recognizable by its cavalier application of historical references and materials to modern steel-frame buildings. Surfaces of stone and mirrored glass are generally more colorful and modulated than their rigid and severe International-style predecessors, and elements of Classical architecture reappear on a grand scale. The AT&T Headquarters (1982, Johnson & Burgee) introduced post-Modernism to the nation with its whimsical "Chippendale" roof, and the style continues with the various rooflines of Cesar Pelli's World Financial Center and the "bright-lights" facades of the new Times Square.

Sports

Since the 1920s New York's teams and its athletes have played in the limelight of the world's media capital. First there was **Babe Ruth** (1895-1948), who came to the city in 1920 as a great ballplayer and in a few years became an immortal. The Babe's **Yankees** are, of course, the prime symbol of the city's dominance, but are only one of a total of nine professional sports teams in the four major sports—baseball, basketball, football, and hockey (Los Angeles and Chicago have five teams apiece). All nine have their fans; all nine have won championships. But the central theme of New York sports life is the power and pressure and scale of the city itself. Gotham is the world's biggest stage, where athletes come to be made or to be broken. To the city's sports fans, who pride themselves to be among the most knowledgeable—and unforgiving—the question is not what a player has done in another city, but rather "can he make it here?"

Baseball – The very first baseball games were played in Manhattan in the 1840s by players such as Alexander Joy Cartwright who formalized the layout of the diamond and the rules of the game. In October 1845, he and others organized themselves as the **New York Knickerbockers**, the game's first team. On June 19, 1846 in Hoboken, New Jersey, the first prearranged contest took place between the Knickerbockers and the New York Nine. After the Civil War, as baseball gained popularity, professional leagues sprouted up around the country. The city entered the big leagues for good with the formation of the **New York Giants** in 1883, and by 1924 the team had won 10 pennants in 20 years under manager John McGraw. The Polo Grounds, their horseshoe-shaped home in upper Manhattan (shared with the Yankees until Babe Ruth's popularity led McGraw to evict them), was the site of one of baseball's enduring moments: "the Catch," made by **Willie Mays**, running full speed, back turned to the plate, in the 1954 World Series. The Giants' nemesis, the **Brooklyn Dodgers**, lost when they were bad and lost in heartbreaking fashion when they were good. No matter. Brooklynites flocked to Ebbets Field to root for "dem bums." In 1947 **Jackie Robinson** (1919-72) broke baseball's color line, heralding the civil rights movement. Robinson, Duke Snider and the Boys of Summer were the class of the league in the 1950s. Noted for their succession of strong arms (Tom Seaver, Jerry Koosman, Dwight Gooden) at pitcher-friendly Shea Stadium, the expansion **Mets** are loved less for their dominance than for their underdog spirit and startling moments of grace—notably their miraculous come-from-behind victory in the "Bill Buckner game" of the 1986 World Series. The **Yankees** (who were, like Babe Ruth, born in Baltimore) moved to New York in 1903, their third season. In 100 years the team has won 39 American League pennants and 26 World Series. Taking advantage of Yankee Stadium's short right-field porch, built to accommodate left-handed Ruth, the "Bronx Bombers" have long relied on the home run. The team's pantheon of sluggers—the Babe, Lou Gehrig, Joe DiMaggio, Mickey Mantle, Yogi Berra, Reggie Jackson—have all achieved a fame that transcends the game. Since the 1996 arrival of manager **Joe Torre** and young shortstop **Derek Jeter**, the latest Yankees dynasty has won six pennants and four World Series.

Football – On November 6, 1869, in New Brunswick, New Jersey, Rutgers and Princeton played the first intercollegiate football game before 100 spectators. Rutgers won, 6-4. New Yorkers didn't catch football fever, however, until 1925, when Tim Mara started the **Giants** in the fledgling NFL. That year, 70,000 filled the Polo Grounds to see the team take on Red Grange and the Chicago Bears. Season tickets to "Big Blue" games, at Yankee Stadium, and since 1976 at Giants Stadium in the Meadowlands, have been handed down through the generations. Fittingly, the team is still owned by Wellington Mara, Tim's son. One of football history's best defensive players, **Lawrence Taylor** led the "Jints" to two titles in 1986 and 1990. The team's loss in the 2001 Super Bowl to the Baltimore Ravens evoked memories of the 1958 Championship Game, "the Greatest Football Game Ever Played," a seesaw battle it lost in overtime to the Baltimore Colts. The underdog **Jets'** 1969 Super Bowl victory over, once again, the Colts, "guaranteed" by flamboyant quarterback "Broadway" **Joe Namath**, legitimized the upstart AFL and paved the way for the leagues' eventual merger. Recent years have been marked by turmoil on the field and in the front office.

Basketball – New York basketball is first and foremost a street game. Only blizzards interrupt half-court games of "21." Winners play; losers sit. And in the city's playgrounds, where legends like **Connie Hawkins** made their reputations, flair counts. Not surprisingly, New York has sent a stream of flashy point guards to the pros, from **Bob Cousy** to **Stephon Marbury**. St. John's has regularly appeared in the NCAA and NIT tourneys since the 1940s and has seen a number of top-notch players turn professional. Atop the city's hoops world sits the **Knicks**, an original NBA franchise whose legendary early-1970s squad, led by Willis Reed, Walt "Clyde" Frazier, and "Dollar" Bill Bradley, twice won championships. After a period of decline, the team rebounded with the hiring of Pat Riley as coach in 1991; fans flocked to Madison Square Garden to cheer (and boo) center **Pat Ewing** and the intimidating, defense-oriented Knicks.

The Subway Series

From 1947 to 1956, coinciding with the city's postwar golden era, the Yankees played seven (and won six) Subway Series (World Series matches involving only NYC teams) against the Dodgers and Giants. In 1951 no fan was left out: Giant Bobby Thomson's "shot heard round the world" off Dodger Ralph Branca decided a three-game playoff for the pennant. Then, in the World Series, with Brooklyn fans' approval, the Yankees beat the Giants. The Dodgers' 1955 victory over the Yanks marked Brooklyn's brightest moment, a mood captured by the *Daily News*' front page: a drawing of an ecstatic hobo under the head-line "Who's a Bum?" The Yankees won the 1956 rematch, and a year later, the Giants and Dodgers moved west, prompting, fans presume, the city's decline. New York's recent resurgence seemed to augur the Subway Series' return. And in 2000 it came to be. The Mets assumed the Dodgers' role of outer-borough underdog, and fans hoped for miracles. Fiery Mets manager Bobby Valentine, son-in-law of Ralph Branca, faced off against his stoic coun-terpart, onetime Mets manager Joe Torre, a Brooklyn kid who saw Don Larsen's perfect game against the Dodgers in the 1956 Series. The city turned inward. A base hit or clean stop cheered on the Grand Concourse was met with stony silence in Astoria and Bensonhurst. And vice versa. The old days had returned to New York. Predictably, the Yankees won in five games.

The Yankees win World Series 2000

Agence France Presse/CORBIS

Born with the ABA in 1967, the **Nets**, featuring the gravity-defying "Dr. J," **Julius Erving**, enjoyed early success and a few ABA titles. The team entered the NBA in 1976, then moved to New Jersey, where they remained on the periphery of the city's sports con-sciousness until 2002, when they rocketed to the NBA finals as the Knicks team disintegrated.

Hockey – One of the NHL's "original six" teams, the **Rangers**, and the team's intensely loyal fans, infamous for their unrelenting and slanderous chants, had suffered through a 54-year drought between championships when **Mark Messier**, exiled from Edmonton, led the squad to a Stanley Cup in 1994. The **Islanders**, an expansion team formed in 1972, quickly assembled a nucleus of eventual Hall of Famers (Bryan Trottier, Mike Bossy, Denis Potvin) whose graceful play won four straight Stanley Cups in the early 1980s and helped transform the game's roughhouse image. In years since, hard times have befallen the Islanders faithful at Nassau Coliseum. The **Devils** moved to New Jersey from Colorado in 1982. Their tenacious defense, spearheaded by goalie **Martin Brodeur**, has brought them two championships and a sizable following.

Boxing – **John L. Sullivan** (1858-1918) fought at the first Madison Square Garden, located in, yes, Madison Square, in 1883. In subsequent years and incarnations, the Garden became the country's boxing mecca. The current Garden was the site of the famous 1971 **Ali-Frazier** fight. Yankee Stadium also hosted key bouts, including **Joe Louis'** (1914-81) victory over German **Max Schmeling**, before 70,000. The ascendance of Las Vegas and Atlantic City as boxing locales spelled the end of the city's preeminence.

Other – The Belmont Stakes, the third leg of thoroughbred racing's Triple Crown, is held at Belmont Park, on Long Island. The National Tennis Center in Flushing Meadows hosts the US Open, a grand-slam event. Lifelong New Yorker **John McEnroe**, famous for his big mouth, short fuse, and quirky, brilliant play, has won the tournament four times, to the delight of local fans. Brazilian soccer legend **Pélé**, playing for the Cosmos, electrified New York in the mid-1970s, though local enthusiasm, and the league itself, petered out a few years later. The famed New York City Marathon, held the first Sunday in November, draws 30,000 runners and more than 2 million spectators.

New York in the Movies

King Kong
(1933) ....Merrian C. Cooper

Miracle on 34th Street
(1947) ....George Seaton

On the Waterfront
(1954)............................Elia Kazan

West Side Story ....
(1961).......R. Wise and J. Robbins

Breakfast at Tiffany's
(1961)....................Blake Edwards

America, America
(1963)............................Elia Kazan

Funny Girl
(1968).....................William Wyler

Midnight Cowboy
(1968)................John Schlesinger

Hello Dolly!
(1969) ....Gene Kelly

The French Connection
(1971) ....William Friedkin

Next Stop, Greenwich Village
(1976) ....Paul Mazursky

Taxi Driver
(1976) ....Martin Scorsese

Hair
(1979).......................Milos Forman

Manhattan
(1979) ....Woody Allen

Arthur
(1981) ....Steve Gordon

Ragtime
(1981) ....Milos Forman

The Cotton Club
(1984) ....Francis F. Coppola

Ghostbusters
(1984) ....Ivan Reitman

Broadway Danny Rose
(1985) ....Woody Allen

Desperately Seeking Susan
(1985) ....Susan Seidelman

After Hours
(1985) ....Martin Scorsese

Hannah and Her Sisters
(1986) ....Woody Allen

Moonstruck
(1987) ....Norman Jewison

Bright Lights, Big City
(1988) ....James Bridges

She's Gotta Have It
(1988)..................................Spike Lee

When Harry Met Sally
(1989) ....Rob Reiner

Crimes and Misdemeanors
(1989) ....Woody Allen

New York Stories
(1989) F.F. Coppola, W. Allen, M. Scorsese

Goodfellas
(1990) ....Martin Scorsese

Jungle Fever (1991)...............Spike Lee

The Fisher King (1991) ......Terry Gilliam

The Wedding Banquet (1993) .....Ang Lee

Bullets Over Broadway
(1994) ....Woody Allen

City Hall (1995).............Harold Becker

Smoke
(1995) ....Wayne Wang

The First Wives' Club
(1996) ....Hugh Wilson

The Mirror Has Two Faces
(1996) ....Barbra Streisand

As Good as It Gets
(1997) ....James L. Brooks

Men in Black
(1997) ....Barry Sonnenfeld

You've Got Mail
(1998)............................Nora Ephron

The Siege
(1998) ....Edward Zwick

Pollock
(2000)..................................Ed Harris

Gangs of New York
(2002) ....Martin Scorsese

Spider-Man
(2002) ....Sam Raimi

Woody Allen and Diane Keaton in a scene from *Manhattan*

Little Italy

CARUSO'S FRUIT

WHOLESALE · CARUSO

SHORT...

SHOES REPAIR

補鞋

© Scott Borrow

Address Book

Where to Eat

Rest assured that the quality and variety of New York City's cuisine equals the city's prestige as a financial and cultural center. While top restaurants command jet-set prices, the city's ethnic restaurants or ubiquitous delis will reward you with reasonably priced delicacies and sandwiches piled high with pastrami, prosciutto or whatever your favorite sandwich filling may be. In a city as well known for its slices of pizza as it is for internationally famous chefs, diners know the pleasure of experiencing some of the world's best cuisine in all its magnificence. New Yorkers wouldn't expect anything less.

The venues listed below were selected for their ambience, location and/or value for money. Rates indicate the average cost of an appetizer, an entrée and dessert for one person (not including tax, gratuity or beverages). Most restaurants are open daily—except where noted—and accept major credit cards. Call for information regarding reservations and opening hours.

Additional restaurants are listed throughout this guide in the form of Digressions. See Index for a complete listing of eateries described in the text.

$$$$ over $50	$$ $15-$30
$$$ $30-$50	$ less than $15

■ The Scoop on New York City Restaurants:

Since April 2003, restaurants, bars and clubs in New York City have been made smoke-free by law. Although **jackets** may not be required, gentlemen might feel more comfortable wearing one in the more expensive establishments. **Reservations** are highly recommended. Gratuities are generally not included on the bill; a **tip** of 15 to 20 percent is considered standard.

Luxury

Fiamma Osteria – *206 Spring St. (between Sixth Ave. & Sullivan St.), SoHo.* ☎ *212-653-0100. www.brguestrestaurants.com.* $$$$ **Italian**. Reflecting its chic location, glass elevators whisk patrons—who have included Harrison Ford, Bette Midler and Billy Joel—to one of the three levels of this tastefully decorated *osteria*. The waitstaff is stylishly outfitted by Nicole Miller. Dishes, prepared with the freshest of ingredients, change seasonally, and the wine list includes more than 475 labels. Homemade pastas are in a class by themselves. Rosemary-accented squab with porcini mushrooms, sautéed loin of lamb wrapped in basil, and *branzino dell'Atlantico* (pan-seared wild striped bass) show off chef Michael White's talents to great advantage. Desserts are irresistibly decadent, and as a special bonus, small boxes of chocolate are offered as a parting gift.

Firebird Russian Restaurant – *365 W. 46th St. (between Eighth & Ninth Aves.), Midtown west side. Closed Mon.* ♿ ☎ *212-586-0244.* $$$$ **Russian**. This block of West 46th Street is known as Restaurant Row, and Firebird is one of its hottest spots. Tsar Nicholas would no doubt feel as comfortable in these three elegantly restored town houses as he did in the Winter Palace, and would probably enjoy the cuisine as much, too—with dishes like Ukrainian borscht, poached sturgeon and chicken Kiev, not to mention seven kinds of caviar. It's a fun place to watch the pretheater crowd before walking over to a Broadway show. Or stay to catch the complementary jazz at the adjacent Firebird Lounge.

Gotham Bar and Grill – *12 E.12th St.(between Fifth Ave. & University Pl.), Greenwich Village.* ☎ *212-620-4020. www.gothambarandgrill.com.* $$$$ **New American**. Gotham is consistently rated one of New York's finest restaurants and for good reason. Executive chef Alfred Portale, who studied in France under Michel Geurard, fits New York to a tee. The pioneer of vertical cuisine, his innovative towering "skyscraper" presentations are a treat for the eye as well as the palate. A seafood salad is a high-rise concoction of lobster, scallops, Japanese octopus, squid and avocado, crowned with a vivid ruffle of purple lettuce. Rack of lamb perches upright on a bed of Swiss chard. Even the rich chocolate desserts stand at attention. The dining room is appropriately high-ceilinged and contains a replica of the Statue of Liberty. The best bargain in town is Gotham's prix-fixe lunch—priced at $25, it's a third of what dinner would cost.

Keens Steakhouse – *72 W. 36th St. (between Fifth & Sixth Aves.), Midtown. Closed Sun. Dinner only Sat & Sun.* ♿ ☎ *212-947-3636. www.keenssteak house.com.* $$$$ **American**. A carnivore's delight, Keens serves up big slabs of prime rib, steaks and lamb in a historic setting. The restaurant opened in 1885,

Bullmoose Room at Keens Steakhouse

when Herald Square—which is around the corner—was still the city's Theater District. Keens started out as a men's dining, drinking and pipe-smoking club for the city's movers and shakers at the turn of the century, and hanging from the ceiling is the world's biggest collection of churchwarden clay pipes.

Le Bernardin – *155 W. 51st St. (between Avenue of the Americas & Seventh Ave.), Midtown. Closed Sun & holidays.*   ✆ *212-554-1515. www. lebernardin.com.* **$$$$ French**. Expect to spend serious money at this spacious, elegant restaurant, widely acclaimed as one of the city's best—it will be worth it. With white tablecloths and white-glove service, Le Bernardin serves a prix-fixe menu that comes almost entirely from the sea. Prepare yourself for delicately orchestrated servings of roast baby lobster tail on asparagus and cèpe risotto, saffron ravioli of herbed crab meat or a pot-au-feu of black bass accompanied by a julienne of fresh ginger. The three-course dinner costs about $79 per person without wine, and six-course tasting menus range from $95 to $130 per person. *Jackets required.*

Next Door Nobu – *105 Hudson St. (at Franklin St.), TriBeCa. Dinner only.*   ✆ *212-334-4445. www.myriadrestaurantgroup.com.* **$$$$ Japanese**. Although it's nearly impossible to get a table at the highly acclaimed Nobu, you can sample essentially the same food at a slightly lower cost at Next Door Nobu located right next to the parent restaurant. The emphasis here is on texture— its well-crafted sushi bar of black river rocks, tables of scorched pine and Indonesian market-basket light fixtures harmonize with the sensual pleasures of clawless lobsters, sea urchins, seafood udon (noodles) and mochi ice-cream balls. Next Door Nobu doesn't take reservations; go early to avoid a long wait in line.

Park Avenue Cafe – *100 E. 63rd St., Upper East Side.* ✆ *212-644-1900. www.parkavenuecafe.com.* **$$$$ American**. Whimsical touches of Americana—a shelf of antique cookie jars, a mural of the US flag, sheaves of wheat—fill this contemporary, Upper East Side restaurant. Chef David Burke's acclaimed menu lists signatures like house-cured pastrami salmon and rack of lamb with potato, leek and goat cheese cannelloni. Don't skip the chocolate Park Bench, complete with lamppost.

San Domenico NY – *240 Central Park South (between Seventh Ave. & Broadway.), Midtown.* ✆ *212-265-5959. www.restaurant.com/sandomenicony.* **$$$$ Italian**. One of your best souvenirs from a visit to New York will be memories of dining at San Domenico. The signature dish, *uovo in raviolo al burro nocciola tartufato* (raviolo of soft egg yolk in truffle butter), delicately satisfies, the popular *branzino all'acquapazza con fregola sarda* (fillet of seabass poached in a fish and tomato broth) reflects the importance placed on the exceptional quality of ingredients, and the remarkable wine list is sure to please the most demanding oenophile. Carrara marble, Poltrona Frau banquettes and Cassina chairs make for a decor so discreetly elegant it takes a moment to realize just how refined it is.

Courtesy San Domenico

Sea urchin ravioli at San Domenico, New York

Mid-Range

The Boathouse at Central Park – *72nd St. & Park Dr. N., Central Park.* ☎ *212-517-2233.* **$$$ New American.** One of the city's best-kept secrets is hidden inside Central Park. The lakeside eatery switches from its outdoor veranda in summer to a ski lodge-style interior room during colder months. Dishes reflect the city's melting-pot culture: Atlantic salmon is pan-seared and jumbo lump crab cakes are served with cornichon and caper remoulade.

Bridge Café – *279 Water St. (at Dover St.), Downtown.* ♿ ☎ *212-227-3344. www.bridgecafe.com.* **$$$ American.** The Bridge Café serves up elegant dishes reflecting the chef's preference for seasonal fare using regional ingredients—pan-roasted lobster with heirloom apple and celery root salad and spicy lobster broth; saffron-poached halibut with puréed and caramelized cauliflower and Osetra caviar. It also serves up lots of history: sitting next to the Brooklyn Bridge and a few blocks from South Street Seaport, this little red wooden building dates back to 1794. The restaurant has been serving customers continuously since 1847, when a pub opened here—making it New York's oldest drinking establishment.

Carmine's – *200 W. 44th St. (between Seventh & Eighth Aves.), Midtown,* ☎ *212-221-3800; 2450 Broadway (between 90th & 91st Sts.), Upper West Side,* ☎ *212-362-2200. www.carminesnyc.com.* ♿ **$$$ Italian.** If you're traveling in a group, this is a good place to come for a hearty dinner of southern Italian favorites like veal saltimbocca, chicken scarpariello and shrimp scampi. Hefty portions are dished up family-style, so sharing is de rigueur at Carmine's. The midtown location, in the heart of the theater district, will only take reservations for groups of six or more after 6pm, and a similar policy is sometimes imposed at the uptown restaurant. But there's plenty of space at the bar if you have to wait.

Cub Room/Cub Room Café – *Prince & Sullivan Sts., SoHo.* ♿ ☎ *212-677-4100 (Cub Room). www.cubroom.com.* **$$$. American.** The Cub Room *(entrance on Sullivan St.)* is the more elegant of this popular dining duo, serving up New American specialties like filet mignon with Cognac, raisin and potato gratin, and seared scallops with beef short ribs, potato cream and onion marmalade. For a more relaxed and less expensive option, walk around the corner to the **Cub Room Café $$** *(entrance on Prince St.)*, a neighborhood spot with sandwiches and other casual fare, along with a busy bar.

E.A.T. – *1064 Madison Ave. (between 80th & 81st Sts.), Upper East Side.* ☎ *212-772-0022. www.elizabar.com.* **$$$ Deli.** This restaurant makes a good lunch stop between visits to nearby museums like the Metropolitan and the Whitney. As an upscale deli befitting its affluent neighborhood, E.A.T. serves excellent—if somewhat pricey—sandwiches and soups. Dinner offerings include cold plates, pasta, seafood, meat and poultry dishes, with a good selection of wines. There's also a full-service deli here, in case you want a picnic lunch to take to Central Park, just a block away.

Josephina – *1900 Broadway (at 63rd St.), Upper West Side.* ☎ *212-799-1000. www.josephinanyc.com.* **$$$ New American.** This pleasant restaurant across the street from Lincoln Center is often crowded before performances *(6pm–8pm)*. The focus here is on healthy, natural cuisine with interesting nondairy, fish and vegetarian options as well as meat dishes. The roasted butternut squash soup is a favorite appetizer, while entrées include items like goat cheese ravioli, pan-roasted farm chicken, sesame-coated yellowfin tuna and standards such as rack of lamb and filet mignon. During summer, try a sidewalk table for Broadway people-watching.

Marseille – *630 Ninth Ave. (at 44th St.), Hell's Kitchen/Clinton.* ♿ ☎ *212-333-2233. www.marseilleny.com.* **$$$ Mediterranean.** This bustling bistro within walking distance of Times Square is a terrific spot for pre-and post-theater dining. Serving French cuisine with Moroccan, Turkish and Tunisian overtones, Marseille's Art Deco setting with its pastel arches, handmade floor tiles and old zinc bar makes you think you're on the set of *Casablanca*. The chef is not afraid to experiment with ingredients: seared Moroccan tuna with a spicy crust of peppercorns, sesame, cumin and pistachio typifies his artistry. And would you believe a crunchy peanut butter tart with celery sorbet for dessert? Broadway headliners often drop by between and after performances.

Mesa Grill – *102 Fifth Ave. (between 15th & 16th Sts.), Union Square/Gramercy Park.* ♿ ☎ *212-807-7400. www.mesagrill.com.* **$$$ Southwestern**. Southwestern cuisine doesn't mean just tacos and burritos, as you'll find in this often-crowded bi-level restaurant. It does mean a hint of spice and Mexican influence, as in the yellow-corn-crusted chile relleno, the New Mexican spice-rubbed pork tenderloin or the crispy whole striped bass, and in side dishes like cilantro-pesto mashed potatoes or sweet potato tamale. Celebrate North America with the all-American wine list and fine selection of Mexican tequilas.

Rock Center Café – *20 W. 50th St. (at Rockefeller Plaza), Midtown.* ♿ ☎ *212-332-7620. www.restaurantassociates.com.* **$$$ American**. Tucked into the recently renovated lower level of Rockefeller Center, the Rock Center Café offers comfortable seating for weary shoppers with its spacious banquettes and upholstered chairs. During winter, it also provides a unique view outside its huge windows: the skaters on the Rockefeller Center rink. The menu lists a selection of pastas as well as American standards like salmon, prime rib, chicken and steaks.

Sushi Samba – *87 Seventh Ave. South (Barrow St.), Greenwich Village.* ♿ ☎ *212-691-7885. www.sushisamba.com.* **$$$ South American**. Brazilian flavors, Japanese technique and Peruvian culinary tradition all on one plate? That's what you'll find at lively Sushi Samba. Join celebs like Gwyneth Paltrow, Tara Reid and Chelsea Clinton and chow down on stellar sushi, South American beef maki rolls filled with hearts of palm, carrots and grilled asparagus, or blue cornmeal-crusted calamari with tamarind sauce, tomato sauce and plantains. Start with a Sakegria, the house cocktail (a punch made with plum sake, red and white wine, champagne and fruit juices), and end with a warm chocolate banana cake topped with maple-butter ice cream. From Thursday to Sunday, you can groove to the live Latin DJ.

Galaxy Global Eatery – *15 Irving Pl. (at E. 15th St.), Union Square area.* ☎ *212-777-3631. www.galaxyglobaleatery.com.* ♿ **$$ International**. This unusual little eatery, with its black decor, sprinkle of stars across the ceiling and statue of Buddha at the entrance, serves up creative and inexpensive dishes with truly international influences. Filipino Pork Adobo to Thai pizza to Native American Hempanadas (that's the correct spelling—the owners have a particular affection for hemp, which finds its way into several menu items like the Hempnut Crusted Catfish and the Hempnut Veggie Burger) are just a few of the unique items on the menu. It's a block east of Union Square.

Heartland Brewery – *1285 Avenue of the Americas (at 51st St.), Rockefeller Center area.* ☎ *212-582-8244; 35 Union Square W. (between 16th & 17th Sts.),* ☎ *212-645-3400. www.heartlandbrewery.com.* ♿ **$$ American**. Typical of the many US microbreweries and brewpubs that have sprung up in the past decade, the Heartland Brewery is best known for its home-brewed American beers and ales, such as Cornhusker Lager, Smiling Pumpkin Ale and Farmer John's Oatmeal Stout. The menu is hearty pub-style food—chicken, burgers, fish, ribs and steaks—with a few unusual touches. Ever had a buffalo burger? You can try one at Heartland.

Macelleria – *48 Gansevoort St. (between Greenwich & Washington Sts.), Meatpacking district.* ☎ *212-741-7455.* **$$ Italian**. Housed in a brick-walled reconstructed butcher shop (or *macelleria* in Italian), this engaging trattoria with its brick-walled wine cellar offers an outstanding variety of salami, homemade pastas, meat dishes and Italian wines. The iceberg lettuce wedge with gorgonzola and peppercorn dressing is unique. The authentic Italian green and white tagliolini with peas and prosciutto, and garganelli with oxtail ragu are two of the most popular pastas. And a secret for those whose itinerary doesn't include a classic New York steakhouse, the prime dry-aged Porterhouse for two (the only really expensive dish on Macelleria's menu) is the same beef that's served at the famous Peter Luger's in Brooklyn.

Noho Star – *330 Lafayette St. (at Bleecker St.), East Village.* ♿ ☎ *212-925-0070.* **$$ International**. Situated where the East Village, West Village, Little Italy and SoHo come together, this pleasant, inexpensive restaurant is a good place to stop during an excursion through the area. ("NoHo" stands for north of Houston Street.) Open for breakfast, lunch, dinner and weekend brunch, Noho Star's menu is hard to describe, ranging from sandwiches and burgers to standard American entrées to Asian-influenced dishes to classic Chinese (available at dinner only)— a little bit of something for everyone, as befits its polyglot neighborhood.

Pearl Oyster Bar – *18 Cornelia St. (between W. 4th & Bleecker Sts.), Greenwich Village. Closed Sun.* ☎ *212-691-8211.* **$$ Seafood**. You can't get fresher fish for the price in Manhattan. Pearl Oyster Bar is a small, friendly eatery that caters to the cognoscenti. There are sixteen seats at a long marble counter, where people talk to each other easily, two windowfront tables and a side room. Owner/chef Rebecca Charles' signature dish, a gargantuan lobster roll (chunks of the fresh crustacean moistened with Hellman's mayonnaise and served on a toasted bun), puts many a Maine lobster shack to shame. The menu is limited; New England clam chowder with bacon, several variations of oysters, and smoked Atlantic salmon with johnnycakes and crème fraiche are three popular selections. Regulars know to check the blackboard specials.

Pó – *31 Cornelia St. (between Bleecker St. & W. Fourth Ave.), West Village. Closed Mon.* ♿ ☏ *212-645-2189. www.po-nyc.com.* **$$ Northern Italian.** Pó is the kind of neighborhood restaurant locals wish they lived around the corner from. Specializing in extraordinary Tuscan fare with a well-selected, moderately priced wine list, this snug Italian trattoria makes diners feel like welcome guests at a delightful dinner party. Its value for the money can't be beat: Dinner pastas (think papparadelle with braised rabbit, onion and sage) are only $13. Innovative fresh fish, veal and chicken preparations range about $17. The chef's six-course dinner tasting menu for $40 (less expensive for lunch) is probably the best deal in town. *American Express and cash only.*

Sammy's Roumanian Steak House – *157 Chrystie St. (at Delancey St.), Lower East Side.* ☏ *212-673-0330.* **$$ Jewish.** You don't have to be Jewish to love Sammy's. Diners of all ages and backgrounds come together nightly at this small cellar restaurant to sing, dance, schmooze, be entertained and above all, to eat. Portions are humungous—one order easily feeds two. Start with the hearty chopped liver with all the fixin's—chopped onions, radishes and schmaltz (chicken fat). The hefty garlic-rubbed Roumanian tenderloin is a must. And what would a dinner at Sammy's be without potato latkes, kasha varnishkes, stuffed cabbage and kishka? Forget about calories and cholesterol—they don't count when you're on vacation. Live music starts at 6pm.

Sarabeth's – *423 Amsterdam Ave. (at W. 80th St.), Upper West Side,* ☏ *212-496-6280; 1295 Madison Ave. (at E. 92nd St.), Upper East Side,* ☏ *212-410-7335. www.sarabeth.com.* ♿ **$$ American.** Although Sarabeth's serves breakfast, lunch and dinner, it is most popular in the morning hours and for midday brunch on weekends. Breakfast fare includes porridge, fluffy omelets with a choice of muffin, pancakes and waffles. Try the Four Flowers juice—a blend of banana, pineapple, orange and pomegranate. Sarabeth's also sells a selection of its own baked goods and preserves, and has branches in the Whitney Museum of American Art and in Chelsea Market.

Tamarind – *41-43 E.22 St. (between Broadway & Park Ave.), Flatiron/Gramercy Park.* ♿ ☏ *212-674-7400. www.tamarinde22.com.* **$$ Indian.** Presented in a sophisticated setting amidst a colorful mix of classic textiles and artifacts, Tamarind specializes in haute Indian cuisine. Popular dishes include she-crab soup with nutmeg, saffron and ginger sauce, and lobster cooked with shitake mushrooms, chopped onions, garlic and Indian spices. Nan bread fresh out of the tandoor oven is stuffed with onions and black pepper or dried fruits and nuts. The bread is just as addictive as the spiced-apple samosas with caramel sauce and ginger ice cream. Request a curved banquette in the back room and you'll be treated to service fit for a maharajah.

Pretzels are available from vendors all over the city

Virgil's Real Barbecue – *152 W. 44th St., Midtown.* ♿ ✆ *212-921-9663.* *www.virgilsbbq.com.* **$$ Barbecue.** Southern US barbecue in all its variety, from Texas to North Carolina, is the specialty here. If it can be barbecued or smoked, Virgil's has it—beef, pork, chicken, shrimp, ham. The restaurant barbecues with a blend of hickory, oak and fruitwoods for the best results. This unpretentious, two-story eatery also serves related regional dishes like chicken-fried steak, fried chicken and fried or grilled catfish, and a good selection of beers.

Zen Palate – *34 Union Square (at 16th St.).* ♿ ✆ *212-614-9291. www.zen* *palate.com.* **$$ Vegetarian.** You won't find any meat in the creative menus of the Zen Palates, but you will find substitutes like soy protein, wheat gluten and portobello mushrooms. With locations throughout Manhattan, the restaurants use innovative combinations of Asian and western vegetables and sauces, and give many of their creations haiku-sounding names such as Red Mist, Rose Petals and Shredded Heaven.

Budget

Dim Sum Go Go – *5 E. Broadway (Chatham Square), Chinatown.* ♿ ✆ *212-732-0797.* **$ Chinese.** Don't let the Chinese take-out name throw you. This sleek restaurant is more sophisticated than many of its Uptown counterparts. New wave dim sum is served to order, not on traditional rolling carts. Mushroom and pickled-vegetable dumplings, duck skin and crabmeat wrapped in spinach dough, or chive and shrimp dumplings in a ginger-vinegar dipping sauce are but three of the more than forty choices. Those with heartier appetites will certainly enjoy the steamed halibut under a bed of braised Chinese leeks and celery, or the signature roast chicken with fried garlic stems.

Gonzo – *140 W. 13th St. (between Sixth & Seventh Aves.), Greenwich Village.* ✆ *212-645-4606.* **$ Italian.** Chef/owner Vincent Scotto is responsible for introducing the grilled pizza craze that is sweeping New York. Gonzo's paper-thin pies are chargrilled, not oven-baked, and use bel paese and romano cheeses in place of the traditional mozzarella. Staples like the classic Margherita pizza, made with fresh tomatoes and basil, are undoubtedly delicious, but toppings like corn and mashed potatoes, cumin-scented ricotta, spicy eggplant purée, even watermelon with prosciutto and arugula, are treats that you won't soon forget. Venetian tapas called cichetti are also served in the noisy bi-level dining space. A full-service bar and a menu of pastas, fresh fish, meat and desserts are also available for those not watching their budget.

It's A Wrap – *2012 Broadway (between 68th & 69th Sts.), Upper West Side.* ♿ ✆ *212-362-7922. www.itsawrap.com.* **$ Wraps.** This small restaurant, with locations throughout Manhattan, offers 17 varieties of wraps, both hot and cold. Similar to sandwiches but rolled up in a laffa flat bread, the wraps include six vegetarian versions. Smaller kids' wraps are also available, along with a morning breakfast menu of egg wraps, a daily selection of soups, and a good selection of "smoothies"— shakes made from various combinations of fruits and/or frozen yogurt.

Jackson Hole – *1270 Madison Ave. (at 91st St.), Upper East Side.* ♿ ✆ *212-427-2820. www.jacksonholeburgers.com.* **$ Burgers.** For your basic American hamburger—weighing in at a hefty 7 ounces—you won't find more choices than at Jackson Hole. Burgers come in 31 versions, depending on the toppings selected, ranging from a Texas Burger (with a fried egg) to the California Burger (lettuce,

A sandwich-board menu beckons diners in Little Italy

tomato and mayo). If beef's not to your taste, the restaurant also offers chicken sandwiches in the same varieties, as well as some Mexican dishes, salads and a breakfast menu. Two of the other four locations in Manhattan are located along Second Avenue.

John's Pizzeria – *260 West 44th St. (between Broadway & Eighth Ave.).* ♿ ☎ *212-391-7560.* **$ Pizza.** New York has hundreds of pizzerias, but John's takes the quality of the product up a notch by baking them in brick ovens, with thin crusts, a light touch on the cheese, and fresh vegetables and other toppings. Pizzas come in six-slice or eight-slice sizes. With several locations in Manhattan, John's also offers a selection of salads, pastas and sandwiches, and a big calzone for two people. The 44th Street location is in the middle of the Theater District.

Second Avenue Deli – *156 Second Ave., East Village.* ♿ ☎ *212-677-0606.* **$ Jewish Kosher.** The smell of pickles wafts through the front door at this East Village landmark. Locals from around the city come to the lackluster room for overstuffed pastrami and corned-beef sandwiches on rye. Chopped liver and matzoh-ball soup are touted as the best in town.

Where to Stay

To accommodate its 35 million visitors a year, New York City boasts over 70,000 hotel rooms. The high price of real estate coupled with tremendous demand makes for what can be astronomical room rates. With this in mind, visitors interested in staying in Manhattan will enjoy tremendous variety, from daringly trendy Ian Schrager-Philippe Starck creations to the tradition and elegance of the Plaza. Budget-minded travelers will have success finding quality rooms for considerably lower rates by using the discount brokers listed below. *For general information about hotel chains in New York, see the Accommodations section in the back of this guide.*

The properties listed below were selected for their ambience, location and/or value for money. Prices reflect average cost for a standard double room (two people) in high season (not including any applicable city or state taxes). Room prices may be considerably lower in off-season, and many hotels offer discounted weekend rates. The presence of a swimming pool is indicated by the ⌇ *symbol. The presence of a full-service spa is indicated by the* Spa *symbol.*

$$$$$	over $300		$$	$75-$125
$$$$	$200-$300		$	less than $75
$$$	$125-$200			

■ The Scoop on New York City Hotels:

Quoted rates do not include the city's substantial **hotel tax** of 13.625 percent (for example, with a quoted room rate of $179, you will actually pay $203.39 for that night's stay).

Rate categories below should be taken as a general guideline only. **Rates** can be higher or lower depending on season, day of the week and volume of advance reservations. Prices are generally lower on weekends and from Christmas through March.

Guest **parking** is usually in a nearby garage, and will cost from $20 to $40 per day. More expensive hotels have valet parking.

For **price-shopping**, and to find available rooms during the high season, consider using a rooms broker like Hotel Reservations Network *(www.hoteldiscount.com),* Express Reservations *(www.express-res.com),* Quikbook *(www.quikbook.com)* or Utel *(www.utell.com).*

In-room **telephone charges** can range from 50¢ to as much as $2 for local calls. Be especially prudent when making calls using the hotel's long-distance provider. Some establishments will charge as much as four to five times the usual rate. Even using a long-distance calling card can sometimes incur connection fees. When checking in, be sure to ask the price for local calls and connection fees for toll-free numbers. When in doubt, use the pay phones in the lobby.

Luxury

The Algonquin – *59 W. 44th St., Midtown.* ✗ ♿ ☎ *212-840-6800 or 800-555-8000. www.algonquinhotel.com. 174 rooms.* **$$$$$** This quiet, elegant hotel is designated a Literary Landmark as the site of Alexander Woollcott's famous Algonquin Round Table. As such, the hotel served as a gathering place for a celebrated clique of writers, including Dorothy Parker, Robert Benchley,

Robert Sherwood and other notables, in the 1920s. A thorough refurbishing in 1998 gave all its guest rooms new (but traditional in style) furnishings and fittings. The Algonquin has a popular if pricey cabaret, the Oak Room; its Roundtable Restaurant offers a moderately-priced pretheater men; and the Blue Bar offers casual dining.

The Four Seasons Hotel – *57 E. 57th St. (between Madison & Park Aves.), Midtown.* ✗ ⟐ 🅿 🆂🅿🅰 ☎ *212-758-5700 or 800-332-3442. www.foursea sons.com. 360 rooms.* $$$$$ Located in the heart of Manhattan's premier shopping and business district, the luxurious Four Seasons Hotel, a soaring 52-story spire designed by legendary architect I.M. Pei, stands out as New York City's tallest hotel. A full-service spa offers cutting-edge relaxation and rejuvenation techniques along with time-honored treatments. Elegant accommodations are done in soothing pastels and earth tones and feature floor-to-ceiling windows, pillow menus (select your favorite degree of firmness), and marble steeping tubs that fill up in 60 seconds. Complimentary car service is available within a 2mi radius. Your pets and children are warmly welcomed here.

The Melrose Hotel New York – *140 E. 63rd St., Upper East Side.* ✗ ⟐ 🅿 ⤢ ☎ *212-838-5700 or 800-635-7673. www.melrosehotel.com. 306 roooms.* $$$$$ Grace Kelly and Liza Minnelli called this 1927 landmark home when it was an "exclusive residence for young women." A recent renovation has refreshed the residential appeal of its spacious rooms with contemporary furnishings, wrought-iron headboards and shuttered windows. Its location on the Upper East Side makes for easy jaunts to fashionable Madison Avenue, the Frick, the Metropolitan and the Guggenheim museums.

The Michelangelo – *152 W. 51st St. (at Seventh Ave.), Midtown.* ✗ ⟐ 🅿 ☎ *212-765-0505 or 800-237-0990. www.michelangelohotel.com. 178 rooms.* $$$$$ The flavor is Italian at The Michelangelo, from the Limoncello restaurant off the lobby to the complimentary Italian breakfast to the Baci Perugina chocolates on the pillows. The only US property of Italy's Starhotels, the Michelangelo has large guest rooms (average size: 475sq ft), bidets and color TVs in the bathrooms and 55-gallon soaking tubs. It's conveniently located between Rockefeller Center and the Theater District.

Millenium Hotel New York U.N. Plaza – *One United Nations Plaza (between First & Second Aves.), East Side.* ✗ ⟐ 🅿 ⤢ ☎ *212-758-1234 or 866-866-8086. www.millenium-hotels.com. 427 rooms.* $$$$$ Directly across from the United Nations with convenient access to the Midtown business district and fashionable East Side restaurants and boutiques, the Millenium's spacious and elegantly appointed guest rooms start on the 28th floor and provide breathtaking views of the New York skyline and the East River. A treasure house of tapestries dating back to the 9C adorns the lobbies, corridors and accommodations. The Millenium is the only Manhattan hotel to have both an indoor tennis court and a glass-enclosed swimming pool. There's also a currency exchange at the front desk, and a full-service health club and fitness center. The hotel's Ambassador Grill serves as a meeting place for many UN dignitaries.

The Plaza – *Fifth Ave. at Central Park South, Midtown.* ✗ ⟐ 🅿 🆂🅿🅰 ☎ *212-759-3000 or 800-759-3000. www.fairmont.com. 805 rooms.* $$$$$ This is the grande dame of New York hotels, and has been since it opened in 1907, accommodating many of the world's rich and famous over the decades. Featured in countless movies, The Plaza is a national historic landmark. Guest rooms, all renovated in 1997 and 1998, still have original crystal chandeliers, and many have fireplaces. Almost as well known as the hotel are its restaurants—the Palm Court and the Oak Room—and its Oak Bar and Oyster Bar.

The Ritz-Carlton New York, Central Park – *50 Central Park South at Sixth Ave., Midtown.* ✗ ⟐ 🅿 🆂🅿🅰 ☎ *212-308-9100. www.ritzcarlton.com. 277 rooms.* $$$$$ With unrivaled views of Central Park and the city skyline, New York's newest Ritz-Carlton provides the ultimate in luxury and service. Amenities especially stand out: complimentary limousine service in the Midtown area; telescopes and birding books in park-view rooms; in-room safes that accommodate laptops; DVD players and a library of Academy Award-winning films; and complimentary use of Burberry trench coats for guests—even dogs—when needed. La Prairie Switzerland has opened its first American full-service luxury day spa here, and **L'Atelier ($$$$)** with its New French cuisine rates as one of the finest restaurants in New York *(jackets required at dinner)*. Put yourself in the hands of acclaimed chef Gabriel Kreuther and go for the chef's eight-course tasting menu.

The Royalton – *44 W. 44th St., Midtown.* ✗ ⟐ 🅿 ☎ *212-869-4400 or 800-635-9013. www.ianschragerhotels.com. 205 rooms.* $$$$$ In contrast to its historic exterior, dating to 1898 (look closely: there's no marquis, awning or even a noticeable sign), the inside of The Royalton is daringly modern. Opened in 1988, it's the first New York product of avant-garde hotelier Ian Schrager and designer Philippe Starck. Sleek, well-appointed guest rooms all have VCRs, CD and cassette players, and refrigerator/minibars. Bathrooms offer slate- and glass-walled showers or wide circular tubs. Ultra-hip staffers dress in black.

SoHo Grand Hotel – *310 W. Broadway (between Grand & Canal Sts.), SoHo.* ⏃ ♿ 🅿 ☏ *212-965-3000 or 800-965-3000. www.sohogrand.com. 369 rooms.* $$$$$ Opened in 1996, the SoHo Grand brought luxurious accommodation to a part of the city that didn't have it before. At the southwest edge of the arty SoHo neighborhood, it's also a short walk from trendy TriBeCa. The Gallery restaurant serves acclaimed contemporary American dishes. Rooms all have VCRs and CD players, minibars and 24-hour room service. The SoHo Grand welcomes pets, and will even provide a goldfish for your room upon request.

Waldorf-Astoria Hotel – *301 Park Ave. (between 49th & 50th Sts.), Midtown.* ⏃ ♿ 🅿 ☏ *212-355-3000 or 800-925-3673. www.waldorfastoria.com. 1,423 rooms.* $$$$$ *(see p 104).* Undergoing a renovation approaching $400 million, the regal Art-Deco building reigns over New York City as one of its most classic symbols. Over the years, this grande dame has hosted the likes of major world leaders and cultural icons. The elegant, marble-floored lobby reflects the opulence worthy of its history. Well-appointed rooms are individually decorated, and units in the exclusive Waldorf Towers are especially known for their exquisite European furnishings, spaciousness and butler service.

Westin New York at Times Square – *270 W. 43rd St. (at Eighth Ave.), Times Square.* ⏃ ♿ 🅿 ☏ *212-201-2700 or 800-WESTIN. www.westinny.com. 863 rooms.* $$$$$ Westin New York is the newest, largest and most dramatically designed hotel to hit New York in a decade. Arquitectonica of Miami's work is, according to critics, either a delight or disaster—you decide. Either way, it's an attention-grabber: The facade of this 45-story prism utilizes more than 1,000 permutations of curtain-wall panels and intricate patterns of colored glass inspired by earth and sky tones. A soaring beam of light curves up the 42nd Street side of the structure at night and appears to pierce the sky. Guest rooms boast sleek furnishings and bold abstract art on muted wall coverings. The health club offers a panoramic view of the city, and "one call does it all" permits guests to dial just one number to have any request fulfilled. **Shula's Steak House ($$$$)** specializes in serving the "biggest and best" certified Angus beef.

The Gorham Hotel – *136 W. 55th St. (between Sixth & Seventh Aves.), Midtown.* ⏃ ♿ 🅿 ☏ *212-245-1800 or 800-735-0710. www.gorhamhotel.com. 115 rooms.* $$$$ The Gorham characterizes itself as an anti-trendy boutique hotel, carrying on the Old World tradition of hospitality and friendly and professional service. Families are warmly welcomed here and guests are remembered by name—close to half are repeat customers. The European-style lobby is intimate and inviting with its heated vestibule, cut-crystal chandelier, Persian rug, original art, complimentary Internet access station, and heaping bowls of fresh fruit and candy. Each room features a fully equipped kitchenette alcove with microwave, refrigerator and wet bar, digital temperature-controlled water faucets and the latest in communications technology. The hotel is an easy walk to Rockefeller Center, Carnegie Hall and Central Park.

Hotel Wales – *1295 Madison Ave. (at 92nd St.), Upper East Side.* ⏃ ♿ 🅿 ☏ *212-876-6000 or 877-847-4444. www.waleshotel.com. 87 rooms.* $$$$ This nicely restored property is situated in a pleasant residential/commercial neighborhood, within walking distance of some top museums like the Guggenheim, the Cooper-Hewitt Design Museum, the National Academy Museum and the Metropolitan Museum of Art. Amenities include a pleasant rooftop terrace, down comforters on the beds, VCRs and CD players in the rooms. **Sarabeth's** restaurant *(see restaurant listings)* and Café 92 are on the premises.

Iroquois Hotel – *49 W. 44nd St. (between Fifth & Sixth Aves.), Midtown.* ⏃ ☏ *212-840-3080. www.iroquoisny.com. 123 rooms.* $$$$ Newly restored to the tune of $14 million dollars, and convenient to Broadway theaters, Radio City Music Hall, Times Square and West 47th Street's Diamond Row, the Iroquois is one of only three hotels in New York belonging to the Small Luxuy Hotels of the World. Bathrooms are outfitted with Italian marble, robes and linens are by Frette, and dataport phones have dual lines. Don't miss the James Dean Lounge, named after the star of *Rebel Without a Cause,* who used to bunk here when he was a struggling actor (and the rates were much lower!). If you order room service, a complimentary film of your choice—either made in New York, directed by a New Yorker, or starring a New Yorker—comes along with your tray. The multilingual staff is eager to please.

Manhattan East Suite Hotels – *371 7th Ave. (and 9 other locations), Midtown/East Side.* ⏃ ♿ 🅿 ☏ *212-465-3690 or 800-637-8483. www.mesuite.com.* $$$$ Especially popular with family travelers, this group of mostly all-suite properties offers more space for the dollar than comparable hotels. Its properties are scattered around from midtown Manhattan to the Upper East Side, and range in size from the 80-suite **Lyden House** *(320 E. 53rd St.)* to the 523-suite **Southgate Tower** *(Seventh Ave. & 31st St.)*. The 201-suite **Benjamin** *(125 E. 50th St.)* has a full-service spa. All suites have kitchens or kitchenettes, and they range in size from studios to two-bedroom units.

The Mayflower Hotel – *15 Central Park West (at 61st St.), Upper West Side.* ✗ ಈ 🄿 ☎ *212-265-0060 or 800-223-4164. www.mayflowerhotel.com. 365 rooms. $$$$* A reasonably priced hotel with a view of Central Park from many of its rooms, the Mayflower is close to Lincoln Center and within walking distance of the Theater District. With more suites than rooms, the hotel offers accommodations equipped with pantries and refrigerators. Guests can get free morning coffee and newspapers in the lobby and apples at the front desk. A small fitness center is available, and the Conservatory Café—also with park views—is open for breakfast, lunch and dinner.

New York Palace – *455 Madison Ave., Midtown.* ✗ ಈ 🄿 ☎ *212-888-7000 or 800-697-2522. www.newyorkpalace.com. 896 rooms. $$$$* The entrance to this 55-story skyscraper is the 19C Villard House opposite Midtown's St. Patrick's Cathedral. Just inside, you'll see the mansion's original molded ceilings before descending the grand staircase into the marble-columned lobby. Pricey oversize guest rooms are adorned with gold-brocade bedspreads. A 7,000sq ft fitness center leaves you physically and spiritually inspired. Famed for its award-winning wine list, contemporary French cuisine and elegant decor, **Le Cirque 2000 ($$$$)** is right downstairs.

W New York-The Court – *120 E. 39th St. (between Park & Lexington Aves.), Murray Hill.* ✗ ಈ 🄿 ☎ *212-685-1100 or 888-625-5144. www.whotels.com. 198 rooms. $$$$* W New York–The Court is set on a quiet tree-lined street three blocks from Grand Central Station. Most of the spacious guest rooms have terraces and provide goose-down comforters and pillows, upholstered chaise lounges, Aveda bath products, high-speed laptop connections, 24-hour room service and W's signature "Whatever, Whenever" button on the phone. Press it to request whatever you want, whenever you want it. **Icon ($$$)**, the hotel's contemporary American restaurant, draws a smart crowd of locals, visitors and of course, icons. The hotel's **WetBar** is the hottest club/lounge in the neighborhood.

Mid-Range

The Avalon – *16 E. 32nd St. (between Madison & Fifth Aves.), Midtown.* ✗ ಈ 🄿 ☎ *212-299-7000 or 888-442-8256. www.theavalonny.com. 100 rooms. $$$* In the shadow of the Empire State Building and a short walk from Macy's, the Avalon opened in 1998 in a building that was totally rebuilt on the inside. Today, it's an elegant, luxurious boutique hotel with traditional comforts and modern technology (all suites have high-speed Internet access). Most guest accommodations are suites, averaging more than 450sq ft. The Avalon Bar & Grill serves New American cuisine, and breakfast is included in the room rate.

Hotel Chelsea – *222 W. 23rd St., Chelsea.* ✗ 🄿 ☎ *212-243-3700. www.hotelchelsea.com. 250 rooms. $$$* The Chelsea's redbrick Victorian structure, with its wrought-iron balconies, dominates its block on West 23rd Street. Rooms all have private baths and cable TV, but otherwise this is a no-frills hotel with a number of permanent residents, including artists, writers and musicians. Once home to Thomas Wolfe, Arthur Miller, Dylan Thomas and other literary luminaries, the hotel is listed on the National Register of Historic Places. The old-fashioned lobby's huge wooden fireplace contrasts with the modern art hanging from every wall—and even the ceiling.

Hotel Pennsylvania – *401 Seventh Ave. (between 32nd & 33rd Sts.), Midtown.* ✗ ಈ 🄿 ☎ *212-736-5000 or 800-223-8585. www.penn5000.com. 1,700 rooms. $$$* Well-located across the street from Madison Square Garden and Penn Station, and a short walk from the shopping mecca of Herald Square, the Pennsylvania is one of New York's largest hotels. It was recently renovated, as seen in its modern, bustling marble-pillared lobby with mirrored walls. The labyrinthine corridors in its 17 floors of guest rooms can be daunting, but the large number of rooms makes the hotel quite affordable by New York standards. There's a sightseeing and airport transportation desk in the lobby.

The Hudson – *356 W. 58th St. (between Eighth & Ninth Aves.), Midtown.* ✗ ಈ 🄿 ☎ *212-554-6000 or 800-444-4786. www.ianschragerhotels.com. 1,000 rooms. $$$* Manhattan's hottest new hotel, the stylish Hudson offers a wide array of services and in-room amenities for a reasonable price. The tradeoff: guest rooms are very small even by New York City standards. A short walk north of the Theater District, The Hudson is another Ian Schrager-Philippe Starck collaboration that has drawn attention for its unique and creative public spaces. Its restaurant, the Hudson Cafeteria, features communal tables; the rooftop garden boasts hot tubs; and the glass-floored Hudson Bar overflows with young, hip customers.

Lobby of The Hudson Hotel

The Lucerne – *201 W. 79th St. (at Amsterdam Ave.), Upper West Side.* ✕ ☎ *212-875-1000 or 800-492-8122. www.newyorkhotel.com. 250 rooms.* **$$$** Occupying a historic landmark property built in 1903, the Lucerne has been transformed into a modern, European-style boutique hotel with spacious guest rooms featuring a full slate of amenities, from in-room movies to marble bathrooms. The hotel also offers a fitness facility and a business center. **Nice Matin ($$$)**, the Lucerne's new restaurant featuring French Mediterranean cuisine, opened in December 2002. Set in the heart of the trendy Upper West Side, The Lucerne is a short walk from the Museum of Natural History and its new Rose Center planetarium.

Maritime Hotel – *363 W. 16th St. (between Eighth & Ninth Aves.), Chelsea.* ✕ ▣ ☎ *212-242-4300. www.themaritimehotel.com. 120 rooms.* **$$$** The Maritime Hotel, new to the exciting Chelsea district—which now houses the greatest concentration of art galleries and dance clubs in the city—has quickly become the favorite of artists, collectors, and fashion and music moguls. Following a seafaring pattern—the white-tiled building was once headquarters to the National Maritime Union. Each "cabin" (or room) features porthole windows 5ft in diameter that face the Hudson River, queen-size platform beds set in burnished teak-paneled nooks, and sleek shelves for luggage. Two restaurants (one serving Japanese cuisine; the other offering Mediterranean fare) are located off the main lobby. A fitness center is scheduled to open in spring 2004.

Le Marquis New York – *12 E. 31st St. (between Fifth & Madison Aves.), Murray Hill.* ✕ ♿ ▣ ☎ *212-889-6363 or 866-627-7847. www.lemarquisny.com. 123 rooms.* **$$$** In close proximity to the Empire State Building, Madison Square Garden, Penn Station and the garment district, Le Marquis New York offers understated elegance at a reasonable price. Black-and-white photographs of New York street scenes decorate the walls of spacious rooms, where the bed is wrapped in Frette linens and the bath is stocked with Aveda products. Other amenities include overnight shoeshine service, a full mini bar with premium liquors, and a fitness center and sauna that are open 24 hours. Relax in the Library Room, which boasts a desktop PC and a 40-inch flat-screen TV. The intimate Bar 12:31 serves breakfast, light lunch and evening snacks and is a favorite gathering place for budding models and moguls.

Washington Square Hotel – *103 Waverly Pl., Greenwich Village.* ✕ ☎ *212-777-9515 or 800-222-0418. www.wshotel. 170 rooms.* **$$$** Across Washington Square Park in Greenwich Village, this intimate 1902 property is introduced by the small, green-and-white marble lobby, with hand-painted tile murals of wildflowers. Most rooms have been updated with a minimalist decor of mustard-colored walls and ebonized-wood night stands. **North Square** restaurant **($$$)**, on the lower level, is a secret neighborhood find.

Budget

Amsterdam Inn – *340 Amsterdam Ave. (at 76th St.), Upper West Side.* ☎ *212-579-7500. www.amsterdaminn.com. 25 rooms.* **$$** For a decent place to sleep at a bargain price try the Amsterdam Inn. A residential building converted to hotel use in 1999, the inn has some rooms with shared baths, some with private facilities. All have color TV, air conditioning, phones and maid service. Be prepared to carry your luggage up a few flights of stairs—there's no elevator. There's no restaurant, either, but the popular Upper West Side neighborhood right outside the door has plenty of them, including a brewpub in the same building. It's a short walk to the Museum of Natural History and Central Park, and a short subway or bus ride to Midtown.

Cosmopolitan Hotel – *95 West Broadway (at Chambers St.), TriBeCa.* ☎ *212-566-1900 or 888-895-9400. www.cosmohotel.com. 115 rooms.* **$$** The longest continually operating hotel in New York City, dating back to 1850, the Cosmopolitan is located in the heart of TriBeCa within walking distance of Ground Zero, the World Financial Center, Wall Street, SoHo, Chinatown and Little Italy. Standard rooms contain a work desk, a standing armoire or clothes rack, a phone dataport, satellite TV and safe-deposit box; young people and businessmen make up most of the clientele. You can overlook the tiny bathrooms in favor of the location; there are over 40 restaurants within a five-block radius, ranging from the tony Bouley, Montrachet and Chanterelle to fast-food joints.

La Quinta Inn Manhattan – *17 W. 32nd St.(between Fifth & Sixth Aves.), Midtown.* ✗ ♿ ☎ *212-790-2710 or 800-567-7720. www.applecorehotels.com. 182 rooms.* **$$** Recently renovated to the tune of $2.5 million and within walking distance of Madison Square Garden, Penn Station and the Javits Convention Center, La Quinta Inn Manhattan appeals to cost-conscious leisure and business travelers. Large, well-appointed guest rooms offer myriad amenities: free high-speed Internet connections, color TV with wireless Web access, telephone with data port and voice mail, coffee maker, iron and ironing board. The dramatic rooftop **Sky Bar** offers libations and light refreshments with breathtaking views of the towering Empire State Building, just one block north.

Mayfair New York – *242 W. 49th St. (between Broadway & Eighth Ave.), Midtown.* ♿ ☎ *212-586-0300. www.mayfairny.com. 77 rooms.* **$$** One of the few family-run hotels in Manhattan, Mayfair New York is located in the heart of Broadway theaters and Times Square nightlife. The entire building is "no smoking." Guest rooms and common areas showcase a collection of rare, historic photos from the Museum of the City of New York. Double-pane windows filter out the street noise. All accommodations come with modern conveniences including high-speed Internet connections, hair dryers and computerized wall safes. Service is extremely friendly.

Pickwick Arms – *230 E. 51st. St. (between Second & Third Aves.), Midtown.* ✗ ♿ ☎ *212-355-0300 or 800-742-5945. 368 rooms.* **$$** You can't find a better East Side hotel bargain than the Pickwick. What the accommodations lack in size they make up for by being in an upscale neighborhood convenient to Saint Patrick's Cathedral, Grand Central Station, the United Nations and most tourist attractions. Safe-deposit boxes are available in the lobby as is Internet access *(25¢ a minute)*. Most rooms have only showers, and you should bring your own shampoo. Weather permitting, spend some time on the charming rooftop garden enjoying the superb view.

West Side YMCA – *5 West 63rd St., Upper West Side.* ✗ ♿ ▣ ⚒ ☎ *212-875-4100. www.ymcanyc.org. 539 rooms.* **$$** You'll find basic, dormitory-style accommodations here, with small, spartan rooms. Many have shared baths, but rooms with private baths are also available, and all have TVs and air conditioning. The West Side "Y" is popular with travelers on a budget, from students to seniors (it hosts the Elderhostel program in New York). For the price, the location is as good as you'll find, with Lincoln Center at one end of the block and Central Park at the other. Another bonus: Guests can use the YMCA's extensive health and fitness facilities and two swimming pools.

Out on the Town

PERFORMING ARTS

Visitors and New Yorkers alike can take their pick from among the city's abundant and diverse performing-arts offerings year-round. Spring brings performances by visiting theatrical companies from around the world; summer offers colorful street fairs and ethnic festivals in the city's parks; during the fall and winter the curtain rises at the city's cultural institutions *(the season runs from mid-Sept–mid-May)*. No visit to New York City is complete without the experience of a Broadway show. Many museums and libraries feature musical evenings, lectures and film shows. In addition, the boroughs are home to various cultural centers. *For a detailed listing of events, call the numbers listed here or consult the arts and entertainment sections of publications listed on p 318.*

USEFUL NUMBERS

The Broadway Line

☎ 212-302-4111

New York City on Stage

☎ 212-768-1818

Music and Dance

Classical Music and Opera Companies	Venue	☎ Information
Metropolitan Opera	Metropolitan Opera House between West 62nd & 65th Sts.	212-362-6000 www.metopera.org
New York City Opera	New York State Theater Columbus Avenue at 63rd Street	212-870-5630 www.nycopera.com
New York Philharmonic	Avery Fisher Hall 65th St. & Broadway	212-875-5656 www.newyorkphilharmonic.org
Performance Spaces		
Alice Tully Hall	65th St. & Broadway	212-875-5050
Brooklyn Academy of Music	30 Lafayette Ave. (Brooklyn)	718-636-4100
Carnegie Hall	57th St. & Seventh Ave.	212-247-7800
Symphony Space	2537 Broadway	212-864-5400

Rock/Pop

Irving Plaza	17 Irving Place	212-777-6800
Madison Square Garden	2 Penn Plaza	212-465-6741
Radio City Music Hall	1270 Ave. of the Americas	212-307-7171

Dance

Alvin Ailey Dance Co.	City Center 130 W. 55th St.	212-581-1212 www.alvinailey.org
American Ballet Theatre	Metropolitan Opera House between West 62nd & 65th Sts.	212-362-6000 www.abt.org
Ballet Hispanico	various locations	212-362-6710 www.ballethispanico.org
Dance Theatre of Harlem	various locations	212-690-2800 www.dancetheatreofharlem.com
Dance Theater Workshop	219 W. 19th St.	212-691-6500 www.dtw.org
Eliot Feld's Ballet Tech Company	Joyce Theater 175 Eighth Ave.	212-242-0800
Martha Graham Dance Co.	various locations	212-838-5886 www.marthagrahamdance.org
New York City Ballet	New York State Theater Columbus Avenue at 63rd St.	212-870-5570 www.nycballet.com

Off Broadway Theaters

The city's most renowned venues are concentrated in the Broadway theater district *(www.broadway.com)*, near Times Square. The following is a selection of Off Broadway *(www.offbroadway.com)* and Off Off Broadway theaters found primarily in Greenwich Village and the Astor Place/East Village neighborhoods. The *Broadway Theater Guide* provides a weekly schedule of Broadway shows *(free, available at visitor centers)*.

Theaters	Address	☎
Cherry Lane	38 Commerce St.	212-989-2020
La Mama, E.T.C.	74A E. Fourth St.	212-475-7710
Pearl Theatre Co.	80 St. Mark's Place	212-598-9802
Wooster Group	Performing Garage 33 Wooster St.	212-966-3651

Tickets

As some of the more popular events sell out months in advance, we recommend you buy tickets early. Note that some performances can be sold out before tickets become available for public sale. Full-price tickets for most venues can be purchased directly from the box office or from one of the following companies; major credit cards are accepted (a service charge of $1–$7 may be added to the ticket price). Tickets for performances at Avery Fisher and Alice Tully halls can be obtained through Lincoln Center Charge (☎ *212-721-6500; www.lincolncenter.org*). For all other performances at Lincoln Center, contact the box office. Ticket brokers sometimes have tickets available when the box office is sold out but a substantial service fee must be paid (up to 25%). Hotel concierges may also be able to help secure tickets.

TKTS *(www.tdf.org)* offers discount tickets *(25% & 50%)* for events on the day of the performance. Purchases must be made in person *(cash or traveler's checks only)* from the booth in Times Square *(Broadway & 47th St.;*

Broadway marquee

© Brigitta L. House/MICHELIN

tickets for evening performances sold year-round Mon–Sat 3pm–8pm, Sun 11am–7pm; tickets for matinees sold Wed & Sat 10am–2pm, Sun 11am–7pm) or at its downtown location at South Street Seaport *(corner of Front & John Sts., at the rear of 199 Water St.; tickets for same-day evening performances & day-before-the-show matinee performances sold year-round Mon–Sat 11am–6pm, Sun 11am–3:30pm)*. Tickets are usually plentiful for less popular shows; the choice of seats, however, is often limited. Vouchers that are redeemable at the theater box office for two tickets for the price of one—**Twofers**—can be obtained free of charge from the Convention & Visitors Bureau. **Ticketmaster** *(☎ 212-307-4100; www.ticketmaster.com)* outlets are found in most locations of Tower Records and Rite-Aid pharmacies, and at Bloomingdale's.

NIGHTLIFE

From listening to rock, western or z to suit anyone's tastes. The city has garnered an excellent reputation for its numerous **jazz clubs** *(see listings p 160 & p 200)* famous

■ On-line Guide to NYC Nightlife

www.allny.com
www.justwearblack.com
www.raveclick.com
www.nytheatre.com

for their impromptu jam sessions. Wind down the evening with a cappuccino in one of New York's cozy coffeehouses *(see listing p 154)*.

Nightclubs

Cabaret	Address	☎
Bar d'O	29 Bedford St.	212-627-1580
Cafe Carlyle	35 E. 76th St.	212-570-7175
Feinstein's	540 Park Ave.	212-339-4095
The Firebird Café	365 W. 46th St.	212-586-0244
Joe's Pub	425 Lafayette St.	212-539-8777
Cocktails		
Bar 89	89 Mercer St.	212-274-0989
The Rainbow Room	30 Rockefeller Plaza	212-632-5100
The Supper Club	240 W. 47th St.	212-921-1940
Vintage	753 Ninth Ave.	212-581-4655

Comedy

Caroline's Comedy Club	1626 Broadway	212-757-4100
Comedy Cellar/ Olive Tree	117 MacDougal St.	212-254-3480
Comic Strip	1568 Second Ave.	212-861-9386
Gotham Comedy Club	34 W. 22nd St.	212-367-9000
New York Comedy Club	241 E. 24th St.	212-696-5233
Stand-up New York	236 W. 78th St.	212-595-0850

Rock/Blues

CBGB & OMFUG	315 Bowery	212-982-4052
Cotton Club	656 W. 125th St.	212-663-7980
Session 73	1359 First Ave.	212-517-4445

Latin

S.O.B.'s	204 Varick St.	212-243-4940
Zinc Bar	90 W. Houston St.	212-477-8337

Dance Clubs

Club NY	252 W. 43rd St.	212-997-9510
Culture Club	179 Varick St.	212-414-2882
Deep	16 W. 22nd St.	212-229-2000
Nell's	246 W. 14th St.	212-675-1567
Roseland	239 W. 52nd St.	212-247-0200

■ The Donkey Show
"I love the Nightlife, I want to Boogie"

The Donkey Show

Hustle over to the El Flamingo Theater *(547 W 21st St., between 10th & 11th Aves.)* in Chelsea to watch Studio 54 and *A Midsummer Night's Dream* converge in *The Donkey Show*, a funky, glittery, disco-queen, dancing-machine rendition of one of Shakespeare's greatest hits. Cross-dressing performers and scantily clad, well-muscled men encourage revelers to become part of the action—though there are places to sit for those who prefer just to observe. If you haven't moved to the rhythms of disco favorites like "Car Wash" and "We Are Family" in a while, strap on those platforms and get ready to board the Love Train. *For tickets, contact Ticketmaster:* ☎ *212-307-4100 or www.thedonkeyshow.com.*

Shopping

The Big Apple is a veritable shopper's paradise—everything from the functional to the bizarre lies within easy reach. Numerous fashionable stores are located on Fifth Avenue *(between 47th & 57th Sts.)* and Madison Avenue *(between 59th & 79th Sts.)*, where window-shopping is a favored pastime. The latest addition to Madison Avenue is the elegant Crystal District *(between 58th & 63rd Sts.)*. Trendy boutiques and art galleries can be found in SoHo, TriBeCa and Chelsea. New York City is also home to the nation's fashion industry, centered in the Garment District on Seventh Avenue, and its diamond wholesale trade, concentrated on Diamond and Jewelry Way *(47th St. between Fifth & Sixth Aves.; www.diamonddistrict.org)*. The *Official NYC Guide*, published by the New York Convention & Visitors Bureau, NYC & Company, offers detailed information on the types of shops, their locations and hours of operation.

New York's neighborhoods offer easy access to shopping

© Scott Barrow

Main Shopping Areas

Fifth Avenue – Most of New York's department stores and major bookstores are located along Fifth Avenue between 34th and 60th streets.

Department stores include:

Bergdorf Goodman	754 Fifth Ave.	☎ 212-753-7300
Henri Bendel	712 Fifth Ave.	☎ 212-247-1100
Lord & Taylor	424 Fifth Ave.	☎ 212-391-3344
Saks Fifth Avenue	611 Fifth Ave.	☎ 212-753-4000
Takashimaya	693 Fifth Ave.	☎ 212-350-0100

Book retailers include:

Barnes & Noble	600 Fifth Ave.	☎ 212-765-0590
Borders	461 Park Ave.	☎ 212-839-8049
Rizzoli	31 W. 57th St.	☎ 212-759-2424

Scattered among the retail giants are world-renowned specialty shops, toy stores and designer boutiques such as:

Banana Republic	114 Fifth Ave.	☎ 212-366-4691
Cartier	653 Fifth Ave.	☎ 212-753-0111
Disney Store	711 Fifth Ave.	☎ 212-702-0702
FAO Schwarz	767 Fifth Ave.	☎ 212-644-9400
Fortunoff	681 Fifth Ave.	☎ 212-758-6660
Gucci	685 Fifth Ave.	☎ 212-826-2600
H&M	640 Fifth Ave.	☎ 212-489-0390
Tiffany & Co.	727 Fifth Ave.	☎ 212-755-8000

Don't miss the elegant **Trump Tower complex** with over 40 upscale shops and restaurants located at 725 Fifth Avenue.

57th Street – Considered one of the most exclusive shopping streets in the world, 57th between Second and Eighth avenues is home to numerous galleries, the **Manhattan Art and Antiques Center** and chic designer boutiques, including **Chanel**

(15 E. 57th St.; ☎ 212-355-5050) and **Louis Vuitton** (19 E. 57th St.; ☎ 212-371-6111). Next to these elegant boutiques lies **NikeTown** (6 E. 57th St.; ☎ 212-891-6453).

Lower Manhattan – Primarily known as the financial center of the city, this area offers a varied shopping experience, including famed discount store **Syms** (42 Trinity Pl.; ☎ 212-797-1199; www.syms.com). Festive **South Street Seaport** incorporates more than 50 boutiques and restaurants, as well as the **Pier 17** shopping center.

Lower East Side/East Village – A bargain hunter's dream, these neighborhoods are chock-full with shops selling discount designer clothing and furnishings and stores specializing in vintage apparel. **Orchard Street** is the heart of the discount area. Note that many shops

Whimsical window displays at F.A.O. Schwartz tempt young and old alike

© Scott Barrow

may close early on Friday and all day Saturday for the Jewish Sabbath.

SoHo/TriBeCa – The trendy and avant-garde prevails in the boutiques and galleries of SoHo, one of the city's best spots for people watching. To the south, artsy TriBeCa is home to hip shops and some of New York's hottest eateries.

Greenwich Village – The city's bohemian enclave is known for its quaint boutiques, specialty shops, jazz clubs and coffeehouses. Bleecker Street is lined with old-world bakeries and Italian grocery stores. NYU students with eclectic tastes flock to the Village's famed music stores, including **Tower Records** (692 Broadway; ☎ 212-505-1500; www.towerrecords.com).

Chelsea/Garment Center – An up-and-coming neighborhood, Chelsea boasts exclusive art galleries and fashionable cafes. Farther north on Seventh Avenue is the heart of the wholesale garment industry (note: some establishments will sell retail). The city's fur district is also located on Seventh Avenue between West 28th and West 29th streets. Moderate chains are clustered on Avenue of the Americas. Chelsea is home to **Manhattan Mall** (Ave. of the Americas & W. 33rd St.; ☎ 212-946-6100; www.manhattanmallny.com) and **Macy's Herald Square** (151 W. 34th St.; ☎ 212-695-4400; www.macys.com), the world's largest department store.

Upper East Side – This area encompasses an interesting mix of upscale fashion boutiques (primarily west of Lexington St.) and funky thrift shops hawking second-hand clothing and other used items. A bastion of high-end shopping, **Bloomingdale's** (59th St. & Lexington Ave.; ☎ 212-705-2098; www.bloomingdales.com) is known for its elaborate window displays.

Madison Avenue Stores	Address	☎
Baccarat	625 Madison Ave.	212-826-4100
Barneys	660 Madison Ave.	212-826-8900
Bebe	1044 Madison Ave.	212-517-2323
Betsey Johnson	1060 Madison Ave.	212-734-1257
Calvin Klein	654 Madison Ave.	212-292-9000
Daum	694 Madison Ave.	212-355-2060
DKNY	655 Madison Ave.	212-223-3569
Emanuel Ungaro	792 Madison Ave.	212-249-4090
Giorgio Armani	760 Madison Ave.	212-988-9191
Polo Ralph Lauren	867 Madison Ave.	212-606-2100
Prada	841 Madison Ave.	212-327-4200
Steuben	667 Madison Ave.	800-424-4240

Swarovski	625 Madison Ave.	212-308-1710
Valentino	747 Madison Ave.	212-772-6969
Versace	815 Madison Ave.	212-744-6868

Trademark Stores

Store	Address	☎
Coca-Cola	711 Fifth Ave.	212-418-9260
Disney	711 Fifth Ave.	212-702-0702
ESPN	1472 Broadway	212-921-3776
Hard Rock Café	221 W. 57th St.	212-489-6565
Kate Spade	454 Broome St.	212-274-1991
NBA Store	666 Fifth Ave.	212-515-6221
NBC Experience Store	30 Rockefeller Plaza	212-664-3700
NikeTown	6 E. 57th St.	212-891-6453
Original Levi Store	750 Lexington Ave.	212-826-5957
Yankees Clubhouse Shop	393 Fifth Ave.	212-685-4693

Auction Houses

Whether you're in the market for a priceless van Gogh or not, these establishments offering fine art, furnishings, books and decorative arts are well worth a visit. Advance viewings of items to be auctioned are usually held 3-5 days prior to the event and are open to the public. Visitors are welcome to participate in or watch the auctions. Advance reservations may be required for some events. Call for schedule of upcoming shows.

Auction House	Address	☎	Web site
Christie's	20 Rockefeller Plaza	212-636-2000	christies.com
Sotheby's	1334 York Ave.	212-606-7000	sothebys.com
William Doyle Galleries	175 E. 87th St.	212-427-2730	doylenewyork.com

Museum Shops

Looking for an unusual gift? Visit the city's numerous museum gift shops where items on sale are fashioned after pieces from the permanent collections and special exhibits—jewelry, sculptures, scarves, stationery, prints, posters and art books. Listed below is a selection of the city's most noteworthy museum gift shops:

Shop	Address	☎
American Museum of Natural History	W. 79th St.	212-769-5100
Brooklyn Museum of Art	200 Eastern Pkwy.	718-638-5000
Cooper-Hewitt National Design Museum	2 E. 91st St.	212-849-8400
The Frick Collection	1 E. 70th St.	212-288-0700
International Center of Photography	1133 Ave. of the Americas	212-860-1777
The Metropolitan Museum of Art	Fifth Ave. at 82nd St.	212-535-7710
Museum for African Art	3601 43rd Ave., Long Island City	718-784-7700
Museum of the City of New York	1220 Fifth Ave.	212-534-1672
Museum of Contemporary Arts & Design	40 W. 53rd St.	212-956-3535
The Museum of Modern Art	11 W. 53rd St.	212-708-9400
Pierpont Morgan Library	29 E. 36th St.	212-685-0610
Solomon R. Guggenheim Museum	1071 Fifth Ave.	212-423-3615
The Studio Museum in Harlem	144 W. 125th St.	212-864-4500
Whitney Museum of American Art	945 Madison Ave.	212-570-3676

Book Shops

Book Shop	Address	☎
Coliseum Books	11 W. 42nd St.	212-803-5890
Complete Traveller	199 Madison Ave.	212-685-9007
Gotham Book Mart	41 W. 47th St.	212-719-4448
Hagstrom Map & Travel Center	57 W. 43rd St.	212-398-1222
Military Bookman	29 E. 93rd St.	212-348-1280
Oscar Wilde Bookshop	15 Christopher St.	212-255-8097
Kitchen Arts & Letters	1435 Lexington Ave.	212-876-5550
Strand Books	828 Broadway	212-473-1452

Books and Music

Venue	Address	☎
Barnes & Noble	600 Fifth Ave.	212-765-0590
	105 Fifth Ave.	212-807-0099
	1972 Broadway	212-595-6859
	2289 Broadway	212-362-8835
	4 Astor Pl.	212-420-1322
	33 E. 17th St.	212-253-0810
	675 Sixth Ave.	212-727-1227
	240 E. 86th St.	212-794-1962
Borders	461 Park Ave.	212-980-6785
HMV	565 Fifth Ave.	212-681-6700
Sony Style	550 Madison Ave.	212-833-8800
Tower Records & Books	692 Broadway	212-505-1500
	725 Fifth Ave.	212-838-8110
	1961 Broadway	212-799-2500
Virgin Megastore	1540 Broadway	212-921-1020

Flower Markets

Take time to browse through the city's markets offering a wide variety of fresh produce, antiques and collectibles. Arrive early for the largest selection. Some of the more popular markets are the **Flower District**, four blocks of wholesale flower dealers (most will sell retail) located at Avenue of the Americas and West 28th Street; **The Annex** *(Ave. of the Americas & W. 26th St., year-round weekends 9am–5pm;* ☎ *212-243-5343)*; **SoHo Antiques Fair, Collectibles & Crafts** *(Broadway & Grand St., year-round weekends 9am–5pm;* ☎ *212-682-2000)*; and **Union Square Greenmarket** *(p 167)*.

Food Markets

The wonderfully popular **Greenmarket** *(above)* in Union Square Park is more than just flowers; it's also a great place to start your gourmet tour of the Big Apple. No trip would be complete without a visit to a few of the city's renowned food markets.

Market	Address	☎
Chelsea Market	75 Ninth Ave.	212-620-7500
Citarella	424 Ave. of the Americas	212-874-0383
Dean & Deluca	560 Broadway	212-226-6800
Eli's Manhattan	1411 3rd Ave.	212-717-8100

© Scott Barrow

Faicco's Pork Store	260 Bleecker St.	212-243-1974
Fairway Fruits & Vegetables	2127 Broadway	212-595-1888
Gourmet Garage	453 Broome St.	212-941-5850
Grace's Marketplace	1237 3rd Ave.	212-737-0600
Vinegar Factory	431 E. 91st St.	212-987-0885
Russ and Daughters	179 E. Houston Street	212-475-4880
Zabar's	2245 Broadway	212-787-2000

Wine and Spirits

Venue	Address	☎
67 Wine & Spirits	179 Columbus Ave.	212-724-6767
Acker, Merrall & Condit (AMC)	160 W. 72nd St.	212-787-1700
Astor Wines & Spirits	12 Astor Pl.	212-674-7500
Chelsea Wine Vault	75 Ninth Ave.	212-462-4244
Garnet Wines & Liquors	929 Lexington Ave.	212-772-3211
Morrell & Company	1 Rockefeller Plaza	212-688-9370
Shapiro's	126 Rivington St.	212-674-4404
Sherry-Lehman	679 Madison Ave.	212-838-7500

Home & Kitchen Furnishings

New Yorkers say **ABC Carpet & Home** *(888 Broadway St.; ☎ 212-473-3000; www.abchome.com)* is the must-do shop of the city. At the **Terence Conran Shop** *(407 E. 59th St.; ☎ 212-755-9079; www.conran.com)* you can find high-fashion bathmats, kitchen knickknacks and gourmet foods. **Bridge Kitchenware** *(214 E. 52nd St.; ☎ 212-688-4220; www.bridgekitchenware.com)* offers a tremendous array of cookware, and SoHo's **Property** *(14 Wooster St.; ☎ 917-237-0123)* gets you out of the kitchen and into a really cool furniture scene. **Move Lab** *(803 Washington St.; ☎ 212-741-5520; www.movelab.com)* in the Meatpacking District offers up unique, modern crafts and furnishings. **Amalgamated Home** *(9-19 Christopher St.; ☎ 212-691-8695)* combines three stores into one, allowing you to find that perfect lamp, unique cabinet hardware or funky furniture.

Sightseeing

VISITOR INFORMATION

Four free publications, *City Guide Magazine (www.cityguidemagazine.com)*, *IN New York Magazine (www.in-newyorkmag.com)*, *Where New York*, and the *Official City Guide*, offer information on events, attractions, shopping and dining. They are available at hotels and visitor information kiosks. The *Official NYC Guide* is available free from New York City & Company (☎ 212-397-8222 or 800-692-8474; www.nycvisit.com). Volunteer New Yorkers take out-of-towners on two- to four-hour visits of city neighborhoods as part of a unique free service called **Big Apple Greeter**. Particular emphasis is placed on matching interests and language requirements of visitors and volunteers *(advance reservations required; Big Apple Greeter, 1 Centre St., Suite 2035, New York NY 10007; ☎ 212-669-8159; www.bigapplegreeter.org)*.

Consider purchasing a **CityPass** booklet *($45 adults; $36 children age 6-17; ☎ 707-256-0490; www.citypass.net)* that includes discounted admission to six major sights in New York (Guggenheim Museum; Empire State Building Observatory and Skyride; Museum of Modern Art; American Museum of Natural History; Intrepid Sea-Air-Space Museum; Circle Line harbour cruise) and allows you to skip most ticket lines. Buy your CityPass online or at any of the participating attractions.

Visitor Centers

NYC & Company Official Visitor Information Center
810 Seventh Ave., between 52nd & 53rd Sts.
☎ *212-484-1222. www.nycvisit.com.*
Open year-round Mon–Fri 8:30am–6pm; weekends & holidays 9am–5pm.

City Hall Park Visitor Information Kiosk
Southern tip of City Hall Park on the Broadway sidewalk at Park Row
Open year-round Mon–Fri 9am–6pm; weekends & holidays 10am–6pm.

Harlem Visitor Information Kiosk
163 W. 125th St., just east of Seventh Ave.
Open year-round Mon–Fri 9am–6pm; weekends & holidays 10am–6pm.

Times Square Visitors Center
1560 Broadway between 46th & 47th Sts.
☎ *212-869-1890.   www.timessquarebid.org/visitor.*

Open year-round daily 8am–8pm. Closed Jan 1 & Dec 25. Free walking tour of Times Square leaves from the visitors center every Fri at noon, rain or shine.

■ NYC Online

In addition to the official visitor center Web sites, the following sites provide a wealth of information about the Big Apple.

www.applevision-nyc.com	*www.in-newyork.com*
www.citidex.com	*www.cityguidemagazine.com*
www.newyork.citysearch.com	*www.newyorkmetro.com*
www.downtownny.com	*www.ny.com*
www.newyorkcityfood.com	*http://gonyc.about.com*

TOURS

For visitors with little time at their disposal, we recommend the two- or four-day itineraries described on pp 18-20. Visitors may also choose from a wide variety of guided tours offered in the city. A selection appears below.

Tours of the City

Double Decker and Trolley Tours – These tours of Manhattan aboard double-decker buses and trolleys allow visitors to board at any of over 40 stops located at major attractions. Most operators split the city into two itineraries, Lower and Upper Manhattan, each lasting about 3–4hrs. Tours run every 30min; the same ticket allows free reboarding for two consecutive days. **Gray Line** *(year-round daily 8:30am–5pm; $49 both loops; tickets sold at Gray Line Visitors Center, Eighth Ave. between 47th & 48th streets.; ☎ 212-445-0848 or 800-669-0051; www.newyorksightseeing.com).*

World Yacht Dinner Cruises

Pier 81, W. 41st St. at the Hudson River. ☎ *212-630-8100. www.worldyacht.com.* Spectacular views of the Manhattan skyline complement an elegant gourmet dinner and dancing to live music aboard World Yacht. The cost per person is about what you'd pay for dinner in a top restaurant (*$69.95 Sun–Thu; $79 Fri & Sat*). Three-hour cruises take place every evening from April through December, with weekend departures from January through March.

Helicopter Tours – Offering a panoramic view of Manhattan, these unforgettable trips last a brief 4–18 minutes. Tours depart year-round, weather permitting. **Liberty Helicopters** *(depart Midtown from heliport at 12th Ave. & W. 30th St. or Downtown from heliport at Pier 6; year-round daily 9am–9pm, Jan & Feb until 7:30pm; $52–$186;* ☎ *212-967-6464; www.libertyhelicopters.com).*

Neighborhood Tours

The following organizations offer a number of different walking tours through New York's distinct neighborhoods, exploring the city's diverse history and architecture:

Adventure on a Shoestring – ☎ *212-265-2663. About 25 tours year-round weekends. Any tour $5.*

Big Onion Walking Tours – ☎ *212-439-1090. www.bigonion.com. Weekend 2hr tours of historic districts and ethnic neighborhoods.*

Grand Tour of Midtown – ☎ *212-883-2468. Year-round Fri 12:30pm. Departs from corner of Park Ave. & 42nd St. by Whitney Museum.*

iMAR – ☎ *212-239-1124. www.imar.com. Insider Marketplace lists more than 300 different tours.*

New York Like a Native – ☎ *718-393-7537. www.nylikeanative.com. Offers a variety of Brooklyn tours year-round. Call or check their Web site for detailed tour and schedule information. $13–$35.*

Radical Walking Tours – ☎ *718-492-0069. www.he.net/~radtours. More than 12 tours year-round. Call for schedule & departure points. $10.*

Harlem Spirituals, Inc. *(see p 193) –* ☎ *212-391-0900. www.harlemspirituals.com.*

Scenic Cruises and Ferries

Tours of New York Harbor with panoramic views of the Statue of Liberty and the city's skyline are offered by the following boat lines:

NY Waterway – Harbor Cruise *(departs from Pier 78, W. 38th St. year-round daily 10am–4pm hourly; no cruises Jan 1 & Dec 25; 1hr 30min; $19)*; **Twilight Cruise** *(departs from Pier 78 May–Sept Mon–Fri 8:45pm, weekends 7:15pm & 8:45pm (Sat at 10:15pm also); no cruises Jan 1 & Dec 25; 1hr 30min; $19)*. Lower Harbor Cruise *(departs from Pier 17, South Street Seaport May–mid-Nov Mon–Fri 11:45am–3:45pm, weekends 11:45am–7:30pm; 50min; $11)*. All cruises: ✗ ♿ ☎ *800-533-3779; www.nywaterway.com.*

Circle Line tour boat

Courtesy New York Cruise Lines, INC

■ TV Show Tickets

Tickets for shows in NYC are free, but are often hard to come by since some shows have waiting lists over a year long. Mail a postcard in advance, submit a request online or call the shows listed below for tickets.

The Late Show with David Letterman – *The Ed Sullivan Theater, 1697 Broadway, NY, NY 10019. ☏ 212-247-6497. www.cbs.com. For stand-by tickets to the Late Show, call the above number at 11am on the day of the show. Phones will be answered as long as tickets are available.*

NBC Studio Show Tickets – *☏ 212-664-3056. www.nbc.com. For stand-by tickets, arrive at the 49th St. entrance of 30 Rockefeller Plaza (under the NBC Studios marquee) before the time listed above on the day of taping.*

      Late Night with Conan O'Brien   *stand-by: 9am*

      Saturday Night Live   *stand-by: 9am*

Live with Regis and Kelly – *For advance tickets, send a postcard to Live Tickets, Ansonia Station, P.O. Box 230777, NY, NY 10023; or try for same-day tickets at ABC Studios on the corner of 67th St. & Columbus Ave. at 7am. ☏ 212-456-3054.*

Who Wants To Be A Millionaire? – *For tickets and taping information, call ☏ 212-479-7755 or www.millionairetv.com. Stand-by tickets are available at the ABC Studios (67th St & Columbus Ave.) at 12:30pm for the 2pm show or at 3pm for the 4pm show.*

Total Request Live – *1550 Broadway, between 44th & 45th Sts. To be part of the studio audience for MTV's hit hosted by Carson Daly, call the hotline at ☏ 212-398-8549 or try for same-day stand-by tickets at the studio beginning at 2pm.*

No Tickets? You can still be on TV!

Several TV shows in NYC use background audiences gathered outside the plate-glass windows of the studio. If you are not able to acquire tickets to be real-life audience members, don't despair—you can still appear on television. Just arrive early outside one of these studios:

The Today Show – *30 Rockefeller Plaza, between Fifth & Sixth Aves.; Mon–Fri 7am–10am. www.nbc.com.*

Good Morning America – *Times Square at 44th St. & Broadway; Mon–Fri 7am–9am. ☏ 212-580-5176. www.abcnews.com.*

TV Tours

New York is the setting for many popular television shows and movies. On average, there are 75 movie or television crews filming daily throughout the city. Call or check Web sites for departure points and additional information.

On Location Tours, Inc. – This company offers six different bus tours, including the three listed below. Reservations are required for all of the On Location Tours (☏ 212-209-3370; www.sceneontv.com). Tours range from 2-4hrs and cost from $15-$35.

Manhattan TV and Movie Tour – Visit the Huxtables' home from *The Cosby Show*, stop by Central Perk where your favorite *Friends* get together and visit the diner where scenes from *Men in Black* were filmed.

Sopranos Tour – Jump into the world of Mafia boss Tony Soprano. Devotees of the popular miniseries, *The Sopranos*, will enjoy seeing sites like the Bada Bing night club and the cemetery where Livia is buried.

Sex and the City Tour – Carrie, Samantha, Charlotte and Miranda from *Sex in the City* have kept viewers entertained season after season with their escapades and antics. This tour will give you an inside-out view of the miniseries that constantly leaves fans wondering, "What could they possibly do next?"

NBC Experience/Studio Tour – Begin with a glimpse of the history of NBC, then see where shows like *NBC Sports*, *Dateline* and *Saturday Night Live* are filmed. Wrap up your tour with a glimpse of things to come with a demonstration of the futuristic look and sound of HDTV technology. *Tours begin and end at the NBC Experience Store (30 Rockefeller Plaza, between Fifth & Sixth Aves.; every 15 min Mon–Sat 8:30am–5:30pm, Sun 9:30am–4:30pm; $17.75; reservations: ☏ 212-664-3700; www.nbc.com; no children under age 6 permitted on tour).*

Circle Line – **Full Island Cruise** *(departs from Pier 83, W. 42nd St. early Mar–Dec; 3hrs; $26)*; **Harbor Lights Cruise** *(departs from Pier 83 early Mar–Nov; 2hrs; $21)*; **Seaport Liberty Cruise** *(departs from Pier 16, South Street Seaport early Mar–mid-Dec; 1hr; $13)*. Beast Speedboat Rides *(departs from Pier 16 and Pier 83 May–Oct; 30 min; $16)*. Call for departure times. No cruises Jan 1, Thanksgiving Day & Dec 24-25. ✗ ♿ 🅿 ☎ 212-563-3200. www.circleline.com.

Spirit Cruises – *All cruises depart from Pier 61, W. 23rd St.* Lunch cruises *(year-round daily 11:30am; 2hrs; $30–$39)*. Dinner cruises *(year-round daily 7pm; 3hrs; $55–$95)*. ✗ ♿ 🅿 (fee) ☎ 212-727-2789. www.spiritcruises.com.

Staten Island Ferry – *See p 282.*

Entertainment Tours

The following tours give visitors a behind-the-scenes look at some of the city's renowned entertainment venues.

Radio City Grand Tour *(p 96)*; **NBC Studio Tour** *(p 96)*; **Lincoln Center Tour** *(departs from the lower-level tour desk year-round; 1hr; $10; ☎ 212-875-5350; www.lincolncenter.org)*; Carnegie Hall Tours *(p 101)*; Madison Square Garden Tour *(tours begin on the hour Mon–Sun 10am–3pm and depart from the box office; $15; ☎ 212-465-5802; www.thegarden.com)*.

TIPS FOR SPECIAL VISITORS

New York for Children – *(See p 79)* In this guide, sights of particular interest to children are indicated with a 🆓 symbol. Many of these attractions offer special children's programs. *New York Family*, a free monthly magazine, includes articles of interest to parents as well as an extensive calendar of family-oriented events, and is available at major attractions and libraries throughout the area *(☎ 914-381-7474)*. The popular Brooklyn Children's Museum and Staten Island Children's Museum feature interactive exhibits designed for children under age 12. Most attractions in New York offer discounted, if not free, admission to visitors under 18 years of age. In addition, many hotels boast special family discount packages and some restaurants provide a special children's menu.

Travelers with Disabilities – In this guide wheelchair access is indicated in admission information accompanying sight descriptions with a ♿ symbol. Most public buildings, attractions, churches, hotels and restaurants provide wheelchair access. All New York City Transit buses and some subway lines are wheelchair-accessible. *For information, contact MTA Customer Assistance: ☎ 718-596-8585 or www.mta.nyc.ny.us.* Discounted fares are available. NYC Transit operates a shared-ride, door-to-door service for people with disabilities who are unable to use public transport; for information about eligibility, call ☎ 718-596-8585. *Access for All* provides a wealth of information about many sights and entertainment venues in New York *(available from Hospital Audiences, Inc., 548 Broadway, 3rd floor, New York, NY 10012; $5; ☎ 212-575-7676; www.hospitalaudiences.org)*.

Sports and Recreation

Spectator Sports

Tickets for sporting events can generally be purchased at the venue or through **Ticketmaster** *(☎ 212-307-7171; www.ticketmaster.com)*. Many sporting events—ranging from boxing to figure skating—take place at **Madison Square Garden**; contact the box office for information *(☎ 212-465-6741; www.thegarden.com)*. When events are sold out, you can sometimes get tickets for a fee through a ticket agency *(see Manhattan Yellow Pages)*.

Horse Racing

Racetrack	Season	Event	☎ Information
Aqueduct	Jan–May	Thoroughbred racing	718-641-4700
Belmont Park	May–mid-Oct Closed Aug	Thoroughbred racing, Belmont Stakes	516-488-6000
Meadowlands	Jan–Aug Sept–Dec	Harness and Thoroughbred racing	201-935-8500
Yonkers Raceway	year-round	Harness racing	914-968-4200

Note that racing seasons may change from year to year.

Professional Team Sports

Sport/Team	Season	Venue	☎ Information
⚾ **Baseball**	Apr–Oct		*www.mlb.com*
NY Mets (NL)		Shea Stadium	718-507-8499
NY Yankees (AL)		Yankee Stadium	212-307-1212
🏈 **Football**	Sept–Dec		*www.nfl.com*
NY Giants (NFC)		Giants Stadium	201-935-8222
NY Jets (AFC)		Giants Stadium	201-935-3900
🏈 **Arena Football**	Sept–Dec		*www.arenafootball.com*
NY Dragons		Nassau Coliseum	866-235-8499
NJ Gladiators		Continental Airlines Arena	866-654-5237
🏀 **Men's Basketball**	Oct–Apr		*www.nba.com*
NY Knicks (NBA)		Madison Square Garden	212-465-5867
NJ Nets (NBA)		Continental Airlines Arena	201-935-8888
🏀 **Women's Basketball**	May–Aug		*www.wnba.com*
NY Liberty		Madison Square Garden	212-564-9622
🏒 **Hockey**	Oct–Apr		*www.nhl.com*
NY Islanders (NHL)		Nassau Coliseum	800-882-4753
NY Rangers (NHL)		Madison Square Garden	212-465-6741
NJ Devils (NHL)		Continental Airlines Arena	201-935-3900
⚽ **Soccer**	Apr–Nov		*www.mlsnet.com*
NY/NJ MetroStars (MLS)		Giants Stadium	888-463-8768

Tennis – The USTA National Tennis Center (☎ *718-760-6200*) in Flushing Meadows-Corona Park, Flushing, is the site of the **US Open Tennis Championships** *(www.usopen.org)* during late August to mid-September. The WTA Tournament **Chase Championships**, a major women's professional event, takes place each year at Madison Square Garden in late November (☎ *212-465-6500*).

Recreation

After **Central Park**, New York City's largest public recreational facility is **Chelsea Piers** *(W. 23rd St & Hudson River;* ✷ ✗ ☎ *212-336-6666; www.chelseapiers.com).* This impressive complex resides on four former ocean liner piers and includes: the Golf Club's heated outdoor driving range with 52 stalls on four tiers *(Pier 59; open daily 6am–midnight; 17¢/ball–25¢/ball;* ☎ *212-336-6400);* Sports Center *(Pier 60; open Mon–Fri 6am–11pm, weekends 8am–9pm; day pass $50;* ☎ *212-336-6000)* housing the world's longest indoor running track, a rock-climbing wall, basketball courts, a swimming pool, aerobics studios, weight deck and spa services; Sky Rink indoor ice-skating arena *(Pier 61; year-round daily noon–5:20pm, extended hours Mon, Wed & Sat; $13; skate rentals available $6;* ☎ *212-336-6100);* outdoor in-line roller rinks & skate park *(Pier 62; weather permitting;* ☎ *212-336-6200);* and the Field House with facilities for gymnastics, soccer, lacrosse and field hockey leagues.

Biking and Jogging – In addition to **Central Park**, popular routes can be found in Riverside Park and along the East River Promenade on the Upper East Side. Contact the New York Road Runners Club *(p 174)* for more information. Bike rentals are available near Central Park; consult the Manhattan Yellow Pages.

Ice-skating in Central Park

Ice-Skating – Enjoy skating among the skyscrapers at the following venues in Central Park and at **Chelsea Piers** *(p 77)*:

The Rink at Rockefeller Plaza – *Open Oct–Apr Mon–Thu 9am–10:30pm, Fri–Sat 8:30am–midnight, Sun & holidays 8:30am–10pm. $13, Mon–Fri; $15, Sat & Sun (rates are higher during Christmas holidays). Skate rentals available, $6.* ☎ *212-332-7654.*

Wollman Skating Rink – *Open Oct–Apr Mon–Tue 10am–2:30pm, Wed–Thu 10am–10pm, Fri–Sat 10am–11pm, Sun 10am–9pm. $8.50, Mon–Fri; $11, Sat–Sun. Skate rentals available, $4.75.* ☎ *212-439-6900. www.wollman-skatingrink.com.*

Lasker Skating Rink – *Open Nov–Mar Mon, Wed, Thu 10am–3:45pm; Tue & Fri 10am–10pm; Sat 12:30pm–10pm; Sun 12:30pm–4:30pm. $4.50. Skate rentals available, $4.75.* ☎ *917-492-3856.*

Where To Get a Workout

The following clubs allow non-members to use their facilities (weight rooms, aerobics classes and pools) for a daily fee *($20–$50)*. Many private fitness centers are available to guests of major hotels; check with the concierge. **YMCA** memberships are valid worldwide *(for the closest YMCA recreation center, call* ☎ *212-630-9600 or www.ymca.net).*

Club *(Location)*	☎
New York Health & Racquet Club	
132 E. 45th St. *(Midtown)*	212-986-3100
20 E. 50th St. *(Midtown)*	212-593-1500
110 W. 56th St. *(Midtown)*	212-541-7200
115 E. 57th St. *(Midtown)*	212-826-9650
39 Whitehall St. *(Downtown)*	212-269-9800
24 E. 13th St. *(Downtown)*	212-924-4600
1433 York Ave. *(Uptown)*	212-737-6666
Crunch Fitness	
54 E. 13th St. *(Downtown)*	212-475-2018
152 Christopher St. *(Downtown)*	212-366-3725
404 Lafayette St. *(Downtown)*	212-614-0120
1109 Second Ave. *(Downtown)*	212-758-3434
162 W. 83rd St. *(Uptown)*	212-875-1902
New York Sports Clubs	
50 W. 34th St. *(Midtown)*	212-868-0820
614 Second Ave., at 34th St. *(Midtown)*	212-213-5999
575 Lexington Ave., at 51st St. *(Midtown)*	212-317-9400
19 W. 44th St., at Fifth Ave. *(Midtown)*	212-768-3535
1601 Broadway, at 49th St. *(15th floor; Midtown)*	212-977-8880
502 Park Ave., at 59th St. *(Midtown)*	212-308-1010
270 Eighth Ave. *(Downtown)*	212-243-3400
151 Reade St., at Greenwich St. *(Downtown)*	212-571-1000
125 Seventh Ave. S., at W. 10th St. *(Downtown)*	212-206-1500
113 E. 23rd St., at Park Ave. *(Downtown)*	212-982-4400
30 Wall St., at Broad St. *(Downtown)*	212-482-4800
151 E. 86th St., at Lexington Ave. *(Uptown)*	212-860-8630
349 E. 76th St., at First Ave. *(Uptown)*	212-288-5700
61 W. 62nd St., at Broadway *(Uptown)*	212-265-0995
248 W. 80th St., at Broadway *(Uptown)*	212-873-1500

Kids in New York City

Where To Eat

New York City offers a wide variety of kid-pleasing eateries, anything from a hot dog or a pretzel from a roadside vendor to lunch at ESPN Zone.

Mars 2112   *Corner of 51st & Broadway*   ☎ 212-582-2112

Take a ride on a UFO to the unknown world of Mars where you will find food, games and even aliens! *www.mars2112.com.*

Hard Rock Cafe   *221 W. 57th St.*   ☎ 212-489-6565

Rock and roll memorabilia is served up with heaping hamburgers and ribs. *www.hardrock.com.*

Planet Hollywood   *1540 Broadway at 45th St.*   ☎ 212-333-7827

Try to dine next to the belongings of your favorite Hollywood action hero or heartthrob. *www.planethollywood.com.*

Stardust Diner   *1650 Broadway & W. 51st St.*   ☎ 212-956-5151

Enjoy this classic 50s diner along with its singing waitstaff. *www.ellensstardustdiner.com.*

The Jekyll & Hyde Club   *1409 Avenue of the Americas*   ☎ 212-541-9517

A real New York favorite, visitors line up for tasty pub-style dining with a haunted house atmosphere. *www.eerie.com.*

Mickey Mantle's   *59th St. between Fifth*   ☎ 212-688-7777
   & Sixth Aves.

Check out the sports memorabilia museum, watch games on the numerous televisions and enjoy a plate of hickory-smoked ribs at this restaurant named after a famous New York Yankee. *www.mickeymantles.com.*

ESPN Zone   *1472 Broadway*   ☎ 212-921-3776

Watch your favorite team in action on one of many televisions, eat in the Studio Grill, then play upstairs in the Sports Arena. *www.espnzone.com.*

Shopping for Kids

FAO Schwarz   *767 Fifth Ave.*   ☎ 212-644-9400
www.fao.com

The Disney Store   *711 Fifth Ave.*   ☎ 212-702-0702
www.disneystores.com

NBA Store   *666 Fifth Ave.*   ☎ 212-515-6221
www.nba.com

NikeTown   *6 E. 57th St.*   ☎ 212-891-6453
www.niketown.com

Pokémon Center NY   *10 Rockefeller Plaza*   ☎ 212-307-0900
www.pokemoncenter.com

The Scholastic Store   *557 Broadway*   ☎ 212-343-6166
www.scholastic.com/sohostore

Toys 'R' Us   *1514 Broadway*   ☎ 646-366-8800
www.toysrustimessquare.com

Places to Play

Broadway City   *W. 42nd St. between 7th & 8th Sts.*   ☎ 212-997 0001

This interactive amusement center off Times Square offers video games and virtual reality galore. *www.broadwaycity.com*

Big Apple Circus   *Damrosch Park at Lincoln Center*   ☎ 800-922-3772

Classical circus acts mix with puppets, parades and floats in this New York favorite. *www.bigapplecircus.org.*

Central Park Carousel   *At 65th St. in Central Park*   ☎ 212-879-0244

The carousel, with its 58 hand-carved and hand-painted horses, has been running since 1870 *(Apr–Nov daily 10am–6pm; rest of the year weekends only, 10am–4:30pm; $1.25).*

Yankee Stadium Tour   *161st St. & River Ave., Bronx*   ☎ 718-579-4531

Visitors get a tour of the dugout, the press box, the clubhouse and Monument Park *(1hr tour offered daily at noon, except when games are scheduled; www.yankees.com).*

The New York Hall of Science   *47-01 111th St.*   ☎ 718-699-0005

A hands-on science museum in Flushing Meadows-Corona Park with over 200 exhibits. *www.nyscience.org.*

Bronx Zoo   *Fordham Rd. & Bronx*   ☎ 718-367-1010
   River Pkwy.

This stellar zoo in Bronx Park features more than 1,800 mammals, 1,200 birds and 1,000 reptiles and amphibians. *www.bronxzoo.com.*

Sony Wonder Technology Lab
   56th St. at Madison Ave.   ☎ 212-833-8100

Located in Sony Plaza, the lab is an interactive learning center that explores the world of electronics. *www.wondertechlab.sony.com.*

Coney Island   *1015 Surf Ave., Brooklyn*   ☎ 718-266-1234

This area offers a variety of activities including an amusement park, a famous boardwalk, an aquarium and the new Keyspan Stadium for professional baseball. A Coney Dog from Nathan's is a local tradition! *www.coneyislandusa.com.*

Madison Square Garden All Access Tour
   W. 32nd St. between Seventh& Eighth Aves.   ☎ 212-465-5800

Get an insider's view of how Madison Square Garden operates. Check out the locker rooms for the Knicks, Rangers and the Liberty, and maybe even get a glimpse of a pre-game practice or a performance rehearsal *(1hr tours available daily 10am–3pm; $16, adults; $12, children; www.thegarden.com).*

Staten Island Ferry   ☎ 718-815-2628

One of the few **free** things to do in NYC, the ferry takes you from the city to Staten Island. The ferry passes right by Ellis Island, giving a nice view of the Statue of Liberty. On the return trip, passengers enjoy a beautiful view of the New York City skyline. *www.siferry.com.*

■ Cyber-Cafés

E-mail withdrawal? Can't live without checking your daily stock quotes or knowing the outcome of the big game last night? Don't worry! The Big Apple offers its visitors many ways to surf the World Wide Web. Some hotels are now offering Web TV, which allows you to surf the net from the comfort of your hotel room. For about $10, you have the world at your fingertips for 24 hours. If your hotel doesn't offer this amenity, have no fear ... cyber cafés are popping up everywhere.

Cyber Cafe – *250 W. 49th St., Times Square. Open year-round Mon–Fri 8am–11pm, weekends 11am–1am.* ☎ *212-333-4109. www.cyber-cafe.com.*

Cyber Cafe SoHo – *273 Lafayette St. at Prince St. Open year-round Mon–Fri 8am–11pm, weekends 11am–1am.* ☎ *212-334-5140. www.cyber-cafe.com.*

Easy Internet Cafe – *Times Square/W. 42nd St. Open year-round daily 7am–1am. $1 for 5hrs (ticket valid for one month).* ☎ *212-398-0775. www.easyeverything.com/usa.*

Alt.coffee – *139 Avenue A. Open year-round Mon–Fri 7:30am–1am, weekends 9:30am–1am. $10/hr prorated).* ☎ *212-259-2233.*

NY Computer Cafe – *247 E. 57th St. Open year-round Mon–Fri 8am–11pm, Sat 10am–11pm, Sun 11am–11pm. $12/hr.* ☎ *212-872-1704. www.nycomputercafe.com.*

The Plaza Hotel overlooks Central Park

© Brigitta L House /MICHELIN

Sights

Manhattan

View south from the Empire State Building

Manhattan

Area: 22 square miles
Population: 1,537,195

Celebrated for its spectacular skyline, Manhattan constitutes the heart of New York City's vibrant cultural and commercial activity. This tongue-shaped island, flanked on the west by the expansive Hudson River and on the east by the Harlem and East rivers, measures 13.4mi in length and 2.3mi at its widest point, making it the smallest of the city's five boroughs. Manhattan, whose name derives from an Algonquian word meaning "island of the hills," was acquired from the Algonquian Indians by Dutch governor Peter Minuit in 1626, in exchange for trinkets valued, during that period, at a mere $24. The Dutch settlement of Nieuw Amsterdam developed on the island's southern tip, giving rise to the irregular street pattern that has prevailed to this day in the Financial District.

After British occupation the town expanded northward, following a neat grid of numbered streets that eventually predominated throughout most of the island.

Today the area south of 14th Street is known as "Downtown"; it is bordered on the north by "Midtown," which in turn gives way to "Uptown" beyond 59th Street at the southern rim of Central Park. Fifth Avenue, one of Manhattan's grand north-south thoroughfares, marks the boundary between the east and west sides.

The following **23 walks** will help you explore the rich variety of Manhattan's sights: busy avenues bordered by luxurious shops; historic and ethnic enclaves; bustling commercial districts; canyons of concrete and glass; airy landscaped plazas; and a multitude of soaring skyscrapers, grand civic structures and elegant mansions. The section on **museums** provides detailed information on more than 50 of New York City's reputed cultural institutions.

1 • FIFTH AVENUE★★★

MTA N, R train to 34th St.
Map pp 88 - 89

New York's most prestigious thoroughfare, Fifth Avenue is studded with striking land-mark skyscrapers, elegant churches, exclusive shops and grand public buildings. The elaborate window displays and the elegance of well-heeled New Yorkers contribute toward making this one of the most fascinating walks in the city.

Historical Notes

Residences were first erected on the lower stretch of Fifth Avenue in 1824, and by 1850 this area had become more fashionable than Broadway. Following the Civil War, a housing boom increased the number of town houses by 350. Each home cost at least $20,000—a small fortune at the time.

By 1880 the avenue was a busy and noisy thoroughfare, teeming with carriages and horse-drawn omnibuses. Scattered among the stately mansions were elegant private clubs and modest brownstones. The first fashionable stores were established in the mid-19C around 34th Street and continued to move northward on the avenue until the middle of this century.

From the very beginning, Fifth Avenue attracted fabulously rich New York society people. A.T. Stewart, a partner in several department stores, erected a splendid marble mansion at Fifth Avenue and 34th Street. The opposite corner was dominated by the huge brownstone of William Astor. Jay Gould, the American railroad tycoon, built a residence on the corner of 47th Street, while the Vanderbilt dynasty established itself around 50th Street. When Mrs. Astor erected a Renaissance palazzo at 65th Street, the city's movers and shakers followed suit and began to gravitate north. Today only a few 19C mansions remain on the avenue, offering a glimpse of the gilded path once known as "Millionaires' Row."

WALKING TOUR Distance: 2mi

Although such mass-market ventures as Disney and Coca-Cola have joined the avenue's famed exclusive jewelers and designers, and tony shoppers rub elbows with camera-toting tourists, Fifth Avenue continues to exude a sense of luxury and elegance unequaled in New York. To escape the clangorous activity, retreat to one of the peaceful church sanctuaries or head for the cafe and sculpture garden at the Museum of Modern Art.

Begin at the corner of Fifth Ave. and W. 34th St.

★★★**Empire State Building** – **Kids** *350 Fifth Ave.* Rising to a height of 1,454ft with a grace, elegance and strength that have made it one of the finest and most breathtaking skyscrapers ever built, the Empire State Building has remained, since its completion in 1931, the most distinctive feature of the Manhattan skyline.

Named for New York, the "Empire State," the sky-scraper was the world's tallest for four decades. Although it has been sur-passed by soaring towers in the US and the Far East, the

Empire State Building

The Complete Traveller

Map p 88. 199 Madison Ave., at 35th St. ☎ 212-685-9007. The oldest travel bookstore in the US, this cozy shop offers a great selection of the latest editions of travel guides from the most unique to the most popular destinations. Voyage into the past with their outstanding collection of antique travel books—with first editions from some of the world's oldest and best-known publishers.

Empire State Building remains the world's quintessential skyscraper. The view from the top is so impressive that it deserves two visits: by day, for an overview of the entire region, and then again in the evening, to enjoy the spectacle of the city's lights.

A Prestigious Site – The edifice occupies the site of two mansions belonging to William Astor and his wife, the former Caroline Schermerhorn, in the late 19C. William's nephew William Waldorf Astor tore down the southern mansion and erected the **Waldorf Hotel** (1893) next to his uncle's house. Within a year Mrs. Astor had moved north to Fifth Avenue and 65th Street, and by 1897 her son John Jacob Astor had razed the other mansion and built the **Astoria Hotel** next to the Waldorf. The hotels were operated together until 1929, when the structures were demolished to make way for the Empire State Building. The "new" Waldorf-Astoria Hotel was erected uptown, on Park Avenue, in 1931.

The Construction – Commissioned by a syndicate headed by Alfred E. Smith, governor of New York (1918-28), the building was completed in May 1931, less than two years after the first excavations began in October 1929. Work progressed at a hectic pace; at times, the building rose more than a floor each day. Since there are only two stories of foundations, 60,000 tons of steel beams—enough to lay a double-track railroad from New York to Baltimore—were added to support the tower. Although there were initial doubts as to the stability of the building, it has proved to be extremely sound. Specialists intended to use the top floor as a mooring platform for dirigibles, but the project was abandoned after one trial in 1932, which nearly resulted in a catastrophe. Tragedy struck the building in July 1945 when an errant bomber crashed into the 79th floor, killing 14 people, including the crew.

Visible for miles, the 203ft television antenna installed in 1985 is 22 stories high. A beacon light at the tip of the antenna serves as a warning signal for aircraft. The top 30 stories of the building are illuminated from dusk to midnight, often in colors that reflect the day or the season, e.g., green for St. Patrick's day; red, white and blue for national holidays such as Independence Day; and red and green at Christmastime. Lights are turned off on foggy nights during the spring and fall migratory bird seasons, lest the birds be confused by the diffused light and crash into the building.

Observatory – *Enter the ticket office from Fifth Ave. Open year-round daily 9:30am–midnight (reduced hours Jan 1 & Dec 24–25). $11.* ✗ ⅙ ☎ 212-736-3100. www.esbnyc.com. *Consult the visibility chart before buying your tickets.* Magnificent **views★★★** of the metropolitan area can be enjoyed from the open-air platform on the 86th floor observatory. On clear days the view extends for 80mi in all directions. Another elevator takes visitors to the glass-enclosed circular observatory on the 102nd floor.

■ How the Empire State Building Stacks Up

Height: 1,454ft (including 203ft antenna)

Weight: 365,000 tons

Materials: 200,000cu ft of limestone and granite, 10 million bricks, 730 tons of aluminum and stainless steel

Cost: almost $40 million

Floors: 102 (the 86th and 102nd are accessible to the public)

73 elevators and 7mi of shafts; the express elevator reaches the 80th floor in less than a minute

1,860 steps (it takes half an hour to walk all the way down); every year, runners have climbed 1,567 of the steps during the Empire State Building Run-Up (record time: 10min 47sec)

6,500 windows, washed once a month

About 15,000 people work here; another 35,000 visit daily

King Kong (1933) is the most famous movie filmed here

New York Skyride – 🎬 *Open year-round daily 10am–10pm. Shows every 10min. $16.50.* 👤 ☎ *212-279-9777. www.skyride.com. Combination tickets are available with the Empire State Building Observatory.* Although not for the fainthearted, this big-screen flight simulation makes for a thrilling ride. Visitors board a specially designed "craft," piloted by a famous New Yorker. Shortly after takeoff an engine failure causes the machine to plunge into the canyons of Manhattan—the beginning of a breathtaking tour of the city.

Continue north on Fifth Ave.

The section of Fifth Avenue between 34th and 40th streets is bordered by several large department stores, including the city's oldest, Lord & Taylor, known for fine clothing and its window displays during the Christmas season. The limestone Renaissance Revival edifice (1906) at 34th Street once housed the venerable B. Altman and Co. store, which closed in 1990. Today part of the grandly renovated interior is home to the Science, Industry and Business Library, one of the New York Public Library's four research branches. Other tenants include Oxford University Press and City University.

★★**New York Public Library Humanities & Social Sciences Library** – *476 Fifth Ave., between W. 40th & 42nd Sts. Open Mon & Wed 11am–7:30pm, Tue, Fri & Sat 10am–6pm. Closed major holidays.* 👤 ☎ *212-340-0830. www.nypl.org.* Founded in 1895 to combine the Astor Library, Lenox Library and Tilden Trust under one roof, this research branch of the New York Public Library is the second-largest research library in the US, after the Library of Congress in Washington, DC. A Beaux-Arts masterpiece by Carrère and Hastings, the imposing marble temple (1911) is midtown Manhattan's most striking public edifice. Two famous marble **lions** (Edward C. Potter), often called Patience and Fortitude, guard the main entrance. On the library's opening day in 1911, President William H. Taft declared, "This day crowns a work of national importance."

Historical Notes – The first American World's Fair took place in 1853 in the **Crystal Palace**, an imitation of the London Crystal Palace completed two years earlier. The domed iron and glass pavilion sheltered a large assortment of works of art and industrial products. A fire destroyed it in 1858, leaving the open space that would become Bryant Park. To the east of the park was the **Croton Distribution Reservoir** (1845), a fortlike building topped by a walkway that surrounded a 4-acre reservoir supplied with water from Croton Lake in Westchester County. It remained in service until 1899 and was replaced 12 years later by the New York Public Library building. A little farther north, set back from 42nd Street, was a pointed tower of timber braced with iron rising more than 300ft. A predecessor of the Eiffel Tower, the **Latting Observatory**, as it was called, had three levels of wooden platforms. The highest one afforded a superb view of New York, with the Croton Reservoir and Crystal Palace in the foreground. The observatory, too, was short-lived; it burned down in 1856, only three years after its completion.

Collections and Library Network – Disseminated in various branches throughout New York City, the library's collection comprises more than 15 million books and more than 48 million manuscripts, maps, phonograph records, tapes, prints and other library materials. The main building itself contains more than 16 million manuscripts, 178,000 prints and 370,000 maps. The Research Libraries, which are privately financed, house 11 million volumes in four locations, including the Center for the Humanities *(main building)*; the Schomburg Center for Research in Black Culture; the New York Public Library for the Performing Arts *(40 Lincoln Plaza)*, featuring collections in the fields of theater, music and dance; and the Science, Industry and Business Library *(above)*.

A network of 86 branch libraries and 4 research libraries serves Manhattan, the Bronx and Staten Island. The largest of the branch libraries are located in the midtown area: the Mid-Manhattan Library *(455 Fifth Ave.)*; the Donnell Library Center *(20 W. 53rd St.)*; and the well-known Andrew Heiskell Braille and Talking Book Library *(40 W. 20th St.)*, containing thousands of braille and recorded materials.

Visit – The library's main entrance at Fifth Avenue opens into the grand, white marble **Astor Hall**, adorned with lavish decorations. Turn to the south corridor, where the newly opened (2002) **South Court**, a dramatic 6-story glass structure with cantilevered floors, holds the visitor center, 2 classrooms, offices and a 178-seat auditorium. A film *(12min)* on the history of the library is shown in the visitor center's screening room. At the corridor's end, the richly paneled **DeWitt Wallace Periodical Room** *(no access from South Court)* contains a series of 13 murals by 20C artist Richard Haas. Behind Astor Hall, the handsome Beaux-Arts **Gottesman Hall**, enhanced by graceful marble arches and a carved oak ceiling, presents major temporary exhibits. *Take the elevator at the far north end of the corridor on the right to the third floor.*

Rotating exhibits, including portraits by noted American artists and printmakers, adorn the walls on the third floor. Selections from the library's special collections are presented in the **Salomon Room**★, a 19C picture gallery. Among the rarities displayed on occasion are a draft of the Declaration of Independence in Jefferson's own hand and an edition of Galileo's works, which can be read only with a magnifying glass. The paintings on permanent display include a group of five portraits of George Washington on the west wall. The large central hall, **McGraw Rotunda**, is decorated with wood paneling and murals depicting the story of the recorded word. Facing the Salomon Room is the **Public Catalog Room**, which contains 800 retrospective volumes with 10 million entries. Beyond is the enormous main reading room, which recently underwent a $15 million renovation; it has 51ft ceilings and covers half an acre. Additional space for library stacks has been created beneath Bryant Park.

Continue west on W. 42nd St. to Bryant Park.

★ **Bryant Park** – *On Avenue of the Americas, between W. 40th & 42nd Sts.* Located behind the library, this formal garden is midtown's only large green space. Built on the site once occupied by the Crystal Palace and Croton Reservoir, the park was named for **William Cullen Bryant** (1794-1878) in 1884 but remained vacant until 1934, when it was given a complete makeover by Parks Commissioner Robert Moses, using plans drawn by Lusby Simpson. Despite endeavors to keep the park a pleasant public space, it soon became a gathering spot for the unemployed and homeless, and in the 1960s it was taken over by drug dealers and panhandlers. The park reopened to the public in late 1991 after undergoing an extensive restoration effort, which included widening the entrances, planting 300ft-long flower borders, and adding hundreds of folding chairs. Today tourists and New Yorkers alike flock to Bryant Park to relax and enjoy concerts of live music and, on occasion, art exhibits. In summer the park becomes an oasis of coolness in sweltering Manhattan, and is host to snack kiosks and informal chess games. On summer evenings, free movies are projected on a huge screen in the park *(call 212-512-5700 for schedule).*

Among the sculptures dotting the landscaped alleys, note the 1911 **memorial (1)** to the park's namesake, a bronze statue sheltered by a marble canopy. Author of the poem "Thanatopsis," Bryant was editor and part-owner of the *New York Evening Post*, an influential paper during the Civil War. He also gained renown

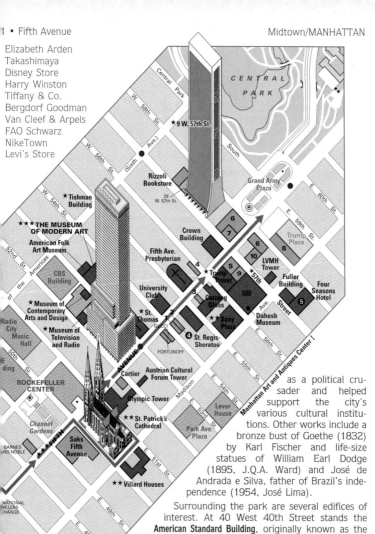

Elizabeth Arden
Takashimaya
Disney Store
Harry Winston
Tiffany & Co.
Bergdorf Goodman
Van Cleef & Arpels
FAO Schwarz
NikeTown
Levi's Store

as a political crusader and helped support the city's various cultural institutions. Other works include a bronze bust of Goethe (1832) by Karl Fischer and life-size statues of William Earl Dodge (1895, J.Q.A. Ward) and José de Andrada e Silva, father of Brazil's independence (1954, José Lima).

Surrounding the park are several edifices of interest. At 40 West 40th Street stands the **American Standard Building**, originally known as the American Radiator Building, designed by Raymond Hood in 1924. Inspired by Gothic tradition, the black brick building is adorned with gold terra-cotta trim.

To the west rises the streamlined form of the **New York Telephone Company Building** *(1095 Avenue of the Americas)*, faced with alternating columns of white marble and dark tinted glass. Dominating the north side of the park, at 1114 Avenue of the Americas, is the **Grace Building** (1974), the hyperbolic lines of its base merging without break into a 50-story tower of travertine and tinted glass. It was erected by the architectural firm of Skidmore, Owings & Merrill, which designed a similar building that same year at 9 West 57th Street. The City University Graduate Center *(33 W. 42nd St.)* is one of 20 individual educational units within the City University of New York (CUNY). The Mall, a pedestrian arcade running from 42nd to 43rd Street between Fifth Avenue and the Avenue of the Americas, hosts art exhibits and occasional free concerts.

Return to Fifth Ave. and continue north.

At the corner of 43rd Street is a branch of **Chase Manhattan Bank** (1954; Skidmore, Owings & Merrill). One of the first banks constructed in glass, it represented a

 Bryant Park Grill
Map p 88. 25 W. 40th St., between Fifth Ave. & Avenue of the Americas.
☏ *212-840-6500.*
www.arkrestaurants.com.
This handsome restaurant, a popular lunch spot for nearby magazine publishers, has made perfect use of the long-empty space behind the New York Public Library. Both the terrace and the airy dining room offer sensational views of Bryant Park and the lunchtime throngs sprawling on the main lawn.

radical departure from the usual thick-walled buildings of masonry. The lobby is decorated with Macassar ebony furniture and Italian marble floors. Among the abstract sculpture, note the spectacular composition (1953, Harry Bertoia) of metallic strips hanging from the ceiling. The door of the main vault is visible through one of the windows.

On the corner of 45th Street, look up to admire the attractive multicolored faience decoration embellishing the upper stories of the **Fred F. French Building** *(551 Fifth Ave.)*. Constructed of masonry and solid in appearance, the ornate building (1927) rises 38 floors in a series of massed setbacks, in typical 1920s fashion.

Turn left onto W. 46th St. and continue west, crossing Ave. of the Americas.

Church of St. Mary the Virgin – *145 W. 46th St. Open year-round Mon–Fr 7am–7pm, Sat 10:30am–5:30pm, Sun 8am–6:00pm, Guided tours available by appointment. ☎ 212-869-5830. www.stmvirgin.com.* Distinguished by a Gothic Revival facade, this Episcopal church was founded in 1868. The present building was completed in 1895. Extensively decorated during the first part of the century, the interior was restored in 1996. Note in the left side aisle the Madonna and Child, a 19C majolica bas-relief from the Della Robbia workshop in Florence, Italy. The murals adorning the Lady Chapel represent the Annunciation and the Epiphany. Admire the colossal pulpit in the nave; and in the baptistery, note the wooden font cover embellished with 73 delicately carved figures. The Chapel of Our Lady of Mercy contains a black marble altar and a 15C plaque depicting the death of St. Anthony. In the apse above the high altar, three large stained-glass lancet windows (early 20C) were crafted by Kempe of England. Located in the rear gallery, the Aeolian-Skinner organ, built in 1932, has nearly 6,000 pipes.

Return to Ave. of the Americas, turn left and then right onto W. 47th St.

★**Diamond and Jewelry Way** – This 750ft block of 47th Street, between Fifth Avenue and Avenue of the Americas, is home to nearly 90 percent of the diamond wholesale trade in America. Carat, cut, color and clarity are discussed in a bewildering variety of languages—Spanish, Yiddish, Armenian, Russian and Arabic. The street is lined with shops, notably the International Jewelers Exchange, the National Jewelers Exchange, the Diamond Center of America and the New York Jewelry Center, all displaying a superb array of precious stones. Much of the trade is carried on in booths located on the upper floors and in the rear of the buildings. Sophisticated security systems protect the dealers from unwelcome intruders.

The merchants usually carry their precious bounty in suitcases, unobtrusive packages or in their coat pockets. The exchanges take place either right on the sidewalk or in one of two private-membership diamond-dealer clubs; major transactions may be sealed simply by a handshake. Offenders transgressing this honor code are reportedly blacklisted throughout the diamond world.

Continue north on Fifth Ave.

Between 48th and 49th streets lies a Barnes & Noble bookstore with its tremendous array of bestsellers. Across the avenue, note the building at no. 601. Designed by Ernest Flagg, who also conceived the Singer Building in SoHo, the edifice (1913) has retained its handsome turn-of-the-century cast-iron facade and genteel interior. Cross 49th Street and enter the shopping emporium of **Saks Fifth Avenue**, an exclusive department store offering designer collections for men and women. Eye-catching window displays are spectacular at Christmastime.

③ Gotham Book Mart

Map p 88. 41 W. 47th St., between Fifth Ave. & Avenue of the Americas. ☎ 212-719-4448. Step off Diamond and Jewelry Way into New York's most beloved bookstore, with its quirky sign that says "Wise Men Fish Here," an allusion to a fairy tale about the three wise men of Gotham. This haven for bibliophiles has been trumpeting the new and modern in literature and poetry since it opened in 1920; today it remains a musty but appealing warren of faded covers, tattered literary magazines and tacked-up flyers for groups like the Yeats Society. There actually is a logic to the shelving of the quarter-of-a-million mostly used books on literature, poetry, film and theater. Just ask the numerous and knowledgeable staff—they will even help you find a used, signed first edition, but you have to know what you want (they keep hundreds in storage).

★★★**Rockefeller Center** – *Description p 94.*

★★**Saint Patrick's Cathedral** – *On Fifth Ave., between E. 50th and 51st Sts. Open year-round Sun–Fri 7am–6pm, Sat 8am–6pm. ♿ ☎ 212-753-2261. www.ny-arch-diocese.org/pastoral.* Designed by renowned architect **James Renwick** (1818-95), New

York City's major Roman Catholic cathedral was one of the first examples of Gothic Revival ecclesiastical architecture in the US. When construction of the cathedral began in 1853, churchgoers complained that it was too far out in the country. However, the city continued its growth northward, and by the time the church was consecrated in 1879, Saint Patrick's dominated the city's most fashionable residential district. Today the slender, balanced proportions seem rather dwarfed by the Rockefeller Center high rises and the Olympic Tower, whose glass wall mirrors the church.

The elegant granite and marble structure, with its 330ft spires (1888), is reminiscent of the cathedral of Cologne, Germany. Missing, however, are the extensive stone carvings (owing partially to the use of granite, a hard stone) and the flying buttresses, hallmarks of Gothic architecture.

Saint Patrick's Cathedral

© Brigitta L. House/MICHELIN

Inside, the cathedral features a typical cruciform plan. Three portals with intricately sculpted bronze doors open into the spacious nave, illuminated by stained-glass windows of the Gothic type, most of which were manufactured in Chartres and Nantes, France. A series of slender marble pillars supports the cross-ribbed vaults, which rise 110ft above the nave. Note also the elegantly designed baldachin over the high altar (Renwick), and the monumental organ. Located behind the apse, the lovely Lady Chapel was added in 1906.

The cathedral is dedicated to the patron saint of the Irish, who constitute a large segment of New York's population. The festivities of St. Patrick's Day demonstrate their veneration for the apostle of Ireland. Each Easter Sunday, Fifth Avenue near Saint Patrick's is closed to traffic and New Yorkers stroll in their spring finery. The event is memorialized in Irving Berlin's song "Easter Parade."

Head east on E. 50th St. to Madison Ave.

Facing Madison Avenue, the apse of Saint Patrick's is flanked by two small town houses: the rectory *(no. 460)* and the residence of the archbishop *(no. 452)*.

★★Villard Houses (New York Palace Hotel) – *451-457 Madison Ave.* This graceful ensemble features a group of six mansions built in 1885 by McKim, Mead and White for Henry Villard, founder of the Northern Pacific Railroad. The brown, Renaissance-style houses appear to be one mansion built in a U-shape around a central courtyard. Inspired by the Palazzo della Cancelleria in Rome, the architects successfully incorporated such elements as window framing and arcades into a 19C North American residential style. Following World War II, several companies used the mansions as office space until the Archdiocese of New York sold them to the Helmsley chain in 1976, on the condition that they be preserved as the hotel's public rooms. Today the town house serves as the entrance for the New York Palace hotel.

Enter the pedestrian courtyard—formerly a carriage yard—through the wrought-iron gates fronting Madison Avenue, and step inside the central mansion. The interior, appointed in an ornate, Italian Renaissance style, features luxuriously restored public rooms which have been luxuriously restored. Now part of **Le Cirque 2000** restaurant, the **Gold Room**, with its barrel-vaulted ceiling, musicians' gallery and lunette paintings by John LaFarge, exudes an aura of 1930s high society. Adorned with Venetian mosaics, the great hallway features a sweeping staircase graced with stained-glass windows by Louis Comfort Tiffany and a gilt and marble zodiac clock by Augustus Saint-Gaudens. The latter also designed the red marble fireplace dominating the second-floor lobby.

Return to Fifth Ave. on E. 51st St. and continue north.

At no. 645 rises the 51-story **Olympic Tower**. This elegant, brown tinted-glass building (1976; Skidmore, Owings & Merrill) houses shops, offices and luxury apartments on its upper stories. Located on the ground floor, H. Stern Jewellers enjoys a worldwide reputation for colored gemstones hailing primarily from Brazil. Olympic Place, an indoor arcade, is a delightful public space, replete with a reflecting waterfall, palm trees and plants *(entrance on Fifth Ave.).*

The Renaissance-style palazzo on the southeast corner of 52nd Street houses the French jewelry firm **Cartier** *(651 Fifth Ave.),* which acquired the building in 1917. The edifice is one of the avenue's few remaining early-20C mansions originally built for the city's moneyed class.

Austrian Cultural Forum Tower — *11 E. 52nd St. Open Mon–Sat 10am–6pm.* ☏ *212-319-5300. www.acfny.org.* Across from Olympic Tower, on the north side of 52nd Street, stands a severe sliver of a building, its sloped glass-wall facade marked by protruding beams and overlapping setbacks. Built for the Austrian Cultural Forum in 2002 by Austrian-born Raimund Abraham (a New York resident since the early 1970s), the 24-story tower announces the forum's touchstone theme of "transforming modernity." The forward-looking programming, which explores the rich legacy of Austrian art and culture in a context of emerging digital culture, furthers that mission. Within, the facilities include a series of connected public spaces for exhibitions and installations, a two-level library, and a bright, cheerful 90-seat theater.

★**Tishman Building** – *666 Fifth Ave.* Built in 1957, the 39-story edifice with its facade of embossed aluminum panels represents a worthy attempt at originality. The interior is equally imaginative, with its unusual ceiling composed of thin wavy hanging strips, and a cascade fountain on one wall. Designed by Isamu Noguchi, the space exudes an air of serenity often found in Japanese gardens.

★**St. Thomas Church** – *At corner of W. 53rd St. Open year-round Mon–Fri 7am–6:30pm, Sat 7am–2pm, Sun 7am–7pm. Guided tours (1hr) available Sun 12:30pm.* ♿ ☏ *212-757-7013. www.saintthomaschurch.org.* Topped by a single tower, this Episcopal church was completed in 1913 by Cram, Goodhue and Ferguson in a flamboyant Gothic Revival style. It replaces a building destroyed by fire in 1905. A wealth of statues and delicate tracery adorns the facade on Fifth Avenue. In the center of the main portal, St. Thomas, flanked by six of the apostles, welcomes the worshipers. The remaining apostles are arrayed overhead in the tympanum. Below the sculptures, bas-reliefs depict the legend of St. Thomas. Step to the left of the main portal to admire the narrow "Brides' Entrance," ornately decorated with symbolically joined hands.

On entering the nave, note the lovely **reredos**★ of Dunville stone that rises to a height of 80ft above the altar. Spotlighted, it forms a light contrast to the dark vault. Numerous recesses shelter statues of Christ, the Virgin Mary, the apostles and other saints, carved by Lee Lawrie. Also of interest are the stained-glass windows in deep reds and blues, the pulpit and the sculptured organ case.

Opposite St. Thomas Church, on the east side of Fifth Avenue, stands Fortunoff, a four-story jewelry and silverware emporium, distinguished by a sleek, stainless steel and glass facade. Adjoining Fortunoff, the Italian fashion and shoe boutique Gucci displays its wares, recognizable by the red and green stripe. Set on the northwest corner of 54th Street, the imposing **University Club** was designed by McKim, Mead and White (1899) in the Italian Renaissance style. Adorning the building's three-tiered granite exterior are the shields of major American universities, all carved by Daniel Chester French.

Between 54th and 55th streets, adjacent to a second Gucci shop, is the famed beauty and fashion salon of **Elizabeth Arden (1)**, heralded by a bright red door. Occupying an elegant tower designed by John Burgee in 1993, **Takashimaya (2)**, a Japanese retail store, offers a luxurious and peaceful retreat from the avenue. The carefully selected merchandise emphasizes Eastern aesthetics as well as Western functionality. At the corner of 55th Street is the elegant **St. Regis-Sheraton Hotel**, designed in 1904 in an ornate, Beaux-Arts style. It was commissioned by John Jacob Astor as one of the first luxury hotels in the city. Note the Maxfield Parrish **mural** in the King Cole Bar.

Fifth Avenue Presbyterian Church – *At corner of W. 55th St. Open Jun–Sept Mon–Fri 9am–5pm, weekends 8am–4pm. Rest of the year Mon–Fri 9am–5pm, Sat 8am–5pm, Sun 8am–4pm. Closed major holidays.* ♿ ☏ *212-247-0490. www.fapc.org.* Erected in 1875 in the Gothic Revival style, this edifice is one of the last churches built in brownstone in the city. The sanctuary, with a seating capacity of 1,800, is notable for its magnificent organ casing and an intricately carved ashwood pulpit.

Facing the church, large figures of Mickey and Minnie Mouse, wielding crayons and paintbrushes, mark the latest mass-market venture to join the avenue once known only for its exclusive boutiques. The **Disney Store (3)** [Kids] stocks merchandise based on popular characters from its famous animation studio.

The southeast corner of 56th Street is occupied by the **Corning Glass Building**, New York City headquarters of one of the world's leading producers of fine glass, including Steuben crystal. Built in 1959, the 28-story building bears the characteristics of skyscrapers from that era: tinted-glass exterior, trim lines and an outdoor plaza with reflecting pool. The Steuben shop on the ground floor presents displays of new or historical designs and examples of crystal ware often chosen as gifts for heads of state. Standing opposite is the small Renaissance-style palace of jeweler **Harry Winston (4)**, who specializes in diamonds and precious stones.

★**Trump Tower** – *725 Fifth Ave.* Rising 58 stories above street level is the exuberant, bronze-mirrored Trump Tower, a luxurious mixed-use structure containing commercial space, condominium apartments and retail stores. Designed in 1983 by Der Scutt, this glass-sheathed tower, with its myriad tiny setbacks often topped by trees and shrubs, is typical of the lively, innovative skyscraper style of the 1980s. The six-story **atrium**★, a lavish pink marble shopping center featuring an 80ft-high waterfall cascading down one side, offers an array of fine boutiques and specialty shops, such as Asprey and Charles Jourdan.

At the corner of 57th Street, stop to gaze at the exquisite window displays at **Tiffany & Co. (5)**, the internationally renowned jewelry store. Visitors can also admire the 128-carat Tiffany Diamond, displayed along the far left wall from the Fifth Avenue entrance. Across the avenue is the **Crown Building** (1921), its chateau-like upper section richly embellished in 23-carat gold leaf. Designed by Warren & Wetmore in the French Renaissance style, the building is named for the gilded crown at its pinnacle. Ferragamo, known for fine shoes and leather accessories, occupies a street-level shop.

 Tea Box Café at Takashimaya
Map p 89. 693 Fifth Ave. between 54th & 55th Sts. ☎ *212-350-0180. Tea served Mon–Sat 3pm–5:45pm (extended holiday hours).* Escape midtown's clamor in this soothing beige basement tea salon in the Takashimaya department store. Nearly 40 kinds of tea are available by the pot, and more by the ounce in loose leaf, as well as delicious pastries and green-tea ice cream. A good choice is the "East-West" tea service, which includes a pot of tea (try the *sen-cha*, a sweet green tea) with a tray of sandwiches (curry crab roe, salmon pressed on rice, wasabi chicken), your choice of desserts (green-tea mousse, panna cotta), sweet-potato chips, fruit and chocolates.

On either side of the avenue between 57th and 58th streets is **Bergdorf Goodman's** legendary emporium **(6)**, a bastion of haute couture. Adjacent to the store, the jewelry boutique of **Van Cleef & Arpels (7)** features a sparkling array of treasures, including the diamond tiara of the Empress Josephine.

Towering over the east side of Grand Army Plaza is the General Motors Building, a 50-story tower (1968) articulated by white marble piers. Enter the renowned **FAO Schwarz** toy store **(8)** 🎈, located within the building, to view the 28ft animated clock tower.

MUSEUMS *(See Museums section)*

★★**Pierpont Morgan Library** – *29 E. 36th St.*

 ★**Museum of Television and Radio** – *25 W. 52nd St.*

 ★**International Center of Photography** – *1133 Avenue of the Americas*

 ★**Museum of Arts & Design** – *40 W. 53rd St.*

  American Folk Art Museum – *45 W. 53rd St.*

  Dahesh Museum – *580 Madison Ave. at 56th St.*

Visitors ogle a Christmas window display at Bergdorf's

© Scott Barrow

2 • ROCKEFELLER CENTER AREA★★★

MTA B, D, F train to Rockefeller Center

Map below

Located in the heart of midtown Manhattan, between Fifth and Seventh avenues and 47th and 52nd streets, Rockefeller Center comprises an imposing group of harmoniously designed skyscrapers dating primarily from the pre-World War II era. Vital, dignified and steeped in an air of festivity year-round, this jewel of an urban complex draws thousands of office workers and tourists daily.

Historical Notes

The Beginnings – In the early 19C, the site now occupied by Rockefeller Center was part of public lands administered by the city. Collectively known as "Common Lands"or "The Fields," the area extended from today's City Hall up to approximately 53rd Street. Dr. David Hosack, a professor of botany, acquired 15 acres from the city for $5,000 to establish a public botanical garden. In 1811 he sold the land to the State of New York, which turned it over to Columbia University. The university then rented parcels to farmers for $100 a year.

The first buildings on the site appeared around 1850, when New York's present gridiron pattern of streets and avenues was laid out. The area soon developed into a fashionable residential district, where splendid mansions stood side by side with modest brownstones. A few of these residences have survived to this day on 53rd Street. In the 1900s the neighborhood began to decline. The area had become noisy, especially after the construction of the Sixth Avenue "El" (the elevated railway) in 1878, and the millionaires and middle class moved away to Fifth Avenue, leaving their fine homes to poorer tenants. Later, during the Prohibition era, this once elegant district became notorious as the "speakeasy belt." Following the repeal of Prohibition, many speakeasies on 52nd Street were converted to jazz clubs, hosting such artists as Count Basie, Harry James and Coleman Hawkins.

The Rockefellers – In 1870 the American oil magnate John Davison Rockefeller (1839-1937) created the Standard Oil Co. of Ohio and soon began dominating the US oil industry. When John Sr. retired in 1911 as a multimillionaire, his son, **John D. Rockefeller Jr.** (1874-1960), took over management of the company. During his tenure, he was known as one of the nation's greatest philanthropists. His most important contributions in New York City helped erect the United Nations Headquarters, the Cloisters and Riverside Church.

"John D.," as he was called, leased the land now occupied by the Rockefeller Center from Columbia University in 1928. With associates from the Metropolitan Opera, Rockefeller planned to erect a colossal new opera house on the site. The initial lease ran 24 years and was renewable until 2015, when the land and the building would revert to the university; however, the crash of 1929 brought this project to an abrupt halt. Left during the Depression days with a long-term lease on this parcel of land and a sizable rent to pay, John D. decided to build a commercial center, a "city within a city." In 1933, when the RCA Building (now the GE Building) was opened, John D. celebrated by moving the Rockefeller family office from 26 Broadway to 30 Rockefeller Plaza.

An Urban Triumph – Over a period of 10 years, 228 buildings were destroyed and 12 edifices erected on an area of approximately three blocks (12 acres). The project's core, including the RCA Building, was completed in 1940. Expected to trigger a boom and bring renewal to the area, the center quickly fulfilled its goal. Seven additional buildings were added between 1947 and 1973. The ensemble was designed by a

eam of seven architects, which included Wallace K. Harrison, who was also responsi-
le for the design of the United Nations Headquarters and Lincoln Center. The primary
ntent of the architects was to provide midtown Manhattan with an urban center that
vould foster a sense of community, openness, beauty and convenience. The result is
a wonderful combination of buildings, open spaces, restaurants, shops and boutiques.
Today 19 buildings cover about 22 acres and house a working population of 65,000.
Add to that the number of tourists who visit the center each day and the result is a
workday population of more than 275,000 persons. The buildings are connected by
a maze of underground passages, the concourse, lined with attractive shops and
restaurants; the concourse also provides access to the subway system.

WALKING TOUR *Distance: 1mi*

Begin in front of Saint Patrick's Cathedral on Fifth Ave.

Rising across the street from St. Patrick's Cathedral, the 41-story **International
Building** (1935) houses consulates, international airlines, travel agencies and a passport office on the mezzanine level. Standing in front of the building is a
monumental bronze statue of Atlas (1937, Lee Lawrie) supporting the world.
Enter the vast lobby, with its piers and walls of marble from the Greek island of
Tinos. The ceiling is covered with very thin gold leaf. If all this gold were removed
from the ceiling, it would weigh about a pound and, melted down, could be held
in the palm of your hand.

Continue to the Channel Gardens.

★★**Channel Gardens** – 🄺🄸🄳🄸 *Fifth Ave. between 49th & 50th Sts.* A relaxing spot, these
gardens separate two low-lying, seven-story structures topped by roof gardens: the

Maison Française (1933) on
the left, and the British Empire Building (1932) on the
right. A series of six pools is
surrounded by flower beds,
which are changed regularly
in season, beginning with
Easter lilies on Good Friday.
The promenade leads down
a gentle slope to the lower
plaza. Centerpiece of Rockefeller Center, it is a sunken
open area rimmed by the
flags of the United Nations
member countries. At the
top of the steps leading to
the lower plaza is a plaque
citing John D.'s credo.

On the north side of the
plaza, note the colorful
limestone screen adorning
the International Building's
south facade. Designed in
1935 by Lee Lawrie, it represents man's progress in
the fields of art, science,
trade and industry. The
west side of the lower plaza
is dominated by the cen-
ter's best-known sculpture,
the gold-leaf bronze statue
of **Prometheus (1)** (1934,
Paul Manship) stealing the
sacred fire for humankind.

© Brigitta L. House/MICHELIN

Channel Gardens in autumn

An outdoor cafe in summer, the plaza serves as a skating rink in winter. Every December, a huge Christmas tree towers 65ft to 90ft above this setting. Visitors come
to admire the spectacular lighting displays and to observe the ice-skaters on the
rink below.

Rockefeller Plaza, a private street running from north to south between 48th and
51st streets, was constructed to provide access to the GE Building. The street is
closed one day each year so that it does not become public property, in accor-
dance with local laws.

★★**GE (General Electric) Building** – *30 Rockefeller Plaza.* Soaring 850ft above street
level, the 70-story GE Building (former RCA Building; renamed in 1990) is the
loftiest of the center's towers and also the most harmonious architecturally. Slight
setbacks in the massing of its slablike form soften the severity of its lines. General
Electric and the National Broadcasting Co. (NBC) are headquartered here.

Rainbow Room

Map p . 44 Rockefeller Plaza.
☎ *212-632-5000.*
www.cipriani.com. It would
be difficult to find a spot
more glamorous, or more
"New York," than the 65th
floor of the GE building. The
place for a drink with a view
is the Rainbow Grill *(open
daily 5pm–11:30pm; jackets
required)* or pull out all the
stops for a romantic evening
at the Rainbow Room *(open
Fri 7pm–1am; black tie).*
Here you can dance cheek to
cheek on the revolving dance
floor, with all of glittering
Manhattan as a backdrop.

A glass and limestone Art Deco panel
(1933) by Lee Lawrie enlivens the main
entrance at 30 Rockefeller Plaza. Step
into the lobby decorated with immense
ceiling and wall murals by the Spanish
artist José Maria Sert depicting America's development and man's progress
through time. These murals are actually
the second series executed for the
building. The first set, designed by
Mexican muralist Diego Rivera, was
considered too radical for this capital-
istic enterprise and was subsequently
destroyed.

On the 65th floor is the **Rainbow Room★**,
the legendary ballroom and restaurant,
which reopened its doors in 1987 after
a two-year restoration effort. Spectacular views can be enjoyed from all sides.

★**NBC Studios** – 🎥 *Visit by guided tour
(1hr) only Mon–Sat 10am–5pm every
hour, Sun 10am–4pm. No tours Thanksgiving Day & Dec 25. $10.* ☎ *212-664-*
7174. *www.nbc.com.* Several floors of the GE Building are devoted to National
Broadcasting Co. television studios. After providing a brief overview of the company's "golden days" in radio, the tour takes visitors through various studio sets,
including *Saturday Night Live.* High-tech equipment, including NBC's "Van Go" mobile units, which monitor all major sporting events, can also be viewed. The tour
ends in a simulated mini-studio where visitors appear on camera and learn a meteorologist's tricks for explaining the weather on television. The new street-level
studio for the *Today Show* draws throngs of tourists every morning.

Across the street at 20 Rockefeller Plaza is a new 300,000sq ft complex completed
in 1999 for **Christie's**, the fine-art auction house founded in 1766 and formerly
located on Park Avenue.

Continue west on W. 50th St. to Radio City Music Hall.

★★**Radio City Music Hall (A)** – *1260 Avenue of the Americas.* ☎ *212-632-4041.
www.radiocity.com.* A treasured New York landmark, Radio City Music Hall is one
of the city's most grandiose Art Deco creations and a spectacular entertainment
venue. The Music Hall opened its doors to the public in 1932, under the direction
of Samuel "Roxy" Rothafel, to present variety shows. At the time, it was the largest
indoor theater in the world. In order to become more profitable, the Music Hall
began operating as a movie house and soon hosted great movie premieres. When
the movie business became unprofitable, plans were made to tear the building
down. Public outcry, including hundreds of signed petitions from all over the
country, put an end to the plan and the building was completely renovated in
1979. Reopened in 1999 after a $70 million restoration, Radio City today is still
famed for the musical spectaculars presented live on its Great Stage and for concerts by top performing artists.

★★★**The Interior** – *Visit by guided tour (1hr) only, year-round Mon–Sat 11am–3pm. Tours
depart from main lobby every 30min. $17.* ☎ *212-632-4041. www.radiocity.com.*
The luxurious Art Deco interior of Radio City Music Hall allows visitors to marvel
at the same architectural splendor that awed the public a half-century ago. As you
enter the Grand Foyer, designed by Donald Deskey, your eyes rise from the plush
carpet, featuring a geometric pattern representing six musical instruments, up to
the sweeping Grand Staircase and three mezzanine levels. Ezra Winter's enormous
60ft-by-40ft mural *Fountain of Youth* adorns the wall behind the staircase.
Magnificent chandeliers, considered among the largest in the world, emit a suffused light overhead. Each weighs two tons—a ton of crystal and a ton of
steel—and can be lowered for cleaning merely by pushing a button. Note also the
immense wall mirrors extending up to the sparkling ceiling, covered in gold leaf.
In the auditorium, note the curved wall-and-ceiling design and the immense **proscenium arch** (60ft high), the most striking feature of the 5,882-seat theater. The stage
itself, a masterpiece of technical expertise, is equipped with complex machinery:
three elevators, a three-section turntable and an orchestra elevator. The musicians
in the orchestra and the two electric organs (with pipes up to 32ft high), complete with their organists, can be whisked away behind the walls or below the floor
when necessary, without interrupting their playing.

On the lower level, the smoking and powder rooms form a striking Art Deco
ensemble.

The Rockettes perform the Radio City Christmas Spectacular

The Rockettes – 🧒 *Major shows are the Spring Spectacular (2 weeks around Easter) and the Christmas Spectacular (mid-Nov–Jan 5). Concerts and special events are presented year-round. For show schedule call ☎ 212-247-4777 or www.radiocity.com. For ticket information contact Ticketmaster ☎ 212-307-7171.* The Rockettes, founded in St. Louis, Missouri, in 1925, have been a star attraction at the music hall since opening night, December 27, 1932. Known originally as the Missouri Rockets, then as the Roxyettes when they were resident performers at New York's Roxy Theater (named for Mr. Rothafel), the troupe was renamed the Rockettes in 1934, the moniker by which they have gained international renown as the world's finest precision dance team.

Upon exiting Radio City Music Hall, turn left onto Avenue of the Americas.

An imposing series of tall office towers with spacious plazas lines the west side of the **Avenue of the Americas★**; aligned like dominoes, these skyscrapers create a breathtaking canyon. Built in the 1950s and 60s, the row of buildings became part of Rockefeller Center but never quite managed to match its elegant style and refined beauty. Peek into the towers' spacious lobbies at your leisure to admire the decor and to view various artworks and temporary exhibits.

■ What Happened to Sixth Avenue?

Visitors may be understandably bewildered when residents direct them to Sixth Avenue. In 1945 New York's most famous mayor, Fiorello La Guardia, signed a bill officially renaming Sixth Avenue the Avenue of the Americas. Even though the busy thoroughfare is decorated with the coats of arms of the nations of the Americas, most New Yorkers still stubbornly cling to the old name and reject La Guardia's grandiose international gesture. The avenue (by either name) runs from TriBeCa to Central Park.

Across 47th Street rises the **Celanese Building** (1973), a 45-story edifice similar in conception to the McGraw-Hill Building and 1251 Avenue of the Americas; the striking trio was designed by Harrison, Abramovitz & Harris.

Backtrack and continue north on Avenue of the Americas.

McGraw-Hill Building – *No. 1221.* Housing the celebrated publishing company, this 51-story building constructed of flame-finished granite and solar bronze glass is surrounded by plazas. The lower plaza in front of the building features a sleek 50ft steel sun triangle, designed by meteorologist Athelstan Spilhaus in 1973. Each side of the triangle points to the seasonal positions of the sun at solar noon in New York during the solstices and equinoxes. This plaza leads to the lower concourse and the McGraw-Hill Bookstore.

Bordering the western edge of the building, a small park features a moon-shaped walk-through waterfall, a tree-shaded mall with an ornamental pool, hanging plants, tables and chairs, and refreshment facilities.

Across the street behind 1251 Avenue of the Americas, another peaceful minipark, replete with flowers, trees, food stands and a cascading waterfall, provides a welcome respite from the busy streets and sidewalks.

1251 Avenue of the Americas – With its 53 stories, this is the second-tallest skyscraper in Rockefeller Center after the GE Building, which it faces across the avenue. Rising 750ft from a landscaped plaza, the edifice (1971), formerly the headquarters for Exxon Corp., is marked by alternating limestone piers, bronze-tinted windows and steel beams.

Time & Life Building – *No. 1271.* Across from Radio City rises the smooth, glistening exterior of the building where *Time*, *Life*, *Money*, *People*, *Sports Illustrated* and *Fortune* magazines are published. Erected in 1959, the building was the first modern skyscraper constructed on the west side of the Avenue of the Americas. Admire the pure vertical lines of the 48-story building, featuring limestone, aluminum and glass. On two sides of the building is the Americas Plaza, paved with a two-toned terrazzo pattern. The undulating design contrasts pleasantly with the rectangular pools and their fountains.

★**Equitable Center** – *On Seventh Ave., between W. 51st & 52nd Sts.* This block-long complex named for the insurance company features as its centerpiece **Equitable Tower** (1985), an elegant 54-story granite, limestone and glass structure designed by Edward Larrabee Barnes. In the tower lobby *(entrance on Seventh Ave.)* is Thomas Hart Benton's expressive 10-part mural *America Today*, depicting life across the nation on the eve of the Great Depression. An atrium, dominated by the bold images of Roy Lichtenstein's 65ft-high *Mural with Blue Brushstroke*, adjoins Equitable Tower on the west; the atrium houses the **Equitable Gallery**, a 3,000sq ft space dedicated to presenting works from all fields of the visual arts *(open year-round Mon–Fri 11am–6pm; Sat noon–5pm; closed Jan 1 & Dec 25–26;* & ☎ *212-554-4818).*

To the east stands the **PaineWebber Building** (1961), presenting changing exhibits on the lobby level *(open year-round Mon–Fri 8am–6pm; closed major holidays & during installations;* & ☎ *212-713-2885).*

★**CBS Building** – *51 W. 52nd St.* Known as the "Black Rock," this abstract structure is the only high-rise building (38 stories) designed by renowned architect Eero Saarinen (1910-61). Completed in 1965, the tower presents a framework of reinforced concrete, covered with dark granite, and triangular columns, exuding the sense of a grid. The building's sunken plaza and its indiscernible entranceways contribute to its aloofness and detachment from the busy thoroughfare.

Behind the CBS Building rises the Deutsche Bank Building *(31 W. 52nd St.),* a post-Modern pile sitting atop large piers of red granite, designed by Roche, Dinkeloo and Assocs. in 1987. In the benched courtyard separating the two buildings, note the large sculpture (1987, Jesús Bautista Moroles) reminiscent of ancient ruins.

Return to Ave. of the Americas and turn left on W. 52nd St.

The tapered form of the **Sheraton Center** (originally known as the Americana Hotel) is particularly elegant seen from the south, where the line is slightly broken. Built almost entirely of glass over a stone framework, it was erected in 1962 and contains 1,828 rooms on 50 floors.

Return to Ave. of the Americas and continue north.

Adorning the plaza fronting the Crédit Lyonnais Building *(between W. 52nd and 53rd Sts.)* are three huge (14ft to 23ft) **bronze sculptures (2)** by Jim Dine, representing the Venus de Milo statue; the ensemble (1989) is titled *Looking toward the Avenue.*

Covered with steel and blue glass panels, the 46-story **New York Hilton and Towers** hotel was completed in 1963. The first four stories house service and reception facilities, while the slablike tower contains 2,034 guest rooms and suites, each designed to have a view of the New York skyline. On the main floor, next to the lobby, is the Promenade Cafe, with its tall glass walls looking out onto the avenue.

Across 54th Street stands the 50-story, brown-tinted Burlington House, which extends the impressive row of tower buildings on the west side of the Avenue of the Americas.

MUSEUMS *(See Museums section)*

★**Museum of Arts & Design** – *40 W. 53rd St.*

★**Museum of Television and Radio** – *25 W. 52nd St.*

★**International Center of Photography** – *1133 Avenue of the Americas*

American Folk Art Museum – *45 W. 53rd St.*

3 • 57th STREET★

One of New York's upscale thoroughfares, 57th Street spans the breadth of upper midtown Manhattan, encompassing some of its most exclusive shops, galleries and office towers. Venerable stores such as Tiffany & Co. and Bergdorf Goodman, along with elegant designer boutiques, vie for the sophisticated shopper's attention, while newcomers such as NikeTown and Levi's attract a younger, more eclectic crowd. Chain restaurants and theme-inspired clubs, including the Hard Rock Cafe, and Jekyll and Hyde, cluster at the bustling artery's western end.

Historical Notes

Once home to the Vanderbilts, Whitneys, Roosevelts and other members of the city's wealthy political elite, 57th Street was a premier residential address in the years following the Civil War. Commercial development after World War I transformed the area into a vibrant shopping district featuring tony department stores and specialty shops. Carnegie Hall's 1891 debut heralded the area's evolution as a center for classical music and the arts.

Today East 57th Street is home to a wide range of art, home furnishings and decorator shops. The **Manhattan Art and Antiques Center** *(1050 Second Ave.)* offers attractive displays of porcelain, jewelry, furniture and objets d'art in an urban bazaar setting. West of Park Avenue, 57th Street is known as a bastion of 20C art, housing one of the world's largest concentrations of art and antique dealers.

WALKING TOUR *Distance: .8mi*

Begin at corner of E. 57th St. and Lexington Ave. and walk west.

Distinguished by the post-Modern *tempietto* fronting its plaza, 135 East 57th Street (1987; Kohn, Pederson and Fox), with its curved facade, presents an original corner treatment for a Manhattan building. Erected in 1975, the Galleria (no. 117), marked by a sharply angled facade, contains an inviting interior shopping mall. The building is flanked by a pleasant public arcade to the east.

Standing between Park and Madison avenues is the elegant **Four Seasons Hotel**. An I.M. Pei creation, this Art Moderne-style tower rises to 52 stories through a series of setbacks. An enormous blind oeil-de-boeuf adds a whimsical touch to the light stone facade. The cavernous sunken foyer, clad in limestone and onyx, presents quite a contrast to the traditional bustling hotel lobby.

Fuller Building – *41 E. 57th St.* Once headquarters of the Fuller Construction Co., the elaborate 1929 Art Deco edifice showcases an assortment of contemporary art and antiques in more than 20 galleries. The elegant black granite building, topped by a limestone tower, encloses a richly ornamented lobby: the bronze elevator doors chronicle the building's construction while the mosaic floor displays other Fuller commissions, notably the Flatiron Building.

LVMH Tower – *17-21 E. 57th St.* North American headquarters for luxury luggage manufacturer Louis Vuitton, this layered 23-story glass composition (1999, Christian de Portzamparc) is indebted to, yet disrespectful of, its post-Modern parentage. Illuminated layers of facade have been pulled back to reveal only more sheets of glass—in disregard of post-Modern solidity. The 103,000sq ft building houses retail space on the first two levels, and offices for Louis Vuitton Moët Hennessy on the upper floors.

Turn right onto Madison Ave. to E. 56th St.

★★Sony Plaza (former AT&T Headquarters) – *550 Madison Ave.* Presenting a radical departure from the metal-and-glass boxlike forms erected in the 1960s and 70s, this 1984 stone building was designed by Philip Johnson and John Burgee in association with Henry Simmons. Distinguished by an unusual roof reminiscent of Colonial furniture design (a triangle split at the peak by a semicircular hollow), the 40-story edifice has been dubbed the first post-Modern skyscraper. To conserve energy, only a third of its pink granite exterior is covered with windows. The building is elevated from the ground by massive, 110ft-high columns that enclose a pleasant outdoor public arcade, lit by oversize portholes and lanterns. The **Sony Wonder Technology Lab** Kids *(open year-round Tue–Wed & Fri–Sat 10am–6pm, Thu 10am–8pm, Sun noon–6pm; closed Jan 1, Easter Sunday & Dec 25; ✕ ᕕ ☎212-833-8100; http://wondertechlab.sony.com)*, an interactive, hands-on learning center, explores the world of electronics, allowing young and old to learn about technological equipment while editing a music video, assisting a doctor with an ultrasound examination or programming a robot.

Enter 590 Madison through the E. 56th St. entrance.

590 Madison (former IBM Building) – Clad in polished black granite, the 43-story high rise (1983, Edward Larrabee Barnes) features an imposing cut-corner overhang above its entrance, defying the visitor to enter the monolith. Strips of windows set flush with the smooth stone exterior wrap around the building, creating a pattern of horizontal bands. A 17ft flame-red, jagged-back stabile by Alexander Calder, *Saurien* (1975), stands sentinel at the doorway. At the 56th Street entrance, a stylized, rough-hewn fountain containing horizontal flowing waters reflects the daily tides of pedestrian and automotive traffic. Cryptic striations at the fountain's edges are coded references to surrounding street addresses. Enlivened by bamboo-filled planters, refreshment kiosks, and tables and chairs, the light and airy four-story atrium hosts installations of rotating sculpture, including pieces by Calder, Nevelson, Lichtenstein, Appel and others. Just off the atrium is the new home of the **Dahesh Museum** *(see Museums)*.

Return to E. 57th St. and continue west.

The stretch of 57th Street between Madison and Fifth avenues contains an array of signature boutiques, including Chanel, Hermès, Louis Vuitton and Burberry's, whose attractive storefronts present the latest in fashion design. The newest rage, however, is **NikeTown (9)** 🔲, showcasing the company's famed footwear and apparel collections. The sporting-goods emporium attracts hordes of tourists hoping to catch a glimpse of Mia Hamm or Michael Johnson.

The intersection of Fifth Avenue and 57th Street is marked by several luxury shops, including jewelers **Tiffany & Co. (5)** and **Van Cleef & Arpels (7)**. Bergdorf Goodman's **(6)** exclusive men and women's department stores flank Fifth Avenue.

Cross Fifth Ave.

The striking and controversial building at **9 West 57th Street★** (1974, Skidmore, Owings & Merrill), a twin to the Grace Building on East 42nd Street, rises on the north side of the thoroughfare. Articulated by tinted glass curtain walls and travertine edges, the 50-story high rise slopes down to plazas on 57th and 58th streets. The slightly distorted images of other buildings reflected in the sloping, curved exterior walls produce unusual visual effects. The award-winning sculptured red "9" sign on 57th Street is the work of graphic designer Ivan Chermayeff. The neighboring building, 29 West 57th Street, is adorned with a colorful sculpted relief of the French Cross of the *Légion d'Honneur* on its tower. Located next door, the **Rizzoli Bookstore** *(no. 31)*, distinguished by a rounded archway, contains wood-paneled shelves lined with fine books.

■ Art Galleries

Midtown anchor of the New York art world, 57th Street features galleries from SoHo as well as older standbys in locations such as the Fuller Building *(41 E. 57th St.)*. A sampling of the more celebrated ones:

■ **Pace Wildenstein** *(32 E. 57th St., 2nd floor;* ☎ *212-421-3292; www.pacewildenstein.com)* is an amalgamation of two of the largest and most prominent galleries in the city. Credited with playing a major role in the American art scene, this gallery represents Robert Rauschenberg, Joel Shapiro, Kiki Smith, Jim Dine, Agnes Martin and Julian Schnabel, among a score of other celebrated contemporary artists.

■ **Tibor de Nagy** *(Entrance at 724 Fifth Ave., 12th floor;* ☎ *212-262-5050; www.tibordenagy.com)* focuses on contemporary American painting.

■ **Gregory Gallery** *(Fuller Bldg., 41 E. 57th St., 8th floor;* ☎ *212-754-2760; www.gregorygallery.com)* often sponsors international contemporary artists.

■ **David Findlay Jr. Fine Art** *(Fuller Bldg., 41 E. 57th St., 11th floor;* ☎ *212-486-7660)* specializes in American 19C and 20C masters, American modernists from 1910-50, and American contemporary art.

■ **Marian Goodman** *(24 W. 57th St., 4th floor;* ☎ *212-977-7160; www.mariangoodman.com)* carries a slate of well-known artists including Jeff Wall, Dan Graham, Gerhard Richter, Lawrence Wiener, William Kentridge and Thomas Struth.

■ **Michael Rosenfeld** *(24 W. 57th St., 7th floor;* ☎ *212-247-0082; www.michaelrosenfeldart.com)* features 20C American art in all media. The gallery specializes in WPA (1930s-40s) realists and modernists.

■ **Marlborough** *(40 W. 57th St., 2nd floor;* ☎ *212-541-4900; www.marlboroughgallery.com)* handles a number of important estates such as those of James Rosati and Jacques Lipchitz, as well as the work of well-known contemporary artists Fernando Botero, Red Grooms and Tom Otterness.

Be sure to pick up a **Gallery Guide** *(available at galleries and visitor centers) for information on the latest exhibits and offerings.*

Continue west. For sights west of Ave. of the Americas, see map p 176.

The fabled **Russian Tea Room** *(no. 150)* was opened in 1926 by Russian émigrés as a gathering spot for expatriate ballet corps members. In July 2002, the tea room sadly closed its doors for good. Golden dancing bears still grace the elegant Art Deco facade of the building, which had been purchased by the U.S. Golf Association. That plan fell through, however, and the Russian Tea Room building, including its four kitchens, the china and silver, and even the staff uniforms, is back on the market.

★**Carnegie Hall** – *154 W. 57th St. Visit by guided tour (1hr) only, Jan–Jun & Sept–Dec Mon–Fri 11:30am, 2pm & 3pm. $6. & ☎ 212-247-7800.* At the corner of Seventh Avenue, majestic Carnegie Hall is regarded as one of the world's most prestigious concert venues. Over the last century, Carnegie Hall has hosted luminaries from Gustav Mahler to the Beatles, Winston Churchill and Dr. Martin Luther King Jr. Faced with orange-colored bricks, the building (1891) was designed by architect and cellist William B. Tuthill in the Italian Renaissance style.

5 **FiftySevenFiftySeven Bar**

Map p 89. 57 E. 57th St., in the Four Seasons Hotel. ☎ *212-758-5757.* All maple, onyx and soaring spaces, this stunning bar has revived the martini in New York City. Choose from a menu of 15 tempting concoctions—including the 007, the Metropolitan and the Cosmopolitan—all poured from individual silver shakers and served with dried cherries. Live piano music is featured on Friday and Saturday nights after 9pm. Designed by Philip Johnson, The Four Seasons' fine-dining restaurant—also called **FiftySevenFiftySeven**—is renowned as one of the most famous locations for deal-making in the city *(reservations and jacket and tie required).*

Originally known as "Music Hall," it was renamed for steel magnate and philanthropist **Andrew Carnegie** (1835-1919), under whose auspices it was built. Carnegie Hall opened in 1891 with Tchaikovsky's American conducting debut. Two additions of studio offices and apartments were added to the original building in 1896 and 1898. After narrowly escaping demolition in the 1960s, the hall was renovated in 1986. A 60-story office tower built on adjoining property to the east in 1990 provided additional backstage and support spaces. Today this landmark recital hall has three performance spaces: the Isaac Stern Auditorium, the largest hall, which seats 2,804 and is well known for its fine acoustics; Weill Recital Hall, an intimate Belle Epoque-style space seating 268; and the new 650-seat Zankel Hall.

The small **Rose Museum at Carnegie Hall** *(access at no. 154; take elevator to second floor; open Sept–Jun daily 11:30am–4pm; may be closed in Aug; closed major holidays; & ☎ 212-903-9629)* features photos, programs and artifacts detailing the history of the hall. The autographs of Irving Berlin, Duke Ellington, The Beatles and others as well as Benny Goodman's clarinet and Toscanini's baton are on display.

Carnegie Hall

At the corner of Seventh Avenue, pause to look north to the ornate **Alwyn Court Apartments** *(182 W. 58th St.)*, built in 1909 by Harde & Short. This flamboyant building is faced entirely with terra-cotta panels decorated with Renaissance motifs.

Between Seventh and Eighth avenues, on the northern side, stands the **Art Students League** *(no. 215)*, founded in 1875 by former students of the National Academy of Design (now National Academy Museum) who wanted to create an independent school that would admit women. Designed by Henry J. Hardenbergh in 1892, the building resembles a 16C hunting lodge built by King François I of France.

Located at no. 221, the London-originated **Hard Rock Cafe** features a vintage Cadillac crashing into its facade. The Hard Rock is noted for its guitar-shaped bar and extensive displays of rock 'n' roll memorabilia.

Bridgemarket

An immense cathedral-like hall under the roadway to the Queensboro Bridge has been restored to its original grandeur after decades in oblivion. Until the 1930s, food vendors sold their goods in the 120ft by 275ft vaulted arcade that became known as Bridgemarket. After the market failed in the Depression, the city's Department of Transportation took the space over and used it for storage.

The impetus to salvage Bridgemarket came when British designer Terence Conran signed on to develop a shop and restaurant on the site. Opened in 1999, Conran's houseware and modern design emporium *(407 E. 59th St; ☎ 212-755-7249; www.conran.com)* presents a modern glass-and-steel entry pavilion in the plaza next to Bridgemarket. An underground level holds the greater part of the shop's 22,000sq ft of floor space.

Under the soaring vaults of Bridgemarket's eastern (and higher) half is **Gustavino's** *(409 E. 59th St; ☎ 212-980-2455; www.gustavinos.com)* a chic American brasserie. The restaurant's name pays homage to Spanish architect Rafael Gustavino and his son, Rafael, who designed the space.

Updating traditional building techniques, they built the 30ft by 30ft "Catalan Vaults" completely from layers of flat rectangular tiles and mortar. Each of the 36 vaults that form the arcade's canopy is faced with about 1,600 tiles; four more layers of tile lie underneath. The strength and lightness of the clay tile allow for broader spans than are possible with stone.

The father and son's work can be seen elsewhere around the city, most notably at the Oyster Bar in Grand Central Terminal and in the Registry Room at Ellis Island. In a return to its roots, Bridgemarket's other tenant is a Food Emporium supermarket.

Museums *(see Museums section)*

Dahesh Museum – *580 Madison Ave. at 56th St.*

> *"I think this city is full of people wanting inconceivable things."*
> John Dos Passos, Manhattan Transfer (1925)

4 • PARK AVENUE★★

MTA 4, 5, 6 train to Grand Central Terminal

Map p 105

A majestic boulevard lined with broad sidewalks and divided by a series of islands embellished with flower parterres, shrubbery and sculpture, Park Avenue is considered one of the most desirable residential and commercial addresses in New York. The midtown section of the avenue, today taken over by corporate America, is the thoroughfare's busiest. Colorful in summer, it is also attractive at Christmastime when the trees are decorated with multicolored lights.

Historical Notes

Park Avenue was not always the tony place it is today. From the 1830s to the 1890s, open railroad tracks ran straight down the thoroughfare, called Fourth Avenue, while bridges carried the crosstown traffic. The resulting smoke and noise made the area almost unbearable.

In 1903 the New York Central Railroad Co. commenced work on Grand Central Terminal and sank the offensive tracks below street level. New engineering techniques made it possible to erect buildings on stilts, thereby isolating them from railroad vibrations. This innovation allowed the company to develop the real estate above both the tracks and the fan-shaped train yards, as far north as 50th Street. The newly named Park Avenue was quickly lined with uniform rows of apartment buildings, and the entire scheme was hailed as one of the great pieces of urban design of the early 20C. During the postwar wave of construction, the original apartment houses were replaced by high-rise offices of varying styles, home mainly to banks, and the former residential elegance of Park Avenue's midtown section gradually vanished. Today current architectural tastes coupled with the prohibitive cost of preserving the outdated glass boxes are threatening the avenue's well-known "corporate canyon" look. While some owners struggle to preserve the original structures, hoping for eventual landmark status, others choose to envelop the buildings in a new shell, giving way to a sometimes incongruous corridor of glass and metal towers.

WALKING TOUR *Distance: 1mi*

Begin at Park Ave. and E. 46th St.

★**Helmsley Building** – *No. 230.* Erected in 1929 to house the headquarters of the New York Central Railroad Co., this distinctive building crowned by a pyramidal roof and cupola straddles Park Avenue. Designed by Warren & Wetmore (the firm responsible for Grand Central Terminal's imposing exterior), the structure sits atop two levels of railroad tracks. Once the dominant centerpiece of the area, the elegant tower is today dwarfed by the MetLife Building (formerly the Pan Am Building) rising behind it. The edifice is pierced by two tunnels reserved for motor traffic and two street-level arcades for pedestrians.

Step inside the opulent lobby to admire the travertine walls and bronze detailing. At the time of construction, the sumptuous decor offered a dramatic contrast to the neighboring, sober office buildings and reflected the grandiose aspirations of the railway company. Acquired by the Helmsley chain in 1977, the edifice was covered with a new coat of gold leaf and is now illuminated at night.

View down Park Avenue toward the Helmsley and MetLife buildings

Scandinavia House

Map p 105. 58 Park Ave. at 38th St. Open year-round Tue–Sat, noon–6pm. $3. ☎ *212-879-9779. www.amscan.org.* The new home of the American Scandinavian Foundation (2000, Polshek Partnership) serves as the cultural headquarters for the five Nordic countries in the US. Uncompromisingly modern, the zinc, glass and spruce edifice rises six stories and features superbly designed facilities—a wood-paneled theater, light-filled galleries, a glass-enclosed gift shop and the **AQ Café** *(open Mon–Sat 10am–5pm),* run by the celebrated Restaurant Aquavit. Changing exhibits, as well as an ambitious roster of films and lectures, reward returning visitors to this architectural gem.

Rising 53 stories from a small pedestrian plaza is **no. 270** *(between E. 47th and 48th Sts.),* a slender tower of contrasting black and white steel, erected in 1960 for Union Carbide Co. by Skidmore, Owings & Merrill. Today it houses the world headquarters of the Chase Manhattan Corp. As is the case for many buildings in the vicinity of Grand Central, the main lobby and elevators are located on the second floor because the elevator shafts cannot be accommodated below ground where the train tracks run.

No. 277, a silver gray tower built in 1962 by Emery Roth & Sons, rises 50 stories on the east side of the street, balancing no. 270 with its similar height and axial alignment.

★**Waldorf-Astoria Hotel** – *No. 301, between E. 49th & 50th Sts.* ☎ *212-355-3000. www.waldorfastoria.com.* This world-famous hotel, designed by Schultze and Weaver in 1931, is the successor to the former Waldorf-Astoria (1897), which stood on the present site of the Empire State Building. The massive structure, occupying an entire city block, is distinguished by its twin chrome-capped towers rising 47 stories from an 18-story granite base, and a series of setbacks in limestone and brick, which contribute to the edifice's demure Art Deco look.

The elegant interior presents an eclectic mix of Art Deco ornamentation and Second Empire furnishings. Of particular interest is the main lobby, with its marble floor embellished by an intricate mosaic known as the *Wheel of Life*. The east lobby is noteworthy for the bronze clock, crafted in London in 1893.

A staff of 1,500 serve the 1,410 guest rooms, including luxury apartments and suites occupied by a succession of celebrities. Several suites are reserved for presidents or heads of state. A protocol service has been organized to decide delicate questions of precedence and etiquette. Thus certain dignitaries who stay at the Waldorf are entitled to see their national flags flying in front of the hotel. The private apartments have been occupied by every US president since Herbert Hoover, and other notables such as Cary Grant, General Douglas MacArthur, the Duke of Windsor, Henry Kissinger and Frank Sinatra.

Lobby, Waldorf-Astoria Hotel

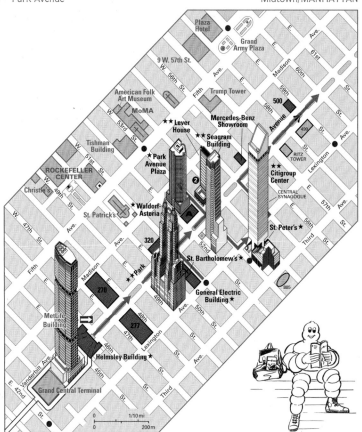

★**St. Bartholomew's Church** – *At the corner of E. 50th St. Open year-round Mon–Wed & Fri 8am–6:30pm, Thu & Sat 8am–7:30pm, Sun 8am–8:30pm.* ✗ ⅃ ☏ *212-378-0222. www.stbarts.org.* Considered one of architect Bertram G. Goodhue's most successful constructions, this Episcopal church illustrates the tenets of the Romanesque style, accentuated with Byzantine details. The edifice is distinguished by a multicolored dome, salmon-colored brick and gray limestone walls. Set in a charming, terraced garden, the church offers a contrast to the surrounding modern skyscrapers.

The elaborate, eclectic front portal (1903), donated by the Vanderbilts, was moved here from the original St. Bartholomew's Church (Stanford White), which stood on Madison Avenue from 1872 to 1918. Its three pairs of sculptured bronze doors depict scenes from the Old and New Testaments. In the richly decorated marble interior, note the mosaic of the Transfiguration located in the apse, above alabaster windows. In the baptistery stands the statue of a kneeling angel, the work of 19C English sculptor James Redfern. The church's Aeolian organ is the largest in the city.

In the late 1980s St. Bartholomew's was the focus of a bitter preservation dispute ultimately settled by the Supreme Court in 1991, which ruled against the church's proposal to demolish its community center. Today the renovated space houses Café St. Barts, a lovely spot for a noontime snack.

Across the street rises **320 Park Avenue**, headquarters for the Mutual of America insurance company. The former ITT Building (1962; renovated 1995) now sports a gray granite base and a double-glazed curtain wall punctuated with stainless steel ornaments. The structure is topped off with a 52ft-high stylized mast.

Turn right on E. 51st St. and continue to Lexington Ave.

★**General Electric Building** – *570 Lexington Ave.* Located immediately behind St. Bartholomew's is this marvelous Art Deco creation (1931, Cross & Cross), its reddish-orange spire topped by a spiky crown. The 51-story octagonal brick tower rising from a square base was designed to be viewed in conjunction with St. Bartholomew's. It was constructed for the RCA Victor Co., which deeded it to General Electric when the former moved to Rockefeller Center in 1931. Decorative features include rays, flashes and lightning bolts, which are particularly appropriate to the building's principal tenant.

Monkey Bar

Map p 105. In the Hotel Elysée, 60 E. 54th St. between Park and Madison Aves. ☎ *212-838-2600. www.theglaziergroup.com.* Try a Sparkling Monkey (champagne and Chambord) in this beautifully restored former haunt of Tennessee Williams and Tallulah Bankhead. The murals of frolicking monkeys, bar stools shaped like olives, live piano music and a chic, attractive clientele make this one of the city's most engaging bars.

Return to Park Ave. and continue north.

★★**Seagram Building** – *No. 375.* The former headquarters of Joseph E. Seagram & Sons, Inc. was designed in 1958 by **Mies van der Rohe** and **Philip Johnson**. Harmoniously proportioned, the 38-story tower is set back on a granite plaza with twin fountains. The subtle color scheme of the exterior bronze panels and the bronze-colored windows, the refinement of the interior lobby with its travertine walls and the continuation of the granite plaza floor give an air of classic distinction to this building. The only edifice in the city designed by Mies, the Seagram Building represents one of the finest International-style skyscrapers in New York.

Facing the Seagram Building, the 1918 Italian Renaissance style "palazzo" housing the exclusive **Racquet and Tennis Club (A)** *(no. 370)* was designed by McKim, Mead and White. The edifice is one of the few survivors of a bygone era when this section of Park Avenue was lined with masonry buildings.

★**Park Avenue Plaza** – *E. 52nd to 53rd Sts., between Park & Madison Aves. Enter on 53rd St.* The massive bulk of this 15-sided green mirror-glass structure rises behind the Racquet and Tennis Club. Designed by Skidmore, Owings & Merrill and opened in 1981, this office building contains a 30ft, double-level pedestrian shopping arcade enhanced by a fountain resembling a wall of water. A monumental work, *Deauville* (1970), by Frank Stella hangs above the main desk on the upper level. Temporary exhibits are displayed in the lobby.

★★**Lever House** – *No. 390. Illustration p 45.* Designed by Skidmore, Owings & Merrill, and influenced by the architectural concepts of Le Corbusier, this building was considered avant-garde when it opened in 1952. The 21-story vertical slab of blue-green glass and stainless steel rising from a two-story horizontal base presented an exciting contrast to the concrete and stone apartment buildings that lined the avenue in the 1950s. The Lever House inaugurated an era of glass-box structures throughout the city and firmly established the International style for commercial constructions.

From Park Ave., turn right on E. 53rd St. and continue to Lexington Ave.

★★**Citigroup Center** – *153 E. 53rd St., at the corner of Lexington Ave.* Citigroup (née Citicorp), parent company of Citibank, is headquartered in this spectacular aluminum and glass-sheathed tower (1978) whose top slopes at a 45° angle. The 915ft tower is Manhattan's fifth-tallest building and one of its most conspicuous landmarks. The success of the complex designed by Hugh Stubbins & Assocs. has led to a surge of high-rise construction in the area between Lexington and Third avenues. The tower stands on four colossal pillars—each nine stories, or 115ft, high and 22ft square—set at the center of each side, rather than at the corners of the building. Beneath these cantilevered corners, which extend 72ft from the central columns, nestle St. Peter's Church and a separate seven-story structure housing the **Market**, an attractive complex of shops and restaurants set around a landscaped atrium. Beneath the vast skylight, through which the main tower can be glimpsed, cafe tables have been placed among trees and shrubs. Popular and full of vitality, the atrium is often the scene of exhibits, concerts and other activities.

★**Saint Peter's Church** – *Access on 54th St. Open year-round daily 9am–9pm. Closed major holidays.* ♿ ☎ *212-935-2200. www.saintpeters.org.* This Lutheran church sold its land to Citicorp on the understanding that a new church would be integrated within the complex. The result is a comparatively tiny structure whose rooflines repeat the angle of the tower above. With its 80ft ceilings, the interior *(viewed from street level gallery)* is dramatic and simple, with stark white walls and granite floors. Roof and sidewall skylights bring natural light into the structure, yet excellent soundproofing makes it an oasis of silence in this noisy corner of Manhattan. The altar, lectern, platform, steps and pews are constructed of red oak.

Upon exiting the gallery, visit the adjoining **Erol Beker Chapel of the Good Shepherd★**, sculpted by Louise Nevelson as a "place of purity" in Manhattan.

The unusual, elliptical building visible at the corner of 53rd Street and Third Avenue *(885 Third Ave.)* was erected by Philip Johnson and John Burgee in 1986. Rising in setback tiers, the flashy brown and pink structure has been dubbed the "Lipstick Building."

Continue north on Lexington Ave. to E. 55th St.

Marking the southwestern corner of 55th Street and distinguished by bronze onion domes, Central Synagogue exemplifies the Moorish Revival style. Completed in 1870 by Henry Fernbach, this landmark structure is the oldest synagogue in continuous use in the city.

Return to Park Ave. on E. 55th St.

Continuing north along Park Avenue, note the **Mercedes-Benz Showroom** *(no. 430)*. Designed in 1953 by Frank Lloyd Wright for Max Hoffman, a distributor of Mercedes automobiles, it is a symphony of ramp and reflection.

At the corner of 57th Street is the Ritz Tower *(no. 465)*, crowned by stepped obelisks, a typical Park Avenue apartment building. It was erected in 1925 by Emery Roth and Carrère & Hastings as part of the Hearst apartment hotel chain. Between 58th and 59th streets, the black, glass and aluminum facade of 499 Park Avenue (1981) reflects the neighboring buildings. Designed by I.M. Pei, the high rise houses the Banque Nationale de Paris. At this point, on either side of the street, the **view**★★ south toward the Helmsley and MetLife Buildings is splendid.

500 Park Avenue – *At the corner of E. 59th St.* Designed by Skidmore, Owings & Merrill, this elegant 11-story structure (1960), formerly the Olivetti Building, seems dwarfed by the 1984 building (500 Park Tower) rising behind it. The geometric rigor of its lines, with glass panels resting on supporting pillars, is impressive. It was given landmark status in 1995.

5 • EAST 42nd STREET★★

MTA 4, 5, 6 train to Grand Central Terminal

Map p 110

Slicing across Manhattan from the East River to the Hudson, 42nd Street is New York's major crosstown artery. Its eastern section, between the United Nations and Fifth Avenue, features a magnificent assortment of distinguished buildings reflecting changing architectural styles since 1900.

Historical Notes

In an attempt to encourage people to move uptown and away from the crowded tenements of lower Manhattan, the city of New York opened 42nd Street to settlement in 1836. However, owing to the noise and pollution from steam trains, only factories and breweries would operate in the area, thereby stunting residential development. By 1860 the district abounded in shanties where newly arrived immigrants eked out an existence.

The construction of Grand Central Terminal in the early 20C created a catalyst for much-needed change. The unsightly railroad tracks were covered up, and following the station's completion in 1913, a boom in real estate opened up the area to office towers, apartment buildings and hotels. To the north, the Waldorf-Astoria Hotel (1931) attracted a wealthy clientele to its high-society events. Erected to the south and east, the Chanin, Chrysler and Daily News buildings inaugurated an era of architectural innovation. When six blocks of slaughterhouses were razed to make room for the United Nations Headquarters in 1946, this area of New York became a recognized district in the city.

WALKING TOUR *Distance: .5mi*
Begin at Grand Central Terminal, at the corner of Park Ave. & 42nd St.

★★**Grand Central Terminal** – *Travel information:* ☎ *718-330-1234; event hotline: 212-340-2210. www.grandcentralterminal.com.* Often referred to as the "gateway to the nation," this world-famous railroad terminal represents a masterpiece of urban planning. Designed by the engineering firm of Reed and Stem and architects Warren & Wetmore, the grand Beaux-Arts edifice has remained a symbol of the city since its inception in 1913. Grand Central recently underwent a $196 million restoration aimed at improving circulation, renovating interior spaces and upgrading amenities.

 Grand Central Oyster Bar and Restaurant

Map p. 110 In Grand Central Terminal, lower level. ☎ *212-490-6650. www.oysterbarny.com.* The Guastavino-tile vaulted ceiling makes for a grand setting and cacophonous sound effects, but New Yorkers and tourists come here for the best selection of fresh seafood in the city. Settle in at the counter and order oysters Rockefeller and clam chowder—it's a tradition. Out of a wine list of some 400 bottles, 80 are available by the glass.

From Depot to Terminal – In the early 19C, the first steam trains in New York chugged down Fourth Avenue (now Park Avenue) to a depot on 23rd Street, where the coaches were hooked up to a team of horses, which pulled them to the end of the line near City Hall. By 1854 an ordinance was passed banning steam locomotives south of 42nd Street to reduce air and noise pollution. The "Commodore" **Cornelius Vanderbilt** (1794-1877), who had acquired and consolidated all the city's railroad companies by 1869, decided to build an enormous iron and glass terminal at the present site of Grand Central.

In 1902 a new state order banned steam locomotives from the city altogether, leaving the New York Central railroad company with the choice of relocating outside city limits or electrifying the line. Under the direction of chief engineer William J. Wilgus, the company chose to cover the tracks and bring trains in on two levels. Today, there is virtually no evidence that a vast underground railroad terminal exists at all. Some 500 trains carrying 500,000 commuters arrive and depart daily via a subterranean tunnel that extends beneath Park Avenue from East 42nd to East 59th streets.

The Building – *Dining concourse open Mon–Sat 10am–9pm, Sun 10am–6pm.* The cavernous **main concourse★**, measuring 375ft long by 120ft wide, soars to a height of 125ft (12 stories). The hall is crowned by a vaulted ceiling decorated with the constellations of the zodiac. (One of the city's least-known oddities is that the zodiac was created backward in 1913; terminal representatives say it will probably never be corrected.) The 60ft-tall arched windows piercing the hall flood the concourse with sunlight. Melon-shaped chandeliers highlight the elegant interior, which is lined with massive square columns. Continuous streams of people flood past the central brass and onyx **clock**, a traditional New York City rendezvous point. During the recent renovation, a marble staircase was added at the eastern end of the concourse. Sculpture and other works of art adorn the interior. Shops and service concessions line the two levels of ramps that lead to the tracks. The terminal is connected to many of the neighboring buildings underground.

Step outside to admire the sumptuous facade designed by Warren & Wetmore, pierced by three massive arched windows separated by an order of double columns. Surmounting the windows are the immense 13ft clock and Jules-Félix Coutan's sculpture *Transportation* (1914), which incorporates the figure of Mercury (commerce) flanked by Hercules (physical energy) and Minerva (intellectual energy). Below the sculpture stands a bronze statue (1869) of Cornelius Vanderbilt.

Towering 59 stories over Grand Central, the **MetLife Building** (1963), formerly the Pan Am Building, was conceived by a group of architects that included **Walter Gropius** of the Bauhaus school. Its nonconforming design and the fact that it blocked the formerly unobstructed view down Park Avenue raised a storm of protest, which still rumbles occasionally today. With 2,400,000sq ft of office space at the time of completion, the edifice was exceeded in size only by the Pentagon building in Washington, DC.

Cross E. 42nd St. to the south side.

Dominating the southwestern corner of Park Avenue and 42nd Street, the sober tower designed by Ulrich Franzen and Assocs. houses the **Philip Morris World Headquarters**. Completed in 1983, the 26-story building is distinguished by a glass facade articulated by vertical strips of granite. Located on the ground floor, the midtown branch of the **Whitney Museum of American Art (M)** *(open year-round Mon–Fri 11am–6pm, Thu til 7:30pm; closed Jan 1, Thanksgiving Day, Dec 25; guided tours available Wed & Fri 1pm; & ☎ 917-663-2453; www.whitney.org)* offers a welcome respite from the crowded sidewalks and traffic-clogged streets. Large 20C American sculptures are displayed in the 42ft-high enclosed sculpture court *(open year-round Mon–Sat 7:30am–9:30pm, Sun & holidays 11am–7pm; &)*, and an adjacent gallery hosts temporary exhibits covering the range of American art.

Continue east on E. 42nd St.

The **Bowery Savings Bank Building** *(no. 110)*, a monumental structure erected in 1923 by York and Sawyers, is well known for its richly ornamented banking hall, clad in marble and mosaic.

Grand Hyatt Hotel – *No. 125.* ☎ *212-883-1234. www.hyatt.com.* Opened in 1980, this immense structure of silver mirrored glass, rising to 30 stories, presents a striking contrast to its neighbors, Grand Central Terminal and the Chrysler Building, which are both reflected in it. Designed by Gruzen and Partners with Der Scutt, the H-shaped structure is actually the former Commodore Hotel, dating from 1920. That masonry building is now sheathed in glass.

★**Chanin Building** – *No. 122.* A prime example of the Art Deco style, this 56-story building (1929) designed by architect and developer Irwin Chanin with Sloan & Robertson, features a series of setbacks topped by a buttressed crown, rising from a massive base. Adorning the first four floors, an exquisite terra-cotta frieze of floral bas-reliefs reflects typical curvilinear Art Deco elements. Step inside the intricately detailed lobby to view the door frames, convector grilles and mailboxes.

★★★**Chrysler Building** – *405 Lexington Ave.* Rising to 1,048ft (77 stories), this famous New York landmark is surmounted by a distinctive spire of radiant stainless steel arches that glimmers in sunlight and glows in the nighttime illuminations. Designed by William Van Alen and completed in 1930, it was briefly the tallest building in the world (the Empire State Building was opened in 1931). It was also one of the first buildings to feature exposed metal as an essential part of its design. The pinnacle resembles a radiator cap from a 1930 Chrysler car. Abundant automotive decorations adorning the various setbacks under the spire include silver hood ornaments, stylized racing cars and the huge radiator-cap gargoyles at the fourth level, modeled after a 1929 Chrysler. (Chrysler no longer has offices in the building.)

The **lobby★**, a superb example of Art Deco, is faced with red African marble. The elevator cabs feature ornate doors and richly paneled interiors. Note also the elaborate ceiling mural by Edward Trumbull.

★ **Mobil Building** – *No. 150.* Erected in 1955, this massive 45-story structure (Harrison & Abramovitz) occupies an entire city block between Lexington and Third avenues. The largest metal-clad office building in the world at the time of construction, it represented an unsuccessful attempt by the steel industry to demonstrate that glass and aluminum were not the trends of the future. The stainless steel skin, backed by a masonry wall, measures about a third of an inch in thickness. The large embossed panels were designed to be self-cleansing—the wind scours the splayed pattern and prevents dirt from building up.

★ **Daily News Building** – *No. 220.* The original building (1930) was designed by Howells and Hood for the *Daily News*, a tabloid that once had the largest circulation of any metropolitan newspaper in the US but has been plagued by labor disputes in recent years. One of the city's first skyscrapers to abandon the Gothic style popular at the time, the Daily News Building features white brick piers alternating with patterned red and black brick spandrels, giving the tower a vertical striped look and an illusion of height greater than its actual 37 stories. A flat roof, a remarkable innovation for 1930, crowns the slablike edifice. The more recent annex (1958, Harrison & Abramovitz), stretching to Second Avenue, repeats the striped pattern.

Note the embellishments above the main entrance; these are typical of the stylized decorative designs of the 1930s. The lobby is famed for its huge revolving **globe** (12ft in diameter) and the clock that gives readings in 17 time zones. The floor is laid out as a giant compass indicating most of the principal cities of the world and their distance, by air, from New York City.

Ford Foundation Building – *320 E. 43rd St.* ☎ *212-573-5000. www.fordfound.org.* This 12-story glass and granite building (1967), designed by Roche, Dinkeloo and Assocs., provides an elegant home for the Ford Foundation, a private, nonprofit institution established in 1936 by Henry and Edsel Ford. The foundation funds support research, training and other activities in the fields of social welfare, human rights, public policy, education, culture and international affairs. To date, the Ford Foundation has assisted more than 9,000 organizations all over the US and in many foreign countries.

The edifice reversed the trend of the 1960s to build in the center of a plaza; instead it encompasses an open green space within the building. Rising to 10 stories and enclosed by a skylight, the interior **garden★**, covering a third of an acre, contains a lush forest of trees, shrubs and flowering plants interspersed with pools and benches.

R. Corbel/MICHELIN

Chrysler Building

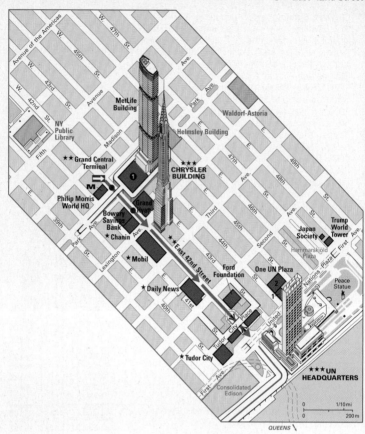

★**Tudor City** – *Tudor City Place*. Erected in the mid-1920s on a bluff overlooking the future sight of the United Nations Headquarters, this group of buildings was designed in the Tudor Gothic style, with such details as quatrefoils, pointed arches, pinnacles and crenellated rooflines. About 1925, the developer Fred F. French began acquiring dilapidated houses on this site with a view to creating a large housing project that would be accessible to the middle class. The complex was developed as a self-contained community with 3,000 apartments, a hotel, shops and parks.

Declared a landmark district in 1989, Tudor City enjoys a level of calm and isolation rare in New York. Facing two private parks to the west, the buildings are almost windowless on their east side because, in the 1920s, the current United Nations plaza was an industrial area of breweries, slaughterhouses, glue factories and a gasworks.

Tudor City Place, which crosses 42nd by a bridge *(access by steps from E. 42nd or 43rd Sts.)*, affords a superb **view**★ of 42nd Street to the west and of the United Nations to the east.

6 • UNITED NATIONS HEADQUARTERS★★★

MTA 4, 5, 6, 7 train to Grand Central Terminal

Map p 110 and p 113

Situated on 18 acres of land on the banks of the East River, between East 42nd and East 48th streets, the United Nations complex comprises four buildings and various gardens that enjoy extraterritorial status. Composed of 191 member states, this international organization pledges to "preserve international peace and security, promote self-determination and equal rights, and encourage economic and social well-being."

Historical Notes

An Ambitious Goal – The United Nations officially came into existence on October 24, 1945, when its charter—which had been signed in San Francisco on June 26 of that year—was ratified by a majority of the 51 founding members. Hoping to provide a framework in which nations could work together for international security and peace, the UN succeeded the League of Nations, created under President Woodrow Wilson following World War I.

The UN Charter's ambitious goals include international cooperation to solve economic, social, cultural and humanitarian problems; peaceful solutions to international disputes; and an end to threats or use of force against any nation. Over the years the UN has authorized several military efforts to repel aggression, beginning with an intervention in 1950 to turn back North Korea's incursion into South Korea and extending through to the Gulf War in 1991, in which Iraqi forces were ousted from Kuwait, and more recent maneuvers in Bosnia. Many of the most heated conflicts were outgrowths of the Cold War between the US and the former Soviet Union.

One of the most striking developments in the UN's evolution has been the increasing influence of the so-called Third World, due to the end of colonial empires and the rapid growth in the number of independent states.

Building the UN – In December 1946 John D. Rockefeller Jr. offered the United Nations a gift of $8.5 million to acquire the present site on the East River. At the time, this area known as Turtle Bay consisted mainly of slums, slaughterhouses and breweries. The construction program, costing more than $67 million, was financed in large part by the US government, which made available an interest-free loan of $65 million that was entirely reimbursed by annual payments. The balance was paid from the regular United Nations budget. The UN buildings were designed by a group of international architects, including Le Corbusier (France), Oscar Niemeyer (Brazil) and Sven Markelius (Sweden), under the direction of the American architect Wallace K. Harrison.

The Secretariat Building opened in 1950, and two years later the first meetings of the Security Council and the General Assembly were held there. The Dag Hammarskjöld Memorial Library (Harrison, Abramovitz & Harris) was completed in 1961.

Organs of the UN – The United Nations, governed by a charter of 111 articles, is composed of six principal organs: the General Assembly, Security Council, Trusteeship Council, Economic and Social Council, Secretariat, and International Court of Justice (also known as the World Court). Working closely with the UN are 14 specialized international agencies such as the United Nations Educational, Scientific and Cultural Organization (UNESCO) in Paris; the Food and Agriculture Organization (FAO) in Rome; and the International Monetary Fund (IMF) in Washington, DC, which helps to stabilize exchange rates. The UN and these specialized agencies make up what is known as "the United Nations family."

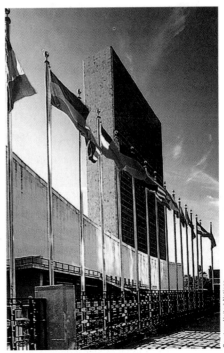

Courtesy United Nations

United Nations Headquarters

The Secretary-General is the organization's chief administrative officer. He or she performs such functions as are necessary to carry out decisions or recommendations adopted by the General Assembly and the councils.

Visiting the UN – *Entrance on First Ave. between 45th & 46th Sts. Buildings open to the public can be visited by 1hr guided tour only, year-round Mon–Fri 9:30am–4:45pm; weekends 10am–4:30pm. $10. ✗ ໄ Call for information about holiday closings. ☎ 212-963-8687; www.un.org. Children under 5 not admitted on tours.* Lines are often long to enter the premises, so it is best to arrive early if you wish to take the first tour. Tours in a language other than English require reservations after 9:30am the day of the visit. Large handbags and backpacks must be inspected at the gate. All visitors pass through a security check upon entering the General Assembly building. Thereafter it is advisable to proceed immediately to the ticket counter to purchase your tour ticket. You can then be seated until your tour is announced. This entry procedure can take 30min or more, if lines are long. Restrooms, eating facilities and the UN bookstore are located in the basement, where the tour ends.

VISIT

The Grounds

The corner of 45th Street and First Avenue offers a fine **view** of the four buildings and the flags of the 189 member states lining the United Nations plaza. These flags are arranged north to south in English alphabetical order, from Afghanistan to Zimbabwe. Delegations seated in the General Assembly follow the same order, although the starting point in the alphabet varies from year to year, depending on which member state is randomly selected to take the first seat.

Diagonally across from the Secretariat and General Assembly Buildings, at the northwest corner of 44th Street and First Avenue, rise the spires of **One United Nations Plaza** (1976), two commercial office buildings. Designed by Roche, Dinkeloo and Assocs., the irregularly shaped towers sheathed entirely in green reflecting glass present an appropriate counterpart to the straight shaft of the Secretariat Building.

Around the corner is Ralph J. Bunche Park, a small relaxing spot honoring the first African-American United Nations official from the US. The park is a frequent rallying point for demonstrations on issues before the UN.

The esplanade near the visitor entrance affords a pleasant **view** of the spacious gardens, dotted with various works of outdoor sculpture. The bronze equestrian statue, *Peace* (1954, Anton Augustincic), was a gift from Yugoslavia. A stairway located nearby leads to a lower terrace and the riverside promenade, which provides good **views★** of the UN complex, the river and buildings lining the bank. Beneath the lawn to the north of the complex, three underground levels are occupied by printing facilities and conference rooms.

The Buildings

General Assembly Building – Forming the heart of the United Nations, this long, low-lying structure topped by an elegantly curved roof contains the vaulted Assembly Hall. Visitors enter through one of the seven doors (donated by Canada) that pierce the huge exterior wall of concrete and glass. Various objects enhance the lobby, including a model of Sputnik I, a Foucault pendulum, a statue of Poseidon and a chunk of moon rock. To the left of the entrance is the information desk, and to the right, the **Meditation Room**, dedicated to those who have died in the name of peace. Just outside the room is a dramatic, 15ft-by-20ft stained-glass window by Marc Chagall. Unveiled in 1964 as a memorial to the former UN Secretary-General Dag Hammarskjöld, the window was contributed by members of the UN staff and the artist.

❶ The World Bar

Map p 113. 845 United Nations Plaza. ☎ 212-935-9361. Sophistication and understatement reign at the World Bar, located in the lobby of Trump World Tower. Its muted golds and Scandinavian light wood evoke the cosmopolitan world of the 1960s international executive set, a nod to its neighbor the United Nations. The room begins to fill in the early evening; comfortable banquettes and low music foster an atmosphere perfect for conducting the most discreet rounds of after-hours diplomacy. Less understated is the lounge's Trumpian signature drink: The World's Most Expensive Cocktail, a $50 amalgam of Remy XO cognac, white grape juice, fresh lemon juice, Angostura bitters, Veuve Clicquot champagne, and real gold (in a liquid and perfectly potable form).

Assembly Hall – Lighted from above, the oval Assembly Hall measures 165ft by 115ft and is 75ft high. The speaker's rostrum is surmounted by a dais on which the president of the General Assembly sits, flanked by the secretary-general and a high-ranking UN official. Above the dais, the emblem of the United Nations hangs between the illuminated boards that indicate members' votes. On either side are glass-enclosed booths

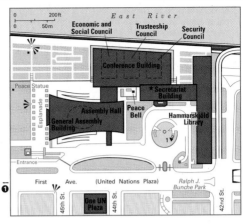

for radio and television, and for the interpreters who work in the six official UN languages (Arabic, Chinese, English, French, Russian and Spanish). The sidewalls are decorated with murals designed by the French artist Fernand Léger.

The General Assembly meets regularly in an annual three-month session, which starts in September. Special sessions may be called at the request of the Security Council or by a majority of the member states. The Assembly may discuss any matters within the scope of the UN Charter, except those under consideration by the Security Council. It also receives and discusses annual reports from the other organs and votes on the UN budget. Decisions on important questions are made by a two-thirds majority of members present and voting; a simple majority suffices for other matters. The Assembly may pass resolutions, initiate studies and make recommendations for the maintenance of peace and security and the promotion of international cooperation. It also elects its own president and vice presidents, admits new members on the recommendation of the Security Council and chooses the nonpermanent members of the Security Council.

Conference Building – Thus named because of its council and committee meeting rooms, this low, rectangular building links the Secretariat and the General Assembly buildings. The five stories of the Conference Building house—from the basement up—technical installations (air conditioning, printing presses, television and recording studios, photographic darkrooms), conference rooms, council chambers, delegates' lounges and the delegates' dining room.

A number of works of art (gifts of member nations) adorn the premises. They include a Persian carpet; a mosaic from Morocco; a Belgian tapestry; two Brazilian murals depicting Peace and War; a painting by Rouault, *Christ Crucified*; an **ivory carving** from China illustrating the Chengtu-Kunming Railway; and a scale model of a Thai royal barge. In the garden, in front of the Conference Building and the Secretariat, is a Japanese **peace bell**, made of copper coins and metal donated by the children of 60 countries, as well as a sculpture by Henry Moore, *Reclining Figure: Hand*.

Security Council – Donated by Norway, this chamber is decorated with gold and blue wall hangings and a mural by Norwegian artist Per Krohg symbolizing Peace and Liberty, Equality and Fraternity. The public gallery seats 200 people *(council sessions are no longer open to the public)*.

The Security Council assumes the primary responsibility for the maintenance of international peace and security. Amendments, which were adopted by the General Assembly and came into force in 1965, have increased the number of members of the Security Council from 11 to 15; 10 are elected for two-year terms, and the other five (China, France, United Kingdom, Russian Federation, US) are permanent. Votes on procedural matters require an affirmative vote of nine members, and for important questions these nine must include the five permanent members. This rule of unanimity for the "great powers" is better known as the veto, but an abstention by a permanent member does not in practice prevent a decision from being adopted. The members of the Security Council preside in rotation; the president changes every month.

Trusteeship Council – The furnishings in this room were donated by Denmark. Precious woods sheathe the walls and provide the backdrop for a large teak statue of a woman releasing a bluebird, which symbolizes Hope and Independence. The Trusteeship Council was created with the goal of helping nonautonomous colonies exercise their right to self-determination and supervising the Trust Territories administered by member states. The original 11 Trust Territories have become independent over the years, with Palau—the last one—achieving self-government in October 1994. Since then the council has formally suspended operations.

Economic and Social Council – This functional room was decorated with funds contributed by Sweden. The plain walls and exposed heating apparatus symbolize the council's never-ending tasks. The 54-member council coordinates the efforts and resources of various UN and affiliated organizations toward the alleviation of economic and social problems. Subjects under consideration include the environment, population, women's rights, health, transportation, human rights, crime prevention and freedom of information. All the decisions of the council are subject to the approval of the General Assembly.

★**Secretariat Building** – *Not open to the public.* Constructed entirely of white Vermont marble, and glass and aluminum panels, this slablike building is architecturally striking for its pure, clean lines. The simple grid pattern of the exterior rises 39 floors without a break. In front of the building lies a circular marble pool donated by American schoolchildren, with black and white stones collected by the children of the Greek island of Rhodes. Highlighting the pool, *Single Form* **(1)**, an abstract sculpture (1964) by Barbara Hepworth of Great Britain, commemorates Dag Hammarskjöld.

The 7,400 international civil servants and other employees who work here are drawn from many of the member nations and include interpreters and translators, experts in international law and economics, press officers, printers, librarians, statisticians, United Nations security officers and other support staff. Young people in uniform or their native dress serve as tour guides for the approximately half-million visitors who come each year.

Hammarskjöld Library – *Not open to the public.* Located on the southwest corner of the complex, the library, a gift of the Ford Foundation *(p 109)*, is dedicated to the memory of the second secretary-general, **Dag Hammarskjöld**, killed in 1961 in a plane crash during a peacekeeping mission to the Congo.

Its marble walls enclose 380,000 volumes for the use of UN delegates, Secretariat staff members and scholars. In addition, there are newspapers, reading rooms, a collection of 80,000 maps, a microfilm laboratory, tape recording services and an auditorium.

Trump World Tower – *845 United Nations Plaza.* Soaring 881ft over the United Nations is Donald Trump's latest contribution to the New York skyline—the world's tallest residential building. The 72-story slender bronze-glass box (2001, Costas Kondylis and Partners) represents a return to modernist simplicity; inside though, more is more. A deal to sell the four top-floor co-ops as a single $38 million 20,000sq ft duplex penthouse fell through. Undeterred, Trump raised the asking price to $56 million. Derek Jeter and Bill Gates are among those who have bought more modestly priced apartments.

MUSEUMS *(See Museums section)*

Japan Society – *333 E. 47th St.*

7 • BROADWAY – TIMES SQUARE★★

MTA any train to 42nd St.
Map p 117

Running the entire length of Manhattan, Broadway, "the longest street in the world," has given its name to the city's famous entertainment district, which extends approximately from 40th to 53rd streets, between the Avenue of the Americas and Eighth Avenue. Times Square, referred to as the "Crossroads of the World," marks the center of this concentration of world-renowned theaters, cinemas, night spots and bars. Broadway lights up at night, and colorful crowds throng beneath its huge illuminated billboards, called "spectaculars."

Historical Notes

Times Square Yesterday – At the end of the 19C, the Times Square district, then named Longacre Square for a similar area in London, was a center for livery stables and harness makers. The American Horse Exchange remained at 50th Street and Broadway—the present site of the Winter Garden Theater—until 1910. The square was renamed in 1904 when the *New York Times* moved its headquarters here.

On the southeast corner of Broadway and 42nd Street stood the ornate Knickerbocker Hotel *(142 W. 42nd St.)*, which housed the fashionable King Cole Bar and its renowned Maxfield Parrish mural. When the hotel was converted to offices, the Parrish mural was rescued and now graces the King Cole Bar at the St. Regis-Sheraton Hotel. The Hotel Astor (1904), one of the grandest in New York, stood on the west side of the square between 44th and 45th streets and was replaced in 1968 by an office building.

In the first decade of the 20C, Times Square abounded with vaudeville houses. The mecca for vaudeville performers was the prestigious Palace Theater *(1564 Broadway)*, now a legitimate theater. As vaudeville waned, live entertainment persisted during the "big band" era of the 1930s and 40s. Opened in 1919, the legendary Roseland Ballroom *(239 W. 52nd St.)* was *the* place for devotees of ballroom dancing, attracting Fred Astaire and Ginger Rogers "wannabes."

Times Square Today – Over the years the area deteriorated, becoming a haven for adult bookstores, X-rated movie theaters, porn shops and other tawdry establishments. Noisy, congested and frequented by shadowy characters, it revealed little of its former glamour, becoming instead a thorn in the city's side. Efforts to revitalize the area began in the mid-1970s with the construction of **Manhattan Plaza** (1977), a complex of shops, restaurants and two residential towers (whose units are primarily reserved for low- and middle-income theater artists) and the reconversion of tenements between Tenth and Dyer avenues into **Theater Row**, a series of Off-Off Broadway theaters on the westerly fringe of Times Square. In the 1980s the completion of the Marriott Marquis Hotel and the restoration of several venues, including the **Ed Sullivan Theater** at 1697 Broadway—now home to *The Late Show with David Letterman*—heralded the area's long-awaited rebirth.

The city gave the oversight of the revamping of Times Square to the Urban Development Corp. (UDC), a public authority created in 1968 with wide powers to condemn land and issue bonds for redevelopment. An ambitious plan to erect four large office towers (designed by Philip Johnson and John Burgee) on all four corners of the square fell through during a real-estate market crash in the early 1990s. Undaunted, the state and the city commissioned architect Robert A.M. Stern and graphic artist Tibor Kallmann to head up a revitalization plan forWest 42nd Street. When giant corporations such as Disney, MTV, Virgin Megastores and Condé Nast agreed to purchase real estate here, Times Square's resurgence as a mecca of entertainment was sealed. After ten years of building, Times Square—though destined to always be a work in progress—stands renewed. New Reuters, Ernst & Young, and Condé Nast skyscrapers surround the square itself; and the striking Westin New York at Times Square (2001, Arquitectonica) at the corner of 43rd Street and Eighth Avenue is a colourful 45-story prism split in two from top to bottom by a curving beam of light. Today the thriving corridors of 42nd Street and 7th Avenue and Broadway, bustling with crowds at every hour, again feel like the crossroads of the world.

© Brigitta L. House /MICHELIN

Legitimate Theaters – *For ticket information, see p 117.* One of the area's first theaters was opened by Oscar Hammerstein in 1899 at the corner of 42nd Street and Seventh Avenue. This far-sighted gentleman was the grandfather of Oscar Hammerstein II, composer of such popular musicals as *Oklahoma!* and *South Pacific*. Many of the early theaters in the Broadway area specialized in vaudeville or burlesque. The 1920s and 30s saw the emergence of the Theater Guild and the Group Theater, which helped promote classic dramas as well as the works of local playwrights. Political and satirical plays popular in the 1960s were often performed in locales situated off Broadway, giving rise to a new category of theaters presenting a varied repertoire.

Times Square

Some 40 theaters are concentrated between 40th and 57th streets and the Avenue of the Americas and Eighth Avenue, an area which has been designated a special theater district to protect its exceptional character. Today most of these establishments present musicals, some of which run many years to sold-out houses. Off and Off-Off Broadway theater developed as a response to the soaring cost of mounting Broadway productions after World War II. The movement encourages experimentation with new talent (authors, directors and performers) and the revival of classic plays.

Movie Theaters – In the 1920s the rise of the film industry was reflected in the number of movie palaces that began to appear in the area. The **Paramount Building** (1926), located between 43rd and 44th streets, was erected to house a movie theater and offices. The theater was gutted and converted to office space in the 1960s, but the building, its symmetrical silhouette culminating in a clock tower crowned with a glass ball, remains as a monument to the movie era. (Ground-floor tenant World Wrestling Entertainment has built a re-creation of the theater's bow-shaped marquee as a grand entrance to its restaurant and shop.) Gone are the scores of movie theaters concentrated in the Broadway area. In their last years, many of them were adult houses and "grinds," open around the clock to screen second-run films.

Farther north on Seventh Avenue and Broadway, larger movie houses were originally built to accommodate two to three thousand spectators at a sitting. On their screens passed such famous figures as Shirley Temple, Gary Cooper, Clark Gable, Doris Day, James Dean and Marilyn Monroe. King of them all was the 6,300-seat Roxy Theater, on 50th Street. Sadly, "The Cathedral of the Motion Picture" was torn down in 1961. The area's other giant prewar houses have met the same fate.

Replacing the old houses big and small are two multiplexes on 42nd Street with more than 30 screens between them. The Loews Astor Plaza, built in the 1970s, is Times Square's only remaining single-screen first-run theater.

SIGHTS

★★Times Square – *Visitor center located at 1560 Broadway between 46th & 47th Sts. Open year-round daily 8am–8pm. Closed Jan 1 & Dec 25.* ♿ ☏ *212-768-1560. www.timessquarebid.org/visitor. Free tours of Times Square leave from the visitors center every Fri at noon.* Located at the intersection of Broadway and Seventh Avenue, Times Square is best known for its **nighttime illuminations★★★**, which generate great excitement: it is here that the quick pulse of the city can best be felt, as the milling theater crowds merge with the thousands strolling under the flashing neon signs. Although the first electric advertising sign in the city was erected on Madison Square in 1892, the sign industry soon moved to Times Square, attracted by its combination of huge crowds and large vistas. In 1916 a city zoning bill formally encouraged large electric signs in Times Square and the "Great White Way" was born. Corporate advertisers still outdo themselves to create eye-catching displays (today spectaculars are required by law in Times Square). Among the best remembered is the smoke-ring sign between 43rd and 44th streets. Sponsored by Camel and later Winston cigarettes, it employed a steam box to produce about 1,000 rings a day through the lips of a gigantic smoker. It began puffing in 1941 and succumbed in 1977.

The Theater District

The telephone number for Telecharge (☎ 212-239-6200) is shown below for theaters that do not have a box-office phone number.

2) Ambassador Theater
219 W. 49th St.
☎ *212-239-6200*

Biltmore Theater
261 W. 47th St.
☎ *212-239-6200*

3) Belasco Theater
111 W. 44th St.
☎ *212-239-6200*

4) Booth Theater
222 W. 45th St.
☎ *212-239-6200*

5) Broadhurst Theater
235 W. 44th St.
☎ *212-239-6200*

6) Broadway Theater
1681 Broadway
☎ *212-239-6200*

7) Brooks Atkinson Theater
256 W. 47th St.
☎ *212-719-4099*

8) Circle in the Square
1633 Broadway
☎ *212-329-6200*

9) Cort Theater
138 W. 48th St.
☎ *212-239-6200*

10) Duffy Theater
1553 Broadway
☎ *212-921-7862*

11) Ethel Barrymore Theater
243 W. 47th St.
☎ *212-239-6200*

12) Eugene O'Neill Theater
230 W. 49th St.
☎ *212-239-6200*

**13) Ford Center for
the Performing Arts**
213 W. 42nd St.
☎ *212-307-4100*

14) Gershwin Theater
222 W. 51st St.
☎ *212-586-6510*

15) John Golden Theater
252 W. 45th St
☎ *212-239-6200*

16) Helen Hayes Theater
240 W. 44th St.
☎ *212-944-9450*

17) Imperial Theater
249 W. 45th St.
☎ *212-239-6200*

18) Lambs Theater
130 W. 44th St.
☎ *212-239-6200*

19) Longacre Theater
220 W. 48th St.
☎ *212-239-6200*

20) Lunt-Fontanne Theater
205 W. 46th St.
☎ *212-575-9200*

21) Lyceum Theater
149 W. 45th St.
☎ *212-239-6200*

22) Majestic Theater
247 W. 44th St.
☎ *212-239-6200*

23) Marquis Theater
1535 Broadway
☎ *212-382-0100*

24) Al Hirschfeld Theater
302 W. 45th St.
☎ *212-239-6200*

32) Plymouth Theater
236 W. 45th St.
☎ *212-239-6200*

33) Richard Rodgers Theater
226 W. 46th St.
☎ *212-221-1211*

34) American Airlines Theater
227 W. 42nd St.
☎ *212-719-1300*

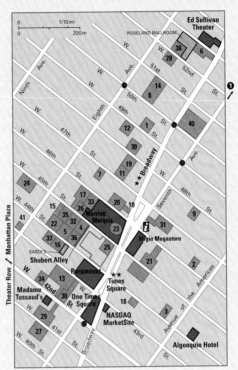

25) Minskoff Theater
200 W. 45th St.
☎ *212-869-0550*

26) Music Box Theater
239 W. 45th St.
☎ *212-239-6200*

27) Nederlander Theater
208 W. 41st St.
☎ *212-921-8000*

28) Neil Simon Theater
250 W. 52nd St.
☎ *212-757-8646*

29) New Amsterdam
*Theater 214 W. 42nd
St.* ☎ *212-282-2900*

30) New Victory Theatre
209 W. 42nd St.
☎ *646-223-3020*

31) Palace Theater
1564 Broadway
☎ *212-730-8200*

35) Royale Theater
242 W. 45th St.
☎ *212-239-6200*

36) Shubert Theater
225 W. 44th St.
☎ *212-239-6200*

37) St. James' Theater
246 W. 44th St.
☎ *212-239-6200*

38) Virginia Theater
245 W. 52nd St.
☎ *212-239-6200*

39) Walter Kerr Theater
*219 W. 48th
St.* ☎ *212-239-6200*

40) Winter Garden Theater
1634 Broadway
☎ *212-239-6200*

41) Second Stage Theater
307 W. 43rd St.
☎ *212-246-4422*

Theaters not appearing on map:

- **Actor's Studio** *(432 W. 44th St.;*
☎ *212-757-0870)*

- **Douglas Fairbanks Theater** *(432 W. 42nd
St.;* ☎ *212-239-4321)*

- **New Dramatists** *(424 W. 44th St.;*
☎ *212-757-6960)*

- **Westside Theater** *(407 W. 43rd St.;*
☎ *212-315-2244)*

Times Square is also often the setting for huge gatherings such as political demonstrations or the annual vigil to celebrate the twelfth stroke of midnight on New Year's Eve. The December 31 celebrations began in 1908 to mark the anniversary of the occupancy of the square's new building by the *New York Times*.

One Times Square – The former Times Tower dominates the southern end of the square; it was erected for Adolph S. Ochs, owner of the *Times* (the paper has since consolidated its operations at 229 West 43rd Street; in 2003 it will begin construction of new headquarters on 8th Avenue between 40th and 41st streets). Rising to 25 stories, the building seemed prodigiously tall at the time of construction. Demolished except for its steel framework in 1964, the edifice was remodeled into a marble-clad structure and is now best known for the lighted ball—today replaced by a big apple—that falls to mark the arrival of the New Year. The famous news "zipper," circling the facade, now operated by Dow Jones, was the world's first moving sign when it was installed in 1928. Atop the zipper, a giant computer-generated display (20ft by 40ft) features a mix of art and advertisements.

NASDAQ Market Site – *Broadway and 43rd St. Open year-round Mon–Fri 9am–8pm (Fri until 10pm), Sat 10am–10pm, Sun 10am–8pm (no tours). $5.* ☎ *877-627-3271. www.nasdaq.com.* The largest LED display in the world fronts this flashy new temple to high-tech stock trading. Some 18 million lights fill the 12,000sq ft billboard, across which the daily share prices and corporate logos of some 5,600 securities are run, ticker-tape style, above a swirling array of text and numbers. A ground-floor studio features live broadcasts, while upper-level interactive exhibits let visitors try their hand at do-it-yourself trading.

Marriott Marquis Hotel – *1535 Broadway.* ☎ *212-398-1900 or 800-843-4898. www.marriott.com.* The futuristic profile of this 50-story glass and concrete structure (1985) towers above the western side of Times Square. Second-largest hotel in Manhattan, the Marriott Marquis hosts conventions and seminars year-round. Designed by John C. Portman and Associates, the 1,874-room hotel has as its centerpiece a 37-story landscaped **atrium**, which ranks among the world's tallest. Note, on the Broadway facade, the four-story electronic billboard.

Virgin Megastore – *1540 Broadway.* ☎ *212-921-1020. www.virginmega-magazine.com.* Occupying the atrium of a 44-story skyscraper, this retail center claims to be the largest music/entertainment emporium in the world with 70,000sq ft of space. The store is one of three tenants at 1540 Broadway, along with Loews movie theaters and the popular Planet Hollywood. Trumping the size of Virgin Megastore, Toys "R" US opened a 110,000sq ft flagship store in 2001, just a block away at 1514 Broadway *(☎ 646-366-8800; www.toysrustimessquare.com).*

West 42nd Street – First target of Times Square's revitalization project, the section of 42nd Street between Broadway and Eighth Avenue has undergone a dramatic transformation. The long-neglected **New Amsterdam Theater (29)**, commissioned in 1903 by Florenz Ziegfeld and host to such stars as French legend Maurice Chevalier and Italian actress Eleonora Duse, has been restored to its Art Deco splendor by the Walt Disney Corp. *(guided tours Mon 11am–5pm; ☎ 212-307-4747).* Across the street stands the **New Victory Theatre (30)** (built in 1900 by Oscar Hammerstein), which reopened as a children's performance venue in December 1995, following a much-acclaimed $12 million renovation. The Lyric (1903) and Apollo (1920) theaters have been combined to become the **Ford Center for the Performing**

Theater Row

Two decades after its role in sparking the Times Square boom, the Off and Off Off Broadway houses of Theater Row, on 42nd Street between Ninth and Tenth avenues, have themselves been entirely rebuilt. A complex of five small houses (with between 88 and 199 seats) reopened in spring 2002; the 499-seat Little Shubert Theatre opened its doors in November 2002; and the neighboring $32 million theater complex of Playwrights Horizon, on the site of its old space, opened in January 2003.

Following is a list of the Theater Row venues. Telecharge (☎ 212-239-6200) handles ticket sales for all theaters except the Little Shubert.

Acorn Theater *(410 W. 42nd St.)*

Harold Clurman Theater *(410 W. 42nd St.)*

Lion Theater *(410 W. 42nd St.)*

Little Shubert Theater *(422 W. 42nd St.; ☎ 212-239-6200)*

Rodney Kirk Theater *(410 W. 42nd St.)*

Playwrights Horizon *(416 W. 42nd St.)*

Sameul Beckett Theater *(410 W. 42nd St.)*

Arts (13)—an 1,800-seat venue, opened in 1998, that preserved and reinstalled the Apollo's oval dome and proscenium arch as well as other architectural details *(guided tours Sat 10:30am & 11:30am, Sun 11:30am;* ☎ *212-307-4100).* Next door, the former Selwyn Theater is now the recently restored American Airlines Theatre, home to the Roundabout Theatre Company. Also new on the block is the 10-story, 84,000sq ft space housing a theater and rehearsal studios built on the site of the demolished Selwyn building (1918).

Madame Tussaud's – [Kids] *234 W. 42nd St. Open year-round daily 10am–8pm (Fri & Sat until 10pm) Occasionally closes early for special events; check website for dates.* 👤 *$25.* ☎ *212-512-9600 or 800-246-8872. www.nycwax.com.* A fitting complement to Times Square's larger-than-life video displays, the London-based wax museum's newest outpost brings celebrity down to size in 200 eerily realistic figures culled from history and popular culture. First stop inside is the ninth-floor "Opening Night Party," a simulated courtyard gala in which wax casts of current celebrities (Ted Turner and Donald Trump; Cybill Shepherd and Hugh Grant; Barbra Streisand and Woody Allen) mingle in casual poses but fancy dress. From the party, visitors go back in time to "Madame Tussaud's Story," a walk-through chamber of horrors featuring the grisly death masks Tussaud (born Marie Grosholtz) made from the guillotined heads of French Revolutionary figures. "Behind the Scenes" describes the painstaking process of making a wax portrait (each one takes up to six months to produce and draws from 250 precise measurements of the model's body). New additions include Julia Roberts, Madonna and NBC weatherman Al Roker.

Shubert Alley – Parallel to Broadway, the alley forms the heart of the theater district. This short private street, reserved for pedestrians, was laid down in 1913, between 44th and 45th streets. The Shubert brothers built the Booth and Shubert theaters, and were required to leave this passage as a fire exit. At intermission or after the show, many theatergoers drop into Sardi's restaurant, well known for the caricatures of celebrated theatrical personalities lining the walls, and their more or less famous successors who gather in the bar or the restaurant.

1 Carnegie Delicatessen and Restaurant

Map p 117. 854 Seventh Ave. between 54th & 55th Sts. ☎ *212-757-2245. www.carnegiedeli.com.* It's hard to tell what this kosher-style deli is more famous for: salty service or mile-high pastrami. At this New York legend, it's best to endure the former for the latter (split one if you want to save room for the famous cheesecake), and be prepared to share your table—it's all part of the fun here. Film buffs will be interested to know that much of Woody Allen's 1983 flick *Broadway Danny Rose* was shot on the premises—there's even a namesake sandwich on the menu.

■ Theater Rules

The "Broadway" theater rules cover all productions in designated "legitimate" houses of more than 500 seats in the areas between Fifth and Ninth avenues, from 34th through 57th streets, and between Fifth Avenue and the Hudson River, from 55th to 72nd streets. (There are currently 39 Broadway houses.) Off Broadway theaters are generally outside this territory and operate with fewer than 500 seats. Union rules are more flexible here. As the Off Broadway theaters flourished (and tickets became more expensive), the more experimental Off-Off Broadway movement took up the avant-garde mantle. These theaters are limited to fewer than 100 seats; they are found in churches, vacant factory lofts and storefronts in many parts of the city.

8 • STATUE OF LIBERTY – ELLIS ISLAND★★★

MTA 4,5 train Bowling Green

Map below

At the entrance to New York harbor stands the Statue of Liberty, her upraised torch lighting the world with the promise of freedom and justice for all. A dignified, stirring reminder of the ideals upon which the nation was founded, "Miss Liberty" has been welcoming travelers arriving by sea for more than a century.

Nearby in the harbor is Ellis Island, the immigration station and entry point for millions during the peak years of immigration.

VISIT

Kids *The Statue of Liberty has been closed to visitors indefinitely. For an update, call or check the Web site listed below. National Park Service Ferry departs from Battery Park South (Manhattan) or Liberty State Park (New Jersey) Jul–Aug daily 8:30am–4:30pm every 30min. Rest of the year daily 9am–3:30pm every 45min. No service Dec 25. $10 (fare includes round-trip and visits to both sights).* ✗ ♿ ⏟ Circle Line ☎ 212-269-5755. www.statueoflibertyferry.com. Manhattan ticket office is located at Castle Clinton National Monument. Park grounds are open year-round daily 9:30am–5pm. Closed Dec 25. D ☎ 212-363-3200. www.nps.gov/stli.

★★★Statue of Liberty

The Birth of an Idea – The idea to present the American people with a memorial commemorating the friendship between France and the US (which dates back to the American Revolution) was first conceived at a dinner party hosted by law professor Édouard-René de Laboulaye in 1865. Six years later, a committee formed under the chairmanship of de Laboulaye selected Alsatian sculptor **Frédéric-Auguste Bartholdi** (1834-1904), who then traveled to America for the purpose of studying and promoting the project.

The Inspiration – Bartholdi had attended the opening ceremonies of the Suez Canal in 1869, in hopes of securing a commission for a huge statue-lighthouse at the entrance to the new canal. Unsuccessful in obtaining the commission, he then turned his energy to creating a similar monument in the US. Entering New York harbor, he was overwhelmed and inspired by the grandeur of the scene before him, and its significance as the main gateway to the New World. Then and there he knew that the monument would be a figure of Liberty, and that one of the tiny harbor islands in this breathtaking setting would be an ideal site for it.

A Franco-American union was established, with de Laboulaye as president, to raise funds and coordinate all matters regarding the statue. The project was to be a joint effort—the French would underwrite the statue itself, and the Americans, the pedestal.

Trials and Tribulations – Bartholdi began work on the sculpture in 1874. He first made a clay figure 4ft high, and then three successively larger working models in plaster, which were corrected and refined before final dimensions were achieved. Turning his attention to the framework that would support the statue, Bartholdi called upon the skill and knowledge of the inventive French engineer **Gustave Eiffel**

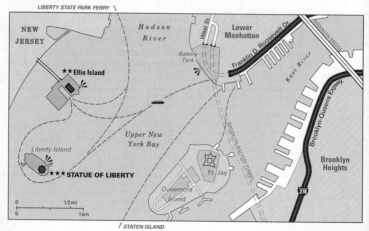

(1832-1923), who was later to build the Eiffel Tower. Employing construction techniques similar to the ones used for the skyscrapers of the 1880s, Eiffel created an intricate iron and steel skeletal frame to which 300 copper plates (each 3/32in thick) forming the skin of Liberty were applied.

As work on the statue progressed, the cost of construction almost doubled. To reach their goal, the French launched a massive fund drive, and by 1884 the statue was complete. At a special ceremony held July 4, 1884, in Paris, the statue was presented to the ambassador of the US as a gift from the people of France. Following the festivities, Liberty was dismantled and packed in 220 crates, in preparation for the ocean voyage to her permanent home across the Atlantic. In the meantime, in the US, little progress had been made in raising funds for the pedestal. At the American centennial exhibit in Philadelphia in 1876, the statue's forearm and torch were displayed to the delight of numerous visitors who took great pleasure in being photographed on its balcony; but purse strings were slow to loosen. Benefit balls, theatrical and sporting events, even a poetry contest were held to support the pedestal campaign.

In 1884, in another effort to raise money, Liberty's arm, complete with torch, was exhibited in the center of Madison Square. By 1885, with the statue awaiting shipment to the US and contributions still not forthcoming, the committee issued an appeal to patriotism, stating: "If the money is not now forthcoming, the statue must return to its donors, to the everlasting disgrace of the American people." As a result, numerous donations were received. The success of the project was due largely to the fund-raising campaign of **Joseph Pulitzer** (1847-1911), the publisher of the *New York World*. In front-page editorials, Pulitzer criticized the rich for not providing the mere "pittance" required, and encouraged all Americans to contribute to the project as the masses of French people had. In addition, he promised to publish in his newspaper the name of every donor, no matter how small the gift. With this, new impetus, contributions began to pour in daily.

© Patti McConville/DPA

The Dedication – In May 1885 the French ship Isère, carrying its precious cargo, set sail from Rouen and approximately one month later dropped anchor in New York harbor. Bartholdi traveled once more to New York to confer with the engineers and the architect chosen to design the pedestal, **Richard Morris Hunt**, one of the leading American architects of the day. Hunt's final design for the pedestal blended in character and scale to form an integrated unit with the statue.

■ Inspired by the spirit of liberty and affected by the persecutions then taking place in Russia, Emma Lazarus (1849-87) wrote her poem, "The New Colossus," in 1883. Included were these memorable lines now appearing on the pedestal:

Give me your tired, your poor,
Your huddled masses yearning to breathe free,
The wretched refuse of your teeming shore,
Send these, the homeless, tempest-tost to me,
I lift my lamp beside the golden door!

The festivities took place on October 28, 1886, declared an official holiday in New York City. Presiding over the unveiling of the statue on Bedloe's Island (renamed Liberty Island in 1956) was President **Grover Cleveland**, who had arrived by boat, accompanied by a 300-ship escort. National and international dignitaries huddled together at the foot of the statue while speech after speech was heard. As the statue was unveiled, foghorns bellowed and the roar of a 21-gun salute sounded from nearby batteries. Liberty's crown was illuminated simultaneously, symbolizing prophetically the beacon of hope she would be to the millions who would flock to these shores.

A Magnificent Restoration – Through the wear and tear of the years, the statue suffered degradation. The idea of restoring Liberty to her former splendor originated in France in 1981. After three years of extensive research and experiments designed to test the statue's soundness, an elaborate restoration effort was begun with the financial assistance of the Statue of Liberty-Ellis Island Foundation, Inc., headed by chairman emeritus Lee Iacocca of Chrysler Corp. The five-year project, costing millions of dollars, involved a thorough cleaning of the statue's copper skin and the replacement of various parts that had been damaged beyond repair: the torch, the flame and the 1,700 iron bars supporting the structure. Additional improvements included the installation of new elevators and staircases and the creation of a museum chronicling the statue's history. Declared a national monument and administered by the National Park Service, the statue receives about five million visitors a year.

Visit – The brief ferry crossing *(15min)* affords magnificent **views★★★** of the lower Manhattan skyline gradually receding into the background, and of the majestic and massive Statue of Liberty standing at the eastern end of the island, above the star-shaped walls of Fort Wood (1808-11). From the ferry slip, walk up the landscaped mall past the visitor center and the cafeteria to the statue. From there visitors may proceed to the pedestal.

The Lowdown on Lady Liberty

Weighing 225 tons, the statue is 151ft high and the head is 10ft by 17ft. The right arm, holding the torch, measures 42ft in length with a diameter of 12ft; the index finger is 8ft long. Liberty represents a crowned woman trampling beneath her feet the broken shackles of tyranny; the seven points in her crown signify liberty radiating to the seven continents and the seven seas. In her left hand she holds a tablet representing the Declaration of Independence and bearing the date of its proclamation, July 4, 1776. Her right hand raises the torch, symbolizing a beacon of hope, 305ft above sea level. The torch and the crown are lit in the evening.

Pedestal – The visitor entrance and a lobby adjoin the pedestal. Dominating the center of the lobby is one of the previous torches (1916, Gutzon Borglum). On the second-floor mezzanine, panels describe the evolution of the torch. In a corner of the lobby, a video *(shown continuously)* provides a preview of the climb to the crown and the views from the observation deck.

Statue of Liberty Exhibit – 2nd level in the pedestal. The badly corroded original torch is featured in this exhibit, which recounts the history of the statue from de Laboulaye's conception to the present. Bartholdi's working models of the statue illustrate the evolution of his ideas, and a cutaway model provides an excellent view of the complex inner structure. The repoussé technique used in forming the copper exterior is explained in a continuous video, and a substantial collection of postcards and souvenirs depicts the statue's role as a symbol of liberty both in America and abroad.

Observation Deck – At the top of the pedestal; access by elevator from the lobby level. This four-sided balcony provides spectacular **views★★★** of New York harbor, lower Manhattan and the Financial District, the Verrazano-Narrows Bridge and New Jersey.

Climb to the Crown – The 354-step climb (22 stories) from the ground to the crown begins just inside the main entrance, off the lobby. A narrow, circular metal staircase *(not for the claustrophobic)* winds its way up through the statue's interior, culminating in a narrow platform from which a view of the New York harbor is visible through the openings in the crown.

Before returning to the ferry pier, stroll along the waterfront **promenade**. As you glance across the harbor, note the contrast between Manhattan's striking high rises and the older, smaller-scale buildings found in Brooklyn. Bordering the walkway near the pedestal are six slender sculptures by Phillip Ratner of key figures in the history of the statue: de Laboulaye, Bartholdi, Eiffel, Hunt, Pulitzer and Lazarus.

★★Ellis Island

Situated in New York harbor, approximately halfway between lower Manhattan and the Statue of Liberty, Ellis Island stands as living testimony to the millions of immigrants who passed through its gates to enter the "land of golden opportunity." A multimillion-dollar restoration project transformed this 27.5-acre parcel of land into a national monument that pays tribute to the ancestors of nearly 40 percent of Americans by commemorating their hope and determination.

America's Great Immigrant Gateway – Inaugurated in 1892 on the site of an abandoned fort, Ellis Island was America's first and most comprehensive immigration facility. It quickly became the main port of entry for newcomers to America, replacing Castle Garden *(p 134)*, which had operated from 1855 to 1890. Until its demise in 1954, Ellis Island received more than 12 million immigrants, attesting to one of the greatest mass migrations in history, which helped shape the face of 20C America. From 1900 to 1924, an average of 5,000 new arrivals were processed daily, the majority in less than half a day. Most immigrants quickly booked passage beyond New York City, joining friends or family already in America; unfortunately, two percent of them were denied admission and shipped back to their country of origin. After World War I, restrictive laws and quotas diminished Ellis Island's importance as a reception site, and by 1954 the island had slipped into decay and was officially closed. In 1984, with funding and supervision by the Statue of Liberty-Ellis Island Foundation, Inc., the main building in the 33-structure complex underwent one of the most elaborate restorations of any public building in the US. It reopened its doors in September 1990 as the Ellis Island Immigration Museum *(it is the only building on the island open to the public)*. Plans are under way to create an immigration history center and Web site to enable visitors to research their family heritage via a computerized database *(www.ellisislandrecords.org)*.

★★Ellis Island Immigration Museum – *On Ellis Island in New York Harbor. Open year-round daily 9:30am–5pm. Closed Dec 25.* ☏ *212-363-3200. www.ellisisland.com. Obtain free tickets to the Island of Hope/Island of Tears film as soon as you enter the main building—shows fill up quickly.* A glass-and-metal canopy leads from the ferry slip to the elegant brick and limestone Beaux-Arts edifice. Completed in 1900 by Boring and Tilton, it replaced an earlier structure that had burned down in 1897. Crowned by four copper-domed towers and pierced by three arched entrance portals, the former processing center has been restored to reflect its appearance from 1918 to 1924, presenting a series of permanent and temporary installations on three floors.

First Floor – Visitors enter the baggage room, where immigrants were separated—sometimes forever—from their precious belongings. The old railroad office, to the north, houses the "Peopling of America" exhibit, which uses statistical displays to chronicle the history of immigration and ethnicity in the US, from the 17C to the present. Highlights include a 6ft globe that traces worldwide migration patterns since the 18C, and the "Word Tree," which explains the origin of many American words. A poignant film entitled *Island of Hope/Island of Tears* portrays the human

Ellis Island Immigration Museum

National Park Service

face of migration: the film is screened in the two theaters located in the eastern wing *(30min, shown every half-hour)*. The western wing houses the American Family Immigration History Center where visitors can research their family heritage via a computerized database.

Second Floor – The sweeping two-story Registry Room/Great Hall was the site of the initial inspection of immigrants, who awaited their fate while queuing behind metal pens. The hall that once accommodated thousands has been left empty, save for a few scattered benches, to serve as a grand, quiet memorial. The pride of the 17,300sq ft hall is its impressive vaulted ceiling, rebuilt in 1917 with interlocking tiles by Spaniard Rafael Gustavino and his son; only 17 of the 28,000 tiles had to be replaced during restoration.

In the western wing, the 14-room exhibit, Through America's Gate, re-creates the step-by-step inspection process that often culminated in the dividing of families at the "Stairs of Separation." The displays in the eastern wing chronicle the immigrants' hopes and hardships through photographs, memorabilia and recorded commentaries. Life-size portraits enliven the hallways in the two wings.

Third Floor – The highlight of this floor, Treasures from Home, presents objects donated by immigrants and their families, from a teddy bear to an elaborate wedding gown. In Silent Voices, large photographs taken before the restoration evoke the eerie feeling of an abandoned place, while furnishings recall the daily routine of processing, registering and caring for immigrants. Another exhibit, tracing 300 years of the island's history, displays five detailed models showing the evolving site plans of the island between 1897 and 1940.

Along the north wall of the mezzanine, a narrow dorm room has been furnished to reflect the cramped living conditions experienced by some of the detainees.

Grounds – Facing Manhattan, a newly rebuilt American Immigrant Wall of Honor serves as a memorial to the nation's immigrant heritage. The 652.5ft-long, double-sided, semicircular wall contains the names of more than 500,000 individuals and families whose descendants have honored them by donating to the Ellis Island restoration project *(for more information on how to add a name, contact the Statue of Liberty-Ellis Island Foundation, Inc.: ☎ 212-883-1986)*. The terrace offers breathtaking **views**★★ of the Manhattan skyline.

9 • FINANCIAL DISTRICT –
LOWER MANHATTAN★

MTA 4, 5 trains to Fulton St.

Map p 126

Site of the city's earliest Dutch settlement, the Financial District today is defined by skyscrapers towering over a maze of narrow streets, creating some of the city's most spectacular canyons. Through the years Wall Street has come to symbolize the nation's financial power. Just a few blocks from the Stock Exchange is "ground zero," where the World Trade Center stood. A rebuilding effort will continue in the district for years to come.

Historical Notes

Birth of a City – The general area now called the Financial District was the birthplace of New York in 1625. Trade flourished under the Dutch West India Company, and the town of Nieuw Amsterdam quickly developed as the center of Dutch hegemony in the colonies. Occupying a limited area, the small town was defended to the south by a fort and to the north by a wall of thick wooden planks constructed in 1653 between the Hudson and East rivers. Erected to protect the town from Indians, the wall (the origin of the name of Wall Street) was instead regularly dismantled by residents, who would take the planks to shore up their houses or heat their homes.

About 1,000 persons occupied the 120 wood and brick houses topped with characteristic Dutch gables and tile roofs. A windmill and a canal, "the Ditch," dug in the middle of Broad Street, attested to the town's Dutch heritage. The inhabitants, however, were of varied origins; in 1642, when the first Stadt Huys (City Hall) was built at 71 Pearl Street, no less than 18 languages were spoken in Nieuw Amsterdam. Governing the town was first a commercial agent of the Dutch West India Company, and later a succession of governors, including Peter Stuyvesant. When the British took over Nieuw Amsterdam in 1664, "the Ditch" was filled in and the wall torn down. During the 18C, colonial Georgian houses, such as Fraunces Tavern, began to replace the narrow Dutch dwellings.

Wall Street: Birth of a Financial Center – Completely dismantled by the British in 1699, the wooden wall was replaced by a new street where, on the corner of Broad Street, the City Hall was built (today the Federal Hall National Memorial). Wall Street became an administrative and residential street, lined with rows of fine houses ornamented with Georgian pilasters and porticos. After the Revolution, the east end of the street harbored a series of coffeehouses and taverns. The famous **Tontine Coffee House**, built in 1792 at the corner of Wall and Water streets, served as the first home of the New York Stock Exchange.

As the area specialized in shipping and warehousing, accounting and banking developed. Following an 1835 fire that destroyed 700 houses in the area, storehouses, shops and banks moved into the reconstructed buildings. Speculation flourished, especially after 1860. On September 24, 1869, the financier **Jay Gould** (1836-92), who had tried to corner the gold market with his associate James Fisk, sold out and brought about the financial panic known as "Black Friday."

Cornelius Vanderbilt (1794-1877), nicknamed "The Commodore" owing to his interests in the shipping industry, began to extend his activities to the railroads in 1862. First the owner of small lines (the Harlem, the Hudson, and New York Central), he launched the famous New York-Buffalo line in 1873. At the same time, banker **J. Pierpont Morgan** (1837-1913) financed the great new industries: steel, oil and railroads. Generous, but a ruthless businessman, the founder of the famous Pierpont Morgan Library was succeeded by his son, John Pierpont Morgan Jr., who was the target of an assassination attempt in 1920. On September 16 a bomb exploded in a cart near the Morgan Guaranty Trust building; it missed Morgan Jr., but killed 38 innocent people caught in the midday rush.

The business activities and interests of the Vanderbilts, Goulds, Morgans and other financiers contributed to the leading position gained by New York in the 1920s. Wall Street gradually replaced London as the financial capital of the world and has maintained this role despite the crash of 1929.

Thousands of jobs were lost after the 1987 stock market crash; office vacancy rates soared to 25 percent and higher. The city intervened with tax incentives designed to encourage the conversion of offices into residences. By 1996 developers had created almost 5,000 new apartment units. The energy from the young professionals who moved in and the bull market of the late nineties revitalized the downtown once again. The September 11 attack prompted Wall Street to consider decentralizing its operations. Moves to Midtown and elsewhere in the city continue, as the Financial District is transformed into a mixed residential and business neighborhood. Nevertheless, Wall Street will reign as capital of the world markets in the years to come.

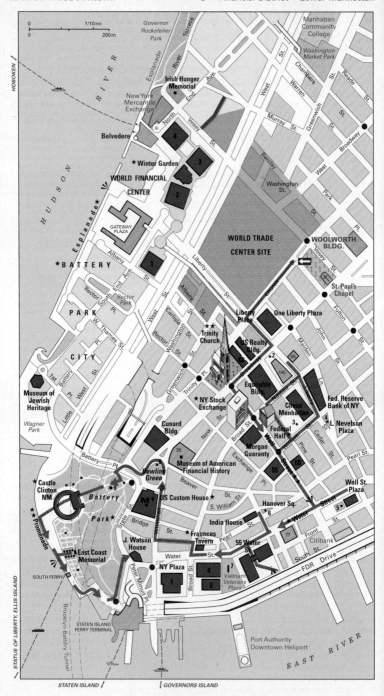

WALKING TOUR *Distance: 2.5mi*

Begin at Church & Fulton Sts. The World Trade Center site (see shaded area of map above) has no pedestrian access.

★**World Trade Center Site** – The seven buildings of the World Trade Center (WTC) stood on a 16-acre site, grouped around the sweeping five-acre **Austin J. Tobin Plaza**. Modeled after St. Mark's Square in Venice, the plaza linked various buildings of the center and interconnected them with other pedestrian systems in the area. Two years after the concept of a trade center was proposed in 1960 by David Rockefeller, head of Chase Manhattan Bank, and supported by his brother Nelson, the governor of New York, legislation was passed authorizing the Port Authority to

126

realize the project. Architects Minoru Yamasaki & Assocs. and Emery Roth and Sons designed the complex whose first buildings opened in 1970. Referred to as a "United Nations of Commerce," it became the central market of world trade. All international business services were concentrated here: exporters; importers; American and overseas manufacturers; freight forwarders; customhouse brokers; international banks; federal, state and overseas trade development agencies; trade associations and transportation lines. Fifty thousand people worked in the center, and its 13.4 million square feet represented 16 percent of the total office space downtown. The complex included a concourse with a PATH (Port Authority TransHudson) railroad terminal, access to the New York subways and eight acres of shops and services.

The two 110-story **Twin Towers**, the second-tallest buildings in the nation after the Sears Tower in Chicago, rose to 1,350ft. In designing the towers, the architects used a new structural design in which the exterior walls would bear most of the load, maximizing open, column-free floor space. Closely spaced steel columns formed the outer walls. The aluminum-clad columns were joined by spandrel beams girdling the towers at every floor. The tight alternation of the columns and recessed floor-to-ceiling tinted windows gave the towers their trademark windowless look.

A Target for Terrorists – On February 26, 1993, a terrorist bomb rocked One World Trade Center, killing six and injuring more than 1,000 persons. The twin towers sustained millions of dollars in damage and were closed for almost a month. On September 11, 2001, two hijacked commercial airliners were crashed into the towers of the World Trade Center. Within an hour and a half, the Twin Towers collapsed, causing approximately 2,800 fatalities and effectively destroying the entire complex. Rescue and recovery efforts began immediately. Workers removed 1.5 million tons of steel and debris in the following months, and in May 2002 the cleanup finished ahead of schedule.

Just months before the attack, developer Larry Silverstein had signed a $3.2 billion contract to lease the center from the Port Authority for 99 years. That lease remains in effect, giving him a leading role in building and managing new office buildings on the site, but power to commission and approve plans for the site remains in public hands. The governor and mayor of New York set up the Lower Manhattan Development Corporation (LMDC) to oversee the planning process for the site itself and the surrounding area.

After a first round of design proposals for the site were roundly criticized as compromises that pleased no one, the LMDC invited six teams of high-profile architects—including such luminaries as Daniel Libeskind and Richard Meier—to submit new proposals. Daniel Libeskind's winning design, chosen in February 2003, preserves the exposed slurry walls of the site's foundation and the 4.7 acre "footprint" of the twin towers as the setting for a memorial garden. The plan also calls for a 1,776ft "Freedom Tower" to rise above the buildings flanking the memorial.

Ground Zero: A Place of Remembrance

As plans for the World Trade Center site are finalized in anticipation of the groundbreaking, set for summer 2004, access to the cleared and excavated site itself remains restricted to authorized workers and officials. To accommodate New Yorkers and the visitors from around the world who have come to witness the extent of the destruction and remember the thousands who died, a viewing wall has been erected along Church Street. Panels mounted along the wall trace the history of the site, in text, photos and maps, from the era before the World Trade Center through its construction and reign over the skyline and into the future. The most complete views of the site can be found along Liberty Street and the connecting South Bridge, which rises above the site's southwest corner. Also, the concourse and track platforms of the recently reopened PATH station, built into the east end of the WTC site, offer commanding views of the slurry wall and the excavated pit from 70ft below street level.

Though a permanent memorial is years from completion, the city has carefully secured the history of September 11 in a number of ways. Many of the city's cultural institutions continue to present works and exhibits related to 9/11. The New-York Historical Society and the Museum of the City of New York have been making substantial efforts to document the events and have both mounted a number of exhibitions and programs. St. Paul's Chapel, just across Church Street, has preserved the impromptu memorial that grew along the wrought-iron fence surrounding its grounds—a year's worth of messages of condolence hand-printed on t-shirts, baseball caps and banners. Fritz Koenig's **Sphere (9)**, the 15ft diameter, 22-ton brass sculpture, once the focal point of the center's plaza, was recovered from the debris and then reassembled by Koenig. It stands dented and punctured along the tree-lined mall at the entrance of Battery Park, accompanied by an eternal flame that was lit on the one-year anniversary of the attack.

The rebuilding of the site, one of the biggest development projects in the city's history and, perhaps, the most emotionally intense, has engaged the city's continuing attention. Silverstein invited a number of renowned architects, including David Childs and Norman Foster, whose master plan lost out to Libeskind's, to design individual buildings within the project. A new round of tussles and turf fights among architects, builders, and politicians has broken out, with the daily papers reporting each blow. Even as key details of the master plan are hammered out, and the public assesses the recently unveiled eight finalist designs for the memorial, the governor has set an ambitious timetable into motion: The cornerstone of the first tower is to be laid in August 2004 (in time for the Republican National Convention, to be held in New York City). The Port Authority signaled its own increasing ambitions, meanwhile, with the announcement that Diego Calatrava, often referred to as the world's greatest transportation architect, would design a permanent PATH commuter station for the site. A temporary station opened in November 2003.

★**Battery Park City** – This vast commercial/residential complex adjoining the World Trade Center rises on 92 acres of landfill edging the Hudson River. An extension of lower Manhattan, Battery Park City has a working population of almost 50,000 and 9,000 residents. Building continues, and the size of the residential community is expected to increase in the years ahead to as many as 25,000.

In the late 1960s Governor Nelson Rockefeller continued his effort to revitalize the area with a proposal to erect a residential complex in lower Manhattan that would provide space away from the city's hustle and bustle. The landfill and infrastructure were completed in the mid-1970s, but the city's faltering finances stalled construction. In 1979, during the administrations of Mayor Ed Koch and Governor Hugh Carey, a barrage of criticism that the complex would be too isolated spurred the adoption of a new master plan to develop the area as an integrated extension of the island—following the same street grid. Construction resumed, and in 1982 the first tenants moved in to Gateway Plaza.

Winter Garden, World Financial Center

© Patti McConville DPA

The Complex – The **World Financial Center** (WFC), designed by Cesar Pelli & Associates, forms the commercial heart of Battery Park City. Its four glass-and-granite-sheathed office towers extending from Vesey to Albany streets encompass 7,000,000sq ft of office space and have served as home to some of the nation's most prestigious brokerage and financial services firms—American Express, Dow Jones, Merrill Lynch. Marked by setbacks and notches, and topped with geometrically-shaped copper roofs, the buildings of the WFC present a graceful blend of traditional and contemporary design elements. Highlighting the WFC is the **Winter Garden★** (1987), a barrel-vaulted glass and steel structure reminiscent of London's 19C Crystal Palace. This attractive space, nestled between the WFC towers, offers performing-arts programs and events, and houses shops and a variety of restaurants. Sixteen 45ft palm trees dot the large plaza, which culminates in the grand central staircase. Weary shoppers can rest on the benches and admire the fascinating play of light on the glass.

Falling debris from the Twin Towers destroyed the Winter Garden; in the course of the restoration—completed on the one-year anniversary of the attack—workers replaced 2,000 broken panes of glass, imported new palm trees and relaid 1.2 million pounds of Italian marble. The towers of the WFC suffered from the collapse of the World Trade Center—a fragment of the wall from the north tower was very visibly embedded high up in the facade of 3 WFC. Luckily, most of the damage was cosmetic, not structural. The complex has been fully repaired and reoccupied.

Just northwest of the WFC, overlooking River Terrace at North End Avenue and Vesey Street, a modest, sloping green field enclosed by low stone walls forms the **Irish Hunger Memorial.** A path curves uphill, past an abandoned stone cottage and along fallow potato fields sprouting clover and other native Irish flora. The memorial's highest point, 25ft above the sidewalk, provides a view of the bay in which the Statue of Liberty and Ellis Island figure prominently. The field, 96ft by 170ft, rests on top of a wedge-shaped base of Irish limestone. Bands of text on the potato famine are worked into the stone—excerpts from letters, newspapers and histories; statistics on the deaths and displacements. Reports on more recent famines are also woven in. The Great Hunger lasted from 1845-52. During that time, one million Irish died of starvation and many more went hungry. Nearly one million Irish arrived in New York City between 1847 and 1851. The memorial, designed by artist Brian Tolle, opened in July 2002.

North of the memorial, stretching uptown along North End Avenue to Chambers Street, rise the buildings of the River Terrace complex, still under construction. One of them, 20 River Terrace *(on Murray St.)*, is touted as the world's first "green" high rise. The environmentally sustainable apartment building will incorporate solar power cells and water recycling, and use the latest energy-efficient technology for both building-wide systems and for electric appliances in individual apartments. Occupancy is scheduled for 2004. Gateway Plaza (1982), the first of Battery Park City's residential developments, is at the head of South End Avenue. Just to the south lies Rector Place, a 10-building ensemble containing 2,200 residential units.

The enormous complex also includes public plazas, outdoor sculpture and landscaped parks, including the 1.6-acre **Belvedere** *(just north of Winter Garden)*, planted with English oaks and honey locusts and marked by two distinctive light pylons sculpted by Martin Puryear. A stroll south along the 1.2mi riverside **esplanade★**—with its cast-iron benches and lampposts, lush trees and flowering shrubs—affords spectacular **views★★** of the harbor. The esplanade's boardwalk leads to the small Robert F. Wagner Jr. Park and the Museum of Jewish Heritage.

Return to the South Bridge and continue east on Liberty St.

Liberty Plaza – *At Liberty St. between Church and Broadway Sts.* This small, pleasant square is surrounded by prestigious buildings. **One Liberty Plaza**, a 54-story building (1974; Skidmore, Owings & Merrill) of thick, horizontal steel beams and tinted gray windows, borders the northeast side. Dominating the east side of the plaza is the slender, dark glass tower at **140 Broadway**. Rising 55 stories without a single setback, this edifice is characteristic of the buildings erected in the 1960s. Isamu Noguchi crafted the reddish-orange **cube (2)** (1967) that enlivens its plaza. Resting solely on one corner, the sharply angled, brightly colored sculpture provides a foil for the stark yet elegant bank building. The **US Realty Building** (1907) stands to the south of the park.

Continue south on Broadway.

The **Trinity Building (G)** is located immediately behind the US Realty Building and is connected to it by a pedestrian walkway on the top floor. The two limestone structures were designed in an elaborate Gothic style to harmonize with neighboring Trinity Church.

Rising across the street, the **Equitable Building** *(no. 120)*, an immense Beaux-Arts edifice (1915), comprises twin towers connected by a recessed central section. Protests over the building's bulk—it encompasses 1,200,000sq ft of office space on an area of less than one acre—gave rise to the city's first zoning resolution *(p 45)*, passed in 1916, which limited the amount of floor space allowed on a particular plot of land.

View of Trinity Church from Wall Street

© Brigitta L. House/MICHELIN

★★Trinity Church – *Open year-round Mon–Fri 7am–6pm, weekends & holidays 8am–4pm. Guided tours (30min) available daily 2pm; reservations suggested. Classical music programs Thu 1pm–2pm. ☎ 212-602-0872. www.trinitywallstreet.org.* Located on Broadway at the head of Wall Street, this lovely Gothic Revival church, now dwarfed by the surrounding high rises, was the tallest building in New York at the time of its construction. It is lined on three sides by a grassy cemetery, where several famous New Yorkers are buried.

The First Anglican Parish of New York – An Episcopal church, Trinity was founded by a charter granted by King William III in 1697. Among the influential local citizens aiding its construction was **William Kidd**, the famous captain-turned-pirate who lived at nearby Hanover Square and was hanged for piracy in London in 1701. The first church building (1698), resembling a country chapel with a spire and narrow, spear-shaped windows, burned in the great fire of 1776 and was replaced by another, the roof of which collapsed in the 1839. The present edifice, designed by Richard Upjohn, was completed in 1846. The Chapel of All Saints was added in 1913, and the Bishop Manning Memorial Wing in 1966.

The Building – The rose sandstone exterior is distinguished by the square bell tower and its 280ft spire, which soared above the nearby houses when it was built. The tower contains ten bells, including eight of the original eight bells dating from 1797. Handsome bronze doors (designed by Richard Morris Hunt), inspired by those of the Baptistery in Florence, Italy, lead to the interior. Note the brightly colored stained-glass windows by Upjohn above the white marble altar (1877), and the elaborate wooden vault and screen of the Chapel of All Saints at the right of the choir.

To the left of the chancel is the **Trinity Museum** *(open year-round Mon–Fri & holidays 9am–3:45pm, Sat 10am–3:45pm, Sun 1pm–3:45pm)*, which presents exhibits portraying the history of Trinity Church and its relationship with the city of New York from colonial days to the present.

The Cemetery – Dotted with old and worn tombstones, the cemetery offers a pleasant, shady green space among the Financial District skyscrapers. The oldest stone marks the grave of Richard Churcher, who died in 1681 *(right of the church)*. Notice also the graves of the publisher William Bradford Jr.; Robert Fulton, the inventor of the steamboat; two secretaries of the Treasury, Alexander Hamilton and Albert Gallatin; and Francis Lewis, a New York signer of the Declaration of Independence.

Turn left on Wall St.

The nation's center of high finance, **Wall Street★★** winds its narrow way in the shadows of the surrounding skyscrapers.

★New York Stock Exchange – *8-18 Broad St. As a security precaution, the Exchange has been closed to all visitors except school groups. Call or check the exchange's Web site for updates. ☎ 212-656-5165. www.nyse.com.* Facing Broad Street, this 8-story building (1903) presents a majestic facade of Corinthian columns crowned by an elaborate pediment with sculpted figures symbolizing Commerce. Marking the entrance, a tree recalls the buttonwood tree at Wall and Williams streets where 24 brokers met to found the forerunner of the New York Stock Exchange in 1792. The traders dealt in stocks and bonds issued by the government and a few private companies; a handshake sealed a deal.

New York Stock Exchange

The stock exchange gained popularity among ordinary folks in the early 20C, particularly following the Liberty Bond campaign of World War I. By the late 1920s, guided by an unshakable feeling of prosperity, over one million Americans invested in stocks listed on the exchange, many buying on credit with as little as 10 percent down. On October 29, 1929, thereafter known as "Black Tuesday," the stock market experienced a financial panic that ushered in the Great Depression of the 1930s. In a matter of weeks, more than nine million savings accounts were depleted and the national income was cut in half.

Today exchange members trade the shares of thousands of domestic and foreign companies listed on the stock exchange, including virtually every leading industrial, financial and service corporation in the US. The value of shares listed for trading is about $9 trillion. On an average day, some 1.4 billion shares are traded, valued at more than $42 billion. Approximately 85 million Americans are shareholders. On the ground floor is the actual trading floor where transactions are completed Mondays through Fridays from 9:30am to 4pm. Staff monitor the sophisticated systems that enable the trading operations from a 3-D, computer-generated trading floor, installed in 1999 as part of the exchange's $2 billion investment in technology during the 1990s.

Exhibits in the **Interactive Education Center** trace the history of the New York Stock Exchange and present the workings of the stock market. The **Members Gallery★** *(3rd floor)* overlooks the hectic trading floor below.

★**Federal Hall National Memorial** – *26 Wall St. Open year-round Mon–Fri 9am–5pm. Closed major holidays.* ♿ ☎ *212-825-6888. www.nps.gov/feha.* This imposing Westchester marble edifice marks one of the city's most historic locations. The site was first occupied by New York's City Hall, construction of which began in 1699 on land donated by Abraham de Peyster; in 1702 the city government moved in. This first City Hall also served as a courthouse and a debtor's prison.

Reconstructed in 1789 under the supervision of **Pierre Charles L'Enfant** (1754-1825), who designed the master plan of Washington, DC, the building became Federal Hall, the first capitol of the US under the Constitution. George Washington took the oath of office as the first president on the balcony of Federal Hall on April 30, 1789. After the federal government was transferred to Philadelphia the following year, the building was used for state and city offices, then torn down in 1812.

The present building (Town & Davis) dates from 1842 and served as the US Custom House until 1862, when it became the US Subtreasury. Occupied by a number of government offices in the years that followed, it was designated as a historic site in 1939 and a national memorial in 1955. Today a towering bronze **statue** of Washington, designed in 1883 by John Q.A. Ward, looks down on the city from atop Federal Hall's wide steps.

The **interior** of Federal Hall is dominated by a splendid central rotunda. Sixteen marble Corinthian columns support the large dome and balconies, embellished with ornate bronze railings. Mementos of George Washington are displayed alongside an exhibit on the Constitution. In the section devoted to the history of the building and New York, dioramas depict the three buildings that have stood on this site.

Morgan Guaranty Trust Company – *23 Wall St., at the corner of Broad St.* Erected in 1913, this austere, white marble building still bears the scars from a bomb explosion that was meant to kill J. Pierpont Morgan Jr. The narrow Beaux-Arts structure with salmon-colored trimmings, adjoining the building on the Wall Street side, also belongs to the Morgan Co.

Continue to William St., turn left, then left again on Pine St.

Chase Manhattan Bank – *On Pine St., between Nassau and William Sts.* Born of the merger between Chase National Bank and the Bank of the Manhattan Co., this institution became, in 1961, the first bank to occupy a prestigious modern building in lower Manhattan. The stately glass and aluminum structure, designed by Skidmore, Owings & Merrill, rises 813ft from a paved plaza enlivened by various sculptural elements.

Historical Notes – In 1798 a yellow fever epidemic, attributed to polluted water, broke out in the city. The following year, **Aaron Burr** (1756-1836) founded the Manhattan Co. to provide and distribute drinking water to the city. The company laid down a network of hollow pine-log pipes, which still come to light occasionally during excavations. Burr then decided to expand the company's activities to the realm of banking and finance. On September 1, 1799, the Manhattan Co. opened its first office of discount and deposit. The extension of its activities was a serious blow to **Alexander Hamilton** (1755-1804), who had political and financial interests in two other banks functioning in New York at the time. The two men's financial differences, reinforced by their long-standing political rivalry, finally led Burr to challenge Hamilton to their historic duel (July 11, 1804), in which Hamilton was fatally wounded.

The Chase Bank was founded in 1877 by John Thompson and his son, who named it in honor of **Salmon P. Chase** (1808-73), US senator and governor of Ohio. Chase also served as Lincoln's secretary of the Treasury and chief justice of the US

Supreme Court. He drafted a bill enacted by Congress as the National Currency Act of 1863, establishing a national currency and the present federal banking system. The portrait of Chase appears on the largest bill in circulation ($10,000).

The Building – The 2.5-acre tract of land purchased by the Chase Manhattan Bank was originally bisected by a street. Under an agreement with the city, the bank was able to acquire the part of the street connecting the two parcels and to build on it. Almost five years were required for the completion of the building, a steel frame structure covered with a glass-curtain wall. One of the largest office buildings in the city, the edifice contains 65 stories (including 5 below street level). The bank vault, located in the fifth basement, is reputed to be the world's largest. Longer than a football field, it weighs 985 tons and has six doors, each 20in thick (four of them weigh 45 tons apiece; the other two weigh 30 tons). Note, on the esplanade fronting the bank, Jean Dubuffet's striking **sculpture (3)** *Group of Four Trees* (1972). The undulating figures present a vivid contrast to the sober Chase tower. To the left, the Plaza Banking Office curves around a sunken Japanese water garden, designed by Isamu Noguchi in 1964.

Continue on Pine St. to Nassau St.; turn right and continue to Liberty St.

Federal Reserve Bank of New York – *33 Liberty St. As a security precaution, visitors must arrive 20min before the start of the tour. All visitors must undergo a screening process. Visit by guided tour (1hr) only, year-round Mon–Fri 9:30am–2:30pm. Closed major holidays. One-month advance reservations required.* ♿ ☎ *212-720-6130. www.ny.frb.org.* Facing Chase Manhattan Bank, this imposing, 14-story masonry edifice, which occupies an entire block, was completed in 1924. The structure's design, distinguished by massive rusticated walls, was inspired by several 15C Italian Renaissance palaces, which were built to house the wealthiest banking and merchant families in Florence. Inside the building, 80ft below street level, is the Federal Reserve's gold vault **Kids**. Stored within are the gold reserves of approximately 80 foreign nations, thought to be the largest accumulation of gold in the world, with a market value (2002) of over $85 billion. The guided tours allow the public to view the gold vault and participate in FedWorks, an interactive exhibit on monetary policy and the role of the Federal Reserve Bank.

Continue east on Liberty St. to William St.

In the small park at the triangle formed by William and Pine streets and Maiden Lane, note the seven huge, black welded-steel **sculptures (4)** crafted in 1977 by **Louise Nevelson**, for whom the space is named.

Turn right on William St. to return to Wall St.

55 Wall Street – This massive Greek Revival temple is distinguished by its double colonnade of Ionic and Corinthian columns. The building, now home to the Regent Wall Street hotel, was occupied by Citibank until 1992. Created in 1812, the City Bank of New York, as it was originally called, succeeded the first financial establishment founded 10 years earlier in New York by Alexander Hamilton. Designed in 1841 by Isaiah Rogers as the Second Merchants Exchange, the building was enlarged and renovated by McKim, Mead and White in 1907.

Especially impressive is the ornate interior, restored to its original Neoclassical appearance. The Great Hall, embellished with arches and colonnades and clad in marble and travertine, culminates in a 72ft coffered and domed ceiling.

60 Wall Street – Designed by Roche, Dinkeloo and Assocs. in 1988 for J.P. Morgan Bank, this giant 47-story tower, rising 750ft, is one of the tallest skyscrapers in the Financial District. Protruding from the granite and reflective glass facade are representations of classical pilasters, replete with base, shaft and capital. The motif recurs on the top 10 stories. The white marble lobby, enlivened with trelliswork and a multitude of mirrors, provides an inviting public space, dotted with ficus trees, flowers, tables and chairs. The building became Deutsche Bank's Manhattan headquarters in 2001.

Continue east to Water St.

Before reaching Water Street, turn around and admire the **vista★** down the celebrated "canyon," which ends with the dwarfed, dark silhouette of Trinity Church.

Turn left on Water St.

Water Street★ reflects the astonishing amount of development in lower Manhattan since the late 1960s, spurred by the need for new office space. Here progressive planning has reestablished the human and recreational elements in the architectural landscape. Laid out on landfill, Water Street is lined with office buildings in a variety of shapes, colors and construction materials, greatly altering the skyline of this seafront area.

At the corner of Water and Pine streets rises the elegant glass and aluminum **Wall Street Plaza**, designed by I.M. Pei in 1973. Highlighting the building's plaza is Yu Yu Yang's tantalizing two-part **sculpture (5)**, consisting of a pierced slab and a disk. Beside it, a plaque commemorates *Queen Elizabeth I*, the largest and fastest ocean liner ever built, whose last proprietor, Morley Cho, owned Wall Street Plaza.

Double back and walk toward Wall St.

Continuing south along Water Street, pass the small, welcoming plaza of 77 Water Street, known as Bennett Park, where pools, fountains, sculpture and benches provide a pleasant recreational ensemble.

Continue south on Water St.

To the right is **Hanover Square**, a quiet little plaza dotted with trees, benches and a bronze **statue (6)** of Abraham de Peyster (1896), a prosperous Dutch merchant and mayor of the city. William Bradford established his first printing press in 1693 in one of the shops originally lining the square. **India House**, a handsome Italianate brownstone erected in 1853, borders the south side of the plaza.

Continue south to **55 Water Street**, a two-building complex flanking a raised plaza *(access by escalator from Water St.)*, which affords an expansive **view★** across the East River to Brooklyn Heights.

At Vietnam Veterans Plaza, a street-level plaza, pause to view the 1985 **Vietnam Veterans Memorial (7)**, a 66ft-by-16ft granite and glass-block wall dedicated to the nation's men and women who served in the conflict. The memorial is inscribed with passages from letters, diary entries and poems written by American soldiers. A redesign of the plaza, completed in 2001, added a ceremonial walk flanked by stone pylons inscribed with the names of the 1,700 New Yorkers who died in the war.

Continue on Water Street as it bears west.

The buildings of **New York Plaza** (nos. 1, 2 and 4) form a varied ensemble, linked by plazas and a ground-level concourse lined with shops and restaurants. Note in particular the 22-story redbrick building of 4 New York Plaza, punctuated by narrow slit windows.

At the corner of Broad St., turn right and continue north to Pearl St.

★**Fraunces Tavern** – *54 Pearl St.* This handsome yellow brick house, with its slate roof, portico and balcony, represents a fine example of Georgian Revival architecture. The original house was built in 1719 as the home of Etienne de Lancey, the ancestor of a prominent New York family, which gave its name to Delancey Street in the Lower East Side.

The house became a tavern in 1763 when Samuel Fraunces acquired the building. Governor George Clinton gave a dinner here, celebrating the British evacuation of New York in 1783, and in December of the same year the tavern was the scene of Washington's farewell to his troops. The present building is a 1907 restoration.

Fraunces Tavern has been preserved by the Sons of the Revolution. A restaurant occupies the main floor. A wooden stairway leads to the **museum** on the upper two floors, where permanent and changing exhibits trace the early history of New York City and the Revolutionary War *(open year-round Tue–Sat 10am–5pm, Thu until 7pm, Sat 11am–5pm; closed major holidays; $3; ☎ 212-425-1778; www.frauncestavernmuseum.org)*. Also in the museum, American decorative arts are displayed in period settings.

Just east of the tavern, note the descriptive panels on the plaza at 85 Broad Street and three glass-covered archaeological sites *(below street level)* that reveal portions of a 17C tavern, a well, and Stadt Huys—the Dutch city hall.

Continue west on Pearl St. Turn right on Whitehall St. and continue to the former US Custom House.

★**Former US Custom House** – *1 Bowling Green.* Erected in 1907 by Cass Gilbert, this magnificent Beaux-Arts building stands on the site originally occupied by a fort and later by the Government House, which served as a residence for state governors until its demolition in 1815. The current imposing edifice presents a monumental gray granite facade adorned with white Tennessee marble sculptures. The lower series, by Daniel Chester French, depicts Asia, America, Europe and Africa. The statues above represent some of the most famous trading cities and nations of the world: Notice a woman depicting Lisbon (to the left of the central shield) by Augustus Saint-Gaudens; and the doge with death's head evoking Venice.

The building was vacated in 1973, when the customs offices moved to the new US Custom House at 6 World Trade Center. In 1994 the **National Museum of the American Indian (M¹)** relocated a large part of its collection from Audubon Terrace to this site. The remainder of the collection will be housed in a newly constructed museum on the Mall, in Washington, DC, to be completed by 2004.

Cunard Building – *25 Broadway, on Bowling Green.* Now converted into a post office, this grand structure, which once housed a steamship ticket office, is noteworthy for its splendid **lobby★**. Designed in 1921 by Benjamin W. Morris, the grand space features a 68ft rotunda and a series of large murals.

Opposite the Cunard, at no. 26 Broadway, stands the former Standard Oil Building (1922, Carrère and Hastings), where John D. Rockefeller Jr. had offices. One of the building's current tenants is the **Museum of American Financial History** *(entrance at 28 Broadway)*.

Bowling Green – Named for the lawn where gentlemen could bowl for the modest annual fee of one peppercorn, this egg-shaped park is surrounded by a 1771 wrought-iron fence. It was here, in 1776, that independence-minded New Yorkers

Sphere by Fritz Koenig now sits in Battery Park

toppled a statue of George III. The prosperous residences that lined the small park in the 19C have since made way for office buildings. A 3.5-ton bronze statue of a **charging bull (8)** (1988), symbolizing a rising stock market, guards the northern entrance to the green.

From Bowling Green, continue southwest to Battery Park.

★ **Battery Park** – On the southwestern tip of Manhattan, the maze of stone and steel monoliths dominating the Financial District suddenly gives way to a vast expanse of greenery, known as Battery Park. Here, strolling along the waterfront promenade, visitors may enjoy one of the most spectacular panoramas on the eastern seaboard. During the 17C and 18C, the shore followed the lines of State Street, between Bowling Green and Pearl Street. To protect the harbor from British invasion during the War of 1812, the military erected the West Battery (Castle Clinton) some 300ft offshore, and the East Battery (Castle Williams) on Governors Island in the years preceding the War of 1812. In 1870 the land was filled in between the West Battery and Manhattan proper, creating a pleasant park subsequently named Battery Park. Today the area encompasses 21 acres extending from Bowling Green to the junction of the Hudson and East rivers. The view of New York Bay, enlivened by the movement of boats of all sizes entering and leaving the harbor, attracts large numbers of tourists year-round. The park, dotted with commemorative monuments, is also the departure point for ferries to the Statue of Liberty and Ellis Island.

The Brooklyn-Battery Tunnel (about 2mi) linking Manhattan to Brooklyn passes under Battery Park.

★ **Castle Clinton National Monument** – *Open year-round daily 8:30am–5pm. Closed Dec 25. Guided tours (25min) available. & ☎ 212-344-7220. www.nps.gov/cacl. The large interior courtyard contains a ticket office for various ferries and boat tours to the Statue of Liberty and Ellis Island.* Built on a small artificial island between 1808 and 1811, the structure known as West Battery was part of a series of forts erected to protect the New York harbor. However, it was never used for its original purpose, and in 1824 the fort (renamed Castle Garden) was ceded to the city and remodeled into a concert hall. That same year a gala evening honoring French general Lafayette was held here. On another grand occasion in 1850, Castle Garden served as the setting for a famous concert promoted by P.T. Barnum—the American debut of the "Swedish Nightingale," Jenny Lind. It was also here that Samuel Morse first demonstrated his revolutionary invention, the telegraph.

In 1855 the former fort and opera house was transformed into an immigrant landing depot. Over seven million immigrants were processed here before the inauguration of the Ellis Island station in 1892. Six years later the New York Aquarium (now located in Coney Island) moved in and occupied the building until 1942. Designated as a national monument in 1950, the structure was restored to its original appearance and reopened to the public in 1975. Today Castle Clinton, named for DeWitt Clinton, governor of New York State in the early 19C, consists of 8ft-thick walls pierced with gun ports for cannons; the entrance is framed by pilasters.

★★ **Promenade** – From Castle Clinton to the Staten Island Ferry Terminal, the walk meanders pleasantly along the shore of New York Bay. South of the fort stands a statue of Giovanni da Verrazano. Near the South Ferry stands the **East Coast Memorial** (1961), dedicated to those who died in the Atlantic during World War II. The powerful statue of a landing eagle with outspread wings is flanked on both sides by four granite columns inscribed with the names of the deceased.

The promenade offers magnificent **views**★★★ of the bay. Among the points of interest that visitors can spot from west to east: **Jersey City**, with its tall Colgate clock; Ellis Island, the former processing center for immigration; Liberty Island, formerly known as Bedloe's Island, home to the colossal Statue of Liberty; and Brooklyn, with its docks at the foot of Brooklyn Heights. Also visible from this vantage point is **Governors Island**, known in Dutch times as Nutten's Island, because of the many nut trees that grew there. The island affords spectacular views of Manhattan and Brooklyn, and is the site of two pre-1800 structures: the Governor's House and Fort Jay. Another fort, Castle Williams, was erected on the island at the beginning of the 19C, at the same time as Castle Clinton. For years the island remained a government reservation and was home to the US Coast Guard. In 2001, the two historic fortifications on the island became a national monument. The National Park Service is in the process of redeveloping the site in anticipation of opening it to the public in 2004 *(for updates, check online at www.nps.gov/gois)*. Farther in the background are Bayonne, New Jersey, with its oil refineries and its naval port; the hills of Staten Island; the Narrows and the cobweb of cables of the Verrazano-Narrows Bridge, half-hidden by Governors Island.

Continue toward the Staten Island Ferry Terminal.

Badly damaged by fire in 1991, the Staten Island Ferry Terminal is currently undergoing a restoration and expansion. A preliminary design by Venturi, Scott Brown was replaced in 1996 by Anderson Schwartz Architects' plan for the construction of a simple glass-walled facade. The $135 million, 200,000sq ft facility will boast a waiting room with a 75ft ceiling and glass-curtain wall, and a redesigned Peter Minuit Plaza (projected completion in spring of 2004). The old terminal continues to be used as the new one is being built.

Turn left on State St. and continue to the corner of State and Water Sts.

At 7 State Street, note the handsome, Federal-style Shrine of St. Elizabeth Seton, one of the few remaining grand mansions erected in the late 18C on the waterfront. The part of the building on the right, the former **James Watson House**, dates from 1792; the graceful Ionic colonnade was added in 1806. Elizabeth Ann Seton (1774-1821), America's first saint, was canonized in 1975.

MUSEUMS *(See Museums section)*

★★ **National Museum of the American Indian** – *1 Bowling Green*

Museum of American Financial History – *28 Broadway*

Museum of Jewish Heritage – *18 First Pl., Battery Park City*

10 • SOUTH STREET SEAPORT★★

12 Fulton St. [MTA] 2, 3 train to Fulton St.
Map p 137

One of New York's leading tourist attractions, South Street Seaport Historic District encompasses an 11-block area fronting the East River, south of Brooklyn Bridge. Heart of the Port of New York and center of its worldwide shipping activities during the early 19C, the South Street port declined after the Civil War, as shipping moved to the deepwater piers on the Hudson River. Its once-busy countinghouses, shops and warehouses, at first converted to a variety of uses, were gradually abandoned and left to decay. In the 1960s efforts to preserve the port's historic buildings, piers, streets and vessels led to the establishment of the South Street Seaport Historic District and the South Street Seaport Museum. A large-scale development project was then launched in the 1980s to revitalize the district. Extensive restoration and new construction have transformed the area bounded by John, South, Water and Beekman streets into a complex of pedestrian malls, restaurants, shops and boutiques animated with a vitality reminiscent of the district's days as a major seaport. During the summer, open-air concerts draw throngs of visitors to the piers.

VISIT

🅺 *Admission is free to the historic district, its shops, restaurants, piers & Fulton Market. Free concerts, festivals, maritime events & holiday celebrations take place throughout the year. For the museum, the $8 general admission fee covers the gallery, historic ships, and the museum's special programs (films) and guided tours (1hr, available year-round daily). Purchase tickets at visitor center located at 12-14 Fulton St. Visitor center open Apr–Sept daily 10am–6pm. Rest of the year Wed–Mon 10am–5pm. Closed Jan 1, Thanksgiving Day & Dec 25. ✗ & 🅿 ☎ 212-748-8600 or 888-768-8478. www.southstreetseaportmuseum.org.*

Museum Block – The block bounded by Fulton, Water, Beekman and Front streets contains a group of fourteen 18C and 19C buildings, many of which have been converted into exhibit galleries. The visitor center *(hours above)*, located at 12-14 Fulton Street, features a permanent exhibit on the history of the seaport. On Water Street three similar edifices—**nos. 207, 211, 215**—house the Bowne & Co.

South Street Seaport

Stationers, a re-creation of a 19C printing and stationery shop; the Chandlery; and the Gallery, which displays changing exhibits related to the history of the South Street district and the waterfront. The **New "Bogardus" Building** *(17-19 Fulton St.)* is a steel and glass low-rise structure (1983) inspired by the cast-iron buildings of James Bogardus.

Schermerhorn Row – Distinguished by a uniform brick facade and sloping roofs, this handsome group of 19C buildings exemplifies the Federal style. Constructed for the ship chandler and developer Peter Schermerhorn between 1811 and 1813, the row was occupied by a string of countinghouses and warehouses during South Street's heyday. A renovation of the upper floors of these buildings, completed in December 2003, created 30,000sq ft of gallery space for the museum's permanent exhibit, **World Port New York**. The ground floor houses a number of specialty shops, as do the Greek Revival structures located across the street in Cannon's Walk Block.

Fulton Market Building – This brick and granite market (1983), designed by Benjamin Thompson & Assocs., is the fourth market to be built on this site since 1822. Formerly sheltering an assortment of food stalls and restaurants, the building is now home to shops, restaurants and a convention center.

Facing the building across South Street are the stalls of the **Fulton Fish Market**, which has been operating at this waterfront site for more than a century and a half.

★**Pier 17 Pavilion** – Rising from a pier that extends 400ft into the East River, the Pavilion (Benjamin Thompson & Assocs.), a three-story glass and steel structure, encompasses more than 100 shops, restaurants and cafes. The spacious public promenade decks overlook the river on three sides, creating the marvelous illusion of being on board a ship. The **views**★★ are magnificent: north to the Brooklyn Bridge, east to Brooklyn Heights and the Brooklyn waterfront, and south to New York harbor.

★**Historic Vessels** – *Pier 16. Same hours as the visitor center (above).* Moored at piers 15 and 16 along South Street is a fleet of historic ships: the **Peking (1)**, a square-rigged, four-masted barque (1911); the **Wavertree (2)**, a square-rigger (1885)

 Fulton Fish Market

Map p 137. Adjacent to Pier 17. Guided tours are available Apr–Oct on the first and third Wed of every month at 6am. Call ☎ 212-748-8786 for information. Adjacent to the historic district, this famous wholesale fish market, located in a building first erected for this purpose in 1869, is one of the last outdoor markets in Manhattan and still the largest in the country. It comes to life every night from midnight to 8am, when refrigerated trucks unload the goods, and local chefs and grocers pick out the catch of the day. Summer 2004 will mark the end of an era: the market will be moving to the Hunts Point section of the Bronx when an $80 million indoor facility is completed.

built for the jute trade between India and Europe;
the *Ambrose* **(3)**, the first
lightship to serve as a
guide to vessels ap-
proaching the entrance to
Ambrose Channel in the
New York harbor; the
Lettie G. Howard **(4)**, one
of the last extant Glouces-
ter fishing schooners
(1893); and the
W.O. Decker **(5)**, a 1935
wooden tugboat.

Harbor Cruises – *Depart
from Pier 16 May–Sept
(call for schedule). 2hrs
round-trip. Reservations
required (minimum 24hrs
in advance). $25.* ☎ *212-
748-8786. www.southst-
seaport.org.* The South
Street Seaport Museum
offers sail cruises of New
York's harbor aboard
the *Pioneer*, an 1885
schooner.

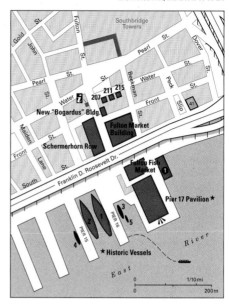

Before leaving the seaport, notice at 41 Peck Slip the trompe l'œil painting *The
Brooklyn Bridge*, one of several outdoor murals in the city by 20C artist Richard
Haas.

11 • CIVIC CENTER –
BROOKLYN BRIDGE★★

MTA N, R train to City Hall

Map p 138

Located at the foot of Brooklyn Bridge, north of the Financial District and west of
Chinatown, the Civic Center area encompasses Foley Square and City Hall Park. Once
covered by swamps and marshland that formed part of the Common Lands *(p 94)*,
the district developed as one of New York's principal gathering places during the 18C;
residents would often assemble to protest or celebrate here. The northern section of
the Common Lands contained a large body of water called the Fresh Water or Collect
Pond, on which John Fitch tried out a prototype of the steamboat in 1796. Located
west of the pond was a burial ground for free and enslaved blacks, who according to
law had to be buried outside the city limits.
After the completion of City Hall in 1811, several federal, state and municipal buildings
were erected in the immediate vicinity. Although the city continued its northward expansion, the area around City Hall remained the heart of government activities. Today it is
a bustling area during the workweek, alive with crowds of office workers. In 1993,
during the course of archaeological excavations, part of the ancient African burial ground
was uncovered and declared a historic landmark by the Preservation Commission.

★CIVIC CENTER WALKING TOUR *Distance: .8mi*

Begin at Foley Square.

Foley Square – This square stands on the former site of the Collect Pond. The
area was drained in 1808 to make room for a recreational center. Owing to inad-
equate drainage and poor foundations, several houses began to sink, and the
structures were quickly abandoned. In the early part of the century, government
buildings sprang up around the square, which was named in 1926 for Thomas
F. Foley (1852-1925), a city alderman, sheriff and saloon-keeper.

Jacob K. Javits Federal Office Building and US Court of International Trade – *26 Federal Plaza*.
The Federal Office Building, a 1967 high rise resembling a checkerboard of granite
and glass, is attached by a bridge to a smaller glass building (the court), which is
suspended from concrete beams.

New York State Supreme Court – *60 Centre St.* Formerly housing the New York County
Courthouse, this granite-faced, hexagonal Classical Revival edifice (1927) is distinguished by its monumental Corinthian colonnade. The imposing interior radiates

from an elaborate central rotunda. Note the rich polychrome marble floor with copper medallions representing the signs of the zodiac, and the murals (1930s) decorating the dome, by Attilio Pusterla.

United States Courthouse – *40 Centre St*. Completed in 1936 by Cass Gilbert, designer of the Woolworth Building, the courthouse presents a curious blend of architectural elements. A square, 32-story tower capped by a pyramidal top bursts through the roof of a Classical Revival temple. Step inside the main hallway, flanked by marble columns, to admire the ceiling murals.

Erected just south of the building is the new US Courthouse, a 27-story gray granite tower designed by Kohn Pedersen Fox in 1994. Adjacent to it, the attractive St. Andrew's Plaza is particularly pleasant in summer, with its tables, umbrellas and food stalls.

Walk south along Centre St.

★**Municipal Building** – *1 Centre St*. Located at the foot of Chambers Street, this 40-story edifice was erected in 1914 by McKim, Mead and White. Rising from a limestone base distinguished by a Neoclassical colonnade, the tower culminates in a gilded finial—the heroic statue *Civic Fame*. Designed by Adolph A. Weinman in 1914, the 25ft statue is the tallest in Manhattan. Weinman was also commissioned to create the carvings adorning the monumental central arch.

A pedestrian walkway leads to Police Plaza and the New York City Police Headquarters, a brick structure completed in 1973. Highlighting the three-acre plaza is Bernard (Tony) Rosenthal's imposing 75-ton rusted steel sculpture, *Five in One* **(1)**, composed of five disks that have come to represent the city's five boroughs.

Surrogate's Court – *31 Chambers St*. This richly ornamented Beaux-Arts structure, completed by John Thomas in 1907, houses the Hall of Records—the city archives. The profusion of sculptural detail embellishing the granite facade includes statues of mythical figures and famous New Yorkers. The central hall features marble walls and floors and a mosaic ceiling.

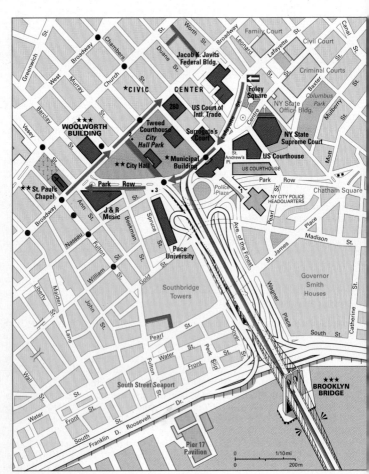

AINAY-LE-VIEIL
(Cher - Berry)

An octogonal enclosure linked by towers, with an imposing postern gate, and protected by a moat of running water, surrounds a gracious Renaissance Dwelling. Leading from the big drawing-room, decorated in honour of the visit of Louis XII and Anne de Bretagne, is a exquisite Renaissance Oratory. The chateau has been owned by the Bigny family and their descendants the Colbert and the d'Aligny who still live there and keep many precious historical souvenirs.

The roses Garden is now open to the public. It presents a collection of old fashion roses, fragrant roses, etc... cultivated in France from 1420 to present days.

Visits : from the first saturday of February Holidays to November, 30 : every day, 10-12 a.m. and 2-7 pm or to nightfall, in autumn, February and March. Closed on tuesday in February, March and November.

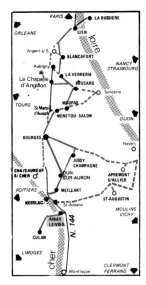

Do not mistake Ainay-le-Château (Allier) for Château d'Ainay-le-Vieil.

AINAY-LE-VIEIL

(Cher - Berry)

«LE PETIT CARCASSONNE»

Monument historique - Meublé et habité
Ouvert au public

Pur joyau renaissance, en son fier écrin féodal

Une enceinte octogonale flanquée de tours et d'une imposante poterne, protégée par des douves d'eau vive, enclôt une gracieuse demeure de la Renaissance. Dans le grand salon, dont la décoration fut conçue en l'honneur d'une visite de Louis XII et d'Anne de Bretagne, s'ouvre un ravissant oratoire Renaissance. Le château appartient depuis 1467 à la famille de Bigny et à ses descendants : ils y résident au milieu de nombreux souvenirs historiques, évoquant Colbert, Marie-Antoinette, Napoléon, etc.......

Vous pouvez y admirer une roseraie de type français présentant une collection de variétés de roses anciennes et odorantes de 1420 à nos jours.

Tél. 48 63 50 67

Visite : tous les jours, du 1er samedi des vacances de Février au 30 Novembre. De 10 h. à midi et de 14 h. à 19 h. ou jusqu'à la tombée de la nuit, en automne et en Février - Mars.

Fermé le mardi en Février, Mars et Novembre.

Ne pas confondre le Château d'Ainay-le-Vieil et Ainay-le-Château (Allier).

Réalisation : Route Jacques-Cœur - C.G.L. BRIARE - Printed in France

City Hall Park

★★City Hall – Surrounded by a pleasant, tree-shaded park, this handsome edifice contains the office of the Mayor and the City Council Chamber.

The present building is New York's third city hall. The Dutch established their "Stadt Huys" in 1653 in a former tavern on Pearl Street (their city council consisted of two burgomasters, a public attorney and five magistrats). During the 18C, the British City Hall stood at the corner of Wall and Broad streets (the present site of Federal Hall National Memorial). Today's city hall, built between 1802 and 1811 at a cost of about $500,000, is the work of architects **Joseph F. Mangin** and **John McComb Jr.**, who won a competition for the design and a prize of $350. Solemnly inaugurated on May 5, 1812, the building has been the scene of several memorable events. In 1824 Revolutionary War hero Marquis de Lafayette was officially entertained here during his triumphal return to America. The first parades on Broadway for visiting dignitaries began at that time.

In the middle of the night of April 9, 1865, the city learned of General Robert E. Lee's surrender at Appomattox, and the following day the city was draped with flags. The gaiety was brief, for less than a week later Abraham Lincoln's assassination plunged the nation into despair. Lincoln's body lay in state at City Hall while 120,000 grief-stricken New Yorkers filed past. Then, on April 25, the hearse, pulled by 16 black horses, proceeded slowly up Broadway to the Hudson River Railroad where the coffin was placed in a special train bound for Springfield, Illinois, Lincoln's home.

The 1860s witnessed less solemn and dignified proceedings at City Hall and nearby Tammany Hall (formerly located at the corner of Park Row and Frankfort Street). The Tammany political machine, founded by Aaron Burr at the beginning of the 19C, flourished under the leadership of **"Boss" William M. Tweed** (1823-78). Once in control of local government, Tweed and his infamous Tweed Ring are said to have filched the city out of approximately $30 million. The pendulum swung against him during the 1870s. Discontented city officials, aided by the incisive cartoons Thomas Nast drew for *Harper's Weekly* and exposés by the *New York Times*, finally brought about his downfall and imprisonment.

The City Hall building was restored in 1956 at a cost of about $2 million. It remains the focus of welcoming ceremonies for visiting dignitaries and the finishing point of ticker-tape parades during which the honoree is deluged with tons of paper shreds.

The Building – *Visit by guided tour (1hr) only on the second & fourth Fridays of the month. Call for reservations:* ☎ *212-788-3000*. Distinguished by a well-proportioned Neoclassical facade and a superb Georgian interior, City Hall ranks among the city's most elegant buildings. It was originally constructed of marble on its downtown side and brownstone on the uptown face. According to tradition, the City Fathers, in an economy drive, decided that since hardly anyone lived north of Chambers Street, no one would notice! City Hall was entirely refaced with Alabama limestone in 1956.

In the central rotunda, note the bronze statue (1860) of George Washington by William James Hubbard, a replica of the original marble work by Jean-Antoine Houdon. A pair of graceful, cantilevered stairs leads to the second floor. The gallery is ringed with slender Corinthian columns, supporting the coffered dome, and a delicate wrought-iron railing. Located at the top of the stairs, the **Governor's Room** consists of a suite of three rooms once used by the governor on official visits. Today it houses a small museum of furniture (note the 18C mahogany writing desk used by George Washington) and paintings including John Trumbull's portraits of Washington, John Jay and Alexander Hamilton.

To the right is a public hearing room, and to the left the City Council Chamber, which features a statue of Thomas Jefferson by David D'Angers and a portrait of General Lafayette by Samuel F.B. Morse, inventor of the telegraph.

The Park – Before the Revolutionary War, this area encompassed a common planted with apple trees. Liberty poles were erected here by the Sons of Liberty, and in July 1776 the Declaration of Independence was read in the presence of Washington, his troops and other patriots. Afterward the crowd rushed down to Bowling Green to attack the statue of the British monarch George III.

A statue (1890) by Frederick MacMonnies, erected on the Broadway side of City Hall Park, commemorates **Nathan Hale (2)**, one of the heroes of the Revolutionary War, whose famous last words were: "I only regret that I have but one life to lose for my country." A statue (1890) of Horace Greeley by John Q.A. Ward and a plaque to Joseph Pulitzer are reminders that this was once the center of newspaper publishing in New York.

Behind City Hall, the old New York County Courthouse, generally known as the **Tweed Courthouse**, stands as a monument to "Boss" Tweed, who allegedly pocketed some $10 million of the building's $14 million construction cost. The edifice contains one of the city's finest 19C interiors. Of particular interest are the cast-iron staircases and the Gothic-style courtroom. After years of neglect, the city undertook an $85 million, two-year restoration of the Tweed Courthouse, which was completed in December 2001; the courthouse is now the headquarters for the newly renamed city Department of Education.

Continue south onto Park Row.

Park Row – The stretch of road bordering the edge of City Hall Park between St. Paul's Chapel and the Municipal Building was a fashionable promenade in the 19C. It became known as Newspaper Row at the end of the century because so many newspapers—including the *Times*, *Tribune*, *Herald*, *World* and *Sun*—had their offices here. The intersection with Nassau Street was called Printing-House Square. No longer the center of journalism in the city, today Park Row is more renowned as home of the electronic and entertainment emporium **J&R Music**, a New York institution that started from a single storefront in 1975. Now its warren of shops extends the length of the block.

Near the bronze statue (1872) of Benjamin Franklin **(3)** holding a copy of his *Pennsylvania Gazette* stands **Pace University** (Civic Center Campus). The main building, adorned with a copper-relief sculpture, surrounds a garden and pool *(visible from Spruce St.).*

Cross Broadway.

★★**St. Paul's Chapel** – *On Broadway, between Fulton and Vesey Sts. Open year-round Mon–Sat 10am–6pm, Sun 9am–4pm. Closed major holidays. &. ☎ 212-233-4164. www.saintpaulschapel.org. Classical music programs Mon 1pm–2pm. $2.* Belonging to the Trinity Church parish, this small chapel constructed of native Manhattan schist is the oldest public building in continuous use in Manhattan. Completed in 1766, it resembles the Church of St. Martin-in-the-Fields in Trafalgar Square, London (its architect, Thomas McBean, studied under James Gibbs, who designed St. Martin's). The lovely spire and the portico on Broadway were added in 1794. Pierced by a Palladian window, the portico contains a memorial to Major General Richard Montgomery, who was killed in Quebec City in 1775. Montgomery is interred under the church.

Visit – The chapel has a surprisingly elegant Georgian interior. Painted in pastel colors and lit by early 19C crystal chandeliers, it was remodeled in the 1790s. The flamboyant altar is attributed to Pierre Charles L'Enfant, who later laid out Washington, DC. Above the cream and gold pulpit, the feathers of the Prince of Wales can be seen, reminding visitors that this was the "Established" church prior to the Revolution. Despite this fact, Washington worshiped here regularly after his inauguration. His pew can be seen in the north aisle, and in the south aisle is the Governor's pew (the arms of the state of New York hang on the wall above it). Today the chapel has become a pilgrimage site for visitors to Ground Zero.

Walk north on Broadway.

★★★**Woolworth Building** – *233 Broadway.* This 1913 skyscraper, Cass Gilbert's masterpiece, was the tallest in the world until the Chrysler Building's completion in 1930. Created for F.W. Woolworth (the founder of the once ubiquitous five-and-ten-cent store), the Gothic-style building cost more than $13.5 million, which Woolworth paid in cash. Soaring without setbacks to a height of 792ft, the tower is ornamented with gargoyles, pinnacles, flying buttresses and finials. At the highlight of the opening ceremony, President Woodrow Wilson pressed a button in Washington that lit up 80,000 light bulbs on the building.

During recent renovation efforts, much of the terracotta facade has been replaced with cast stone; the top 27 stories are being converted to condominium apartments. An ornate entrance leads to the spectacular **lobby★★**. Rising to three stories, it features a barrel vault covered with Byzantine-style mosaics and second-floor balconies decorated with frescoes. A marble stairway, bronze furnishings, plaster grotesques and ornate gilt decoration complete the Gothic theme. Note the six whimsical caricatures, among them Woolworth (counting his nickels and dimes) and Gilbert (clutching a model of the building), under the supporting crossbeams on the Barclay Street side.

Continue north on Broadway to Chambers St.

280 Broadway – When it opened in 1846, A.T. Stewart & Co.'s emporium

Woolworth Building

(Trench & Snook) at 280 Broadway pushed redbrick Manhattan into the shadows with the structure's gleaming white marble Italianate facade. Filling an entire city block, the building housed the world's first department store. From 1919 to 1950, the building served as publishing offices for the now-defunct *Sun* newspaper; the building's brass clock, perched above Broadway and Chambers Street, still bears the motto "The Sun: It shines for all." The city's Department of Buildings moved into the structure's upper floors in 2002 after a $26 million renovation that scrubbed "the marble palace" white again.

★★BROOKLYN BRIDGE

The pedestrian walkway can be reached by crossing Park Row from City Hall Park, or from the Brooklyn Bridge–City Hall subway station. The walkway begins near the Municipal Building. The Brooklyn side is accessible from the High St.–Brooklyn Bridge subway station. Allow 30min to cross the bridge on foot. If walking from Manhattan to Brooklyn, continue on to nearby Brooklyn Heights.

Looking across Brooklyn Bridge to the Financial District

141

The first bridge to link Manhattan and Brooklyn, this famed structure was one of the great engineering triumphs of the 19C and the world's longest suspension bridge for 20 years. Its graceful silhouette set against the New York skyline has inspired many artists, writers and poets. The stroll across the bridge is one of the most dramatic walks in New York. The **view★★** of the city and harbor through the filigree of cables is magnificent, especially as the sun sets.

Construction – In 1869 German-born **John Augustus Roebling**, a pioneer bridge builder responsible for the Niagara Falls and Cincinnati, Ohio suspension bridges, was commissioned to design a bridge linking Manhattan and Brooklyn. Shortly after the plans were approved, Roebling's foot was crushed while he was taking measurements for the piers. Despite an amputation, gangrene set in and he died three weeks later. His son, Washington Roebling, carried on his work, adopting new methods in pneumatic foundations, which he had studied in Europe.

> **■ Just the Facts**
>
> The bridge has a total length of 3,455ft with a maximum clearance above water of 133ft. The central suspended span between the two stone towers is 1,595ft long. The span is made of steel—the first time this metal was used for such a mammoth undertaking—and it is supported by four huge cables (15 3/4in thick) interconnected by a vast network of wires.

To construct the foundations, workers used caissons immersed in water and then filled with compressed air to prevent water infiltration. In order to adapt to the air pressure, the workmen underwent periods of gradual compression before going down to work, and decompression afterward. Despite these precautions, a few had burst eardrums or developed the "bends," which causes convulsions and can bring on partial or total paralysis. Washington Roebling himself was stricken with the bends. Confined to his sickbed, he nevertheless continued to direct the operation from his window overlooking the bridge. Finished in 1883, the bridge cost $25 million. With its intricate web of suspension cables and its majestic, pointed arches, the bridge represents an aesthetic and technical masterpiece. In 1972 the cables and piers were repainted in their original colors—beige and light brown. The walkway was rebuilt in 1983. The cables undergo regular maintenance.

History and Legend – The bridge immediately became the busy thoroughfare its planners had foreseen. On opening day, 150,000 people walked across it. However, less than a week after its inauguration by President Chester Arthur, tragedy struck. A woman fell on the stairway and her screams set off a panic killing 12 persons and injuring many more.

Fifteen years after the inauguration of the bridge, the city of Brooklyn was incorporated into New York. The bridge played a significant role in the development and growth of Brooklyn, the city's most populous borough.

Monumental and awe-inspiring, the Brooklyn Bridge has fascinated, obsessed and haunted New Yorkers. Immortalized in the works of Walt Whitman, it has also been painted on canvas by numerous artists. Colorful, cubist renditions of the bridge, created in the 1920s by Joseph Stella, are among the best-known depictions of the monument.

Some people have felt compelled to jump from the bridge, not all of them in despair. New Yorker Steve Brodie purportedly jumped off Brooklyn Bridge in 1886 without harm; leapers have been said to "do a Brodie" ever since. (Brodie later gained fame as an actor on Broadway.)

Since the end of the 19C, the bridge has provided an opportunity for confidence men to fleece strangers to the city by extorting exorbitant "tolls" (the original toll, now abolished, was one cent for pedestrians), or by "selling" it to the gullible.

12 • CHINATOWN – LITTLE ITALY★★

MTA B, D, Q train to Grand St.
Map p 144

Situated on the western edge of the Lower East Side, Chinatown and Little Italy form the other two neighborhoods in New York City's immigrant-filled East Side district. Sprawling China-town is a veritable city within a city. The narrow streets lined with colorful shops and restaurants teem with people, particularly on weekends. Little Italy, con-centrated on Mulberry Street, draws crowds to its neighborhood stores, plen-tiful restaurants and pastry shops, and annual feasts.

★★CHINATOWN

Trains and Tongs – The first Chinese to settle in New York came via the western states, where they had worked in the Califor-nia gold fields or on the transcontinental railroad. The majority were men who had no intention of staying, unlike other immi-grants. They just wished to make their fortunes and re-turn to a comfortable life in China. By the 1880s the community numbered about 10,000. The Chinese Exclusion Act passed in 1882 stopped further im-migration, and growth was

Shopping for produce on Pell Street

© Patti McConville /DPA, Inc.

effectively halted. By the turn of the century, Chinese immigrants began to form **tongs**, or associations designed to ease their adaptation to American culture. Or-ganized gambling and prostitution eventually sprang up in Chinatown, and the tongs fell into conflict with each other. During the resulting tong wars, accounts were often settled with hatchets and revolvers, giving rise to the term *hatchet men*.

---

① Dim sum
Map p 144. After plunging into bustling Chinatown, take time to sample the district's renowned dim sum eateries. Pick from a variety of delicious appetizers circulating the room, including *bao* (steamed buns), *wonton* (dumplings filled with fish) and *harkow* (steamed shrimp dumplings). Among the best bets: **Nice Restaurant** *(35 E. Broadway between Catherine and Market Sts.; ☎ 212-406-9510)*, at its liveliest during the lunchtime rush; and **H.S.F.** *(46 Bowery at Canal St.; ☎ 212-374-1319)*, where a pic-ture chart helps you identify more than 75 offerings.

② Food Markets
Map p 144. Chinatown teems with tiny, cramped shops hawking every-thing from exotic produce to jade souvenir pendants and kitschy snow globes. **Ten Ren Tea and Ginseng Co.** *(75 Mott St.; ☎ 212-349-2286)* sells Chinatown's traditional beverage in an amazing variety, ranging from the pricey $125-per-pound handpicked green oolong to the more af-fordable jasmine tea. The tea is measured out by the ounce from beau-tiful old canisters. Around the corner is **Kan Mam Food Products** *(200 Canal St.; ☎ 212-571-0330)*, a Chinese supermarket that also features a wide selection of Oriental porcelain plates and teapots. Note on the staircase the intriguing display of Chinese pharmaceuticals used to treat every mal-ady imaginable.

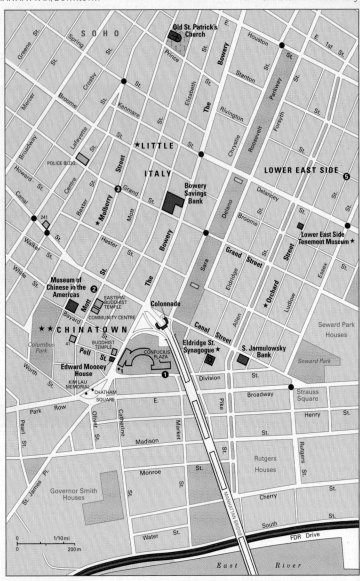

Present-day Chinatown – Following the 1943 repeal of the Chinese Exclusion Act, New York experienced a new influx of immigrants from Taiwan and Hong Kong, as well as from mainland China. Once bounded by Baxter, Canal and Worth streets and the Bowery, Chinatown is rapidly encroaching on Little Italy and the formerly Jewish Lower East Side, both of which now contain a multitude of Chinese factories and laundries. The present-day Asian community of New York has been estimated at 700,000, of which roughly three-fourths are Chinese. The majority of Manhattan's 110,000 Asians live in Chinatown.

Chinatown comes to life with a bang for the Chinese New Year *(the first full moon after January 19)*, when dragons dance down the streets accompanied by banner-carrying attendants while evil spirits are driven away by displays of fireworks.

Visit

Canal, **Mott**, Bayard and **Pell** streets form the heart of Chinatown. Strung with colorful banners and sporting signs in Chinese calligraphy, Catherine Street and East Broadway are especially lively. Columbus Park, located on the former site of a large slum area, provides much-needed green space in this congested part of the city. A stroll through the heart of Chinatown leads past stalls and shop windows piled high with displays of exotic herbs and condiments, snow peas, bean curd, dried fungi, duck eggs, real birds' nests for soup and bundles of Chinese mushrooms resembling strange marine plants. Other shops offer jade and ivory carvings, brocade dresses, silks, fans, "Chinese" lanterns and tea sets. Elements of Chinese architecture grace the otherwise undistinguished tenement buildings, and several telephone booths are crowned with mini-pagoda roofs. Note the gaily ornamented pagoda-roofed structure at 241 Canal Street.

At the corner of the Bowery and Division Street, adjacent to Confucius Plaza, stands a bronze **statue (1)** of the Chinese philosopher (551-479 BC). Just across the inter-section, traffic flows past the 1962 Kim Lau Memorial *(on Chatham Square)*, which honors those Chinese Americans killed in US conflicts. The Chinese culture is kept alive here by a number of Chinese film theaters, by Buddhist temples (Buddhist and Eastern Buddhist) and by the local community center on Mott Street. The red-brick **Edward Mooney House** *(18 Bowery)* is reputed to be the earliest surviving row house in Manhattan. Dating from the Revolutionary era (1785-89), it reflects both Georgian and Federal styles.

A visit to Chinatown is of course not complete without a meal in a Chinese restau-rant. The cuisine of China is as varied as the country is large, and many different regional specialties are available, including Cantonese, Hunan, Mandarin and Szechuan.

★LITTLE ITALY

Roughly bounded by Canal, Lafayette and Houston streets and the Bowery, this district was populated by Italian immigrants who arrived at Ellis Island between the 1880s and the 1920s. Hailing primarily from southern Italy and Sicily, the

Little Italy

Map p 144. This small (and getting smaller) neighbor-hood is still one of the most wonderful corners of the city, with countless cafes for cappuccino and cannoli, and decent red-sauce joints everywhere you look. On a summer evening, snag an outdoor table and watch the locals play bocce and converse in Italian while watching the world go by from lawn chairs placed right on the sidewalk. Have one of the de-lectable pastries and a mochaccino and enjoy the scene at the original **Ferrara Café and Bakery** *(195 Grand St.; ☎ 212-226-6150; www.ferraracafe.*

com). Locals opt for **Caffé Napoli** *(191 Hester St.; ☎ 212-226-8705)* or **Caffé Roma** *(385 Broome St.; ☎ 212-226-8413),* which are smaller and less touristy cafes. Join the exuberant crowd lining the long tables at **Puglia's** *(189 Hester St.; ☎ 212-966-6006; www.littleitaly.com),* known for its generous portions of veal parmigiana and its singing waiters. A true neighborhood institution, **Vincent's Clam Bar** *(119 Mott St.; ☎ 212-226-8133)* features fresh raw seafood and a great selection of sauces, rang-ing from mild to hot (and they mean hot!). And seafood lovers will ap-preciate **Umberto's Clam House** *(178 Mulberry St.; ☎ 212-431-7545; www.umbertosclamhouse.com).* **Le Mela** *(167 Mulberry St.; ☎ 212-431-9493)* has no menu—the waiter chooses for you, but the outcome is al-ways delicious, and deliciously cheap. A little out of the way, but worth it for coal-oven-baked pizza and homemade sauces, is **Lombardi's** *(32 Spring St.; ☎ 212-941-7994).*

immigrants were fleeing their country's rampant poverty and epidemics. Although many Italians have left the neighborhood, they return for family gatherings, marriages, funerals, festivals and saints' days. The friendly atmosphere of neighborhood grocery stores displaying their wares of pastas, salamis, olives and cheeses, and the inviting smells drifting from the cafes have turned this area into a popular tourist attraction.

Visit

The hub of Little Italy centers on **Mulberry Street★**, sometimes called the Via San Gennaro. During the feast of San Gennaro *(mid-September)*, the patron saint of Naples, the street is a vast alfresco restaurant.

At the corner of Prince and Mulberry streets stands **Old St. Patrick's Church** (1815, Joseph F. Mangin), New York's Roman Catholic Cathedral until 1879, when it was replaced by the larger Gothic Revival structure on Fifth Avenue. Marking the corner of Grand and Centre streets, the Police Building, a massive Renaissance palazzo (1909), served as the city's police headquarters until 1973. Neglected for more than a decade, it was restored in the late 1980s and converted into cooperative apartments.

MUSEUMS *(See Museums section)*

Museum of Chinese in the Americas – *70 Mulberry St., 2nd floor*

13 • LOWER EAST SIDE

MTA 4, 5, 6 or N, R trains to Canal St.

Map p 144

Encompassing the area below Houston Street bounded by the Bowery and the East River, the Lower East Side is best known historically as a melting pot for newly arrived immigrants. Once primarily home to Jewish and Ukrainian families, the neighborhood has undergone continual change as successive waves of immigrants have staked their claim to it. Lining the narrow streets, an eclectic ensemble of tenement buildings, bustling open-air markets and grand houses of worship combine to create one of America's landmark ethnic neighborhoods.

Historical Notes

The Governor's Farm – The last Dutch governor of Nieuw Amsterdam from 1647 to 1664, **Peter Stuyvesant** (1592-1672) established a farm (*bouwerie* in Dutch) on the land he wrested from the Indians between Broadway and the East River and the present 5th and 17th streets. In order to facilitate transport to his farm, Stuyvesant laid out a broad, straight road, known today as the Bowery. His own home was located near a small chapel—rebuilt in 1799 by one of his descendants—the present-day St. Mark's-in-the-Bowery Church.

Neighborhood of Beginnings and Dreams – The first mass migration to the Lower East Side occurred in the mid-1800s with the arrival of Irish immigrants seeking relief from famine. From the late 19C until World War I, millions of southern and eastern Europeans arrived via Ellis Island, America's great immigrant gateway. After being processed at Ellis Island, these new arrivals were diverted to the Lower East Side by "street birds" who directed them to neighborhoods already populated by other recently arrived immigrants. The tide of immigration was halted in the 1920s with the passage of restrictive legislation.

UPI/Corbis-Bettmann

Lower East Side in 1926

Katz's Delicatessen

Map p 144. 205 E. Houston St. at Ludlow St. ☎ 212-254-2246. www.katzdeli.com. Yes, this is where that scene from *When Harry Met Sally* was shot, and yes, this is where the original "Send a Salami to your Boy in the Army" sign hangs, but there's more to Katz's than clichés. New York's oldest Jewish, but not kosher, deli has been curing and hand-carving its own pastrami (ask for moist) since 1888, when it was often the first stop for Eastern European immigrants right off the boat. Yiddish theater memorabilia and other bric-a-brac abound, but you're just as likely to be seated next to hipsters or rap record producers as old-time locals. Go for the fun, and for the huge portions, which are more than anyone could possibly eat.

 Jewish tradition

Map p 144. This neighborhood still bears traces of its former role as the center of a thriving Eastern European immigrant community in the late 19C and early 20C. **The Pickle Guys** *(49 Essex St.; ☎ 212-656-9739 ; www.nycpickleguys.com)* offer a full line of traditional kosher pickles (sour, half-sour, and even hot) and plenty more, including olives, peppers, pickled tomatoes and horseradish. Pick up some of the city's best smoked salmon or sturgeon and a full array of traditional delicacies at **Russ and Daughters** *(175 E. Houston St.; ☎ 212-475-4880)* or watch conveyor belts full of freshly made matzohs at **Streit's Matzoh Co.** *(150 Rivington St. at Suffolk St.; ☎ 212-475-7000).*

The neighborhood still contains many of the cramped tenement buildings that were constructed specifically to house immigrants. Entire families were often crowded into one-room apartments under oppressive living conditions. Reformers such as **Jacob Riis** (1849-1914) chronicled the plight of the immigrant through photographs, while service groups were established to ease the assimilation process.

Although many second-generation immigrants moved away as they prospered, the Lower East Side today remains a neighborhood of ethnic contrasts where visitors are likely to hear Chinese, Spanish and Yiddish as well as English. As one strolls along the narrow streets, it is easy to conjure up the sights and smells encountered by late-19C residents. Open markets selling exotic fare and buildings with multilingual signs bear witness to the successive waves of immigrants who have made the Lower East Side their home. In recent years, storefront boutiques, small bistros, and nightspots have become a common sight in the neighborhood, as the young bohemian crowd has pushed south from an increasingly gentrified Alphabet City.

VISIT

It is best to visit the area on Sundays, when most stores are open and the neighborhood becomes a lively and colorful bazaar. We recommend walking south on the Bowery, then turning onto Grand and Orchard streets, and completing the walk along Canal Street.

The Bowery – Once a notorious entertainment center where vaudeville became fashionable and risqué revues flourished, the Bowery was nicknamed "the poor man's Broadway." After World War I the area degenerated into an undesirable neighborhood frequented by vagrants and alcoholics. Although the street is still home to shelters and soup kitchens, it is also known for its stores specializing in electrical goods—especially lighting fixtures—and wholesale restaurant equipment. Designed in 1895 by McKim, Mead and White, the Beaux-Arts **Bowery Savings Bank** *(no. 130, near Grand St.)* is distinguished by imposing Corinthian columns and opulent detailing, making it one of the most striking buildings on the Lower East Side. The interior features an ornate coffered vault marked in the center by a large, opaque skylight.

Grand Street – In past years this thoroughfare was known for its shops selling wedding gowns and linens. Today fresh fish stalls, bustling open-air vegetable markets and small restaurants support the growing Asian communities that have spilled into this area north of Chinatown.

★Orchard Street – Once jammed with pushcarts and street vendors, this bustling artery and its surrounding streets are closed to traffic on Sundays, becoming a veritable mecca for those seeking bargains on clothing and accessories. More than 300 tiny stores display their wares on stalls in the street. Enthusiastic merchants and street hawkers vie for the customer's attention with colorful invitations to inspect their merchandise. At no. 97 stands the Lower East Side Tenement Museum.

Canal Street – This busy east-west thoroughfare separates SoHo and Little Italy to the north from TriBeCa and Chinatown to the south. The eastern end is noted for its jewelry and diamond merchants. Once the tallest structure on the Lower East Side, the **S. Jarmulowsky Bank** *(nos. 54-58, at Orchard St.)* was established in 1873 to cater to newly arrived Jewish immigrants.

A short detour on Eldridge Street leads to the **Eldridge Street Synagogue★** *(nos. 12-16)*, the first great house of worship built by Eastern European Jews in America. The Eldridge Street Project, a nonprofit organization, is restoring and transforming the landmark into a cultural and heritage center. A Herter Brothers commission, the 1887 building displays a striking rose window set against an ornate Moorish facade. Inside, hand-stenciled walls rise to a 70ft vaulted ceiling *(visit by 1hr guided tour only, year-round Tue & Thu 11:30am & 2:30pm, Sun 11am–4pm; closed major & Jewish holidays; $5; ☎ 212-219-0888; www.eldridgestreet.org)*.

At the base of the Manhattan Bridge linking Manhattan with Brooklyn stands the sorely neglected **Manhattan Bridge Colonnade** (1915, Carrère and Hastings). Designed as part of the City Beautiful movement, the gateway features an arch flanked by curved colonnades. Heavy traffic at its base coupled with vandalism and graffiti have taken their toll on this once-noble civic commission.

MUSEUM *(See Museums section)*

★**Lower East Side Tenement Museum** – *90 & 97 Orchard St.*

14 • SOHO – TRIBECA★★

MTA 1, 9 train to Prince St., or N, R train to Spring St.
Maps pp 151 and 153

The heart of Manhattan's fashionable downtown art scene, **SoHo** (an acronym for South of Houston—pronounced Howston—Street) is New York at its trendiest and most colorful. This once largely industrial area is now an international center for artists and collectors, and the place where the hottest fashions in clothing, collectibles and home furnishings are likely to appear first. Declared a historic district in 1973, the 26 blocks bounded by Canal, West Houston and Crosby streets and West Broadway also boast the largest concentration of 19C cast-iron buildings in the US.

Just to the southwest lies **TriBeCa**, an intriguing district of commercial warehouses, art space and chic restaurants that gained its acronym (for Triangle Below Canal) in the 1970s from a real estate agent hoping to create an identity for the area as trendy as SoHo's. TriBeCa is also notable for its impressive 19C and early-20C commercial architecture, ranging from cast-iron warehouses to Art Deco office towers from the 1920s.

Historical Notes

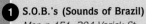

Rural Beginnings – While SoHo's lively facade makes it hard to imagine a quieter past, the area was actually remarkably rural from the early Dutch colonial period well into the 1800s. The site of the first free black community in Manhattan, this area was settled in 1644 by former slaves of the Dutch West India Company who were granted the land for farms. Serious development did not begin until the early 19C, when the city drained and filled the area's badly polluted waterways.

By 1809 Broadway was paved and a number of prominent citizens, including James Fenimore Cooper, had moved in, bringing considerable cachet to the new residential district. In the late 1850s, large stores, including Tiffany & Co., E.V. Haughwout, Arnold Constable and Lord & Taylor, began lining Broadway, soon joined by grand hotels like the St. Nicholas, which occupied most of a city block. Theaters, casinos and the numerous brothels found on Crosby, Mercer and Greene streets offered still more diversion. As the area grew increasingly commercial in character, respectable middle-class families began to

1 S.O.B.'s (Sounds of Brazil)
Map p 151. 204 Varick St.
☎ 212-243-4940.
www.sobs.com.
Reservations suggested.
New York's premier world-music venue has a tropical decor, a cabana-like bar, and a menu featuring tasty Brazilian and Portuguese specialties. When the music starts pumping, the mixed crowd often ends up dancing. Every Monday is Latin dance night (a free lesson is included); on Saturdays, nightcrawlers with real endurance stay for the late-night performances of *capoeira*, a mesmerizing Brazilian martial art accompanied by live drumming and chanting.

Construction in Cast Iron

Although cast iron has a long history of use for tools and household utensils, it was not exploited as a building material until the late 1700s, when the English developed a novel iron framing technique used in spinning and textile mills that would be the prototype for commercial buildings in the US some 50 years later. Among the material's two greatest American proponents were Daniel Badger and James Bogardus, both of whom established foundries in New York in the 1840s.

Limited primarily to the front, beams, and interior columns of a building, cast iron had many virtues. Sold through catalogs, the prefabricated parts were relatively easy to produce and assemble. Moreover, the columns, which eliminated the need for interior load-bearing walls and allowed much more open space, were ideal for warehouses. Formed in molds, the material introduced an

New York Convention & Visitors Bureau

inexpensive way to reproduce the elaborate stone balustrades, cornices and columns that distinguished the architectural styles of the day. Using cast iron, which cost far less than carved granite or marble, a style-conscious merchant could turn a suitably grandiose facade to the street with a Second Empire design like the elaborate confections of architect Isaac F. Duckworth or the elegant compositions of Richard Morris Hunt.

Used for both full and partial facades, cast iron remained extremely popular until the 1890s, when it was eclipsed by a new taste for styles better interpreted in brick or stone. At the same time, the development of steel framing and elevators made possible taller buildings, which were more difficult to face with cast-iron units.

Finished with paint, cast iron can look remarkably like stone, another widely used building material in SoHo. Apart from telltale signs of rust, the only sure way to identify the metal is to use a magnet.

move uptown and the district evolved into a thriving industrial dry-goods center during the second half of the 19C. SoHo's remarkable cast-iron and stone commercial buildings date from this period.

Art Brings a New Start – By the 1950s the district became known as "Hell's Hundred Acres" and was threatened with decimation by a proposed Lower Manhattan expressway. After fierce local opposition, the scheme was abandoned. During the 1960s SoHo came to life as an artistic community. Painters began moving into the old warehouses, or lofts, attracted by low rents and huge, open spaces that could accommodate enormous canvases. Although the area was zoned for manufacturing, a 1971 provision allowed artists to legally convert the lofts into living/working quarters. Uptown galleries arrived, and as the area became desirable, real estate values skyrocketed. While affluent professionals moved in, many artists were priced out, drawn to cheaper warehouse space in Brooklyn, Queens and New Jersey. However, scores of aspiring and struggling artists still work and live here.

Today SoHo, with its smart restaurants, trendy coffee bars and pricey boutiques, caters primarily to the well-heeled. It has also become a popular weekend destination for tourists and out-of-towners. Yet here, where "shabby chic" is the epitome of style, light manufacturing still exists and dumpsters and loading docks are still to be found, especially in the more industrial area south of Broome Street.

■ **Art Galleries**

The largest concentration of galleries is found on Broadway between nos. 594 and 560. Another cluster is located on Greene and Wooster streets. Try **Ronald Feldman Fine Arts** *(31 Mercer St.; ☎ 212-226-3232; www.feldmangallery.com)* for major installation art with a focus on Russian artists such as Komar and Melamid, and Ida Applebroog. **Sperone Westwater** *(415 W. 13th St.; ☎ 212-999-7337; www.speronewestwater.com)* offers a first-rate selection of contemporary artists both European and American, including Susan Rothenberg.

Take a respite from gallery hopping at the coffee bar at **Dean & Deluca** *(560 Broadway; ☎ 212-226-6800; www.deandeluca.com)*. The store also features a wonderful selection of pastries, imported specialties, cheeses and organic vegetables.

Be sure to pick up a **Gallery Guide** *(available at galleries and visitor centers) for information on the latest exhibits and offerings.*

Trendy TriBeCa – Visitors looking for an even more authentic edge will find it in the less gentrified district of TriBeCa. During the latter half of the 19C, much of the shipping and warehousing industry formerly located at the South Street Seaport moved to deepwater piers on the Hudson River. As activity on the East River declined, this western flank of lower Manhattan—known as the Lower West Side—became the center of New York's most important wholesaling district for its produce, meat and dairy products. In addition, dozens of "store and loft" buildings for fruits and vegetables served nearby Washington Market. (In the 1960s, produce wholesalers relocated to the Hunts Point market in the Bronx.)

Though textile jobbers still deal in odd lots and remnants from their cast-iron warehouses, the area's industrial component has been diminishing since the real-estate boom of the 1980s. Much of the commercial loft space has been converted to luxury co-ops. Despite high-priced galleries and apartments, TriBeCa and SoHo remain home to several early outposts of experimental film and video, dance and drama. Indeed, both districts are thoroughly incongruous areas, but that is precisely their attraction.

★★SOHO

The best way to experience SoHo is to wander at will, taking time to window-shop, browse in galleries and boutiques, and engage in one of the most popular downtown rituals of all: people-watching. Note that most galleries and museums are closed on Monday and many shut down for part or all of the summer.

★ **Broadway** – Overflowing with traffic, pedestrians and sidewalk vendors, this lively thoroughfare is a street of contrasts, where hardware stores and bargain outlets are sandwiched between galleries and museums such as the **New Museum of Contemporary Art** *(see Museums section)* and tony emporiums selling everything from antiques to Armani. Modern signs obscure some of the proud old storefronts, but there are still many outstanding architectural landmarks.

The impressive brick-and-stone building at no. 575, dating to 1882, houses the new 24,000sq ft **Prada** store, designed by Rem Koolhaas. In a neigborhood where designer boutiques have proliferated (Vivienne Westwood, Marc Jacobs, Louis Vuitton have all opened shops, and Armani has not one but two), the Prada opening may mark the advent of a new era in retail decadence. Inside, a cylindrical glass elevator occupied by a headless mannequin wearing a clear plastic raincoat, ubiquitous video panels, and a floor that falls away to the lower level in a 16ft wave of zebrawood set the tone. Downstairs, where white, translucent and brushed metal surfaces predominate, the "smart" dressing rooms are the main attraction. One floor button closes the clear sliding door; another renders the door opaque. Lucite cubicles embedded in the dressing-room wall scan clothing tags, activating a flat-panel touch-screen display with information about the selected items.

The 1903 **Singer Building** *(nos. 561-563)*, designed by Ernest Flagg, is a handsome example of the new skyscraper architecture that emerged in the early 20C. Twelve stories high, it features a fireproof facing of brick and terra-cotta, but wrought-iron tracery and expanses of glass keep the tall office building from appearing heavy. The remarkable **E.V. Haughwout Building★** *(nos. 488-492)*, on the northeast corner of Broome Street, boasts the oldest complete cast-iron facades in the city, produced by Daniel Badger's ironworks in 1857. With its rhythmic pattern of arched windows, balustrades and Corinthian columns—repeated 92 times—this "Venetian palace" proved a suitably pretentious setting for the cut-glass chandeliers, silver and clocks originally sold here. Inside is the country's first safety passenger elevator, installed by Otis Elevators.

On the southwest corner of Broome Street, at no. 487, stands a handsome example of the tall, brick-and-stone office buildings that appeared in SoHo in the 1890s. Across Broadway, at 435 Broome Street, is an unusual building, designed in 1873 in a Victorian Gothic style, seldom used for commercial cast-iron architecture; the tracery arches, typical of the style, would have been extremely expensive to produce in stone. Farther south on Broadway is the elegant facade of 478-480 Broadway (1874, Richard Morris Hunt), distinguished by slender colonnettes, large plate-glass windows and an unusual concave cornice.

★ **Greene Street** – One of the richest collections of cast-iron building facades in SoHo is found on this thoroughfare, where the original cobblestones and wide granite sidewalks accentuate the 19C atmosphere. The notable facade at 112-114 Prince Street on the southwest corner of Greene may look like cast iron, but it is actually a trompe l'œil design painted on brick by artist Richard Haas in 1975. The "King" of Greene Street is located at **no. 72**, a grandiose composition with massive projecting bays designed by Isaac F. Duckworth in 1872. Around the corner at 469-475 Broome stands the Gunther building; this impressive 1871 creation by Griffith Thomas features a curved corner bay and curved plate-glass windows. Located nearby is another architectural gem, 91-93 Grand Street. This building, dating to 1869, appears to be two stone row houses; closer inspection, however, reveals that the facade is actually cast iron, complete with imitation mortar joints. Called the "Queen" of Greene Street, the six-story warehouse at **nos. 28-30** was built the same year as the "King" and is also the work of Isaac F. Duckworth; the enormous mansard roof, projecting central bay and ornate dormers are hallmarks of the Second Empire style.

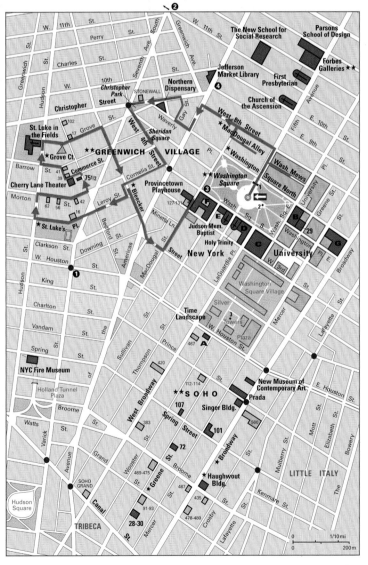

Taking a break from gallery shopping

© Brian McGillivray /Robert Holmes Photography

Spring Street – This vibrant shopping street is notable for its mix of clothing boutiques, galleries and antique stores. The oldest building in the district is located at **no. 107**. Completed prior to 1808, the corner house has been faced with stucco, but its small scale is immediately apparent, recalling the pre-cast-iron days of SoHo, when the neighborhood was primarily residential. With its large expanses of glass and slender columns, the 1870 building at **no. 101** is among the most distinguished cast-iron structures on the street.

West Broadway – Lined with T-shirt shops and expensive clothing boutiques alike, this busy avenue comes alive on weekends, as it is also home to some of SoHo's best-known galleries, including Leo Castelli *(no. 420)*, Sonnabend *(no. 420)*, and OK Harris *(no. 383)*.

Canal Street – Forming the boundary between SoHo and TriBeCa, this wide, vibrant thoroughfare teems with people drawn to its hardware stores, plastic wholesalers and art supply shops. Completed in 1996, the SoHo Grand Hotel *(310 W. Broadway)* features a high-style lobby dominated by a cast-iron stairway.

★TRIBECA *Map p 153.*

Roughly bounded by Broadway and Canal, Chambers and West streets, the wedge-shaped district is characterized by an asymmetrical streetscape of small parks and interesting nooks and crannies. The name Washington Market came to be applied to the region extending south along Greenwich to Chambers streets, where the rich aroma of imported cheeses and nuts, dried fruits and spices once permeated the air. More recently, the food sellers have been displaced from their loft buildings by high-profile restaurants (such as Robert De Niro's Tribeca Grill). Large office and residential buildings add to TriBeCa's own peculiar mix, which also includes some of New York's trendiest restaurants. Several street segments are contained in a New York City historic district.

Walking Tour *Distance: .8mi*

Begin at the corner of White and Church Sts. and walk west.

At the corner of White and Church streets, note the **Let There Be Neon Gallery** *(no. 38)*, featuring the creations of founder Rudi Stern and other American neon artists. White Street is lined with buildings reflecting TriBeCa's commercial and industrial history; crowned by a mansard roof, the cast-iron example at **nos. 13-17** on the southwest corner of the Avenue of the Americas now contains several galleries.

Walk north on Ave. of the Americas.

At 32 Avenue of the Americas stands the **New York Telephone Company Building**, an ornate Art Deco tower with brick setbacks designed by Ralph Walker in 1918 as one of several AT&T Long Lines buildings. Be sure to step into the lobby, where the original terrazzo floor and intricate wall and ceiling mosaics have been beautifully preserved.

Walk west on Walker St., then south on West Broadway to Finn Square; turn right on Franklin St.

A fine example of the Romanesque Revival style, the six-story building of rose-colored brick at no. 143, notable for its whimsical arched windows detailed with human faces, houses **Urban Archaeology**, a well-known gallery dealing in salvaged building parts. (The store operates a second location on Lafayette Street.)

Continue west to Hudson St., turn left and continue south to Harrison St.

At the northwest corner *(2-6 Harrison St.)* is the 1884 **New York Mercantile Exchange**, which once housed the offices of food brokers for the Washington Market; the polychrome tile floor and elaborate cast-iron staircase in the vestibule are original. The ground floor houses one of the city's most acclaimed restaurants, Chanterelle.

Continue west on Harrison St. to the corner of Greenwich St.

A group of restored 19C Federal-style row houses, **Harrison Street Row** *(nos. 37-41)* is the last remnant of merchant homes once common to this area.

Continue south on Greenwich St.

A holdover from TriBeCa's past, nut and candy distributor **A.L. Bazzini Co.** *(339 Greenwich St.)* has been in the neighborhood since 1886. Though the company moved processing operations to Hunt's Point and converted the upper floors to apartments in the 1990s, it operates a specialty food store and deli on the ground floor, where Bazzini pistachios, peanuts and cashews are sold in traditional tins or from barrels by the pound.

Continue south to Washington Market Park.

A cast-iron fence in a repeating Gothic-arch pattern encloses the **Washington Market Park**, an oasis of flower gardens and neatly trimmed lawns embellished with a Victorian-style gazebo.

Walk east on Duane St. and north on Hudson St.

At 60 Hudson Street stands the **Western Union Building**. Erected in 1928 as the company headquarters, the massive brick-clad Art Deco building, which occupies an entire block, originally held corporate offices as well as an auditorium, shops, a cafeteria and classrooms for Western Union messengers; several communications businesses are located here today.

MUSEUMS *(See Museums section)*

New Museum of Contemporary Art – *583 Broadway*

New York City Fire Museum – *278 Spring St.*

15 • GREENWICH VILLAGE★★

MTA A, C, E or 6 trains to Spring St., or N, R train to Prince St.

Map p 151

Greenwich Village occupies the area bounded by Houston and 14th streets, between Greenwich Street and Broadway. The heart of this heterogeneous district is Washington Square and the area just to the west of it. Here Federal and Greek Revival town houses line narrow streets that play havoc with Manhattan's grid system. Restaurants and coffeehouses abound, interspersed with craft shops, boutiques, theaters and galleries.

During the day, a serene small-town atmosphere pervades, enlivened on Sunday afternoons by strollers who gather to hear street musicians or have their portraits painted. The night, however, reveals a countenance reminiscent of Montmartre and Saint-Germain-des-Prés in Paris: a cosmopolitan tourist crowd rubs shoulders with artists, intellectuals and students. People flock to theaters and movie houses, and folk, rock and jazz musicians perform in dimly lit nightclubs and cafes.

Historical Notes

A Country Village – In 1609, when Henry Hudson sailed up the river that was later named for him, the countryside that was to become Greenwich Village was covered with woods and streams and sheltered an Algonquian Indian settlement called Sapokanikan. Later, British colonists settled here, and in 1696 a village sprang up, named after the English town Greenwich (actually, the name "Greenwich Village" is redundant, since *wich* means "village" or "town"). Between rows of wooden houses ran Greenwich Street, then the main street of the village overlooking the Hudson River.

During the 18C wealthy landowners such as the de Lanceys, Van Cortlandts, Sir Peter Warren and Abraham Mortier built estates in the area, which became a settled and well-known part of the city, with good taverns and even a road that led directly out of town. Thomas Paine, the famous revolutionary figure and pamphleteer, lived in Greenwich Village for a time. After the Revolutionary War, six parallel streets south

---

Coffeehouses

No visit to New York is complete without lingering over cappuccino at one of Greenwich Village's innumerable cafes. While there has been an invasion of Starbucks and other Seattle-style coffee bars all over town, the New York coffeehouse remains an institution to be experienced at leisure.

The late, late weekend hours *(some coffeehouses may stay open until 5am)* make them perfect spots to wind up a Village evening.

• **Caffé del Artista** – *46 Greenwich Ave.* ☎ *212-645-4431.* The tiny candlelit back rooms are the coziest in this bohemian haunt, where a good accompaniment to café au lait is the pistachio gelato with an almond biscotti.

• **Caffé Sha Sha** – *510 Hudson St.* ☎ *212-242-3021.* The added attraction of this classic Village coffeehouse is a pleasant back patio, where folks idle away the summer hours over fine coffee, ice cream and pastries. Brunch is served on weekends *(11am–4:30pm).*

• **Caffé Raffaella** – *134 Seventh Ave. South.* ☎ *212-929-7247.* It feels like the mad tea party with oversized chairs and lamps scattered all about. Check out the wonderful selection of pastries.

• **Caffé Reggio** – *119 MacDougal St.* ☎ *212-475-9557. www.cafereggio.com.* New York's oldest cafe hasn't changed much since 1927, except half of it is no longer a barber shop—now the whole place is devoted to coffee and conversation. Outdoor tables are perfect for summer sipping.

• **Caffé Vivaldi** – *32 Jones St.* ☎ *212-929-9384.* Vivaldi's is one of the few cafes with a real fireplace and authentic fin-de-siècle Vienna coffeehouse atmosphere. A lounge ambience prevails in the evening thanks to a full-service bar.

• **Caffé Dante** – *79 MacDougal St.* ☎ *212-982-5275.* This easygoing cafe claims some of the strongest coffee around—and the waitresses speak Italian!

---

of the area that became Washington Square Park were named for Revolutionary officers. The "Streets of the Six Generals," from west to east, are (Major General Alexander) MacDougal, (Brigadier General John) Sullivan, (Brigadier General William) Thompson, (Brigadier General David) Wooster, (Major General Nathanael) Greene and (Brigadier General Hugh) Mercer.

The early 19C saw recurrent outbreaks of smallpox and yellow fever ravaging the downtown area; residents thus sought the healthy country air of Greenwich Village. The present Bank Street, in the northern part of the Village, was named for the Wall Street banks that took temporary refuge here in 1822, during the city's most virulent yellow fever epidemic. In the 1830s prominent families brought cachet to the area by constructing elegant town houses, but they moved farther north when industry developed near the waterfront. Irish and Chinese immigrants, as well as free blacks, came to live in the Village, and Italian immigrants settled in the area south of Washington Square Park, creating Little Italy. Lower rents attracted artists and writers following the example of **Edgar Allan Poe** (1809-49), who took up residence at 85 West 3rd Street in 1845, where he wrote *Gordon Pym* and *The Fall of the House of Usher*.

Village Bohemia – During the early 1900s Greenwich Village became New York's bohemian enclave. Intellectuals, social reformers and radicals descended in droves to join the writers and artists, and it seemed as though the entire avant-garde of the US was concentrated in these few streets. *The Masses*, a publication founded in 1910, was the mouthpiece of radicals who attacked the complacency of American society and its Victorian morality. The favorite haunt of the Village rebels was the **Liberal Club**, frequented by such social critics as **Upton Sinclair** (1878-1968). At its headquarters, at 133 MacDougal Street, the club organized Cubist art exhibits, lectures and debates, and all-night dances called "Pagan Routs." There were soon so many "Pagans" that the festivities had to be moved to other quarters. Polly Holliday's restaurant, located below the Liberal Club, became the favorite meeting place of anarchists.

Ferment also swept the arts. A new group of painters known as **The Eight**—or the Ashcan school—challenged established academic concepts and was instrumental in organizing the 1913 Armory Show. Literary salons helped to create an intellectual climate in the Village, which stimulated such writers as Walt Whitman, Mark Twain and Henry James. Theodore Dreiser, Richard Wright, O. Henry and Stephen Crane also lived here for a time. Not surprisingly, the Village attracted the theater. In 1915 the **Washington Square Players** ensemble, later to become the Theater Guild, was founded at the Liberal Club. In the following year the **Provincetown Players** made their New York debut on the ground floor of a bottling plant, after a summer season in Provincetown on Cape Cod. Among the members of the company was poet and playwright Edna St. Vincent Millay. It was in Greenwich Village that Eugene O'Neill first gained recognition, and where **F. Scott Fitzgerald** (1896-1940) played a key role in the revelry and creativity of the Roaring 20s and the Jazz Age.

The Village has historically been the stomping ground for the city's large gay population. Although the Village still claims an active gay community, other sections of the city, including the Upper West Side and Chelsea, are also home to a growing population of gays.

Today Greenwich Village remains a hive of nonconformism and originality, but it is not as radical, bohemian and avant-garde as it once was. High rents have driven away struggling and would-be artists to cheaper areas (such as the East Village and TriBeCa). Nonetheless, scattered among the small houses in the narrow streets, high-rise buildings accommodate New Yorkers who prefer the vitality of the Village to the conventionality of suburbia and who are attracted by a community that welcomes talent, offers serious and light entertainment, caters to the bibliophile and to the gourmet, and cherishes diversity of lifestyle.

WALKING TOUR *Distance: 2mi*

Map p 151. Begin at Washington Square.

★**Washington Square** – Forming the heart of present-day Greenwich Village, this large square is the main gathering place for Villagers and visitors alike. It stands at the foot of Fifth Avenue, its monumental arch a fitting entry to this famous thoroughfare. Originally a marshland and favorite hunting ground of the early colonists, the site of the present square became a potter's field in the 18C (skeletons of about 1,000 early New Yorkers were found during the renovation of the square in the 1960s). It was also popular as a dueling ground and a site of public hangings. Following its transformation into a park in 1826, it served as a military parade ground and later spurred the growth of a fashionable residential enclave of redbrick town houses. **Henry James'** novel *Washington Square* (1881), later adapted for stage and screen as *The Heiress*, depicts the life of the local aristocracy. Mark Twain, O. Henry, Walt Whitman and the painter Edward Hopper also frequented Washington Square and evoked it in their works.

After the founding of New York University, Washington Square became the university's unofficial campus, and a large number of the surrounding buildings now belong to NYU. Today the park is a veritable people-watcher's paradise: throngs of visitors stop to listen to impromptu performers and soapbox orators, admire skateboard and Frisbee enthusiasts or gaze at the eclectic mix of people dressed in all sorts of wild and wonderful outfits. Radiating from the central fountain, the park offers entertainment for young (children's park) and old (large chess tables). Even dogs can frolic in their own little play area. Twice a year for three weeks the square and surrounding streets are the scene of the **Washington Square Outdoor Art Exhibit**. More than 500 emerging artists display their work, many for the first time.

Washington Square

★**Washington Arch (1)** – Designed by Stanford White in 1892, this white marble triumphal arch replaced a temporary wooden one commemorating the centennial of President Washington's inauguration. The arch, 30ft across and 77ft high, is best viewed from Fifth Avenue. Gracing this side are two sculptures of Washington—as a soldier (by Herman MacNeil) and as a civilian (by A. Sterling Calder, father of the renowned 20C sculptor Alexander Calder). On the south side, note the frieze with the American eagle, the W for Washington at the center, and the trumpet-blowing statues. Located east of the arch, the 1888 bronze **statue of Garibaldi (2)** forms a rallying point for the inhabitants of Little Italy. A hero of the Italian struggle for independence, Garibaldi stayed in New York in 1850.

Walk to the north side of the square.

★**Washington Square North** – Often referred to as "the Row," this is the most attractive side of the square. Two blocks of Greek Revival town houses *(nos. 1-13 and 21-26)* remain from the 1830s, suggesting what the entire square once looked like. The residences have housed such renowned individuals as Richard Morris Hunt, Henry James, Edward Hopper and John Dos Passos, who wrote *Manhattan Transfer* while living at no. 3. Doric or Ionic columns grace the entrances, which are topped by flat lintels, and elaborate cast-iron railings separate the redbrick houses from the sidewalk. Some of the residences *(nos. 7-13)* retain only their original facades, as the interiors have been gutted and converted into an apartment complex *(entrance on Fifth Ave.)*.

Continue up Fifth Ave. to Washington Mews.

Washington Mews – Behind Washington Square North, this secluded alley once contained stables and servants' quarters for the town houses on Washington Square North. The charm and intimacy of this street, with its whitewashed and brick facades, climbing shrubs and cobblestone pavement, have long attracted artists, writers and actors.

Continue north on Fifth Ave. and turn left on W. 8th St.

West Eighth Street – This lively artery caters to a motley crew of regulars and tourists, who enjoy browsing in the shoe stores and vintage-clothing boutiques that line this street.

③ Chess, Anyone?

Map p 151. Southwest corner of Washington Square Park. Chess lovers and kibitzers alike should check out the action here. Bring your own set and prepare to challenge the old-timers. Nearby, the venerable **Marshall Chess Club** *(23 W. 10th St.;* ☎ *212-477-3716; www. marshallchessclub.org)* has played host to some of the most famous chess contests of the century, including the 1956 tournament in which Bobby Fischer defeated David Byrne. You don't have to go inside; just peek in the windows.

Turn left on MacDougal St. to MacDougal Alley.

★**MacDougal Alley** – Yet another picturesque lane, similar to Washington Mews, this alley was inhabited by sculptor Gertrude Vanderbilt Whitney (1875-1942), who opened a gallery in a converted stable that was the precursor to the Whitney Museum of American Art. Lit by gas street lamps, the row houses have been converted into private studios.

Return to W. 8th St., turn left, continue to Ave. of the Americas and glance north to the corner of W. 10th St.

Renowned as one of the Village's more eccentric landmarks, **Jefferson Market Library** *(425 Avenue of the Americas)*, a castlelike redbrick structure (1877, Frederick Clarke Withers and Calvert Vaux), was modeled after King Ludwig II's Neuschwanstein Castle in Bavaria, Germany. Designed in an ornate Victorian Gothic style, the building is adorned with pinnacles, gables, turrets, arches and traceried windows, and is dominated by a whimsical clock tower.

2 The Art Bar
Map p 151. 52 Eighth Ave. between Jay and Horatio Sts. ☎ *212-727-0244.* Don't be fooled by first impressions— go all the way to the back and through the curtain. Behind it there's an inky dark treasure land of antique couches, velvet curtains, candles and even a blazing (gas) fireplace for extra warmth and atmosphere. And, of course, the eponymous art on the walls. Good food and a decent jukebox make this a perfect place to decompress after a day of walking, or if you're intrepid—a spot to wind up an evening. The crowd's young and funky, but not too concerned with who's sharing the chairs.

Originally used as a courthouse, the building was threatened with destruction in the 1960s. At the urging of the local populace, the building was considered for adaptive reuse and today houses a branch of the New York Public Library.

Continue south on Ave. of the Americas, turn right on Waverly Pl. and right again on Gay St.

Lined with quaint, Federal-style brick houses, charming Gay Street bears no trace of its past as a ghetto.

Continue to the end of Gay St. and turn left on Christopher St.

Historically the center of the city's gay population, **Christopher Street** is lined with an array of eccentric shops. Occupying the intersection with Waverly Place is the imposing, triangular **Northern Dispensary** (1831), New York's oldest medical clinic, established in 1827 to dispense free medical care to the poor; now it is being refurbished as a residence for homeless people with AIDS. A little farther down the street, at the intersection with West 4th Street, **Christopher Park**, a small square, became the focus of controversy in the early 1990s owing to the installation of a sculpture by George Segal that depicts two gay couples. On the north side of the park stands the Stonewall Bar *(no. 51)*, scene of the historic 1969 riot between police and gays that sparked the Gay Liberation movement.

Turn left on W. 4th St.

A lively artery, **West 4th Street** is jammed with restaurants, coffeehouses and craft shops. Take a minute to admire the splendid assortment of shrubs and flowers in the viewing garden at **Sheridan Square**, a welcome spot of greenery on this commercial street.

© Martha Cooper

Hudson Street mural by Chico

Chumley's

86 Bedford St. at Barrow.
☎ *212-675-4449.* The Village's best-known secret, this friendly former speakeasy has been serving up top-notch pub grub and microbrews since 1922. Such upscale fare as grilled salmon and Chumley's famous lobster special are now featured on the menu as well. Step through the arched doorway down into the cozy burnished-wood-and-brass interior, the set for movies including Warren Beatty's *Reds* and Woody Allen's *Sweet and Lowdown*. Black-and-white photos of some of the city's most famous bar-crawling scribes (Arthur Miller, Jack Kerouac, Lillian Hellman) decorate the walls, attesting to Chumley's long history of entertaining the crème de la crème. Just remember to take note of the address—there's no sign outside.

Turn right on Cornelia St., left on Bleecker St. and right on Leroy St. Cross Seventh Ave. and continue on Leroy St. to St. Luke's Place.

West of Seventh Avenue, the Village presents a series of charming, tree-lined streets, quaint houses and a few choice restaurants. Exuding a quiet, residential atmosphere, this area provides a peaceful retreat from the more vibrant section centering around 8th and Bleecker streets. Lining the winding streets, two-and-a-half-story Federal houses, topped by slate roofs and brick chimneys and enlivened with elaborate wrought-iron gates and railings, recall the area's 19C elegance.

★**St. Luke's Place** – Located across from a public swimming pool and park, this attractive street of brick and brownstone residences from the 1860s is shaded by gingko trees and fragrant wisteria. It was here, at no. 16, that Theodore Dreiser wrote *An American Tragedy*. South of this area, near Charlton and Vandam streets, an elegant estate known as Richmond Hill served as a headquarters for General Washington, and later as a residence for both John Adams and Aaron Burr.

Turn right on Hudson St. and right again on Morton St.

Lined with lovely trees, curving Morton Street features stately homes, some adorned with elaborate doorways, especially nos. 42, 56 and 62. As you continue left on Bedford Street, note **no. 75 1/2** (1873), reputedly the narrowest house in the city (9.5ft wide by 30ft long). Edna St. Vincent Millay lived here from 1923 to 1924.

From Bedford St. turn left on Commerce St.

A charming, rambling residential alley, **Commerce Street** well represents the "village" feel of West Greenwich. Housed in an old barn at no. 38, the **Cherry Lane Theater**, a venue for Off Broadway productions since the 1920s, has hosted the American premieres of plays by Samuel Beckett, Eugene Ionesco and Edward Albee. Around the corner, at nos. 39 and 41, rise two handsome brick houses (1832), called "The Twin Sisters"; legend has it that they were built by a sea captain for his two daughters who could not live together under the same roof.

Greenwich Village

Turn left on Barrow St., continue to Hudson St. and turn right.

On the west side of Hudson Street stands the **Church of St. Luke in the Fields**, an austere brick structure erected in 1822 and reconstructed following a fire in 1981. A little farther north, Hudson Street is lined with cafes, boutiques and bookshops.

Turn right onto Grove St. across from St. Luke's.

Grove Street, like Bedford, is a peaceful byway that seems miles away from feverish Manhattan. At nos. 10-12, peek through the gate of **Grove Court★**, an attractive fan-shaped cul-de-sac surrounded by brick-fronted Federal houses of the 1850s. A three-story wood-frame house *(no. 17)*, unusual for New York, marks the northern corner of Grove and Bedford streets. Don't miss the "twin peaks" of 102 Bedford Street, an eccentric 1925 renovation of a traditional Village house.

Continue to Bleecker St., turn right and continue to Ave. of the Americas.

★Bleecker Street – This is one of the most active commercial thoroughfares in the Village, along with West 8th and Hudson streets. Part of an old Italian neighborhood, Bleecker is famed for displays of fruits and vegetables, specialized grocery stores and pastry shops, and coffeehouses for espresso lovers.

The four-block stretch of Bleecker between the Avenue of the Americas and La Guardia Place is an old 1960s stomping ground. Today the stretch still abounds with small cabarets, music clubs and bars.

Continue on Bleecker St. and turn left on MacDougal St.

Erected for Aaron Burr, Federal-style residences *(nos. 127-131)* dominate the west side of the street. At no. 133 is the **Provincetown Playhouse**, one of the oldest Off Broadway theaters.

NEW YORK UNIVERSITY

Visitor information: ☎ *212-998-4636; www.nyu.edu.* The largest private university in the US, NYU was founded in 1831 by **Albert Gallatin**, secretary of the Treasury under Jefferson. Today NYU has 13 colleges, a staff of 14,500 and more than 45,000 students. The principal campuses are: Washington Square (Sciences, Arts and Letters, Business, Law, Education), the Medical Center on First Avenue (Medicine and Dentistry), the School of Continuing Education on Trinity Place in the Wall Street area, the Real Estate Institute on West 42nd Street and the NYU Institute Of Fine Arts on Fifth Avenue.

Main Building (B) – *100 Washington Square East.* Built in 1895, this Neoclassical structure replaced the original building erected in 1836. An impressive row of four paired Doric columns adorns the facade fronting Washington Square. The ground floor houses the **Grey Art Gallery**, which features changing exhibits encompassing various aspects of the visual arts, including painting, sculpture, photography, decorative arts and video *(open Sept–July Tue, Thu & Fri 11am–6pm, Wed 11am–8pm, Sat 11am–5pm; closed major holidays; $2.50 contribution requested;* ♿ ☎ *212-998-6780; www.nyu.edu/greyart).*

Elmer Holmes Bobst Library (C) – *70 Washington Square South. Not open to the general public.* This imposing red sandstone cube on the southeast corner of the square was designed by Philip Johnson and Richard Foster in 1972. Rising to 150ft, its 12 stories house over two million books.

The **Loeb Student Center (D)** (1959, Harrison & Abramovitz) stands on the site of a boardinghouse known as the House of Genius, which had been home to Herman Melville, Stephen Crane and Eugene O'Neill. It features an aluminum-panel sculpture (1960, Reuben Nakian) on its facade, representing birds in flight. Adjacent to it, the triangular-shaped Roman Catholic **Holy Trinity Chapel** is distinguished by modern stained-glass windows.

Judson Memorial Baptist Church – *55 Washington Square South.* Providing a marked contrast to Holy Trinity Chapel, this distinctive structure of mottled yellow brick and white terra-cotta presents an eclectic mix of Greco-Romanesque and Renaissance motifs. Built in 1893, it is considered one of architect Stanford White's finest designs in the city. Inside, note the superb stained-glass windows by John LaFarge. The separate, 10-story campanile now houses a student dormitory.

Hagop Kevorkian Center for Near Eastern Studies (E) – *At corner of Washington Square South & Sullivan St.* Dominating a small corner lot, this stark granite building was designed by Philip Johnson and Richard Foster in 1972. It contains a surprising and delightful **entrance hall★** *(on Sullivan St.)*, a reconstruction of a Syrian courtyard complete with tiled floor, fountain, moldings and door panels. The various pieces came from a merchant's house (1797) in Damascus.

The 1951 redbrick Georgian Revival **Vanderbilt Hall (F)**, which houses NYU's School of Law, features a pleasant courtyard at its entrance on Washington Square South.

Tisch School of the Arts (G) – *721 Broadway.* The recycled NYU loft building is where such well-known movie directors as Spike Lee, Martin Scorsese and Oliver Stone learned their trade.

Sylvette (3) – *In Silver Towers Plaza located on Bleecker St., between La Guardia Pl. and Mercer St.* Located in the center of the Silver Towers complex (designed for NYU by I.M. Pei in 1966) stands this 36ft-high bust of Sylvette David, a young woman Picasso met in the 1950s. The original Picasso sheet-metal sculpture was enlarged in concrete and stone by Carl Nesjar and Sigurd Frager in 1968.

ADDITIONAL SIGHTS

Time Landscape – *At corner of La Guardia Pl. and W. Houston St.* Designed by environmental sculptor Alan Sonfist, this patch of greenery represents the vegetation found on the island of Manhattan prior to the arrival of Europeans. Planted in 1978, the garden includes oaks, sassafras, maples, wild grasses and flowers.

29 Washington Place East – *At northwest corner of Washington Place E. & Greene St.* In 1911 a Saturday afternoon fire in the workrooms of the Triangle Shirtwaist Co. on the top three floors of this 10-story industrial building killed 145 people, most of them women and young girls. Many leapt to their deaths into Washington Place. The outcry led to the passage of the first factory safety laws. A modest plaque commemorates the disaster, and the International Ladies Garment Workers Union marks the event every March 25 with an on-site memorial service.

Church of the Ascension – *At Fifth Ave. and W. 10th St. Open year-round Mon–Fri noon–1pm, Sun for services only.* & ☎ 212-254-8620. www.ascensionnyc.org. Built of local brownstone, this Gothic Revival Episcopal church (1841) was designed by Richard Upjohn during the Village's first wave of development, which included the construction of prominent institutional buildings. Of particular interest is the soaring interior, remodeled by Stanford White in 1888, is John LaFarge's superb **mural** of the Ascension over the altar, the stained-glass windows and the box pews.

Located one block north, at the corner with West 11th Street, the **First Presbyterian Church** (1845, Joseph C. Wells), topped by a square, pinnacled tower, exemplifies a more elaborate Gothic Revival style.

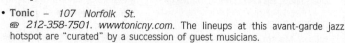

Jazz Clubs

An evening of jazz in New York is a must on everyone's list. All but the last three of these are in Greenwich Village. See the chapter on Harlem for clubs in that neighborhood.

R. Corbel/MICHELIN

- **Blue Note Jazz Club** – *131 W. 3rd St.* ☎ *212-475-8592. www.bluenote.net.* Incredible acoustics and a stellar lineup (often two top artists in one evening) make this the city's premier jazz club.

- **Fat Cat** – *75 Christopher St.* ☎ *212-675-7369.* The owner of the sorely missed Small's is now booking Fat Cat, just around the corner.

- **Tonic** – *107 Norfolk St.* ☎ *212-358-7501. wwwtonicny.com.* The lineups at this avant-garde jazz hotspot are "curated" by a succession of guest musicians.

- **Village Vanguard** – *178 Seventh Ave. S.* ☎ *212-255-4037. villagevanguard.com.* As New York's oldest jazz club, this dark, smoky basement reverberates with history and the music of today's top acts.

- **Cajun** – *129 Eighth Ave. at W. 16th St.* ☎ *212-691-6174. www.jazzatthecajun.com.* A Manhattan slice of New Orleans Dixieland Jazz from regulars Joe Muranyi (clarinetist for Louis Armstrong), pianist Chuck Folds (accompanist to Doc Cheatham) and others.

- **Iridium Jazz Club** – *1650 Broadway, at 51st Ave.* ☎ *212-582-2121. www.iridiumjazzclub.com.* Here you'll find serious jazz in the most playful setting imaginable. Two shows a night, plus midnight sets on the weekend draw large crowds.

- **Birdland** – *315 W. 44th St.* ☎ *212-581-3080. www.birdlandjazz.com.* A classy, ultra-cool midtown venue, the Birdland serves up down-home Southern cuisine with some of the best jazz in town.

New School University – *Main building at 66 W. 12th St.* ☎ *212-229-6500. www.newschool.edu.* The New School for Social Research, founded in 1919 by historians Charles Beard and James Harvey Robinson and philosophers John Dewey and Thorstein Veblen, was originally conceived as a small informal center for adults, where a broad range of economic and political issues could be discussed. Over the years the New School has evolved into a diversified institution of higher learning and today, with its six divisions and total enrollment of more than 30,000 students, it is one of the nation's most innovative universities. In 1970 it joined with the **Parsons School of Design** *(66 Fifth Ave. between 12th & 13th Sts.)* to broaden its curriculum. The Parsons School, founded in 1896 by William Merritt Chase, has garnered a worldwide reputation in the fields of fine arts, photography, illustration, design marketing, and the design of interiors, fashions and products. Some 1,800 undergraduate students attend the school. In 1989 the Mannes College of Music, a distinguished classical music conservatory founded in 1916 by violinist David Mannes, joined the New School.

MUSEUM *(See Museums section)*

★★**The Forbes Galleries** – *62 Fifth Ave.*

16 • ASTOR PLACE – EAST VILLAGE★

MTA 4, 5, 6 train to Astor Place

Map p 166

This somewhat seedy but lively district, bounded by Houston and 14th streets east of Broadway, is an active center for dance, theater (Off-Off Broadway) and visual and performance art. Trendy bars and restaurants abound in the **NoHo** (North of Houston) and Astor Place neighborhoods; to the east, toward Second Avenue and Avenue A, secondhand shops, ethnic boutiques, bakeries, restaurants and coffeehouses are an adventure to explore, especially in the evening.

Historical Notes

In the 17C the area was part of a 600-acre farm tract owned by Gov. Peter Stuyvesant. Briefly in the early 1800s, the now-commercial district west of Second Avenue boasted fashionable town houses; the working-class neighborhoods farther east were home to Polish, Ukrainian and German immigrants until the early 20C. In the 1950s low rents and an air of romantic seediness attracted such beat-generation writers as Jack Kerouac and William S. Burroughs. In the 1960s and 70s came the "hippies," then the "punkers" and eventually every other imaginable layer of New York's counterculture. The glory days were the 1980s, when rock bands like the B-52's and Talking Heads made their name at the **CBGB Club** *(315 Bowery)*, still a center of the underground music movement; transvestites danced on the bars of popular nightspots like the Pyramid *(101 Ave. A)*; and storefront galleries and performance spaces appeared, and often disappeared, overnight. In 1985 the **Palladium** *(126 E. 14th St.)*, housed in the 1920s Academy of Music building converted by Arata Isozaki and decorated by artists Francesco Clemente and Keith Haring, opened as one of the city's most popular discotheques. A magnet for the homeless, the run-down Tompkins Square Park *(east of Ave. A)*, once the center of a German neighborhood known as Kleindeutschland, was the scene of riots during the financial panic of 1873, and again in 1991, when the police uprooted a colony of homeless people from the park, leading to its temporary closing. While the district has become somewhat gentrified, the area is still home to urban housing projects, mainly in Alphabet City, and retains much of its avant-garde flavor.

■ Off-Off Broadway

The East Village is a prime location for Off-Off Broadway theater. In addition to the **Public Theater**, the following venues are of note. **Theater for the New City** *(155 First Ave. at 10th St.;* ☎ *212-254-1109; www.theaterforthenewcity.net)* produces experimental and new work by American playwrights, including full-length plays, musicals and community festivals. The legendary **La Mama etc.** *(74A E. 4th St. between Second and Third Aves.;* ☎ *212-475-7710; www.lamama.org)*, run by Ellen Stewart, often features groups from around the world. Such major plays as *Torch Song Trilogy*, *Godspell* and *Blue Man Tubes* were launched here. A former school building converted to a cultural center some 20 years ago, **P.S. 122** *(150 First Ave.;* ☎ *212-477-5288; www.ps122.org)* remains the granddaddy of performance art. Be sure to stop by the two galleries: one showcasing curated works of cutting-edge artists from around the globe, the other displaying works of the currently featured performance artist.

ASTOR PLACE

The restored 1904 Astor Place subway kiosk is the pride of this busy street connecting Third Avenue to Broadway. Below ground, the station has also been restored to its former glory; note in particular the bas-relief beavers celebrating John Jacob Astor's primacy in the 19C beaver trade. Located opposite the kiosk is Bernard (Tony) Rosenthal's sculpture *Alamo*, popularly known as the "black cube."

 Ethnic fare

Map p 166. Although the Ukrainian population in the East Village is in decline, the area still boasts some of the city's best Ukrainian restaurants, which ladle out bowls of borscht (thick beetroot soup topped with a dollop of sour cream), hearty portions of pierogis (dumplings filled with cheese, meat or cabbage) and blintzes (crêpes filled with fruit or cottage cheese). A neighborhood landmark, **Kiev** *(117 Second Ave.;* ☎ *212-420-9600)* is open 24 hours a day, and the menu will please your palate as well as your wallet. **Veselka** *(144 Second Ave.;* ☎ *212-228-9682)* offers hearty Eastern European fare at rock-bottom prices to a motley crew of East Villagers.

Cooper Union for the Advancement of Science and Art – Located between Third and Fourth avenues, the Cooper Union comprises three colleges emphasizing architecture, engineering and art. This free institution was founded in 1859 by Peter Cooper (1791-1883), a self-made industrialist who wanted to provide working-class students with the formal education he himself never had. Art shows, dance performances, literary evenings and lectures—open to the public—occur regularly in the main **Cooper Union Foundation Building★**, the oldest extant steel-frame structure in the US. Noted figures who have delivered speeches here include Gloria Steinem, Jimmy Carter, Susan B. Anthony and Abraham Lincoln, who gave his famous "right makes might" antislavery speech here in 1860.

Lafayette Street – In the early 1800s this area was the site of Vauxhall Gardens, a popular pleasure ground of outdoor cafes and bars. It was developed as a fashionable residential neighborhood in 1825 by John Jacob Astor, then the richest man in America. **Colonnade Row**, the marble-columned houses at nos. 428-434, features the remnants of nine magnificent Greek Revival manses erected in 1833. Originally called La Grange Terrace, after Lafayette's country estate near Paris, this was a coveted address for such society members as Cornelius Vanderbilt and Warren Delano (grandfather of President Franklin Delano Roosevelt).

The monumental brick and stone building across the street was originally the Astor Library, funded by John Jacob Astor and opened in 1854. Offering about 100,000 volumes without charge—a revolutionary idea at the time—it eventually formed the nucleus of the New York Public Library. In 1967 the late impresario Joseph Papp converted the then-abandoned building into the **Public Theater** *(no. 425)*. Home of the New York Shakespeare Festival, the Public also screens films and hosts new plays in its six theaters; *Hair* (1967) and *A Chorus Line* (1975) were both launched here.

A block west of Lafayette Street, at 700 Broadway, stands the **National Audubon Society** (c.1892, George Brown Post), the eight-story headquarters of the famed environmental concern. In renovating this handsome Romanesque structure in the early 1990s, the society created an ecologically informed edifice that set a new standard for environmental responsibility in building design.

EAST VILLAGE

The main artery of this lively and colorful district is **Second Avenue**, the spine of the Jewish intellectual community during the first half of the 20C. The Entermedia Theater *(189 Second Ave.)*, originally the Yiddish Art Theater, is located here, along with an astounding variety of inexpensive ethnic eateries offering Caribbean, Ukrainian, Russian, Chinese, Yemenite, Italian, Japanese, Tibetan, Mexican and Israeli food. Indian restaurants line both sides of East 6th Street between Second and First avenues; the block is now known as "Curry Lane" or "**Little India.**" **St. Mark's Place** between Second and Third avenues is packed with shops and stalls where you can buy everything from vintage hats and comic books to leather goods.

St. Mark's-in-the-Bowery Church – *E. 10th St. and Second Ave.* This Georgian-style Episcopal Church, crowned by a Greek Revival steeple (added in 1828), was built in 1799 on the site of Peter Stuyvesant's 1660 family chapel and is the second oldest church in Manhattan after St. Paul's Chapel. Damaged by fire in 1978, the church was restored and rededicated in 1983. Seven generations of Stuyvesants

2 Little India
Map p 166. 6th St. between Second and First Aves. Whiffs of curry and sounds of sitars waft from the numerous Indian restaurants lining this colorful street. Although most are run by immigrants from Bangladesh, all offer spicy and delicious Indian food and a festive, inexpensive dining experience. Try **Mitali** *(334 E. 6th St.;* ☏ *212-533-2508)*, which pioneered this location and receives raves for its lamb vindaloo. Just up the street, **Gandhi** *(345 E. 6th St.;* ☏ *212-614-9718)* offers wonderful breads (poori, naan and parathas). If you're not shy, celebrate your birthday at **Rose of India** *(308 E. 6th St.;* ☏ *212-533-5011)*; as poker-faced waiters whisk a bowl of mango ice cream or honey cake topped by a candle to your table, strobe lights surge and Indian disco music blares for about 10 seconds.

3 McSorley's Old Ale House
Map p 166. 15 E. 7th St. ☏ *212-473-9148.* Once known as McSorley's Saloon, this tavern was opened in 1854 and is celebrated in the paintings of John Sloan and the short stories of Joseph Mitchell. For years the establishment was off-limits to women. Today crowds of coeds and post-college pub crawlers keep the place busy. Try McSorley's house ale—choose light or dark—that predates trendy microbrews.

are buried under the building. The church hosts literary readings and a resident theater company.

Nearby in the St. Mark's Historic District are the **Nicholas William Stuyvesant House** *(44 Stuyvesant St.)*, built in 1795, and the 1804 **Stuyvesant-Fish House** *(no. 21)*, among the finest and very few surviving Federal-period town houses in the city. Also on Stuyvesant Street, the **Renwick Triangle** *(23-25 Stuyvesant St. and 114-128 E. 10th St.)*, an ensemble of five-story row houses (1861) attributed to James Renwick, once shared a large garden with the Stuyvesant-Fish House.

MUSEUM *(See Museums section)*

★**Merchant's House Museum** – *29 E. 4th St.*

17 • GRAMERCY PARK –
UNION SQUARE AREA★

MTA N, R train to 23rd St.

Map p 166

Located north of the East Village and east of Chelsea, this vibrant area extending from 26th Street south to 14th Street between Second and Fifth avenues comes as a pleasant surprise in an otherwise undistinguished section of the city. The area encompasses remnants of an elegant neighborhood that became engulfed by commercial structures at the turn of the century. Today the district's old-fashioned residential charm is again in vogue, attracting young professionals in search of moderate rents. The once-quiet streets, lined with eclectic, mid-19C buildings, now play host to ad agencies and publishing houses, popular restaurants and nightclubs, and fashionable shops and boutiques.

WALKING TOUR *Distance: 2mi*

Begin walk at Madison Square.

Madison Square – *E. 23rd to 26th Sts., between Madison & Fifth Aves.* Created in 1847 on a patch of swamp-infested land, Madison Square originated as a military parade ground. Following on the heels of its southern neighbor, Union Square, it became an elegant residential enclave during the second half of the 19C, when it was surrounded by fashionable hotels, fine restaurants and expensive shops.
The square was long associated with sporting events. In 1845 it was the site of the city's first baseball games. From 1853 to 1856, a type of circus called the Hippodrome was housed in a converted railroad depot just northeast of the square, attracting as many as 10,000 spectators at a time. In 1879 the structure was renamed Madison Square Garden. Then, at the end of the 19C, it was replaced by an ornate sports arena with room for 8,000 spectators, designed by Stanford White, architect and man about town. White was murdered on the roof garden in 1906 by Henry K. Thaw, whose wife, starlet Evelyn Nesbitt, had had an affair with the architect before her marriage. Destroyed in 1925 to make room for the New York Life Insurance Building, the "Garden" was relocated to a site on West 49th Street, between Eighth and Ninth avenues. In 1968 a new Madison Square Garden opened at its current location.
Although no longer at the height of its glory, this pleasant spot of greenery is still surrounded by several noteworthy buildings. At the northeast corner, between East 26th and 27th streets, where the "Garden" once stood, stands the New York Life Insurance Building (1928), designed by Cass Gilbert in the Gothic style and embellished with impressive gargoyles. Marking the corner of East 25th Street, the elegant white marble building (1899) fronted by Corinthian columns houses the **Appellate Division of the Supreme Court** of New York State. The roof balustrade depicts symbolic figures and great teachers of law (including Moses, Justinian and Confucius). Formerly on the far right, the statue of Muhammad has been removed at the request of the city's Islamic community, since the Koran forbids the corporeal representation of the Prophet. The vestibule inside features a gilded ceiling supported by yellow marble columns. Farther south, between East 24th and 23rd streets, the 700ft **Metropolitan Life Insurance Company Tower** (1909, Le Brun & Sons) resembles the campanile of St. Mark's in Venice, Italy. Note the enormous clock with its four faces: the minute hands each weigh 100lbs and the hour hands 700lbs.

★**Flatiron Building** – Standing on the south side of the square, this striking 22-story brick and limestone structure (1902, Daniel H. Burnham) has an unusual, triangular shape, resembling an iron. One of the city's first skyscrapers, it was originally erected for the Fuller Construction Co. (which also commissioned the Fuller Building on East 57th Street). The Renaissance-style edifice, with its three-tiered palazzo format and articulated cornice, was soon dubbed the Flatiron Building and later adopted its nickname as its official title.

Walk east on E. 23rd St. to Park Ave. and turn right.

Dominating the northeast corner of Park Avenue and East 21st Street, the red sandstone Calvary Episcopal Church (1846) was designed in the Gothic Revival style by James Renwick, architect of St. Patrick's Cathedral.

Turn left on E. 21st St. and continue east.

★**Gramercy Park** – This attractive square and its immediate surroundings form an elegant and tranquil residential enclave in a largely commercial area of the city. The patch of greenery was laid out in 1831 by Samuel B. Ruggles, who drained an old marsh—Gramercy is a corruption of the Dutch for "little crooked swamp"—and patterned the area after London's residential squares. Ruggles sold more than 60 lots surrounding the square on the understanding that each owner would have access to the park at the center. He also laid out Irving Place, named for his friend

164

Washington Irving, and Lexington Avenue, as extensions of the park. The first grand homes appeared in the 1840s, and the area quickly attracted prosperous residents. Following several decades of high life, the district's prestige began to wane and apartment houses were erected. By the early 20C, artists and intellectuals moved into the town houses, many of which were converted into cooperatives and duplexes.

Today surrounded by an 8ft-high cast-iron fence, Gramercy Park remains private— the only such square in New York. Access (by key) is restricted to owners and tenants. A statue (1916, Edmont Quinn) of actor Edwin Booth, dressed in his favorite role of Hamlet, stands at its center.

Walk around the park.

Gramercy Park West, the most attractive side of the square, presents a harmonious front of redbrick town houses. **Nos. 3** and **4**, designed by Alexander Jackson Davis, boast elaborate cast-iron porches, reminiscent of New Orleans architecture. No. 4, the former home of James Harper, mayor of New York in 1844 and one of the founders of Harper & Bros. publishers, is flanked by a pair of iron lanterns, called "mayor's lamps": the mayor could request to have such lamps installed in front of his house to facilitate locating him in case of nighttime emergencies.

The south side features two distinguished clubs. **No. 15**, the present site of the National Arts Club, was the home of Samuel Tilden, an opponent of Tammany Hall, governor of New York State from 1874 to 1876, and unsuccessful Democratic nominee for the presidency in 1876. Designed in 1884 by Calvert Vaux in a Victorian Gothic style, the building is embellished with sculptural detailing ranging from flowers and birds to famous authors and thinkers. Fearing for his life after having destroyed the Tweed Ring, Tilden had an underground passageway built to 19th Street as a possible escape route. Located next door at **no. 16**, the Players Club was founded in 1888 by Edwin Booth, the brother of John Wilkes Booth, President Lincoln's assassin. Booth commissioned Stanford White to renovate the facade. Note the ornate, wrought-iron street lamps and the elaborate ironwork of the two-story porch. No. 19 was the domain of Mrs. Stuyvesant Fish, grande dame of New York society, whose innovations included reducing the time for a formal dinner from several hours to 50 minutes.

At the east end of the square stand two apartment buildings. Dating from 1883 the redbrick **no. 34** is marked by an octagonal turret corner. Adjacent to it, the white terra-cotta building at no. 36 (1910) represents the Gothic Revival style; two concrete knights in armor flank the entrance way.

Follow E. 20th St. west and cross Park Ave.

★**Theodore Roosevelt Birthplace National Historic Site** – *28 E. 20th St. Visit by guided tour (30min) only, year-round Tue–Sat 9am–5pm. Closed major holidays. $2. ☎ 212-260-1616. www.nps.gov/thrb.* This reconstructed Victorian brownstone stands on the site of the home of Theodore Roosevelt (1858-1919), who lived here until he was 14 years of age. Harvard graduate, rancher in the Dakota Territory, colonel in the Rough Riders, hunter-naturalist and author of some 30 books, "Teddy" Roosevelt—who gave his name to teddy bears—was a colorful personality and a dynamic force in US politics for 40 years. McKinley's vice president in 1901, he succeeded to the Oval Office on the assassination of the president. Elected in his own right in 1904, he declined to run for reelection in 1908 and failed in an attempt for the presidency in 1912. He received the Nobel Peace Prize for his mediating efforts between Russia and Japan.

The 32nd US president, Franklin Delano Roosevelt was a fifth cousin of Theodore and married the latter's niece, Eleanor Roosevelt, in 1905.

Visit – Erected in 1848 the original three-story brownstone was torn down in 1916 and replaced by a two-story commercial building. Three years later, prominent New York citizens acquired that structure and the adjacent building (which once belonged to Teddy's uncle, Robert) and rebuilt the house as a memorial. Opened to the public in 1923, the museum features five period rooms adorned with family heirlooms and the original color schemes, selected by interior designer Leon Marcotte in 1865. The room located to the right of the entrance contains exhibits tracing Roosevelt's career through letters, mementos, cartoons and other memorabilia. On the second floor are the parlor, library and dining room. The master bedroom and nursery occupy the third floor. The "lion's room," which showcases Roosevelt's hunting trophies and his large writing desk, can also be found on this floor. The house was donated to the park service in 1963 and has been designated a National Historic Site.

Return to Park Ave., continue south one block and turn left on E. 19th St.

Lined with graceful trees, the stretch of East 19th Street between Irving Place and Third Avenue is known as the "block beautiful." Renovated in the 1920s by Frederick J. Sterner, the houses present a curious yet harmonious blend of stuccoed facades. Note in particular no. 141 with its jockey hitching posts. The artist George Bellows (1882-1925) lived at no. 146 from 1910 until his death.

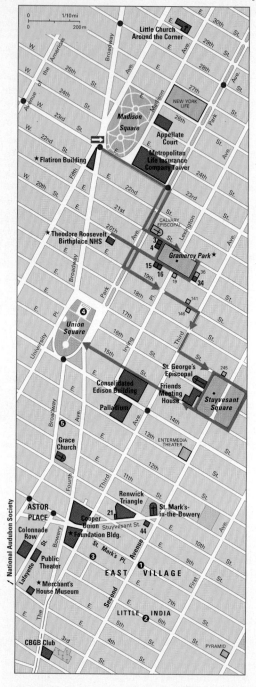

Turn right on Third Ave. and left on E. 17th St.

Stuyvesant Square – A gift to the city from the Stuyvesant family in 1836, the square formed part of an elegant residential quarter in the 19C. Today, unfortunately, the fenced-in park is bisected by Second Avenue, thereby losing much of its original charm. Hospitals surround the east side, and the towers of Stuyvesant Town, a middle-income housing project built by the Metropolitan Life Insurance Co., are visible beyond. On the north side, at no. 245, the Sidney Webster House (1883) is reputedly the only surviving residential structure in New York designed by Richard Morris Hunt. The west side of the square attests to the area's former elegance. Located on Rutherford Place, the austere, red-brick **Friends Meeting House** and Seminary (1860) and the neighboring **St. George's Episcopal Church** (1856) lend the square the appearance of a "village green." St. George's, a Romanesque brownstone edifice constructed in 1856 by Blesch and Eidlitz, was known as "Morgan's Church" when the elder J.P. Morgan was a parishioner here. Its massive, round arches represent an early Romanesque Revival style. Destroyed by fire in 1865, the church was rebuilt to the original specifications. Crafted by Gertrude Vanderbilt Whitney, a 1936 bronze statue of Gov. Peter Stuyvesant, easily recognizable by his peg leg, stands in the square, facing St. George's church.

Walk west on E. 15th St. to Union Square.

At the intersection with Irving Place rises the **Consolidated Edison Building**, headquarters of the company that provides gas, electricity and steam for most of the city. Designed in 1915 by Henry Hardenbergh, who also drew plans for the Dakota and the Plaza Hotel, the tower is crowned by a landmark clock.

Union Square – *E. 17th to 14th Sts., between Park Ave. & University Pl.* This grassy park was created in the early 19C as a stopover point on the post road to Albany. In 1836 the garden at the center of the square was enclosed by iron grillwork and locked at night. At the time, the square marked the northern border of the city. By the mid-19C, it had become a fashionable address for New York's finest families, rivaling Astor Place. As the city spread northward in the late 19C, wealthy residences gave way to theaters, the Academy of Music (now converted into the Palladium), commercial establishments such as Tiffany's and Brentano's, and restaurants like Delmonico's. During the first decades of the 20C, Union Square became the scene of political gatherings—a New York equivalent of London's Hyde Park where political radicals indulged in soapbox oratory—and witnessed mass demonstrations such as the one on August 22, 1927, when convicted murderers Sacco and Vanzetti were executed in Boston. Today the square is best known for its popular Greenmarket.

Three statues of interest grace the park: George Washington *(south)* and Abraham Lincoln *(north)*, both by Henry Kirke Brown, and Lafayette *(east)* by Bartholdi, better known as the sculptor of the Statue of Liberty.

ADDITIONAL SIGHTS

Grace Church – *802 Broadway at E. 10th St. Open Sept–Jun Tue–Fri noon–1pm. Rest of the year Wed noon–1pm. Open Sun for services only. Closed major holidays.* ♿ ☎ *212-254-2000. www.gracechurchnyc.org.* Founded by the Trinity Church parish in 1808, this Episcopal church was erected in 1846 by James Renwick, who later designed Saint Patrick's Cathedral. Distinguished by an elegant spire, the church

④ Union Square Greenmarket
Map p 166. In Union Square, E. 17th to 14th Sts., between Park Ave. & University Pl. www.cenyc.org. On Monday, Wednesday, Friday and Saturday mornings, upstate New York's farm bounty is exhibited in this bustling, colorful market. The display of fresh produce varies by season but is sure to include a wonderful assemblage of tubers and herbs, fresh poultry and eggs, dazzling flowers and dried arrangements, and succulent preserves, pastries and breads.

⑤ Strand Books
Map p 166. 828 Broadway. ☎ *212-473-1452. www.strandbooks.com.* Behind the unassuming facade you'll find New York's largest used-book store. The Strand stocks more than two million new and secondhand books, all available at great prices. The third floor is the place to search for a rare first edition. Don't miss the basement for art books and history specials.

is a fine example of the Gothic Revival style. In 1863 P.T. Barnum arranged for the rector to marry two midgets from his circus: Charles S. Stratton, better known as Tom Thumb, and Lavinia Warren.

Located to the left of the church, the rectory (also by Renwick) is one of New York's earliest Gothic Revival residences.

© Martha Cooper

Union Square Greenmarket

Little Church Around the Corner (Church of the Transfiguration) – *1 E. 29th St. Open year-round daily 8am–6pm. Guided tours (30min) available Sun 12:30pm.* ⚿ ☎ *212-684-6770. www.littlechurch.org.* This charming Episcopal church with its peaceful garden seems dwarfed by the surrounding skyscrapers, especially the Empire State Building. Built of redbrick in the mid-19C, the edifice reflects the 14C Gothic style and is sometimes referred to as an example of "English Cottage Gothic."

The church earned its nickname in 1870, when the pastor of a nearby church refused to hold funeral services for an actor; at that time, those associated with the theater were not looked upon favorably. The cleric did, however, suggest that the actor's friends try "the little church around the corner" where a monument still commemorates its pastor's charitable decision. It has remained a favorite parish for theater people, and also one where many weddings are held.

The interior is remarkable for its luminous stained-glass windows dedicated to great New York actors; note the window depicting Edwin Booth as Hamlet, designed by John LaFarge, and the one in the vestibule *(leading to the south transept)*, which is studded with raw diamonds. It is dedicated to the memory of the Spanish actor José Maria Muñoz. The Transfiguration, designed by Frederick Clark Withers, adorns the high altar reredos.

Museums *(See Museums section)*

★**Merchant's House Museum** – *29 E. 4th St.*

★★**The Forbes Galleries** – *62 Fifth Ave. at 14th St.*

18 • CHELSEA – GARMENT CENTER★

MTA 1, 9 train to 23rd St.

Map p 170

Situated roughly west of the Avenue of the Americas between 14th and 30th streets, Chelsea is a multifaceted neighborhood that combines refurbished industrial buildings and busy commercial avenues with a quiet residential district of historic brownstones. A thriving arts scene and increasingly upscale air make a distinct contrast to the commercial grit of the Garment Center just to the north.

Historical Notes

Named after the London neighborhood of the same name, Chelsea traces its roots to a country home staked out in 1750 along the Hudson River by Capt. Thomas Clarke. In 1813 the property passed to Clarke's grandson Clement Clarke Moore, an erudite scholar and literary figure who nevertheless remains best remembered for his famous poem, "A Visit from St. Nicholas." By 1820 the bucolic nature of the area began to fade as Eighth and Ninth avenues were laid out and a grid plan of cross streets added. Moore, who used the estate as a summer residence, deplored the change but soon gave in to progress and devised a plan to redevelop his land as an elegant residential neighborhood. Key to its design were parklike squares and row houses set back behind spacious front yards; required by deed covenants, these yards still exist today. Despite Moore's plans, the neighborhood remained largely middle class. The Hudson River Railroad opened along Eleventh Avenue in 1851, spawning slaughterhouses, breweries and tenements. From about 1905 to 1915, the area was a center of the new moviemaking industry, which attracted a vibrant artistic community that still flourishes today.

Rejuvenation of the area is especially evident along the industrial west side, where many 19C warehouses have been converted to galleries, theaters and performance venues such as **The Kitchen** *(512 W. 19th St.)* and a branch of the Dia Center for the Arts. Overlooking the Hudson River, the reconverted **Chelsea Piers** now house a massive recreational venue, offering sports enthusiasts a wide range of facilities, including a golf course and a rock-climbing wall. A historic district, located roughly between 19th and 23rd streets and Ninth and Tenth avenues, preserves one of the largest concentrations of Greek Revival and Italianate row houses in the city; in recent years this beautifully restored area has become an enclave for New York's well-heeled gay community. Eighth Avenue features the dance-oriented **Joyce Theater** *(no. 175)*; Seventh Avenue is lined with smart bistros and shops.

Just north of Chelsea lies the **Garment Center**, a largely commercial area, which runs from West 29th to 40th streets between Broadway and Eighth Avenue, occupying the former Tenderloin, a notorious late-19C bordello district. The garment industry relocated here from the Lower East Side in the 1920s. Shops for fabric and trimmings (mostly wholesale, but some retail) line streets jammed with trucks, while workers crowd the sidewalks with racks of clothing. Rush-hour traffic and the mass exodus at quitting time add to the dizzying hubbub; by early evening the area is eerily deserted.

WALKING TOUR *Distance: 1.8mi*

Dia: Chelsea – *548 W. 22nd St. Open mid-Sept–mid-Jun Wed–Sun noon–6pm.* $6. ✗ ☎ *212-989-5566. www.diaart.org.* Originally based in SoHo, this center for the arts opened exhibition galleries in Chelsea in 1987, luring several other galleries from SoHo—including Paula Cooper—to the area. This unusual exhibition space is situated in a renovated warehouse on Chelsea's west side. Each of four stories is devoted to a large-scale, single-artist project installed for a minimum of a year. The roof features an intriguing long-term installation by Dan Graham comprising a pavilion made of two-way mirrored glass, along with a coffee bar, video room and great views up and down the Hudson River.

In 2003 Dia opened a 300,000sq ft gallery in an old Nabisco factory 60mi north of the city in Beacon, New York. Dia: Beacon houses large-scale works from the center's collection.

Continue east on W. 22nd St.

West 22nd Street – Characterized by the ample front courts distinctive to the area, the block east of Tenth Avenue—part of the Chelsea historic district—features several Greek Revival buildings dating from the neighborhood's early development, including no. 444, built for Clement Clarke Moore in 1835. The large houses at nos. 414-16 and nos. 436-38 are two of four original mansions designed to face the then-open grounds of the old Clarke estate, "Chelsea," which stood just west of Ninth Avenue between 22nd and 23rd streets. At nos. 400-12 is an 1856 line of narrow Italianate row houses featuring their original bracketed cornices and low "English" basements. At Ninth Avenue, take a peek south to the L&S Dairy and adjacent buildings *(nos. 183-187 1/2)*, examples of the few remaining one-story wooden homes that once abounded in the neighborhood.

Continue south on Ninth Ave. to W. 20th St.

General Theological Seminary – *175 Ninth Ave.* The seminary occupies an entire city block between Ninth and Tenth avenues. Along the Ninth Avenue entrance, the library/administration building offers a nondescript, modern facade (1960). The seminary's brick and brownstone buildings, grouped around a green quadrangle and enclosed by a tall iron gate, evoke a traditional English university campus. Note especially the 1836 fieldstone **West Building**, one of the oldest Gothic Revival structures in New York.

West of the seminary, well-preserved Greek Revival houses notable for their 10ft-deep front yards and cast-iron railings are found along **Cushman Row** *(406-18 W.*

---

① Le Gamin Cafe

Map p 170. 183 Ninth Ave. ☎ *212-243-8864. www.legamin.com.* Paris Metro maps and vintage French advertisements decorate the walls of this funky Chelsea cafe, where croque-monsieur and crêpes fill the menu. Have the café au lait—it's made the authentic way: espresso and lots of foamy milk in an enormous bowl. The mostly French staff can be lax, but on the other hand, you're free to linger as long as you like.

② Art galleries

Map p 170. Recently gentrified Chelsea is the latest neighborhood to attract art galleries to its garages and lofts. The trend was launched by the **Dia Center for the Arts** *(548 W. 22nd St.)*, which moved here in 1987. One of the first galleries to open in SoHo and an early homesteader in Chelsea, the **Paula Cooper Gallery** *(534 W. 21st St.;* ☎ *212-255-1105)* has long been a champion of conceptual and minimalist art. Another large gallery, with two locations, **Matthew Marks** *(522 W. 22nd St. & 523 W. 24th St.;* ☎ *212-243-0200; www.matthewmarks.com)* presents big names in contemporary painting, sculpture and photography. Slightly north of the gallery strip on 22nd Street is **Greene Naftali** *(526 W. 26th St., 8th floor;* ☎ *212-463-7770)*, which showcases contemporary international art. In big, new quarters, another SoHo émigré, **Barbara Gladstone Gallery** *(515 W. 24th St.;* ☎ *212-206-9300)* shows work by top video and conceptual artists. Galleries open here regularly, so keep your eyes peeled for the latest chic newcomer.

③ El Cid Tapas

Map p 170. 322 W. 15th St. ☎ *212-929-9332.* Family-owned and run, this unprepossessing spot is the best place in the city to get tapas (small portions of Spanish dishes) and fresh sangria. The dozen tables are jammed together and the bar is crowded, so make reservations to sample unforgettable dishes like white asparagus in vinaigrette, shrimp grilled in garlic, and tortilla (a potato, cheese and ham concoction). A complimentary glass of sherry is served after dinner.

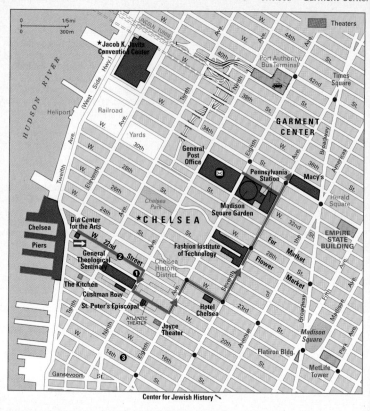

Center for Jewish History ↘

20th St.), built in 1840 by Alonzo Cushman, a friend of Clement Moore, who made a fortune investing in Chelsea's early speculative development.

Continue east on W. 20th St.

St. Peter's Episcopal Church – *346 W. 20th St.* Built the same year as the seminary's West Building (1836), St. Peter's is the first of the 19C English parish Gothic churches built in America and a model for many others in the style. The earlier 1832 rectory (which was the original chapel) represents an adaptation of the Greek Revival style. Located next door at no. 336, the Off Broadway Atlantic Theater, occupying the church's 1854 brick parish house, specializes in new American plays.

Continue east to Eighth Ave., turn left and continue to W. 23rd St.; turn right.

Hotel Chelsea – *222 W. 23rd St. between Seventh & Eighth Aves.* ☎ *212-343-3700. www.hotelchelsea.com.* Located in the center of New York's former theater district, the eclectic Hotel Chelsea (1884, Hubert, Pirrson & Co.) is festooned with cast-iron balconies patterned with sunflowers, a hallmark of the Queen Anne style. One of the very first cooperative apartment houses in the city, the Chelsea became a residential hotel in 1905. It has served as a part- or full-time home to writers and artists from Dylan Thomas and Mark Twain to Jackson Pollock and Andy Warhol, whose cult classic *Chelsea Girls* was filmed here. The somewhat shabby lobby features works by various residents past and present.

Continue east to Seventh Ave., turn left and continue north to W. 27th St.

On the west side of Seventh Avenue, between 26th and 28th streets, is the **Fashion Institute of Technology** (☎ *212-217-7675; www.fitnyc.edu*), a mecca for students aspiring to careers in fashion or the garment industry. 28th Street marks the center of the colorful wholesale **Flower Market**, busy from dawn to mid-morning with delivery-truck traffic taking cut flowers to outlying areas. Farther north, at 29th Street, is the heart of the largest **Fur Market** in the world. Beyond these storefronts, New York furriers create luxurious hats, coats and jackets in the latest designer styles.

Continue north on Seventh Ave. to W. 33rd St.

Madison Square Garden and Pennsylvania Station – On this spot stood the original 1906 Pennsylvania Station designed by McKim, Mead and White. Considered the greatest New York work of this famed architectural firm, the cast-iron and glass structure was torn down in the 1960s and replaced by the existing banal design. (The enormous controversy over the project precipitated New York City's first landmark legislation, which remains one of the strongest local preservation laws in the country.) Currently, Penn Station accommodates trains from three lines—Amtrak, New Jersey Transit and Long Island Railroad—running through tunnels under the Hudson and East rivers. Plans are under way to transform the adjacent General Post Office into a new Penn Station to accommodate increasing passenger volume and to right an infamous civic wrong.

Above ground, the complex includes the cylindrical **Madison Square Garden Sports Center**, located on the upper five tiers of the nine-story structure. This is the fourth successor to the original 1879 Madison Square Garden on Madison Avenue and 27th Street. The 20,000-seat "garden" is today home to the New York Knickerbockers basketball team and the New York Rangers hockey team. It is also the site of international horse and dog shows, rock concerts, skating exhibitions, circuses, boxing matches and tennis tournaments. *For tour information, check online at: www.thegarden.com.*

Continue west on W. 33rd St. to Eighth Ave.

General Post Office – *At the corner of Eighth Ave. & 33rd St.* Covering two full blocks, this vast granite structure (James A. Farley Building) was designed in 1908 by McKim, Mead and White as a companion to the original Penn Station and features a colonnade of 20 Corinthian columns, each 53ft high. The cornice bears the well-known inscription "Neither snow nor rain nor heat nor gloom of night stays these couriers from the swift completion of their appointed rounds." It is a rather free translation of the Greek historian Herodotus and, ideally, describes the round-the-clock task of the post office. No longer fully occupied by the Postal Service, the building is expected to serve as the new Penn station after extensive renovation *(projected completion 2008).*

Return to Seventh Ave. and continue north to 34th St.

Macy's – *Bounded by Broadway, Seventh Ave., 34th & 35th Sts.* ☎ *212-695-4400. www.macys.com.* Covering an entire city block, the "world's largest store" consists of two parts: the 1901 classically inspired eastern section and the newer western wing, added in the Art Deco style in 1931. In addition to selling almost every imaginable item—from sensible shoes to gourmet chocolates—Macy's sponsors many seasonal events that have become New York institutions, including the annual spring flower show, Fourth of July fireworks and the renowned Thanksgiving Day parade. During the Christmas season, children may have a personal chat with Santa Claus, a tradition recalling the famous film *Miracle on 34th Street*, in which both Macy's and Kris Kringle had starring roles.

■ 26th Street Flea Market

On Saturday and Sunday, scores of amateur dealers gather in a vacant lot between 26th and 27th streets on the Avenue of the Americas and display an amazing collection of junk, antiques, and odds and ends. One of the city's largest outdoor markets draws an eclectic crowd of both the serious and the barely browsing. Try your luck and look for a silver frame or a vintage hat, but be sure to bargain and check the merchandise before paying.

© Martha Cooper

ADDITIONAL SIGHTS

*★*Jacob K. Javits Convention Center – *655 W. 34th St.* New York's convention center, a low-rise building stretching along the Hudson River from West 34th to West 39th streets, is named for Jacob K. Javits (1904-86), the former US senator from New York. Designed by I.M. Pei & Partners in 1986, the center has 1,800,000sq ft of enclosed space, including two main exhibit halls, more than 100 meeting rooms, and restaurant and service areas; it can accommodate 85,000 persons daily.

Of special architectural interest is the enormous exposed-steel space frame that shapes the main exhibit hall. Some 76,000 tubes, containing tension rods, and 19,000 nodes were used in constructing the space frame, giving it the appearance of an assemblage of gigantic tinker-toy components. Extremely flexible from a structural point of view, the frame serves as beams, walls and roof of the hall and is supported by columns rising 90ft.

Center for Jewish History – *15 W. 16th St. Open year-round Mon–Thu 9am–5pm, Fri 9am–4pm, Sun 11am–5pm. Closed major & Jewish holidays. Yeshiva University Museum open Tue–Thu & Sun 11am–5pm; $6.* ✕ & ☎ *212-294-8301. www.cjh.org.* This facility, the result of the artful merging and reconfiguration of four Chelsea brownstones, opened in 2000. Home to five organizations—the YIVO Institute for Jewish Research, the Yeshiva University Museum, the Leo Baeck Institute, the American Jewish Historical Society and the American Sephardi Federation—the center contains the largest collection of Jewish cultural and historical material outside of Israel. Some 100 million archival documents, manuscripts and photos; 500,000 library volumes; and tens of thousands of artifacts, works of art, and ritual objects are available to scholars and displayed on a rotating basis in the attractive central atrium and in galleries throughout the center. Also on the premises are a reading room, a kosher cafe and a theater. *Call ahead for current exhibitions.*

19 • CENTRAL PARK★★★

Map p 176

A sweeping, rectangular greensward located in the geographical center of Manhattan, Central Park provides a haven of greenery, light and air to the more than 20 million people who flock to the park each year. Covering 843 acres and measuring 2.5mi long by .5mi wide, the man-made park extends from 59th to 110th streets, and Fifth Avenue to Central Park West. Framed by the silhouettes of surrounding buildings, the park offers a quiet oasis in the heart of bustling Manhattan, with many opportunities for recreation.

Historical Notes

An Idea Takes Shape – Foreseeing the need for recreational open spaces in the fast-growing city, the editor and poet **William Cullen Bryant** launched the idea of Central Park in 1850 through a press campaign in his newspaper, the *New York Evening Post*. With the aid of two well-known authors, Washington Irving and George Bancroft, and other public-minded New Yorkers, Bryant urged the city government to acquire a "waste land, ugly and repulsive," located well beyond 42nd Street, which marked the northern border of the city at that time. It was in fact a swamp inhabited by squatters, who raised pigs and goats. After acquiring the land, the city held a competition for the design of the park. The $2,000 prize was awarded to landscape architects **Frederick Law Olmsted** (1822-1903) and **Calvert Vaux** (1824-95). Clearing began in 1857 with a labor force of 3,000 mostly unemployed Irish workers and 400 horses.

In spite of fierce resistance by the squatters who bombarded the workers with stones, the project got underway and proceeded at a steady pace. The workers moved an estimated billion cubic feet of earth, and after 19 years of extensive drainage, planting, road and bridge building and ingenious landscaping, the park emerged essentially as we now know it.

Using nature as their main source of inspiration, Olmsted and Vaux skillfully blended natural and man-made elements to create a park inspired by the "picturesque," or Romantic style that was highly favored in the mid-19C. Sparse vegetation in parts of the park, where the thin layer of top soil barely covers outcropping rocks, accentuates the rugged character of the topography. In the northern part, hills and dales, rocky crags, trees, bushes and shrubs produce a landscape of great scenic beauty. Wide open spaces and meadows, where sheep grazed until 1934, lend other sections a rural charm, unimpaired by asphalt-covered roads. Over 185 acres were set aside by the designers for lakes and ponds. A formal atmosphere prevails at the Mall and in the Conservatory Garden.

A Popular Park – From its beginnings Central Park enjoyed great popularity among New Yorkers. Soon after its completion it became the testing ground for the finest equipages. On sunny afternoons carriages lined up at the park entrance were avidly eyed by the populace. Victorias, broughams, phaetons and barouches carried society ladies, who pitilessly judged the rigs of their rivals.

Visiting Central Park   Area Code: 212

Getting There – There is no parking available in Central Park. Subway lines B & C stop at 59th, 72nd, 81st, 86th, 96th and 103rd Sts. and Cathedral Pkwy. on the west side of the park. Lines 1 & 9 go to 59th St. at Columbus Circle. Lines N & R stop at 57th St. and Fifth Ave. Buses M¹, 2, 3 & 4 run along the eastern edge of the park.

Getting Around – More than 25mi of paved paths wind through the park passing over four transverse roads (65th, 79th, 85th & 97th Sts.). East and West drives are closed to motor traffic on weekends and holidays and certain hours during the week. The first two digits of number plates on lampposts throughout the park indicate which cross street you are nearest.

Safety – Central Park is patrolled by the police and park enforcement patrol rangers in vehicles, on horseback and on skates. Direct-line emergency call boxes are located throughout the park. *Always explore the park during day-light hours and refrain from visiting alone.*

Visitor Information – For information on special events, public programs, sports and recreation facilities, visitors can call ☎ 360-3444 *(recording)* or visit the park Web site *(www.centralparknyc.org)*. Park maps and activity calendars are available at the following visitor centers *(call for seasonal hours)*: **The Dairy** *(65th St; ☎ 794-6564)*, **Belvedere Castle** *(79th St.; ☎ 772-0210)*, **North Meadow Recreation Center** *(97th St.; ☎ 348-4867)* and the **Charles A. Dana Discovery Center** *(110th St. & Fifth Ave.; ☎ 860-1370)*. For additional information, call the Central Park Conservancy *(☎ 310-6600)*.

Recreation – **Running** is the most common sport in the park. The NY Road Runners Club can provide information on races and group runs *(☎ 860-4455; www.nyrrc.org)*. Public sports and recreation facilities include baseball/softball fields converted for soccer/football in fall and winter *(located throughout park; available by permit only; $8; ☎ 408-0209; www.nycparks.com)*; **tennis courts** *(mid-park at 94th & 96th St.; open Apr–Nov; $5/day; ☎ 360-8133)*; and skating rinks. **Ice-skating** lessons and skate rentals are available in season at Wollman Rink *(east side between 62nd & 63rd Sts.; Mon–Fri $8.50, weekends $11; ☎ 439-6900; www.wollmanskatingrink.com)* and at Lasker Rink *(mid-park between 106th & 108th St.; $4.50; ☎ 534-7639)*. **In-line skate** rentals are offered at Wollman Rink for use in the park *($15/day includes safety equipment; $100 security deposit; lessons available; ☎ 396-1010)*. Loeb Boathouse rents **bicycles** *(Mar–Oct daily 10am–7pm; $10–$15/hr; ☎ 517-2233)* and **rowboats** *(Mar–Oct daily 10am–5pm; $10/hr)*; they also offer **gondola rides** *(May–Sept Mon–Fri 5pm–9pm; weekends 2pm–9pm; $30/30min; reservations suggested; ☎ 517-2233)* on the lake. Over 4mi of bridle paths lace the park; **horses** can be rented at Claremont Stables *(175 W. 89th St.; year-round Mon–Fri 6am–10pm, weekends 6am–5pm; $50/hr; English riding proficiency required; ☎ 724-5100)*.

Tours – Free **walking tours** sponsored by the Central Park Conservancy highlight the park's history, design, wildlife and botany *(for schedule, call ☎ 360-2726)*. **Bike tours** combine exercise with exploration *(daily 10am, 1pm & 4pm; $35 includes bike rental & tour guide; ☎ 212-541-8759; www.centralparkbiketour.com)*. **Horse-drawn-carriage rides** are available at Central Park South near the Plaza Hotel and at Tavern on the Green *(year-round daily 24hrs/day unless temperature is below 18°F or above 89°F; 1-4 passengers; $34/per carriage for 20min, $54 for 50min; ☎ 246-0520; www.centralpark.org)*.

Just For Kids – Popular destinations for children include the **Wildlife Center** *(open Apr–Oct daily 10am–5pm; rest of the year 10am–4:30pm; $6 adults, $1 children 3-12; ☎ 439-6500)*, the **carousel** *(open May–Oct daily 10am–6pm, rest of the year weekends only 10am–4:30pm; ☎ 879-0244)*, the **Swedish Cottage Marionette Theatre** *(year-round Tue–Fri 10:30am & noon, Sat 1pm; $6 adults, $5 children; reservations required; ☎ 988-9093)* and the many playgrounds found throughout the park. Natural history exhibits and children's programs are available at **Henry Luce Nature Observatory** *(Belvedere Castle)* and **Charles A. Dana Discovery Center**. Indoor and outdoor activities including wall climbing, challenge courses and adventure programs for youth are offered year-round at **North Meadow Recreation Center** *(mid-park at 97th St.; ☎ 348-4867)*. **Summer** activities include swimming at Lasker Pool *(daily 11am–3pm & 4pm–7pm)*, the catch-and-release fishing at Harlem Meer *(bamboo poles and bait available at the Dana Discovery Center)* and storytelling sessions at the Hans Christian Andersen statue.

Special events – Free entertainment in summer includes the popular **Shakespeare in the Park** festival, Metropolitan Opera performances, New York Philharmonic concerts, **SummerStage** *(www.summerstage.org)* popular music concerts and a variety of light entertainment.

Trotters too were in great favor, and they whipped through the park to the speedways of Harlem. In 1875 it became fashionable for gentlemen to drive their own four-in-hands. A year later Leonard Jerome, the maternal grandfather of Sir Winston Churchill, founded the select Coaching Club together with the financier and sportsman August Belmont. Bicycle riding, which became popular in the 1890s, was denounced as unbecoming for young ladies because it encouraged undue freedom of dress and movement. However, the trend was too strong to resist, and before long the curved paths of Central Park were teeming with cycling women.

In the early 1930s Central Park served as a camping ground for victims of the Great Depression. The emptied reservoir sheltered a "Hooverville"—a cluster of shanties. Following several decades of peace and prosperity, the city entered the "flower child" era of the 1960s, and the park became a gathering place for the counterculture and a haunt of hustlers and drug dealers. Owing mainly to a shortage of city funds, the park gradually fell into a state of neglect. In 1980 a private nonprofit organization, the Central Park Conservancy, was created to launch a large-scale renovation effort. Contracted by the City of New York, the conservancy has raised more than $300 million to renovate the park and return its green space to their former splendor.

VISIT

Enter Central Park South at Fifth Ave. and 60th St. from Grand Army Plaza.

As you approach the Scholars' Gate from Grand Army Plaza, note the bronze sculpture titled *Standing Figure* (1984) by Willem de Kooning near the park entrance.

Walk north to the entrance of the Wildlife Center.

Just before the Wildlife Center, pause and look west to glimpse Wollman Memorial Rink, a popular spot for ice-skating in winter and in-line skating in summer. To the south a crescent-shaped **pond**, surrounded by luxuriant vegetation, borders the bird sanctuary situated atop a rocky outcrop.

Enter the Wildlife Center.

★**Central Park Wildlife Center** – 🄺🄳🄱 *East side between 63rd & 66th Sts. Map available at entrance. Open Apr–Oct Mon–Fri 10am–5pm, weekends & holidays 10am–5:30pm. Rest of the year daily 10am–4:30pm. $6 (includes admission to children's zoo).* ✗ ⚹ ☎ *212-439-6500. www.centralparknyc.org.* Occupying 5.5 acres, this zoo houses more than 450 animals of 100 species in a newly renovated naturalistic habitat that represents three distinct climatic regions: the tropical zone, the temperate regions and the polar circle.

Following a $6 million renovation, the **Children's Zoo** reopened in the summer of 1997 and features domesticated animals *(feed available for purchase)* and some wildlife. Be sure to see the Delacorte Clock over the entrance arch, with its moving bronze animal figures holding musical instruments *(figures rotate on the hour and half hour 8am–6pm)*.

On the Fifth Avenue side of the zoo stands a severe, massive building in gray stone and red brick. Built in the 1840s in the Gothic Revival style, the Arsenal of the State of New York now serves as the headquarters of the New York City Parks and Recreation Department.

Exit the children's zoo at the north end and walk under 65th St. Bear left at the fork, then left again to take the wide steps to cross East Dr. Enter the southern end of the Mall at the statue of Shakespeare.

---

1 **Tavern on the Green**

Map p 176. West side of Central Park at W. 67th St. ☎ *212-873-3200. www.tavernonthegreen.com.* The famed tavern is a perfect Sunday brunch spot (be sure to reserve), with stained-glass windows, sand-carved mirrors and glittering crystal chandeliers to brighten even the gloomiest day. Weather permitting, head for the outdoor cafe, lit by thousands of colored lights strung through the branches, and enjoy the view of the park. The site of innumerable film and television scenes, this restaurant also serves as the finish line for the New York Marathon.

Courtesy NYC & Co.

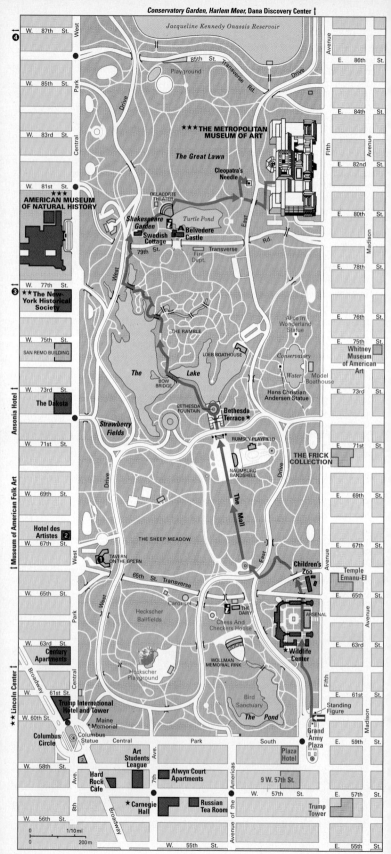

Jacqueline Kennedy Onassis Reservoir

4 W. 87th St. West

W. 85th St.

85th St. Transverse Rd.

Playground

W. 83rd St. Central

E. 86th St.

E. 84th St.

★★★ THE METROPOLITAN MUSEUM OF ART

The Great Lawn

Fifth Avenue

E. 82nd St.

Cleopatra's Needle

W. 81st St.

★★★ AMERICAN MUSEUM OF NATURAL HISTORY

DELACORTE THEATER

Turtle Pond

E. 80th St.

Shakespeare Garden

Swedish Cottage

Belvedere Castle

79th St.

Transverse

Fire Dept.

E. 78th St.

Madison

West

Transverse Rd.

3 W. 77th St.

★★ The New-York Historical Society

E. 76th St.

W. 75th St.

SAN REMO BUILDING

THE RAMBLE

Alice In Wonderland Statue

E. 75th St.

Whitney Museum of American Art

LOEB BOATHOUSE

Conservatory

Ansonia Hotel

W. 73rd St.

The Dakota

The Lake

BOW BRIDGE

Water

Model Boathouse

Hans Christian Andersen Statue

E. 73rd St.

W. 71st St.

Strawberry Fields

BETHESDA FOUNTAIN

Bethesda Terrace ★

RUMSEY PLAYFIELD

THE FRICK COLLECTION

E. 71st St.

Museum of American Folk Art

Drive

NAUMBURG BANDSHELL

E. 69th St.

W. 69th St.

Hotel des Artistes **2**

W. 67th St.

THE SHEEP MEADOW

The Mall

E. 67th St.

Temple Emanu-El

1 TAVERN ON THE GREEN

West

E. 65th St.

W. 65th St.

65th St. Transverse

Children's Zoo

Carousel

THE DAIRY

ARSENAL

E. 65th St.

W. 63rd St.

Century Apartments

Heckscher Ballfields

Chess And Checkers House

★ Wildlife Center

E. 63rd St.

Avenue

Lincoln Center

W. 61st St.

Heckscher Playground

WOLLMAN MEMORIAL RINK

Broadway

Trump International Hotel and Tower

Bird Sanctuary

The Pond

E. 61st St.

Standing Figure

Madison

W. 60th St.

Maine Memorial

Columbus Circle

Columbus Statue

Central

Park

South

Grand Army Plaza

E. 59th St.

W. 58th St.

Art Students League

Ave.

Plaza Hotel

Americas

Hard Rock Cafe

7th

Alwyn Court Apartments

9 W. 57th St.

W. 57th St.

E. 57th St.

W. 56th St.

8th

★ Carnegie Hall

Russian Tea Room

Avenue of the Americas

Trump Tower

W. 55th St.

E. 55th St.

0 1/10mi
0 200m

The Mall – One of the few formal areas in the park, the Mall consists of a straight, wide path lined with handsome elms and sculptures depicting famous writers. At the north end of the Mall is the small Naumburg Bandshell, once a popular concert site and now unused. Summer evening concerts are performed at the Rumsey Playfield, east of the band shell. (Occasionally, large public-benefit concerts and rallies take place on the Great Lawn, behind the Metropolitan Museum of Art.) Lying to the west of the Mall, the Sheep Meadow attracts throngs of people to its rolling hills, which also offer superb views of the city skyline.

Located to the far west of the Sheep Meadow, near the West 66th Street entrance, stands the renowned restaurant, Tavern on the Green, housed in a former sheep barn (1870).

From the Mall, take the steps down to Bethesda Terrace.

★**Bethesda Terrace** – Considered the centerpiece of the park, this lovely sandstone plaza resembles a Spanish courtyard with its arcaded bridge adorned with ornate marble panels, Minton ceiling tiles *(under restoration)*, sweeping stairs and central fountain. Crowning the fountain is a statue by Emma Stebbins titled *Angel of the Waters* (1868).

From the fountain, take the pathway to the left.

The Lake – Steps, banks and irregular shores make the lake seem almost transplanted from some far-off mountains. Located a short distance from Bethesda Fountain, Bow Bridge—a graceful iron bridge—has been reproduced innumerable times in engravings and photographs.

To the west lie the **Strawberry Fields** and the International Garden of Peace honoring the late musician John Lennon, a member of the Beatles. The three-acre garden, containing 161 species of plants representing the various nations of the world, is steps away from New York's first luxury apartment house, the Dakota, where Lennon lived and was murdered.

Bordering the lake to the east is the Loeb Boathouse, a popular eating spot in summer. Between the lake and Fifth Avenue, Conservatory Water attracts young mariners with model sailboats. North of the lake, the Ramble is a heavily wooded hill interrupted by a meandering brook and crisscrossed by hidden paths that seem to wind aimlessly.

Enter the Ramble. To reduce your chances of getting lost, stay on paths on the west side of the Ramble, keeping the lake waters in view as much as possible. You will cross two bridges before you reach West Dr. Then turn northward on West Dr.

Swedish Cottage – 🧒 A model of a Swedish schoolhouse, this delightful log structure was fabricated abroad and shipped to the US in sections. Erected in Central Park in 1877, the cottage was renovated in 1998 and now serves as home to the **Marionette Theatre**, which presents puppet shows throughout the year *(p 174 for hours & admission)*.

Take a moment to wander the paths of the **Shakespeare Garden**, located adjacent to the cottage. Here can be found several species of flowers, herbs, trees and shrubs mentioned in the works of the Bard. Small plaques display quotes from the playwright pertinent to a garden setting; spacious benches offer visitors rest and refreshment.

Proceed up the stairs to Belvedere Castle.

Henry Luce Nature Observatory (A) – 🧒 *In Belvedere Castle. Open year-round Tue–Sun 10am–5pm. Closed major holidays.* ☎ *212-772-0210. www.central-parknyc.org.* Opened in May 1996, this nature education center hosts hands-on exhibits on the city's flora and fauna. It occupies two floors of the **Belvedere Castle**, an imitation medieval Scottish castle (1872) complete with merlons and crenels, created by Vaux. Don't miss the tree loft with its papier-mâché reproductions of birds found in Central Park. From its site atop Vista Rock, the castle overlooks the entire northern part of the park, affording good views of the park and neighboring parts of the city. From the observatory, a Naturalists' Walk points out geologic features as it winds its way to the American Museum of Natural History.

Just north of Belvedere Castle lie Turtle Pond and the Delacorte Theater. Beyond, the **Great Lawn** occupies the site of the Receiving Reservoir, dug in 1862 to supply the city water system. Today it is best known as the setting for performances by such artists as Elton John and Pavarotti.

From Belvedere Castle walk northeast toward the Metropolitan Museum, whose massive silhouette appears through the

 Café des Artistes

Map p 176. 1 W. 67th St. ☎ *212-877-3500. Jacket required at dinner.* With one of the city's most romantic interiors and fashionable addresses (it's on the ground floor of the legendary Hotel des Artistes), this elegant restaurant caters to the well-heeled and the famous. Designed by Howard Chandler Christy in 1934, the murals of female nudes are a must-see, as are the many celebrities who drop in regularly. Spare your wallet and stop by just for the lavish desserts—you won't regret it.

Exercising in Central Park

trees. Just before reaching the museum, note **Cleopatra's Needle**, a 77ft pink-granite obelisk (16C BC) from Heliopolis, given to the City of New York in 1880 by the Khedive Ismael Pasha. Translated hieroglyphs tell the story of Pharaoh Thutmose III.

ADDITIONAL SIGHTS

North of 96th Street lies the Upper Park, long considered foreboding and unsafe. In recent years, numerous improvements and upgraded security have contributed to a renewal of this section of the park. Just south of 96th Street, the 107-acre Jacqueline Kennedy Onassis Reservoir is rimmed by a popular running track and a bridle path.

Conservatory Garden – *Enter at E. 103rd St., opposite El Museo del Barrio.* Step into Central Park's only formal garden through the ornate wrought-iron Vanderbilt Gate (1894), crafted in Paris for the Vanderbilt Mansion on Fifth Avenue. Created in 1936, the six-acre garden soon gained enormous popularity, especially as a spot for weddings. A 12-year restoration project gave it its present luster. Opposite the entrance is the half-acre Central Garden, flanked by two crab apple alleys and ending in a wisteria pergola. The South Garden, known as "The Secret Garden" after Frances Hodgson Burnett's children's classic, is graced with 175 varieties of perennials. The French-style North Garden features two dazzling annual displays—20,000 spring tulips and 5,000 chrysanthemums in fall.

Harlem Meer – *E. 110th St. at Fifth Ave.* Once a beautiful lake with coves and inlets, Harlem Meer (Dutch for "lake") was surrounded by a concrete rim in the 1940s and almost abandoned. In recent years the 11-acre lake was dredged and is now well stocked with largemouth bass and bluegills. Lasker Pool and Skating Rink (1964) mark the lake's west end. Located at the north end of the Meer, **Charles A. Dana Discovery Center** Kids features nature exhibits and serves as a starting point for exploring the park's northern end.

MUSEUMS *(See Museums section)*

★★★**American Museum of Natural History** – *Central Park West between W. 77th & W. 81st Sts.*

★★★**The Frick Collection** – *5th Ave. at E. 70th St.*

★★★**Metropolitan Museum of Art** – *Fifth Ave. at E. 82nd St.*

★★**Guggenheim Museum** – *1071 Fifth Ave.*

★★**Museum of the City of New York** – *Fifth Ave. at 103rd St.*

★★**The New-York Historical Society** – *2 W. 77th St. at Central Park West.*

★**Cooper-Hewitt National Design Museum** – *2 E. 91st St.*

★**Jewish Museum** – *1109 Fifth Ave.*

★**Neue Galerie** – *1048 Fifth Ave., at 86th St*

20 • UPPER EAST SIDE★★

Known primarily as an enclave for the wealthy and fashionable, the area between Central Park and the East River, stretching from 59th Street to 97th Street, actually represents a broad cross section of New York neighborhoods. In the most desirable areas near the park, you'll find some of the city's great museums and an impressive concentration of galleries, along with elegant shops, restaurants, clubs and residences. East of Lexington Avenue, the atmosphere becomes more casual. Here, modern high rises dominate, sharing space with a variety of delis, bars, pizza joints and parking garages.

Historical Notes

Dotted with squatters' shanties and a few farms, the East Side remained largely rural until the 19C. One of the first sections to be developed was **Yorkville**, a hamlet just south of Harlem centering on present-day 86th Street, east of Lexington Avenue. Several prominent families of German descent, including the Schermerhorns, Astors and Rhinelanders, built country estates here in the late 18C. Along with its **Carnegie Hill** neighbor to the west *(between 86th and 96th Sts., east of Fifth Ave.)*, Yorkville soon became a suburb for middle-class Germans, many of whom worked in nearby piano factories and breweries.

New horsecar lines established on Madison, Second and Third avenues in the 1860s spurred development south of 86th Street after the Civil War. By the 1880s speculative builders had lined the streets with rows of brownstones. Churches, synagogues, armories and charitable institutions soon followed.

Attracted by large lots on and near Fifth Avenue, New York's high society also continued the migration uptown, gradually extending "Millionaires' Row" northward with lavish mansions and club buildings. The boldest, Andrew Carnegie, purchased land in the remote area of East 90th Street and Fifth Avenue in 1898. Other prominent financiers, including Otto Kahn, bought land from Carnegie north of 90th Street, while Mrs. Caroline Astor, the Goulds and the Whitneys built homes down between 60th

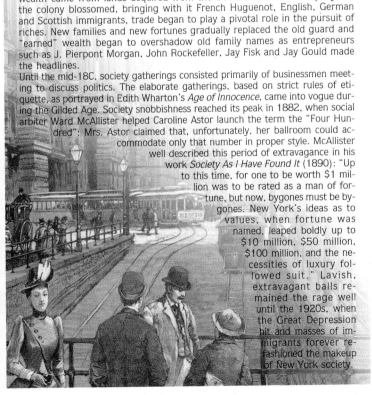

New York Society

Early New York society revolved around established Dutch families whose wealth came from lands acquired from the Dutch East India Company. As the colony blossomed, bringing with it French Huguenot, English, German and Scottish immigrants, trade began to play a pivotal role in the pursuit of riches. New families and new fortunes gradually replaced the old guard and "earned" wealth began to overshadow old family names as entrepreneurs such as J. Pierpont Morgan, John Rockefeller, Jay Fisk and Jay Gould made the headlines.

Until the mid-18C, society gatherings consisted primarily of businessmen meeting to discuss politics. The elaborate gatherings, based on strict rules of etiquette, as portrayed in Edith Wharton's *Age of Innocence*, came into vogue during the Gilded Age. Society snobbishness reached its peak in 1882, when social arbiter Ward McAllister helped Caroline Astor launch the term the "Four Hundred"; Mrs. Astor claimed that, unfortunately, her ballroom could accommodate only that number in proper style. McAllister well described this period of extravagance in his work *Society As I Have Found It* (1890): "Up to this time, for one to be worth $1 million was to be rated as a man of fortune, but now, bygones must be bygones. New York's ideas as to values, when fortune was named, leaped boldly up to $10 million, $50 million, $100 million, and the necessities of luxury followed suit." Lavish, extravagant balls remained the rage well until the 1920s, when the Great Depression hit and masses of immigrants forever refashioned the makeup of New York society.

and 80th streets. In the 1920s stylish apartment buildings replaced many of the town houses. Over the years the posh East Side neighborhoods have continued to attract celebrities—Greta Garbo, Andy Warhol, Richard Nixon and Woody Allen among them—as well as old New York families and young Wall Streeters. Perhaps most changed is the Yorkville region, which has lost much of its old European flavor. Most of the area's German residents, along with Hungarians and Czechs who arrived in the mid-1900s, have been replaced by an influx of young urban professionals.

Today the Upper East Side is synonymous with wealth and culture; an air of luxury and refinement prevails throughout the neighborhood. A stroll along its great avenues—Fifth, Park, Madison and Lexington—and quiet side streets reveals a rich assemblage of elegant homes, exclusive galleries, European-style boutiques and trendy eateries.

★★FIFTH AVENUE

Sights on the following avenues are described from south to north.

The section of Fifth Avenue bordering Central Park has long been New York's most prestigious residential area. Luxury apartments abut former mansions, most of which have now become museums, consulates, clubs or cultural institutions.

Surrounded by distinguished hotels, **Grand Army Plaza★★**, a large and flowered square, marks the division between Fifth Avenue's luxury shopping area and its residential section. Highlighting the plaza is the **Pulitzer Fountain** (1915) with its gracefully cascading waters. Just to the north, the statue of Gen. William Tecumseh Sherman on horseback (1903, Augustus Saint-Gaudens).

The **Plaza Hotel★** (1907), designed by Henry J. Hardenbergh in the French Renaissance style, is a New York institution of elegance and standing where coming-out parties and charity balls draw the cream of New York society. Nearly as celebrated as the Plaza, the Hotel Savoy stood across the square until 1966, when it was replaced by the General Motors Building. Across 59th Street stands the Sherry-Netherland Hotel (1927), its graceful tower overlooking the park. The south corner of 61st Street is dominated by the Hotel Pierre (1930), the last of the grand hotels erected around the plaza.

At the corner with 62nd Street rises 810 Fifth Avenue, former home of such famous personalities as William Randolph Hearst, Richard Nixon and Nelson Rockefeller. On the south corner of 64th Street, note the Tuscan Renaissance mansion built in 1896 for the coal baron Edward J. Berwind. On the same street, at 3 East 64th Street, is the **New India House**, headquarters of the Consulate of India and the Indian delegation to the United Nations. Built in 1903 by Warren and Wetmore (architects of Grand Central Terminal) as a private residence for Mrs. Caroline Astor's daughter

Jacqueline
Kennedy Onassis
Reservoir

National Academy
Museum
★★ Solomon R.
Guggenheim
Museum

Museum Mile

E. 88th St.
E. 87th St.

★★★ THE METROPOLITAN
MUSEUM OF ART

Neue Galerie ★

E. 86th St.

Avenue

E. 85th St.

E. 84th St.

998

E. 83rd St.

CAMPBELL FUNERAL CHAPEL

CENTRAL PARK

E. 82nd St.

Ukrainian Institute of America

Avenue

E. 81st St.

972

NYU Institute of Fine Arts

E. 80th St.

Park

Harkness House

in Wonderland
Statue

vatory

E. 79th St.

Carlyle Hotel

E. 78th St.

Avenue

E. 77th St.

E. 76th St.

★ Madison

French
Consulate

Whitney Museum of
American Art ★★

E. 75th St.

GERTRUDE RHINELANDER
WALDO HOUSE

E. 74th St.

St. Jean Baptiste

E. 73rd St.

❶

Asia Society
and Museum ★

E. 72nd St.

Lexington Avenue

E. 71st St.

Third Ave.

E. 70th St.

nter
College

147-149

Carl Schurz Park / Islamic Cultural Center /

0   1/10mi
0   150m

Carrie, its exterior features a
lavish entranceway, tall second-
story windows and a dormered
mansard roof.

Located on the site of Mrs. Astor's
former mansion, **Temple Emanu-El★**
(1 E. 65th St.) was completed in 1929 in
the Byzantine Romanesque style. It is the leading Reform synagogue in New York and the
largest in the world. The majestic main sanctuary,
rising to 103ft, can welcome 2,500 worshipers. The
ceiling, the marble columns in low relief and the great
arch covered with mosaics are reminiscent of the basilicas
of the Near East. The sanctuary harbors the Holy Ark, which
contains the Torah scrolls *(call for hours:* ☎ *212-744-1400;
www.emanuelnyc.org).*

Occupying the block between 70th and 71st streets, Henry C. Frick's
former mansion, surrounded by terraced flower beds, now houses a
world-class assemblage of Old Masters (the Frick Collection).

At the corner with 75th Street, an attractive wrought-iron fence protects
Harkness House (1900), an Italian-style palace built for Edward S. Harkness, son
of a partner of John D. Rockefeller. Today Harkness House serves as headquarters of the Commonwealth Fund, a philanthropic foundation.

The renowned **New York University Institute of Fine Arts** *(1 E. 78th St.)*, a division of New York University, is located in the James B. Duke House (1912), built for one of the founders of the American Tobacco Company. Architect Horace Trumbauer's Neoclassical design for the house was modeled after a Louis XV-style chateau in Bordeaux. Duke's wife donated the splendid mansion to New York University in 1957. The institute offers graduate courses in art, architecture, conservation and museum curating.

The cultural and press services of the French consulate are housed in the former Payne Whitney home *(no. 972 Fifth Ave.)*, designed by McKim, Mead and White in 1906. The turreted mansion on the southeast corner of 79th Street, the former Stuyvesant Fish house, now serves as the home of the **Ukrainian Institute of America**.

Looking north up Fifth Avenue

On the northeast corner of 80th Street is one of the first and most luxurious apartment houses erected on Fifth Avenue—**no. 998**. Completed in 1914 by McKim, Mead and White, the Renaissance-style building attracted a wealthy clientele and inspired the creation of countless similar structures on Fifth, Madison and Park avenues. Dominating the Central Park side of Fifth Avenue between 80th and 84th streets is the imposing facade of the Metropolitan Museum of Art.

★MADISON AVENUE

Lined with exclusive stores, galleries and haute couture boutiques, this is a street for moneyed shoppers, where the pedestrians often look as chic as the window displays. Most of the small designer boutiques are concentrated south of 79th Street, but the stretch north to 96th Street, with its neighborhood bookstores, shops and trendy bistros, also has great appeal.

Many of the fine brownstones that made the avenue a choice residential district in the late 19C remain, now remodeled with stylish storefronts at street level. Several early prestigious apartment buildings and apartment hotels, including the 1929 **Carlyle Hotel** *(35 E. 76th St.)*, also enhance the street's genteel character. Note the 1895 French Renaissance Gertrude Rhinelander Waldo house *(no. 867)*, built for an eccentric dowager who never lived in it; the mansion now houses Polo Ralph Lauren.

The rich and famous not only come to Madison to shop, but some—including Tennessee Williams, Judy Garland, John Lennon and Arturo Toscanini—have even passed on to their next lives by way of the prestigious Frank E. Campbell Funeral Chapel, located at 81st Street. At no. 945 stands the renowned Whitney Museum of American Art.

 Madison Avenue Shopping

Map p 181. Madison Avenue between 72nd and 59th streets has become synonymous with designer boutiques and glamorous shops. The Polo look is alive and kicking at **Polo Ralph Lauren** *(867 Madison Ave.; ☎ 212-606-2100; www.polo.com)*. Interested in European couture? Try **Emanuel Ungaro** *(792 Madison Ave.; ☎ 212-249-4090)*, **Valentino** *(747 Madison Ave.; ☎ 212-772-6969; www.valentino.it)* or **Giorgio Armani** *(760 Madison Ave.; ☎ 212-988-9191; www.giorgioarmani.com)*—the ready-to-wear selections are appealing if not always affordable. Farther south you'll find **Barneys**, a nine-story fashion emporium specializing in designs for men and women *(660 Madison Ave.; ☎ 212-826-8900; www.barneys.com)*. American icon **Calvin Klein** sells his popular clothing as well as home furnishings at this uptown location *(654 Madison Ave.; ☎ 212-292-9000)*.

★PARK AVENUE

A meticulously landscaped mall and dignified apartment houses define this European-style boulevard, originally called Fourth Avenue. Although the two-way street is now a highly coveted address, the first occupants were not society members, but hospitals and educational institutions that took advantage of the inexpensive land adjacent to the Fourth Avenue railroad tracks *(p 103)* in the 1870s and 1880s. Among these was the Normal College for Women at 68th Street, founded in 1870 to train teachers and renamed **Hunter College** in 1914. When New York Central Railroad covered the tracks as far north as 96th Street early in the century, Park Avenue was born. It quickly became fashionable and prosperous as New Yorkers erected grand residences there. The splendid block of Georgian buildings on the west side between 68th and 69th streets *(nos. 680-686)* provides some notable examples: all four structures were built as private homes between 1909 and 1926 and now contain diplomatic or cultural institutions.

The area is home to many respected organizations, including the **Grolier Club** *(47 E. 60th St.)*, founded in 1884 and named for 16C French bibliophile Jean Grolier. The 90,000 volumes of this private library are for scholars only, but the club regularly mounts public shows relating to the book arts in the first-floor exhibit hall *(open Sept–Jul Mon–Sat 10am–5pm;* ♿ ☎ *212-838-6690; www.grolierclub.org).* The stately brick town house at 125 East 65th Street serves as headquarters for the **China Institute**, which offers a broad range of classes, public lectures and changing exhibits about China. The first-floor galleries are open to the public *(year-round Mon–Sat 10am–5pm; closed major holidays; $5;* ☎ *212-744-8181; www.chinainstitute.org).*

Designed by Charles W. Clinton, the monumental fortress occupying the block between 66th and 67th streets houses the **Seventh Regiment Armory** (1877), headquarters of the New York National Guard.

LEXINGTON AVENUE

With its mix of apartment houses, brownstones, coffee shops and bookstores, this busy thoroughfare has a neighborhood feel and a pleasant scale unbroken by high-rise buildings. A famous landmark is the Art Deco-style **Bloomingdale's** department store at 59th Street. Here, high fashion applies not only to clothes but to all the merchandise, from designer bonbons to trendy shower curtains.

Located at no. 869, the **Church of St. Vincent Ferrer** *(open year-round daily 7:30am–6:30pm; holidays 7:30am–3pm; guided tours available;* ♿ ☎ *212-744-2080),* designed by Bertram Goodhue and completed in 1918 for the Dominican order, features a lovely rose window dominating the granite facade adorned with carvings by Lee Lawrie. Note also the 1880 Victorian Gothic priory just to the south.

At East 76th Street and Lexington rises the imposing Roman Catholic **St. Jean Baptiste Church** *(open year-round Mon–Fri 7:30am–6:30pm, weekends 8am–6:30pm;* ☎ *212-288-5082),* founded by French Canadians in 1913. Its gold-leaf interior contains a handsome altar.

---

① Payard Patisserie & Bistro
Map p 181. 1032 Lexington Ave. ☎ *212-717-5252. www.payard.com.* A most welcome respite for that badly needed, mid-shopping-spree jolt, this classy French bistro boasts superb pastries, handmade chocolates, contemporary bistro fare (bouillabaisse, homemade foie gras), plus delicious coffees and teas. Open for breakfast, lunch and dinner, including afternoon tea *(Mon–Sat).*

● Fauchon
1383 Third Ave. at 78th St.; ☎ *212-517-9600. www.fauchon.com.* Legendary French food emporium and gourmand's delight, Fauchon recently opened its third outlet on Manhattan's fashionable Upper East Side. Among its 1,200 offerings, you'll find such unique items at pâté de legumes intensely flavored with beets, red peppers, fennel or carrots; lemon-basil or chocolate dulce de leche sorbets; and cognac marrons glacés. And then there's the 98 different varieties of preserves, not to mention preserved duck à l'orange, and goose, duck or Sichuan-peppercorn foie gras. Everything, including flaky croissants, decadent bonbons and mouthwatering pastries, can be packaged to go. You'll find other locations at 424 Park Ave. at 56th St. *(☎ 212-308-5919)* and 1000 Madison Ave. at 77th St. *(☎ 212-570-2211).*

ADDITIONAL SIGHTS

Islamic Cultural Center of New York – *1711 Third Ave. at 96th St. Open by ap pointment only.* & ☎ *212-722-5234. Women are requested to cover their heads with a scarf and wear long sleeves.* Completed in 1991 from designs by Skidmore, Owings & Merrill, this pink-marble center for Muslim worship is the first major mosque built in New York City. The two-story domed prayer hall, where light streams through a curtain wall of windows distinguished with Eastern motifs, is particularly stunning. Designed to serve the city's 400,000 Muslims, the mosque is flanked by a 12-story minaret, from which the faithful are called to prayer.

Kitchen Arts & Letters
435 Lexington Ave.; ☎ *212-876-5550.* An intriguing little spot, **Kitchen Arts & Letters** only stocks books on food and wine—some 12,000 titles ranging from traditional recipe compilations to out-of-print rarities, antique food advertisements and cooking memorabilia.

Carl Schurz Park – *Located along East End Ave. from 84th to 90th Sts.* This appealing sliver of green, completed in 1891 and remodeled in 1938, stretches along East End Avenue, capturing fine East River views from the promenade. It is named for a famous 19C German immigrant who served as US senator and as secretary of the Interior under President Hayes and who lived nearby in Yorkville. At the northern end stands Gracie Mansion, official residence of New York's mayor. Fronting the park across East End Avenue at 86th Street is the **Henderson Place Historic District**, comprising 24 turreted houses (1881) designed in the Queen Anne style.

Roosevelt Island – *Access by subway (**MTA** S train from 63rd St. & Lexington) or tramway: departs from Second Ave. and 59th St., year-round daily 6am–2am (weekends 3:30am) every 15min. $1.50 one-way.* & ☎ *212-832-4543. www.rioc.com. A walking-tour map (25¢) is available at the tram booth in Manhattan. The island is also accessible by car from the borough of Queens across the bridge at 36th Ave. Because vehicular traffic is restricted on the island, all cars are required to park at the Motorgate Garage, just across the bridge on the island or on Main St. From there, visitors can take a minibus to the center of the island.* Roosevelt Island is located in the East River, 300 yards off the shore of Manhattan. Formerly the site of various public health facilities, and therefore known as "Welfare Island," it is now the home of a residential "town-in-town" built by the New York State Urban Development Corp. in the 1970s. Politically a part of the borough of Manhattan, the island is 2.5mi long and 800ft wide at its broadest point, encompassing 147 acres. It is linked to Manhattan by bridge, by subway, and by an aerial tramway that provides a 4min ride across the East River with views in each direction.

The buildings in the first phase of the Roosevelt Island Community—designed by the noted architectural firms Johanson & Bhavnani and Sert, Jackson and Assocs.—were based on a master plan by Philip Johnson and John Burgee, while Gruzen Sampton Steinglass conceived the Manhattan Park complex, containing 1,108 units. Southtown, a development of 2,000 units near the island's tramport, began construction in 2001. The community includes mixed-income housing, retail shops, schools, two city hospitals, parks and other recreational facilities. Several of the island's landmarks have been restored, including the **Chapel of the Good Shepherd**, erected in 1889; the **Blackwell Farm House** (1796), one of the oldest farmhouses still standing in New York City; and the **Lighthouse**, built in 1782 under the supervision of James Renwick. Octagon Tower, the remains of the New York City Lunatic Asylum, the city's first mental health institution, is currently being restored. A waterfront promenade on both sides of the community affords wonderful views of river traffic and the Manhattan skyline.

MUSEUMS *(See Museums section)*

Fifth Avenue between 70th and 103rd streets is known as **Museum Mile**.

★★**Whitney Museum of American Art** – *945 Madison Ave.*

★**Asia Society and Museum** – *725 Park Ave.*

★★★**Frick Collection** – *1 E. 70th St.*

★★★**Metropolitan Museum of Art** – *Fifth Ave. at E. 82nd St.*

★★**Museum of the City of New York** – *Fifth Ave. at 103rd St.*

★★**Solomon R. Guggenheim Museum** – *1071 Fifth Ave.*

★**Cooper-Hewitt National Design Museum** – *2 E. 91st St.*

★**Neue Galerie** – *1048 Fifth Ave., at 86th St.*

★**Jewish Museum** – *1109 Fifth Ave.*

El Museo del Barrio – *1230 Fifth Ave.*

National Academy of Design Museum – *1083 Fifth Ave.*

This ethnically diverse area reaching northward from Columbus Circle to West 125th Street between the Hudson River and Central Park is home to many of the city's great cultural institutions, including Lincoln Center, Columbia University and the American Museum of Natural History. Relatively free of modern high-rise development, it also boasts numerous historic districts and some of the most harmonious blocks of row-house architecture in Manhattan.

Historical Notes

From Wasteland to Wealth – In the late 19C, development reached the rural area of Bloomingdale, dotted with shantytowns and saloons and populated by stray goats, when New York's first luxury apartment house was erected on West 72nd Street and Central Park West in 1884. Even then, the building was considered to be so far out west in the middle of nowhere that it was dubbed the "Dakota."

From the late 1880s onward, middle-class tenements and flats began to appear along Amsterdam and Columbus avenues, with stylish row houses lining the cross streets. In the 1890s the area also gained numerous studio buildings designed specifically for artists, along with another late-19C innovation: **apartment hotels**. These featured fancy suites with parlors, dining rooms, bedrooms and baths, but no kitchens; residents brought meals up from a main kitchen via a dumbwaiter or ate downstairs in the main dining room.

The fine residences of the West Side were home to bankers, lawyers and other well-to-do professionals. After the 1930s, prosperous Jewish families began arriving from the Lower East Side. In the 1960s low rents in the old tenement buildings attracted

3 Food Markets

Map p 176. The Upper West Side is renowned for its purveyors of special-ty foods. Among the most celebrated is **Zabar's** *(2245 Broadway; ☎ 212-787-2000; www.zabars.com)*, which features a stupendous selection of unusual food from around the globe as well as a fine selection of cookware. Zabar's has come a long way since its beginnings as a Jewish deli: today the store sells more than 1,000lbs of smoked salmon per week. The adjoining cafe may look plain, but it serves one of the best cappuccinos in town. Across the street is **H&H Bagels** *(2239 Broadway; ☎ 212-595-8003; www.hhbagels.com)*, which receives FedEx orders from around the globe and churns out more than 50,000 bagels a day. For a wonderful selection of fresh produce, stop by **Fairway Fruits and Vegetables** *(2127 Broadway; ☎ 212-595-1888; www.fairwaymarket.com)*; the supply of mushrooms alone is worth the trip. **Citarella** *(2135 Broadway; ☎ 212-874-0383; www.citarella.com)* features a variety of seafood salads for take-out as well as an outstanding range of fish.

Zabar's is a feast for the senses

© Brigitta L. House/MICHELIN

an element of bohemia, while urban renewal projects brought further diversity to the area. Recent gentrification of the older row houses has made the cross streets quite desirable, particularly among young professionals drawn to the area by the friendly neighborhoods.

The tree-lined residential blocks provide a quiet contrast to the bustle of Broadway, the area's commercial spine, which features everything from discount shoe stores to gourmet food shops.

Famous Buildings and Famous Residents – Some of New York's best-known apartment buildings are found on the West Side and have long attracted a famous clientele. At 1 West 72nd Street stands the 1884 **Dakota**, whose ornate finials and Gothic gables made it a suitable setting for the film *Rosemary's Baby* (1968, Roman Polanski). The work of Henry Hardenbergh, who also created the Plaza Hotel, it contains apartments with as many as 20 rooms. Well-known residents have included Leonard Bernstein, Lauren Bacall and John Lennon, who was killed just outside the 72nd Street entrance in 1980.

Dominating the Central Park West skyline are the twin-towered 1931 **Century Apartments** *(no. 25)*, a superb Art Deco design by Irwin Chanin, and the elegant San Remo *(nos. 145-146)*, home to Dustin Hoffman, Paul Simon and Diane Keaton. Featuring one of the first drive-in courtyards in the city, the ornate 1904 **Ansonia Hotel** *(2101-2119 Broadway)* was a fashionable apartment hotel that attracted residents such as Babe Ruth and Arturo Toscanini. Norman Rockwell, Rudolf Valentino and Noel Coward, in turn, all lived at the popular **Hotel des Artistes** *(1 W. 67th St.)*, erected in 1907. Its duplex studio spaces are lit by huge two-story windows.

SIGHTS

The far-flung sights described below do not lend themselves to a walking tour; begin by visiting the Lincoln Center area, then head north to the Cathedral of St. John the Divine and Columbia University. End your day with a stroll along Columbus or Amsterdam Avenue. Both thoroughfares have enjoyed a renaissance as lively districts for shops and nightspots, in particular the stretches below 86th Street.

Not as elegant as its counterpart across Central Park, the Upper West Side nevertheless encompasses a wealth of attractions, such as Lincoln Center, Columbia University and Grant's Tomb. As young singles moved to the Upper West Side in the 1970s, **Columbus Avenue**, once lined with local hardware stores, laundries and markets, became almost overnight the site of dozens of specialty shops and sidewalk cafes. In the past few years **Amsterdam Avenue** has followed suit and is now the setting for several popular bars, coffeehouses and bistros.

Columbus Circle *Map p 176*

The focal point of this busy traffic circle is the 1894 statue of Christopher Columbus. Three bronze ships' prows represent his famous fleet: the *Niña*, the *Pinta* and the *Santa Maria*. At the entrance to Central Park is the Maine Memorial (1913), dedicated to the 260 men who lost their lives when the battleship *Maine* was destroyed in Havana Harbor in 1898.

This busy intersection has undergone considerable redevelopment in recent years. The 1956 New York Coliseum, formerly located on the circle's west side, was torn down in 2000. It will be replaced in 2003 by the new twin-towered AOL Time Warner Center, which will encompass a high-end mall and hotel, luxury apartments and Jazz at Lincoln Center.

Dominating the northern end is the glitzy **Trump International Hotel and Tower**, housing luxury condominiums as well as hotel rooms; the 45-story edifice—formerly the Gulf and Western Building—has been given a new skin of flashy, gold-tinted glass designed by Philip Johnson and Costas Kondylis.

On the south side of the circle stands 2 Columbus Circle (1965), a 10-story white-marble structure vaguely reminiscent of a Venetian palazzo. Recently, the Museum of Contemporary Arts and Design announced it would move into the building—originally designed by famed architect Edward Durell Stone—after a $30 million renovation that could result in changes to a facade that has become a neighborhood icon.

Across Eighth Avenue, the **Time Warner Center** continues to rise. When completed in early 2004, its twin towers will reach a height of 750ft. The building will house the headquarters of Time Warner Inc., a hotel, luxury apartments, an upscale retail gallery, and a $128 million, 100,000sq ft performance complex that will be the new home of Jazz at Lincoln Center.

★★Lincoln Center *Map p 11*

On Broadway between W. 62nd & W. 67th Sts.

Devoted to drama, music and dance, Lincoln Center for the Performing Arts is a 16-acre complex comprising five major theater and concert buildings, a library, a band shell and two outdoor plazas *(free performances held in summer)*. It is home to 12 constituent companies including the Metropolitan Opera, New York Philharmonic, New York City Ballet, New York City Opera, the Chamber Music Society of Lincoln Center, the Film Society of Lincoln Center, Jazz at Lincoln Center, the Juilliard School, Lincoln Center for the Performing Arts, Inc., Lincoln Center Theater, the New York Public Library for the Performing Arts and the School of American Ballet.

The idea for such a grand cultural center, where operas, ballets, plays and concerts could take place simultaneously, originated in 1955, and two years later the city bought the necessary land in what was then a run-down neighborhood (the setting for the film *West Side Story*). Despite considerable controversy—the new complex prompted the demolition of 188 buildings, forcing some 1,600 residents to relocate—the project proceeded, with John D. Rockefeller III chairing the building committee. A board of architects headed by Wallace K. Harrison, who had helped design the United Nations and Rockefeller Center, went to work, analyzing some 60 theater designs in 20 countries. Construction finally began in 1959 with Avery Fisher Hall and continued over the next 10 years, ending with the Juilliard School. Private contributions largely accounted for the total budget (about $350 million). In 1991 the Samuel B. and David Rose Building, a multipurpose structure, was added to the complex, northwest of the Juilliard School. The sleek rectangular buildings of glass and Italian travertine marble can accommodate 13,666 spectators at a time.

Visit – *Visit of performance spaces by guided tour (1hr) only, year-round daily 10am–5pm. No tours Jan 1, Thanksgiving Day & Dec 25. Visit includes Metropolitan Opera House, the New York State Theater and Avery Fisher Hall. $9.50. Advance reservations recommended. Tours depart from the concourse level under the Metropolitan Opera House.* ✕ ♿ 🅿 ☎ *212-875-5350. www.lincoln-center.org.*

Metropolitan Opera House – *Backstage tours (1hr 30min) depart from main lobby Oct–Jun Mon–Fri 3:30pm. $10. Advance reservations required.* ♿ 🅿 *(fee).* ☎ *212-769-7020. www.operaed.org.* Distinguished by a 10-story colonnade, this opera house, which opened in 1966 with Samuel Barber's *Anthony and Cleopatra*, forms the centerpiece of the main plaza. Designed by Wallace K. Harrison with seating for 3,788 persons, it replaced the celebrated "Met" at Broadway and 39th Street, which closed in April 1966 and was later demolished. The building hosts both the Metropolitan Opera and the American Ballet Theater and contains seven rehearsal halls and storage space for six opera sets. In the lobby hang large murals by Marc Chagall, *The Sources of Music* and *The Triumph of Music*. The double staircase carpeted in red is accentuated by crystal chandeliers, donated by Austria.

© Jon Ortner/Courtesy NYC & Co.

Metropolitan Opera House, Lincoln Center

Music to your ears

Map p 176. Home to some of the country's most accomplished musicians, the Upper West Side offers a range of performances year-round. For live classical music, stop by the **Manhattan School of Music**, which occupies the former premises of the Juilliard School *(120 Claremont Ave. at 122nd St.; ☎ 212-749-2802)*. Most evening concerts and all student recitals are free. Another local institution worth a visit is **Symphony Space** *(2537 Broadway at 95th St.; ☎ 212-864-1414; www.symphonyspace.org)*. The programming here is extremely varied and includes the annual 12-hour Wall to Wall, a celebration of works by a specific composer (Miles Davis, Joni Mitchell and Ravel have been featured in past years) as performed by a variety of musicians; and the literary performance series, where noted Broadway and Hollywood actors read classic and new short stories.

Levain Bakery

167 W. 74th Street at Amsterdam Ave. ☎ *212-874-6080. www.levain-bakery.com.* Possibly the largest, most delectable chocolate-chip cookies in Manhattan are baked at the ovenful at this cheerful basement bakery. Crisp on the outside, chewy within and dense with gooey chips, they're irresistible to chocoholics. For others, there are oatmeal-raisin cookies and basketfuls of scones, brioches and specialty sandwiches to gobble on the spot or take to go.

Avery Fisher Hall – Originally called Philharmonic Hall, this concert hall, designed by Max Abramovitz and set to the right of the main plaza, was renamed in 1973 in recognition of a gift from Avery Fisher, the founder of Fisher Radio. The 2,742-seat auditorium is home to the New York Philharmonic, the country's oldest orchestra, which previously played at Carnegie Hall.

New York State Theater – Designed by Philip Johnson, this theater is home to the New York City Opera and the New York City Ballet. The City Center of Music and Drama, which oversees the two companies, operates the theater, owned by the City of New York. Completed in 1964, it seats 2,792 people.

The Lincoln Center complex also includes the Guggenheim Bandshell (in Damrosch Park, behind the opera house to the south), the site of free concerts. Behind the opera house to the north is the **New York Public Library for the Performing Arts** *(open year-round Mon–Sat noon–6pm, Thu until 8pm; closed major holidays; 1hr guided tours available Tue 2pm; ☞ ☎ 212-870-1630; www.nypl.org)*. This building (1965; Skidmore, Owings & Merrill) houses a museum of the performing arts, a 200-seat auditorium and a wonderful music library whose extensive collections include original manuscripts, diaries, recordings, photographs and costumes. Two small stages are located in the recently renovated Vivian Beaumont Theater and the Mitzi E. Newhouse Theater. Built according to plans by Eero Saarinen, these are home to the Lincoln Center Theater Company, which opened in 1980. A footbridge leads across West 66th Street to the Juilliard Building (1968; Pietro Belluschi, Catalano and Westerman), which contains the Juilliard School (for musicians, actors and dancers) and Alice Tully Hall, used by the Chamber Music Society of Lincoln Center. The New York Film Festival *(p 308)* is also held here every fall.

★★Cathedral of St. John the Divine *Map p 190*

On Amsterdam Ave. at W. 112th St. Open year-round daily 9am–5pm. Guided tours (1hr) available Tue–Sat 11am, Sun 1pm. $5. ☞ ☎ 212-316-7540. www. stjohndivine.org.

Seat of the Episcopal Diocese of New York, this is reputedly the largest cathedral in the world built in the Gothic style. The massive stone edifice—begun in 1892 and still under construction—can welcome up to 3,000 worshipers at a time and is also the setting for frequent dance, music, film and drama performances, many of them free. The 13-acre area on Amsterdam Avenue between Cathedral Parkway and West 113th Street contains seven ancillary buildings and gardens.

A Challenging Task – Although the idea for a monumental cathedral in the city dates back to 1828, the building was not conceived until 1872, when Horatio Potter, then bishop of New York, presented a proposal to the diocesan convention. After several delays, the bishop's nephew and successor, Henry Potter, settled on this site in Morningside Heights *(western fringe of Manhattan between Cathedral Pkwy. & 125th St.)*, and construction began in 1892. From the start, excavation and structural problems plagued the builders. Twenty-five years into the project, the original 1888 Romanesque design by Heins and LaFarge was scrapped for a revised plan in the Gothic style by Ralph Adams Cram. The choir and sanctuary were completed in 1916, and construction of the nave began in 1925. Another century is needed to finish the towers, central spire, transepts and portal carvings, and limestone interior facing.

Visit – Two square Gothic towers (to reach 266ft when completed) flank the symmetrical west facade, where the central **Portal of Paradise★** features a double set of bronze doors bearing scenes from the Old *(left doors)* and New *(right doors)* Testaments. The doors, each weighing three tons, were produced in Paris by Ferdinand Barbedienne, who also cast the Statue of Liberty. Between the doors is the carved figure of St. John the Divine surmounted by a tympanum adorned with a Christ in Glory.

The portals open into the narthex, or vestibule, where striking stained-glass windows from the studio of Ernest W. Lakeman represent the Creation

Portal carvings, Cathedral of St. John the Divine

© Brigitta L. House /MICHELIN

(on the left) and scenes from the Old Testament *(on the right)*. Note also the Greek icons and 15C paintings of the Virgin and Child. The majestic **nave** measures 248ft long and is as wide as 112th Street. Along the flanking side aisles are 14 bays honoring as many prominent institutions in the fields of education, art, medicine and religion. The aisles are also the setting for a group of 17C tapestries depicting the Acts of the Apostles, woven in Mortlake, England, after cartoons painted by Raphael in 1513.

The 100ft-wide crossing, a holdover from the original Heins and LaFarge design, features a second set of 17C tapestries, woven on papal looms founded by Cardinal Barberini in Rome; these scenes are from the New Testament. The crossing offers an excellent view back to the great rose window in the narthex, which was made by the Connick studios in the 1920s and contains 10,000 pieces of glass.

A semicircle of eight granite columns (each weighing 130 tons) encloses the sanctuary, containing the great choir and the high altar. Niches in the marble parapet fronting the altar hold statues of notable figures, including St. Paul, Abraham Lincoln and George Washington; a stone block representing the 20C is carved with the images of Gandhi, Dr. Martin Luther King Jr., Albert Einstein and Susan B. Anthony.

The apse aisle, or ambulatory, contains seven chapels and, on the south side, displays several paintings of the 16C Italian school, a glazed terra-cotta Annunciation (15C, Della Robbia school) and a 16C silk-embroidered cloth, representing the Adoration of the Magi.

The domed baptistery, located to the north of the choir, is decorated with eight niches holding figures associated with the early history of Nieuw Amsterdam, including Peter Stuyvesant, depicted with his wooden leg. In the gift shop, located in the south tower, you may purchase books and souvenirs.

To the east of the south transept lies the small Biblical Garden, planted with flora mentioned in the Bible. The distinctive **Peace Fountain (1)**, which celebrates the triumph of good over evil, was executed by Greg Wyatt, artist-in-residence at the cathedral. It dominates the children's sculpture garden to the south, where animal sculptures by local youths have been cast in bronze.

★Columbia University *Map p 190*

W. 114th to 120th Sts., between Amsterdam Ave. & Broadway. Main entrance at W. 116th St. The visitor center (open year-round Mon–Fri 9am–5pm) is located in Low Memorial Library. Visitors may stroll around the campus at their leisure. Guided tours (45min) that access the interior of many of the buildings are available year-round (Mon–Fri 11am & 2pm). ✗ ♿ ☎ *212-854-4900. www.columbia.edu.*

★ General Grant National Memorial

The first college in New York and the fifth oldest in the nation, Columbia is one of the country's most distinguished Ivy League universities, with almost 22,000 students. Located on the site of the former Bloomingdale Insane Asylum, Columbia's main campus occupies 36 acres in Morningside Heights. Its formal axial arrangement is typical of the turn-of-the-19C Beaux-Arts movement. Charles McKim envisioned Low Memorial Library as the focus of his 1894 design, which encompasses the area north of 116th Street. Added in 1934, Butler Library faces Low Library across a majestic mall, while handsome limestone and brick classroom buildings define the quadrangles. The university began expanding outside the old campus in the early 20C, adding the 1926 Casa Italiana by McKim, Mead and White, and the more recent Law School building and School of International and Public Affairs, all on Amsterdam Avenue.

From King's College to Columbia University – Founded in 1754 by a charter from George II, King's College was first located in lower Manhattan, where the original class of eight men met in the schoolhouse of Trinity Church. Among the early students at King's College were Alexander Hamilton, aide-de-camp to General Washington and later secretary of the Treasury; and John Jay, first chief justice of the US. After the Revolution, the school reopened in 1784 under a new name—Columbia College. In 1897 it moved to the present site after 40 years at Madison Avenue and East 49th Street. It was during the 20C that the university earned its reputation for excellence, claiming among its noted administrators Dwight D. Eisenhower, who served as Columbia president from 1948 to 1953, when he left to become president of the US.

Today the coeducational university has an endowment of $4.3 billion and boasts 69 academic departments and some 5,000 faculty. Its 16 schools include 13 graduate and 3 undergraduate schools. Affiliated with the university are Columbia's Business College and Barnard College. Founded in 1889, Barnard is a liberal arts school for women located on the west side of Broadway between 116th and 120th streets.

★ **Low Memorial Library** – The gift of Seth Low, president of Columbia from 1890 to 1901, this elegant Neoclassical building, completed in 1897, was the first major structure on the campus. Designer Charles McKim modeled the library on the Roman Pantheon. Since 1934 the building has served as an administrative center and exhibit hall. Step inside to view the magnificent marble rotunda, with its 130ft dome and 16 colossal columns.

❶ Hungarian Pastry Shop

Map above. 111th St. & Amsterdam Ave. ☎ *212-866-4230.* Since 1961 this bohemian, family-owned cafe has been *the* place for Columbia and Barnard students to study, debate and hang out. The moody burgundy-walled interior is appropriately studious and smoky—you might be inspired to deconstruct Kafka over that *caffé Viennese* (order it topped with whipped cream). The pastry selection includes brioches, strudel and an assortment of Eastern European standards. Outdoor tables offer a nice perspective on Morningside Park.

Temple Hoyne Buell Hall – The only building remaining from the former Bloomingdale Insane Asylum, this 1878 edifice is the oldest structure on campus and now serves as a center for the study of American architecture. Frequent exhibits are mounted in the first-floor galleries *(open to the public)*. La Maison Française, the university's French cultural center, is located on the upper floor.

★**St. Paul's Chapel** – This elegant structure (1907), a Northern Italian Renaissance design by Isaac Phelps Stokes, features a beautiful vaulted interior with salmon-colored Guastavino tiling and striking cast-iron chandeliers. The carved pulpit, choir stalls, and organ front recall those in the Church of Santa Croce in Florence, Italy. Because of the chapel's excellent acoustics, many concerts are held here.

Schapiro Center – Completed in 1992 for $62 million, this Neoclassical building was designed by Hellmuth, Obata and Kassabaum and contains state-of-the-art laboratories for research in microelectronics, video imaging and other technologies. A glass-enclosed skyway connects it to the 1927 Pupin Physics Laboratories; the Manhattan Project, which pioneered the development of atomic energy in the US, originated there.

Outdoor Sculpture – A number of sculptures by European and American artists also distinguish the campus. Fronting Low Library is the regal *Alma Mater* **(2)** designed by Daniel Chester French in 1903; the Neoclassical bronze figure, emblem of the university, survived a bombing during the 1968 student riots. Admire Rodin's famous bronze *The Thinker*, cast from the 1880 model in 1930, in front of Philosophy Hall *(east of Low Library)*; and the *Great God Pan* (1899) by George Grey Barnard, originally intended for the Dakota *(west of Low Library)*. Modern works include *Bellerophon Taming Pegasus* **(3)** by Jacques Lipchitz (1967), mounted over the entrance to the Law School; *Tightrope Walker* (1979) by Kees Verkade and *Three Way Piece: Points* (1967) by Henry Moore, both on the Amsterdam Avenue overpass; and *Curl* (1968) by Clement Meadmore, fronting the Business School *(Uris Hall, behind Low Library)*.

★RIVERSIDE PARK AND RIVERSIDE DRIVE *Map p 190*

Designed as a single entity in 1875 by Frederick Law Olmsted (the creator of Central Park), Riverside Drive and Park take advantage of the beautiful views and sloping topography along the Hudson River. The traditional home of artists and musicians, the curving drive is complete with majestic elms, walkways and scenic overlooks, boasting fine 19C row houses, turn-of-the-century mansions and elegant early-20C apartment buildings. The park, in turn, extending from West 72nd to 155th streets *(recommended area: below 100th St.)*, contains some of the city's most important monuments, including Grant's Tomb; the 1902 Soldiers' and Sailors' Monument at West 89th Street; the Joan of Arc Statue at West 93rd Street; and the Firemen's Memorial at West 100th Street. The latest addition, erected as part of an extensive renovation of the park's southern entrance, is an 8ft bronze statue of Eleanor Roosevelt (1996); the sculptor, Penelope Jencks, captured the famous first lady in a pensive pose. The 91st Street garden, a beautiful English garden maintained by local residents, is also noteworthy. Together, the park and drive are a designated New York City Historic Landmark.

★Riverside Church *Map p 190*

On Riverside Dr. between W. 120th & 122nd Sts. If west portal is closed, use entrance at 91 Claremont Ave. Open year-round daily 9am–5pm. Guided tours Sun 12:30pm; reservations required. ✗ ♿ ⏚ ☎ *212-870-6700.*

With its soaring 400ft tower—containing the largest carillon in the world—this streamlined Gothic Revival building is a dominant Upper West Side landmark. It is also an important community center offering a broad range of social services and cultural programs. Founded before 1850 as a small Baptist congregation in the Lower East Side, the church is associated with the American Baptist Churches and the United Church of Christ. Interdenominational and interracial, it is perhaps best known for its liberal stance on social issues. John D. Rockefeller Jr. helped fund the present 1927 building of limestone, designed by Allen and Collens and Henry C. Pelton (the south wing was added in 1960).

Visit – The magnificent west portal faces Riverside Drive and recalls the sculptures at Chartres Cathedral in France. Prophets from the Old Testament are carved into the columns on the left, with New Testament figures on the right. The tympanum above features a Christ in Glory and symbols of the Four Evangelists.
In the narthex you will see two striking **stained-glass windows**★ depicting the life of Christ, made in the 16C for the Cathedral of Bruges in Belgium. From the narthex, enter the nave, which is 100ft high and 215ft long, with space for 2,500 worshipers. The clerestory windows are modeled after those at Chartres, while the chancel screen is notable for 80 panels depicting figures whose lives embodied Christian ideal—among them Luther, Milton, Lincoln and Pasteur. A passage from the narthex leads to a small, very lovely Romanesque **chapel**. You may visit the observation deck *(Tue–Sun 11am–4pm)* by taking an elevator to the 20th floor. Ascending the final 147 steps, you will pass the chambers of the 74-bell carillon. A stunning **panorama**★★ from the summit encompasses Riverside Park, the Hudson River and the New Jersey shore.

★General Grant National Memorial *Map p 190*

On Riverside Dr. at W. 122nd St. Open year-round daily 9am–5pm. Closed Jan 1, Thanksgiving Day & Dec 25. Guided tours (40min) available. ☎ 212-666-1640. www.nps.gov/gegr.

Popularly known as Grant's Tomb, this Neoclassical monument is the final resting place of Ulysses Simpson Grant (1822-85) and his wife, Julia Dent Grant (1826-1902). Grant was commander of the Union Army during the Civil War and president of the US from 1869 to 1877.

The white granite mausoleum, crowned by a stepped cone, was designed in 1890 by John H. Duncan and took six years to build. The tablet above the Doric portico bears the words "Let us have peace"; the words were part of Grant's written reply to the Republican Party in 1868, in which he accepted his nomination as presidential candidate. Gold-tinted clerestory windows create a soft glow in the marble interior, which recalls Napoleon's tomb at the Invalides in Paris. A dramatic coffered dome is suspended directly over the sunken crypt, where niches contain busts of Grant's comrades-in-arms: Sherman, Sheridan, Thomas, Ord and McPherson. Two small rooms display photographs illustrating Grant's life and achievements. The free-form mosaic benches flanking the tomb outside were designed by Pedro Silva in the early 1970s as part of a community project to involve neighborhood youths with the monument.

MUSEUMS *(See Museums section)*

★★★**American Museum of Natural History** – *Central Park West, between 77th & 81st Sts.*

★★**New-York Historical Society** – *2 W. 77th St.*

Eva and Morris Feld Gallery of the Museum of American Folk Art – *2 Lincoln Square.*

22 • HARLEM★

MTA any train to 125th St.

Map p 10

Embracing most of northern Manhattan above 106th Street in the east, and 110th Street and 125th Street in the west, Harlem is home to a fairly sizeable segment of New York's African-American and Hispanic communities. The story of Harlem could best be told as the tale of two Harlems. East of Fifth Avenue and north of 106th Street lies East Harlem, or "El Barrio," with its distinctively Puerto Rican flavor; west of Fifth Avenue is central Harlem, bound by 110th Street to the south and Morningside Avenue, St. Nicholas Avenue and Edgecombe Avenue to the west and the Harlem River to the north. No other area in New York City has fascinated, inspired and perplexed as has Harlem. To many, Harlem is the symbol of African-American culture and a center of this rich heritage; to others Harlem came to be a symbol of urban blight and failed social policies. To most who visit it, though, Harlem is much more—it is a community that celebrates its history and its culture, and has struggled for its place in the world. The architectural treasures alone warrant a visit to this incredibly diverse neighborhood.

Historical Notes

Nieuw Haarlem – Established in 1658 by the Dutch governor Peter Stuyvesant in northern Manhattan, Nieuw Haarlem was mostly farmland and remained largely rural until the New York and Harlem Railroad inaugurated service along Fourth Avenue (Park Avenue) in 1837. Most of the development occurred in the latter part of the 19C with the construction of the elevated rail lines in the western part of the valley. By the early 1890s, Harlem had become one of the most fashionable residential areas in New York City, with its fine department stores, Opera House, Symphony Hall and Yacht Club. By the beginning of the 20C, as the real-estate market went through a slump due largely to overbuilding, speculators were going bankrupt and landlords began to rent to working-class black families in search of better living conditions than those on the West Side of midtown Manhattan. By 1920 the black population of Central Harlem was estimated at about 60,000.

Harlem Renaissance – Harlem experienced its heyday in the 1920s. As bootleg liquor flowed, popular nightspots including the original Cotton Club on Lenox Avenue drew nightly crowds (some white-only) with performances by jazz greats Duke Ellington, Count Basie and Cab Calloway. Dubbed at the time the New Negro Movement, the era also provided a serious cultural forum for emerging writers and artists, and a haven for prosperous middle-class black families. Today this period is known as the Harlem Renaissance—writers such as Langston Hughes and Zora Neale Hurston celebrated their "blackness," and artists and musicians inspired by African imagery created some of the most important works of the 20C. Popular expressions such as "I'd rather be a lamppost in Harlem than gobnor of Georgy (Governor of Georgia)" expressed the energy and magnetism of the neighborhood. The Renaissance came to an end with the Great Depression, however. While a wave of newcomers from the American South and the Caribbean contributed to the growth and unity of the black community, after World War II jobs were scarce. Though the jazz scene remained active, artists began gravitating to Greenwich Village, and by the 1960s Harlem's celebrities were more likely to be civil rights activists such as Malcolm X, who worked with the Black Muslims' Temple of Islam at 116th Street and Lenox Avenue. In 1965 he was assassinated at the Audubon Ballroom on West 166th Street. More recently, Harlem has been the home of prominent public officials, including the city's first black mayor, David Dinkins. Former president Bill Clinton established his office on 125th Street, an easy commute from his new home in Westchester County.

■ Harlem Slang of the 1920s

The Big Apple	New York City
Dig	Understand
First thing smoking	A train
Out this world	Beyond belief
Astorperious	Haughty, high hat (from the wealthy Astor family)
Brick presser	An idler, loiterer, one who literally walks the pavement

Harlem Today – By the 1960s, the population of Harlem was decreasing rapidly. Hard hit by inflation, rent control and vandalism, some landlords simply abandoned their buildings or torched them for insurance money, leaving behind a bleak landscape of rubble-strewn lots and public housing projects. The climate of violence and uncertainty forced many middle-class families to move to the suburbs. In recent years the city has acquired thousands of buildings for nonpayment of taxes and has initiated several rehabilitation programs, including the 1992 renovation of the 19C Astor Row Houses at nos. 8-62 West 130th Street. Other historic districts also recall Harlem's glory days, including Hamilton Heights, Audubon Terrace, Mount Morris Park and the elegant brick houses on West 139th Street known as **Strivers Row**. ("Strivers" refers to the prominent middle-class blacks who moved in during the 1920s.)

Today central Harlem is experiencing an extraordinary economic revitalization. Many of the abandoned buildings are being renovated for affordable housing; private funds are being invested in new shops, restaurants and businesses; and old landmarks are being restored. The legendary **Apollo Theater** *(see p 194)*, famous for its all-black revues of the 1930s, now hosts a variety of shows including Wednesday's Amateur Night, which still draws would-be stars to the stage. As development continues and national retail chains such as Starbucks, H&M, and Disney arrive, some longtime residents believe Harlem's next challenge is to maintain its historic identity as the symbol of the celebrations, struggles, joys and achievements of the African-American community.

125TH STREET AND ENVIRONS

A main thoroughfare and bustling commercial artery of fashion boutiques, discount stores and street vendors, 125th Street, also called Martin Luther King Jr. Boulevard, was the site of marches, rallies and protests during the civil rights movement. Development at a pace unseen in generations, from storefront renovations to large-scale commercial projects, is underway along the length of 125th Street, the heart of Harlem.

Touring Harlem

Although many parts of Harlem are safe, it is advisable to limit your visit to daylight hours as most of the side streets are not well lit at night. Take a taxi if you plan to visit a jazz club or restaurant at night. Not all sights mentioned appear on the Map of Principal Sights. Because of the distance between sights, we recommend visiting the area by guided tour.

Harlem Spirituals, Inc. offers various guided tours of Harlem. Here are some of the more popular ones: evening visit of Harlem including soul food and jazz *(5hrs; Mon, Thu & Sat 7pm; $99)*; Sunday visit with gospel and soul-food brunch *(5hrs; Sun 9:30am; $79)*; mid-week visit of Harlem with gospel *(4hrs; Wed 9am; $44)*. *All tours depart year-round from office at 690 Eighth Ave. between 43rd & 44th Sts. Reservations required. No tours Jan 1. Thanksgiving Day or Dec 25.* ♿ ☎ *212-391-0900. www.harlem-spirituals.com.*

Harlem Tourist Center and Harlem Gift Shop – *2224 Frederick Douglass Blvd., between 119th & 120th Sts. Open year-round daily 10am–7pm. Closed Dec 25.* ♿ ☎ *212-749-5700. www.hatt.org.* The Tourist Center provides visitors with up-to-date information on the neighborhood, maps, brochures and a schedule of community events. Peek into the gift shop for a variety of crafts designed by Harlem-based artists or sign up for a walking tour *($15)*.

Franco's Boulevard – Colorful murals executed by Franco Gaskin, a self-taught artist in Harlem, decorate the storefront iron gates of the shops lining 125th Street. Be sure to admire his work in the morning before the stores open at 10am.

Apollo Theater – *253 W. 125th St., between Frederick Douglass & Adam Clayton Powell Jr. Blvds.* ♿ ☎ *212-531-5337. www.apollotheater.com.* The Apollo opened in 1914 as Hurtig & Seamon's New Burlesque Theatre, where black audiences were excluded. Two decades later, under a new name and management, the Apollo Theater became a mecca of black entertainment. In 1934 the Apollo launched the "Amateur Night at the Apollo" contest where such music legends as Ella Fitzgerald, Sarah Vaughan, James Brown and pop icon Michael Jackson were discovered. The tradition continued through the 1960s with the "Motown Revue." The theater closed in the 1970s and reopened in 1981 when it was designated a National Landmark. Today, "Amateur Night" continues and is considered one of the most prestigious performance opportunities in the US. In 2003 a $12 million refurbishing of the theater's exterior and historic marquee was completed.

Harlem USA – *W. 125th St. at Frederick Douglass Blvd.* A major multimillion-dollar commercial venture, this shopping center counts among its many tenants a Disney Store, HMV Records and the Magic Johnson Theaters. Since opening in spring 2000, the center has played an important role in the revitalization of Harlem's economy.

Theresa Hotel – *2082-2096 Adam Clayton Powell Jr. Blvd. at the corner of 125th St.* This elegant white brick, masonry and terra-cotta building was constructed in 1913 by George & Edward Blum. Note the triangle-shaped roof that hides the unsightly water tower. The Theresa became a social center for black celebrities and politicians in the 1940s. It was also home of the late Secretary of Commerce **Ronald H. Brown**, former chairman of the Democratic Party. In 1960 the Theresa gained national fame for welcoming Fidel Castro as a guest. The hotel also housed community-based groups such as the Organization for African Unity led by Malcolm X, and the March on Washington headed by A. Philip Randolph. Today the hotel functions as an office building.

> **■ Pig Foot Mary**
>
> Lillian "Pig Foot Mary" Harris came to New York in 1901 as an illiterate immigrant and began selling boiled pigs feet from a baby carriage on the West Side of Manhattan, where most African Americans then lived. As Harlem grew, she established a food stand at 135th Street and Lenox Avenue where she continued serving the people of her community and intelligently investing her profits. At the time of her death, it was said that Ms. Harris was worth half a million dollars in real estate.

Looking north along Lenox Avenue from West 132nd Street (c. 1928)

R. Corbel /MICHELIN

Ephesus Seventh Day Adventist Church – *267 Lenox Ave. at 123rd St.* Until 1930 the building housed the Reformed Low Dutch Church of Harlem. The Ephesus Seventh Day Adventist Church then leased the premises, purchasing it in 1939. Walter J. Turnbull founded the **Boys Choir of Harlem** here in 1968 as the Ephesus Church Choir of Central Harlem. Established as a vehicle to help lower-income children succeed, the choir has become one of the most famous singing groups from Harlem, achieving international fame as well as a run on Broadway. The Choir Academy was founded in 1986 and graduated its first class in 1996.

Strivers Row and Environs

This area of central Harlem around 135th Street became active during the Harlem Renaissance as a cultural and social center. Named after Strivers Row, the historic district of beautiful 19C town houses lies on West 138th and West 139th streets between Adam Clayton Powell Jr. and Frederick Douglass boulevards. A highlight of the neighborhood is the row of brown brick buildings by New York architect Stanford White located on the north side of 139th Street.

Schomburg Center for Research in Black Culture – *515 Malcolm X Blvd. Open year-round Tue–Wed noon–8pm, Thu–Fri noon–6pm, Sat 10am–6pm. Special collections open Mon–Wed noon–5pm, Fri & Sat 10am–5pm. Closed major holidays.*

  ✆ *212-491-2200. www. nyplorg.* This branch of the New York Public Library system contains one of the world's largest archives relating to black heritage. **Arthur Schomburg** (1874-1938), a black Puerto Rican who was an influential cultural leader during the Harlem Renaissance of the 1920s, began the collection in an effort to discredit the contemporary belief that African Americans had no history. Today more than five million books, photographs, manuscripts, films, recordings and works of art are kept in the center, which is housed in a 1905 landmark library building designed by McKim, Mead & White (restored in 1990) and a modern 1980 annex. Not to be missed are the Pietro Calvi bust of Ira Aldridge, the great black Shakespearean actor of the 19C depicted in the role of Othello; and the art installation *Rivers*, a tribute to Langston Hughes and Arthur Schomburg, located in the vestibule. The center also presents exhibits, screenings and educational forums throughout the year.

 ① Sylvia's

Map p 10. 328 Lenox Ave. between 126th & 127th Sts. ✆ *212-996-0660. www.sylviassoulfood.com.* The most celebrated soul-food restaurant in Harlem, Sylvia's is also the place for important political and cultural gatherings for the Harlem community. Order the delicious greens, candied yams and southern fried chicken. For a special treat, come for the Sunday gospel brunch *(noon–4pm)*.

Harlem YMCA – *180-181 W. 135th St.* Literary greats Langston Hughes, Richard Wright and Ralph Ellison were only a few of the artists of the 20C to make a home at the Harlem YMCA. Originally called the Colored Men's Associated, the organization got its start in a small room in Greenwich Village in 1867. Although denied branch status until 1901, the Association was supervised by the New York City YMCA. Through the efforts of Dr. C.T. Walker of the Mount Olivet Baptist Church, the Colored branch of the YMCA then moved to new quarters on West 53rd Street in the area of Manhattan known as Black Bohemia in the West Fifties. The Harlem YMCA opened at 181 West 135th Street in 1919. By the late 1920s it had outgrown its new facility and a new imposing Colonial Revival building was constructed in 1932 across the street at 180 West 135th Street.

African American Walk of Fame – *W. 135th St., between Adam Clayton Powell Jr. & Frederick Douglass Blvds.; located mid-block on both sides of the street.* Commissioned by the Harlem Chamber of Commerce in 1995 as part of the redesigning of the streetscape of 135th Street, the African American Walk of Fame is a series of imbedded bronze plaques crafted by New York sculptors Otto Neals and Ogundipe Fayoumi. The plaques honor people of African descent who have made significant contributions in music, science, the arts and community service. Start at no. 236 West 135th Street, walk west towards Frederick Douglass Boulevard, then cross the street. Plaques resume at no. 219 West 135th Street.

Harlem street scene in 1935 (135th St. and Lexington Ave.)

Florence Mills Home – *220 W. 135th St.* This white masonry building, condemned since the early 1990s, was home to Florence Mills (1896-1927) from 1910 until her death nearly two decades later. One of the most famous performers of the Harlem Renaissance, Mills appeared in numerous musical revues including *Shuffle Along*, the first all-black revue to play on Broadway.

Small's Paradise – *2294 1/2 Adam Clayton Powell Jr. Blvd. at 135th St.* Small's opened in 1925 and soon became "The Hottest Spot in Harlem." Patrons were required to follow strict rules of conduct: no loud speaking and no bottles of liquor set on the floor. Anyone who broke the rules was evicted with a simple glance from the head waiter. Unlike the Cotton Club, Small's was fully integrated; white and black patrons mixed freely and danced to the music of Harlem's top-notch bands including pianist Charlie Johnson's orchestra. Work is underway to transform the building into the Thurgood Marshall Academy, the first high school to be built in Harlem in 50 years.

Mother A.M.E. Zion – *140-148 W. 137th St., between Adam Clayton Powell Jr. & Malcolm X Blvds.* ☎ *212-234-1544.* Mother Zion, as it is affectionately called, is the oldest black church in New York State, founded in 1796 by dissatisfied congregants of the John Street Methodist Church. As a center of strength for the community, Mother Zion established itself wherever the African-American community would migrate; from Leonard and Church streets (now TriBeCa), to West 10th and Bleecker streets in Greenwich Village, to its final home in 1925 on West 137th Street in Harlem. The Neo-Gothic structure was designed by George W. Foster Jr., one of the first African-American architects to be registered in New York. During the 19C Mother Zion was referred to as a "freedom church," reflective of its role as a station on the Underground Railroad.

Abyssinian Baptist Church – *132 W. 138th St.* Designated a New York City landmark in 1993, this 1923 Gothic Revival church is home to New York's oldest black congregation, founded in 1808. It was built during the tenure of Adam Clayton Powell Sr. and became prominent in the 1930s under the leadership of **Adam Clayton Powell Jr.** (1908-72), the controversial pastor and civil rights advocate who was elected to Congress in 1944. Under financial investigation, Powell was stripped of his congressional office in 1967 but was reinstated two years later. Clippings and photos in the memorial room trace his career.

Renaissance Theater and Renaissance Ballroom & Casino – *2341-2359 Adam Clayton Powell Jr. Blvd.* The entire block between 137th and 138th streets is occupied by the Renaissance, or "Renny." The theater opened in 1921 and the ballroom

② **Londel's**
Map p 10. 2620 Frederick Douglass Blvd., between 139th & 140th Sts. Open Tue-Sat 11:30am-4pm for lunch; 5pm-11pm for dinner; Sun 9am-noon for breakfast and noon-5pm for brunch. ☎ *212-234-6114.* Nestled in the Strivers Row area, this upscale Harlem restaurant has become a meeting place for local celebrities and political figures. Ask for the house specialty, Atlantic salmon in a champagne sauce. Londel's also features live jazz on Friday and Saturday evenings.

③ **Home Sweet Harlem Cafe**
Map p 10. 270 W. 135th St. between Adam Clayton Powell Jr. & Frederick Douglass Blvds. Open Mon-Fri 7:30am-7:30pm; Sat 10am-7:30pm; Sun 10am-4pm. ☎ *212-926-9616.* This quaint little cafe offers the weary visitor a variety of baked goods, coffees, teas and light fare all served in a cozy setting.

■ **Spirituals**

Until the mass conversion of blacks to Christianity in the late 1700s, very few practiced western religions. By the end of the 18C though, spirituals, often referred to as slave songs, were becoming an integral part of the African-American worship experience. Although the harmonies are based on Protestant hymns, the rhythms reflect ancestral African musical traditions such as the call and response where a primary singer's verses are echoed by a chorus. Text and harmonies are simple while emotion is at the core of every song; melodies are lined with "blue" notes (flat notes) that would later become an important part of blues and jazz compositions. Spirituals are food for the soul as well as an important repository of the oral history of blacks in the days of slavery. Among some of the best known spirituals: *Nobody Knows the Trouble I've Seen, Go Down Moses, Joshua Fit the Battle of Jericho, Roll Jordan Roll.*

■ **Photographing History**

Harlem was home to a number of successful artists who today are highly regarded visual historians. **James Van Der Zee**, one of Harlem's most revered and respected photographers, established his first studio in 1916 on West 135th Street, a few doors away from the Public Library. He eventually moved to 272 Lenox Avenue. **Austin Hansen**, a native of St. Croix, served as a war photographer in the US Navy during World War II. After the war, Hansen settled in Harlem and opened a studio at 232 West 135th Street. His extensive photographic archive has been donated to the Schomburg Center. The identical twin brothers **Morgan and Marvin Smith** moved to New York in 1933 from their native Kentucky to study art with the Renaissance-era sculptor Augusta Savage and renowned painter Romare Bearden. In 1939 the brothers opened their first studio at 141 West 125th Street, then moved next to the Apollo Theatre at 253 West 125th Street.

and casino in 1923. Some of the biggest names in jazz were featured at the Ballroom—bands like the Fletcher Henderson Orchestra and the Chick Webb Orchestra. Black professional basketball got its start at The Renaissance; known as the "Rens" or "Rennies," the team played exhibition games on the floor of the casino's ballroom and even had a friendly rivalry with the Boston Celtics until the 1940s. Plans for the rehabilitation of the building are under consideration.

Hamilton Heights/Sugar Hill and Environs

This elevated area, which encompasses the historic district east of Amsterdam Avenue between West 140th and West 145th streets, was once part of a 35-acre estate owned by statesman **Alexander Hamilton** (1757-1804). The picturesque gabled row houses on Hamilton Terrace and Convent Avenue include some unusual Dutch and Flemish Revival residences dating from the 1880s, when the district was developed as a suburb for prosperous New Yorkers. Note the imposing brownstone, St. Luke's Episcopal Church *(285 Convent Ave.)*, designed in the Romanesque Revival style in 1892.

On the heights between Edgecombe and St. Nicholas avenues lies **Sugar Hill★**. This affluent black neighborhood of elegant four-story houses was home to such famous residents as Cab Calloway, Duke Ellington, Thurgood Marshall and Langston Hughes between the 1920s and 1950s. Just to the south is City College's campus, begun in 1897. Some 14,000 students, mainly African-American, Hispanic and Asian, are enrolled here.

★**Morris-Jumel Mansion** – *W. 160th St. and Edgecombe Ave. Open year-round Wed–Sun 10am–4pm. Closed major holidays. $3.* ☎ *212-923-8008. www. morrisjumel.org.* Occupying a hilltop site with a superb view of the Harlem valley, this handsome Georgian mansion is the only colonial home to survive in northern Manhattan. Col. Roger Morris built the house (originally known as Mount Morris) in 1765, but a decade later he fled to England, where his Loyalist sentiments were better appreciated. During the Battle of Harlem Heights in 1776 the estate served as General Washington's headquarters, and in 1810 it passed to Stephen Jumel, a wealthy French wine merchant. Jumel's wife, Eliza Bowen, was never fully accepted in New York society, and the Jumels set sail for France in 1815, where they traveled more comfortably in Napoleonic circles. Jumel died in 1832 and, a year later, his widow married Aaron Burr, the third vice president of the US, in the front parlor of her mansion. After a year of marriage the couple separated. Their divorce was granted on the day Burr died, in 1836.

While constructed of brick, the mansion features wood facades, corner quoins and a lovely two-story Federal-style portico. The interior is particularly noteworthy for the rear drawing room on the first floor—possibly the first octagonal room in the US. The front parlor contains a fashionable Empire-style settee and chairs, and a French chandelier that belonged to Madame Jumel. On the second floor, Madame Jumel's bedroom and dressing room feature Empire furniture that once belonged to the Bonaparte family; note especially the 19C mahogany slipper chairs.

The mansion is part of the **Jumel Terrace Historic District**, which also includes 20 simple two-story row houses built in the 1880s on the original carriage drive, now known as Sylvan Terrace. The homes are among the few surviving wood-frame structures that once proliferated in the region.

Ralph Ellison Apartment – *749 St. Nicholas Ave., between 147th & 148th Sts.* Ellison was one of the post-Renaissance-era writers who moved to Harlem in the 1930s. At the Harlem YMCA he met Langston Hughes, who introduced him to Harlem literary circles and encouraged him to write. His novel *Invisible Man*, which won the National Book Award in 1952, was written while he was living in this building.

Dining Room, Morris-Jumel Mansion

Courtesy of Morris-Jumel Mansion

Duke Ellington Apartment – *935 St. Nicholas Ave. at 157th St.* One of America's greatest and most influential composers, Duke Ellington moved to Harlem in 1923 and took over the band at the Cotton Club where he eventually conducted a live radio broadcast. Ellington went on to compose and record some of the most recognizable music in jazz history—"Mood Indigo" (1931) and "It Don't Mean a Thing If It Ain't Got That Swing" (1932). Ellington lived here until 1961. **Billy Strayhorn**, his pianist, arranger and co-composer who also lived nearby, wrote "Take the A Train," one of Ellington's most recognizable pieces, for the A train that runs under St. Nicholas Avenue.

Hamilton Grange National Memorial – *287 Convent Ave.* Designed in 1801 by John McComb Jr. (architect of City Hall), this Federal-style clapboard residence was Alexander Hamilton's country estate and his principal residence when he was killed in a duel with Aaron Burr in 1804. In 1889 the house was moved about 100 yards to its current location and altered; the rear facade now faces the street. The building was later used as a rectory for St. Luke's Church and is now owned by the National Park Service.

555 Edgecombe Avenue – *Southwest corner of 160th St.* This imposing white-brick and terra-cotta building was once owned by Bishop Charles Emmanuel "Sweet Daddy" Grace, founder of the United House of Prayer for All People. Designated a landmark in 1993, it was home to prominent African Americans such as Olympian **Jesse Owens**, tennis champion **Althea Gibson**, arctic explorer **Mathew Henson**, jazz great **Count Basie**, and stage legend **Paul Robeson**.

409 Edgecombe Avenue – *Corner of 155th St. viaduct & St. Nicholas Pl.* Originally known as the Parkway Apartments, this elegant and imposing building atop Coogan's Bluff was the most prestigious address in Sugar Hill and was home to many of Harlem's most prominent intellectuals. Residents include **Thurgood Marshall**, first black Supreme Court Justice; **W.E.B Dubois**, historian, editor of *The Crisis*, cofounder of the National Association for the Advancement of Colored People (NAACP) and one of the fathers of the Harlem Renaissance; and **Walter F. White**, executive director of the NAACP. It was designated a historic landmark in 1995.

MUSEUMS *(See Museums section)*

★**Audubon Terrace** – *On Broadway between 155th & 156th Sts.*

★**Studio Museum in Harlem** – *144 W. 125th St.*

Jazz in Harlem

Duke Ellington and Band (1945)

Harlem's first dance hall was the Manhattan Casino at 155th Street and Eighth Avenue where James Reese Europe's band was usually the main feature. In the years that followed World War I, New York City was swept up in jazz mania. The night scene in Harlem took on a life of its own: clubs like Small's Paradise opened to sell-out crowds; and bands like Duke Ellington and his Washingtonians moved up to The Big Apple. Harlem became the undisputed Capital of Jazz, and remained a fertile ground for the development of a new breed of artists and a new brand of jazz, born in the 1940s with the arrival of innovators such as Miles Davis, Charlie Parker and John Coltrane. The jazz scene remained active until the early 1960s when musicians began working more in Greenwich Village and touring Europe. Today the jazz scene is experiencing another renaissance. Visit the clubs listed below for an authentic look at Harlem's jazz scene.

St. Nicks Pub – *773 St. Nicholas Ave., between 148th & 149th Sts. Open nightly.* ☎ *212-283-9728.* A tradition at the Pub since the 1920s, the nightly jam sessions *(Mon–Fri)* are particularly lively, attracting locals as well as the downtown crowds.

Showman's – *375 W. 125th St., between St. Nicholas & Morningside Aves. Open Mon–Sat.* ☎ *212-864-8941.* A steady presence on the Harlem music scene since 1942, this club features a mix of jazz and blues. The crowd is definitely local and everyone seems to know each other. Visitors are greeted like old friends.

The Lenox Lounge – *288 Lenox Ave., between 124th & 125th Sts. Open nightly.* ☎ *212-427-0253. www.lenoxlounge.com.* When film producers search for an authentic Harlem club of the 1920s, they need not look further than the Lounge, as it is commonly known to musicians and locals. Although recently renovated, the club has preserved its Art Deco features. Patrons include both downtowners and locals.

The Cotton Club – *656 West 125th St. at Riverside Dr. Open nightly.* ☎ *212-663-7980. www.cottonclub-newyork.com.* The original Cotton Club opened in 1923 on Lenox Avenue as an elegant place to entertain white downtowners and as an East Coast outlet for the renowned beverage Madden's #1 beer. Club owner Owney Madden, a prominent gangster and bootlegger, hired former prizefighter Jack Johnson as his manager. Segregation was strictly enforced at the door, but the Cotton Club soon became Harlem's hot spot, reputed for its "Colored Revues," its chorus line, and by 1927 its new bandleader Duke Ellington. Some of the biggest names in jazz have played the Cotton Club—Lena Horne, Josephine Baker, Cab Calloway and Louis Armstrong. After the lifting of prohibition and the economic gloom of the Great Depression, the Cotton Club moved downtown where it eventually closed its doors in 1940, marking the end of an era. Under new ownership, the Cotton Club reopened in its Harlem location in the late 1970s.

23 • THE CLOISTERS★★★

MTA A train to 190th St.–Overlook Terrace;
or bus no. 4 to Fort Tryon Park–The Cloisters
Map p 205

Isolated on a hill in Fort Tryon Park, The Cloisters re-creates a fortified monastery, a part of the Old World transplanted to the New. Housed in four reconstructed medieval cloisters and part of a fifth, its collections, which include innumerable sculptures, stained-glass windows, tapestries and other objects spanning over centuries, enjoy an unrivaled reputation among lovers of medieval art.

Historical Notes

The core of the collection is made up of medieval sculptures and architectural remains assembled by the American sculptor **George Grey Barnard** (1863-1938), during his frequent trips to Europe. When the collection was opened to the public in 1914 in a special brick building on Fort Washington Avenue, it already included large sections of the cloisters of Saint-Michel-de-Cuxa, Saint-Guilhem-le-Désert, Bonnefont-en-Comminges, and Trie, all from regions in southern France.

In 1925 **John D. Rockefeller Jr.** granted a large sum to the Metropolitan Museum of Art to purchase the Barnard collection and to improve its presentation. At that time, the Rockefellers also donated more than 40 sculptures from their collection. Five years later Rockefeller presented the City of New York with an estate he owned in the area that is now Fort Tryon Park. He stipulated that the northern part be reserved for the new Cloisters, today home to this extraordinary institution. Designed by **Charles Collens** of Boston, also responsible for Riverside Church, the Cloisters complex was completed in 1938. Considerably enriched by gifts and acquisitions, the museum has remained administratively a part of The Metropolitan Museum.

VISIT

Open Mar–Oct Tue–Sun 9:30am–5:15pm. Rest of the year Tue–Sun 9:30am–4:45pm. Closed Jan 1, Thanksgiving Day & Dec 25. $12. Guided tours available Tue–Fri 3pm, Sun noon. ✕ (May–Oct) 🅿 ☎ 212-923-3700. www.metmuseum.org.

The central structure, containing a group of cloisters, chapels and halls, is arranged around a square tower inspired by that of Saint-Michel-de-Cuxa in the Pyrenees Mountains in southern France. There is little unity of style because both Romanesque and Gothic elements are incorporated, as was often the case in European monasteries. The weathered stone and pleasing proportions, however, combine to create a harmonious ensemble. A stroll along the rampart wall affords various views of the building, the park and the Hudson River. On the east side of the building, a postern serves as the entrance. As you exit the building, note the driveway paved with Belgian blocks—originally from New York streets—reminiscent of European cobblestones.

Main Floor *See floor plan, p 203*

Fuentidueña Chapel – This "chapel" is largely devoted to Spanish Romanesque art. The apse comes from the Church of San Martin at Fuentidueña in Old Castile, Spain, and dates from about 1160. Notice the capitals depicting Daniel in the Lion's Den *(right side)* and the Adoration of the Magi *(left side)*, and pier figures of the Annunciation *(right side)* and St. Martin, bishop of Tours *(left side)*. The two niches in the wall probably contained the cruets of water and wine used during mass and held the ewer for the priest's ceremonial hand washing.

The semidome bears a fresco of the Virgin and Child with the three wise men and the archangels Michael and Gabriel. It once graced the apse of the small Catalan Church of San Juan de Tredos in the Spanish Pyrenees.

In the nave of the chapel is a Romanesque doorway from San Leonardo al Frigido in Tuscany, carved from Carrara marble around 1175. Just to its left, a Tuscan marble holy-water font depicts Raynerius, patron saint of Pisa, who is believed to have performed miracles such as separating water from wine. The font was carved in 1160, the year of Raynerius' death. Suspended from the ceiling of the apse hangs a well-preserved 12C crucifix from the Convent of Santa Clara in Spain.

Romanesque Hall – The entrance features a round-arched doorway characteristic of the Romanesque style. On the left side, the capitals are carved with graceful birds feeding on acanthus plants. The capitals on the right bear carvings of imaginary animals surmounted by a delicate acanthus motif. The doorway is believed to come from Poitou, France.

The portal leading to the Saint-Guilhem Cloister is from a church in Reugny, in the upper Loire Valley, and dates from the late 12C; it represents a transitional style between the Romanesque and Gothic styles. The Gothic portal (13C) leading to the Langon Chapel was the entrance to a transept of the former Abbey of Moutiers-

Pontaut Chapter House

Saint-Jean in Burgundy. The statues might represent Clovis *(on the left)*, the first Christian French king, and his son Clothar *(on the right)*, who protected the abbey after its founding by his father at the end of the 5C.

Saint-Guilhem Cloister – The covered walkway contains a magnificent series of columns and capitals from the Benedictine abbey of Saint-Guilhem-le-Désert, near Montpellier, France. The property was sold during the French Revolution; some of the columns were being used to support grape vines when George Grey Barnard acquired them in 1906. Admire the intricately carved capitals (12C–13C), adorned with plants and figures; a number of the capitals reflect Roman inspiration. Several columns are also decorated with stylized patterns of vegetation.

The fountain in the center of the cloister was once a Romanesque capital in the Church of Saint-Sauveur in the Auvergne region of France. The grotesque corbels supporting the transverse arches and cornice of the gallery vaults hail from the Abbey of Sauve-Majeure, near Bordeaux.

Langon Chapel – The original parts of this chapel came from the choir of the Romanesque Church of Notre-Dame du Bourg at Langon, near Bordeaux, which was used as a Jacobin club during the French Revolution and later transformed into a dance hall and movie theater. A 12C Italian marble ciborium (tabernacle) symbolically protects a poignant 12C Virgin Mary carved in birch from Autun, Burgundy.

Pontaut Chapter House – Notre-Dame-de-Pontaut was first a Benedictine and later a Cistercian abbey in Gascony, France. Its chapter house, where the monks met every morning to discuss community affairs, exemplifies both the late-Romanesque style and the transition to Gothic with rounded-arch windows and doors and a rib-vaulted ceiling. On the other side of the open arches, lay brothers gathered in the cloister to follow the debates, while monks were seated along the wall. The capitals are particularly worth noting for the simple but forceful carving of ornamental geometric or plant forms.

Cuxa Cloister – Although this is the museum's largest cloister, it represents only half the size of the original structure. The various elements came from the Benedictine monastery of Saint-Michel-de-Cuxa, near Prades, in the French Pyrenees, an active center of art and learning in the 12C. Abandoned during the French Revolution, the monastery was sold in three parts, and during the 19C its elements were widely scattered. In 1913 Barnard was able to bring together about half of the original Romanesque capitals, 12 columns, 25 bases and 7 arches. Rose-colored Languedoc marble was cut from original quarries to complete the reconstruction. Note the capitals carved with plants, grotesque personages and fantastic animals possibly inspired by motifs from the Near East; curiously, there are very few that bear any clear religious significance.

Early Gothic Hall – *This room has been closed indefinitely.*

Nine Heroes Tapestries Room – The doorway from the Cuxa Cloister is capped by ornamental ogee arches, exemplary of the Flamboyant Gothic style. Contained within this room is part of a set of **tapestries**★ (1410) that are among the oldest in existence, along with the Apocalypse tapestries in Angers, France. The theme of the Nine Heroes, very popular in the Middle Ages, includes three pagans (Hector,

Alexander, Julius Caesar), three Hebrews (David, Joshua, Judas Maccabeus) and three Christians (Arthur, Charlemagne, Godfrey of Bouillon). Their feminine counterparts were the Nine Heroines.

The surviving tapestries on display depict five of the nine Heroes. David is recognizable by his golden harp, and Arthur by his banner with three crowns representing England, Scotland and Brittany. Joshua, Alexander and Caesar are also portrayed. A number of lesser personages escort the Heroes, giving an edifying view of the medieval social structure. The arms of Berry, with golden fleurs-de-lis above the Hebrew heroes, indicate that the tapestries may have been woven for Jean, Duke of Berry, a patron of the arts and brother of the French king Charles V. Before continuing into the next room, pause to admire the 16C Gothic stone doorway from Auvergne, carved with unicorns.

Unicorn Tapestries Hall – The magnificently colored **Unicorn tapestries**★ are among the most exceptional of the golden age of tapestry, which flourished at the end of the 15C and the beginning of the 16C. Admire the fine craftsmanship and attention to detail with which the artist has depicted the people and animals, their expressions and poses. The set of seven tapestries originally hung in the Château de Verteuil in Charente (southwestern France), the home of the well-known La Rochefoucauld family. Six of the tapestries were acquired by John D. Rockefeller Jr. in 1922; the seventh was added in 1938. A narwhal tusk, strongly resembling a unicorn's horn, is mounted adjacent to a 15C limestone fireplace from Alençon, Normandy.

Boppard Room – This room is named for the German town of Boppard on the Rhine, where the six stained-glass panels were created for the Carmelite church (late 15C). There is also a Spanish alabaster altarpiece (15C) and a brass eagle lectern (16C) from Belgium.

Burgos Tapestry Hall – *This hall is closed for renovation.*

Campin Room – This room, with its painted Spanish ceiling, has been furnished with medieval domestic objects including a table and benches, a bronze chandelier and a 15C iron bird cage (the only one known to have survived from the Middle Ages). Above the chest is the famous **Annunciation Triptych** by 15C Flemish artist Robert Campin. The central panel represents the Annunciation. The side panels depict the donors, on the left, and on the right, St. Joseph in his workshop; notice the mousetrap on St. Joseph's workbench and the painstakingly reproduced details of the town square in the background.

Late Gothic Hall – This large gallery, designed to resemble a monastery refectory, is lighted by four 15C windows from the convent of the Dominicans at Nivernais (Yonne), in Burgundy. There is a remarkable example of a Spanish 15C altarpiece, in painted, carved and gilded wood. You may also admire the pure lines of a kneeling Virgin (late 15C, Italy) and the Adoration of the Magi (late 15C, Swabia, Germany). In an effort to re-create the original positioning, the statues of God, the Father; Christ; and the Virgin (15C, Austria) have been placed over a console above the doorway.

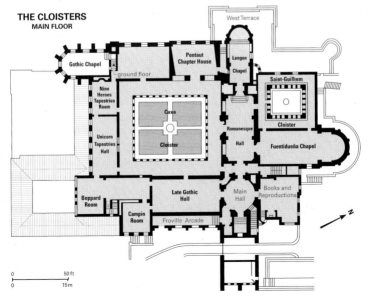

THE CLOISTERS
MAIN FLOOR

Ground Floor *See floor plan, below*

Gothic Chapel – Inspired by a chapel in the Church of Saint-Nazaire at Carcassonne and by the church at Monsempron, both located in France, this structure provides a superb setting for an interesting collection of tomb effigies and slabs. Among the former, note the effigy of Jean d'Alluye (13C) and four monumental Catalan sarcophagi of the Counts of Urgel (14C). The tombs come from the Premonstratensian monastery of Santa Maria de Bellpuig de las Avellanas, north of Lérida in Spain. The apsidal windows are now glazed with 14C Austrian stained glass, mostly from the pilgrimage Church of St. Leonhard in Lavanthal.

Bonnefont Cloister – This cloister is bordered on two sides by twin columns. Their double capitals in gray white marble, from the quarries of Saint-Béat, come from the cloister (13-14C) of the former Cistercian abbey at Bonnefont-en-Comminges in southern France.
The other two sides of the cloister form terraces offering a view of Fort Tryon Park and the Hudson River. A garden of medieval herbs and flowers adds to the charm of this spot.

Trie Cloister – Because of its small size, this cloister evokes in an especially pleasant manner the atmosphere of serenity and meditation associated with a monastery. Its capitals, dating from the late 15C, are decorated with coats of arms or religious scenes; note those on the south arcade, which illustrate the life of Christ. The central fountain is a composite of two 15-16C limestone fountains discovered in France's Vosges region.

Glass Gallery – This room is named for the roundels and panels of stained glass (15-16C) representing scenes from the Old and New Testaments. A fine selection of 15C and 16C statues in wood, alabaster, stone and ivory is gathered here along with a Nativity altarpiece painted in the workshop of 15C Flemish artist Roger van der Weyden. At the far end of the gallery, note the intricately carved wooden panels that originally surrounded the courtyard staircase of a 16C house in Abbeville, in northern France.

Treasury – The Cloisters' collection of smaller objects of exceptionally fine quality is displayed in this hall. The most outstanding piece is a walrus-ivory cross from the 12C, the so-called Cloisters Cross, which has been traced to the monastery of Bury St. Edmund's in Suffolk, England. Both the front and back of the cross are covered with figures, inscriptions and minuscule scenes from the Old and New Testaments that have been skillfully carved with great attention to detail. Note the expressiveness of the hands and, on the back of the cross, the individuality of the 12 figures set in frames. The facial expression of each of these figures is different, and no two hold the scroll in the same manner.
Also of interest are the enamels (13C, Limoges, France) and reliquaries used for private devotions, and a rosary bead of boxwood with a tiny representation of the Passion inside (16C, South Lowlands). Superb wall hangings embroidered with silk and gold threads depict biblical scenes. Note the late-14C German hanging with scenes from the life of Christ and the Old Testament.

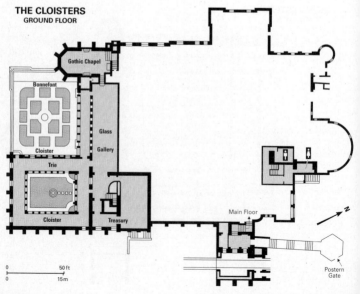

THE CLOISTERS
GROUND FLOOR

Gothic Chapel

Bonnefont

Glass

Cloister

Gallery

Trie

Cloister   Treasury

Main Floor

N

Postern
Gate

0   50 ft
0   15m

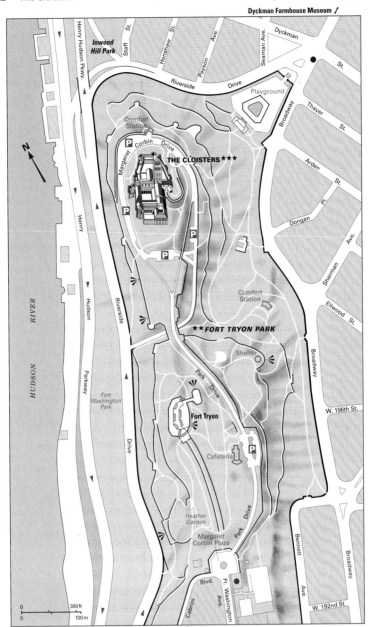

Dyckman Farmhouse Museum /

/ George Washington Bridge ★★

A group of 37 carved wooden panels is believed to have been part of a set of choir stalls, probably from the royal abbey of Jumièges in Normandy (early 16C). The panels are decorated in the late-Gothic style with scenes from the life of the Virgin and Christ. The wall case contains the magnificent *Belles Heures* (Book of Hours) manuscript, which belonged to Jean, Duke of Berry, who also might have commissioned the Nine Heroes Tapestries.

ADDITIONAL SIGHTS

★★ **Fort Tryon Park** – *Map above.* Covering 62 acres of wooded hills above the Hudson River, this peaceful green space, landscaped by Frederick Law Olmsted Jr., seems miles away from the bustle of the heart of the city. Although fairly small, the terrain is varied with hills, dales and cleverly arranged terraces overlooking the river. In the 19C the area was covered with farms and pastures, replacing earlier Indian camps. John D. Rockefeller Jr. acquired the site in 1909 and donated it to the city in 1930.

A lookout built on the site of **Fort Tryon** caps a hill 250ft above the river. The fort, named for the last English civil governor of New York, William Tryon, was an outpost of Fort Washington, which was the last fort to resist the British invasion of Manhattan during the American Revolution. It was here that American heroine Margaret Corbin replaced her husband—who had been killed in action—and fought until severely wounded. With the fall of Fort Washington on November 16, 1776, the British occupied all of New York City, which remained in their hands for seven years.

The lookout point affords fine **views**★ of the Hudson River and the George Washington Bridge to the west, and the East River to the east.

Between Fort Tryon and Margaret Corbin Plaza to the south is the three-acre Heather Garden planted with colorful and ornamental flower beds.

Inwood Hill Park – *It is unwise to walk in the park alone.* Set at the northwestern tip of Manhattan, this park is separated from Fort Tryon Park by a ravine dotted with several apartment houses. Wooded and hilly, the terrain seems to have altered very little since the Algonquins inhabited the area, then known as *Shora-Kapkok*. During the Revolution, British and Hessian troops were quartered here. Today the park is quite empty on weekdays, but on Sundays New Yorkers in search of greenery come to the park to picnic and relax. Located northeast of the park along the Harlem River is Columbia University's ballpark, Baker Field. To the east of the park, on the corner of West 204th Street and Broadway, stands **Dyckman Farmhouse Museum** *(open year-round Tue–Sun 10am–4pm; closed major holidays; $1; ☎ 212-304-9422; www.dyckman.org)*, the only extant 18C Dutch Colonial farmhouse in Manhattan. Appointed with period Dutch and French furniture, and bordered by a charming herb garden and a smokehouse, the structure illustrates life in colonial America.

★★**George Washington Bridge** – *Toll charged (toll booth on New Jersey side only; ☎ 800-221-9903)*. A tremendous feat of engineering, this toll bridge, which links 179th Street in Manhattan to Fort Lee in New Jersey, was for a number of years the longest bridge in the world and is still the only 14-lane suspension bridge. Designed by **O.H. Amman** (an American engineer of Swiss origin, who also conceived the Verrazano-Narrows Bridge) and architect Cass Gilbert, the bridge was opened on October 25, 1931, and cost about $59 million. In 1959 the growing volume of traffic required the construction of a lower level, opened in 1962. At the same time, an intricate system of interchanges was installed.

> ■**A few facts**
>
> The bridge spans the Hudson River in one pure line 3,500ft long. The towers are 604ft high, and the supporting cables have a diameter of 36in. The upper level, 250ft above water, holds eight lanes; the lower level is divided into six lanes.

The best view of the George Washington Bridge may be had from the sightseeing boats *(p 75)* that circle Manhattan, or from the Henry Hudson Parkway along the Hudson River. To the north, note the **Little Red Lighthouse** on Jeffrey's Hook, a point of land on the Hudson near 178th Street. The only lighthouse on Manhattan, this cast-iron structure was moved here from New Jersey in 1921 to alert seacraft to the treacherous surrounding waters. After construction of the George Washington Bridge—equipped with special lighting to direct river traffic—the lighthouse was decommissioned *(visit by appointment only Apr–Oct; ☎ 212-304-2365)*.

Museums in Manhattan

(in alphabetical order)

AMERICAN FOLK ART MUSEUM

45 W. 53rd St. **MTA** E, F train to 53rd St.
Map p 89

Open year-round Tue–Sun 10am–6pm (Fri until 8pm). Closed major holidays. $9. ✗ ♿
☎ 212-595-9533. www.folkartmuseum.org.
Quartered across from Lincoln Center and housed in a recently completed structure near
the Museum of Modern Art, this museum was founded in 1961 to preserve and present
American folk art from the 18C to the present. Opened in late 2001, the new eight-
story building, designed by Williams, Tsien and Associates, was conceived to display—on
seven atrium-lit levels—about 500 of the 4,000 works in the museum's permanent collection. The Lincoln Center site continues to host temporary and traveling shows
(2 Lincoln Sq.; open daily 11am–7:30pm, Mon til 6pm; ☎ 212-595-9533).
The artists represented in the permanent collection are mainly self-taught, their work
functional and, for the most part, handmade. Holdings include 19C weather vanes; a
whirligig depicting Uncle Sam riding a bicycle; the lovely portrait *Girl in Red Dress*
with Cat and Dog by Ammi Phillips; and a number of paintings and manuscript pages
by the Chicago-based fantasist Henry Darger.

AMERICAN MUSEUM OF NATURAL HISTORY★★★

Central Park West, between 77th and 81st Sts.

MTA B, C train to 81st St. or 1, 9 train to 79th St.
Map p 176

One of New York's most venerated establishments, this institution ranks among the
largest of its kind in the world. Dealing with all facets of natural history, its outstanding collections range from minerals and gems to dinosaurs, and from Indian
totem poles to Tibetan gowns.

Historical Notes

The Building – Founded in 1869 by Albert S. Bickmore, the museum was initially
installed in the Arsenal, in Central Park. Calvert Vaux designed the first building of the
present structure to be erected on a swampy area north of the Dakota. Construction of
the colossus, today composed of 23 interconnected buildings, began in 1874, when Gen.
Ulysses S. Grant, then president of the US, laid the cornerstone. It was formally opened
three years later by his successor, Rutherford B. Hayes. Finally completed in the 1930s,
the complex is a curious mixture of styles, the result of its being worked on by various
architects at different periods. Designed by John Russell Pope, the grand, rotunda-
topped Theodore Roosevelt Memorial Hall was dedicated in 1936 as the state's official
memorial to the nation's 26th president. Roosevelt's boyhood interest in taxidermy and
collecting resulted in his giving the museum some of its earliest acquisitions, namely: a
bat, a turtle, 4 bird eggs, 12 mice and the skull of a red squirrel. His enthusiasm lasted
a lifetime as did his generosity in donating specimens from his worldwide expeditions.
A 1996 renovation restored the fourth floor exhibition halls to their former grandeur,
revealing windows, arches and cast-iron columns that had been hidden for years. It was
the February 2000 opening of the **Rose Center for Earth and Space★★** on the museum's north
side (West 81st Street) that brought much-deserved national attention. Increasing the
museum's square footage by 25 percent, a glittering, seven-story-high glass box contains
state-of-the-art exhibits and a gargantuan sphere, inside of which stargazers can enjoy the
Hayden Planetarium's new, turbo-charged space show. Views of the eye-catching center,
a replanted Theodore Roosevelt Park, and the old apartment buildings of 81st Street can
be enjoyed from the Arthur Ross Terrace, a vast, 47,000sq ft public space built above a
new sunken parking lot. To the west (Columbus Avenue), the new Weston Pavilion, a glass-
walled little sibling to the Rose Center, houses a suspended 18ft aluminum-and-steel
spherical armillary that demonstrates New York's exact position in the cosmos on
January 1, 2000. In an added millennial touch, the museum and the *New York Times*
planted a time capsule in the stone court outside the pavilion. A plaque instructs future
generations that the capsule not be opened until January 1, 3000. On West 77th Street
an eight-story library holds the museum's 450,000 volumes on natural history.

The Collections – Culled from more than 1,000 expeditions since 1869, the museum's
holdings include over 30 million artifacts and specimens, only a small part of which are
on view in some 40 exhibit halls on four floors. The various displays include life-size
dioramas of animals shown in their natural habitats: the ground and vegetation are

faithfully reproduced, and the background scenes are effectively painted by artists using sketches made at the original sites. The lighting contributes to the realism of the scenes. The latest scientific information and interpretive techniques inform the design of the new galleries.

Visiting the Museum

Kids *Open year-round daily 10am–5:45pm. Closed Thanksgiving Day & Dec 25. $12 adults; $7 children (includes admission to Rose Center exhibits). Combination tickets including the museum, the Rose Center and the Hayden Planetarium Space Show are available for $22 adults; $13 children.* ✗ ♿ ☎ 212-769-5100. www.amnh.org.

Because the museum's collections are numerous, it is impossible to see every exhibit in a single day. You may wish to budget two days and take a break by exploring adjacent Central Park, or having a meal at a restaurant on nearby Amsterdam Avenue. The museum offers four eateries: in the **Museum Food Court** (lower level; *open daily 11am–4:45pm*) you can get anything from hot entrées to sushi; next to the food court, **Big Dipper Ice Cream Café** *(seasonal hours)* features classic sundaes and cones as well as egg creams, floats and malteds; sandwiches and salads are available at **Café On 4** *(4th floor, Central Park West side; open Sat & Sun 11am–4:45pm)*; **Café Pho** *(77th St. lobby; seasonal hours)* serves traditional Vietnamese fare in a re-created Asian marketplace setting.

The following description presents the highlights of each floor. To plan an itinerary that suits your interests, stop by the information desk to pick up the museum's detailed floor plan. Some halls may be devoted to temporary exhibits or closed for renovation; check at the information desk. Located throughout the halls, touch screens provide directions to, and descriptions of, each exhibit.

VISIT

Main Entrance – On the Central Park side is the main entrance, which opens onto the main lobby of the museum *(2nd floor)*, part of a majestic 800ft-long facade. (Another entrance, on West 77th Street, leads to the first floor and the IMAX Theater.) Before entering, note the Ionic colonnade of Theodore Roosevelt Memorial Hall bearing the statues of explorers and naturalists Daniel Boone, John James Audubon, and Lewis and Clark. An equestrian statue (1940, James Earle Fraser) featuring Roosevelt flanked by a Native American and an African American, stands sentinel at the entrance to the hall.
Begin in the Theodore Roosevelt Memorial Hall on the 2nd floor.

Second Floor – Posed with some imagination, protecting its young from an allosaurus, a replica of a huge **barosaurus** looms over the central rotunda. Rising to five stories (50ft), the skeleton of this Jurassic herbivore is a resin-and-foam replica of the original fossilized bones, which are too fragile to be mounted for display. Just west of the rotunda is the spectacular **Hall of African Mammals★** dedicated to Carl Akeley, who revolutionized museum display with his realistic dioramas in the early 20C. Highlighted by an impressive herd of African elephants on the alert, dioramas present zebras, antelopes, gorillas, lions and gazelles in their natural surroundings. In the galleries on the third-floor level of this hall, other dioramas depict various species of monkeys, rhinoceroses, leopards and hyenas. To the north of the Central Park West entrance is the **Hall of Oceanic Birds**. Winged creatures from New Guinea to New Zealand are represented in dioramas, while albatrosses fly overhead, set off by a light blue sky (through May 2004, the hall is home to a special exhibit, The Butterfly Conservatory).
The **Hall of African Peoples** traces the development of complex human culture on the African continent. The **Hall of Mexico and Central America** displays an outstanding pre-Columbian collection. Of special interest are the exhibits related to the Aztec and Mayan civilizations, gold ornaments of the ancient Americas and stone and clay sculptures from central Veracruz. The **Hall of South American Peoples** exhibits Andean and Amazonian treasures, including the 2,500-year-old Paracas mantle, that are testimony to the religious beliefs and social organization of the ancient, recently extinct and existing cultures of this continent.
The **Hall of Asian Peoples★** features a comprehensive exhibit of life from prehistoric times to the late 19C, when Western technology began to influence the traditions of the Orient. Daily life in Asian trading cities and villages from Arabia to Japan and Siberia to India, and colorful ceremonies and rituals are portrayed by life-size displays and dioramas. The Asian collection comprises more than 60,000 artifacts, making it one of the largest such assemblages in the Western hemisphere.

First Floor – The 77th Street foyer is dominated by a seagoing Haida war canoe from the Queen Charlotte Islands, in British Columbia. Carved out of one piece of cedar in 1878, the craft can hold more than 30 passengers. The **Hall of Northwest Coast Indians★** presents superb totem poles, American Indian and Inuit tools and handicrafts. To the left of the foyer is the **Hall of Mollusks and Our World**, covering the many uses of mollusks and their shells by past and present cultures around the globe. The **Hall of Human Biology and Evolution★** strives to place humans in the context of the natural world. The first section of the hall explores the biology we share with life around us and the characteristics that make us unique. Blending whimsy (one "diorama" poses a family of skeletons in front of the TV), frankness (straightforward discussions of bodily functions), and aesthetics (a video interprets the body's workings using dance, music and graphics), lively displays contrast human and nonhuman biology. The second section, devoted to evolution, explains the confusing array of early human ancestors through dioramas and fossil exhibits. A fascinating holographic diorama explains the work of archaeologists at LaMicoque in France. The final section explores the emergence of human creativity at the end of the ice ages. As a whole, the hall conveys the wonder and complexity of life across time and the animal kingdom.

Ahnighito, a 34-ton meteorite fragment found in Greenland in 1895, forms the focal point of the newly renovated **Hall of Meteorites★**. The hall incorporates more than 130 meteorite specimens in its investigaton of the nature and history of meteorites and their role in unlocking the history of the solar system. Among the meteorite "greatest hits" documented are the one that produced a 185mi crater in the Yucatan peninsula some 65 million years ago and is credited by some with killing off the land dinosaurs.

In the **Halls of Minerals and Gems★★**, you may feast your eyes on more than 4,000 specimens of rocks, minerals and gems, including rubies, emeralds and diamonds. Here you'll find the Star of India, the world's largest star sapphire (weight: 563 carats). The first floor **Hall of Biodiversity★** bustles with an array of life-forms intended to convey the variety and interactivity of life on earth. The exhibit also communicates a strong environmental message about human impact on biodiversity worldwide. The west wall displays 1,500 specimens and models that illustrate the wonders of biodiversity. The heart of the exhibit, however, is the walk-through **diorama** of the Dzanga-Sangha rain forest in Africa. This lush setting includes 160 replica species and more than 500,000 carefully crafted leaves. Also of interest are the North American Mammals and North American Forests halls.

An immense (94ft long) model of a blue whale, suspended in a dive position, dominates the two-story **Hall of Ocean Life★**, which reopened in summer 2003 after a $25 million renovation. Shimmering lights and an underwater soundscape "immerse" visitors in the whale's ocean home. Traditional dioramas—notably the two-story Andros Coral Reef—have been restored and improved. On the mezzanine, the museum took the opportunity to update the traditional diorama display with eight new exhibits that explore ocean ecosystems (such as estuaries, polar seas, the deep-sea floor). They incorporate historical models with fiber-optic lighting, embedded text and graphics, touch screens, and high-definition video of the actual environments. Films on different subjects are shown in the IMAX Theater, a 996-seat auditorium equipped with a gigantic movie screen four stories high and 66ft wide.

Third Floor – The **Hall of Reptiles and Amphibians** features the world's largest living lizard, the 10ft Komodo dragon. The **Hall of Primates** displays animals from the same biological order as man, beginning with the tree shrew. To the west of the primates, displays on the lifestyles of the Eastern Woodlands and Plains Indians include model houses, weapons, tools and utensils. In the **Hall of North American Birds**, you'll find a variety of birds from all corners of the country, including the wild turkey, which Benjamin Franklin wanted to designate America's national bird.

The **Hall of the Pacific Peoples★**, inspired by the work and ideas of Dr. Margaret Mead (1901-78), contains exhibits related to six cultural areas of the Pacific: Australia, Indonesia, the Philippines, Melanesia, Micronesia and Polynesia. A large display case near the center of the hall holds sacred masks, carved figures and boldly decorated shields illustrating the rich and diverse art of the peoples of the Sepik River basin.

Barosaurus skeleton

Fourth Floor – *Begin your visit in the orientation center.* Completed in 1996, the six **fossil halls**★★ on the top floor represent a visual and intellectual tour de force, but visitors should be prepared for an overwhelming experience. Curators have attempted a stunning departure from the usual presentation of this type of material by arranging the familiar fossil remains and interpretive exhibits along a cladogram, or "branching evolutionary tree." Such an arrangement is intended to depict evolutionary relationships among contemporaneous creatures as well as through time. These galleries are dense with information, making a preliminary visit to the orientation center essential. Then, beginning with the **Hall of Vertebrate Origins**, the visitor navigates along the branches of the tree, following the development of vertebrates from the earliest jawless fishes to dinosaurs and mammals. As the cladogram progresses, "advanced" features emerge (jaws, four limbs, grasping hands, and so on) to create the branching effect that furthers evolution. Specimen alcoves on either side of the main branch explore groups of related animals in detail. The museum has the largest collection of fossil vertebrates in the world, and visitors scouting out skeletal remains will not be disappointed. In the **Hall of Saurischian Dinosaurs** (distinguished by grasping hands), huge apatosaurus and *Tyrannosaurus rex* tower over tiny *Archaeopteryx lithographica*. In the **Hall of Ornithischian Dinosaurs** (whose pubis bones point backward), note the "mummy," really a fossilized imprint of a duck-billed dinosaur carcass. Discovered in 1908, the fossil is so detailed that it has even preserved the texture of the animal's skin. Together the two dinosaur halls present more than 100 specimens, 85 percent of which are real fossils. The final wing showcases "Mammals and Their Extinct Relatives," including ancient mammoths, mastodons, saber-toothed cats and giant sloths.

★★ **Rose Center for Earth and Space** – *Open year-round daily 10am–5:45pm (Fri until 8:45pm). Closed Thanksgiving Day & Dec 25. Museum admission includes space center exhibits. $12 ($22 including show). Audio tours (75min; free with admission) are available. Space shows are shown in the Hayden Planetarium Mon–Fri 10:30am–4:30pm (Fri until 7:30pm), Sat 10:30am–4:30pm. Advance tickets: ☏ 212-769-5200 or www.amnh.org.* Accessible via the museum (first and second floors), or through its own arched entrance on West 81st Street, the center blends cutting-edge science with high-impact visuals to describe the mysteries of the cosmos. A good place to start is with a star show at the acclaimed **space theater**,

● **Starry Nights: Under the Sphere**

On the first Friday of every month, the Rose Center hosts live jazz performances. On these nights you can sip sangria (or Spanish sherry or wine) and nibble Spanish tapas (small plates) from the Tapas Bar while you enjoy the music. *Performances at 5:30pm–6:30pm and 7pm–8pm.*

located inside the Hayden Sphere. The most advanced of its kind, the digital program takes spectators on a virtual ride through the Milky Way Galaxy to the edge of the observable universe, using 3-D maps developed with the help of NASA.

Outside the theater, a 400ft-long display, Scales of the Universe, demonstrates the enormity of space with scale models, touch screens and text panels. Dangling from the ceiling above it are models of the planets of our solar system—all except Pluto. In a controversial decision, the center has demoted the ninth planet to asteroid status.

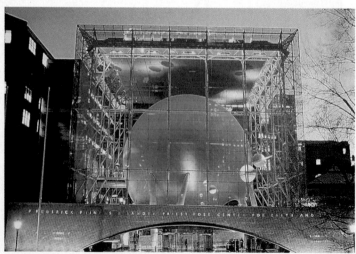

Rose Center for Earth and Space

A two-minute presentation on the Big Bang uses lasers and SurroundSound to conjure the birth of the universe. Upon exiting, visitors descend a spiral ramp to the first-floor **Hall of Planet Earth★**, where exhibits focus on geologic and climatic features of our own planet. Down on the lower-level, the **Hall of the Universe★**, sparkles and hums with up-to-the-minute video from the Hubble Telescope; towering models of cosmic phenomena; and artifacts including the 15-ton Willamette Meteorite.

ASIA SOCIETY AND MUSEUM★

725 Park Ave. **MTA** 6 train to 68th St.
Map p 181

Open year-round Tue–Sun 11am–6pm (Fri until 9pm). Closed major holidays. $7. ✗ &
☎ *212-517-2742. www.asiasociety.org.*

This intimate museum was founded in 1956 under the guidance of John D. Rockefeller III, with a view to promoting an increased understanding and appreciation of Asian cultures. In addition to providing an elegant setting for showcasing Asian art, the Asia Society offers lectures, films and performances year-round.

Designed by Edward Larrabee Barnes in red granite and sandstone, the distinguished headquarters building (1981) rises to eight stories. A major renovation, conceived by New York architect Bartholomew Voorsanger and completed in 2001, doubles the interior public and exhibit space and includes a glass-enclosed, sky-lit Garden Court. In the new Visitor Center and Asian Arts Learning Center, interactive terminals provide in-depth information on Asia Society exhibits and programs as well as links to resources on Asian art.

The new exhibit space houses Mr. and Mrs. John D. Rockefeller III's outstanding collection of Asian art, donated to the society in 1978. Objects on view include lively animated Indian bronzes, Chinese and Japanese ceramics, exquisite screen paintings and hanging scrolls, wood carvings and manuscripts. Also of interest are the three-dimensional and low-relief stone sculptures from Southeast Asia.

AUDUBON TERRACE★

On Broadway between 155th and 156th Sts.
MTA 1 train to 157th St. or B train to 155th St.

Grouped around a wide, barren plaza located to the northwest of Harlem stand some of the city's lesser-known museums and cultural institutions. Naturalist John Audubon once had a country house named Minniesland on the site. The present buildings were erected at the beginning of the 20C in the Neoclassical style by Charles Pratt Huntington, nephew of Archer M. Huntington, who conceived the Audubon Terrace project in 1908 and provided the financial backing.

★★**Hispanic Society of America** – *Open year-round Tue–Sat 10am–4:30pm, Sun 1pm–4pm. Closed major holidays.* ☎ *212-926-2234. www.hispanicsociety.org.* This small yet fascinating museum, which offers a panorama of Spanish civilization from pre-Roman times to the present century and houses a collection of high-quality Old Masters, comes as quite a surprise in this part of the city. Located opposite a bronze statue of El Cid (1927, Anna Hyatt Huntington), the two-story edifice contains a lavish and well-appointed interior. Designed as an interior courtyard in the Renaissance style, the first-floor gallery presents a large selection of traditional and ritual objects such as choir stalls, exquisite silverware, Paleolithic tools, Renaissance tombstones, tabernacles, silk brocades and altar frontals. Upon entering, notice two life-size portraits by 18C Spanish artist Francisco de Goya, including one of the Duchess of Alba. To the right of the gallery, note the 15C Mudejar door surrounded by colorful tiles. The Sorolla room *(far right)* features an ensemble of paintings by Sorolla y Bastida titled *Provinces of Spain*. A research library is also located on the first floor.

The second-floor balustrade contains a rich collection of earthenware, ceramics, metalwork, porcelain, lusterware and jewelry displayed in glass cases. Portraits by renowned artists El Greco, Morales, Ribera, Velázquez and Goya line the walls.

★**American Numismatic Society** – *Open year-round Tue–Sat 9:30am–4:30pm. Closed major holidays.* ☎ *212-234-3130.* Founded in 1858, this small museum houses one of the world's foremost collections of coins and medals, as well as a comprehensive research library and archives. Two galleries on the first floor display medals of historic or artistic interest and rotating exhibits on the history and various uses of coins throughout the world. A major exhibit, "The World of Coins," traces the history of money as a medium of exchange from ancient to modern times.

American Academy of Arts and Letters – *Open during exhibitions Mar & mid-May–mid-Jun Thu–Sun 1pm–4pm.* ☎ *212-368-5900.* This is the nation's highest honor society for the arts, with a membership of 250 of America's foremost artists, architects, writers and composers. Art and manuscript exhibits are held twice a year *(call ahead for schedule).*

COOPER-HEWITT NATIONAL
DESIGN MUSEUM★

2 E. 91st St. MTA 4, 5, 6 train to 86th or 96th Sts.
Map p 11

Founded in 1897 by New York socialites **Sarah**, **Eleanor** and **Amy Hewitt**, this museum of the decorative arts is devoted to historical and contemporary design, with a focus on its uses in industrial and interior design, architecture, fashion and advertising. Affiliated with the Smithsonian Institution since 1967, the museum reopened as the National Design Museum in 1976.

Historical Notes

The Complex – The Cooper Union of New York—the college of art, architecture and engineering founded by the Hewitt sisters' grandfather Peter Cooper—first housed the museum's holdings. In 1972 the collection was transferred to this Beaux-Arts mansion (1898), built by wealthy industrialist **Andrew Carnegie** (1835-1919). Surrounded by a wrought-iron fence and an inviting garden, the Chateau-style residence once contained 64 rooms on six stories. A $20 million renovation, aimed at updating the landmark mansion and renovating gallery space, was begun in 1995 and completed in 1998. A large **Design Resource Center**, housed in two adjoining 19C town houses and linked to the original mansion via a two-story bridge, opened in mid-1998. The permanent collection is stored in the resource center.

The Collection – The Cooper-Hewitt's extensive collection encompasses some 250,000 objects representing artists from around the world and spanning more than 3,000 years. Among the highlights are 50,000 original **prints** and **drawings**, ranging from works by 15C Italian master Andrea Mantegna to Americans Frederic Church and Winslow Homer to 20C Italian Surrealist painter Giorgio de Chirico. The museum's rich holdings also include delicate textiles dating from the 3C BC; decorative arts including silver, bronze and wrought-iron metalwork; examples of jewelry and goldsmiths' work; wallpaper samples; bandboxes; porcelain, glass and earthenware; furniture; woodwork; and hardware (18C and 19C Chinese bird cages and splendid clocks).

VISIT

Open year-round Tue–Fri 10am–5pm (Fri until 9pm), Sat 10am–6pm, Sun noon–5pm. Closed major holidays. $10 (free Tue 5pm–9pm). ✗ ♿ ☎ 212-849-8400. www.si.edu/ndm. Note: The permanent collection may be viewed by advance appointment only. The library may be visited by appointment only (same day).

Exhibits change regularly. Each focuses on a particular aspect of design or a type of decorative or functional object, using a selection of objects from the permanent collection as illustration. Located on the third floor, the library includes a picture reference section and archives of color, pattern, textiles, symbols and interior design. At the rear of the mansion, the terrace overlooks a spacious outdoor garden of seasonal plantings.

Cooper-Hewitt Museum

DAHESH MUSEUM

580 Madison Ave. at 56th St. **MTA** 6 train to 51st St.
Map p 89

Open Tue–Sun 11am–6pm. Open until 9pm the 1st Thu of every month. Closed major holidays. $9. ♿ ☎ 212-759-0606. www.daheshmuseum.org.

Located since 1995 on Fifth Avenue in the heart of midtown Manhattan, the Dahesh is slated to move to Madison Avenue at 56th Street in spring 2003. The museum houses a collection of European Romantic and academic art amassed earlier in the 20C by an influential Lebanese writer and philosopher whose pen name, Dr. Dahesh, means "wondrous." Shows presented each year draw from the museum's own holdings, including works by Rosa Bonheur, John Ward, Adolphe Bouguereau and Constant Troyon, as well as related 19C and early-20C art and photography from other museums. Lunch-hour gallery talks, music performances and evening lecture series are also offered.

EL MUSEO DEL BARRIO

1230 Fifth Ave. **MTA** 6 train to 103rd St.
Map p 10

Open year-round Wed–Sun 11am–5pm. Closed major holidays. $6. ♿ ☎ 212-831-7272. www.elmuseo.org.

Housed in the left wing of an imposing U-shaped building fronting Fifth Avenue, this small museum (1969) serves as the leading cultural center for "El Barrio," the Hispanic—predominantly Puerto Rican—community of Spanish Harlem. Devoted to the arts and culture of Puerto Rico and other Latin American countries, the museum presents changing displays of Caribbean artifacts and contemporary painting and sculpture, as well as a permanent exhibit of hand-carved statuettes, known as Santos de Palo (saints). The museum plays an active role in the Latin American community, sponsoring lectures and various workshops.

THE FORBES GALLERIES★★

62 Fifth Ave. **MTA** 4, 5, 6 train to 14th St.
Map p 151

Housed in the ground-floor galleries of the Forbes Building (1925, Carrère and Hastings), home of the well-known business biweekly, an eclectic collection gathered by publisher Malcolm Forbes (1919-1990) and his sons has been on view since 1985. Best known for their beautiful Fabergé pieces, the galleries also feature thousands of toy soldiers, fine art and autograph memorabilia.

VISIT

Open year-round Tue–Sat 10am–4pm. Closed major holidays. ♿ ☎ 212-206-5548.

Highlighting the collection of more than 200 objets d'art created by jeweler and goldsmith Peter Carl Fabergé are the **Imperial Easter Eggs★**, produced by Fabergé workshops for the Russian royal family between 1885 and 1916. The museum owns 12 of the 45 such eggs known to exist today. Forbes encountered the work of Fabergé when he purchased a gold cigarette case for his wife. Gold, silver, precious stones and enameling decorate these exquisite fantasies, several of which conceal hidden surprises: note the mechanical bird that emerges and sings when a certain orange is rotated (Orange Tree Egg); the bejeweled replica of the royal coronation coach (Coronation Egg); and the chanticleer that appears on the hour, crowing and flapping its wings (Chanticleer Egg).

The Spring Flowers Easter Egg by Peter Carl Fabergé

Forbes bought his first lead soldier at an auction in the 1960s (only memories of his childhood toy figures survived). Some 12,000 of the more than 100,000 **toy soldiers** in the Forbes collection are on view. Arranged in scenes dramatizing historic events, miniature soldiers depict famous battles such as the Trojan War and Alexander the Great's defeat of the Persians as well as encounters between cowboys and Indians.

The Forbes flotilla of over 500 miniature watercraft ranges from Noah's ark to riverboats and ocean liners. Begun in 1970, the collection consists of toy boats manufactured in tin and cast iron from 1870 to 1955.

THE FRICK COLLECTION★★★

1 E. 70th St., between Fifth and Madison Aves. **MTA** 6 train to 68th St.
Map p 180

One of the world's most distinguished small museums, The Frick Collection, displayed in a luxurious private mansion, constitutes an exceptional trove of Old Masters, furnishings and decorative arts acquired by a single collector over a period of 40 years.

Historical Notes

A Pittsburgh coke and steel industrialist, **Henry Clay Frick** (1849-1919) began collecting works of art on his first trip to Europe, which he took in the company of his friend Andrew Mellon, the primary benefactor of the National Gallery of Art *(see Michelin Green Guide Washington DC)*. First concentrating on 18C English paintings, Frick later ventured into sculpture, in particular bronzes, then prints and drawings, enamels, furniture, porcelain and rugs. In 1913 he commissioned this 40-room mansion, designed by Carrère and Hastings (also responsible for the New York Public Library) and erected on the site of the former Lennox Library, to display his holdings. Frick bequeathed the mansion and the collection to a board of trustees, with a mandate to transform the building into a museum after his death. Following a renovation and extension project undertaken by John Russell Pope, the residence reopened as a museum in 1935. Today the rich collection contains works ranging from the 14C to the 19C.

VISIT

Open year-round Tue–Sat 10am–6pm (Fri until 9pm), Sun 1pm–6pm. Closed major holidays. $12. Children under 10 not admitted; children 10-16 must be accompanied by an adult. Audio tours available at no charge. & ☎ 212-288-0700. www.frick.org. Before touring the mansion, we recommend viewing the orientation film shown on the half hour in the Music Room.

Entrance Hall – A bust of Henry Clay Frick (1922) by Malvina Hoffman is displayed in a niche on the right of the marble-floored hall.

Boucher Room – Reminiscent of an 18C boudoir, with its intimate and refined atmosphere, this room contains eight paintings by French Rococo painter François Boucher (1703-70). Commissioned by Louis XV's favorite consort, Madame de Pompadour, in 1752, they represent the Arts and Sciences. Among the 18C French furniture are pieces by Carlin and Riesener.

Anteroom – This room features Hans Memling's *Portrait of a Man* (c.1470), the Flemish artist's earliest known portrait with a landscape background.

Dining Room – The spacious room, decorated with 18C English paintings in delicate colors, includes portraits by Hogarth, Romney and Reynolds, and a masterpiece by Gainsborough, *St. James' Park*. Also of note are the 18C English

Fragonard Room

silver-gilt wine coolers and the Chinese porcelain, in particular the pair of cobalt-blue vases adorning the mantelpiece.

West Vestibule – Here you will find the series of the *Four Seasons* (1755, Boucher), commissioned by Madame de Pompadour as overdoors for her residence. A marquetry-veneered clock by Balthazar Martinot sits atop the splendid marquetry desk crafted in the workshop of André-Charles Boulle. Also note the terra-cotta bust of the Swedish miniature painter Peter Adolf Hall, executed by French sculptor Boizot in 1775.

Fragonard Room – The room is named for the 11 decorative paintings by Jean-Honoré Fragonard (1732-1806). Four of the large panels were commissioned by Madame du Barry, a mistress of Louis XV. They recount the various stages of a romantic encounter: *The Pursuit*, *The Meeting*, *The Lover Crowned* and *Love Letters*. Exquisite furnishings add to the total effect: sofas and armchairs covered in Beauvais tapestry after designs by Boucher and Oudry; a Louis XVI commode by La Croix; two delicate tripod tables, one covered in lapis lazuli and the other in Sèvres porcelain plaques; and a marble bust of the *Comtesse du Cayla* (1777) by Houdon on the mantel.

South Hall – Highlights among the furniture include the Louis XVI drop-front secretary and chest of drawers crafted for Queen Marie Antoinette by Jean-Henri Riesener. Among the paintings, note Boucher's portrait of his wife and two rare works by the 17C Dutch master Vermeer, one of which, *Officer and Laughing Girl*, is remarkable for its radiant luminosity. At the foot of the stairs is a 30-day Louis XV calendar clock, which also contains a barometer. Note also the Aeolian pipe organ and its elaborate marble and gilded screen, installed in 1914.

Living Hall – Furnished with a desk by André-Charles Boulle and a pair of marquetry cabinets in the style of this famous 17C French cabinetmaker, this room displays 16C masterpieces. The Venetian school is represented by Giovanni Bellini's *St. Francis in the Desert* set against a finely rendered landscape, and by two Titian portraits, one depicting the sensual features of a young man in a red cap and the other of *Pietro Aretino*. The commanding figure of *St. Jerome* as cardinal, by El Greco, represents the Spanish school. Typical of the best of the German school, two celebrated portraits by Hans Holbein the Younger depict Sir Thomas More and Thomas Cromwell.

Library – Dominated by a portrait of Henry Clay Frick (1943, John Johansen) over the mantel, this wood-paneled room houses an array of art books, fiction and volumes of poetry. Enlivening the stately decor are lovely pieces of Chinese porcelain and several small Italian and French bronzes from the 16C and 17C. Among the English paintings of the 18C and 19C, note in particular John Constable's *Salisbury Cathedral from the Bishop's Garden*.

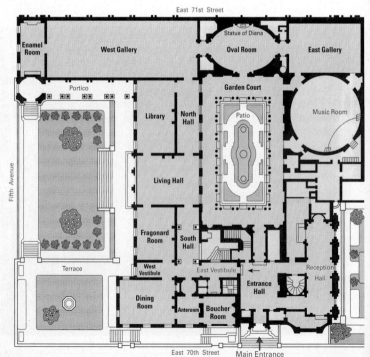

North Hall – Above the superb blue marble Louis XVI table hangs Ingres' renowned portrait of the *Comtesse d'Haussonville*, granddaughter of Madame de Staël, who hosted an influential literary and political salon in Paris in the late 18C. The marble bust by Houdon represents the Marquis de Miromesnil, minister of justice under Louis XVI. The remaining works range from the newly acquired *Portal of Valenciennes* by Jean Antoine Watteau to Monet's *Vétheuil in Winter* and Degas' *The Rehearsal*.

West Gallery – In this room, decorated with 16C Italian furniture, are portraits and landscapes of the Dutch, French, Spanish and British schools. Among the portraits, notice *Lodovico Capponi*, a page in the court of Duke Cosimo I de Medici, by 16C Florentine artist Bronzino; an El Greco of the Italian period *(Vincenzo Anastagi)*; works by Frans Hals; three splendid Rembrandts of great intensity of expression *(Self-Portrait, Nicolaes Ruts* and *Polish Rider)*; two famous works by Van Dyck (of the Antwerp still-life painter Frans Snyders, and of Snyders' wife, Margareta); and *Philip IV of Spain*, by Velázquez. Other well-known pieces include *The Forge* by Goya and two large allegorical paintings by Veronese.

Particularly noteworthy among the landscapes are Van Ruisdael's *Landscape with a Footbridge*, Hobbema's *Village with Water Mill Among Trees* and *The Harbor of Dieppe* by Turner. A 17C work by Étienne de la Tour, *The Education of the Virgin*, formerly attributed to his father Georges, also deserves attention.

Enamel Room – Several Italian Primitive and Renaissance works form an appropriate backdrop to the splendid collection of Limoges painted enamels of the 16C and 17C in intense blues and greens. Many of the pieces are labeled Léonard Limosin, the leading enameler and painter at the 16C Limoges school. Paintings of interest include *St. John the Evangelist* by Piero della Francesca, *Madonna and Child with Saints Lawrence and Julian* by Gentile da Fabriano and *Coronation of the Virgin* by Veneziano.

Oval Room – A life-size terra-cotta figure of Diana the Huntress by 18C French sculptor Jean-Antoine Houdon graces this gallery. It is a version of a statue executed for the Duke of Saxe-Gotha and acquired by the Russian empress, Catherine the Great.

East Gallery – This room presents a fine assortment of paintings from different schools and periods. Claude Lorrain's dramatic *Sermon on the Mount* dominates the gallery. Other works on display include Greuze's genre painting *The Wool Winder*; *Quay at Amsterdam*, by Jacob van Ruisdael, in which the sail of the boat on the left seems to capture all the light; and a portrait by Jacques Louis David of *Countess Daru*, the wife of Napoleon's quartermaster general. Chardin's *Still Life with Plums* represents the collection's only still-life work. Portraits by Gainsborough, Van Dyck and Goya also grace the gallery.

Garden Court – One of the most delightful parts of the museum, the court provides a cool haven in summertime thanks to its marble floor, fountain and pool, tropical plants and flowers. Originally used as a carriage court, the space was redesigned by John Russell Pope during the 1935 renovation. From the south colonnade you can view the entire court and the statue of Diana, by Houdon, in the Oval Room beyond. Among the works of sculpture, note the 15C bronze *Angel* by Jehan Barbet and the bronze *Marine Nymph* by Stoldo Lorenzi. Among the paintings, look for Edouard Manet's *The Bullfight* on the west wall and *Symphony in Gray and Green: The Ocean* by Whistler, on the north wall.

GRACIE MANSION★

East End Ave. at 89th St. **MTA** 4, 5, 6 train to 86th St.
Map p 11

Visit by guided tour (1hr) only, late Mar–mid-Nov Wed 10am, 11am, 1pm & 2pm. Reservations required. $4. ☎ 212-570-4751. www.nyc.gov.

Located in the northern section of Carl Schurz Park, a sliver of greenery bordering the East River, this 1799 country manor is the official residence of the mayor of New York. The Federal-style mansion, painted in buff yellow with white trim and adorned with green shutters, bears the name of Archibald Gracie, a merchant who entertained many dignitaries here, including Alexander Hamilton and John Quincy Adams. After passing through several hands, the house was eventually acquired by the city in 1896, falling into neglect until the Museum of the City of New York took it over in 1924. In 1942 it became the official home of the mayor. The current restoration by the Gracie Mansion Conservancy—created under the administration of former mayor Edward Koch—features a striking marbleized entry floor and fine Federal- and Empire-style furnishings.

INTERNATIONAL CENTER
OF PHOTOGRAPHY★

1133 Avenue of the Americas **MTA** Any train to 42nd St.
Map p 11

Open year-round Tue–Fri 10am–5pm (Fri until 8pm), weekends 10am–6pm. Closed major holidays. $10. ✗ ♿ ☎ *212-857-0000. www.icp.org.*

Founded by Cornell Capa in 1974, the International Center of Photography (ICP) mounts major exhibits of work by photographers and photojournalists who engage in "concerned photography," as well as those exploring the relationship between photographic representation and politics, memory, or popular culture.

The Midtown gallery space was opened in 1989 as a satellite of the original museum at 5th Avenue and 94th Street, but it became the ICP's sole exhibition area after a major renovation and expansion in 2000 and the closing of the uptown site in June 2001. Today it boasts more display space than the two sites formerly did combined, as well as a cafe and a well-stocked gift shop. About a dozen shows per year are drawn from the museum's own collection of 60,000 prints, as well as from holdings of other museums and partner facilities like the eminent George Eastman House in Rochester, New York. Recent shows have featured work by William Henry Fox Talbot, W. Eugene Smith and Garry Winogrand.

INTREPID SEA-AIR-SPACE MUSEUM

Pier 86 at W. 46th St. and 12th Ave. **MTA** any train to 42nd St.,
then take the M⁴2 bus to the 42nd St. Pier.
Map p 110

Kids *Open Apr–Sept Mon–Fri 10am–6pm, weekends 10am–7pm. Rest of the year Tue–Sun 10am–5pm. Closed Jan 1, Thanksgiving Day & Dec 25. $14. Guided tours (30min) available.* ✗ ♿ ☎ *212-245-0072. www.intrepidmuseum.org.*

Berthed at a pier in the Hudson River is the aircraft carrier USS *Intrepid*, a veteran of World War II and the Vietnam War, a NASA recovery vessel on two occasions for Mercury and Gemini space missions, and a participant in the blockade of Cuba during the 1963 Cuban Missile Crisis. Built in 1943 at a cost of $44 million, the ship was decommissioned in 1974 and now serves as a museum dedicated to the history of sea, air and space warfare.

The main attraction is the 898ft-long, 42,000-ton carrier itself, a veritable floating city—equipped with 1,600 hatches and doors and 20,000mi of electric cable—where a member of the 3,500-man crew could once get anything from a haircut to an ice cream sundae. The main museum entrance leads to the Hangar Deck, divided into four exhibit areas devoted to navy, aviation, space and carrier technology. The east (bow) end features a film titled *Air Power at Sea (17min)* on day-to-day operations aboard an aircraft carrier; Intrepid Hall contains exhibits on Pearl Harbor and World War II (the ship was hit by two kamikaze attacks on Thanksgiving Day, 1944); Pioneer Hall includes the video presentation, *The Fighting I (12min)* on the history of the *Intrepid* itself; rockets, complex weaponry, shipwrecks and space missions are covered in Technologies Hall (stern end), which houses a full-scale mock-up of the Gemini capsule. Topside on the vast Flight Deck—large enough to accommodate three simultaneous football games—aircraft appearing ready for takeoff on a moment's notice may be viewed close up. Highlights include the sinister-looking Lockheed **A-12 Blackbird**, the world's first cruise avenger equipped to fly at Mach 3 (three times the speed of sound), and a Concorde supersonic jet, retired by British Airways in 2003. Above this deck, visitors are free to explore the maze of corridors and ladders leading to the navigating bridge. Admission to the *Intrepid* also includes tours *(20min each)* of the fleet destroyer **USS Edson** and the 1958 guided missile submarine **USS Growler** *(tours accommodate a limited number, so expect a wait)*. Simulated flights aboard an F-18 fighter jet are available at an additional cost *($5)*.

JAPAN SOCIETY

333 E. 47th St. **MTA** any train to Grand Central Terminal
Map p 11

Open during special exhibits only, Tue–Fri 11am–6pm, weekends 11am–5pm. $5. ♿
For schedules: ☎ *212-752-3015 or www.japansociety.org.*

This black, low-rise building, located a short walking distance from the United Nations, houses the headquarters of the Japan Society, a cultural and educational organization. Designed in contemporary Japanese style, the interior contains a bamboo pool, exhibit gallery, auditorium, library, language center, conference rooms and garden, all of which blend together gracefully to create a simple and tranquil effect. Temporary exhibits of Japanese art, films, music and dance are presented here.

THE JEWISH MUSEUM★

1109 Fifth Ave. at 92nd St. **MTA** 4, 5, 6 train to 86th St.

Map p 11

Open year-round Sun–Thu 11am–5:45pm (Thu until 8pm), Fri 11am–3pm. Closed major & Jewish holidays. $10. ✗ ♿ Guided tours (45min) available. ☎ 212-423-3200. www.thejewishmuseum.org.

Founded in 1904 as part of the Jewish Theological Seminary of America *(3080 Broadway)*, this beautifully presented collection of Judaica offers insight into 4,000 years of Jewish history through historical and literary materials, ceremonial objects, Zionist memorabilia, ancient and contemporary art and braodcast media materials.

The more than 28,000 pieces are housed in the 1908 French Gothic-style mansion (donated to the seminary in 1947 by Frieda Warburg), which underwent an impressive renovation by architect Kevin Roche in 1993.

The centerpiece of the expanded interior is the permanent installation Culture and Continuity: The Jewish Journey, mounted in 17 galleries, beginning on the fourth floor and continuing on the third. Built on the recurrent themes of Covenant, Exodus, Law and Land, the exhibit traces the evolution, scope and diversity of Jewish culture throughout the world from antiquity to the present. Among the highlights are ancient ritual vessels and cult images, a carved-wood Torah Ark from the 12C, mosaics from a 16C Persian synagogue, rare embroidered synagogue textiles and a collection of exquisite Torah finials, crowns, shields and binders handworked in silver and gold. The final gallery showcases contemporary works by artists (both Jews and non-Jews) grappling with issues of the Jewish experience. Audio and video presentations exploring Zionism, ritual and identity—including an interactive Talmud debate—are featured throughout.

The Goodkind Resource Center *(3rd floor)* offers visitors access to television and radio tapes from the National Jewish Archive of Broadcasting. The museum also presents a hands-on **children's gallery** **Kids** *(4th floor)* as well as rotating exhibits, special events, lectures, films, performances, readings and book signings.

LOWER EAST SIDE TENEMENT MUSEUM★

90 and 97 Orchard St. **MTA** F train to Delancey St.

or B, D train to Grand St.

Map p 144

The visitor center and gift shop (90 Orchard St. at Broome St.) are open year-round daily 11am–5pm. ♿. The tenement building can be visited by guided tour only; tours depart every half hour from visitor center Tues–Fri 1pm–4pm (Apr–Nov Thur 6pm & 7pm), weekends 11am–4:30pm. Confino Family Apartment tour weekends only at noon, 1pm, 2pm & 3pm. ☎ 212-431-0233. www.tenement.org.

Created in 1988, this museum preserves and interprets immigrant life at 97 Orchard Street, a five-story tenement building (now a National Historic Landmark) in the heart of what was once the most densely populated neighborhood in the US. Between 1863

Baldizzi Apartment

and 1935 some 7,000 people lived in this structure alone, many of them working long hours in nearby factories and sleeping in shifts to accommodate large families. Their history emerges through stories, keepsakes, photographs, newspaper clippings and architectural details presented during guided tours of three cramped apartments and the dark, evocative hallways and staircases that joined them. Though structurally similar, the dwellings have been restored to reflect alterations made by their residents—the Gumpertz family (1878), the Rogarshevsky family (1921), and the Baldizzi family (1935)—who hailed from Germany, Lithuania, and Sicily, respectively.

On a separate, often more intimate "living-history" tour **Kids**, visitors can explore the apartment once occupied by the Confino family, Sephardic Jews who emigrated from Turkey in the early 1900s. On hand to answer questions and tell amusing stories is a guide acting as Victoria Confino, the family's teenage daughter. An aspiring performer herself, she relates in witty detail how work was parceled out, how marriages were arranged and how much rent her family paid—$15 a month, coal included.

Before or after guided tours, visitors can get a historical overview of the neighborhood from videos shown continually in a small theater adjoining the visitor center. The museum also offers an ambitious schedule of walking tours, art exhibits and site-specific performances *(call for schedule)*.

MERCHANT'S HOUSE MUSEUM*

29 E. 4th St. **MTA** 6 train to Astor Pl. or R, N train to 8th St.
Map p 166

Open year-round Thu–Mon 1pm–5pm. Closed major holidays. $6. Guided tours (1hr) available on weekends. ☎ *212-777-1089. www.merchantshouse.com.*

Erected in 1832, this redbrick town house, with its Greek Revival doorway, has been transformed into a museum that illustrates the lifestyle of an affluent 19C family.

Joseph Brewster built the structure as one of six identical row houses. It was sold in 1835 to Seabury Tredwell, a prosperous merchant. The house remained in the Tredwell family for nearly 100 years, and it is the only 19C house in Manhattan to survive intact with its original furniture and family memorabilia. Today renovated into a museum, the house is a characteristic period piece.

Just up the street, at no. 37, is another Greek Revival house, built for Samuel Tredwell Skidmore. Unfortunately, this structure has not been restored and is in a dilapidated state.

■ LOUIS ARMSTRONG HOUSE MUSEUM

34-56 107th St. **MTA** 7 train to 103rd St./Corona Plaza

Open year-round Tue–Fri 10am–5pm, weekends noon–5pm. $5. The inside of the house can only be visited by guided tour, limited to 8 people. Tours begin on the hour. ♿ ☎ *212-478-8274. www.satchmo.net.*

Located in a residential section of Corona, Queens, not far from Shea Stadium, this two-story, redbrick house was home to jazz great Louis Armstrong from 1943 until his death in 1971. After the death of Armstrong's wife Lucille in 1983, the property came into the hands of the city. In September 2003, the house opened to the public as a museum.

The house—furnishings, personal effects and all—provides a window into the domestic life of Louis Armstrong and reveals one of America's most important musical artists as modest, fun-loving and without pretension. (Armstrong and his wife had enough money to live in the toniest of suburbs.) An extraordinary time capsule of post-World War II decoration, the interior represents the work and taste of Lucille and her decorator—who show a predilection for beiges, creams and textured wallpapers. Though Louis was on the road up to 300 days a year, his presence can be clearly felt here. He recorded more than 1,000 hours of his home life on his ever-present reel-to-reel tape players. Snippets from the tapes are played during the tour—in the dining room, you'll hear Armstrong riff on brussels sprouts as he eats his dinner.

The museum's entrance and gift shop are built into the house's ground-level garage, as is a changing exhibit of items from the Louis Armstrong archives, which are held at Queens College.

METROPOLITAN MUSEUM OF ART★★★

Fifth Ave. at E. 82nd St. **MTA** 4, 5, 6 train to 86th St.
Map p 181

A world-renowned institution, the Metropolitan Museum of Art houses a veritable encyclopedia of the arts covering 5,000 years, from prehistory to the 20C. Richly endowed and supported, "The Met" has grown to be the largest museum in the Western hemisphere, attracting more than five million visitors a year.

Historical Notes

The Building – Founded on April 13, 1870, by members of New York's Union League Club, the museum first opened in the former Dodsworth's Dancing Academy at 681 Fifth Avenue in 1872. In 1880 the museum moved to its present location. Designed by Jacob Wrey Mould and **Calvert Vaux**, the landscape artist who collaborated with Frederick Law Olmsted in the creation of Central Park, the first building—a Gothic-style, redbrick edifice—stood on land belonging to the City of New York. Incorporated into the present building, the western facade of the original brick structure is visible from the Lehman Pavilion.

Entrance to the Met

© Brigitta L. House /MICHELIN

The monumental Beaux-Arts facade facing Fifth Avenue, built in gray Indiana limestone, was designed by Richard Morris Hunt and completed in 1902, although the sculptural decoration has never been finished. The southwest wing was added in 1888, while the north and south side wings, designed by McKim, Mead and White, were completed in 1911 and 1913 respectively. The privately endowed Thomas J. Watson Library (designed by Brown, Lawford & Forbes), founded in 1881, was finished in 1965, with room for 300,000 volumes. Now the library holds a collection half again as large, and it plans to expand into an adjacent courtyard. On the occasion of the museum's centennial celebrations in 1970, a comprehensive architectural plan was devised to bring the entire museum to physical completion. This master plan included a series of new wings: the Robert Lehman Wing (1975), the Sackler Wing (1978) with its Temple of Dendur, the American Wing (1980), the Michael C. Rockefeller Wing (1982), the Lila Acheson Wallace Wing (1987) and the Henry R. Kravis Wing (1991), all of which were designed by the architectural firm of Roche, Dinkeloo & Associates. Connecting the main building and the Lila Acheson Wallace Wing, the Carroll and Milton Petrie European Sculpture Court, completed in 1990, is a skylit, sun-drenched area dotted with benches, greenery and statuary. A 1997 reconstruction nearly doubled the exhibition space for Chinese art, and in mid-1998 a new permanent gallery for the arts of Korea opened as part of the Met's presentation of Asian art. The second phase of a three-part renovation and expansion of the Greek and Roman Art Galleries was completed with the unveiling of the new Cypriot Galleries in April 2000. In the third phase, now under way, the main museum cafe is being turned into a 40,000sq ft Roman sculpture court with a mezzanine gallery for Etruscan art. The project is scheduled to be completed in 2005.

The Collections – The first gift to the museum was a Roman sarcophagus. Soon thereafter, General di Cesnola, a former consul in Cyprus, sold the trustees his collection of more than 6,000 antiquities (mainly Cypriot glass and stone objects). In

1877 Catherine L. Wolfe donated 143 paintings, representing the Dutch and Flemish schools. Since then the collection has grown considerably, either through purchases or by bequests and gifts from wealthy benefactors, including the Astor, Morgan, Rockefeller, Marquand, Hearn, Altman, Bache, Lehman and Wrightsman families. Today the museum owns nearly three million objects, a fourth of which are on display at any given time in the Met's two million square feet of space. In addition to special exhibits and concerts, the museum offers a comprehensive program of classes, gallery tours, lectures, courses and films through its Ruth and Harold D. Uris Center for Education.

Principal Sections of the Museum *Plan p 223*

We have organized the museum's 19 departments into 15 selected headings.

American Wing★★★	*(p 222)*	Arts of Africa, Oceania and the Americas★★	*(p 238)*
Ancient Art★★★	*(p 227)*	Arms and Armor★	*(p 239)*
European Sculpture and Decorative Arts★★★	*(p 230)*	Asian Art★★	*(p 239)*
13-18C European Paintings★★★	*(p 232)*	Costume Institute★	*(p 240)*
19C European Paintings and Sculpture★★★	*(p 235)*	Islamic Art★	*(p 240)*
Lehman Pavilion★★	*(p 237)*	Musical Instruments★	*(p 241)*
Medieval Art★★	*(p 237)*	20C Art★	*(p 241)*
		Drawings, Prints and Photographs	*(p 241)*

Collection highlights are indicated in tan boxes in the order of the visit.

Visiting the Museum

Open year-round Tue–Sun 9:30am–5:30pm (Fri & Sat til 9pm). Open holiday Mondays: Columbus Day, Christmas week, Martin Luther King Jr. Day, Presidents Day & Memorial Day. Closed Jan 1, Thanksgiving Day & Dec 25. Suggested contribution $12 (includes same-day admission to the Cloisters, p 201). Guided tours (1hr) available. ✗ ও ▯ ☎ 212-879-5500. www.metmuseum.org.

The main entrance to the Met is on Fifth Ave., across from East 82nd St. You will enter the Great Hall, which houses an information desk, checkrooms and gift shops. In 1999 the Met introduced the *Key to the Met Audio Guide*, an updated self-guided audio tour that provides commentary on selected works of art throughout the museum. A special feature of the *Guide*, the "Director's Selections" tour, available in six languages, traces the history of art through 58 masterworks. Equipment *($6)* may be rented in the Great Hall and at the entrances to special exhibitions. From Tue–Thu, a number of galleries are open on a rotating schedule, either mornings or afternoons, and some galleries might be closed or specific works of art temporarily removed or exhibited in locations other than those indicated here *(inquire at the information desk in the Great Hall or check the visitor information page on the museum's Web site for details)*.

If entry lines are long, use the street-level entrance at 81st St. that takes you to the Uris Center for Education *(ground floor of the museum)*, where there is an information/ticket desk. Then take the elevator to the first floor.

On the ground floor, below the Medieval Hall, you'll find the new museum cafeteria. There's also a small cafe along the west end of the Englehard Court in the American wing, and the Petrie Court Café now offers sit-down dining *(reservations recommended, ☎ 212-570-3964)*. During the warm months, visit the Roof Garden Café for a light snack, contemporary sculpture and dazzling views. The Great Hall Balcony Bar is open Fridays and Saturdays from 4pm until closing. Several galleries are furnished with benches, but for pleasant spots for a rest on the first floor, keep the Temple of Dendur and the Great Hall in mind. The Lehman Pavilion offers a secluded patio. On the second floor, the Astor Court in the Chinese galleries makes a peaceful stop.

★★★AMERICAN WING *First, second & third floors. Floor plan p 225.*

Spanning three centuries, the American collection of paintings, sculpture and decorative arts and 25 full-scale room interiors occupy first-, second-, mezzanine and third-floor galleries neatly stacked in the northwest corner of the museum. Small orientation exhibits on each floor explain evolutions in style; surrounding period rooms and galleries present representative furniture, architectural elements and decorative arts. Paintings from the 18C to the early 20C reside en masse on the second floor. Sculpture, stained glass and architectural fragments occupy the stunning Charles Engelhard Court on the first floor. Delicate glass, ceramics, pewter and silver pieces encircle the second-floor balcony. *For a chronological excursion through American interior design and art, begin on the third floor.*

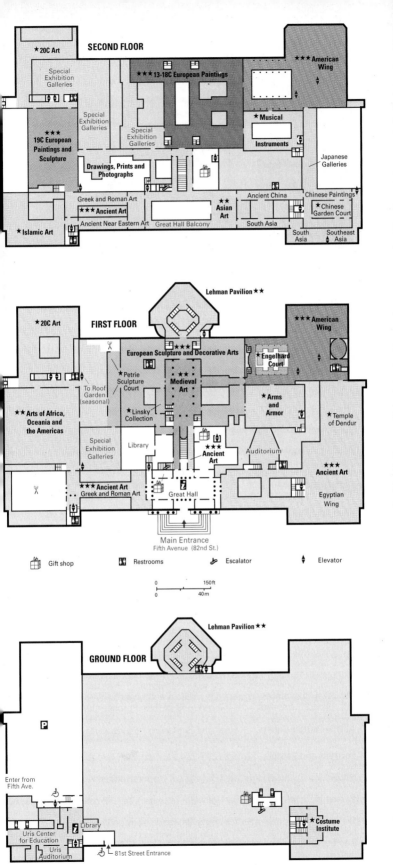

SECOND FLOOR

★ 20C Art

Special Exhibition Galleries

Special Exhibition Galleries

★★★ 13-18C European Paintings

Special Exhibition Galleries

★★★ 19C European Paintings and Sculpture

Drawings, Prints and Photographs

★ Musical Instruments

★★★ American Wing

Japanese Galleries

Greek and Roman Art

★★★ Ancient Art

Ancient Near Eastern Art

Great Hall Balcony

★★ Asian Art

Ancient China

South Asia

Chinese Paintings

★ Chinese Garden Court

★ Islamic Art

South Asia

Southeast Asia

Lehman Pavilion ★★

FIRST FLOOR

★ 20C Art

European Sculpture and Decorative Arts

★★★ American Wing

★ Engelhard Court

To Roof Garden (seasonal)

★ Petrie Sculpture Court

★★ Medieval Art

★ Arms and Armor

★ Temple of Dendur

★★ Arts of Africa, Oceania and the Americas

★ Linsky Collection

Special Exhibition Galleries

Library

★★★ Ancient Art

Auditorium

★★★ Ancient Art

★★★ Ancient Art Greek and Roman Art

Great Hall

Egyptian Wing

Main Entrance
Fifth Avenue (82nd St.)

Gift shop   Restrooms   Escalator   Elevator

0 ———— 150 ft
0 ———— 40 m

Lehman Pavilion ★★

GROUND FLOOR

P

Enter from Fifth Ave.

Library

Uris Center for Education

Uris Auditorium

81st Street Entrance

★ Costume Institute

Engelhard Court, American Wing

Third Floor

At Home in the Colonies – *Galleries 301-312*. Colonial domestic style encompasses a succession of furniture design ranging from simple "pilgrim," or Jacobean, pieces to the elegance of Chippendale. The museum's earliest period rooms, tucked away on the third floor, bear a distinctly medieval look, their sturdy furnishings characterized by turned spindles and square angles. Subsequent interiors exude an increasing refinement of form and finish, blending English, Dutch and French elements. By 1690 the style known today as William and Mary (named for the reigning English monarchs) had introduced slightly more comfort and several new forms. High chests of drawers replaced stocky cupboards and board chests, and upholstered "easy," or "wing," chairs kept drafts away. Chinese motifs and innovations begin to appear, by-products of burgeoning contact with the Far East. Compare the austere and practical 1674 Hart Room *(gallery 303)* with the 1695 Wentworth Room *(gallery 312)*, where furnishings and architecture mark the transition into the 18C.

Orientation Gallery   Meetinghouse Gallery

Second Floor

A Flowering Elegance – *Galleries 201-216*. By 1725 the curvaceous cabriole leg distinguished chairs and tables in the Queen Anne, or Baroque style, to which mid-century designers added claw-and-ball feet and other florid Rococo embellishments based on the design catalog of Englishman Thomas Chippendale. Interiors glowed with the reflected light of mirrors, crystal and polished metals; hand-painted pictorial wallpapers added color and refinement to the homes of the wealthy. American cabinetmakers introduced undulating fronts to desks and chests, and Boston, New York City, Philadelphia and other centers of furniture manufacture developed their own signature styles, which you can compare in galleries 204 and 205. Georgian Colonial architecture added pedimented porticos and Palladian windows to building facades, foreshadowing the Neoclassical styles yet to come. In the countryside, vernacular and folk traditions flourished among German, Dutch and other immigrants who sought freedom and opportunity in the new land but surrounded themselves with the comforts of their European homes.

Orientation Gallery   Alexandria Ballroom   Pennsylvania German Room

Portraits and Patriots – *Galleries 217-224 and mezzanine*. Like its furniture and architecture, America's painterly tradition had its origins in the practical and Puritan. Early colonists, with little time or need for any but the most utilitarian artistic expressions, valued portraiture above all. From the flat, primitive works of itinerant portaitists evolved the fuller, more effulgent canvases of painters such as John Singleton Copley. Revolution moved American painters to employ the sweeping allegories of Neoclassicism to record the events and heroics of war (ironically, many of those painters migrated to London to study with countryman Benjamin West). Yet portrait painting prevailed, as if to personify the nation's new identity. Most recognizable, perhaps, is **Gilbert Stuart's** portrait of George Washington—one of at least 114 that Stuart made of him.

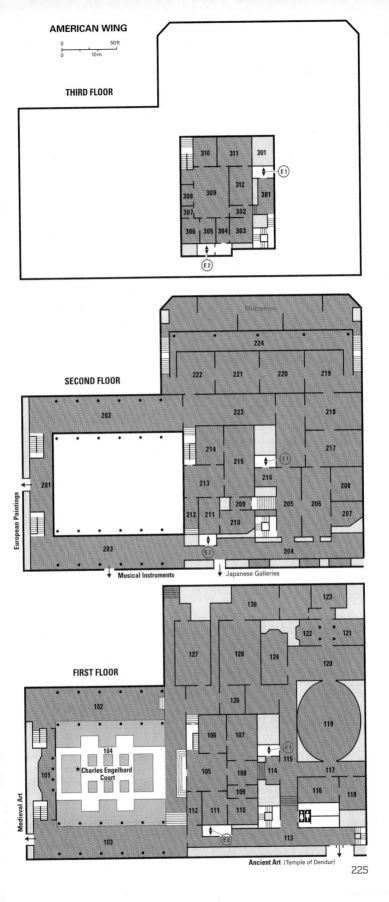

As settlement pushed west, artists turned their eyes to the unfolding breadth of th continent. William Sidney Mount and **George Caleb Bingham** rendered lucent scenes of American life with classical rigor. The drama of light and a heroic sense landscape captured the imagination of painters of the Hudson River school. **Thom Cole**, **Frederic Church** and Albert Bierstadt exulted in the wonder of primordial natur and galleries 220 and 221 virtually glow with the luminescence of their work.

For **Winslow Homer** and Eastman Johnson, heroism came with human endeavo American painting of the late 19C took many forms, informed by currents in Europ where several influential American artists studied, lived and worked. James Abbo McNeill Whistler, an expatriate since 1855, renounced realism to experiment wit compositions of light and color, an effort the titles of his works reflect. The fla tering high-society portraits of **John Singer Sargent** contrast with the penetratin realism of Thomas Eakins. Mary Cassatt, a protégé of Edgar Degas in France, bathe her intimate views of women and children in the light and color of Impressionism Located on the mezzanine, the Henry R. Luce Center for the Study of American Art presents study collections of fine and decorative American art that is current not on display in the main galleries and period rooms. An elaborate compute network (AWARE—American Wing Art Research) provides information on 8,50 paintings, sculptures, pieces of furniture, and decorative objects which a arranged for viewing in rows of tall glass cases.

Gilbert Stuart	*George Washington*, 1795
Thomas Cole	*View from Mount Holyoke ... (The Oxbow)*, 1836
George Caleb Bingham	*Fur Traders Descending the Missouri*, c.1845
Asher B. Durand	*The Beeches*, 1845
Frederic Church	*The Heart of the Andes*, 1859
Thomas Eakins	*Max Schmitt in a Single Scull*, 1871
Winslow Homer	*Snap the Whip*, 1872
John Singer Sargent	*Madame X*, 1884

First Floor

Furnishing America – *Galleries 101-124, 126-128, 130.* In their homes, post Revolutionary Americans adopted English Neoclassicism, calling it Federalism t honor the new Republic. On the museum's first floor, orientation galler 109 describes Federal furniture and architecture. Popularized in England by Georg Hepplewhite and Thomas Sheraton, the style tends toward fine proportions, clea lines and classical motifs. Swags, urns and pilasters decorate furniture, mantel pieces and building facades. Another Neoclassical movement, known as Empire came by way of Napoleonic France, its massive forms and heavy antique flourishe replacing the delicate shapes of Federalism.

American Neoclassicism reached its apex in the New York shop of cabinetmake **Duncan Phyfe**, whose work furnishes the Richmond Room and can also be found i gallery 121, a Greek Revival parlor. After 1820 the rage for reviving antique style escalated, and designers and architects plundered a rich array of historic motifs an forms from ancient Egypt, the Gothic era, the Renaissance and the Rococo period The Industrial Revolution soon made possible the mass production of heavily deco rated furniture in the eccentric shapes and materials that so delighted Victorians Gallery 120 presents a selection of furniture from the various revival movements tha came and went between 1820 and 1900. In the late 19C such excesses gave rise t a shift away from historicism and exorbitance in favor of simplicity and handcrafting The "art furniture" of this era features Japanese elements and delicate, naturalisti surface designs. Proponents of the British Arts and Crafts movement, with its two best-known American offspring, the Mission style and the Prairie school, created sturdy, functional furniture with strong lines. Gallery 130, the DeeDee Wigmore

■ Night Lights

One story up, a three-sided balcony crowns the spacious Charles Engelhard Court like a jeweled tiara. During the day, a flood of sunlight plays over the antique glass and silverware on exhibit here. At night, the space shimmers with exceptional beauty; cut and engraved glass objects (including Mrs. Lincoln's compote) reflect light off every surface, and Tiffany art-glass lamps glow warmly. Spotlights illuminate polished silver tankards, porringers and salvers of the 17C and throw the lushly textured surfaces of extravagant Victorian tureens, ewers and epergnes into high relief. In the courtyard below, backlighting enhances the rich colors of the stained glass, and sculptures settle into the shadows of surrounding greenery. Beyond the glass-enclosed space, city lights imitate the sparkle.

Gallery, has a fine selection of these styles, along with work by the Herter Brothers, Stickley, Van Erp and others. An addition to the Wigmore gallery dedicated to the works of Louis Comfort Tiffany opened in 2002. Ample evidence of the breadth of his work is on display: two impressive windows; a number of Favrile vases, lamps, jewelry; and a rotating selection of paintings and drawings. The adjacent McKim, Mead and White Stair Hall (1884), taken from a Queen Anne House in Buffalo, New York, features similarly dazzling craftsmanship. **Frank Lloyd Wright** referred to his furniture as "architectural sculpture," which echoed in miniature the geometry of Prairie school buildings. This harmony can be seen clearly in **gallery 127**, which contains a room designed inside and out by Wright for Francis Little in 1912.

Orientation Gallery	Richmond Room
Frank Lloyd Wright	Francis Little Living Room, 1912-14

Sculpture – *Charles Engelhard Court.* Many pieces in this lovely **court★** date to the late 19C and early 20C, a prolific period for American sculptors like Augustus Saint-Gaudens, Daniel Chester French and Frederick MacMonnies who used Neoclassical allegory to convey the ennobling power of art and the glory of the Republic. It was also an age that reveled in lush organic decoration, epitomized by the stained glass and mosaic work of **Louis Comfort Tiffany** and the architectural ornamentation of **Louis Sullivan**.

Martin E. Thompson	Facade of United States Bank, 1824
Louis Comfort Tiffany	*Grapevine* stained-glass window
Louis Sullivan	Staircases from Chicago Stock Exchange, 1893

★★ANCIENT ART
First and second floors.

Rich collections from four wellsprings of civilization—ancient Egypt, ancient Greece and Rome, and the ancient Near East—offer a wealth of viewing possibilities.

Egyptian Wing *Galleries 1-32*

The arrangement of these galleries, which cover 69,000sq ft, closely follows the chronology of Egyptian history from the Predynastic period (c.5000-3000 BC) through 30 dynasties (c.3100-342 BC) and the eras of foreign influence, and culminating with the end of the Coptic period in AD 41.

Because the Egyptians believed in life after death, funerary rituals included burying the dead with provisions they might need in the afterlife. From temples and tombs, therefore, come a wealth of objects and wall paintings that reveal the richness and complexity of Egyptian life. Through excavation, purchase and donation since 1874, the museum has amassed a collection of 36,000 such objects, virtually all of which are on exhibit. In addition to traditional displays, several "study galleries" present objects in densely packed wall cases.

Begin your expedition in gallery 1, an orientation space that presents background information, a timeline and a wall map, along with Predynastic artifacts and sculpture. Enter the mastaba of Perneb, a dignitary of the fifth dynasty. While the pyramid is the best-known form of Egyptian tomb architecture, mastabas like this were popular with royal relatives and the elite.

The Metropolitan Museum of Art, gift of Ruth and Frank Stanton

Grapevine by Tiffany Studios

227

The galleries that follow are organized according to dynasty. The Egyptians measured time and calculated dates by the reigns of their kings, who ruled in patrilineal
succession; scholars have since subdivided the dynasties into logical periods.
Ancient Egyptian history alternates between periods of strong pharaonic rule and
the confused decentralization of foreign domination. Amazingly, the material
culture maintained an incredible continuity throughout the centuries.

Archaic Period (Dynasties I and II) – Egypt emerged from prehistory with the uni-
fication of the Upper and Lower Kingdoms. Although connected by the lifeblood
of the Nile River, the two cultures differed greatly. Around the delta to the north
lived the farmers of Lower Egypt. To the south, in Upper Egypt, existed a nomadic
culture whose ambitious princes eventually extended their power throughout the
Nile Valley to unify the "Two Lands." Although a cohesive culture emerged, the
artistic, religious and political distinctions between north and south would continue
to inform Egyptian history.

Old Kingdom (Dynasties III-VIII) – This 500-year period encompasses the era of
pyramid building that produced, among others, the immense structures at Giza.
The scale and splendor of these monuments indicate the power of the pharaohs
and the widespread belief in their divinity. One pyramid alone might comprise more
than two million blocks of limestone, each weighing in excess of two and a half
tons. Pyramid building would crumble under its own weight, as the labor and logis-
tics required to carry out such construction became unsustainable. By the fifth
dynasty (c.2500 BC), the divine status of royalty fell victim to a new belief that
kings, though descended from the sun god Ra, were at least partly human. Collapse
of the central government ensued, and rule passed to local governors for over a
century (Dynasties IX-X).

Middle Kingdom (Dynasties XI-XII) – Theban king Nebhepetra Mentuhotpe once
again united Egypt around 2133 BC, stimulating a golden age of culture and prosperity that lasted 350 years. Funerary practices intensified during this time: grave
goods proliferated and mummification became an art. Sculpture took on an increasingly naturalistic, less idealized look; note the vigorous humanity in the faces of
figures and statues. The cache of **models** *(gallery 4)* from the tomb of Meketre
—one of the richest and most complete sets ever discovered—convey in miniature
a sense of the active bustle of daily life. The painted figures repeat in the wall
paintings of Old Kingdom tombs. Artisans of the day produced the quality of work
represented by the **royal jewels** *(gallery 8)* of Princess Sithathoryunet. The
stunning pectoral, a gift from her father, is considered among the finest examples of ancient
Egyptian jewelry. The strength of the twelfth dynasty had dwindled by around
1800 BC, allowing an intermediate period of foreign rule (Dynasties XIII-XVII).

New Kingdom (Dynasties XVIII-XX) – Once more leaders rose up in the south and
reestablished Egyptian rule around 1570 BC. After a period of expansion and con-
quest, the kingdom grew to encompass the area from Nubia to the upper
Euphrates Valley. Many of the most familiar and interesting monarchs reigned
during this lush age, including Queen Hatshepsut, Akhenaton and his beautiful wife
Nefertiti, young Tutankhamun and a succession of Ramseses. Gallery 12 showcases

Temple of Dendur

figures of **Hatshepsut**, one of few queens to ascend the throne. Sculptors accorded her the full regalia of her office, and often a beard, without disguising her womanly features. Hatshepsut built her monumental funerary temple complex at Deir al Bahri, a true ancient wonder completed around 1500 BC. Akhenaton believed himself to personify the solar deity and attempted to initiate monotheism on that basis. His successor and half-brother, King Tut, made short work of that idea and restored polytheism. The wives of Tuthmose III must have looked stunning in the afterlife in golden sandals and bracelets *(gallery 14)* that embody the luxuriance of the time. Indeed, these were years of superb craftsmanship in gold, bronze, alabaster, ivory, faience and, for the first time, glass. Although Ramses III successfully held off foreign invasions in the twentieth dynasty, civil strife and marauders led to the final waning of Egyptian sovereignty. Throughout Dynasties XXI to XXX, Ethiopians, Assyrians, Persians, Greeks and, occasionally, Egyptians controlled the land.

Ptolemaic and Roman-Coptic Periods (305 BC-AD 641) – Galleries 26 and 29 are devoted to the museum's rich collection of color facsimiles of **tomb and temple paintings**. The Macedonian Ptolemies ruled Egypt for three centuries, until Cleopatra's death in 30 BC brought the Hellenistic monarchies to an end. The Roman empire under Augustus then absorbed the country. Gallery 25 houses a magnificent installation of the **Temple of Dendur**★, built south of Aswan during the Roman period; it was among monuments rescued from submersion by the creation of Lake Nasser. Adjacent study galleries contain a stunning collection of mummies, funerary art, papyrus and faience figurines. The remarkable **Fayum portraits** *(gallery 31)*, made of pigment mixed with hot wax (known as encaustic), date back to the 2C. Crafted as mummy masks by Greeks living in Fayum, they represent the first introduction of European-style painting techniques into Egypt. The Copts—direct descendants of pharaonic Egyptians—many of whom were Christians, produced distinctive pieces that combined elements from disparate mythologies with early church symbolism. Because the Copts were instigators of Christian monasticism, many of their artifacts originated in that context.

Greek and Roman Art

Eight newly renovated galleries for ancient Greek art stand south of the Great Hall. The first, Belfer Court, presents objects dating from the Neolithic period up to the 6C BC, including terra cotta pots, marble figurines, inscribed gemstones and sculpture. The grand, barrel-vaulted Jaharis Gallery and six surrounding rooms feature a roughly chronological progression of 6C BC–4C BC works in all media. With its soaring height, skylights and new limestone walls, the Jaharis Gallery provides a grand setting for large-scale sculpture, including oversize statues of a wounded Amazon and the Greek hero Protesilaos. At the far end of the hall stands a stunningly huge Ionic capital from the 4C BC.

Opening off the hall to the left, the Steinhardt Gallery contains an outstanding collection of Athenian funerary monuments from the 6C BC. The marble statue of a nude youth (kouros) in the center of the gallery is one of the earliest known kouroi to have survived complete. Another monument, an attic Greek stela more than 13ft tall and topped by a sphinx, is the best extant example of its type. Painted terracotta vases from the same period can be found across the hall in Bothmer Gallery I. Their black-figured designs tell stories from mythology and daily life. Bothmer Gallery II presents vases and pots decorated with the red-figure technique that emerged around 530 BC.

In the Wiener Gallery across the hall stand some of the museum's finest marble grave markers, dating from the mid-5C BC to the early 4C BC. The detail of the reliefs gives a sense of the unprecedented flowering of art that took place during this period. Painted vases produced around the same time are presented in the Stavros and Danaë Costopoulos Gallery and the Spyros and Eurydice Costopoulos Gallery, the latter of which also displays Macedonian jewelry and other work made on the eve of the Hellenistic era. A collection of Roman portrait busts from AD 100 to AD 200 reside in a final gallery. Previously home to the museum cafe, the adjacent hall is being transformed into a new Roman sculpture court. The work, which will take several years, marks the last phase of a decade-long renovation of the Greek and Roman galleries.

Second Floor – Four new Cypriot galleries display some 600 works from the island of Cyprus dating from the Neolithic era (c.7000 BC) to the end of the Roman period (AD 800). Most of the works derive from the famed Cesnola Collection, a 35,000-object trove purchased between 1873 and 1876 from the Italian-born general and antiquarian Luigi Palma di Cesnola, who served as the Metropolitan's first director. Though some of the pieces were later found to be either fraudulent or overvalued, the collection is nonetheless considered the finest of its kind outside of Cyprus. It is particularly strong in sculpture, bronze, terra-cotta and precious metals.

The Prehistoric gallery's earliest works show Cypriot artists working in relative isolation on such fanciful objects as zoomorphic terra-cotta vessels, but by the late Bronze age the island had become an important center of copper production as well as a hub of trade in the eastern Mediterranean. Faience vases, gold and silver jewelry, terra-cotta figurines and especially bronze work show a proliferation of adopted styles as well as the continuation of local traditions. Cyprus during the archaic period was occupied by a succession of foreigners—first Greeks, then Phoenicians, Assyrians, Egyptians and Persians, each of whom left their mark on the island's culture and art. Particularly striking are the sarcophagus from Amathus, with its well-preserved polychromy, and the two Graeco-Phoenician sarcophagi from the late 5C BC that flank the door.

The gallery of classical Cypriot art (5C and 4C BC) contains sculpture, terra cotta figures, vases, jewelry and coins, as well as funerary art, much of which was increasingly influenced by Greek models. During the Hellenistic and Roman eras, Cyprus was recognized as the birthplace of Aphrodite. Accordingly, the gallery devoted to this period contains a wide range of votive art, including the cherub-like limestone "Temple Boys."

Ancient Near Eastern Art *Second floor*

The collections of this department, formed in 1956, cover a vast region of southwestern Asia that today reaches from Turkey to Afghanistan and the Indus Valley, and from the Caucasus Mountains in the north to the Arabian Peninsula. Sculpture, pottery and metalwork date from 6,000 BC to the beginning of Islam.

The profusion of cultures that inhabited this region produced finely wrought artifacts of great beauty and sophistication, from intricate Achaemenian (an Iranian empire) gold and silver work to the massive winged lions of Assyria. Other strengths of the collection include stone sculptures from Sumer, the cradle of Mesopotamian (Iraqi) civilization as early as 3000 BC; ivories from ancient Anatolia (Turkey); and bronzes from Iran. As part of a reorganization of the collection completed in 1999, the Sackler Gallery, just east of the Great Hall Balcony, has been reconstructed to mimic the proportions of an audience hall of the palace built by Assyrian king Ashurnasirpal II at Nimrud (in what is now Iraq), in the 9C BC. Extraordinary monumental reliefs and statuary from the palace line the gallery walls. Of equal splendor are 6C BC Mesopotamian reliefs—colorful, glazed brick lions that once decorated the processional way from Ishtar Gate to the Temple of Marduk in the Babylon of Nebuchadnezzer.

***EUROPEAN SCULPTURE AND DECORATIVE ARTS

First floor.

This is one of the museum's largest departments, comprising more than 60,000 works of art ranging from the Renaissance to the early 20C. Pieces include sculpture, furniture, ceramics, woodwork, glass, metalwork and textiles, with an emphasis on French and English furniture and French and German porcelain, exhibited in exquisitely re-created **period rooms★★**.

Northern Renaissance and Italian Galleries – *Galleries 1-3, 5, 8-10.* These galleries include the interior of a chapel faced with marquetry paneling, modeled after the one in the French Château de la Bastie d'Urfé (1550); a paneled room with a ceramic stove from Flims in Switzerland; and a Rococo bedroom from the Sagredo Palace in Venice (early 18C). Most astonishing is the tiny *studiolo* from the palace of Federico da Montefeltro at Gubbio in Italy. Crafted as a personal retreat for the duke in the 1470s, the room is a masterpiece of linear perspective, a novel concept at the time. Intricate inlaid wood paneling, illustrating the art of intarsia, creates the illusion of depth and gives overall perspectival unity to the trapezoidal space. Tableaux depicted relate to the duke's intellectual interests. In the center of gallery 2 stands a monumental table inlaid with alabaster and semiprecious stones; it was designed by the architect Jacopo Barozzi da Vignola for the Farnese Palace in Rome, in the 16C. Faience on display includes Italian majolica from Urbino, Gubbio and Deruta (16C), as well as later productions of the Delft and French workshops.

English Galleries – *Galleries 14-20.* To follow the development of English decorative arts from 1660 to 1840, begin in gallery 19. A staircase from Cassiobury Park, Hertfordshire, by Gibbons, represents the decorative arts of the 17C *(gallery 19)*, while the Rococo style of the mid-18C is reflected in the stucco decoration of a dining room from Kirtlington Park, Oxfordshire *(gallery 20)*. The Tapestry Room *(gallery 17)*, formerly at Croome Court, Warwickshire, was designed by Robert Adam (1728-92), who gave his name to the Adamesque style. The crimson wall coverings and upholstery, ordered by Lord Coventry, were drawn by François Boucher and made at the Gobelins factory. Also designed by Adam is the refined dining room *(gallery 16)* from Lansdowne House, London. Pastel colors, pilasters, niches for ancient statues, and "Pompeian" stucco decoration stand in delicate contrast to the deep tones of the mahogany table and chairs; the Lamerie silver and an elaborate chandelier complete the arrangement. Galleries 15 and 18 present a varied collection of 18C English decorative arts.

French Galleries – *Galleries 23-30 and 32-35*. These galleries of 18C period rooms and settings present a rich panorama of the French decorative arts. The introductory gallery 33 contains a Paris shopfront of 1775. Embellished with pilasters and fancifully carved garlands, this charming boutique facade is typical of the Louis XVI style. Adjacent to the gallery are two small, elegant rooms *(galleries 34, 35)*: the boudoir from the Hôtel de Crillon is graced with pieces of furniture from the chateau of St.-Cloud, including a daybed made for Marie Antoinette, while the Bordeaux Room is a delicately paneled circular salon decorated and furnished in the Neoclassical style.

Hung in the Louis XV Room *(gallery 23)* is a replica of the famous *Portrait of Louis XV as a Child* painted by Rigaud and hanging at Versailles. The Sèvres Alcove Gallery displays pieces in the delicate turquoise blue for which Sèvres was famous. Beyond the alcove is a graceful room *(gallery 23a)* from the Hôtel Lauzun in Paris, the setting for an exquisite collection of French furniture inlaid with Sèvres porcelain plaques. Masterpieces by the cabinetmakers Carlin, Weisweiler and Bernard II Van Risenburgh (B.V.R.B.) are also displayed.

Four 18C rooms open into the Louis XVI gallery *(no. 24)*, furnished with European and Japanese lacquered furniture. The white and gold paneled salon *(gallery 25a)* from the Hôtel de Varengeville contains magnificent Louis XV furniture, particularly the king's own desk from his study at Versailles. In the room from the Palais Paar in Vienna *(gallery 25b)*, a late Rococo room in blue and gold tones, note the writing table by Van Risenburgh and a rock-crystal chandelier. The Neoclassical, oak-paneled reception room *(gallery 25c)* from the Hôtel de Cabris in Grasse still retains the original gilding on the paneling. Among the treasures in the room is a *nécessaire de voyage*, a collapsible table used for traveling, dressing and eating. The Hôtel de Tessé Room *(gallery 26-28)*, with its gray and gold Neoclassical paneling, displays a rare 17C Savonnerie carpet and furniture made for Marie Antoinette by Jean Henri Riesener.

The final galleries highlight art from the reigns of Louis XIII and Louis XIV. The Louis XIV-style state bedchamber *(gallery 30)* features a set of hangings embroidered with allegories of the Seasons and the Elements, several pieces of furniture by André-Charles Boulle (appointed cabinetmaker to the king in 1672) and a monumental carved chimneypiece designed by Jean le Pautre.

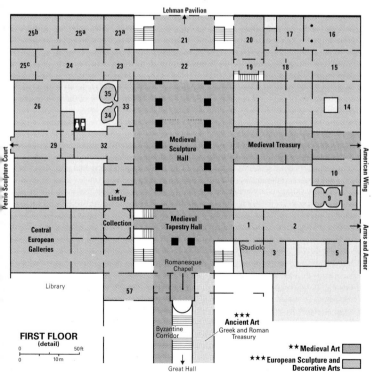

Central European Galleries – Ceramics on display include 18C faience pottery, enameled Zwischengold glass (1730) from Bohemia and a large assemblage of Meissen stoneware and porcelain. The floral garden-room furniture was commissioned by Prince Bishop Adam Friedrich von Seinsheim for his Franckenstein Pavilion at Schloss Seehof near Bamberg, Germany.

EUROPEAN PAINTINGS
SECOND FLOOR

★**Jack and Belle Linsky Collection** – Opened in 1984, these galleries present the private art and artifacts compiled by the Linskys over a period of 40 years. Approximately 375 works of art are displayed in seven rooms designed to create the intimate setting of a private residence. Praised for its beauty as well as its quality, the collection comprises paintings by early European masters, Renaissance and Baroque bronzes, European porcelains, 18C French furniture, jewelry and fine examples of goldsmiths' work.

Among the paintings representing the Italian, Flemish, French, Dutch and German schools, note the *Madonna and Child* by the Venetian artist Carlo Crivelli (15C), and the earliest dated work (1597) by Rubens, a portrait of an architect or geographer painted on copper. The expressive bronzes include *Monk Scribe on a Dragon* (12C) and Antico's *Satyr* (16C). Exhibited in a late-18C period room are an 18C commode by David Roentgen and a writing table inlaid with exquisite marquetry crafted by Jean-François Oeben for Madame de Pompadour. More than 200 Rococo porcelain figures, from the factories of Meissen and Chantilly, do the various rooms. Equally noteworthy are the porcelain figures depicting Russia national types made at the Imperial Porcelain Manufactory in St. Petersburg (lat 18C).

★**Petrie European Sculpture Court** – One of the museum's beautiful converted courtyards, this airy space displays monumental Italian and French sculpture ami fountains and greenery. A new full-service café has opened at the far end of th court, with a view of Central Park and Cleopatra's Needle—the obelisk given t the city by the pasha of Egypt. Adjacent galleries in the Kravis Wing pick up th threads of European decorative arts with 19C and early 20C objects and furniture

★★★13C-18C EUROPEAN PAINTINGS *Second floor. Plan above.*

Arranged by national schools, this collection begins at the head of the grand stair case on the second floor. It is particularly strong in works from Italy, northern Europe and France, with several galleries representing the English and Spanish Religion, history, portraiture, mythology, still life and landscape fill these canvases which together demonstrate the evolution of media and style from the early Renaissance to the Age of Reason.

The Italian Schools – *Galleries 1, 3-9, 19, 20, 22, 29 & 30.* As the Middle Age waned after 1300, Europeans began to broaden their horizons beyond the Church and the arts and sciences flourished. The early Renaissance had Northern Italy a its epicenter, specifically the city of Florence, where Giotto had broken the Byzantine bonds of two-dimensionality to give his figures heft and volume in space Florentines experimented with perspective, and the flat landscapes of medieva painting gave way to works with depth and dimension. By contrast, sixty mile away in Siena, artists such as Giovanni de Paolo and **Sassetta** continued to work in the flattened spatial field of their predecessors. By the 15C, Florence teemed with artists cultivating new approaches to light, form and subject, and in 1504 thre of the greatest and most fertile Renaissance minds worked in that city: Leonard da Vinci, Michelangelo and **Raphael**. Other cities around Italy hatched regional styles borne along by the creative tide of the Renaissance, but by the 16C—the high Renaissance—Venice came to dominate. There, **Titian**, Tintoretto and Verones composed huge, active canvases characterized by vivid colors, large foreground figures and realistic landscape backgrounds. Their work anticipated the Baroqu sense of the picture as a whole, of surface versus line, of a continuous rhythm rather than objects set against a backdrop, as would later be seen in 18C Venetia master **Giovanni Battista Tiepolo's** luminous canvases. At the threshold of this grea movement, however, Italy's artistic supremacy began to slacken even as her influ ence resounded across Europe.

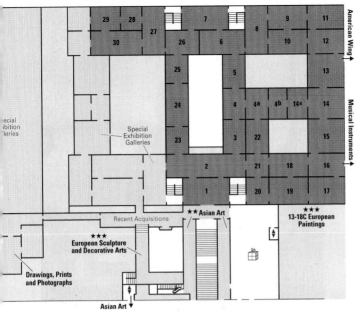

Giotto	The Epiphany, c.1320
Sassetta	The Journey of the Magi, c.1435
Fra Filippo Lippi	Man and Woman at a Casement, c.1435
Sandro Botticelli	The Last Communion of St. Jerome, c.1491
Raphael	Madonna and Child Enthroned with Saints, c.1505
Titian	Venus and the Lute Player, c.1565
Tiepolo	The Triumph of Marius, c.1729

Northern Europe – *Galleries 11-14, 23-28.* North of Italy, other artistic sensibilities stirred. The Catholic Church persisted in its influence over painters of the early Netherlandish school *(galleries 23-25)*, and their work reflects that curious Gothic mixture of the devout and the macabre. In Flanders, a part of present-day Belgium, artists discovered that oil, as a painting medium, imparted to their work a translucent warmth missing in the bright and distinct colors of egg tempera, which remained popular in Italy for some time. Oil paint made possible the rendering of nuance, and the northerners—the earliest of them being **Jan van Eyck** in the 15C—became masters of observing and recording detail. A century later, the genre paintings of **Pieter Brueghel the Elder** represent the last of the northern Gothic works, in temperament if not subject. Compare his satiric, though medieval eye with the soft Baroque luxuriance of **Peter Paul Rubens**, who broke the Church's spell over artistic content and expression. In Holland, 17C painters celebrated their recent independence from Spain with landscapes, portraits and scenes of everyday life. Dark and quiet, Dutch (indeed European) painting reached its apex at the hand of **Rembrandt van Rijn**, who set the dusky Dutch palette aglow. In **Gallery 13★** his portraits of ordinary faces seem to radiate their own light. The museum owns 20 works by Rembrandt. **Johannes Vermeer**, interested less in personality than in composition, focused on the play of light across surfaces and textures to create cool and seamless paintings of extraordinary detail. A meticulous worker, he painted only about 35 canvases throughout his life.

Jan van Eyck	The Crucifixion and The Last Judgment, c.1425
Pieter Brueghel	The Harvesters, 1565
Peter Paul Rubens	Venus and Adonis, c.1635
Rembrandt van Rijn	Aristotle with a Bust of Homer, 1653
Johannes Vermeer	Young Woman with a Water Jug, c.1660

The Metropolitan Museum of Art, Henry G. Marquand Collection

Young Woman with a Water Jug (c.1660) by Johannes Vermeer

The French – *Galleries 2, 10, 17, 18.* Relatively short, the golden age of Dutch painting coincided with the ascendancy of the French school. Although France had produced masterpieces of ecclesiastical art and architecture during the Middle Ages, it took some time before a Gallic style in painting blossomed. French kings of the 15C and 16C recognized the genius of Italy and introduced Italian artists into their courts, thereby discouraging native creativity. In the 17C, Frenchman **Nicolas Poussin** lived and worked in Rome, rendering Classical splendor with Baroque drama. As the 18C dawned, a stylistic ostentation inspired by the opulence and ceremony of the pre-Revolutionary monarchy was becoming fashionable in France. Largely popular for their applications in interior design, ornate Rococo forms found expression in the fanciful pastoral worlds painted by **François Boucher**, **Jean Antoine Watteau** and Jean-Honoré Fragonard. Jean Simeon Chardin painted ordinary people and objects with all of the grandeur and none of the grandiosity of his contemporaries. And, finally, in the revolutionary atmosphere of the late 18C, artists fully rejected the ornate traditions that had come to represent the hated exorbitance of the nobility. Led by Jacques-Louis David, the Neoclassicists viewed the republican virtues and precise proportions of antiquity as fitting counterpoints to the petty dalliances of their Rococo predecessors.

Nicolas Poussin...................*Rape of the Sabine Women,* c.1636
Jean Antoine Watteau ....*Mezzetin,* 1717-19
François Boucher ....*The Toilet of Venus,* 1751
Jacques-Louis David.............*The Death of Socrates,* c.1787

The Spanish Realm – *Galleries 16, 21, 29.* Perhaps the most intriguing and intensely personal artist of the 16C was a Greek who studied in Italy and lived much of his life in Spain. **El Greco** (Doménikos Theotokópoulos) imbued his work with a mystical expressiveness; his brooding palette and distorted figures look distinctly modern. Contrast his work with that of **Diego Velázquez**, Bartolome Murillo and Francisco de Zurbaran, whose academic and workmanlike renderings remain solidly earthbound. In the 18C **Francisco Goya** painted realistic and penetrating portraits that would inspire French painters of the 19C. He is regarded by some as the last of the Old Masters and the first of the moderns.

El Greco ....*View of Toledo,* c.1597
Diego Velázquez...................*Juan de Pareja,* c.1648
Francisco Goya ....*Don Manuel Osorio Manrique de Zuñiga,* c.1786

The English – *Gallery 15.* Because court painters—among them German Hans Holbein—were generally imported from the continent, native British painting had little opportunity to take root. It wasn't until the 18C that William Hogarth, best known for his satirical prints, conceived an English style that rejected the grand manner of contemporary European painters. Renowned primarily for their elegant portraits, **Sir Joshua Reynolds**, **Thomas Gainsborough** and Sir Thomas Lawrence epitomized the academic tradition. But in John Constable's landscapes of the English countryside hints of the sparkle of light that would so intrigue 19C painters can be seen.

Thomas Gainsborough ....*Mrs. Grace Dalrymple Elliott*, c.1778
Sir Joshua Reynolds ....*Colonel George K.H. Coussmaker*, 1782

★★19C EUROPEAN PAINTINGS AND SCULPTURE
Second floor. Plan p 232.

In addition to a generous pledge, Walter Annenberg's sizable bequest of 19C French paintings in the early 1990s crystallized plans for the reconfiguration of the 19C European galleries. Completed in 1993, these 21 galleries now closely reflect the settings the artists themselves might have expected. Designed in the Beaux-Arts style of the 19C, the rooms have been arranged by artistic movements, from the Salon through post-Impressionism. At the same time, they showcase the museum's strengths (Degas bronzes, for instance) and honor various benefactors throughout the years.

The Salon – To understand why Impressionism and other 19C movements created such controversy, it is helpful to view works that were then accepted by the art establishment. These are presented, along with a selection of sculpture, in the long hallway outside the galleries. Representing the conventional aesthetics of form, line and subject by which all work was judged, these paintings won ready entry into the annual juried exhibitions of the Paris Salon. Governed by the standards of the conservative French Academy, the Salon rejected Impressionism and other "avant-garde" movements. Although the Salon's influence on 19C public opinion was strong, the modern viewer cannot fail to note the ultimate success of those artists it shunned. Also on view here are works by **Auguste Rodin**, the finest 19C sculptor. His treatment of surface and concern with light link him with the Impressionist painters who were his contemporaries.

Rosa Bonheur ....*The Horse Fair*, 1852
Gustave Moreau ....*Oedipus and the Sphinx*, 1864
Auguste Rodin ....*Hand of God*

Neoclassicism, Romanticism, Realism – Out of the humanitarian ideals of the Enlightenment grew two major schools of artistic thought: Neoclassicism and Romanticism. In very different languages, both sought to express the idealism and nationalism of the new world order. Inspired by archaeological discoveries at Pompeii and Herculaneum in the mid-18C, the Neoclassicists—preeminently Jacques-Louis David *(gallery 2, 13C-18C European Paintings)*—turned to ancient Greece and Rome for new inspiration. **J.A.D. Ingres** was the finest portait painter of the era, due to his superb draftsmanship and crisp, classical lines. Rejecting such precision, the painters of the Romantic movement reveled in a freer attitude toward brush stroke and color, relying on historic events and settings for their exoticism, drama and allegory. In a portent of Impressionism, Eugène Delacroix, master Romantic, declared, "I do not paint a sword but its sparkle." The treatment of atmosphere and light by Englishmen John Constable and **J.M.W. Turner** is also prophetic. Toward the middle of the 19C, a new movement grounded in reality began to emerge. Forsaking Classical ideals and Romantic bravura, the Realists observed and recorded the world around them. One contingent of Realists, known as the Barbizon school because they painted the landscape around this French town, was inspired by Camille Corot, who painted directly from nature. Their palette tended to be dark and, as in the work of Gustave Courbet and **Jean-François Millet**, their subjects ordinary people. The leaves and landscapes they rendered reveal an interest in light and shade that would blossom with the Impressionists.

J.A.D. Ingres ....*Madame Leblanc*
J.M.W. Turner ....*The Grand Canal, Venice*, c.1835
Eugène Delacroix ....*Abduction of Rebecca*, 1846
Jean-François Millet.............*Autumn Landscape with a Flock of Turkeys*

Impressionism – The segue from Realism to Impressionism took place at the hand of **Edouard Manet**, who employed the dark tones and ordinary subjects of his con temporaries to explore the opposition of light and shadow. Indeed, as it evolved Impressionism sought to define its subjects in terms of their color and reflected light, thereby dissolving the hard outlines that traditionally delineated the painted form and, in the extreme, recasting subjects as an arrangement of color and light The Impressionists understood the ephemeral nature of their quest and painted rapidly to record moments in time with quick brush strokes that would give a spontaneous "impression" of a scene. They often worked outdoors, attempting to capture the fleeting effects of sunlight, and the movement acquired its name, coined derogatorily by an unimpressed critic, from **Claude Monet**'s 1872 painting *Impression: Sunrise* (housed in Paris' Musée Marmottan). So radical did these works seem in subject, palette and technique that they were refused admission to the annual exhibitions of the conservative Paris Salon. Undaunted, the Impressionists mounted eight of their own exhibitions between 1874 and 1886 eventually gaining critical acclaim. From the sunny facade of the Rouen Cathedral and the rugged seaside cliffs of Monet to the graceful young women of Pierre Auguste Renoir, the Impressionists observed and painted a colorful, luminous world.

Edouard Manet ....*Boating*, 1874

Claude Monet ....*Garden at Sainte-Adresse*, 1867

Pierre-Auguste Renoir ....*Madame Charpentier and Her Children*, 1878

Edgar Degas.....................*Little 14-Year-Old Dancer*, original modeled c.1880

Post-Impressionism – Because of its very nature and the diversity of its practi-tioners, the Impressionist phenomenon, though short-lived, opened the floodgates of artistic interpretation. Arising both out of and in opposition to its precepts, post-Impressionism pushed the formal aspects of painting in new emotional, com-positional, coloristic, symbolic and scientific directions. At the heart of the activity were **Paul Cézanne, Paul Gauguin** and **Georges Seurat**, who had practiced as Impressionists. In general, they shared a desire to turn from the spontaneity of Impressionism to explore more enduring forms of expression. Individually, each came to represent a different artistic vision. Cézanne's interest in structure and composition strongly influenced the Cubist artists of the next generation, earning him the epithet "the father of modern painting." Tahitian symbolism lends the work of Paul Gauguin a spirituality, and his bold planes of color bespeak perma-nence rather than impression. Seurat reduced his images to nearly a molecular level, only to build them up again using dot patterns of color. Pointillism had its basis in the idea that points of color mixed more brilliantly in the observer's eye than did paint on the artist's palette. Other post-Impressionist directions can be seen in the tempestuous work of **Vincent van Gogh** and the caricatures of Henri de Toulouse-Lautrec.

Paul Cézanne ....*The Cardplayers*, 1890

Paul Gauguin......................*La Orana Maria*, c.1891

Georges Seurat ....*Study for a Sunday Afternoon on the Island of LaGrande Jatte*, 1884

Vincent van Gogh ....*Cypresses*, 1889

⋆⋆LEHMAN PAVILION

Considered one of the finest private art collections in the US, the Robert Lehman Collection was compiled by financier Philip Lehman and his son, Robert. Ringing a stark central garden court are eleven galleries, seven of which are appointed to re-semble rooms in Robert Lehman's residence on West 54th Street. Some 3,000 works of art are shown here and in additional basement galleries.

Shown in rotating exhibits, the collection is most famous for its Italian paintings of the 14C and 15C, including works by Sassetta *(St. Anthony in the Wilderness)*, di Paolo *(Expulsion from Paradise)*, Botticelli *(Annunciation)*, Bellini *(Madonna and Child)* and Crivelli *(Madonna and Child)*. Representing the Northern Renaissance are Petrus Christus *(St. Eligius)*, Gerard David, Memling and Cranach the Elder. Works by Rembrandt, El Greco *(Christ Carrying the Cross)* and Goya exemplify the 18-19C Dutch and Spanish schools. French masterpieces of the 19C and 20C include Ingres' *Portrait of the Princesse de Broglie* and Renoir's *Young Girl Bathing*, as well as numerous works by Bonnard and Vuillard.

In addition to the artwork, the period rooms contain magnificent examples of the decorative arts, including tapestries, furniture, Venetian glass, bronzes and enamels.

⁑★MEDIEVAL ART *First floor. Plan p 231*

Tracing the development of art from the fall of Rome (4C) to the Renaissance (16C), the museum's extensive collection in medieval art comprises more than 4,000 works from the early Christian, Byzantine, Migration, Romanesque and Gothic periods. Among the treasures not to be missed are some exquisite pieces of Byzantine silver, Romanesque and Gothic metalwork, and Gothic stained glass and tapestries. *Additional medieval art objects are exhibited at The Cloisters p 201.*

Secular and liturgical artworks spanning the Byzantine Empire's 1000-plus-year reign from Constantinople line the corridors flanking the main staircase and reclaimed space underneath and behind the stairs. The north corridor, to the right of the staircase, holds early secular art of the Byzantine Empire and works by the Franks, the Goths and other peoples at the fringes of the empire. Note the representative ivories and enamels and the six silver plates engraved with scenes from the early life of David, all part of the Second Cyprus Treasure (7C). The south corridor, dedicated to liturgical art of the Byzantine Church and middle- and late-Byzantine secular art, features among its devotional objects the Antioch Chalice, said to have been used by Christ in the Last Supper. Among the fine examples of metalwork from the early medieval period are the chip-carved silver-gilt and niello pieces from the Vermand Treasure (northern France). Opening off the left side of the south corridor is the patio from the castle of Vélez Blanco in Spain, completed c.1515. The recently refurbished marble arcades were moved piece by piece to New York in the mid-20C. Underneath the stairs, a cryptlike gallery features Byzantine Egyptian art under a series of low brick arches. Walls built behind the stairs in the 1950s were removed to reveal the original apselike space that connects the corridors. A striking lion (AD 1000-1100), one of the few remaining bronze monumental sculptures from the period, guards the area. Note the leftmost of the three arches leading to the main hall, a marble, Italian Romanesque portal from San Gemini, in Umbria.

Medieval Tapestry Hall – Hung along the walls of this small hall is an ensemble of tapestries, dating from the 14C to the early 16C, woven principally in the workshops of Flanders (Arras, Brussels and Tournai). At that time, the tapestries were as practical as they were ornamental, serving to temper drafts and dampness. The *Annunciation*, begun early in the 15C, is related to a painting by Melchior Broederlam, a court painter in Burgundy. An interesting series of tapestries, commissioned by Charles the Bold, Duke of Burgundy, depicts the arming of Hector during the Trojan War.

Dating from the late Gothic period, large panels of stained glass from Cologne, Germany, and England fill two walls of the gallery.

Medieval Sculpture Hall – This large hall was built to evoke the ambience of a church, with a nave separated from the side aisles by massive columns. Stretching between two columns, a splendid wrought-iron, Baroque **choir screen★** rises almost the full height of the hall. Begun in 1668 for the Cathedral of Valladolid, in Spain, it was completed in 1764. At Christmastime, the museum exhibits a magnificent tree and an 18C Neapolitan Nativity scene in front of the choir screen.

A large collection of sculpture and bas-reliefs, mainly from Burgundy, Italy and Germany, traces the development of Gothic sculpture from the 13C to the 16C. Note especially the 15C Burgundian Virgin and Child from Poligny, France. Also on display is a rare group of panels representing Baptism, Marriage and Extreme Unction.

Medieval Treasury – In addition to portable shrines, reliquary caskets and sacramental objects, the Treasury also contains two fine sculptural groups (early 16C) of the Entombment and Pietà, from the Périgord region of France. The wall and central glass cases display an assemblage of precious objects, including an Ottonian ivory *situla* (holy-water bucket); a 13C Limoges enamel shrine decorated with scenes from the life of Christ in copper gilt; the silver reliquary head of St. Yrieix (13C, Limousin), which once held fragments of his skull; and a processional cross covered in silver (12C, Spanish). The richness of the collection of Romanesque and Gothic enamels rivals that of the French ivories of the 13C to 15C, which include a rosary with beads in the form of skulls.

On the way to the American Wing, note an unusual German saddle of bone housed in a glass case. The decoration, in low relief, depicts scenes of courtly love.

★★ARTS OF AFRICA, OCEANIA AND THE AMERICAS

First floor.

Artworks from sub-Saharan Africa, the Pacific Islands, and North, Central, and South America are located in the museum's south wing, which was named in honor o' Nelson Rockefeller's son, Michael, who died while on an expedition to the island o New Guinea in 1961. The core of the collection encompasses approximately 3,500 works donated to the museum by Nelson Rockefeller in the late 1970s. The depart ment now owns about 8,000 objects spanning a period of 3,000 years. Among the most impressive objects on display are the towering memorial poles (called *mbis* and attractively decorated shields of the Asmat of Irian Jaya (Western New Guinea collected by Michael Rockefeller. *Galleries are arranged to form a loop. The fol lowing description starts from the entrance nearest the Greek and Roman gallerie. and ends at the exit leading to European Sculpture and Decorative Arts.*

Africa – Sculpture, primarily ritualistic masks and figures carved in wood, domi nates the art of Africa, which is essentially religious. The first gallery contains a collection of monumental sculpture by the Dogon of Mali. Note the 7ft-high elon gated male figure standing with arms raised.

Adapting animal traits to headdresses and masks, the Bamana people created ante lope headdresses with extremely slender vertical lines. Ferocious-looking Senufc helmet masks incorporate the jaws and teeth of a crocodile, the horns of an ante lope and the tusks of a warthog. Among the Bamana figures, note a Mother and Child sculpture, one of several in the collection.

To the left of the entrance, the adjacent gallery displays figures, masks and the chief's ceremonial stool carved by the Buli Master; the small ivories and wooden figures from Zaire, notably an ivory mask from the Lega people, are also of interest The serene Fang reliquary head was carved to protect a box that contained the skulls of honored ancestors.

Highlighting this area is a collection of dark brass items—plaques, animals, figures and heads—from the royal court of Benin. Dating from the 16C to the 19C, the heads are adorned with caps and chokers of the type still worn by the king today. A precious **ivory mask**, a royal ornament also from Benin, is displayed in a separate case. Carved into the hair of the mask are mudfish, symbolic of wealth and royalty, and faces that represent the Portuguese merchants who arrived in Nigeria in the 15C.

When leaving this section, pause to admire the naturalistic double headdress of the Ekoi people of Nigeria and the wooden mask (from a triple mask) carved by the Ibibio people.

Oceania – A masterfully carved tall drum from the Austral Islands and a ceremo nial **shield** inlaid with shells (Solomon Islands) reflect the ornamental as well as utilitarian purpose most objects served in cultures from the Pacific Islands. The first gallery presents objects from New Guinea, including elaborately decorated shields, masks, fence posts, ceremonial boards and *slit-gongs* (drums); paintings etched on sheets of bark, re-creating the roof of a ceremonial house, are displayed overhead.

Gold funerary mask (Peru)

This gallery opens onto a long, spacious glass-walled hall that has as its focal point a remarkable group of nine delicately carved **poles** *(mbis)*, ranging up to 20ft in height. These Asmat *mbis* serve as a centerpiece for the other objects arranged in this hall: carvings with intricate openwork from New Ireland, figures sculpted from fern wood, a standing *slit-gong* from New Hebrides and a 25ft-long crocodile effigy from Papua New Guinea.

Americas – The first gallery houses the Jan Mitchell Treasury, where exhibits of gold ornaments, vessels and masks from South and Central America include a pair of Mochica shell-and-stone-mosaic ear spools (3C-6C AD); a pendant (Colombia, 13C-16C AD) in the form of a figure wearing an elaborate headdress; and a boldly painted Sicán **funerary mask** (Peru, 11-9C BC). Also from Peru are the luxurious yellow and blue feathers (late 7C-8C AD) hanging on the far right wall, a group of silver vessels and ancient Peruvian pottery.

The adjacent gallery features the arts of Mesoamerica. Here, note especially the Mayan **seated figure** (6C AD), one of the few extant three-dimensional Mayan pieces in wood. Cases mounted along the wall contain "smiling figures" (7C-8C AD) from Veracruz, characterized by their broad faces and wide grins; and ornamented stone objects *(palmas, hachas)* associated with an ancient ritual ball game. The superb relief carving of the Maya is exemplified by a stone stele from Mexico. A refined jade mask illustrates the artistry of the ancient Olmec civilization (13C-5C BC) of Mexico.

★ARMS AND ARMOR *First floor.*

Displayed in ten recently renovated galleries, this encyclopedic collection comprises more than 14,000 arms, designed mainly for display rather than for actual military use. Surrounding a vast central hall, the western galleries feature European arms—including rare pieces commissioned by various kings and rulers—while the eastern galleries focus on articles from China, Japan, India, Turkey and Iran.

Dominating the vast hall is a striking display of parade armor, replete with suits of armor and horses, designed by Wolfgang Grosschedel and Kunz Lochner in the 16C. Surrounding glass cases display finely chiseled and embossed arms while colorful flags and banners hang overhead.

In the western galleries, arms and armor predating the 16C include pieces from the Crusades, a helmet said to be Joan of Arc's and a group of shields for battle and tournament. Among the most arresting pieces of the collection are the parade helmet of François I, by renowned Milanese armorer Filippo Negroli; the embossed shield (1555) designed by Étienne Delaune for Henry II of France; and the three-quarter armor of Anne de Montmorency, High Constable under Henry II. Arms of tempered steel, predominantly made in Germany and Italy, include daggers, swords and rapiers, halberds, lances and pikes; especially handsome is the sword with the chiseled cup hilt, which belonged to the Marquis of Spinola (16C). Among the firearms, note the pair of flintlock pistols (1786) belonging to Empress Catherine the Great. A double-barreled pistol (c.1540) by Peter Peck of Munich made for Emperor Charles V is one of the earliest in existence.

The eastern galleries present articles from the Far and Near East ranging from small arrowheads to elaborate suits of armor. Of particular interest are the late-15C helmets from Iran, which adopt the shape of a turban, and various sabers and their scabbards intricately decorated with inlaid emeralds, diamonds and other precious stones. Highlighting the Japanese collection is a medieval *yoroi* (14C)—or armor—composed of a leather cuirass and a four-sided skirt.

A small gallery on the north side displays firearms from Europe and America.

★★ASIAN ART *Second floor*
(also accessible by elevator or stairway in the Egyptian Wing) and third floor.

Occupying the Great Hall balcony and the northeast corner and north end of the second floor, the Asian art galleries trace the development of Chinese, Japanese, Korean, Southeast and South Asian art, from the second millennium BC to the present, through ceramics, metalwork, paintings and sculptures, bronzes, jades and textiles. The collection is the largest of its kind in the West. The opening in 1998 of a gallery showcasing Korean art from the Neolithic to the 19C in rotating exhibits marked the completion of the 64,500sq ft wing.

China – Twenty-five hundred years of Chinese ceramics are represented along the perimeter of the Great Hall Balcony. Highlighting the north wall of the Arthur M. Sackler Gallery, a huge mural from Shansi in northern China (14C) depicting Buddha and his assembly forms a magnificent background to the monumental collection of Chinese Buddhist sculpture of the 5C and 6C. Ancient Chinese art is displayed in a series of galleries to the left of the wall mural. Spanning the period from the Neolithic (early 2,000 BC) through the Tang dynasty (10C AD), these galleries include jades, ceramics, bronze ritual vessels and tomb art. Recent renovation has nearly doubled exhibition space for Chinese painting, calligraphy and decorative arts. Rotating exhibits span at least four dynasties—Sung (960-1279), Yuan (1279-1368), Ming (1368-1644) and Ching (1644-1911)—as well as the modern era, and illustrate a wide range of subject matter from landscapes and flower paintings to Buddhist and Taoist themes. In the center of the painting galleries is the **garden court★** *(Astor Court)*, a reproduction of a Ming dynasty courtyard and scholar's study in Soochow, China. Principal features of the courtyard, set apart from the mainstream of museum traffic and meticulously landscaped with Chinese plantings, are the moon-viewing terrace, half-pavilion and opposite walkway, the latticed windows, and formal rock arrangement. The study, built with traditional mortise-and-tenon joining techniques, contains handsome furniture of the era.

On the third floor, several quiet rooms contain elegant Chinese decorative arts: textiles, ivory work, bamboo and boxwood items, red lacquerwork and jades.

Korea – The gallery surveying Korean art, reached from within the ancient Chinese art corridor, near the Sackler Wing, holds a collection that includes earthenware and Bronze Age pieces, Buddhist paintings and ceramics. Note the series of lacquered wood boxes with intricate inlay.

South and Southeast Asian Art – These 18 stunning galleries were opened in 1993 to display some 1,300 works, from Nepal to Burma. The first rooms, running from the right of the wall mural in the Sackler Gallery, trace the history of art in the subcontinent—India, Pakistan and Afghanistan— showcasing a rich diversity of works, including depictions of Buddha, Shiva, Vishnu and other lesser-known deities. Chola dynasty (9-13C AD) bronzes and statuary from the golden age of the Gupta dynasty (4-6C AD) highlight the Indian objects. Among the delightful bronzes are fan-shaped Shivas and a pot-bellied four-armed "Standing Ganesha." Three connected galleries on the third floor house Indian court paintings and religious imagery from Tibet and Nepal. Among the rooms devoted to Southeast Asia (Cambodia, Thailand, Vietnam and Indonesia), a skylit gallery of monumental Khmer sculptures from the Angkor period (8-14C AD) stands out. The collection constitutes one of the largest of its kind outside Cambodia.

Japan – The second-floor galleries dedicated to Japanese art feature changing exhibits of paintings, sculpture, lacquer, wood-block prints, scrolls, screens and kimonos from the museum's collection. This section also includes a *shoin*-style reception room modelled on a room in the Onoji temple (17C) outside Kyoto, and *Water Stone*, a sculpture by Isamu Noguchi.

★COSTUME INSTITUTE *Ground floor.*

This center for costume research and study was created in 1937, with a view to collecting and preserving costumes past and present. Today, the 40,000-article collection of regional garb includes costumes from five continents, ranging from the elegant wardrobes of ancient royalty to chic fashions by the most distinguished contemporary American and French couturiers. Changing exhibits explore topics related to fashion, history and society.

★ISLAMIC ART *Second floor.*

The Islamic Art galleries are closed for renovations until spring 2007. Selected items from the museum's collection can be seen in an installation on the Great Hall balcony.

This section traces the development of Islamic art, beginning with the founding of Islam in the 7C and ending in the early 19C. Encompassing works from various geographical regions, including Mesopotamia, Persia, Morocco, Egypt, Syria and India, the collection is particularly known for its displays of glass- and metalwork, miniatures and classical carpets.

In the first gallery, a map and descriptive text introduce the visitor to the diversity and range of Islamic culture. The opulence of an 18C Syrian house is reflected in the richly paneled reception room decorated with an ornamented ceiling, painted and gilded walls, a marbled fountain and a magnificent marble floor. Gallery 2, devoted to the museum's excavations in Nishapur, a thriving Persian city (9C-12C), contains rare wall paintings and a collection of objects in metal, stone, glass and ceramics; some are engraved with inscriptions and the famous arabesque motifs. Presented in chronological order, the objects on display gain refinement as the centuries unfold. In gallery 4b, admire the colorful tile panels and the intricate wood-and metalwork from the Mamluk period. The early-16C wood **ceiling** hails from Moorish Spain. A pair of Egyptian doors (14C) bearing a kaleidoscopic pattern carved in wood and ivory illustrates the Muslim mastery of intricate design.

Further displays include ivory carvings, artfully painted ceramic bowls, decorated glass mosque lamps, bottles and jugs from Iran, and jade vessels and jewelry from 17C India. In gallery 4c, note the 1354 **mihrab** (prayer niche indicating the direction of Mecca), an exquisite 11ft-high mosaic from Isfahan, composed of glazed ceramic tiles laid in geometric and floral patterns and inscribed with passages from the Koran.

Painting, which found a lively expression in the illustration of manuscripts, is represented by the delicate art of **miniatures** as practiced in Persia, India and Ottoman Turkey. Highlighting the collection is an ensemble of miniatures depicting episodes from the great Persian literary work known as the *Shahnama* or Book of Kings *(gallery 6)*. An array of sumptuous carpets *(galleries 7 and 8)* attests to the level of carpet-weaving mastery achieved in the workshops of Egypt, Persia, Turkey and India. Also in gallery 8, note the gilded Ottoman helmet and a rare Ottoman Court prayer rug from the late 16C.

★MUSICAL INSTRUMENTS *Second floor.*

Audio equipment enables visitors to hear instruments play period music (available at Acoustic Guides Desk, 1st floor).

This section presents an original and rare collection of more than 4,000 musical instruments from all periods and all parts of the world. The western galleries focus on European instruments, including the oldest extant piano (1720); three Stradivarius violins, crafted by the famous violin maker of Cremona; two classical guitars belonging to Andrés Segovia made out of rosewood, spruce and mahogany; and an outstanding series of keyboard instruments decorated with marquetry, sculpture and paintings, including the spinet made in 1540 in Venice for the Duchess of Urbino. Other interesting instruments include a Flemish double virginal of the 16C decorated with musical scenes; lutes, zithers and guitars from the 17C; and wind instruments made of shell, bone, goatskin and Meissen porcelain. The eastern galleries highlight instruments from the Near and Far East, the Americas and Africa, including seldom-seen pieces such as an Indonesian *sesando*, a type of zither made from palm leaves, and an Indian *mayuri*, or bowed sitar. Often selected for their role in society as well as for their tonal qualities, most of the instruments are in working order and are used for occasional concerts.

★20C ART *Lila Acheson Wallace Wing.*

Devoted to art forms from 1900 to the present, the Lila Acheson Wallace Wing displays more than 8,000 paintings, sculptures, works on paper and decorative arts on its three floors and in the skylit sculpture court on the mezzanine level. Located on top of the wing, the **rooftop garden**★ offers a superb setting for contemporary sculpture while affording splendid **views** of Manhattan's midtown and uptown skylines *(open May-Nov)*.

The museum's holdings encompass works by European artists such as Bonnard, Matisse and Picasso *(Gertrude Stein)*, including the Berggruen collection of 90 works by Paul Klee, donated in 1984. However, the strength of the collection lies in American art, in particular works by the Group of Eight, Abstract Expressionists and Minimalists. Recent bequests by Florene May Schoenborn and Klaus G. and Amelia Perls increased the museum's Cubist holdings with several works by Picasso, Braque, Brancusi and Gris. In 1998 trustee Natasha Gelman bequeathed 85 masterworks to the collection, a gift that rounds out the Met's modern holdings with works by Matisse, Picasso, Braque and Modigliani, among others. To show selections from the bequest, in 2001 the museum opened the Gelman Galleries, at the west end of the wing. The galleries, arranged chronologically, include studies of Fauvists and Cubism, notably companion pieces by Braque *(Still Life with a Pair of Banderillas)* and Picasso *(Still Life with a Bottle of Rum)* painted the same week in 1911 while the artists were in the French Pyrenees. Surrealist paintings and works from after 1940 round out the rooms.

Among the early-20C paintings are Marsden Hartley's *Portrait of a German Officer;* Georgia O'Keeffe's *Cow's Skull: Red, White and Blue;* and Florine Stettheimer's *Wall Street, Appropriately Gilt.* In the post-World War II period, New York developed as the center of the contemporary art world and witnessed the development of Abstract Expressionism with such artists as Jackson Pollock *(Autumn Rhythm)*, Willem de Kooning *(Easter Monday)* and Mark Rothko *(Untitled Number 13)*. More recent works by Roy Lichtenstein *(Stepping Out)*, James Rosenquist *(House of Fire)*, David Hockney, Clyfford Still, Frank Stella, Ellsworth Kelly and other important American and European painters continue the survey of 20C art through the 1970s and into the 1990s. Sculptural works include creations by Archipenko, Giacometti, Kiki Smith and Isamu Noguchi.

DRAWINGS, PRINTS AND PHOTOGRAPHS *Second floor.*

At the top of the main staircase, to the left. Presented in the form of temporary exhibits; check on schedules at information desk.

The collection of more than 4,000 drawings focuses on Italian and French artists from the 15C to the 19C, including Michelangelo, Pietro da Cortona, Romanino di Brescia, Poussin, David and Delacroix. The Dutch and Spanish schools are also represented with works by Rubens, Rembrandt and Goya.

Highlighting various techniques, including woodcutting, lithography and other forms of engraving, the Met's assemblage of prints focuses on 15C German, 18C Italian and 19C French images. Among the most memorable early works are: *Battle of the Ten Naked Men* by Antonio Pollaiuolo, *Bacchanal with a Wine Vat* by Andrea Mantegna, *The Four Horsemen of the Apocalypse* by Albrecht Dürer, and Rembrandt's *Faust in His Study*.

The 18C artists represented include Hogarth of England, Piranesi of Rome, Fragonard of France and Goya of Spain. Particularly noteworthy among 19C works are Daumier's *Rue Transnonain* and Toulouse-Lautrec's *Aristide Bruant*.

Forming the core of the museum's holdings in photography is a large collection of Alfred Stieglitz photographs, acquired between 1928 and 1949, and the Walker Evans Archive acquired in 1994. Diane Arbus, Cindy Sherman, and Shirley Levine are among the postwar photographers whose work may be on view. To house and maintain its growing collection, the museum is planning to build a $16-million Center for Imaging and Photography.

MOUNT VERNON HOTEL
MUSEUM AND GARDEN

421 E. 61st St. **MTA** 4, 5, 6, R or N trains to 59th St.
Map p 11

Visit by guided tour (1hr) only, year-round Tue–Sun 11am–4pm (Tue until 9pm June & July only). Closed Aug & Jan 1, Thanksgiving Day & Dec 25. $4. ☎ 212-838-6878.

This 1799 Federal-style stone building, now located in a largely commercial part of midtown Manhattan, is among the few surviving 18C residences in the city. The house was designed to be part of a 23-acre estate acquired by Col. William Smith and his wife, Abigail Adams Smith, daughter of President John Adams. The couple, however, soon encountered financial trouble and had to sell the property to a merchant, William T. Robinson, who in turn erected a manor house and various outbuildings, including this structure, a former coach house and stable. Fire destroyed the manor house in 1826 and the coach house-stable was converted the same year to an inn and tavern, the Mount Vernon Hotel. The Colonial Dames of America purchased the building in 1924 and restored it to its mid-19C appearance. Nine period rooms, appointed with 18C and 19C antiques, as well as a neatly manicured garden, are open to the public.

MUSEUM OF AMERICAN
FINANCIAL HISTORY

28 Broadway. **MTA** 4, 5 train to Bowling Green
Map p 126

Open year-round Tue–Sat 10am–4pm. Closed major holidays. $2. ☎ 212-908-4110. www.financialhistory.org.

Located in the center of America's financial heartland, this small affiliate of the Smithsonian Institution has occupied quarters in John D. Rockefeller's former Standard Oil Building (1928, Carrère and Hastings) since 1988. The museum's mission is to preserve and exhibit financial artifacts and educate the public about the history of finances. Changing exhibits present the nation's financial development via documents, objects and photographs from the permanent collection and from the archives of the Smithsonian Institution. For example, an exhibit entitled High Notes, which includes the highest denomination currencies ever printed, features a $100,000 bill. Don't miss the upstairs museum shop where you can buy an early-19C stock certificate or a vintage annual report.

MUSEUM OF ARTS DESIGN★

40 W. 53rd St. **MTA** E, V trains to 5th Ave.
Map p 89

Open year-round daily 10am–6pm (Thu til 8pm). Closed major holidays. $8 (Thu after 6pm by donation). ♿ ☎ 212-956-3535. www.americancraftmuseum.org.

Housed in a mottled-pink granite office tower (1986; Roche, Dinkeloo & Assocs.) and flanked by stylized columns and 20ft smoked-glass windows, this delightful museum displays contemporary crafts with an eye toward both traditional craftsmanship and ant-garde materials. reated in 1956 by the merican Craft Council, e museum presents ro-ting selections from ermanent and traveling ollections emphasizing e scope and spirit of OC crafts. In late 2005, e museum is slated to ove to a much larger uilding at Two Colum-us Circle, at the south-est corner of Central ark.

side, the gracefully rching, four-story trium features a uggenheim-inspired oiral stairwell leading to alleries that highlight ematic exhibits as well s recent acquisitions. xecuted by interna-onal and American rtists, the works range rom fiber art, glass, /ood and ceramics to ynthetic and mixed-edia creations.

Moon Viewing Chair (1999) by Clifton Monteith

MUSEUM OF CHINESE IN THE AMERICAS

70 Mulberry St., 2nd floor. **MTA** J, M, N, R,Q, W or 6 trains to Canal St.
or B, D trains to Grand St.
Map p 144

Open year-round Tue–Sun noon–5pm. Closed major holidays and Chinese New Year's Day. $3. ☎ 212-619-4785. www.moca-nyc.org.

Created in 1980, this small museum presents the history and culture of Chinese people n New York and promotes awareness of Chinese communities throughout the Americas. Designed by Chinese-American architect Billie Tsien, the main gallery showcases the permanent exhibit, which explores the Chinese American experience using the museum's collection of artifacts and oral histories. In the second gallery, rotating exhibits focus on related themes such as the arts and culture. The museum maintains an annual program of events open to the public and conducts walking tours of Chinatown.

MUSEUM OF JEWISH HERITAGE

18 First Place, Battery Park City. **MTA** 4, 5 train to Bowling Green
Map p 126

Open year-round Sun–Thu 10am–5:45pm (Wed until 8pm), Fri 10am–5pm during daylight savings. Closed Thanksgiving Day & Jewish holidays. Closes 3pm on the eve of Jewish Holidays and Fri. $7. ♿ ☎ 212-509-6130. www.mjhnyc.org.

Overlooking the Statue of Liberty and Ellis Island from the southern tip of Battery Park, the museum is a fitting complement to its eminent neighbors, joining them in 1997 as a testament to humanity's struggle for freedom. Representative of the points of the Star of David, the structure's six planar facades, topped by six tiers of roofline, also symbolize the nearly six million people who lost their lives during the Holocaust. Designed by Roche, Dinkeloo and Assocs., the modest 30,000sq ft building (85ft in height) helps scale down the city along the Battery Park waterfront, while providing a cultural and historical reference in a district known for its commercial might. Inside, three floors of artifacts, photographs and video and audio presentations document Jewish culture from the 1880s to the 1930s; the horrors of the Holocaust; and modern Jewish renewal, symbolized by a massive Torah dominating the third-floor skylit gallery. In October 2000 construction began on a new 70,000sq ft east wing. Plans include a theater, a library, additional exhibit space, a cafe, offices and classrooms. A newly created memorial garden will border New York Harbor *(project completion is slated for early 2004)*.

MUSEUM OF MODERN ART★★★

45-20 33rd St. at Queens Blvd. in Queens. **MTA** 7 local train to 33rd St. Station
Map p 89

One of the world's preeminent cultural institutions, the Museum of Modern Art
(MoMA) offers an unparalleled overview of the modern visual arts. The rich collection
includes not only painting, drawing and sculpture, but also photography; decorative,
graphic and industrial art; architectural plans and models; video; and the most comprehensive film archive in the US.

Historical Notes

Famous Founders – The founding of the museum dates back to 1929, when three
private benefactors—Abby Aldrich Rockefeller, Lillie P. Bliss and Mary Quinn Sullivan—
launched a campaign to promote the modern arts in the US. The first show, of the
then little-known post-Impressionists, opened in temporary quarters that fall. Over the
next decade, founding director **Alfred H. Barr Jr.** shaped the museum's philosophy, which
emphasizes ideas as much as objects, and introduced the novel concept of a multi-
departmental museum of art. Among Barr's pioneering exhibits were shows of
photography, design and architecture, none of which were acknowledged as legitimate art forms at the time.

The Building – *The museum's permanent home at 11 W. 53rd Street in Manhattan
is undergoing extensive renovation and expansion. The Midtown facility closed in 2002
for approximately three years, and MoMA moved to temporary quarters in a former
stapler factory in Long Island City, Queens.*
The original 1939 marble and glass museum building by Philip Goodwin and Edward
Durell Stone was one of the first examples of the International style in the US. (The
term "International Style" came from Barr's groundbreaking 1932 show, "Modern
Architecture: International Exhibition," organized by Philip Johnson and Henry Russell
Hitchcock.) The sculpture garden and east wing are 1964 additions by Philip Johnson.
A 1979 renovation by Cesar Pelli more than doubled the gallery space and included
the addition of the glass-faced Garden Hall and a 44-story residential tower to the west.
In 1997 Yoshio Taniguchi was selected by MoMA to design the museum's latest expansion and renovation. Some 230,000sq ft of new construction to the northwest will be
devoted to additional gallery space; eastern portions will be reconfigured for educational and research needs. Highlights of the new plan include a grand pedestrian
thoroughfare joining 53rd and 54th streets; larger, more flexible spaces for contemporary art; and architecturally distinctive galleries for the museum's masterpieces.

MoMA in Queens: The Building – The old Swingline stapler factory, a low rectangular building off Queens Boulevard, opened to the public as "MoMA QNS" in June
2002. The museum retained the robin's egg blue of the building's stucco exterior that
had long made it a local landmark. Visitors arriving by the 7 train enjoy a trompe l'oeil:
a set of painted equipment boxes on the roof appear in an abstract arrangement, briefly
coalesce to spell "MoMA," then fall again into abstraction. Inside, the 25,000sq ft exhibition space is split between temporary exhibits and a selection of masterworks from
the museum's collection, arranged by period and style (Van Gogh, Matisse, Seurat,
Picasso, Pollock, Rauschenberg and Warhol are represented). The building also houses
museum offices and conservation work and storage space. MoMA will expand these
functions when the viewing galleries move back to Manhattan in 2005.

The Collections – From an initial 1931 bequest by Lillie P. Bliss of 235 works
—including key paintings by Cézanne, Gauguin, Seurat and Redon—the museum's
holdings have grown to encompass more than 100,000 pieces and 14,000 films. There
are six divisions: painting and sculpture (major Western artists from the 1880s to the
present); drawings (Dada, Surrealist, Cubist, school of Paris, Russian avant-garde and
American artists); prints and illustrated books (bibliographic arts and printmaking,
including the graphic arts of Picasso); photography (masters from the 1840s to the
present, including Stieglitz, Cartier-Bresson, Weston, Kertész, Lange and Friedlander);
architecture and design (Frank Lloyd Wright and Mies van der Rohe models, Bauhaus
furniture, Tiffany glass, Russian Constructivist posters); and film and video (silent,
experimental, animated, documentary and feature films and stills from around the
world).

Visiting the museum

*Open year-round Thu–Mon 10am–5pm (Fri until 7:45pm). Closed Thanksgiving Day
& Dec 25. $12. Guided tours (1hr) available. ✗ ⚐ 212-708-9400. www.moma.org.*

During the expansion and renovation, major temporary exhibits as well as "Collection
Highlights," a sampler of MoMA's masterworks, will be on display (with some addi-
tions) at MoMA's Queens facility. Until the expansion is completed, MoMA's Design
Store *(44 W. 53rd St.)* will continue to do business at its Manhattan address, but the
MoMA bookstore wil be closed. MoMA's film program is being held temporarily in the
Gramercy Theatre *(127 E. 23rd St., between Lexington & Park Aves.).*

On weekends a free Queens Artlink shuttle bus takes visitors from West 53rd Street to MoMA QNS every hour on the hour from 10am to 4pm, and returns every hour on the half hour from 10:30am to 5:30pm. A second shuttle loops from MoMA QNS to P.S.1, SculptureCenter, Socrates Sculpture Park, American Museum of the Moving Image, the Noguchi Museum and the Museum for African Art. It leaves MoMA QNS every hour from 10:45am to 4:45pm.

The following paragraphs offer an overview of the major artists, schools and movements represented in MoMA's permanent collection; note that only a small fraction of these works will be on view until the grand reopening of the Midtown facility in 2005. Contact the museum or access its Web site for a current schedule of exhibitions and events.

VISIT

Post-Impressionism – This term refers to several movements that emerged in Europe between about 1880 and 1905 in reaction to French Impressionism. Defining color through the interplay of reflecting light, the Impressionists sought to create a naturalistic "impression" of their subject (Claude Monet's *Waterlilies*, 1899-1926) instead of a literal rendering. By contrast, the post-Impressionists, including Paul Cézanne, Vincent van Gogh *(The Starry Night)* and Henri de Toulouse-Lautrec, emphasized form, rendered through simplified shapes and expressive line; many also embraced symbolism and religious themes. Pierre Bonnard, Paul Gauguin and Édouard Vuillard, members of the Nabis, a group of French painters who favored flat areas of pure color, are also considered post-Impressionists, as is the Pointillist painter Georges Seurat *(Evening, Honfleur)*, known for expressing form with small dots of color.

Fauvism and Early Picasso – When a group of painters, including Henri Matisse *(The Red Studio)* and André Derain *(Bathers)*, mounted a show of dazzling canvases splashed with impulsive brush strokes of color at the 1905 Salon d'Automne in Paris, the critic Louis Vauxcelles was so stunned by the violent appearance of the works that he called the artists *les fauves*, or wild beasts. While the movement lasted only until 1907, its characteristically bold, spontaneous compositions, in which form was analyzed through color, had a strong impact on the development of European Expressionism. The same period marks the proto-Cubist explorations of renowned Spanish artist Pablo Picasso. The two primary sources of Cubism—African sculpture and the later work of Cézanne—were first combined in Picasso's 1907 painting *Les Demoiselles d'Avignon*.

Cubism – Pablo Picasso and Georges Braque pioneered this influential modern movement in 20C painting and sculpture, marking a radical departure from traditional Western art. In an effort to understand the problems of spatial construction, the artists reduced their subjects to apparently abstract geometrics, in which solids became transparent and convex planes concave. The fractured planes in works by Braque, as in *Man with a Guitar* (1911), show a characteristic emphasis on the relationship of shapes rather than on the shapes themselves. Cubism influenced many other early-20C artists, including Juan Gris *(Guitar and Flowers)*, and is considered the forerunner of abstract art.

Expressionism – This emotional approach, which held that art was valid only if it sprang from the artist's "inner necessity," was dominant in Germany from about 1905 to 1925. Following on the heels of Symbolists Edvard Munch and Gustav Klimt *(Hope II)*, and influenced in part by medieval woodcuts and African tribal art, Expressionist works embraced distorted forms, violent stylization and harsh color combinations in an effort to reject the "superficiality" of naturalism. At the core of the movement was Die Brücke, a group of Dresden artists formed in 1905 and led by Ernst Kirchner *(Street, Dresden* and *Street, Berlin)*, and a group of Munich Expressionists known as Der Blaue Reiter, which included Wassily Kandinsky, whose *Picture with an Archer* represented the artist's early experimentation with abstraction, and Paul Klee. One of the major and most individualistic Expressionists was the Austrian Oskar Kokoschka, known for his powerful portraits and self-portraits.

Futurism and Early Abstract Art – The poet F.T. Marinetti founded the Futurist movement in 1909, declaring that "the splendor of the world has been enriched with a new form of beauty, the beauty of speed." The Futurists demanded that all aspects of art and culture, including film, architecture, music and literature, reject the numbing confines of tradition and embrace the dynamism of modern technology. Under the influence of Cubism, the movement swung toward abstraction, producing the tense, turbulent energy of Umberto Boccioni's paintings *(Dynamism of a Soccer Player)* and cast-bronze sculptures *(Development of a Bottle in Space* and *Unique Forms of Continuity in Space)*.

The prismatic breakdown of light and spatially abstract planes of Cubism also influenced the early dreamlike compositions of the Russian-born French painter Marc Chagall, and had a strong impact on Robert Delaunay, Fernand Léger and Kasimir

245

Malevich *(Woman with Water Pails: Dynamic Arrangement)*, one of the great masters of early Abstract art. Pure Abstract, or nonrepresentational, art—in which color, line and form express reality through intuitive suggestions originating in the mind—emerged in Russia before World War I. Around 1914 Kandinsky explored his ideas in related compositions of surging and retracting color shapes *(Four Seasons Series)*, producing what many believe to be the first modern paintings with no references to recognizable objects or situations.

Giorgio de Chirico – Although he would later reject Modernism, the Italian painter Giorgio de Chirico spent his early career exploring disturbing artistic imagery that turned reality inside out. From 1911 to 1915, the artist, considered a forerunner of the Surrealists, resided in Paris. There he produced a series of "enigma" paintings in which lone figures or statues are juxtaposed with symbols of modern progress, set against the melancholy backgrounds of abandoned Italian towns. In 1915 de Chirico returned to Italy, where he founded the short-lived Metaphysical school with Futurist Carlo Carrá. His increasingly surreal canvases began to feature odd, often unidentifiable objects skewed in uneasy perspective and set off by a sharply lit chiaroscuro of light and shadow.

Collage and Dada; Picasso, Duchamp – Continued contemplation of the relationship between actual objects and the perceived reality of the imagination is reflected in the exploratory constructions, known as *papiers collés*, of Picasso, Braque and Juan Gris. In such works, cutout shapes become metaphors for everyday objects, which are taken apart, reconsidered, then reduced to basic elements in unpretentious materials like paper and corrugated cardboard.

Collage, and the underlying idea of juxtaposing odd objects and unexpected materials, also became a centerpiece medium of Dada. Lasting from 1915 to about 1923, this protest movement was an indictment of bourgeois values and the senseless brutality of World War I. The nihilist members, including Americans and Europeans, rejected all established values, creating instead a "non-art" designed to shock and provoke. (The French word *dada*, meaning "hobbyhorse," was picked at random from a dictionary.) A typical Dada collage was made of torn bits of paper, ripped from ads and catalogs; a sculpture might consist of a snow shovel or toilet bowl. Jean Arp, Marcel Duchamp *(The Passage from Virgin to Bride* and *Bicycle Wheel)* and Francis Picabia were all proponents of the movement, which also attracted the German Kurt Schwitters and the American expatriate Man Ray.

Mondrian – Although the early art of this leading Dutch abstract painter focused on landscapes, Piet Mondrian was deeply influenced by Cubism and soon turned away from representational subjects. In 1917 he founded the De Stijl movement with a group of artists, poets and architects. De Stijl (meaning "the style") derived from neo-Plasticism, Mondrian's concept of a new abstract art of "pure plastics" that expressed the truth of contemporary life through the ordered harmony of straight lines, right angles, squares, rectangles, pure colors and neutrals. Many of the artist's early works were done with simple black marks, as in the charcoal *Pier and Ocean* (1914), while his later paintings of the 1940s *(Broadway Boogie Woogie)* are charged with the energy of primary hues worked in precisely syncopated strips of color, evoking an enthusiasm for modern jazz and the sharp rhythms of city street life.

Russian Constructivism and Suprematism – Russian Constructivism (1917-20) was founded by sculptors Naum Gabo, Antoine Pevsner and Vladimir Tatlin, whose highly structural works in wood, glass, metal and plastic embodied the progress of a new industrialized era. Among the influential members of the movement was the graphic designer and photographer Alexander Rodchenko, known for minimalist linear compositions and hanging sculptures *(Oval Hanging Construction Number 12)*. Constructivist ideas were disseminated in Europe through the paintings, book designs and gelatin silver prints of El Lissitzky. This Russian artist inspired the abstract sculpture of the Hungarian-born artist László Moholy-Nagy *(Nickel Construction)*, an early teacher at the Bauhaus.

Concurrent with the development of Constructivism, Kasimir Malevich unveiled his famous Suprematist series, including *White on White*, reducing pictorial references to basic geometric shapes. In contrast to the external concerns of Constructivism, Suprematism was founded on a search for honesty and inner spiritual meaning in nonrepresentational images—"the supremacy of pure feeling or perception"—that was seen to embody the ideals of a new socialist society.

Matisse – Underlying Matisse's works of the Fauvist period were principles of order and composition that the artist explored in the years after the 1905 Salon d'Automne show. Among his early patrons were two successful Russian merchants, Ivan Morosov and Sergei Shchukin, who both formed important collections of modern art in the years before World War I. Matisse's joyous circle of nudes, *The Dance* (1909), is a study for one of two murals created for Shchukin's Moscow apartment. Exemplary of Matisse's later work is *Memory of Oceania* (1952), a vivid collage that expresses the artist's personal response to shape, light and color.

Brancusi and Picasso – One of the most inventive and influential Modernists was Constantin Brancusi, a Romanian-born sculptor who trained in Bucharest but spent his most productive years in Paris. After working briefly with Rodin, Brancusi moved away from academic Realism toward the reduction of forms into pure, mystical shapes—often studies from animals and birds—that seem to emerge effortlessly from wood *(The Cock)*, stone *(Fish)* and metal *(Bird in Space)*. Brancusi's search for elemental forms sometimes led him to create the same sculpture in different materials; the bronze *Bird in Space* (1928), for example, also exists in black, gray and white marble.

Picasso's 1921 painting *The Three Musicians* represents a mature Cubist phase, while *Three Women at the Spring* shows a new exploration of the female figure, now rendered as a robust, even grotesque, form that moves deliberately away from the abstract planes of Cubism.

Klee and Schwitters – A fascination with abstract spaces and chromatic construction infuses the work of Paul Klee, a Swiss artist who became involved with Der Blaue Reiter in 1911 and taught at the Bauhaus from 1920 to 1930. Linked to Surrealism, Symbolism, Expressionism and Constructivism, his witty compositions cut across a broad range of movements from abstract to figural, but are nearly always suffused with a certain joyous insight. Klee's contemporary, the Dadaist Kurt Schwitters, was a painter, poet and sculptor perhaps best known for his *Merz* constructions. In true Dada spirit, Schwitters chose the syllable randomly from the German word *kommerzial* (commercial) and used it as a kind of catchall description for his life and work. The collages *Merz Picture 32A* and *Merz 458* were apparently haphazardly conceived of odd scraps and bits of trash, but they convey a wit similar to that of Klee.

Surrealism – Led by the poet André Breton, the French avant-garde movement of Surrealism in the 1920s and 30s was deeply influenced by Dadaist nihilism and French Symbolism, a poetic tradition based on irrational associations. A friend and admirer of Breton, Picasso was influenced by the movement, which inspired a new surge of inventive power in his paintings *(Seated Bather* and *Girl Before a Mirror)* and distorted, oversize plaster sculptures *(Head of a Woman* and *Head of a Warrior)* of the period. Picasso, however, was never a full subscriber to Surrealism, which developed into two schools. One group, including Joan Miró *(Hirondelle/Amour)*, Jean Arp *(Bells and Navels)* and Max Ernst *(Rendezvous of Friends)*, employed symbols and hallucinatory images. The other, including René Magritte *(The False Mirror)* and Salvador Dalí *(The Persistence of Memory)*, used realistic images—although in dreamlike and often macabre compositions. Among the most memorable Surrealist sculptures are Alberto Giacometti's *Woman with Her Throat Cut* (1932), which embodies the striking sense of violence that underlaid the imagery of the movement, and Meret Oppenheim's *Object* (1936), a fur-covered cup, saucer and spoon.

Beckmann and Orozco – After World War I, the issues of human suffering and social protest became recurring themes in modern art. *Neue Sachlichkeit*, a German term meaning "new objectivity" that was coined in 1923, referred to a trend among such artists as George Grosz and Max Beckmann toward distorted compositions that were meant as scathing comments on the spiritual emptiness of German society and the effects of war. The Mexican Mural Renaissance, founded by painters Diego Rivera *(Flower Festival: Feast of Santa Anita)*, David Alfaro Siqueiros *(Collective Suicide)* and José Clemente Orozco, lasted from about the 1920s to the 1940s, glorifying folk traditions, the common man and the ideals of the Mexican Revolution. While never a muralist, the painter Frida Kahlo *(Self-Portrait with Cropped Hair)* blended a rough-hewn folk style with elements of Surrealism.

Painting and Sculpture in the 1940s – After World War II the search for contemporary expression swung away from Realism toward intuitive modes of painting and sculpture in an effort to convey the postwar themes of spiritual emptiness and isolation. Among the important figures then working in Paris were the Swiss sculptor Alberto Giacometti, whose attenuated human and animal figures *(Man Pointing* and *Dog)* evoke a strong sense of alienation and dissipation, and French painter Jean Dubuffet. Dubuffet's deliberately "anti-fine art" approach was evident in bloblike figures *(Joe Bosquet in Bed)* worked in a purposely crude impasto of paint mixed with mud, plaster, sand and gravel. Randomly textured paint surfaces incorporating pigment, sand and glue were also explored by such artists as André Masson *(Meditations on an Oak Leaf)* and Francis Bacon, a British painter who often based his disturbing compositions on newspaper photos of horrific events. The amorphous figures and fluid paint washes of works by Arshile Gorky *(Summation)* made this American painter, strongly influenced by Picasso, Miró and Roberto Matta Echaurren, a leading forerunner of Abstract Expressionism.

American Art 1920–1945 – The best-known members of the conservative Regionalist movement, associated with the Great Depression, are Thomas Hart Benton and Grant Wood, who both painted realistically rendered, folksy paintings of small-town America as a deliberate reaction to the sophisticated art of the previous decades. Working in the Southwest, Georgia O'Keeffe represented the natural world in increasingly isolated symbolic fragments *(Abstraction Blue)*. Edward Hopper *(House by the Railroad)* and Andrew Wyeth rank among the leading figurative painters, known for realistic, often melancholy renderings of American scenes and moody landscapes like Wyeth's *Christina's World* (1948). Less sentimental are the sharply focused, hard-edged compositions of Charles Sheeler and Precisionist Stuart Davis, whose works of the period *(Visa* and *Lucky Strike)*, presage Pop Art.

Early Abstract Expressionism – Based on a search for artistic and social truths through the use of pure line, form, color and texture, Abstract Expressionism emerged in the late 1940s. The extremely influential movement began when a group of New York sculptors and painters responded to Surrealist and Expressionist influences; styles varied considerably, but all eschewed traditional values and figurative representation, emphasizing spontaneous, emotional expression. In the enigmatic "assemblages" of Joseph Cornell *(Roses des Vents* and *Taglioni's Jewel Casket)*, objects relate through repeated shapes, textures and shadows. Evocative of Surrealism, Arshile Gorky's eerie painting *Agony* (1947) is pervaded by a sense of both passion and emptiness. Jackson Pollock, Mark Rothko and Willem de Kooning were also leaders of the early movement.

Jackson Pollock – A leading figure of Abstract Expressionism, Jackson Pollock is the celebrated American virtuoso of Action Painting, in which paint was vigorously streamed, splashed and spattered onto large canvases in an effort to make a kinetic connection between the work and its viewer. Pollock began laying his mural-size canvases on the floor in 1947, dripping and sprinkling paint from above them in order to exercise some control over the emerging patterns; instead of artist's oils, he used commercial enamels *(Echo)* and metallic paints better suited to pouring. The impulse was to freely create, inventing and improvising as the sinuous web of color and texture built up on the canvas in a dynamic, energized composition that could never be exactly duplicated.

The 1950s – Abstract Expressionism continued to flourish into the 1950s, spawning a broad range of styles. The term Color Field was used to describe work by such painters as Mark Rothko, Clyfford Still and Barnett Newman, whose lyrical canvases explored the subtle relationships of large planes of color. Ad Reinhardt reduced his geometric abstractions to monochrome compositions (usually red or blue), as did Robert Motherwell *(Elegy to the Spanish Republic, 108)*, who combined planar explorations with the aggressive slashes of Action Painting; Franz Kline's works were more calligraphic *(Chief)*. Sculptors of the period include Louise Nevelson, whose *Sky Cathedral* (1958) consists of 38 wooden boxes stuffed with machine-line forms painted black, and David Smith, who focused on nonrepresentational forms with dynamic compositions in rough, burnished and painted metal.

Johns, Rauschenberg and Twombly – Although Robert Rauschenberg and Jasper Johns (who had studios in the same New York loft building) continued the search for expression through the innovative use of surface textures, they rejected the perceived limitations of pure abstraction. In the early 1960s, Rauschenberg, a continuously experimental painter, produced large-scale silk screens and collage-like canvases incorporating paint, newspaper and cloth with mundane objects such as quilt fragments *(Bed)* and license plates *(First Landing Jump)*. Playing reality off illusion, Jasper Johns also drew on familiar objects and symbols, experimenting with such images as flags, targets and numbers. Cy Twombly's large-scale works feature random drips, childlike scrawls and paint blobs *(The Italians)*; while reminiscent of Abstract Expressionism, his art has an ironic edge that relates this painter more closely to Johns and Rauschenberg.

Abstract and Pop Art – During the 1960s and 70s, the search for essentials and spatial relationships characterized the severely minimalist work of such artists as Kenneth Noland, Frank Stella, Helen Frankenthaler *(Mauve District)*, Ellsworth Kelly and Agnes Martin, who reduced their compositions to deceptively simple arrangements of color and line. Celebrating the images of mass media and popular culture, Pop Art—a send-up of the self-conscious seriousness of Abstract Expressionism—emerged in Britain and America in the mid-1950s and lasted to the early 1960s. Adherents included Andy Warhol *(Gold Marilyn Monroe* and *Campbell's Soup Cans)*, James Rosenquist *(F-111)*, Claes Oldenburg and Roy Lichtenstein *(Girl with Ball)*.

MUSEUM OF TELEVISION AND RADIO★

25 W. 52nd St. **MTA** E, F train to 53rd St. or 6 train to 51st St.
Map p 89

Kids *Open year-round Tue–Sun noon–6pm (Thu until 8pm). Theaters open Fri until 9pm. Closed major holidays. $10. Guided tours (1hr) available.* ♿ ☎ *212-621-6800. www.mtr.org.*

Created by CBS chairman William S. Paley with a view to preserving two increasingly popular fixtures of 21C American culture—radio and television—this museum (1975) is the first of its kind in the world. Originally located on East 53rd Street, the museum moved to its new location in 1991. Designed by John Burgee and Philip Johnson, the 17-story structure sheathed in limestone houses several theaters, screening rooms, individual listening-viewing consoles, three public galleries and an extensive library with a computerized card catalog *(4th floor).*

The museum's collection comprises tapes of more than 110,000 radio and television programs and commercials that visitors can request and listen to or view in the consoles. Major public events from war reportage to presidential elections are represented along with dramatic and comedy productions from the past 70 years of broadcasting. The museum also mounts programs on changing themes in its theaters and screening rooms.

MUSEUM OF THE CITY OF NEW YORK★★

Fifth Ave. at 103rd St. **MTA** 6 train to 103rd St.
Map p 10

Founded in 1923 as America's first institution dedicated to the history of a city, this museum chronicles the changing face of New York from a modest Dutch trading post to a thriving international metropolis. Originally housed in the Gracie Mansion, it moved to the present Georgian Revival building fronting Central Park in 1929. The museum's rich collections span three centuries of New York memorabilia, decorative arts, furnishings, silver, prints and paintings. Plans to move to the refurbished Tweed Courthouse fell through at the last minute, and the museum continues its search for a downtown location.

VISIT

Kids *Open year-round Wed–Sun 10am–5pm. Closed major holidays. $7.* ♿ ☎ *212-534-1672. www.mcny.org.*

Basement – The Volunteer Fire Gallery depicts the history of fire fighting through prints, texts and artifacts, including a horse-drawn double-decker Big Six model. The adjacent hall and small gallery feature temporary exhibits.

First Floor – *Main entrance.* A lofty rotunda, dominated by a graceful, spiraling staircase, bisects two long galleries displaying rotating exhibits. The information desk is located to the right of the entranceway and the museum shop to the left.

Second Floor – Six **period alcoves** ranging from a traditional Dutch living room (17C) to a late-19C drawing room contain appropriate furnishings and costumes reflecting the evolution of New York interiors. Highlighting the gallery, the luminous stained-glass window was crafted in Paris for the H.G. Marquand House. Examples of three centuries of **silver**, including tea services and monogrammed tankards, are displayed in the New York silver collection. Parlor furnishings found in various galleries include a cabinet-bookcase given to songstress Jenny Lind that contains seven volumes of Audubon's *Birds of America.* Other galleries present the marine history of New York through model ships, carved figureheads and paintings.

Third Floor – The Toy Gallery features a delightful selection of playthings from the museum's collection of more than 10,000 items. Arrayed thematically, the objects range from plush teddy bears to intricate mechanical banks. The exquisite series of **dollhouses★** includes the rare 1769 Ann Anthony Pavilion noted for its "shadow box" style and primitive wax figures. Other elaborately crafted houses reflect the predominant domestic styles at various periods. The Stettheimer House re-creates a 1920s New York brownstone complete with artwork by Marcel Duchamp and other avant-garde artists.

Lining the walls of the main hall, paintings of New York cityscapes provide a pictorial history of the changing urban scene from 1800 to 1900.

Fifth Floor – Two ornate rooms from John D. Rockefeller's 1860s residence—formerly located on the site of the Museum of Modern Art's sculpture garden—reflect the opulent tastes of the late-Victorian era. The master bedroom features heavy damask furnishings and forest-green walls hung with gilt-framed paintings from Rockefeller's private collection. The American Renaissance-style dressing room contains inlaid-pearl rosewood furnishings by master woodworker George Schasty.

NATIONAL ACADEMY
OF DESIGN MUSEUM

1083 Fifth Ave. **MTA** 4, 5, 6 train to 86th St.
Map p 181

Open year-round Wed & Thu noon–5pm, Fri–Sun 11am–6pm. Closed Jan 1, Thanksgiving Day & Dec 25. $8. ⟡ ☎ 212-369-4880. www.nationalacademy.org.

Established in 1825 as the National Academy of Design by eminent American artists Thomas Cole, Samuel F.B. Morse, Rembrandt Peale and others "to sustain an association of artists for the purpose of instruction and exhibition," the institution is among the oldest art organizations in the country governed by artists. Its School of Fine Arts and permanent collection were forged in the tradition of the august art academies of Europe. Located in a small, rounded Beaux-Arts town house, the museum has amassed one of the country's finest collections of American art. The practice of requiring candidates for membership to present a portrait of themselves and a representative example of their work led to the growth of the academy's rich holdings of 19C and 20C American art and brought to the collection the works of such famous members as Winslow Homer, John Singer Sargent, Augustus Saint-Gaudens, Isabel Bishop, Thomas Eakins, N.C. Wyeth and Andrew Wyeth. Today exhibits of 19C and 20C painting (works by Chuck Close, Jasper Johns and Jim Dine for example), sculpture, engraving, print-making and architecture are mounted regularly.

The first floor features a charming, wood-paneled bookshop that leads into a marble entrance foyer dominated by a gracefully sweeping staircase. The statue of *Diana* was sculpted by Anna Hyatt Huntington, wife of Archer M. Huntington, who resided in the building from 1902 and turned it over to the academy in 1940. The second floor is devoted to traveling exhibits. The newly renovated fourth-floor galleries exhibit rotating selections from the Academy's collection of 19C, 20C and 21C American art. Through its School of Fine Arts, the oldest art school in the city, the museum offers programs in drawing, painting, sculpture and graphics.

NATIONAL MUSEUM
OF THE AMERICAN INDIAN★★

1 Bowling Green. **MTA** 4, 5 train to Bowling Green
Map p 126

The 1907 US Custom House is the splendid setting for the Heye Center of the Smithsonian Institution's National Museum of the American Indian, inaugurated in 1994. (A sister museum in Washington, DC is scheduled to open in 2004.) The collection, culled from about one million objects amassed during the first half of the century by New Yorker George Gustav Heye, represents the history and cultures of indigenous peoples living in North, Central and South America from prehistoric times to the present.

VISIT

Kids *Open year-round daily 10am–5pm (Thu until 8pm). Closed Dec 25. Guided tours available Mon–Fri 2pm. ⟡ ☎ 212-514-3767. www.americanindian.si.edu.*

Flanking a magnificent domed **rotunda★**, the museum's three refurbished galleries hold a changing calendar of exhibitions, dedicated to presenting and preserving the living culture of America's native peoples. The Heye collection provides the prime, but not the only, resource for exhibitions that explore all avenues of cultural practice—including contemporary art, traditional crafts and historical surveys—of the diverse Native American peoples across the Western hemisphere.

National Museum of the American Indian, photo by Pam Dewey

Haida Hat

A resource center located on the main floor includes a library, hands-on displays and interactive computer activities. The museum, which serves as an education center and encourages participation by visitors, also sponsors programs on music, dance, storytelling, media arts and theater throughout the year. Two gift shops sell jewelry, crafts and an extensive selection of books by and about Native Americans.

NEW MUSEUM OF CONTEMPORARY ART

583 Broadway. **MTA** 6 train to Spring St. or N, R train to Prince St.
Map p 151 .

Open year-round Tue–Sun noon–6pm (Thu until 8pm). Closed major holidays. $6 ($3 Thu after 6pm). ☦ ☏ *212-219-1222. www.newmuseum.org.*

Founded in 1977, this museum is an international forum for contemporary artists engaged in innovative and experimental work. While there are no permanent exhibits, the museum mounts some 15 to 20 temporary shows a year, including eye-catching (and often ear-catching) installations in the streetfront window. Many invite visitor participation and are often designed to provoke.
The museum shop stocks exhibition catalogs and museum publications as well as books, games, jewelry and other merchandise.

NEW YORK CITY FIRE MUSEUM

278 Spring St. **MTA** 1, 9 train to W. Houston St.
or C, E train to Spring St.
Map p 151

Kids *Open year-round Tue–Sat 10am–5pm, Sun 10am–4pm. Closed major holidays. $4 contribution requested.* ☦ ☏ *212-691-1303. www.nycfiremuseum.org.*

Located in a 1904 firehouse, this colorful museum displays the most comprehensive collection of fire-related art and artifacts in the US, from the mid-18C to present time. The collection includes an intriguing array of badges, buckets, pump wagons, fire sleighs, trumpets, helmets and fire insurance marks. Also featured are a fire hydrant (the first in New York was installed in 1818) and a sliding pole (invented in Chicago in 1858). Among the most unusual exhibits is a dog that served between 1929 and 1939 as an honorary member of Company 203 in Brooklyn; now preserved, the courageous canine resides within a glass case.
A new permanent exhibit opened on September 11, 2002, the first anniversary of the terrorist attack on the World Trade Center. Highlights include a 6ft by 9ft memorial wall that commemorates the 343 firefighters who lost their lives in the aftermath of the attack, and a photographic timeline documenting the heroic rescue efforts.

NEW-YORK HISTORICAL SOCIETY★★

2 W. 77th St. **MTA** B, C train to 81st St. or 1, 9 train to 79th St.
Map p 176

Open year-round Tue–Sun 11am–6pm. $8. The collection of architectural drawings, prints and photographs (3rd floor) is open by appointment only. ☏ *212-873-3400. www.nyhistory.org.*

Despite the slightly fussy appearance of its Neoclassical edifice (1908) fronting Central Park, the New-York Historical Society approaches its rich trove of material with a keenly modern curatorial eye. Best of all, its large, attractive displays can often be enjoyed without the crowds that throng the city's larger institutions.
The city's oldest museum, it was chartered in 1804 with a view to preserving the history of the US, and since then has amassed a collection that embraces three centuries of Americana. Thanks to a recent $10 million renovation and the November 2000 opening of the **Henry Luce Center for the Study of American Culture★**, today the museum's holdings are presented in a more complete format than ever before. In its latest role, the society is serving as the repository of artifacts relating to the September 11, 2001, terrorist attack on the World Trade Center.
The four main galleries on the first floor hold large temporary exhibits of art and artifacts, many of which are culled from the society's archives. Some paintings from the permanent collection are hung outside the galleries in the Great Hall, but most are exhibited on a rotating basis in the Luman Reed Gallery and Dexter Hall *(second floor)*. Here, Thomas Cole's *The Course of the Empire* and other works from the Hudson River school are displayed along with smaller landscapes and portraiture by Rembrandt Peale and others. A renowned research library features the society's print and photographic collection *(3rd floor; open by appointment only)*.
The Luce Center *(4th floor)* presents a mesmerizing array of nearly 40,000 objects,, in what it calls a "working storage" format. Floor-to-ceiling glass cases are packed with board games, spectacles, Tiffany lamps, fire-fighting equipment, clocks, china— you name it—all organized by type and described in fascinating detail.

NEUE GALERIE★

1048 Fifth Ave. at 86th St. **MTA** 4, 5, 6 trains to 86th St.
Map p 181

Open year-round Fri–Mon 11am–6pm (Fri until 9pm). Closed major holidays. $10. &
☏ *212-628-6200. www.neuegalerie.org.*

The latest addition to Fifth Avenue's Museum Mile, the Neue Galerie was founded in 2001 by cosmetics mogul Ronald Lauder to house his own collection of early twentieth century Austrian and German Art and that of his friend, art dealer Serge Sabarsky, who died in 1996.

The museum's home, a Louis XIII-style Beaux-Arts mansion built in 1914 by Carrère and Hastings, was once the residence of Mrs. Cornelius Vanderbilt III. It retains much of the charm and grandeur of its society days. The Cafe Sabarsky, in the lobby, recreates a Viennese coffeehouse of the period. Second-floor rooms (one wood-paneled, another entirely marble) arranged around a central staircase and landing provide a complementary setting for the artwork. The second floor is devoted to Austrian art. Works by Gustav Klimt (*The Black Feather Hat*, 1910) and Egon Schiele form the heart of the collection. There are also fine examples of decorative art and furniture by members of the Wiener Werkstatte. The third-floor houses the German collection, focusing on members of the Blaue Reiter, Neue Sachlickkeit and Bauhaus (Wassily Kandinsky, Paul Klee, George Grosz). During spring and fall, however, the museum uses the floor for special exhibitions.

PIERPONT MORGAN LIBRARY★★

29 E. 36th St. **MTA** 4, 5, 6 train to 33rd St.
Map p 88

A cultural treasure trove, this venerable institution houses an outstanding collection containing some 350,000 works: rare books, manuscripts, drawings, prints and artworks assembled by **J. Pierpont Morgan** (1837–1913), an inveterate collector whose interest in art, literature and history resulted in an unusually broad and varied accumulation of objects.

Historical Notes – In 1902 Morgan commissioned the firm of McKim, Mead and White to erect a permanent home for his collection that would be accessible to the public following his death. The Italian Renaissance-style main building *(33 E. 36th St.)* was completed in 1906 after several tempestuous tugs-of-war between Morgan and Charles McKim. The annex *(main entrance)* on the corner of Madison Avenue was added by Morgan's son in 1928. Both edifices house a museum and a research library filled with rare and exemplary items attesting to the development of Western civilizations. The annex is connected to a large brownstone building on the corner of Madison Avenue and East 37th Street—the younger Morgan's former residence—by a glass-enclosed court, which houses an airy restaurant *(lunch & afternoon tea)*. The brownstone contains the museum's well-stocked bookshop and, on the fourth floor, the new Thaw Conservation Center, a $10 million state-of-the-art facility dedicated to the preservation and conservation of works on paper.

To accommodate its growing collection, the Morgan Library is embarking on a major expansion project that will close its facilities to the public for several years. Designed by Pritzker Prize-winning architect Renzo Piano, the plan calls for construction of three steel-and-glass pavilions that will integrate the existing buildings into a single complex while preserving their historic character. The expanded complex will have twice the exhibition space, a larger auditorium for concerts, lectures and readings, and enlarged research and storage facilities. The largest of the pavilions will provide a new main entrance on Madison Avenue.

VISIT

The Morgan Library closed to the public in May 2003 to undergo a major expansion of its facilities; it is scheduled to reopen in fall 2006. ☏ 212-685-0610. www.morganlibrary.org. While the library is being renovated, parts of its collection will tour the US beginning in fall 2003 in the exhibit Facets of the Morgan. Pieces from the Morgan's holdings of medieval art will be on view in the Metropolitan Museum of Art's Tapestry Hall until June 2005.

West Room – The opulence of Mr. Morgan's former study is enhanced by a painted and carved wood **ceiling** (16C), red damask hangings, 15-17C stained-glass windows and massive black wood furniture. Paintings and statuettes, enamels and metalwork from the Middle Ages and the Renaissance blend harmoniously with the decor. Above the marble mantel attributed to 15C Florentine sculptor Desiderio da Settignano is a portrait of Morgan by Frank Holl. Among the works of art, note Tintoretto's *Portrait of a Moor* (1570), *Madonna and Saints Adoring the Child* by Perugino, the wedding portraits of Martin Luther and his wife by the workshop of the 16C German artist Lucas Cranach the Elder, and a small portrait attributed to the François Clouet school of painting.

East Room/Library – Lined with three-tiered, floor-to-ceiling bookshelves, this solemn room showcases Morgan's world-acclaimed collection. On display are illuminated medieval and Renaissance manuscripts, dating back to the 5C; thousands of letters and autographed works; a superb assemblage of gilded and bejeweled book bindings; drawings by such artists as Dürer, Rembrandt and Rubens; and a wide selection of music manuscripts including scores by Mozart, Beethoven, Haydn and Mahler.

On rotating display is one of the library's three **Gutenberg Bibles** (mid-15C). Works of art embellishing the room include a 16C Flemish tapestry, representing the Triumph of Avarice, hanging above the marble fireplace. The carved ceiling sports a series of lunettes and painted spandrels featuring the signs of the zodiac.

SOLOMON R. GUGGENHEIM MUSEUM★★

1071 Fifth Ave. **MTA** 4, 5, 6 train to 86th St.
Map p 181

This spiraling concrete monument to Modernism, located on Fifth Avenue between 88th and 89th streets, is among the most original and widely recognized structures in the US. Visited more than any other building designed by Frank Lloyd Wright, it is as much a work of art as the sculptures and paintings it contains.

Historical Notes

Benefactors – **Solomon R. Guggenheim** (1861-1949) came from a family of German-Swiss immigrants who made a vast fortune mining precious metals in the 19C. Long a supporter of the arts, he and his wife, Irene Rothschild, originally collected Old Masters. In the early 20C they began concentrating on nonrepresentational, or "non-objective," works—especially those by Kandinsky, Mondrian and Moholy-Nagy—at the urging of their artistic adviser, Hilla Rebay. In 1937 the Solomon R. Guggenheim Foundation was established to encourage art and art education. Six years later, Rebay commissioned Frank Lloyd Wright to design a permanent home for Guggenheim's collection. Unfortunately, Guggenheim died before he ever saw his museum, finally begun in

Solomon R. Guggenheim Museum

David Heald/Solomon R. Guggenheim Museum

1956. However, the foundation continues to support the museum holdings. These holdings were enlarged in 1963 with 75 Impressionist and post-Impressionist paintings given to the museum by **Justin K. Thannhauser**, an art dealer who helped pioneer the Modern movement. In 1975 Solomon's niece Peggy Guggenheim also left a collection of Dada and Surrealist works, still housed in her Venetian palazzo on the Grand Canal, to the foundation. In 1992 the museum opened a downtown branch in SoHo *(now closed)*. In 1997 the Guggenheim opened sister museums in Bilbao, Spain and in Berlin, Germany, and in 2001, two museums in Las Vegas, one of which is in partnership with the State Hermitage Museum in St. Petersburg, Russia.

"My Pantheon" – The father of modern American architecture, **Frank Lloyd Wright** (1867-1959) revolutionized the field in the early 20C with his natural, organic designs based on geometric forms. Best known for his work with the Chicago school, he was an outspoken critic of New York architecture. The Guggenheim Museum (1956-59) was his only major commission in the city. Calling it "my Pantheon," after the domed Roman monument, Wright considered the idiosyncratic building, based on a complex trigonometric spiral, his crowning achievement. From the start, however, the museum was controversial. It clashed with its surroundings, was a nightmare to construct and, with its interior ramp and sloping walls, proved a difficult place either to view or to display art. As a result, there have been many alterations; most recently, in 1992, the firm of Gwathmey Siegel & Assocs. added a 10-story annex and restored much of Wright's original design. The museum expanded its teaching mission with the 2001 opening of the 8,200sq ft Sackler Center for Arts Education. The center is outfitted with studio-art, computer and multimedia labs as well as exhibition space, a resource center and the New Media Theater.

Collections – The Guggenheim Foundation's holdings comprise more than 6,000 paintings, sculptures and works on paper. The core collection includes 195 works by Kandinsky—the largest assemblage in the US—and more than 75 pieces by Klee, Chagall, Delaunay, Dubuffet and Mondrian. The Cubists Léger and Gris are featured as well. Acquired in 1990, the Panza di Biumo collection has amplified the holdings with more than 300 contemporary pieces, primarily from the 1960s and 1970s, by such Minimalists as Carl André, Dan Flavin and Robert Morris. In 1993 the museum received a $5 million gift from the Robert Mapplethorpe Foundation, including more than 200 works by the famed photographer. Most recently, the Bohen Foundation gave the Guggenheim some 275 works of contemporary art by known and emerging artists in media such as video, photography, painting, sculpture and installation art.

VISIT

Open year-round Fri–Wed 10am–5:45pm (Fri until 8pm). Closed Dec 25. $15 (Fri 6pm–8pm by donation). Guided tours available. ✗ ♿ ☎ *212-423-3500. www.guggenheim.org.*

The Central Park side of Fifth Avenue offers a good view of the entire museum, dominated by a four-tiered spiraling cone, or "nautilus." The smaller, round wing, or "monitor" stands to the left, with the new limestone tower just behind. Inset metal circles in the sidewalk pavement echo the circle motif of the building and continue on the travertine floor inside.

Few public spaces in New York rival the drama of the main gallery, encircled by the famous spiraling ramp. Depending on the current show, you can start your visit at the top or bottom; either way, it will be a journey of discovery as Wright's kaleidoscopic composition of rounded forms—repeated in the railings, furnishings and elevator banks—unfolds and changes at every level. More than a quarter mile long, the ramp now opens on four levels to the new annex galleries. Additional galleries are found on the top three floors of the monitor building, lined with plate-glass windows offering tantalizing views of the museum's exterior and Central Park. Outside, off the fifth floor, is a terrace garden featuring the David Smith sculpture *Cubi xxvii.*

A selection from the **Thannhauser collection**★, located on the second floor of the monitor building, is the only permanent display. The earliest work is a pre-Impressionist landscape by Pissaro, *Les Coteaux de l'Hermitage à Pontoise* (c.1867). There are also canvases by Renoir *(Woman with a Parrot)* and Manet *(Before the Mirror, La Comtesse Albassi)*, van Gogh *(The Viaduct, Mountains at Saint-Rémy)* and Toulouse-Lautrec *(Au Salon)*. You will also find still lifes by Cézanne and small sculptures by Degas and Maillol. Picasso is especially well represented, with early works *(The End of the Road, Le Moulin de la Galette)* and the 1931 painting *The Craft Jug and Fruit Bowl.* The museum offers continuously changing shows in the main gallery and adjacent annex.

STUDIO MUSEUM IN HARLEM★

144 W. 125th St. **MTA** 2 train to 125th St.

Map p 10

Open year-round Wed–Fri noon–6pm (Fri until 8pm), weekends 10am–6pm. Closed major holidays. $7. &. ☎ 212-864-4500. www.studiomuseum.org.

Established in 1968 to provide studio space for African-American artists, this small museum has expanded and grown into a major cultural center. Another major expansion is currently underway and, upon completion in 2003, will add 2,500sq ft of gallery space, an auditorium and a museum cafe. The museum mounts about eight temporary shows a year. Selections from the permanent collection of 1,600 works by prominent and emerging artists of African descent—including Romare Bearden, Alvin Loving, Faith Ringgold and Betye Saar—rotate every 18 months. Jewelry, crafts and books fill the ground-floor gift shop.

WHITNEY MUSEUM OF AMERICAN ART★★

945 Madison Ave. **MTA** 6 train to 77th St.

Map p 181

Dedicated to the advancement of contemporary artists, this museum holds one of the world's foremost collections of 20C American art, housed in a stark granite building designed by Marcel Breuer and Hamilton Smith. Rising above a sunken sculpture garden in a series of inverted stairs, the cantilevered edifice (1966) represents a striking example of the Brutalism style of architecture.

VISIT

Open year-round Tue–Thu & weekends 11am–6pm, Fri 1pm–9pm. Closed Jan 1, Thanksgiving Day & Dec 25. $12 (Fri 6pm–9pm by donation). Guided tours (1hr) available. ✗ &. ☎ 212-570-3676 or 800-944-8639. www.whitney.org. The museum also operates a branch in midtown Manhattan in the Philip Morris Building.

Founded in 1931, the museum grew out of the Greenwich Village studio of sculptor and art collector **Gertrude Vanderbilt Whitney** (1875-1942). After founding the Whitney Studio Club, Whitney began acquiring works by living American artists, creating the core of today's collection of more than 10,000 works by painters such as Hopper, de Kooning, Kelly, Gorky, Prendergast, Demuth and Motherwell, and sculptors such as Calder, Nevelson, Noguchi and David Smith. The museum moved to the current building, its third home, in 1966. From its inception, the museum has provided a unique venue for American artists and played a special role in the development of contemporary art. The museum's frequently changing exhibit programs have been known to explore daring, innovative and often controversial topics. The film and video department presents works by independent American film and video artists. The museum is also known for its invitational biennials, held since 1932, which attempt to offer the public a representative cross section of the current American art scene.

The **permanent collection** is displayed on a rotating basis in galleries on the second and fifth floors. Masterworks of American art from the first half of the 20C are continuously on view, including the work of Marsden Hartley, Georgia O'Keeffe, Stuart Davis and Arshile Gorky. Also featured is a new selection of postwar and contemporary works by such artists as Philip Guston, Jasper Johns, Alex Katz, Lee Krasner, Jackson Pollock, Kiki Smith and Andy Warhol.

Early Sunday Morning (1930) by Edward Hopper

The Bronx

Peggy Rockefeller Rose Garden

The only New York borough located on the mainland, the Bronx exemplifies the contradictions of a mature urban environment. Marked by run-down apartment buildings and massive projects, the southern part of the borough is mainly inhabited by low-income groups. To the north, prosperous sections such as Riverdale are characterized by grand mansions and lush gardens. To the east lies the largest park in New York City, Pelham Bay Park, with its popular sandy beach, Orchard Beach. Today private foundations and grassroots citizen movements are struggling to recreate the Bronx, and a new, vibrant community is emerging.

Area: 42 square miles
Population: 1,332,650

The Bronx was named after Jonas Bronck, a Swedish émigré, who arrived here in June 1639. The borough developed in the late 1800s around the village of Morrisania (**AZ**), which now forms the section of the Bronx around Third Avenue and 161st Street. Two members of the Morris family, for whom the village was named, were prominent during the Revolutionary period: Lewis Morris, a signer of the Declaration of Independence, and Gouverneur Morris, member of the US Constitutional Convention.

As settlement of the Bronx blossomed, journalist John Mullaly led a movement to buy inexpensive land parcels and preserve them as parks; as a result, almost 25 percent of the borough today consists of parkland. In 1891 New York University opened a campus near Morris Heights. The campus was later acquired by the Bronx Community College. Today the borough boasts 11 colleges and universities.

The Bronx was a part of Westchester County until 1898, when it was incorporated into New York City. In 1904 the first subway line connecting the Bronx to the island of Manhattan opened, causing significant migration to this outlying borough. Jews from Eastern and Central Europe settled here en masse, and by 1949 almost 50 percent of Bronx residents were Jewish. During the 1950s and 60s, blacks and Puerto Ricans relocating from slums in Manhattan moved into the Hunts Point and Morrisania areas of the South Bronx; today Hispanics make up about half of the Bronx's population.

BRONX PARK *Map below*

★★**Bronx Zoo** – 🄺🄸🄳🄸 *Bronx River Pkwy. at Fordham Rd.* 🄼🄣🄰 *2 train to Pelham Parkway to reach Bronx Parkway entrance to the zoo. Open Apr–Oct Mon–Fri 10am–5pm, weekends & holidays 10am–5:30pm. Rest of the year daily 10am–4:30pm. $8 (Wed free). Guided tours available, reservations required. Many exhibits close 15-30min before zoo closes.* ✗ ♿ 🄿 *($7)* ☎ *718-367-1010. www.bronxzoo.com.* Covering 265 acres of woodland, this popular zoo is located in Bronx Park, a vast expanse of land laid out in the late 19C on both banks of the Bronx River. Opened in 1899 by the New York Zoological Society, the zoo has grown to encompass the largest urban wildlife park in the country. Over the years

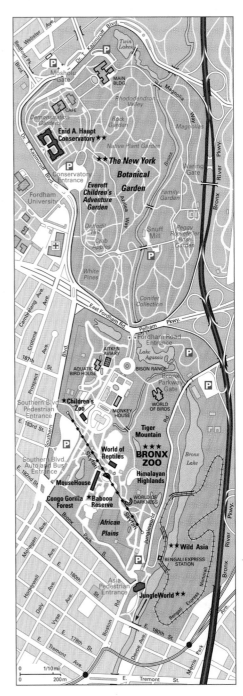

it has changed its focus to concentrate on conservation, a trend marked by the New York Zoological Society's name change to the Wildlife Conservation Society (WCS). Today the zoo exhibits more than 2,000 mammals, 1,000 birds, 1,000 reptiles and amphibians, in addition to more than 2,000 invertebrates, in a series of realistic exhibits that make every effort to replicate the animals' natural habitats. It is ranked among the leading zoos in the country for its exhibit technology and captive management techniques.

Visit – For an overview of the zoo, take the Zoo Shuttle *(departs, weather permitting, from Zoo Terrace and Wild Asia May–Oct; 20min one-way; commentary; $2 one-way)*, a tractor train that travels from one end of the zoo to the other; or the Skyfari aerial tramway *(departs, weather permitting, from Zoo Terrace and African Plains same season & fee as shuttle)*, which offers expansive views of the site. Visitors may also stroll through the zoo at their leisure. Opened in 1941 as the first naturalistic exhibit here, **African Plains** includes a collection of nyala, blesbok, giraffe, gazelles and other plains creatures separated by an invisible moat from a den of lions; the African Market sells concessions and souvenirs. The **Baboon Reserve**★ re-creates the highlands of Ethiopia for troops of gelada baboons, ibex and rock hyrax. Replicating the remote mountaintops of Asia, the **Himalayan Highlands Habitat** is home to

Snow Leopard

snow leopards as well as red pandas, pheasants and cranes. The Bengali Express monorail *(departs from Wild Asia same season & fee as shuttle)* passes through 38 acres of hilly, wooded land on its journey into **Wild Asia★★**, home to IndoChinese tigers, gaur cattle from Thailand, red pandas and Asian rhinoceroses. The one-acre indoor exhibit at **JungleWorld★★** re-creates an Asian rain forest where birds such as the Bali mynah fly among white-cheeked gibbons, Malayan tapirs and Indian gharials. Also on view are black leopards, tree kangaroos and silvered leaf monkeys. **World of Reptiles** is housed in one of the oldest buildings still in use for exhibits.

Other areas of interest include the Aitken Aviary and the Aquatic Bird House, the World of Darkness *(closes 15min before zoo closes)* and the World of Birds, where hundreds of exotic birds can be observed in natural surroundings. Stop by the **MouseHouse**, which contains only rodents—more than 30 species of them—to view the infamous Norwegian rat, a New York City native. Among the animals not to be missed are the American bison (Bison Range), and the Mongolian wild horses and the Pere David deer, both extinct in nature. Covering more than three acres of marsh, prairie and wooded land, the **Children's Zoo★** *($3)* houses more than 500 animals shown in re-creations of their natural habitats, and features a fun prairie dog exhibit, a rope spider web and a farmyard where kids can feed domestic animals. The 6.5-acre **Congo Gorilla Forest** *($3)*, which opened in summer 1999, is home to western lowland gorillas, pygmy marmosets, okapi and mandrills, as well as DeBrazza's and black-and-white colobus monkeys. Visitors here can choose which WCS conservation program they want their entry fee to fund.

In spring 2003, the zoo opened **Tiger Mountain**, a re-creation of the Amur Valley between China and Russia, where the zoo's group of Siberian tigers now resides. Here, visitors can see tigers up close in the Tiger Valley habitat and watch the big cats frolic in the pool at Tiger Ridge. An interactive theater uses film and interactive stations to show how WCS is working to save the endangered Siberian tigers.

★★The New York Botanical Garden – *200th St. & Kazimiroff Blvd.* **MTA** *D or 4 train to Bedford Park Blvd.; walk east to Garden Gate. Or take Metro North train from Grand Central Station to Botanical Garden Station. Open Apr–Oct Tue–Sun 10am–6pm. Rest of the year Tue–Sun 10am–4pm. Closed Thanksgiving Day & Dec 25. $6 (additional fees for tram & some gardens). Guided tours available.* ✗ ♿ 🅿 *($5).* ☎ *718-817-8700. www.nybg.org.* Located directly to the north of the zoo, this is one of the largest and oldest gardens (1891) in the country. Numerous walking trails wind through its 250 acres, past thousands of flowering trees, shrubs and plants that reach their peak in spring and early summer. Favorite attractions include the Rose Garden, Rock Garden, Native Plant Garden and Daylily Collection. The site also features a Home Gardening Center and 50 acres of one of the city's last remaining original forests.

Built in 1901, the glass **Enid A. Haupt Conservatory★★** is modeled after the crystal palaces of the 19C. This glorious Victorian structure presents A World of Plants, a global ecotour showcasing biomes from rain forests to deserts. Opened in 1998, the eight-acre **Everett Children's Adventure Garden** *($3)* allows visitors to investigate how plants live and function. A new International **Plant Science Center**, opened in 2002, incorporates the Beaux-Arts main building and a five-story 70,000sq ft addition designed by James Polshek. Within the redesigned century-old building, the library's reading room and rare book room, an exhibition gallery and a lovely orchid rotunda are open to the public. The addition houses the heart of the new research center, a herbarium containing 7 million plant specimens, the largest such collection in the Western Hemisphere. Located near lush display gardens, the Garden Cafe and Terrace Room offers a restful place to enjoy lunch and snacks.

AROUND THE BRONX *Map pp 260-261*

★**Yankee Stadium** (AZ) – 🧒 *161st St. & River Ave.* 🚇 *4 or D, C trains to 161st St. Tour information:* ☎ *718-579-4531 or www.yankees.com.* This famous baseball stadium, affectionately referred to as "the house that Babe Ruth built," was erected in 1923 by brewery magnate Col. Jacob Ruppert for the team he owned, the Yankees. The stadium's first years saw the heyday of George Herman "Babe" Ruth, one of the outstanding athletes of all time. The 60 home runs Babe Ruth hit in a season and the 714 in his career were hallowed records that stood for decades. When Ruth died in 1948, 100,000 fans came out to pay their respects. Monument Park, behind the left-centerfield fence, commemorates past Yankee greats with a series of bronze plaques—Babe Ruth, Lou Gehrig, Joe DiMaggio and Mickey Mantle among them. The 57,545-seat stadium underwent a massive remodeling program between 1974 and 1976 and now features sets of escalators serving the upper tiers of the grandstands, an unobstructed view of the playing field and an electronically controlled scoreboard. In 2002 a record 3.4 million fans attended Yankee games, squelching, at least temporarily, team owner George Steinbrenner's perennial cries for a new stadium.

Valentine–Varian House (BX) – *3266 Bainbridge Ave. at E. 208th St.* 🚇 *D train to 205th St., or 4 train to Mosholu Pkwy. Open year-round Tue–Fri 9am–5pm, Sat 10am–4pm, Sun 1pm–5pm. Closed major holidays & mid-Dec–mid-Jan. $3.* ☎ *718-881-8900. www.bronxhistoricalsociety.org.* This fieldstone house originally stood on the opposite side of the street, on land acquired in 1758 by Isaac Valentine. The scene of many skirmishes during the Revolution, the area was purchased in 1791 by Isaac Varian, a prosperous farmer whose son later became the 63rd mayor of New York City. Situated on its present site since 1965, the house now contains the **Museum of Bronx History**, featuring a fine collection of prints, lithographs and photographs.

Poe Cottage (AY) – *E. Kingsbridge Rd. and Grand Concourse.* 🚇 *D or 4 train to Kingsbridge Rd. Open year-round Tue–Fri 9am–5pm, Sat 10am–4pm, Sun 1pm–5pm. Closed major holidays & mid-Dec–mid-Jan. $3.* ☎ *718-881-8900. www.bronxhistoricalsociety.org.* From 1846 to 1849 this little wooden house (1812) was the home of author **Edgar Allan Poe** (1809-49), who wrote "Annabel Lee," *The Bells, Ulalume* and *Eureka* during his stay here. Poe moved to this cottage and away from the noise and congestion of New York City in the hope of saving his wife, Virginia Clemm, from tuberculosis; however, she died in 1847. The author died two years later in Baltimore, while on a return trip to the cottage from Virginia. The cottage was moved across the street in 1913 and transformed into a museum in 1917. Today the restored house contains displays of memorabilia and manuscripts, and an audiovisual slide show *(20min).*

★**Van Cortlandt House Museum** (AX) – *Enter Van Cortlandt Park at Broadway & 246th St.* 🚇 *1 train to 242nd St.–Van Cortlandt Park. Open year-round Tue–Fri 10am–3pm, weekends 11am–4pm. Closed major holidays. $2.* ☎ *718-543-3344.* Built in 1748, this colonial plantation house has been admirably preserved by the city and the National Society of Colonial Dames. It is believed that George Washington used the house as headquarters before making his triumphant entry into New York City in November 1783. The manor, appointed with furnishings in the Colonial style, reflects a refinement and style of living typical of 18C and 19C New York gentry. Among the nine rooms open to the public, note the Dutch room, the kitchen and the nursery, which contains one of America's oldest dollhouses.

① Arthur Avenue

Map p 260. This petite stretch of red-sauce joints and pungent food markets is known affectionately by New Yorkers as the real Little Italy, partly because it's still an Italian-American (and not Chinese) stronghold, and partly because it's not as touristy as Manhattan's version. Start out at the **Arthur Avenue Retail Market** *(no. 2344),* which is crammed with stalls hawking everything from wheels of Parmigiana Reggiano to eggs and sliced veal. Some of the best stalls are **Mike & Sons** for cheese and the **Terranova Bakery** for the crustiest loaves. For a meal you'll never forget, get in line at **Dominick's** *(no. 2335;* ☎ *718-733-2807),* the legendary Southern Italian joint where the waiters tabulate the bills in their heads (no menu, no checks) and the crowd is always lively. For seafood antipasto of mussels, squid and lobster in a spicy tomato sauce, settle in at the slightly fancier **Mario's** *(no. 2342;* ☎ *718-584-1188),* a 1919 institution made famous in Mario Puzo's book *The Godfather.*

Hudson River Museum

Bronx Community College (AY) – *University Ave. & W. 181st St.* MTA *4 train to Burnside Ave.; walk 4 blocks west to University Ave., then north to campus.* www.cuny.edu/bcc. Founded in 1891 as the Bronx campus of New York University, this institution, now occupied by the Bronx Community College, comprises 18 buildings lining the banks of the Harlem River.

★**Hall of Fame for Great Americans** – *Hall of Fame Terrace at W. 181st St. Open year-round daily 10am–5pm.* ✗ ὑ ⚑ ☎ *718-289-5161.* Completed by Stanford White in 1900, the Beaux-Arts complex, the first American pantheon, consists of an outdoor colonnade, 630ft in length, surrounding three buildings. This unique sculpture museum honors outstanding Americans in many fields. Candidates, chosen at least 25 years after their death, are selected by an electoral committee in each of the following categories: arts, sciences, humanities, government, and business and labor. Elections were temporarily suspended in 1979, but since then the structure has undergone restoration, and plans are under way to reinstate the election process.

The 102 selected honorees include Harriet Beecher Stowe, George Washington Carver, Edgar Allan Poe, Walt Whitman, John James Audubon, Susan B. Anthony, the Wright brothers, Henry Wadsworth Longfellow, Washington Irving, and presidents Ulysses S. Grant, Thomas Jefferson and Abraham Lincoln.

Pelham Bay Park (CXY) – ⬛MTA *6 train to Pelham Bay Park.* The largest park in the city offers a variety of outdoor activities including golfing, hiking, cycling, tennis, horseback riding, ball playing and fishing. Providing a welcome refuge for swimmers on hot summer days, popular Orchard Beach features one mile of sandy shore.

★ **Bartow-Pell Mansion Museum** (CY) – *Open year-round Wed & weekends noon–4pm. Closed Jan 1, Easter Sunday, Thanksgiving weekend, Dec 25 & last 3 weeks in Aug. $2.50.* ⓟ ☏ *718-885-1461.* The history of this site dates to 1654, when Thomas Pell purchased the land from the Siwanoy Indians. Robert Bartow, a descendant of Pell's, erected the Neoclassical stone mansion overlooking Long Island Sound between 1836 and 1842. The elegant interior contains Greek Revival detailing, including a freestanding elliptical staircase, and furnishings in the American Empire style. A restored 1840s stone carriage house *(open Apr–Oct)* serves as an interpretive center.

★**Wave Hill** (AX) – *675 W. 252nd St.* MTA *1 or 9 train to 231st St., then bus 7 or 10 to 252nd St; cross parkway bridge, turn left on 249th St., then turn right on 252nd St. Open mid-Apr–mid-Oct Tue–Sun 9am–5:30pm (Wed until 9pm). Rest of the year Tue–Sun 9am–4:30pm. Closed major holidays. $4 (free Tue & mid-Nov–mid-Mar).* ✗ ᕃ 🅿 ☏ *718-549-3200. www.wavehill.org.* Opened to the public in 1965, this enchanting 28-acre estate comprises award-winning gardens and greenhouses, rolling meadows and lush woodlands, all overlooking the Hudson River. Built as a country home by William Lewis Morris in the 1840s, the main mansion was later owned by wealthy publisher William Appleton. Theodore Roosevelt's family occupied it in 1870 and Mark Twain leased the estate in 1901. Other celebrity residents include conductor Arturo Toscanini and George Perkins, J.P. Morgan's business partner. The building was restored in the 1960s and now serves as a visitor center.

The great attraction of Wave Hill is its spectacular **site**★★ overlooking the Hudson. Some 18 acres of wonderfully landscaped gardens contain more than 3,000 species of plants and a variety of trees. Of special interest are the greenhouses, the lovely aquatic garden and fragrant herb garden. Today the garden focuses on nature appreciation and education, offering programs in landscape history, horticulture, land management and the arts.

Brooklyn

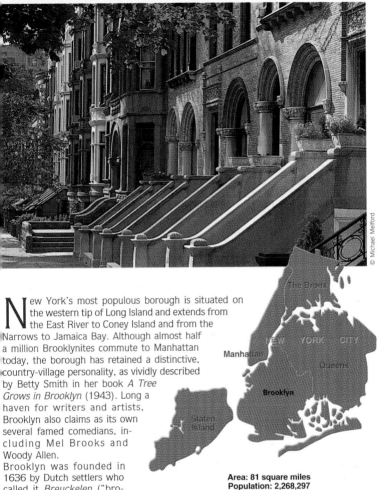

© Michael Melford

N ew York's most populous borough is situated on the western tip of Long Island and extends from the East River to Coney Island and from the Narrows to Jamaica Bay. Although almost half a million Brooklynites commute to Manhattan today, the borough has retained a distinctive, country-village personality, as vividly described by Betty Smith in her book *A Tree Grows in Brooklyn* (1943). Long a haven for writers and artists, Brooklyn also claims as its own several famed comedians, including Mel Brooks and Woody Allen.

Brooklyn was founded in 1636 by Dutch settlers who called it *Breuckelen* ("broken land") after a small town near Utrecht. The present borough of Brooklyn was made up of six small towns. Gradually the settlements spread westward along the river, and by the late 18C, regular ferry service to Manhattan was established. By the early 19C, Brooklyn had become a pleasant residential area. Prosperous New Yorkers established their homes here and commuted to Manhattan for work.

Area: 81 square miles
Population: 2,268,297

In 1834 Brooklyn became an incorporated city with about 30,000 inhabitants. It developed as an important industrial and trading center and was integrated into New York City in 1898, after absorbing a number of villages whose names still designate various sections of the borough.

By 1883 the Brooklyn Bridge formed the first direct link with Manhattan; the Williamsburg Bridge followed in 1903, and the Manhattan Bridge in 1909. The first subway connection dates from 1905. More recently, the Brooklyn-Battery Tunnel, completed in 1950, and the Verrazano-Narrows Bridge, opened in 1964, have further facilitated travel between Brooklyn and the other boroughs.

A visitor passing through Brooklyn is first impressed by its huge size and its labyrinth of streets and avenues lined with neat, straight rows of houses. A closer look, however, reveals a great variety of neighborhoods, such as Park Slope, a choice residential neighborhood; Brooklyn Heights, a charming enclave that is still the refuge of a few "old families"; Williamsburg, containing Hasidic Jewish, Hispanic and Italian communities; Brighton Beach, a thriving Russian neighborhood; Flatbush, with fine private homes and lively commercial streets; Bensonhurst, a predominantly Italian section; and Bedford-Stuyvesant, an African-American neighborhood notable for its many streets lined with fine old brownstones.

★★**BROOKLYN HEIGHTS** *Map below*

Heavily fortified during the Revolution, Brooklyn Heights was the site of General Washington's headquarters during the Battle of Long Island. In the mid-19C this section of Brooklyn developed into a choice residential area, owing largely to its proximity to the city. Brooklyn Heights enjoys a distinct identity, with a serenity often likened to that of a small countrified town. Its narrow, tree-shaded streets are lined with brownstones and town houses that represent almost every style of 19C American architecture.

Walking Tour

Distance: 2.8mi. Begin at Monroe Pl. **MTA** *2, 3 train to Clark St.*

Leaving the subway station, walk toward Monroe Place. At the corner of Clark and Henry streets stands the Hotel St. George, once the largest hotel in New York City. Most of the building has been converted into co-ops and luxury apartments, while an unrenovated section facing Henry Street still functions as a hotel.

Turn onto Monroe Place.

At **46 Monroe Place**, a brick and brownstone Greek Revival dwelling, note the decorative wrought-iron basket urn set on stone pedestals. The pineapple topping the baskets was a symbol of hospitality during the shipping era.

Turn left at Pierrepont St.

The **Brooklyn Historical Society** *(no. 128)* is the primary source of material related to the history of the borough. It contains a large collection of books, documents and artifacts on Brooklyn; features special exhibits, educational programs, concerts and walking tours; and houses the borough's only history museum. Its 1881 Queen-Anne-style building, a national historic landmark, reopened in spring 2003 after a three-year renovation *(open Wed–Sat 10am–5pm—Fri until 8pm, Sun noon–5pm; $6;* ☎ *718-222-4111; www.brooklynhistory.org).*

Backtrack on Pierrepont St. and continue to the corner of Henry St.

82 Pierrepont Street represents a splendid example of the Richardsonian Romanesque style, with its bulky massing and its rough, unfinished masonry surfaces, rounded arches and bas-relief carving. Built in 1890 as a private residence, it was later enlarged and converted into apartments.

Turning onto Willow Street, note **nos. 155, 157 and 159**, three Federal-style houses sporting handsomely detailed entranceways. A skylight in the pavement in front of no. 157 allows daylight to filter down into a tunnel that connects no. 159 to **no. 151**, formerly a stable and now an apartment. Farther up the street, on the opposite side, **nos. 108–112** illustrate the picturesque Queen Anne style, with their great variety of building materials and blend of elements of the Romanesque, Gothic and Renaissance styles.

Continue on Willow St. and turn right onto Orange St.

On Orange Street stands the **Plymouth Church of the Pilgrims** *(visit by 1hr 30min guided tour only, year-round Sun 11am–2pm; advance reservation required;* ☎ *718-624-4743).* The first Congregational Church in Brooklyn, this simple brick meetinghouse dating from 1846 served for 40 years as the pulpit for Henry Ward Beecher, who is well remembered for his anti-slavery efforts and other progressive sentiments. President Lincoln wor-

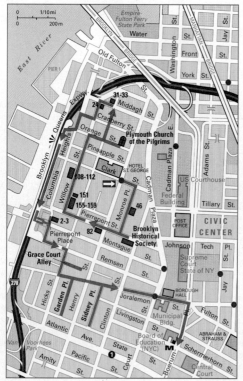

shiped here on two occasions in 1860, and many eminent authors and statesmen have spoken here over the years. In Hillis Hall, the fellowship hall, note the large stained-glass windows by Tiffany.

Backtrack to Hicks St. and continue two blocks north; turn left onto Middagh St.

Several Federal-style clapboard houses, built in the 1820s, line the street. Among the best preserved are the double frame house at **nos. 31-33** and the charming dwelling at **no. 24**.

Take Willow St. to Cranberry St. and continue toward the East River to the Brooklyn Heights Esplanade.

Overlooking the harbor, the esplanade offers magnificent **views★★★** of the Financial District; the view is especially impressive in the early evening when the lights glimmer across the river. Behind the terrace lies a series of houses with lovely private gardens.

Walk along the esplanade; turn left onto Pierrepont St. and right onto Pierrepont Pl.

Note **nos. 2** and **3 Pierrepont Place**, two of the most elegant brownstones in New York.

Continue on Pierrepont Pl., which becomes Montague Terrace; turn left onto Remsen St. and right onto Hicks St.

Off to the left is **Grace Court Alley**, a picturesque mews that was the stable alley for the fine homes on Remsen Street.

Continue along Hicks St. and turn left onto Joralemon St.

The intersection of Hicks and Joralemon streets was the location of the country home of Philip Livingston, a signer of the Declaration of Independence. It is reported that on August 29, 1776, General Washington met at Livingston's home with his chiefs of staff to plan the evacuation of his army.

Continue east on Joralemon St. to Court St.

The Civic Center area presents a contrast to the residential section, with its massive public buildings such as Borough Hall, the former Brooklyn City Hall and the massive Richardsonian Romanesque central post office. Farther down Fulton Street is Brooklyn's center, including the famous department store Abraham & Strauss.

Continue on Joralemon St. to Boerum Pl. and turn right.

★New York Transit Museum (M) – *Boerum Pl. & Schermerhorn St. Open year-round Tue–Fri 10am–4pm, weekends noon–5pm. $5. ☔ ☎ 718-694-1600. www.mta.info/mta/museum.* Located in the refurbished 1930s Court Street shuttle station, this popular attraction reopened in September 2003 after a two-year renovation. Down on the tracks, the museum's collection of vintage subway and el cars dates back to the system's beginnings, a century ago. Along the platform, the subway system's history is told

❶ Atlantic Avenue

Map p 264. The main thoroughfare of Brooklyn's Lebanese and Middle Eastern populations has become one of New York's most popular culinary destinations. Sample delicacies like lamb kabobs and stuffed grape leaves, but try to resist snapping up little bags of every spice imaginable. Some of the avenue's highlights include **Tripoli** *(no. 156; ☎ 718-596-5800; www.tripolirestaurant.com),* a campy two-level restaurant (check out the sea mural on the main level) that serves up hummus, falafel and honeyed desserts. If you want to take something home with you, visit **Sahadi's Importing Co.** *(no. 187; ☎ 718-624-4550; www.sahadis.com)* for Lebanese pistachios, feta, spices and coffee. End your walk at the **Waterfront Ale House** *(no. 155; ☎ 718-522-3794)* for a restorative gulp of one of the 50 varieties of bottled beer.

in text, pictures and maps. At the working signal tower *(near the end of the platform),* flashing lights represent working trains making their way under downtown Brooklyn on the connecting track. Exhibits on the upper level feature Steel, Stone and Backbone, a look at the building of the subways. A new permanent exhibit, On the Streets, gives buses and trolleys their proper due. At a simulated intersection, visitors can take a turn behind the wheel of two city buses, one new, one vintage 1960s.

The walls of the R-46 Gallery display posters of films set in the subways. A program of transit-related films and lectures is scheduled for the gallery. The museum also operates a Gallery Annex and store in Grand Central Terminal and a Museum Store and Travel Information Kiosk in the Times Square Visitor Center *(Broadway between 46th & 47th Sts.).*

BROOKLYN HEIGHTS \ MANHATTAN BRIDGE

PROSPECT HEIGHTS

PROSPECT PARK AND VICINITY *Map above*

★**Prospect Park** – **MTA** *2, 3 train to Grand Army Plaza. Free trolley (weekends & holidays noon–5pm) departs Wollman Rink parking lot on the hour; trolley can be boarded at any of 10 stops.* ♿ ☏ *718-965-8967. Once part of an estate belonging to the Litchfield family, the 526-acre tract of land was purchased by the city in piecemeal fashion between 1859 and 1869. Encompassing rolling meadows and wooded bluffs, streams and a lake, the park was designed by Frederick Law Olmsted and Calvert Vaux (architects of Central Park) in 1860. A network of paths and roadways winds through the park, linking its various sections.*

Brooklyn Botanical Gardens

The main entrance of the park is at Grand Army Plaza, a majestic oval plaza embellished with a monument to President John F. Kennedy and a triumphal arch dedicated to the Civil War dead.

Lefferts Homestead – **Kids** **MTA** *D or S train to Prospect Park. Open Jul–Aug Wed–Fri 1pm–4pm, weekends 1pm–5pm. Mid-Apr–Jun & Sept Thu–Fri 1pm–4pm, weekends 1pm–5pm, Oct–Nov Fri–Sun 1pm–4pm. Guided tours (1hr) available. &* ☎ 718-965-6505.* A graceful gambrel roof crowns this 18C colonial farmhouse, which was moved to the park in 1918. The interior now features a children's museum.
Take time to take a ride on the **carousel** **Kids** located nearby *(operates mid-May–late-Oct Thu–Fri 11am–4pm, weekends & holidays 11am–6pm; 50¢; %* &* ☎ 718-965-8999).*

★★**Brooklyn Botanic Garden** – *900 Washington Ave.* **MTA** *2, 3 train to Eastern Pkwy. or Q train to Prospect Park. Open Apr–Sept Tue–Fri 8am–6pm, weekends 10am–6pm. Rest of the year Tue–Fri 8am–4:30pm, weekends 10am–4:30pm. Closed major holidays. $5 (free Tue & 10am–noon Sat). Guided tours available weekends 1pm. %* &* 🅿(fee) ☎ 718-623-7200. www.bbg.org.* Located to the east of Prospect Park and to the south of the Brooklyn Museum, this outstanding botanical garden contains a great variety of vegetation, including one of the finest assemblages of roses in the country. Covering 52 acres, this refreshing oasis invites visitors to explore its rows of cherry trees and its well-kept gardens: Shakespeare, Children's, Rose, Herb, Rock, Native Flora, Lily Pool Terrace, Japanese Hill and Pond, and the Fragrance Garden for the blind.
Divided into six areas—including a Tropical Pavilion, Aquatic Exhibit and the country's largest bonsai collection—the **Steinhardt Conservatory** complex *(open Apr–Sept Tue–Sun 10am–5:30pm; rest of the year Tue–Sun 10am–4pm)* houses numerous varieties of flora.

Central Library – **MTA** *2, 3 train to Eastern Pkwy. or D train to 107th Ave. Open year-round Mon, Fri–Sat 10am–6pm, Tue–Thu 9am–8pm, Sun 1pm–5pm. Closed major holidays. %* &* ☎ 718-230-2100. www.brooklynpubliclibrary.org.* Occupying a triangular plot, this monumental building was completed in 1941. The main branch of the Brooklyn Public Library system contains about 1.6 million volumes, nearly all of which can be borrowed; 58 library branches are located throughout the borough.

Park Slope – Situated just west of Prospect Park, this residential area is one of the most desirable addresses in Brooklyn. Rows of handsome town houses, punctuated by church spires, line the wide, shaded streets, presenting a picture of the borough as it existed in the 19C. The buildings sport architectural styles typical of the period between the Civil War and World War I.

 Tom's Luncheonette
Map p 266. 782 Washington Ave. at Sterling Pl. ☎ 718-636-9738. This 62-year-old Brooklyn institution is the great all-time breakfast spot—it's open from 6am to 4pm Monday through Saturday. It's also a family affair with Tom, his wife and their kids all tending shop. As son Gus says, "We don't have customers, we have friends." Stop in for a cherry-lime rickey or a real egg cream after your visit to the Brooklyn Museum of Art or Botanic Garden.

Montauk Club – *Northeast corner of Lincoln Pl. & 8th Ave.* This brownstone and brick mansion was constructed in 1891 in a style reminiscent of a Venetian palace. Of particular interest are the friezes, which depict historic scenes associated with the Montauk Indians.

★★BROOKLYN MUSEUM OF ART *Map p 266.*

200 Eastern Pkwy. **MTA** *2 or 3 train to Eastern Pkwy.*

Housed in a monumental Beaux-Arts building designed by McKim, Mead and White, the Brooklyn Museum owns a rich collection of more than 1.5 million works of art, ranging from Egyptian antiquities to contemporary American art. Opened to the public in 1897, the building was never completed to its original specifications —although construction continued through the early 20C. Various elements, such as the central facade with its pediment and peristyle, and the east wing, were added in the early 1900s, but in 1934 the architectural firm canceled its contract and work on the building came to a halt. In 1986 the architectural team of Arata Isozaki and James Stewart Polshek was selected to complete the structure in phases while redesigning, expanding and improving the existing gallery space. The first phase, completed in 1993, resulted in a refurbished west wing—the Morris A. and Meyer Schapiro Wing—with 30,000sq ft of gallery space on three floors, as well as new storage space and the 460-seat Iris and B. Gerald Cantor Auditorium. In the project's second phase, now under way, the museum is building a glass entrance pavilion in front of the Beaux-Arts facade along Eastern Parkway, doubling the existing entrance space. The pavilion, schedule to be completed in April 2004, will radiate outward from the main facade, finally replacing grand entrance stairs that were removed in the 1930s (they were too challenging a climb for many visitors).

Visit

Open year-round Wed–Fri 10am–5pm, weekends 11am–6pm (first Sat of month until 11pm). Closed Jan 1, Thanksgiving Day & Dec 25. $6 (free first Sat of month after 5pm). Guided tours available, reservations required. ✗ ઙ. **P***(fee).* ☎ 718 638-5000. www.brooklynmuseum.org. *Some galleries may be closed and works mentioned may not be on view or may be exhibited in locations other than those indicated because of ongoing renovation and the museum's practice of rotating works of art. The front entrance to the museum will be closed until April 2004 while a new glass entrance pavilion is constructed. In the meantime, visitors can enter through the South Entrance in the parking lot or through the walkway on the side of the building.*

First Floor – On the first floor is the Grand Lobby, in which rotating exhibits of contemporary art are displayed year-round. The Blum Gallery that branches off to the south is reserved for special exhibitions. (The lobby and the Blum Gallery are closed to accommodate construction of the new main entrance).

Devoted to the primitive arts, this floor presents an eclectic collection of artifacts gathered, for the most part, by curator Stewart Culin in the early part of the century. The African gallery displays ritual and household objects, among them handsome wooden statuettes, witch doctors' wands, masks and ceremonial shields. Art from the Americas ranges from pre-Columbian artifacts to magnificent totem poles from the Haida Indians of the Northwest Coast. Oceanic art includes sculptures, musical instruments and headdresses from Papua New Guinea, New Zealand and the Solomon Islands.

Second Floor – A series of galleries showcases art from China, Korea, Japan, Southeast Asia, India and the Islamic world. The Chinese gallery features bronzes, jades, porcelain and paintings; Korea and Japan are represented with sculpture, ceramics, paintings, metalwork and prints. Terra-cotta and ceramic figures are prominent among the works from India, Nepal and Tibet. Islamic art includes works of calligraphy, carpets and objects from the Persian city of Nishapur.

Third Floor – This floor presents the museum's newly installed **Egyptian collection★★**, one of the finest in the world. The exhibits along the Schapiro Wing are arranged in two sections: one traces the development of the Nile civilization from the reign of Amunhotep IV (1350 BC) through the Ptolemaic and Roman periods; the other focuses on the themes of temples, tombs and the Egyptian universe. Admire the sarcophagi and vividly decorated mummy cases. Also of note are the limestone bust of Ptolemy II, as well as a curious sarcophagus for a sacred ibis in gilded wood and silver, and small precious objects in alabaster or stone.

With the opening of newly refurbished rooms in 2003, the Egyptian galleries on the third floor span the full length of the museum. The number of objects on view has doubled, to more than 1,100, many of which have not been exhibited before. The new galleries follow the same arrangement: a chronological section examines early Egyptian history, from the Predynastic period (beginning in 4400 BC) through the reign of Amunhotep III; a thematic section explores questions of

Egyptian religion, culture and technology, stressing the theme of permanence and change. Impressive bas-reliefs from the palace of Assyrian king Ashur-nasir-pal II at Nimrud hang in the recently renovated Kevorkian gallery.

The museum's collection of European paintings, recently reinstalled in the Beaux-Arts Court, has been organized as an exploration of the concept of time, divided into four themes: portraiture, landscape, narrative, and rural and urban life. The Impressionists are well represented with works by Degas, Monet, Morisot, Sisley and Pissarro.

Fourth Floor – Devoted largely to the decorative arts, this floor presents a fascinating collection of **American period rooms** ranging from the 17C to the present: parlors, sitting rooms and dining rooms from both modest and wealthy homes, including an old Dutch home, the Jan Martense Schenck House (c.1625), moved from a street in the Flatlands section of Brooklyn. Displayed within the various interiors are pieces of furniture, glass, silver, pewter and ceramics from the museum's holdings. (A number of period rooms, including the Schenck House, are closed for renovations until 2006.)

The costumes and textiles collection contains outstanding American and European fashions of the past and present. This collection is only on occasional public display, though, because of conservation concerns.

Fifth Floor – Exhibits here focus on sculpture and **American painting**★★ and sculpture. The Iris and B. Gerald Cantor **rotunda gallery**★ displays 58 sculptures by **Rodin**, including portraits, partial figures, erotic and mythological subjects, and groups of works related to his best-known commissions: *The Gates of Hell*, *The Burghers of Calais* and *Balzac*. The expressive figures of Eustache de St.-Pierre, Pierre de Wiessant and Andrieu d'Andres represent three of the citizens of Calais who offered themselves in the 14C to the English king to save their city from starvation. Larger than life-size, they are displayed to allow visitors to walk among them and view them from any angle. Equally powerful are the virile *Age of Bronze* figure, which Rodin was accused of casting from life, and the elderly *Helmet Maker's Wife*. Stop by the small gallery adjacent to the rotunda to see the museum's fine collection of early Italian Renaissance paintings. Note, in particular, a splendid *St. James the Major* by 15C Venetian artist Carlo Crivelli, and works by Sano de Pietro, Alvise Vivarini and Maso di Banco.

The Brooklyn Museum has garnered international renown for its fine collection of **American painting**★★. Its collection includes works by Copley, Cole *(The Pic-Nic)*, Eakins, Homer *(In the Mountains)*, Bierstadt *(A Storm in the Rocky Mountains, Mt. Rosalie*, completed in 1866), Sargent *(Paul Helleu Sketching, and His Wife)*, Cassatt, Chase, Durand *(First Harvest in the Wilderness)*, Saint-Gaudens and Bellows. The Lowenthal bequest has increased the museum's holdings of modern American paintings and sculptures, with 31 works by such well-known artists as Georgia O'Keeffe, Max Weber, Stuart Davis and Marsden Hartley.

With the creation of the Luce Center for American Art in 2001, the museum completely reorganized its display of the collection. The new installation—which integrates paintings with selected sculptures and decorative artworks and embraces historical and stylistic juxtapositions—investigates a series of eight themes (landscape, the Civil War, the modern world, daily life, among others) gathered under the mantle "American Identities." A public study center, to be completed in fall 2004, will open up some 3,000 objects from the museum's American collection to public view.

Throughout the years the museum has gathered an important and fascinating collection of architectural ornaments salvaged from demolished buildings, displayed in the **sculpture garden** (behind the main building beside the parking area).

AROUND BROOKLYN *Map pp 270-271*

★**Shore Parkway (ACYZ)** – This pleasant drive follows the coast from Bay Ridge all the way to Queens and John F. Kennedy Airport, affording successive views of the Verrazano-Narrows Bridge and Staten Island, the Rockaways and Jamaica Bay. On bright, sunny days, when superb views extend across the glittering water, Shore Parkway offers a refreshing respite from the bustle of Manhattan.

★★**Verrazano-Narrows Bridge (AZ)** – *Toll: $7 per car, paid only on west-*

> ■ **Just the Facts**
>
> The bridge boasts a total length of 6,690ft. The main span between the towers (rising 690ft above water) extends 4,260ft. The main cables are 3ft in diameter. The bridge, which is high enough to allow the largest ocean liner to pass, supports two levels for car traffic (six lanes each) but no sidewalk for pedestrians.

bound crossing. **MTA** *R train to 95th St. & Fourth Ave.* The spiderweb silhouette of the Verrazano-Narrows Bridge, the longest suspension bridge in the US, links Brooklyn to Staten Island above the Narrows (the entrance to New York Harbor). The bridge bears the name of Italian explorer **Giovanni da Verrazano**, a Florentine merchant in the service of French king François I who discovered the site of New York in 1524. At the Brooklyn entrance to the bridge stands a monument composed in

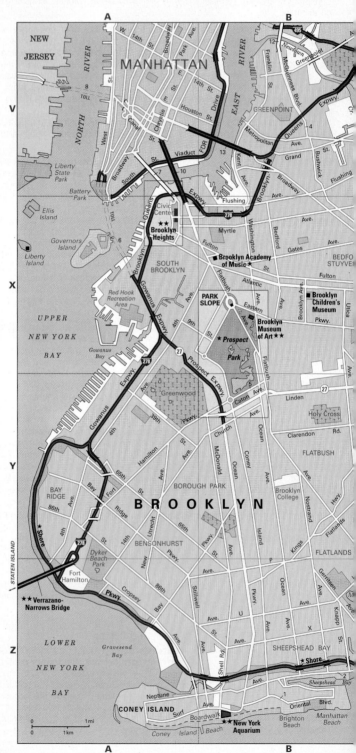

part of stones from the castle of Verrazzano in Tuscany, and from the beach of Dieppe, the French port from which the pilot sailed.

The Triborough Bridge and Tunnel Authority began work on the bridge in January 1959. The project cost $305 million. On November 21, 1964, the bridge was inaugurated in the presence of Gov. Nelson Rockefeller and the bridge's engineer, O.H. Amman, who also designed the George Washington Bridge.

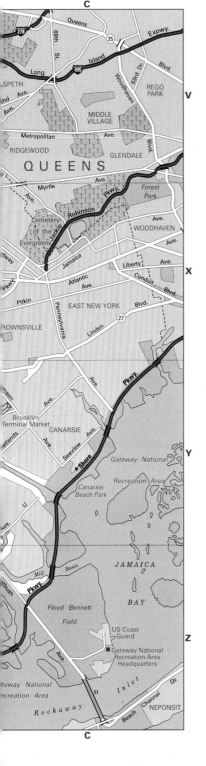

Coney Island's annual Mermaid Parade

Coney Island (ABZ) – *1015 Surf Ave.* ☎ *718-266-1234. www.coneyislandusa.com.* 🚇 *B, N, F or D trains.* Located to the south of Brooklyn and bathed by the Atlantic Ocean, this beach resort and amusement area attracted over a million people on busy summer Sundays in the 1900s.

In Dutch times, this sandy island was inhabited only by rabbits, who left it their name (*Konijn Eiland* meant "Rabbit Island"). This title was soon transformed into its rough English "sound-alike," Coney Island. In the 1830s the broad beaches lining the island began attracting well-to-do city dwellers. Coney Island developed into a fashionable resort and became the site of elegant hotels, hippodromes and casinos. Fifty years later, the resort gained fame as a popular amusement area and the clientele began to change. The first roller coasters appeared in 1884, followed some years later by a merry-go-round and a huge Ferris wheel (George W.G. Ferris built the first one for the Chicago World's Fair in 1893). The Ferris wheel still operates, as does the terrifying wood-frame Cyclone roller coaster.

Today the grand facilities are gone, and Coney Island is no longer the attraction it once was. But between the cool surf and the ramshackle charm of the carnival booths and rides like the 1927 wood-framed rollercoaster, Cyclone, the crowds still turn out on hot summer days. More than half a million spectators attend the colorful and risqué **Mermaid Parade**, held in late June each year.

The Resort – The great attraction of Coney Island was its amusement parks, where scenic railways, loop-the-loop roller coasters and Ferris wheels competed with phantom trains, interplanetary rockets, merry-go-rounds and shooting galleries. For many years the star attraction was the **parachute jump**, still standing but now no longer used, erected during the World's Fair of 1939-40; the lover of thrills could drop in a chair, which was attached to a parachute and guided by cables. Coney Island's heyday lasted into the 1940s. Then, through the 1950s, the crowds diminished and, owing to a lack of prosperity, the area began to decline. Buildings grew shabby and were allowed to deteriorate, while restaurants and other establishments were permanently closed. Today all but a small section of the once-gigantic amusement area has fallen into disuse. For many New Yorkers and out-of-towners, however, a stroll on Coney Island's **boardwalk** along a 3.5mi stretch of sandy beach, the hot dog and cotton candy stands and a handful of attractions still remain a pleasant diversion on a warm summer day.

★★ **New York Aquarium** (BZ) – 🚸 *W. 8th St. & Surf Ave.* 🚇 *W train to Stillwell Ave.–New York Aquarium. Open year-round daily 10am–5pm (weekends until 5:30pm); closing times vary seasonally. $11.* ✗ & 🅿 *(fee).* ☎ *718-265-3474. www.nyaquarium.com.* Opened in 1896 in what is now Castle Clinton National Monument, the aquarium was reputedly the first public aquarium in the US. It has been located at the corner of the Boardwalk and West 8th Street since 1957. In large outdoor pools, whales, seals, sea lions and Pacific walrus go through their paces. Not to be missed are the penguin colony and a 90,000-gallon shark tank holding stingrays and five types of free-swimming and bottom-dwelling sharks. Indoor aquariums, some decorated with live corals, exhibit more than 10,000 specimens and 300 species from the world over, including Pacific reef fish, primitive fish, piranhas, chambered nautilus, clownfish and anemones. The New York Aquarium was the first to exhibit and breed beluga whales in captivity. **Explore The Shore**, a 20,000sq ft educational center, features 65 exhibits including a 400-gallon wave tank showing subtidal, intertidal and upper tidal zones; a reproduction of a living coral reef where jewel-like small fish dart among anemones and barnacles; and a New England lobster boat in its own saltwater dock. In fall 2002 the aquarium unveiled the new **Alien Stingers Exhibit**. Located next to Explore The Shore, Alien Stingers showcases dozens of species of sea jellies, corals and anemones from around the world. At the Sea Cliffs exhibit you'll discover a 300ft-long rocky coast habitat for walrus, sea otters, fur seals and penguins. *Check at entrance for schedule of sea lion shows.*

Brooklyn Children's Museum (BX) – Kids *145 Brooklyn Ave. at the corner of St. Mark's Ave.* MTA *3 train to Kingston Ave.; walk one block west on Eastern Pkwy.; turn right onto Brooklyn Ave.; continue 6 blocks north to St. Mark's Ave. Open Jul–Aug Mon & Wed–Fri noon–5pm (Fri until 6:30pm), weekends 10am–5pm. Rest of the year Wed–Fri 2pm–5pm, weekends 10am–5pm. Closed major holidays. $4.* ♿ ☎ *718-735-4402. www.bchildmus.org.* Founded in 1899 in Brower Park, this institution was one of the first museums designed especially for children. Painted with bright, bold colors, the four-story building has housed the museum since 1977. Interactive, hands-on exhibits cover the areas of cultural and natural history, the sciences and the performing arts. The museum invites active participation, offers family workshops and presents special performances year-round.

★**Brooklyn Academy of Music** (BX) – *30 Lafayette Ave. Check local newspapers for a listing of events.* ✗ ♿ 🅿 ☎ *718-636-4100. www.bam.org.* The Brooklyn Academy of Music is widely regarded as New York's premier venue for avant-garde performance, and a wealth of new programming in recent years ensures BAM's continued vibrancy. Founded in 1859, it is the city's oldest continually operating performing-arts center. After its original Brooklyn Heights premises burned down in 1907, it moved to its Fort Greene home. Behind its imposing brick Beaux-Arts facade lies an elegant 1,100-seat opera house that has hosted Enrico Caruso, Isadora Duncan, Arthur Toscanini, Paul Robeson and, more recently, Philip Glass, Laurie Anderson, and the Merce Cunningham Dance Company; belying its old-fashioned appearance, its technical capabilities and acoustics are first-rate. A second venue, the 900-seat Harvey Theater (formerly the Majestic), is located a block and a half away at 651 Fulton Street and is home to the Brooklyn Philharmonic Orchestra. In addition to live performances, BAM has offered an eclectic program of independent and classic film since 1998, when the four-screen BAM Rose Cinemas opened.

Queens

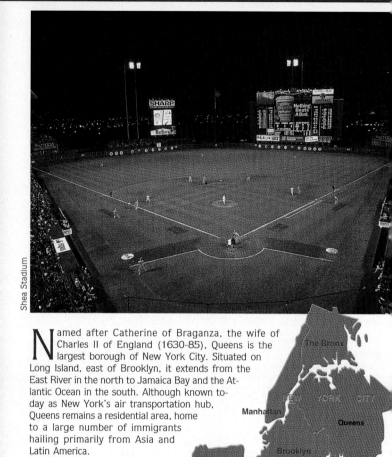

Shea Stadium

Named after Catherine of Braganza, the wife of Charles II of England (1630-85), Queens is the largest borough of New York City. Situated on Long Island, east of Brooklyn, it extends from the East River in the north to Jamaica Bay and the Atlantic Ocean in the south. Although known today as New York's air transportation hub, Queens remains a residential area, home to a large number of immigrants hailing primarily from Asia and Latin America.

In 1642 a Dutch settlement was founded at Maspeth, but it was not until 1645 that Queen's first permanent settlement, at Vlissingen (Flushing), was established. Clashes between English and Dutch settlers over freedom of worship marked the borough's early years. In 1662 the Dutch arrested John Bowne *(p 279)* for allowing Quaker gatherings in his home. Bowne appealed his case, paving the way for religious freedom in the colonies.

Area: 120 square miles
Population: 2,229,379

Until the mid-19C, Queens remained a sparsely populated neighborhood of small villages and farms. As New York City blossomed, urbanization of Queens accelerated, attracting successive waves of German and Irish immigrants. By the end of the 19C, when Queens became incorporated into New York City as a borough, some 150,000 people lived here. In the 1920s Queens attracted the silent film industry, which operated some 20 studios in Astoria before relocating to sunny Hollywood. On the heels of the 1939 World's Fair, the borough developed a reputation as a haven for sports and recreation, an image it still claims today.

The 1970s witnessed the development of an active political machine; from its ranks rose Mario Cuomo, governor of New York from 1982 to 1994. Today a cluster of factories in the Long Island City area, where artists have renovated lofts into studios and living spaces, gives way to more residential sections to the southeast, such as Forest Hills and Jamaica. Queens continues to draw sports fans to its Aqueduct Race Track (**CZ**), Shea Stadium (**BX**) and USTA National Tennis Center (**BX**), while nature enthusiasts flock to the Gateway National Recreation area.

AROUND QUEENS *Map pp 276-277*

Due to the distances between sights and their remote locations, we advise visiting Queens by car. However on weekends a free Queens Artlink shuttle bus takes visitors from West 53rd Street to MoMA QNS every hour on the hour from 10am–4pm, and returns every hour on the half hour from 10:30am–5:30pm. A second shuttle loops from MoMA QNS to P.S. 1, SculptureCenter, Socrates Sculpture Park, American Museum of the Moving Image, the Noguchi Museum and the Museum for African Art. It leaves MoMa QNS every hour from 10:45am–4:45pm.

★★ **Isamu Noguchi Garden Museum** (AX) – *32-37 Vernon Blvd. The museum is closed for renovation until April 2004. It has temporarily relocated to 36-01 43rd Ave., 2nd floor.* **MTA** *7 local train to 33rd St. Station; walk east to 36th St., then left one block to 43rd Ave. Open year-round Mon, Thu, Fri 10am–5pm, weekends 11am–6pm. Closed major holidays. $5.* ✗ & ☎ *718-204-7088. www.noguchi.org.* Conflicting and harmonious relationships between nature and the man-made are a recurrent theme in the sculpture of **Isamu Noguchi** (1904-88), the renowned Japanese-American artist whose works include public spaces (Detroit's Hart Plaza), playgrounds (Atlanta's Playscapes), gardens and fountains. In addition to works in stone, wood and metal, Noguchi created ethereal-looking *akari* light sculptures; he also designed stage sets for choreographers Martha Graham and George Balanchine.

The Isamu Noguchi Garden

Here at this temporary site, rotating exhibits of Noguchi's works illustrate various aspects of his career. When it opens in April 2004, the permanent facility will present changing exhibits relating to Noguchi, as well as a gallery devoted to the artist's interior design work.

★ **American Museum of the Moving Image** (AX) – **Kids** *35th Ave. & 36th St. in Astoria.* **MTA** *R, V or G train to Steinway St.; walk south on Steinway St. and turn right on 35th Ave. Open year-round Wed & Thu noon–5pm, Fri noon–8pm, weekends 11am–6:30pm. Closed Memorial Day, Labor Day, Thanksgiving Day & Dec 25. $10.* ✗ & ☎ *718-784-0077. www.movingimage.us.* Located on the former site of the Astoria Film Studios (built by Paramount Pictures in the 1920s), this unique museum (1988) is devoted to the history, technology and the art of film, television and digital media. Visitors can make their own short animations, experiment with sound effects, or dub their voices into a famous movie. The collection encompasses portrait and scene-still photographs, special effects materials and production equipment; costumes, props and memorabilia from the television and film industries; and clips from movies, videos and advertisements. Screenings and discussion programs are presented frequently throughout the year.

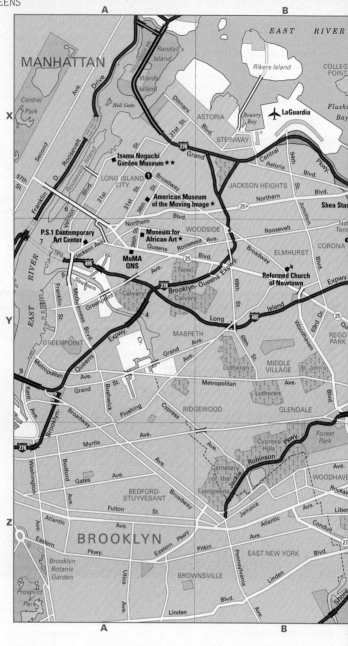

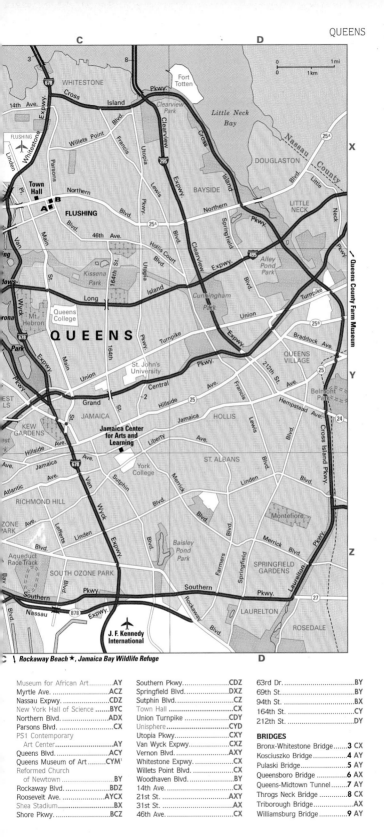

1 Astoria

Map p 276. Astoria is a predominantly Greek enclave of Queens; in fact, this neighborhood is so insular that many of its citizens speak no English. You'll hear plenty of Greek spoken in **Omonia** *(3220 Broadway;* ☎ *718-274-6650),* a coffeehouse and bakery that serves baklava and other assorted pastries. **Karyatis** *(3503 Broadway;* ☎ *718-204-0666), one of the best restaurants in Astoria, features grilled seafood along with classic Greek fare such as lamb and veal dishes and moussaka.* **Elias Corner** *(24th Ave. and 31st St.;* ☎ *718-932-1510) offers a* wide range of Greek specialties including lamb chops, seafood and chicken kabobs. Before leaving the neighborhood, stop in at the **Titan Deli** *(2556 31st St. at 28th Ave.;* ☎ *718-626-7771) to stock up on olives,* feta cheese and pita bread.

★**Museum for African Art** **(AY)** – *36-01 43rd Ave. at 36th St.* MTA *7 local train to 33rd St. Station; walk east to 36th St., then left one block to 43rd Ave. Open year-round Mon, Thu & Fri 10am–5pm, weekends 11am–5pm. Closed major holidays. $6.* ☎ *718-784-7700. www.africanart.org.* This museum is one of only two in the US devoted exclusively to African art. While there is a limited permanent collection for study, broad-based changing exhibits feature both contemporary and historical pieces, including painting, sculpture, textiles and masks.

Since opening as the Center for African Art in 1984, the museum has mounted more than 40 major traveling shows exploring Africa's artistic traditions and cultural heritage. In 1993 it moved from the Upper East Side to SoHo, where architect Maya Lin, best known for the Vietnam Veterans Memorial in Washington, DC, designed the museum's interior. In September 2002, the museum relocated to an interim space in Queens in anticipation of the construction of a permanent museum building at 110th and Fifth Avenue in Manhattan.

Inaugural exhibits on masks are presented in the main gallery, while recent acquisitions are on view in the Focus Gallery. A colorful shop sells traditional crafts, including pottery, clothes, baskets and jewelry from villages across the African continent. The museum also offers music, dance and performance-art programs.

MoMA QNS **(AY)** – *45-20 33rd St. at Queens Blvd. For description, see the Museum of Modern Art in the Museums section.*

P.S.1 Contemporary Art Center **(AY)** – *22-25 Jackson Ave. at 46th Ave.* MTA *7 local train to Courthouse Sq. Open year-round Thu–Mon noon–6pm. Closed Jan 1, Thanksgiving Day & Dec 25. $5 contribution requested.* ✗ ☎ *718-784-2084. www.ps1.org.* Housed in a former public school building—hence the initials P.S.—this center is devoted to the exhibition of contemporary works in virtually all media by new and emerging artists. The fully renovated five-level complex includes a gallery for presentation of films and videos, as well as artists' studios and outdoor exhibit space. In early 1999 merger plans were announced between the Museum of Modern Art and P.S.1, whose cutting-edge exhibits will enable MoMA to expand its presentation of up-to-the-minute art.

Jamaica Bay Wildlife Refuge **(CZ)** – MTA *A train to Broad Channel. From the subway station, take Noel Rd. to Cross Bay Blvd. and turn right (.8mi). A visitor center is on the left (daily 6am–5pm). Open year-round daily dawn–dusk.* ▣ ☎ *718-318-4340.* Located just south of JFK Airport, this peaceful wildlife refuge is a major migratory haven for birds, attracting a wide variety of waterfowl and land and shore birds. It forms part of the Gateway National Recreation Area, one of the nation's largest urban parks. A self-guided **nature trail**★ through the marshes affords pleasant views of the Manhattan skyline to the west *(1.8mi; 1 1/2hrs, request free permit at the visitor center).*

Farther south on Cross Bay Boulevard, beachfront communities dot the five miles of **Rockaway Beach**★ *(access from* MTA *A, C and H trains at stations between 25th and 116th Sts.).* On sunny days, New Yorkers stroll up and down the wide boardwalk, enjoying splendid breezes and splendid ocean views.

Jamaica Center for Arts and Learning **(CY)** – *161-04 Jamaica Ave.* MTA *E, J or Z train to Jamaica Center stop; walk one block north to Jamaica Ave., then east to 161st St. Open year-round Mon–Fri 9am–6pm, (Wed until 8pm), Sat 10am–5pm. Closed major holidays.* ♿ ☎ *718-658-7400.* Founded in 1972, this center operates as a community cultural center, offering educational programs, exhibits, workshops and classes in the performing and visual arts.

Reformed Church of Newtown **(BY)** – *85-15 Broadway, Elmhurst.* MTA *R or G train to Grand Ave.–Newtown. Open Tue–Sun 10am–5pm, Sun 8:45am–4pm. Closed major holidays.* ☎ *718-592-4466.* In 1731 this church was organized as a congregation of the Dutch Reformed Church. It was entirely rebuilt in the Greek Revival style in 1831.

Flushing (**CX**) – A small settlement named Vlissingen was established on this site in 1645; the Dutch name was eventually transformed into Flushing. The town soon became associated with the **Quakers**, or Society of Friends. Believers in a simple way of life, tolerance toward others and pacifism, the Quakers were often persecuted. John Bowne, an Englishman who settled in Flushing, allowed Quakers to hold meetings in his home. His arrest and ultimate acquittal for permitting the meetings helped establish religious freedom in the US. Flushing still has one of the oldest Friends' Meeting Houses in America (on Northern Blvd. near Linden Pl.). At 137-15 Northern Boulevard stands the old Flushing **Town Hall**, a Romanesque Revival building (1862) that has been restored to its original appearance and now hosts art exhibits and concerts on its first floor.

Bowne House (**CX A**) – 37-01 Bowne St. **MTA** 7 train to Main St. Visit by guided tour (2hrs) only, year-round Tue & weekends 2:30pm–4:30pm. Closed mid-Dec–mid-Jan & major holidays (except Jul 4). $4. & ☎ 718-359-0528. The oldest structure in Queens, this house (1661) was inhabited by nine successive generations of the Bowne family, including John Bowne. The house contains a collection of 17C and 18C furniture as well as pewter, paintings and documents, all of which belonged to the Bowne family.

Kingsland Homestead (**CX B**) – 143-35 37th Ave., Flushing. Open year-round Tue, Sat & Sun 2:30pm–4:30pm. Closed major holidays. $3. 🅿 ☎ 718-939-0647. www.queenshistoricalsociety.org. Erected in c.1785, this two-and-a-half-story edifice presents a mix of Dutch and English traditions; note in particular the divided front door and central chimney. The former farmhouse now serves as the headquarters of the Queens Historical Society and houses the local history museum.

Flushing Meadows-Corona Park (**BCXY**) – Once a swamp favored by ducks and then a sanitary landfill, this 1,275-acre park was developed in the 1930s to accommodate New York's first World's Fair (1939). Designs for the park included the creation of **Meadow Lake**, measuring .8mi in length, and the **New York City Building**, which housed the United Nations General Assembly between 1946 and 1949 and now contains the Queens Museum of Art, as well as an ice-skating rink.

Queens Museum of Art (**CY M¹**) – In the New York City Building (located next to the Unisphere). **MTA** 7 train to Willets Point/Shea Stadium; follow signs to museum. Open Wed–Fri 10am–5pm, weekends noon–5pm. Closed major holidays. $5. & 🅿 ☎ 718-592-9700. www.queensmuseum.org. Originally conceived as an arts center for the borough of Queens, the museum today features 20C and contemporary art exhibitions with a diverse global outlook. Don't miss the highlight—an enormous architectural model of New York City built for the 1964-65 World's Fair at a scale of 1in to 100ft. Covering more than 9,335sq ft, the **Panorama of New York City★** presents a detailed model of the five boroughs, including thousands of buildings, parks and an extensive infrastructure. The history of the New York City Building is recounted through photographs and other memorabilia.

New York Hall of Science (**C**) – **Kids** Open Jul–Aug Mon 9:30am–2pm, Tue–Sun 9:30am–5pm. Rest of the year Mon–Wed 9:30am–2pm, Thu–Sun 9:30am–5pm. Closed major holidays. $9. ✗ & 🅿($5) ☎ 718-699-0005. www.nyhallsci.org. A vestige of the 1964-65 World's Fair, this museum of science and technology delights young and old alike. The museum's collections are also strong in microbiology and quantum physics. Walk through the "World of Microbes," then pedal an airplane propeller before heading to the multimedia Science Center. Don't miss the 140ft-high **Unisphere** (**D**) located near the museum.

To the north of Flushing Meadows-Corona Park, **Shea Stadium** (**BX**) also dates from the 1964-65 World's Fair. Home of the New York Mets baseball team, the 55,300-seat venue drew throngs of fans for the famous 1965 Beatles concert as well as for Pope John Paul II's visit in 1979.

Queens County Farm Museum (**CD**) – **Kids** 73-50 Little Neck Pkwy. in Floral Park. Take Long Island Expwy. to Exit 32; continue south on Little Neck Pkwy. (10 blocks to museum entrance). **MTA** E, F trains to Kew Gardens, then Q46 bus to Little Neck Pkwy.; walk north 3 blocks. Open year-round Mon–Fri 9am–5pm, weekends 10am–5pm. Closed major holidays. & ☎ 718-347-3276. www.queens-farm.org. This 47-acre tract of nature trails, fields and farm buildings provides a refreshing change from the bustle of the city. The 18C Flemish-style farmhouse (visit by 30min guided tour only, weekends noon–5pm), replete with its original furniture, and the greenhouses, barns, sheds and petting zoo provide visitors, especially children, with an informative glimpse of Queens County's agrarian origins.

John F. Kennedy International Airport (**CZ**) – 15mi southeast of Midtown (for access, see p 310). ☎ 718-244-4444. www.panynj.gov. One of the busiest airports in the world, JFK Airport covers 4,900 acres in the southeast corner of Queens, along Jamaica Bay—an area the size of Manhattan Island from midtown to the Battery. Construction, begun in 1942 on the site of the Idlewild Beach golf course, was placed under the jurisdiction of the Port Authority of New York and

New Jersey in 1947. Opened as the New York International Airport at Idlewild a year later, the airport was renamed in 1963 to honor the late president. The Kennedy air cargo center, the fourth busiest in the US, handled some 1.7 million tons in 1997. As part of a $10 billion airport improvement plan, a new building Terminal 1 (Bodouva & Assocs.), was completed in 1998 on the site of the former Eastern Airlines terminal and services four foreign airline companies. The new $1.4 billion Terminal 4 opened in 2001, incorporating separate levels for departing and arriving passengers, retail shops and eateries in a mall-like setting. In 1999 American Airlines began construction of a new complex to replace Terminals 8 and 9. The new 2.2-million-square-foot building, which will include 220 check-in counters and a customs and immigration facility, will be the largest terminal at JFK when it opens in 2007.

International Arrivals Building – An arched pavilion forms the center of this 2,000ft long structure (Skidmore, Owings & Merrill), which houses the arrival hall and, in its wings, a number of airline terminals.

Adjacent to the building, an 11-story air traffic control tower rises to 321ft, making it the tallest such tower in North America.

★**TWA International Terminal** – Evoking a huge bird with outspread wings, this soaring structure (1962) is a masterpiece of the architect Eero Saarinen. The building is composed of four intersecting vaults rising from four load-bearing points.

LaGuardia Airport (BX) – *8mi northeast of Midtown (for access, see p 310)*. ☎ *718-533-3400. www.panynj.gov*. Located close to Manhattan, this major airport bordering Flushing and Bowery bays was established in 1939 and named after **Fiorello H. La Guardia**, mayor of the city from 1934 to 1945. Affectionately known as "the Little Flower," Mayor La Guardia was himself a pilot and recognized the importance of air travel to New York. Despite its relatively small size—one-ninth of JFK airport—LaGuardia is capable of handling the bulk of the area's domestic flights. A recent expansion and modernization of the Central Terminal Building included a redesign of the center section to improve pedestrian traffic flow.

"Over the great bridge, with the sunlight through the girders making a constant flicker upon the moving cars, with the city rising up across the river in white heaps and sugar lumps all built with a wish out of non-olfactory money. The city seen from the Queensboro Bridge is always the city seen for the first time, in its first wild promise of all the mystery and the beauty in the world.

F. Scott Fitzgerald, *The Great Gatsby* (1926)

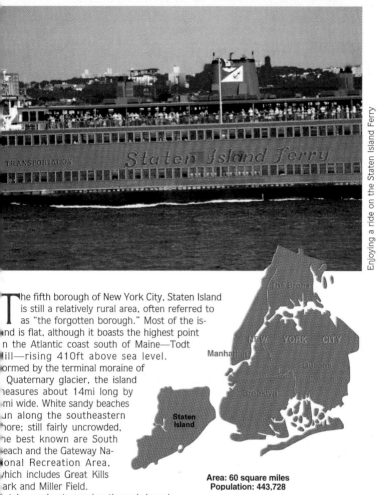

Enjoying a ride on the Staten Island Ferry

The fifth borough of New York City, Staten Island is still a relatively rural area, often referred to as "the forgotten borough." Most of the island is flat, although it boasts the highest point on the Atlantic coast south of Maine—Todt Hill—rising 410ft above sea level. Formed by the terminal moraine of a Quaternary glacier, the island measures about 14mi long by 7mi wide. White sandy beaches run along the southeastern shore; still fairly uncrowded, the best known are South Beach and the Gateway National Recreation Area, which includes Great Kills Park and Miller Field.

Area: 60 square miles
Population: 443,728

Dutch merchants passing through here in the early 1600s named the island after the Dutch States General. The first permanent settlement was established at Oude Dorp by Dutch and French Huguenot families in 1661. Over the next two centuries the island thrived on farming and agriculture, ferrying goods to Manhattan and New Jersey. Staten Island acquired its alternate name (Richmond) in honor of the Duke of Richmond, brother of Charles II, king of England. It grew considerably after integration with the other boroughs in 1898, attracting hard-working immigrants to its farms and factories and hard-playing society folk to its resort hotels. The boom went bust after World War I, when many residents left the island to make their fortunes on the mainland. The borough blossomed once again when the Verrazano-Narrows Bridge opened in 1964, bringing an influx of Manhattanites, seeking to escape the bustle of New York.

Today Staten Island is primarily a bedroom community, culturally and economically related more to New Jersey than to New York. Plagued by urban problems in recent years, its residents created a commission to study the possibility of seceding from Manhattan, and in 1993 they voted in favor of secession. Though the idea has fallen from the forefront of politics in the last few years, the matter would have to be decided by the state legislature in Albany.

AROUND STATEN ISLAND Map p 283

To visit the sights described below, visitors may take buses from the ferry termina at St. George or, in some cases, the Staten Island Rapid Transit.

★**Staten Island Ferry** – 🧒 *Ferry departs from Whitehall Terminal in Manhattan fo the St. George Ferry Terminal on Staten Island year-round daily 24hrs/day abou every 30min (hourly after 11pm). 30min. $3/car (free for pedestrians).* 🍴 ♿ 🅿️ *(a St. George terminal only, $5.50).* ☎ *718-815-2628. www.siferry.com.* Any visi to New York should include a trip on the Staten Island Ferry. On the windy voyage which covers 5mi and takes 30min, the ferry skirts the Statue of Liberty, affordin magnificent **views★★★** of Manhattan and the bay. The ferry that was the start o Cornelius "Commodore" Vanderbilt's fortune now runs night and day, transportin some 20 million passengers a year.

St. George (BY) – Facing lower Manhattan across the bay, this small town is sur rounded by suburban homes and gardens. In the waters near St. George quarantine was imposed on ships arriving from overseas in the 1850s. St. Georg has been the seat of the county and borough government since 1920. In 2003 the St. George terminal building will be revamped with a 40ft-tall glass viewin wall, shops, restaurants and an outdoor plaza.

Staten Island Ferry Collection of SIIAS (BY M¹) – 🧒 *In main waiting room of th St. George terminal. Open year-round daily 9am–3pm. Closed major holidays. $1* 🍴 ♿ ☎ *718-727-1135.* This small exhibit explores the history of the Staten Islan ferry line through photographs and such artifacts as ships' wheels and whistles an elaborate scale models. A well-stocked store carries ferry souvenirs and nautical art

Staten Island Institute of Arts and Sciences (BY M²) – 🧒 *75 Stuyvesant Pl. From th Staten Island ferry terminal walk one block west to Wall St. Turn left on Wall St and walk one block to the museum at Stuyvesant Pl. Open year-round Mon–Sa 9am–5pm, Sun 1pm–5pm. Closed major holidays. $2.50 contribution requeste* ♿ 🅿️ ☎ *718-727-1135.* Founded in 1881, Staten Island's oldest cultural institu tion features a variety of exhibits illustrating the history, geology, flora and faun of the island as well as frequent shows of painting, sculpture, graphics, furnitur and photography.

Alice Austen House

★**Alice Austen House Museum (BY A)** – *2 Hylan Blvd. From the Staten Island ferr terminal take S51 bus. Open Mar–Dec Thu–Sun noon–5pm. Closed Easter Sunda Thanksgiving Day & Dec 25. $2.* ♿ ☎ *718-816-4506.* A pioneer photographe **Alice Austen** (1866-1952) captured turn-of-the-century life in New York City, fron exclusive society gatherings to poignant scenes of immigrant life. Restore according to her photographs, this picturesque Victorian-style cottage—known a "Clear Comfort"—displays changing exhibits, including prints from her glass-plat negatives. Trimmed in gingerbread, the porch affords superb **views★★** of the harbo and Manhattan in the distance.

Snug Harbor Cultural Center (BY) – *1000 Richmond Terrace. From the State Island ferry terminal take S40 bus. Open year-round daily dawn–dusk. Close Jan 1, Thanksgiving Day & Dec 25. Guided tours (45min) available weekends 2pr*

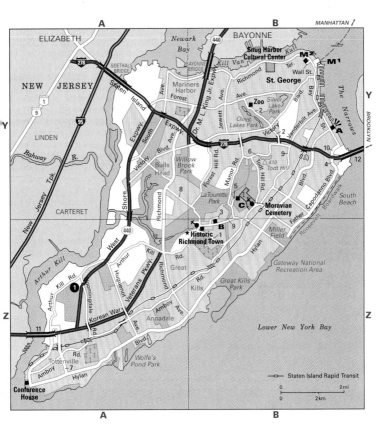

except in winter. ✗ ♿ 🅿 ☎ *718-448-2500.* Founded in 1801 as the first maritime hospital and retired sailors' home in the US, the 83-acre park and its 28 buildings are being restored and converted to a center for the visual and performing arts. Architectural treasures include a row of Greek Revival buildings overlooking the Kill van Kull. Arts organizations at the center include the **Newhouse Center for Contemporary Art** *(Bldg. C; open year-round Wed–Sun 11am–5pm, Sat til 7pm; $2),* which mounts exhibitions in 15,000sq ft of gallery space as well as creating a home for 30 artist's studios. Besides offering a botanical garden and a children's museum, Snug Harbor also hosts concerts, art shows and special events year-round.

Staten Island Botanical Garden – *Open year-round daily dawn–dusk.* ✗ ♿ 🅿 ☎ *718-273-8200. www.sibg.org.* A stroll through this lovely garden reveals an English perennial garden, an herb and butterfly garden designed to attract these colorful insects, and a greenhouse sheltering orchids and other tropicals.

Staten Island Children's Museum – 🄺🄸🄳🄻 *Open Jul–Aug Tue–Sun 11am–5pm. Rest of the year Tue–Sun noon–5pm. Closed 2nd–4th weeks of Sept & major holidays. $4.* ✗ ♿ 🅿 ☎ *718-273-2060.* Interactive exhibits, creative workshops and field trips encourage children to learn by doing. Most activities are designed for children between the ages of 2 and 12.

Old Bermuda Inn Restaurant

Map p 283. 2512 Arthur Kill Rd. (Bloomingdale Rd. & Rossville Ave.). ☎ *718-948-7600.* This stately 1830 Victorian mansion-turned-restaurant has five working fireplaces, servers in period garb, museum-quality antiques, oil portraits of old Staten Island families and even a friendly ghost (allegedly the former mistress of the house, Martha Mesereau, waiting for her husband to return from the Civil War). The slightly stodgy continental menu and the fact that Thursday is Ladies' Night won't let you completely forget you're in New York's most maligned borough, but the food is well prepared and a good bargain. Try the Sunday brunch—it's worth the ferry ride.

Staten Island Zoo (BY) – 🄺 *614 Broadway. From the Staten Island ferry terminal take S48 bus to Forest Ave. & Broadway. Turn left on Broadway and walk 2 1/2 blocks. Open year-round daily 10am–4:45pm. Closed Jan 1, Thanksgiving Day & Dec 25. $5 (free Wed after 2pm).* ✗ ⅃ ☐ ☎ *718-442-3100. www.statenislandzoo.org.* Located in Barrett Park, this small zoo, opened in 1936, is especially known for its comprehensive collection of snakes and reptiles.

★**Jacques Marchais Museum of Tibetan Art (BZ B)** – *338 Lighthouse Ave. From the Staten Island ferry terminal take S74 bus to Lighthouse Ave. Turn right and walk up the hill. Open year-round Wed–Sun 1pm–5pm. Closed Thanksgiving Day & Dec 25–Jan 1. $5. Guided tours available.* ☎ *718-987-3500. www.tibetanmuseum.com.* Laid out on Lighthouse Hill in enchanting terraced gardens, the museum displays a rare collection of art covering the culture, religion and mythology of Tibet, Nepal, China, Mongolia and India. The museum buildings were constructed to resemble a small Buddhist mountain temple. Highlights of the collection include an authentic three-tiered Buddhist altar and a large Tibetan *thangka,* or scroll painting, depicting the Green Tara, goddess of universal compassion. The *thangka,* which was painted in the 17C, has been painstakingly restored by Tibetan artist Pema Wangyal using only traditional techniques and materials.

Greenbelt Environmental Education Dept./High Rock Park (BY C) – *200 Nevada Ave. From the Staten Island ferry terminal take S62 bus to Victory Blvd. & Manor Rd. Transfer to S54 bus to Rockland Ave., then walk 3 blocks and turn right on Nevada Ave. Open year-round daily 9am–5pm.* ☐ ☎ *718-667-2165. www.sigreenbelt.org.* Marking the center of the island, this 90-acre forest preserve with its varied topography and wide range of flora and fauna provides an attractive spot for hiking on more than 30mi of trails. Playing fields, an 18-hole golf course and a replica early 20C carousel round out the center's offerings. The Greenbelt also conducts environmental educational programs and workshops *(by appointment)* and sponsors a variety of special events. In 2003, the park added a new 5,000sq ft nature center.

★**Historic Richmond Town (BZ)** – 🄺 *441 Clarke Ave. From Richmond Rd. turn on St. Patrick's Pl., then right on Clarke Ave.; or take S74 bus from the Staten Island ferry terminal. Open Jul–Aug Wed–Fri 10am–5pm, weekends 1pm–5pm. Rest of the year Wed–Sun 1pm–5pm. Closed Jan 1, Easter Sunday, Thanksgiving Day & Dec 25. $5.* ✗ ☐ ☎ *718-351-1611. Tickets may be purchased at the visitor orientation center in the County Courthouse.* Located on the site of one of the earliest settlements on Staten Island and the island's geographic center, this historic village traces the evolution of community life in Richmond Town from the 17C to 19C through a variety of buildings, furnishings, gardens and implements. The village comprises 27 structures, including private dwellings, craft shops, a schoolhouse and municipal buildings that have been restored and opened to the public. Staff members dressed in period costumes reenact everyday chores, and artisans occasionally demonstrate the crafts of yesteryear.

Visitor Center – The imposing Greek Revival structure containing the center was the third **County Courthouse** (1837) to be built between the 18C and early 20C when Richmond Town was the seat of county government.

Staten Island Historical Society Museum – Some parts of this attractive redbrick building date back to the middle of the 19C when it served as the Surrogates Court and the office of the county clerk. Changing exhibits and documents relate the history of the island.

Stephens-Black House – Facing the visitor center, this building was the residence of the Stephen D. Stephens family, who operated the adjoining general store until 1870. Today the house is decorated with furnishings of the mid-19C, and the store is stocked with goods that would have been sold around the time of the Civil War. The **Print Shop** and the **Tinsmith Shop** *(located on either side of the Stephens-Black House)* are original structures that were moved to this site in the 1960s. They are furnished to represent shops of their trades; seasonal demonstrations of the crafts of printing and tinwork are offered here. The dolls, games and toys on display on the upper floors of the **Bennett House** are nostalgic reminders of the joys of childhood in days gone by. Located across Richmond Road, the Dutch Colonial **Guyon-Lake-Tysen House** was erected in the mid-18C; the interior furnishings reflect this time period. Domestic skills such as spinning and weaving are demonstrated seasonally.

Treasure House – A tannery was established here at the beginning of the 18C. A century later, the house's owner discovered $7,000 in gold hidden in a wall.

Voorlezer House – Built at the end of the 17C, this building served as a church and schoolhouse (reputedly the oldest elementary school in the US), as well as a residence for the church clerk *(voorlezer)*.

Moravian Cemetery (BY) – This peaceful, gardenlike cemetery is affiliated with the Moravian church located at the entrance. Adorned with a columned portico, the white church was constructed in 1845 by the Vanderbilt family, one of whose ancestors belonged to the sect in the 17C. The original church, a Dutch Colonial-style structure erected in 1763, now serves as the cemetery office.

The Moravian denomination, founded in the 15C as an evangelical communion in Bohemia (Moravia), accepted Protestantism in the 17C. Ascetic in its beliefs, the church adhered to strict observance of the teachings of the Bible.

Conference House (AZ) – *7455 Hylan Blvd. From Staten Island ferry terminal, take S78 bus to Craig. Ave.; walk one block south to Satterlee, turn right and continue half a block. Open May–Dec Fri–Sun 1pm–4pm. $2. ☎ 718-984-6046. www.nycparks.org.* Situated at the southwestern tip of Staten Island, Conference House is named after the negotiations between the British and Americans (including John Adams and Benjamin Franklin) that took place here on September 11, 1776 in a futile attempt to end the emerging Revolutionary War. The 17C fieldstone manor house has been restored and now contains a historic museum. The interior, furnished with 18C pieces, interprets the life and times of Col. Christopher Billtop, the house's original owner. The waterfront site affords fine **views** across the river and the bay to New Jersey.

Kykuit, Hudson River Valley

Excursions

VISITING HUDSON RIVER VALLEY AND LONG ISLAND

Getting There

By Train – New Jersey Transit *(p 311)* and Amtrak provide access to many cities in the Hudson River Valley; both depart from Penn Station in Manhattan. Metro-North trains depart from Grand Central Terminal and make stops throughout the valley. Long Island Rail departs from Penn Station.

General Information

Visitor Information – Contact the following agencies to obtain maps and information on accommodations, recreation and seasonal events: **Historic Hudson Valley** *(☎ 914-631-8200; www.hudsonvalley.org)*; **Hudson Valley Tourism** *(☎ 800-232-4782; www.travelhudsonvalley.org)*; **Long Island Convention & Visitors Bureau** *(☎ 631-951-3900 or 877-FUN-ONLI/ toll-free in US; www.licvb.com)*.

Accommodations – **Hotels** and **motels** can be found in Poughkeepsie, Newburgh, Rhinebeck and Tarrytown in the Hudson River Valley, and in Bay Shore or Montauk on Long Island. **Bed and Breakfasts** can also be found in Cold Spring, Warwick or Rhinebeck (Hudson River Valley) or Shelter Island and the Hamptons (Long Island). **Reservation services** for B&Bs include: American Country Collection *(1353 Union St., Schenectady NY 12308; ☎ 518-370-4948 or 800-810-4948; www.bandbreservations.com)* and A Reasonable Alternative *(117 Spring St., Port Jefferson NY 11777; ☎ 631-928-4034; www.areasonablealternative.com)*.

Camping – State parks *(www.nysparks.com)* that offer camping in the Hudson River Valley include: Harriman *(Bear Mountain; ☎ 845-786-2701)*, Fahnestock *(Carmel; ☎ 845-225-7207)* and Mills-Norrie *(Staatsburg; ☎ 845-889-4646)*. Long Island's state parks with camp sites include: Hither Hills *(Montauk; ☎ 631-668-2554)*, Heckscher *(East Islip; ☎ 631-581-2100)* and Wildwood *(Wading River; ☎ 631-929-4314)*. Camping is also available at many privately owned campgrounds in both areas.

Recreation

Cruises – Companies offering cruises on the lower section of the Hudson River include: **Great Hudson Sailing Center** *(sailboat cruises depart from Haverstraw Apr–Oct; 2hrs; ☎ 845-429-1557 or 800-237-1557; www.greathudsonsailing.com)* and **Hudson Highlands Cruises** *(cruises depart from West Haverstraw & West Point May–Oct; 1hr–3hrs; ☎ 845-534-7245; www.commanderboat.com)*. **Whale-watching cruises** depart from Montauk on Long Island July through August *(Viking Fleet; ☎ 631-668-5700; www.vikingfleet.com)*.

Hiking, Biking and Horseback Riding – Many trail systems lace the region, crossing through state and local parks, providing opportunities for all three activities. The **Rails-to-Trails Conservancy** *(☎ 202-331-9696; www.railstrails.org)* maintains several former railroad tracks throughout the Hudson River Valley that have been converted into paved and dirt paths for bikers and pedestrians. Contact the following organizations for maps and trail information: **New York-New Jersey Trail Conference** *(☎ 201-512-9348; www.nynjtc.org)* or **Long Island Greenbelt Trail Conference** *(☎ 631-360-0753; www.hike-li.com/ligtc)*. Bike rentals are available in many towns; contact the agencies listed under Visitor Information *(above)* for more information. **Horseback Riding** is a popular activity on Long Island; horses can be rented in most towns. Public riding stables can be found in Stanfordville and Peekskill in the Hudson River Valley.

Beaches – The beaches of Long Island offer an enchanting combination of wild sea grasses and sandy shores. The water is usually warm enough for swimming from July through September. State parks with public beaches include: **Heckscher** in East Islip *(☎ 631-581-2100)*; **Hither Hills** in Montauk *(☎ 631-668-2554)*; **Jones Beach** in Wantagh *(☎ 516-785-1600)*; **Orient Beach** in Orient *(☎ 631-323-2440)*, **Robert Moses** on Fire Island *(☎ 631-669-0449)*; **Sunken Meadow** in Kings Park *(☎ 631-269-4333)*; and **Wildwood** in Wading River *(☎ 631-929-4314)*.

HUDSON RIVER VALLEY★★★

Originating high in the Adirondacks, the Hudson River flows 315mi to the sea. Navigable as far as Albany, it was linked in 1825 to the Great Lakes by the Erie Canal, once a busy waterway between Albany and Buffalo. On its journey south to New York City, the majestic Hudson flows between rocky crags and wooded peaks, a romantic and even grandiose landscape. The river has often been celebrated in literature and art, especially by the painters of the Hudson River school, whose best-known representatives were Thomas Cole, Albert Bierstadt and Frederic Edwin Church.

DRIVING TOUR *Distance: approximately 180mi round-trip*

This trip covers only the southern part of the Hudson River Valley, which is best seen in the fall, when Indian summer gilds the forests lining the river banks. If you have only one day available, we recommend driving north on the east bank in the morning and returning on the west bank in the afternoon. Route 9, heading north, and Route 9 West, for the return, afford occasional views of the river.

East Bank

Leave Manhattan via Henry Hudson Pkwy., which turns into the Saw Mill River Pkwy. heading north. Take Exit 9/Executive Blvd. and continue to its end. Turn left on Broadway, then next right on Odell Ave. Follow Odell to the end and turn left on Warburton Ave. Continue south for 1.3mi.

Hudson River Museum – *511 Warburton Ave. in Yonkers. Open year-round Wed–Sun noon–5pm (May–Sept Fri until 9pm). Closed major holidays. $5.* ✗ ♿ ▣ ☎ *914-963-4550. www.hrm.org.* This combination historic house, art and history museum and planetarium offers a little something for everyone. Glenview, the stone mansion, was built on the banks of the Hudson for local financier John Trevor in 1876. Late Victorian in style, the house features Eastlake and Gothic Revival-style interiors, including several rooms that have been restored to depict the lifestyle of an upper-class 19C family. The modern wing, added in 1969, displays changing exhibits of art, history and science. Artist Red Grooms created the fanciful bookstore space in the new wing in 1979, a decided contrast to the Victorian interiors of the mansion.

In the **Andrus Planetarium**, shows on the planets are presented using the museum's Zeiss M¹015 star machine *(Fri until 7pm, free; weekends 1:30pm, 2:30pm & 3:30pm, $5).*

Past Yonkers, exit from Saw Mill River Pkwy. at Ashford Ave.–Dobbs Ferry. Follow Ashford Ave. west, then turn right on Broadway (Rte. 9). Beyond Irvington, turn left on W. Sunnyside Lane.

★**Sunnyside** – *W. Sunnyside Lane, off Rte. 9 in Tarrytown. Visit of house by guided tour (1hr) only, Apr–Oct Wed–Mon 10am–5pm. Nov–Dec Wed–Mon 10am–4pm. Mar weekends only 10am–4pm. Closed Jan–Feb, Thanksgiving Day & Dec 25. $9. Combination tickets are available for 2 or 3 houses (Sunnyside, Philipsburg and Van Cortlandt).* ▣ ☎ *914-591-8763. www.hudsonvalley.org.* Located on the east bank of the

Washington Irving's Sunnyside

The Castle at Tarrytown

*400 Benedict Ave.,
Tarrytown.* ☎ *914-631-
1980 or 800-616-4487.
www.castleonthehudson.
com.* Resembling a medieval
castle—with towers and
arched windows—this
mansion sits on a hilltop
overlooking the Hudson
River 25mi north of New
York City. Inside, stained-
glass windows, Oriental rugs
and period tapestries soften
beamed ceilings and stone
walls. Hand-carved four-
poster beds draped in
goose-down comforters, and
custom-made chandeliers
decorate the 31 rooms. Be
sure to have dinner at **Equus**
in the historic Oak Room,
where you'll sup on
memorable dishes such as
seared turbot with fricassee
of baby artichokes, and
roasted veal loin with baby
swiss chard, wild mushroom
strudel and shallot sauce.

Hudson River, Sunnyside was the home of
author-humorist and scholar
Washington Irving (1783-1859), who purchased the cottage in 1835. Author of
*Diedrich Knickerbocker's History of New
York* and chronicler of Rip van Winkle and
Sleepy Hollow, Irving lived here intermit-
tently for the last 25 years of his life, transforming the original stone cottage into what
he called his "snuggery," a picturesque blend
of Dutch, Scottish and Spanish elements. A
historic house museum since 1947, the
home displays furniture and family belongings. Of particular importance is the library,
appointed largely as Irving left it.

Landscaped in the romantic style favored
during the mid-19C, the surrounding 20-
acre grounds offer good views of the Hudson River.

Continue north on Rte. 9.

★**Lyndhurst** – *On Rte. 9 in Tarrytown. Open
mid-Apr–Oct Tue–Sun 10am–5pm. Rest of
the year weekends 10am–4pm. Closed
Jan 1, Thanksgiving Day & Dec 25. $10.
Guided tours available.* ✗ *(in summer)* ▯
☎ *914-631-4481. www.lyndhurst.org.*
Perched on a wooded bluff above the Hudson River is the picturesque Lyndhurst
mansion, resembling from the distance a
baronial castle on the Rhine. Originally a
two-story villa designed in 1838 by Alexan-
der Jackson Davis for William Paulding, a former mayor of New York City, the house
was enlarged by Davis for the subsequent owner, George Merritt, in 1865. In 1880
financier and railroad tycoon Jay Gould acquired the 67-acre estate and its mansion. Lyndhurst remained in the family until the death of Gould's daughter, the
Duchess of Talleyrand-Périgord, in 1961. The house is an outstanding expression
of the Gothic Revival style applied to domestic architecture. A profusion of peaks,
pinnacles, porches and turrets embellishes the exterior, accenting the mansion's irregular shape. In the interior the Gothic mood dominates, exemplified by ribbed
and vaulted ceilings, pointed arches, stained-glass windows and imposing Gothic
furnishings. In the dining room, note the simulated marble colonnettes and leather
wall coverings popular in the 19C. Many other examples of marbleization and simulated masonry can be found throughout the house. A stroll or drive around the
grounds affords striking views of the mansion and its park-like 19C landscaping.

Continue north on Rte. 9 to Sleepy Hollow (formerly North Tarrytown).

★**Philipsburg Manor** – *On Rte. 9 in Sleepy Hollow. Visit of house by guided tour
(1hr) only, Apr–Oct Wed–Mon 10am–5pm. Nov–Dec Wed–Mon 10am–4pm. Mar
weekends only 10am–4pm. Closed Jan–Feb, Thanksgiving Day, & Dec 25. $9.
Combination tickets are available for 2 or 3 houses (Sunnyside, Philipsburg and
Van Cortlandt).* ✗ ▯ ☎ *914-631-3992. www.hudsonvalley.org.* The site conveys
a sense of the manor system under which much of the Hudson River Valley was
settled. At its zenith, the powerful Philips family controlled 52,000 acres of land
along the river by royal charter. The family erected a stone manor by the Pocantico
River to function largely as a business office and a grist mill to grind the grains
that tenant farmers brought as payment of their rent. Their three mills formed the
basis of the successful trading network and shipping business that helped make
them the richest family in the colonies. Today a working mill has been reconstructed on the site, and the house has been furnished with the help of a 1750
probate inventory. A barn and tenant farmhouse add to the ambience of the manor.

★★**Kykuit** – *On Rte. 9 North. Tours depart from Philipsburg Manor Visitor Center.
Visit by guided tour (2hrs) only, May–Oct Wed–Mon 9am–4pm. Closed Nov–Apr.
$22. Reservations suggested.* ✗ ♿ ▯ ☎ *914-631-8200, ext. 619. www.hudson-
valley.org.* One of the last grand homes to be built in the Hudson River Valley,
Kykuit (Dutch for "lookout," pronounced Kye-cut) offers a glimpse into the lives
of four generations of Rockefellers. Built between 1906 and 1913 by **John D.
Rockefeller Jr.**, for his father, patriarch of Standard Oil, the estate suffered from
several shortcomings; a major redesign included the addition of the present-day
Beaux-Arts facade. The new plan better complemented the interior spaces, which
represent fine examples of the Neoclassical style typical of English country homes
(note especially the decorative plasterwork).

Philipsburg Manor

Today, furnishings and room arrangements date to the residency of New York state governor **Nelson Rockefeller** and his wife, Happy, who moved into the house (formerly inhabited by Nelson's parents, Junior and Abby) in 1963. By then the house brimmed with antique furniture, lovely Chinese porcelain of the Han, Tang and Ming dynasties, an assortment of china services and Nelson's burgeoning modern **art collection★**. He acquired his love of contemporary art, particularly sculpture, from his mother Abby Aldrich Rockefeller, a founder of the Museum of Modern Art in New York. His basement art galleries contain many treasures, including one-of-a-kind tapestries by Picasso.

The **gardens★** and terraces of Kykuit, designed in the orderly, Beaux-Arts fashion by William Welles Bosworth (who also redesigned the facade), take their inspiration from Italian hilltop gardens. Nelson's careful siting of more than 70 modern sculptures around the grounds only enhances the beauty of the landscaping. Lovely **views★** across the Hudson, particularly from the west porch, blend with gardens and art to form breathtaking vistas and painterly tableaux.

Located just north of Kykuit on Bedford Road *(Rte. 448)* is the lovely **Union Church of Pocantico Hills★**, a nondenominational Protestant church erected on Rockefeller lands in 1921 *(open Apr–Dec Mon & Wed–Fri 11am–5pm, Sat 10am–5pm, Sun 2pm–5pm; closed Jan–Mar, Thanksgiving Day & Dec 25; $4;* ⬥ 🅿 ☎ *914-332-6659; www.hudsonvalley.org).* Its primary attraction is the **stained-glass windows★** designed by Henri Matisse and Marc Chagall and commissioned by the Rockefellers. The Matisse rose window, completed two days before the artist's death, glows with shades of clear blue, bright yellow and deep green. Chagall designed the eight side panels, representing Old Testament themes, as well as the large window at the rear of the church. It is the only such assemblage created by Chagall in the US.

■ Lords of the Manor

In 1629, to encourage the settlement of New Netherland with private rather than company money, the Dutch West India Company granted estates, each measuring 16mi along the river, to its shareholders. Called "patroons" (patrons), these landholders agreed to send 50 tenant farmers within four years to cultivate the land. Unique in America, this feudal system worked poorly as the absentee patroons mismanaged their estates and attracted few settlers. Even so, when the English took over in 1664, they converted the patroonships into manors and continued to grant lands up and down the river to wealthy families. As freehold lands grew scarcer, more farmers began to settle as tenants on the manors of such families as the Van Rensselaers, Beekmans and Livingstons, who formed the upper crust of the valley's "nobility." Violent tenant uprisings led to a new state constitution in 1846 outlawing "feudal tenures." Soon, however, new generations of American aristocracy— Vanderbilts, Goulds and Rockefellers among them— would flock to the river's edge to build their mansions amid those of the venerable families of the Hudson Valley. Today a remarkable concentration of historic homes and properties remains the lingering legacy of this centuries-old Dutch settlement pattern.

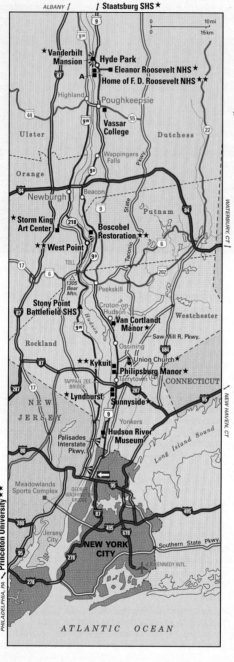

Return to Rte. 9 and con
tinue northward, passin
through Ossining, site c
the Ossining Correction
Facility, formerly known a
"Sing Sing" prison. Tak
the Croton Point Ave. exi
Turn right, then right agai
on South Riverside Ave.

★**Van Cortlandt Manor** –
Off Rte. 9 on S. Riversic
Ave., in Croton-on-Hudsor
Visit of house by guide
tour (1hr) only, Apr–Oc
Wed–Mon 10am–5pm
Nov–Dec weekends on
10am–4pm.   Close
Jan–Mar, Thanksgivin
Day & Dec 25. $9. Comb.
nation tickets are availabl
(Sunnyside, Philipsbur
and Van Cortlandt).   [
☎   914-271-8981
www.hudsonvalley.org
Another of the great Huc
son Valley mansions an
home to the Van Cortlanc
family for 260 years, th
house has been restored t
its appearance during th
tenure of Pierre Van Cort
landt, patriot and the firs
lieutenant-governor of Nev
York State who presidec
over 86,000 acres. Legenc
has it that such notabl
personalities as Benjamir
Franklin, the Marquis d
Lafayette,   Count   d
Rochambeau and John Ja
visited the manor.
The house contains origina
family furnishings, paint
ings and pewter. Don'
miss the large kitchen, re
plete with its origina
hearth, Dutch oven an
cooking utensils. Locatec
on the property, fields, gar
dens and the ferry house
and kitchen evoke 18C life
in the Hudson Valley.

Continue on Rte. 9 North t
Peekskill, then bear lef
onto Rte. 6/202 West; a
Bear Mountain Bridge fo
low Rte. 9D North.

This drive offers beautifu
views of the river and the New Jersey Palisades as the road dips into the valley
and then rises into the hills.

★★**Boscobel Restoration** – On Rte. 9D, 4mi north of junction with Rte. 403. Visi
by guided tour (45min) only, Apr–Oct Wed–Mon 9:30am–5pm. Nov–Dec
Wed–Mon 9:30am–4pm. Closed Jan–Mar, Thanksgiving Day & Dec 25. $10. [
☎ 845-265-3638. www.boscobel.org. Set back from the road and overlookinc
the Hudson River, Boscobel, a handsome example of Federal domestic architecture, was conceived by States Morris Dyckman (1755-1806) in 1804 and
completed after his death by his wife, Elizabeth.
In the 1950s the property on which Boscobel originally stood was sold and the
mansion was almost destroyed. Preservationists acquired the building and moved
it piece by piece to Garrison, where it was reconstructed on grounds high above
the Hudson. Rebuilt and refurbished, Boscobel opened to the public in 1961.

The overall appearance is one of Federal elegance and refinement. The recessed central portion of the facade, with its slender columns and carved trim, contrasts with the otherwise unadorned exterior. The restored interior features graceful arches, fireplaces embellished with classical motifs, delicately carved woodwork and a freestanding central staircase lit by a tall Palladian window. Furnishings include many pieces by leading New York craftsman Duncan Phyfe. A gallery in the basement thoroughly explains the essence of the Federal style.

Follow Rte. 9D North to Rte. 9 North and continue to Poughkeepsie. Head east on Rte. 44/55, then turn right onto Raymond Ave. (Rte. 376).

Vassar College – *Raymond Ave. in Poughkeepsie.* ☏ *845-437-7000. www.vassar.edu.* Vassar is one of the best-known private liberal arts colleges in the US. Founded as a women's college in 1861, it became coeducational in 1969 and now has 2,500 students, 48 percent of whom are men. The buildings reflect traditional American and European styles, as well as modern trends in architecture: notice Ferry House (Marcel Breuer) and Noyes House (Eero Saarinen), dormitories erected in 1951 and 1958, respectively. The library, expanded in 1976, houses 700,000 volumes.

Marc Chagall's *The Good Samaritan* window at Union Church

© Scott Barrow

Return to Rte. 9 and continue north.

Before entering the village of Hyde Park, note, on the left, the 150-acre campus of the **Culinary Institute of America (A)**, an educational institution that prepares men and women for careers in the food service industries.

Hyde Park – *Located 6mi north of Poughkeepsie on Rte. 9.* Once a resort for wealthy New York families, Hyde Park gained renown during Franklin D. Roosevelt's presidency as the location of his "summer White House."

★★**Home of Franklin D. Roosevelt National Historic Site** – *On Rte. 9 in Hyde Park. Visit by guided tour (1hr) only year-round daily 9am–5pm. Grounds open 7am–sunset. Closed Jan 1, Thanksgiving Day & Dec 25. $14.* & 🅿 ☏ *845-229-9115. www.nps.gov/hofr.* Today a National Historic Site, the estate was acquired by

---

■ Culinary Institute of America

1946 Campus Dr., Hyde Park. ☏ *845-471-6608. www.ciachef.edu. Reservations required.* On the premises of a former Jesuit seminary reside the four restaurants of The Culinary Institute of America (CIA). Here, 2,100 chefs-in-training gain practical experience in preparation, cooking and serving under the watchful tutelage of CIA's world-renowned faculty. Each of the restaurants offers a different—and excellent—dining experience. Here you'll find the food and atmosphere are outstanding, and the students friendly and earnest. **St. Andrew's Café** *(Mon–Fri)* serves contemporary fare emphasizing fresh seasonal ingredients; **American Bounty** *(Tue–Sat)* focuses on the bounty of the Hudson River Valley; the elegant **Escoffier** *(Tue–Sat)* will please the Francophile with its light take on classic French cuisine; and **Ristorante Caterina de Medici** *(Mon–Fri)* serves authentic regional Italian dishes. The casual **Apple Pie Bakery Café** *(Mon–Fri 8am–6:30pm),* opened in 2000, offers soups, salads, sandwiches, artisanal breads and pastries (eat-in or take-out) prepared by CIA's baking and pastry arts majors. *All CIA restaurants, except the Bakery Café, are open for lunch and dinner. Dress is "country club casual"—no jeans or sneakers.*

President and Mrs. Franklin D. Roosevelt (1941)

Franklin Delano Roosevelt's father in 1867; FDR was born here in 1882. The mansion, Springwood, dates back to the early 19C but has since been remodeled and enlarged, and more recently, refurbished. Springwood is unique among historic homes for the exceedingly personal experience it offers. Memorabilia of the late president (1882-1945) and his family can be found in the house, library and museum. Exhibits trace the transformation of a "charming New York socialite into one of America's great statesmen." One gallery is devoted entirely to FDR's wife, Eleanor, a prominent international figure in her own right. Also on the grounds, FDR's 1938 retreat, Top Cottage, is now open for tours *(depart from FDR Home; May–Oct, Thu–Sun).*

In the rose garden, a simple monument of white Vermont marble marks the final resting place of Franklin and Eleanor Roosevelt.

★ **Eleanor Roosevelt National Historic Site** – *Rte. 9G. Visit by guided tour (35min) only, May–Oct daily 9am–5pm. Rest of the year Thu–Mon 9am–4:30pm. Closed Jan 1, Thanksgiving Day & Dec 25. $8.* & ☐ ☎ *845-229-9422. www.nps.gov/elro.* The Roosevelts often came to this tranquil corner of the estate on the Fall Kill for family outings and picnics. FDR built a stone cottage on the property in 1925, and a year later a factory workshop was erected to house an experimental business operated by Eleanor Roosevelt (1884-1962) and her friends. After the business folded in the mid-1930s, the building was remodeled and eventually became Eleanor's beloved Val-Kill cottage, named for the stream that flowed close by. Mrs. Roosevelt considered Val-Kill her only true home, and after the president's death, she chose to spend her remaining years there working, entertaining her friends and receiving foreign dignitaries.

★ **Vanderbilt Mansion** – *On Rte. 9, 2mi north of FDR National Historic Site. Visit by guided tour (45min) only, year-round daily 9am–5pm. Closed Jan 1, Thanksgiving Day & Dec 25. $8.* & ☐ ☎ *845-229-9115. www.nps.gov/vama.* Located just north of the FDR mansion, this sumptuous Beaux-Arts residence was erected by McKim, Mead and White between 1896 and 1898 for Frederick W. Vanderbilt and his wife, Louise. Now a National Historic Site, it bears witness to a bygone age of opulence. Before the Vanderbilts bought the property in the early 19C, it belonged

● **The Beekman Arms & Delamater Inn**
6387 Mill St., off Rte. 9 in the Village of Rhinebeck. ☎ *845-876-7077 (Beekman Arms) or* ☎ *845-896-7080 (Delamater Inn). www.beekman-delamaterinn.com.* Wide plank floors, an inviting stone fireplace, and the Tap Room (with its full-service bar) recall the days when the inn welcomed travelers on horseback along the King's Highway (Route 9). Today the 1766 inn, which once hosted George Washington and Alexander Hamilton, offers 63 rooms—all with the contemporary conveniences of private baths, air conditioning and telephones with dataports.

Take some time to prowl through the **Beekman Arms Antique Market** (just behind the inn), featuring 30 dealers whose wares run the gamut from pimitive furniture to estate jewelry and antique prints. Then sit down for dinner at the inn's **Traphagen Restaurant**, where updated comfort food (grilled Smithfield pork tenderloin, slow-roasted Long Island duckling, turkey pot pie) will satisfy your appetite.

One block north of the Beekman Arms, its sister property, the 1844 **Delamater Inn**, typifies the American Carpenter Gothic style. Seven different buildings here—some old, some new—harbor an additional 40 rooms. All accommodations come with refrigerators, and more than half have working fireplaces.

to famed botanist Dr. David Hosack. He and other earlier owners of the estate were exceedingly interested in landscaping; as a result, the grounds represent one of the greatest intact surviving examples of the Romantic style of landscape architecture in the US. The lavish interior contains art and furniture befitting America's "nobility" and ranging from Renaissance to rococo in style.

Walking trails along the river, below the mansion, afford scenic **views** to the north and south.

Continue north on Rte. 9 through Rhinebeck to Staatsburg.

★**Staatsburgh State Historic Site** – *Off Rte. 9 on Old Post Rd., in Staatsburg. Visit by guided tour (1hr) only, Apr–Labor Day Tue–Sat 10am–5pm, Sun noon–5pm. Labor Day–Oct Tue–Sun noon–5pm. $5. ▣ ☎ 845-889-8851. www.nysparks.com.* Built on land that had been in **Ruth Livingston Mills'** family since 1792, this 79-room Beaux-Arts mansion engulfs a Greek Revival home constructed in 1832. Improvements were made by Ogden and Ruth Mills, who inherited the property in 1890 and selected architects McKim, Mead and White to transform the home into a "palace royale" for autumn and winter entertaining. They added the two side wings along with the decorative embellishments popular at the time. Part English baronial hall (note the heavily wooded entryway), part French palace (the Louis XVI **dining room** rivals any in the Hudson River Valley for its scale, luster and view), the home boasted 14 bathrooms and other accommodations, indoors and out, for weekend visitors. Indeed, its lavish public and guest areas overwhelm the private family rooms, emphasizing the mansion's primary purpose. Mrs. Mills' furnishings remain in situ, and her personal touches demonstrate pride in her colonial and Revolutionary War heritage as a member of the ubiquitous Livingston family. She considered herself heiress, as well, to Mrs. Astor as queen of American society.

Hiking trails on the grounds offer rare access to the Hudson's edge, as the railroad runs slightly inland along this small stretch of river.

West Bank

Return to Poughkeepsie, cross the Hudson River and continue south on Rte. 9 West.

★**Storm King Art Center** – *Take Rte. 9 West to the Cornwall Hospital Exit, then bear left onto Rte. 107; at the intersection turn right and follow Rte. 32 North over the bridge, turning left immediately after the bridge onto Orr's Mill Rd. Open Apr–Oct daily 11am–5:30pm, late Oct–mid-Nov 11am–5pm. Closed mid-Nov–Mar. $9. ▣ ☎ 845-534-3115. www.skac.org.* This unique outdoor museum of contemporary sculpture covers 500 acres of meadow, hillsides, forest, lawns and terraces. Large-scale works by such artists as Alexander Calder *(The Arch)*, Mark diSuvero, Alexander Liberman *(Iliad)*, Henry Moore, Louise Nevelson, Isamu Noguchi *(Momo Taro)* and David Smith are installed on the grounds, most of them in settings that have been specially landscaped for the sculpture. Changing exhibits of paintings, graphics and smaller sculptures from the center's collection are presented in the Normandy-style museum building (1935), formerly a private residence.

★**West Point** – *10mi southeast of Storm King Art Center on Rte. 218 South. Guided tours (1hr) depart approximately every 45min from the visitor center Apr–Oct Mon–Sat & holidays 10am–3:30pm, Sun 11am–3:30pm. Rest of the year daily 11:15am & 1:15pm. No tours Jan 1, Thanksgiving Day, Dec 25, on football Saturdays or during Graduation week. $7. ♿ ▣ ☎ 845-446-4724. www.usma.edu.* Overlooking the Hudson River, West Point is renowned as the site of the United States Military Academy. Fortress West Point was established in 1778 as a series of fortifications to protect the strategically important Hudson at this most defensible location. After the war the grounds became a repository for trophies and captured equipment. It was not until 1802 that the US Military Academy, the oldest of the nation's service academies, was established by Congress, and West Point selected as its site. In the academy's first year, five officers trained and instructed the ten students; there are now more than 4,200 men and women cadets. Among its graduates West Point counts generals MacArthur (1903), Patton (1909), Eisenhower (1915) and Schwartzkopf (1956); and astronauts Borman (1950), Aldrin (1951), Collins (1952), White (1952) and Scott (1954).

The Buildings – In the **visitor center**, films and exhibits introduce visitors to the history and sights of West Point and the life of a cadet *(open year-round daily 9am–4:45pm; closed Jan 1, Thanksgiving Day & Dec 25; ☎ 845-938-2638; www.usma.edu).*

The chapels, monuments and museum are open to the public and include the **Cadet Chapel** *(visit by guided tour only)*, an example of the "military Gothic" style, built in 1910; 18C **Fort Putnam**★ *(open only for Saturday football games)*, partially restored in 1907 and completed in 1976; the **Battle Monument**, commemorating victims of the Civil War; and **Trophy Point**. Among the Revolutionary War relics at Trophy Point are links of the great chain that was strung across the Hudson River to prevent British ships from passing.

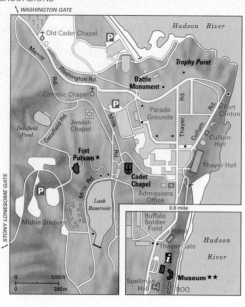

The **museum**★★ *(ope
year-round dail
10:30am–4:15pm
closed Jan 1, Thanks
giving Day & Dec 25
👤 �P 📞 845-938
3590)* thoroughly ex
amines the history o
the military, the acad
emy, warfare an
weapons using diora
mas, print materials an
artifacts, includin
Napoleon's sword an
Goering's jewel-en
crusted marshal's ba
ton. Its collection o
arms, which traces th
development of auto
matic weapons from th
Civil War to the present
began with ordnanc
captured at the Battle o
Saratoga in 1777.

The Parades – *These fa
mous reviews, know
for their precision of movement, are held from early September until November
and late April through May. For schedules:* 📞 *845-938-2638 or www.usma.edu*

Continuing south, Route 9 West passes **Bear Mountain**, the highest point (1,305ft
in Palisades Interstate Park.

Stony Point Battlefield State Historic Site – *Park Rd., off Rte. 9 West. Ope
Apr–Oct Mon–Sat 10am–4:30pm, Sun 11am–4:30pm. Rest of the year Mon–Fr
10am–4pm, weather permitting.* 👤 �P 📞 *845-786-2521
www.nysparks.state.ny.us.* The British wrested this rocky, strategic promontory
from the Americans in 1779, thereby gaining control of the entrance to the Hud
son Highlands and safeguarding Kings Ferry, which connected the east and wes
banks at this narrow stretch of river. Anxious to retrieve it, General "Mad Anthony
Wayne mounted a surprise attack on the point in July of that year, fording th
marshes below at midnight and overcoming the British in less than an hour. The
battle would be the last in the north and a tremendous morale-builder for Conti
nental troops. Now a state historic site, the rugged, windswept terrain is studded
with interpretive signs that describe the fighting and with picnic spots that afford
fine views over the Hudson. In the **museum** *(weekdays $2; on weekends the $5 park
ing fee includes museum admission)*, exhibits and a 12min video offer further de
tails of the battle. The oldest **lighthouse** on the Hudson River, built in 1826 on the
site of the central powder magazine, has been restored to working order with a
19C Fresnel lens *(visit by 30min guided tour only, Apr–Oct weekend
1:30pm–4:15pm; Wed & Thu 10am–4pm by appointment)*.

Continue the drive south on **Palisades Interstate Parkway**—offering superb **views**★★ o
Yonkers, the Bronx and Manhattan—to the George Washington Bridge, which leads
back to Manhattan.

LONG ISLAND★★

Covering an area of 1,723sq mi, Long Island has a population of approximately 6,878,000 and measures 125mi long and 20mi at its widest point. Although Long Island is often misleadingly said to include only Nassau and Suffolk counties, it actually comprises four counties: the other two are Queens (Queens County) and Brooklyn (Kings County), boroughs of New York City.

Owing to its proximity to New York City, the western part of the island has developed into a suburban area while the eastern part has remained more rural. The North Shore became known as the "Gold Coast" as wealthy landowners from the city began building residences here. The South Shore, with its miles of white sandy beaches, developed into a vacation and resort spot for New Yorkers. Long Island includes numerous attractions: small quiet lanes, rustic villages, a countryside flecked with golf courses and tennis courts, wildlife refuges and palatial Gold Coast mansions.

The economy is quite diversified, encompassing light manufacturing, service industries and agriculture. Suffolk County is the largest producer of agricultural products in the state of New York, and a number of farms are engaged in truck farming (fruits and vegetables) and dairy and livestock farming. Ducklings and potatoes are noted area products. Enjoying an ever-increasing reputation for fine merlots and chardonnays, Long Island **wineries** cover hundreds of acres on the North and South forks. Seafood is particularly abundant on the eastern end of the island: oysters, clams, scallops and lobsters have a well-deserved reputation. Commercial and chartered deep-sea fishing boats leave daily from South Shore communities and Montauk Point.

NORTH SHORE

Facing Long Island Sound, the North Shore features rocky necks and beaches, thick woodlands, hilly coves, bays, inlets and steep bluffs; the northern peninsula, extending 25mi, culminates at Orient Point. *Attractions are presented west to east.*

★**Sands Point Preserve** – *95 Middleneck Rd., Port Washington. Grounds open year-round Tue–Sun 10am–5pm. $6 ($2 May–Oct).* 🅿 ☎ *516-571-7900. www.co.nassau.ny.us/parkmuse.html.* This former Gold Coast estate, purchased by railroad tycoon Jay Gould in 1900, features two grandiose mansions, reflecting the styles and aspirations of New York society during the Gilded Age. **Castlegould**, originally planned as stables and servants' quarters, houses an information center and rotating exhibits. The Tudor-style main residence,

Hempstead House – *Visit by guided tour only May–Oct Wed–Sun noon–3pm.* Built in 1912, Castlegould's main residence was sold by Gould to Daniel Guggenheim in 1917. The US Navy operated a naval training center here from 1946 to 1967. Today the massive granite Tudor-style mansion contains an impressive collection of 18C and 19C **Wedgewood china**.

★**Falaise** – *Visit by guided tour (1hr) only, May–Oct Wed–Sun noon–3pm.* Precariously perched on a cliff (*falaise* in French), this Normandy-style manor house (1923) was erected by Capt. Harry F. Guggenheim, son of Daniel. A courtyard leads to the mansion, embellished with a wonderful collection of 16C and 17C French and Spanish artifacts. An arcaded loggia at the rear of the house overlooks the sound, affording spectacular **views**★★.

Nassau County Museum of Art (M) – *In Roslyn Harbor. Take Rte. 25A East, cross the Roslyn Viaduct and turn left on Museum Dr. Open year-round Tue–Sun 11am–5pm. Closed major holidays. $6. Guided tours available Tue–Thu & Sun at 2pm.* ✗ 🅿 ☎ *516-484-9338. www.nassaumuseum.com.* The museum is headquartered on the grounds of a late-19C estate built for Lloyd Bryce, the paymaster-general of New York, and acquired in 1919 by Childs Frick, the son of Henry Clay Frick. Changing art exhibits covering all periods are presented in the elegant Georgian Revival mansion, which has been converted into eight galleries. The attractively landscaped lawns, ponds and gardens, covering 145 acres, offer an ideal outdoor setting for various sculpture shows. Also on the grounds is the Tee Ridder Miniatures Museum, opened in 1995.

Oyster Bay – Renowned as a vacation spot and for its sheltered pleasure-craft harbor, this picturesque town offers historic landmarks, quaint shops and tree-shaded streets lined with Victorian and Colonial homes. Oyster Bay's most famous resident was **Theodore Roosevelt**, who spent some 20 years at Sagamore Hill; his grave **(A)** is located in Young's Cemetery.

★★**Planting Fields** – *Planting Fields Rd., Oyster Bay. Grounds open year-round daily 9am–5pm. Closed Dec 25. $6/car.* ♿ 🅿 ☎ *516-922-9200. www.plantingfields.com.* Formerly the private estate of the financier William Robertson Coe, the 409 acres of planting fields contain 160 acres that have been developed as an arboretum; the remaining land has been kept as a natural habitat. The plant collections include more than 600 rhododendron and azalea species (*in bloom May–June*); the Synoptic Garden, comprising approximately five acres of selected ornamental shrubs for Long Island gardens; the camelia collection, the oldest and largest of its kind under glass *(blooming period: Feb–Mar);* and greenhouses filled with orchids, hibiscus, begonias and cacti. Amid these landscaped gardens and spacious lawns stands **Coe Hall**, a fine example of the Tudor Revival style *(visit by 1hr guided tour only, Apr–Sept daily noon–3:30pm; closed Dec 25; $5;* P ☎ *516-922-9210).*

★**Sagamore Hill National Historic Site** – Kids *Cove Neck Rd. Visit of mansion by guided tour (45min) only, late May–Labor Day daily 9am–5pm. Rest of the year Wed–Sun 9am–5pm. Closed major holidays. $5.* P ☎ *516-922-4447. www.nps.gov/sahi.* Located east of the village of Oyster Bay, this gracious mansion (1885) is maintained as it was during Theodore Roosevelt's presidency (1901-09), housing more than 90 percent of the family's original furnishings. Guided tours through the 23-room Queen Anne structure offer humorous anecdotes on Teddy's life and presidential pursuits. Of special interest is the library, which Roosevelt used as an office and study; note the rhinoceros-foot inkstand—a trophy of his hunting days—and the bronze *Paleolithic Man* by Frederic Remington. After the tour, take a seat on the wide piazza and enjoy sweeping views of the grounds. In the **Old Orchard Museum**, exhibits and a 20min biographical film trace Roosevelt's public and private life. The Georgian-style mansion (1938) was built by Theodore Roosevelt Jr.

Raynham Hall Museum – *20 W. Main St. Open Jul–Labor Day Tue–Sun noon–5pm. Rest of the year Tue–Sun 1pm–5pm. Closed Jan 1, Thanksgiving Day & Dec 25. $3.* ☎ *516-922-6808. www.raynhamhallmuseum.org.* This old farmhouse played an important role during the American Revolution. It was the home of Samuel Townsend, whose son, Robert, was Washington's chief intelligence agent in New York City. The interior contains period furniture and memorabilia dating from the 1770s through the 1870s.

Cold Spring Harbor – From 1836 to 1862 the Cold Spring Harbor whaling fleet of nine ships sailed to every navigable ocean in search of whale oil and bone. The commanders of these vessels came from established whaling centers such as New Bedford and Sag Harbor.

★**Whaling Museum** – Kids *On Main St. (Rte. 25A). Open Memorial Day–Labor Day daily 11am–5pm; rest of the year Tue–Sun 11am–5pm. $3.* ♿ ☎ *631-367-3418. www.cshwhalingmuseum.org.* Dedicated to the preservation of the town's history as a whaling port, this museum features several outstanding exhibits, including a fully equipped 19C whaleboat, looking just as it did aboard the whaling brig *Daisy* on the vessel's 1912 voyage. Located nearby, the detailed diorama of Cold Spring Harbor represents village houses, whaling company buildings and wharves as they appeared in the 1850s, the heyday of the whaling industry. Other permanent

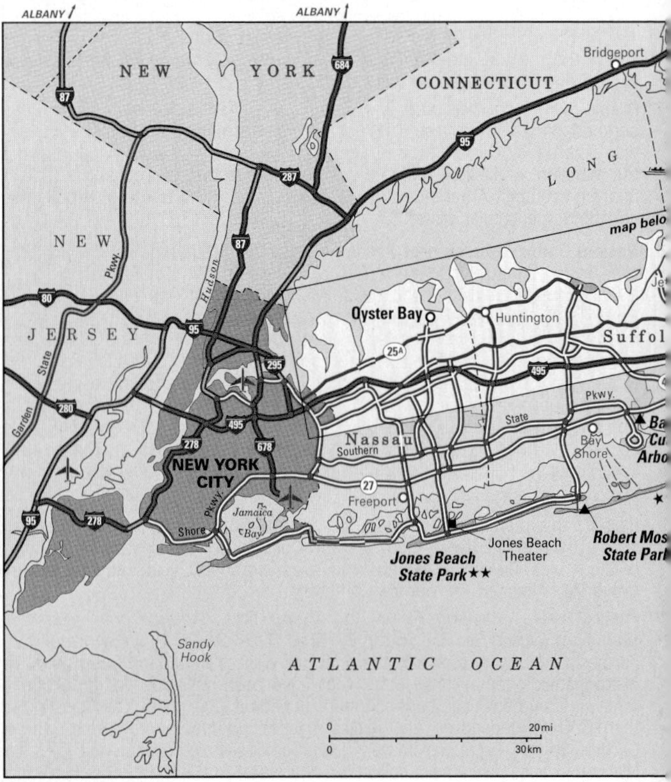

exhibits chronicle Long Island's illustrious whaling history and allow visitors to listen to the sounds of the humpback whale and marvel at the size of an orca (or killer whale) skull. Dispersed throughout the museum are examples of whalecraft: harpoons, navigational instruments and whaling-ship models. Note especially the extensive collection of scrimshaw (carvings of ivory tusks or whale jawbones and teeth), the whaler's folk art.

★**Vanderbilt Museum** – 🧒 *Little Neck Rd., Centerport. Visit of house by guided tour (1hr) only, year-round daily noon–4pm. Closed Jan 1, Thanksgiving Day & Dec 25. $8. Grounds only, $5.* 🅿 ☎ *631-854-5579. www.vanderbiltmuseum.org.* Overlooking Northport Harbor, this 43-acre estate comprises the Vanderbilt Mansion, a marine museum and a planetarium. The grandiose Spanish Revival main structure belonged to William K. Vanderbilt Jr., great-grandson of the Commodore. The 24-room mansion features original family furnishings as well as natural history collections on view in the house's Habitat Wing. The elaborately carved marble and woodwork is especially beautiful.

Also on the grounds is the **Marine Museum**, a showcase for artifacts gathered by William during his travels, including ship models, arms and weaponry, and birds. The **Vanderbilt Planetarium** presents a variety of shows throughout the year *(for schedule: ☎ 631-854-5555).*

★**Sunken Meadow State Park** – *Open year-round daily dawn–dusk.* 🍴 ♿ 🅿 *($5)* ☎ *631-269-4333. www.nysparks.com.* Bordering Long Island Sound, this park offers a wide range of recreational activities, including golfing (27 holes), swimming, nature trails and bike paths. Sunken Meadow refers to the large, fine-sand beach lining the sound.

★★**Stony Brook** – A typical Federal-style village of 18C and 19C America, Stony Brook contains a number of reconstructed buildings in a charming rural setting. Situated within this idyllic hamlet is the **Long Island Museum of American Art, History and Carriages**★★ 🧒, a complex founded in the 1930s that comprises history, art and carriage museums as well as several period buildings, including a blacksmith shop, schoolhouse and barn *(open year-round Wed–Sat 10am–5pm, Sun noon–5pm; closed major holidays; $5;* ♿ ☎ *631-751-0066; www.longislandmuseum.org).*

History Museum – Housed in a renovated 19C lumber mill, the visitor center offers changing exhibits drawn from the museum's collections and those of other institutions. Displays focus on American life from the 18C to the 1900s. There is also a permanent display of antique wildfowl decoys and a gallery of **miniature period rooms** (1in to 1ft scale) depicting interiors from the colonial period to the 1930s.

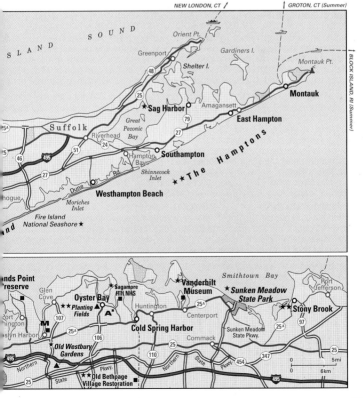

■ Clamming

No visit to Long Island is complete without a stop at a dockside clam shack to sample the region's famous seafood. Clams come in several varieties traditionally prepared in different ways. **Steamers**, with a long neck and thin shell, are served steamed with broth and melted butter. Hard-shelled **littlenecks** and **cherrystones** are types of tender young quahogs (KOE-hogs), typically eaten raw, on the half shell, with lemon and a dab of cocktail sauce. Mature quahogs, which can be fist-sized, are reserved for chowder. If you know the difference between Manhattan (tomato-based) and New England (milk-based) **chowder**, no one will peg you for a tourist.

Carriage Museum – An exceptional collection of some 250 horse-drawn carriages is presented in thematic displays tracing the history of horse-drawn vehicles. Centerpiece of the two-story gallery space is the c.1880 "Grace Darling" omnibus, decorated with carefully conserved landscape paintings. On the upper level, galleries showcase ornate European vehicles from the 18C and 19C, as well as early American gigs, coaches and wagons. The lower level features American coachman-driven carriages; pleasure vehicles; sporting rigs; trade vehicles, including hay, milk, grocery, tea and mail wagons; sleighs; children's vehicles (pulled by goats and dogs); and gaily painted 19C American gypsy wagons. Among the highlights of the horse-drawn fire-fighting equipment also featured is an elegant silver-plated hose carriage made in 1875.

Art Museum – The **paintings and drawings** of **William Sidney Mount** (1807-68) and other 19C and 20C artists are presented in changing exhibits. Mount settled at Stony Brook, where he painted anecdotal records of his rural surroundings. Among the works owned by the museum, the best-known include *Farmer Whetting His Scythe*, *Dancing on the Barn Floor* and *The Banjo Players*.

SOUTH SHORE

Long Island's famed beaches dot this scenic shoreline, which fronts the Atlantic Ocean and also faces the Great South Bay. *Attractions are presented west to east.*

★★Jones Beach State Park – *Off Wantagh Pkwy., in Wantagh.* ☎ *516-785-1600. www.nysparks.com.* A series of sandy beaches, 6.5mi long, makes up this bathing resort, with its double exposure to the ocean and bay. Jones Beach includes the well-known **Jones Beach Theater**, a nautical stadium, heated pools, sports fields and play areas. The water tower, modeled after the bell tower of St. Mark's Church in Venice, rises above a freshwater well.

Bayard Cutting Arboretum – *Rte. 27A. Open year-round Tue–Sun 10am–dusk. Closed major holidays. $5/vehicle.* ✗ ♿ 🅿 ☎ *631-581-1002. www.nysparks.com.* Created in 1887 by William Cutting in accordance with plans by Frederick Law Olmsted, the arboretum covers 690 acres of woodlands and planted areas. Many of the specimens in the pinetum date back to the original plantings of fir, spruce, pine and other evergreens. Rhododendrons and azaleas *(in bloom May–June)* border the walks and drives; wildflowers add blazes of color throughout the park.

★Fire Island – Measuring 32mi long and .5mi to less than 200yds wide, the island boasts more than 1,400 acres of **National Seashore★**. The island, which has no roads for automobile traffic, emanates an air of relaxed informality. National Seashore programs at Watch Hill and Sailors Haven feature interpretive walks and special events. Facilities at both areas include a guarded swimming beach, snack bar and marina. Ferry service connects Patchogue, Sayville and Bay Shore to the Fire Island communities and the main developed areas of the National Seashore: Watch Hill and Sailors Haven. *Ferry to Watch Hill departs from Patchogue near train station May–late Sept daily. First part of Oct Fri–Sun only. 30min. $5.50.* ♿ 🅿 *Call for schedule: Davis Park Ferry Co.;* ☎ *631-475-1665. www.pagelinx.com/dpferry.*

★Robert Moses State Park – ☎ *631-669-0470. www.nysparks.com.* The western part of Fire Island is named for Robert Moses, the former superintendent of Long Island parks. Its dunes and sea grasses provide refuge for myriad waterfowl. The Atlantic coast is excellent for surf casting, a method of fishing in which bait is tossed into the ocean at a site where waves break on the beach.

★★The Hamptons – *www.thehamptons.com.* Dominating a 35mi stretch of Long Island's South Shore, the Hamptons comprise a chain of vacation colonies beginning at Westhampton Beach, which rims Shinnecock Bay, and ending at Amagansett. Once a summer playground for the rich, the Hamptons continue to attract hordes of tourists to their picture-perfect downtowns, exclusive boutiques and first-rate restaurants.

Westhampton Beach – Formerly a seafaring community, Westhampton is a lively resort where New Yorkers—among them musicians, writers and artists—like to spend their weekends or take up summer residence. The annual Westhampton Beach Outdoor Art Show takes place in early August.

A drive along Dune Road, on the narrow barrier beach, leads past numerous houses exemplifying a variety of styles, from the New England home—brown-shingled and trimmed with white—to the bungalow. A 15mi-long beach extends from Moriches

Inlet to Shinnecock Inlet. *Note: sections of Dune Rd. are extremely narrow and may be impassable following a storm.*

★**Southampton** – *Self-guided walking-tour brochures are available from the Chamber of Commerce (76 Main St.; ☎ 631-283-0402; www.southamptonchamber.com).* This famous resort is the largest of the Hampton communities and the home of superb estates. On Jobs Lane, the **Parrish Art Museum** focuses on American art of the 19C and 20C, with major holdings of works by William Merrit Chase and Fairfield Porter. Changing exhibits and selections from the permanent collection are presented *(25 Jobs Lane; open mid-Jun–mid-Sept Mon–Sat 11am–5pm, Sun 1pm–5pm; rest of the year Mon, Thu–Sat 11am–5pm, Sun 1pm–5pm; closed major holidays; $5; & ☎ 631-283-2118; www.thehamptons.com).*

Coast Guard Lighthouse, Fire Island

© Scott Barrow

East Hampton – This town's quaint charm has long attracted writers and artists; indeed, several artists are buried here, including Childe Hassam, Jackson Pollock and Stuart Davis. **Main Street**, lined on both sides by magnificent elm trees, boasts several historic structures, including Mulford Farm and Clinton Academy. At the north end of the street sits Hook Mill, an 1806 windmill. The village green, featuring a central pond flanked by fine old houses, gives East Hampton the appearance of an English country town.

★**Sag Harbor** – *Tourist information: ☎ 631-725-0011 or www.sagharborchamber.com.* This charming sea town with its docks and deep-water harbor nestled in a sheltered cove was named port of entry for the US by George Washington. With its fine colonial homes and saltbox cottages, Sag Harbor still preserves the nostalgic flavor of yesteryear. Considered an outstanding example of the Egyptian Revival style of architecture, the **Whalers Presbyterian Church** was erected in 1918 on Union Street. Its original steeple (destroyed in 1938) rose to 185ft and could be seen miles away at sea. Stop by the **Custom House**, the first customhouse established in New York State *(Main & Garden Sts.; open July–Aug daily 10am–5pm, Jun & Sept weekends only 10am–5pm; $3; ☐ ☎ 631-692-4664).* Designed as a whaling captain's home, the Greek Revival **Sag Harbor Whaling and Historical Museum** on Main Street features exhibits relating to the town's whaling days *(open mid-May–Sept Mon–Sat & holidays 10am–5pm, Sun 1pm–5pm; Oct Sat 10am–5pm, Sun 1pm–4pm; $3; & ☎ 631-725-0770; www.sagharborwhalingmuseum.org).*

A short ferry ride from Sag Harbor lies peaceful **Shelter Island**, a wonderful spot for biking and hiking—nearly one-third of the island's 8,000 acres are owned by the Nature Conservancy.

Montauk – *Whale-watching cruises, p 288.* Located on the easternmost tip of Long Island and encompassing a 10mi strip of natural woodlands, stark cliffs, dunes and white beaches jutting into the ocean, Montauk is a favorite center for deep-sea fishing. Built in 1795, the Montauk Point Lighthouse, rising at the tip of the peninsula, is located in Montauk State Park.

ADDITIONAL SIGHTS

★★**Old Bethpage Village Restoration** – 🖼️ *1303 Round Swamp Rd. Open May–Oct Wed–Sun 10am–5pm. Nov–Dec & Mar–Apr Wed–Sun 10am–4pm. Closed Jan–Feb. $7. ☐ ☎ 516-572-8400. www.oldbethpage.org.* Nestled in a 200-acre valley, Old Bethpage is an active farm community that re-creates a pre-Civil War American village. More than 55 historic buildings reflecting the architectural heritage of Long Island have been moved to the site of the former Powell Farm. Take a leisurely stroll through the village to observe the weaver making cloth, the farm wife preparing a meal and farmers working their fields. Depending on the time of year, sheepshear-

Lobster Roll – 1980 *Montauk Hwy., Amagansett. Closed Nov–mid-Apr.* ☎ *631-267-3740.* Sand dunes surround this highway shanty on Long Island, midway between Amagansett and Montauk. Regulars, including Barbra Streisand, Kathleen Turner and Alec Baldwin, have taken to calling it "lunch" thanks to a neon sign above the outdoor patio. The restaurant's famous lobster rolls, deep-fried Atlantic cod, and crab cake platter make it more than just a roadside pit stop.

ing, cider making and other seasonal activities may also be viewed.

★**Old Westbury Gardens** – *71 Old Westbury Rd. Open mid-Apr–Oct Wed–Mon 10am–5pm (no entry after 4:15pm). Nov Sun 10am–5pm. Dec call for hrs. $10. Guided tours (30min) available.* ✗ 🅿 ☎ *516-333-0048. www.oldwestburygardens.org.* Occupying grounds formerly belonging to John S. Phipps, sportsman and financier, this 160-acre estate contains woods, meadows, lakes and formal gardens. The stately Charles II mansion has been preserved as it was during the family's occupancy in the early 20C. The interior features antique furnishings, paintings by Thomas Gainsborough and John Singer Sargent, gilded mirrors and objets d'art.

PRINCETON UNIVERSITY★★

Map p 303
Tourist Information ☎ 609-258-3000 or www.princeton.edu

Situated in the central part of New Jersey, in a charming residential town, Princeton University is one of the nation's prominent Ivy League schools. Despite the widespread development of office and research complexes in the area, the town of Princeton remains a desirable place to live.

Access – *110mi round-trip. A bus line connects Princeton to New York; information is available at the Port Authority Bus Terminal in Manhattan (42nd St. & Eighth Ave.; ☎ 212-564-8484). If you drive, leave Manhattan via the Lincoln Tunnel and take the New Jersey Turnpike south to Exit 9. Turn right and cross the Lawrence River, then take Rte. 1 toward Penns-Neck. Turn right at the sign for Princeton-Hightstown. Princeton can also be reached by train (New Jersey Transit) from Penn Station.*

Historical Notes

In 1746 a small group of Presbyterian ministers founded a college for the middle American colonies and named it the College of New Jersey. First established at Elizabeth, and then at Newark, it moved to the present site in 1756, after the completion of Nassau Hall. At that time, Nassau Hall was the largest educational building in North America and could accommodate the entire college. During the Revolution, the college served as barracks and hospitals, successively, for British and American troops. Its capture by General Washington on January 3, 1777, marked the end of the Battle of Princeton, a victory for the colonists. In 1783 the college housed the Continental Congress for six months, and the final treaty of peace was signed here. On its 150th anniversary, the College of New Jersey (already called Princeton College) became Princeton University. Since the 18C, Princeton has been noted for its teaching in political science and its programs of scientific research (the first chair of chemistry in the US was created here in 1795). Beginning with Woodrow Wilson's presidency of the university, from 1902 to 1910, Princeton has emphasized individual research and small seminars. An honor system prevails for examinations.
The university has a full-time faculty of about 680 and about 6,300 students; 42 percent of the undergraduates hold scholarships or receive special loans. Formerly all-male, Princeton became coeducational in 1969, and women now make up over one-third of the undergraduate population.
Known more for academics than for sports, Princeton nonetheless competes in 38 varsity sports. The 28,000-seat stadium (1998, Rafael Viñoly Architects) can accommodate football, soccer and lacrosse games as well as track-and-field events.

VISIT

Free guide service is offered by students year-round Mon–Sat 11am, 11:30am, 1:30pm & 3:30pm, Sun 1:30pm & 3:30pm. No tours during winter recess and holiday breaks. Information and maps are available at the Orange Key Guide Service at Frist Campus Center (☎ 609-258-1766).

The 135 buildings of the university are scattered over the 600-acre campus. The more important ones are described below.

★**Nassau Hall** – Named for the Nassau dynasty of Orange, which reigned in England at the time of the founding of the college, this majestic edifice now holds administrative offices. Around Nassau Hall stretches the shady green campus.

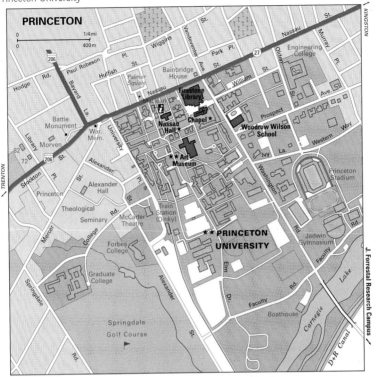

Harvey S. Firestone Library – Containing some five million volumes, the library also provides 850 individual carrels for students and lecture rooms for 12 disciplines.

★**Chapel** – This small chapel can accommodate a congregation of 2,000. Of note in the interior is a 16C wooden pulpit from the north of France.

★★**Art Museum** – *Open year-round Tue–Sat 10am–5pm. Sun 1pm–5pm. Closed major holidays. Guided tours (30min) available Sat 2pm.* ♿ ☎ *609-258-3788. www.princeton.edu.* The university's art museum is particularly strong in Italian and Northern Renaissance and Baroque paintings; prints, drawings and photographs, which are exhibited on a rotating basis; and Ancient, Far Eastern and pre-Columbian works, displayed on the lower level. Impressionist and 20C French paintings from the Henry and Rose Pearlman Foundation are on long-term loan to the museum.

Woodrow Wilson School – This noted school of public administration and international affairs was created in 1930.

James Forrestal Research Campus – Located to the east of Princeton proper, this campus was opened in 1951 for research in applied mathematics, physics and chemistry. It houses the Plasma Physics Laboratory, the university's center for fusion research.

On Campus

Grand Central Station

London

When a man is tired of London, he is tired of life;
for there is in London all that life can afford.

Dr Samuel Johnson 1777

The capital of the United Kingdom, once the capital of a worldwide empire, is composed of many villages fused into a vast conurbation, where tradition contrasts with cosmopolitan modernity. The city was founded on the country's major river; "every drop of the Thames is liquid history" from the old docks below the city to the greener reaches upstream.

Successive styles of architecture are represented in the churches and palaces, public buildings and private houses. Between Westminster and the City, the twin poles of government and commerce, are the major theatres and concert halls. The museums and art galleries display rich collections of treasures from all over the world. The parks and gardens and the extensive open acres of Hyde Park, Hampstead Heath and Richmond Park provide recreation and relaxation for all.

The pace of change, however, has quickened all over the capital. Exciting new attractions, innovative building and renovation projects and a vibrant scene in the worlds of art, fashion, music and cinema attest to a dynamic outlook to mark the third millennium. London also boasts restaurants and entertainment venues reflecting its multicultural population.

Practical
Information

Calendar of Events

Listed below is a selection of New York's many popular annual events; some dates may vary each year. For more information about events in New York City consult the periodicals listed on p 318 or contact the New York Convention & Visitors Bureau (☎ 212-484-1222 or 800-692-8474; www.nycvisit.com).

Date	Event/*Location/Web site*	☎
January–February		
Jan	**New York National Boat Show** *Jacob K. Javits Center* www.discoverboating.com	212-984-7000
mid–late Jan	**Winter Antiques Show** *7th Regiment Armory, 67th St. & Park Ave.* www.winterantiquesshow.com	718-292-7392
late Jan–Feb	**Chinese New Year Celebrations** *Chinatown;* www.chinatowninfo.com	212-625-9977
early Feb	**Empire State Building Run-Up** *350 Fifth Ave.;* www.nyrrc.org	212-860-4455
all Feb	**Black History Month** *various locations*	212-484-1222
mid-Feb	**Westminster Dog Show** *Madison Square Garden* www.westminsterkennelclub.org	212-465-6741
March–April		
early Mar	**Art Expo New York** *Jacob K. Javits Center*	888-322-5226
Mar 17	**St. Patrick's Day Parade** *Fifth Ave. from 44th to 86th Sts.*	718-793-1600
Mar–Apr	**Macy's Spring Flower Show** *Macy's*	212-494-4495
Mar–Jun	**Biennial Exhibit** *Whitney Museum of American Art*	212-570-3676
late Mar–Apr	**NY International Auto Show** *Jacob K. Javits Center* www.autoshowny.com	718-746-5300

Macy's Thanksgiving Day Parade

New York Convention & Visitors Bureau

	Ringling Bros. and Barnum & Bailey Circus *Madison Square Garden* *www.barnumandbailey.com*	800-755-4000
Easter Sunday	**Easter Sunday Parade** *Fifth Ave. between 49th & 57th Sts.*	
late Apr	**Cherry Blossom Festival** *Brooklyn Botanic Garden; www.bbg.org*	718-623-7333

May–June

May	**Spring Flower Exhibition** *NY Botanical Garden, Bronx* *www.nybg.org*	718-817-8700
mid–May	**Ninth Avenue International Food Festival** *Ninth Ave. from 37th to 57th Sts.* *www.9th-ave.com*	212-581-7029
late May	**Washington Square Outdoor Art Exhibit** *Greenwich Village*	212-982-6255
early Jun	**National Puerto Rican Day Parade** *Fifth Ave. from 44th to 86th Sts.* *www.nationalpuertoricandayparade.org*	718-401-0404
early Jun	**Roses, Roses, Roses** *NY Botanical Garden,* *Bronx; www.nybg.org*	718-817-8700
	Museum Mile Festival *www.museummilefestival.org*	212-606-2296
Jun–Jul	**Metropolitan Opera Parks Concerts** *various locations*	212-362-6000
	NY Philharmonic Summer Parks Concerts *various locations*	212-875-5709
	Mid-Summer Night Swing *Fountain Plaza, Lincoln Center* *www.lincolncenter.org*	212-875-5766
Jun–Aug	**SummerStage in Central Park** *Rumsey Playfield;* *www.summerstage.org*	212-360-2777
	Street Performers and Evening Concerts *South Street Seaport* *www.southstreetseaport.org*	212-732-7678
mid–late Jun	**JVC Jazz Festival New York** *Carnegie Hall, Lincoln Center* *and other venues* *www.festivalproductions.net*	212-501-1390
late Jun	**Lesbian and Gay Pride Week Celebrations** *various locations; www.nycpride.org*	212-807-7433
	Mermaid Parade *Coney Island* *www.coneyislandusa.com/mermaid.sthml*	718-372-5159

July–August

July	**Lincoln Center Festival** *Alice Tully Hall; www.lincolncenter.org*	212-875-5127
	NYC Tap Festival *citywide; www.nyctapfestival.com*	646-230-9564
July 4	**Macy's Fireworks Celebration** *East River from 23rd to 42nd Sts.*	212-494-4495
Aug	**Lincoln Center Out-of-Doors** *outdoor plazas; www.lincolncenter.org*	212-546-2656
	Mostly Mozart Festival *Lincoln Center; www.lincolncenter.org*	212-546-2656
	Harlem Jazz & Music Festival *Harlem; www.harlemdiscover.com*	212-862-8473

Labor Day	**West Indian American Day Carnival Parade** *Eastern Pkwy. from Utica Ave.* *to Grand Army Plaza, Brooklyn*	718-773-4052
early Sept	**US Open Tennis Tournament** *USTA National Tennis Center, Flushing* *www.usta.com*	718-760-6200
mid-Sept	**Feast of San Gennaro** *Mulberry St., Little Italy* *www.sangennaro.org*	212-768-9320
	Race for Mayor's Cup *New York Harbor* *www.southstreetseaport.org*	212-748-8738
late Sept–Oct	**New York Film Festival** *Alice Tully Hall, Lincoln Center* *www.filmlinc.com*	212-875-5610
Oct	**Bonsai Festival** *NY Botanical Garden, Bronx* *www.nybg.org*	718-817-8700
mid-Oct	**Columbus Day Parade** *Fifth Ave. from 44th to 72nd Sts.*	212-249-9923
late Oct– early Jan	**Big Apple Circus** *Damrosch Park, Lincoln Center* *www.bigapplecircus.com*	800-922-3772
Oct 31	**Halloween Parade** *Greenwich Village; www.halloween-nyc.com*	212-475-3333

early Nov	**New York City Marathon** *Verrazano-Narrows Bridge to Central Park* *www.nyrrc.org*	212-860-4455
Nov–Dec	**The Rockettes – Christmas Spectacular** *Radio City Music Hall; www.radiocity.com*	212-307-7171
Thanksgiving Day	**Macy's Thanksgiving Day Parade** *Central Park West to Herald Square*	212-494-4495
late Nov–Dec	**The Chorus Tree** *South Street Seaport* *www.southstreetseaport.org*	212-732-7678
late Nov– early Jan	**The Nutcracker** *NY* *State Theater, Lincoln Center* *www.lincolncenter.org*	212-870-5570
	A Christmas Carol *Madison Square Garden*	212-465-6080
	HolidayFest *American Museum of Natural History* *www.amnh.org*	212-769-5100
	Christmas Tree and 18C Neapolitan Baroque Crèche *Metropolitan Museum of Art* *www.metmuseum.org*	212-535-7710
early Dec	**Lighting of the Giant Chanukah Menorah** *Grand Army Plaza, Fifth Ave. at 59th St.*	212-736-8400
	Christmas Tree Lighting Ceremony *Rockefeller Center;* *www.rockefellercenter.com*	212-632-3975
late Dec	**Kwanza Fest** *Penn Plaza Pavilion,* *Seventh Ave. at 33rd St.*	718-585-3530
Dec 31	**New Year's Eve Ball Drop** *Times Square* *www.timessquarebid.org/new_year/index.htm*	212-768-1560
	Midnight Run *Central Park; www.nyrrc.org*	212-860-4455

Planning the Trip

Consult p 288 for detailed practical information about visiting the Hudson River Valley and Long Island.

Visitors can contact the following agencies to obtain maps and information on points of interest, accommodations and seasonal events. NYC & Company, the city's convention and visitors bureau, also publishes the annually updated *Official NYC Guide*, which is available free of charge.

For a list of visitor centers in New York City, see Sightseeing in the Address Book section in the front of this guide.

NYC & Company
810 Seventh Avenue
New York NY 10019
www.nycvisit.com
☎ 212-484-1200
or 800-692-8474

New York State Division of Tourism
1 Commerce Plaza
Albany NY 12245
www.iloveny.com
☎ 518-474-4116
or 800-225-5697

New York's Seasons

New York's four distinct seasons each lend a particular character to the city. The mild months of April, May, September and October are especially pleasant. Hotels are heavily booked during these times and advance reservations are recommended.

© Martha Cooper

Spring – A brief and generally unpredictable season, spring brings New Yorkers out of doors to enjoy the mild temperatures (42° to 62°F). From late March through May, sunny days may give way to rain or to snow showers (not uncommon in April).

Summer – The weather can be unpleasantly muggy in the summer and many New Yorkers head out of town, leaving the city calmer and less crowded. Daytime temperatures can reach into the 90s, especially in July and August. The many shady green parks throughout the city, alive with free summer events, provide a welcome respite from the heat.

New York City Temperature Chart
(recorded at Central Park)

	average high	average low	precipitation
January	38°F (3°C)	26°F (-3°C)	3.9 in (9.9 cm)
April	61°F (16°C)	44°F (7°C)	3.9 in (9.9 cm)
July	85°F (29°C)	70°F (20°C)	4.5 in (11.4 cm)
October	66°F (19°C)	50°F (10°C)	4.5 in (11.4 cm)

Fall – Warm temperatures (47° to 68°F), crisp, clear days and the brilliant colors of the trees (especially the reds and oranges of the maples) make this a favored time to visit New York. Fall also heralds the opening of the city's renowned cultural season.

Winter – Although winds blowing in off the Hudson and East rivers can cause bitterly cold days, New York's winters are usually not too severe. Temperatures hover around 32°F, and the days are short but often clear and bright. Sudden heavy snowfalls and frequent snow accumulation can cause chaos in the city. The holiday season in New York is festive, indoors and out, with seasonal performances and decorations.

What To Wear

As a rule, New Yorkers like to dress up. Jackets and ties are required in some restaurants, but the trend overall is toward business-casual attire. Women should bring dresses, skirts or slacks; men, slacks, sports coats and ties. Avoid wearing expensive-looking jewelry on the street and public transportation; otherwise, you may be a target for thieves. For sightseeing and casual dining, jeans and sneakers are acceptable. In **winter**, be sure to bring gloves, a scarf, an overcoat, boots and an umbrella; in **summer**, pack lightweight cotton clothing and a sweater or jacket for heavily air-conditioned places. In **spring** and **fall**, a sweater, a raincoat and an umbrella come in handy. Remember to always pack comfortable walking shoes.

Getting There

PLANES

New York City is served by three airports, two in the borough of Queens and one in New Jersey. They are all run by the Port Authority of New York and New Jersey. In all three airports, ground transportation and information booths are located on the baggage-claim level. Plan to arrive at the airport at least two hours before flight departure time for domestic flights and three hours ahead for international flights. Due to increased security measures, it takes longer to get through airline security.

John F. Kennedy International Airport (JFK) – ☎ *718-244-4444. www.panynj.gov. 15mi from Midtown (allow 1hr driving time).* Most international flights arrive and depart from Kennedy. Airport information counters are located in all terminals. Departing passengers should allow themselves the maximum amount of time recommended by their airline. Restaurants with sit-down service are located in all terminals. Most modes of transportation depart outside of each terminal. A 24hr full-service medical clinic is located in Cargo Area C.

LaGuardia Airport (LGA) – ☎ *718-533-3400. www.panynj.gov. 8mi from Midtown (allow 30min driving time).* LaGuardia is serviced by most domestic and North American air carriers. The airport information counter is located between concourses C and D on the departure level. Restaurants with sit-down service are located in the USAir and Delta terminals *(free shuttle service available).* Most modes of transportation depart outside of each terminal.

Newark Liberty International Aiport (EWR) – ☎ *973-961-6000. www.panynj.gov. 16mi from Midtown (allow 45min driving time).* Many travelers find this airport easier to navigate; flights include both international and domestic air carriers. The airport information counter is located on the lower level of Terminal B. Restaurants with sit-down service are located on the concourse level of all terminals. Intra-airport monorail stations are available at each terminal. Most modes of ground transportation depart outside of each terminal.

Airport Ground Transportation

It is advisable to accept rides only from authorized ground-transportation agents; contact ground-transportation information counters for agent listing. For additional information on transportation to and from John F. Kennedy, LaGuardia and Newark airports, contact the Port Authority of New York & New Jersey *(☎ 800-247-7433; www.panynj.gov).*

Taxis – Taxi service is available outside each terminal. Only yellow taxi cabs with roof medallions showing the taxi number are authorized by the City of New York to pick up passengers on the street. Passengers at Kennedy and LaGuardia Airports should wait in line and allow a uniformed dispatcher to hail the next available cab. Fares to Manhattan: from JFK, $35 flat rate to any point in Manhattan (tolls not included); from LGA, $18–$26 *(average metered rate plus tolls)*; from EWR, $60–$75 *(average metered rate plus tolls)*. A 50¢ surcharge is added to all metered fares nightly 8pm–6am.

Shuttles & Limousines – **Air Train Newark** is a new airport rail service that provides a rail connection from Newark to Amtrak, New Jersey Transit and PATH existing rail systems *(operates daily 5am–2am; $8–$12;* ☎ *800-247-7433; www.airtrainnewark.com).* The new **Air Train JFK** light-rail system, which began running in December 2003, link JFK's eight terminals to PATH subway and bus lines to New York City and Long Island *(*☎ *877-535-2478; www.panynj.com/airtrain).* **Super Shuttle** offers interairport service as well as service to and from Manhattan 24hrs daily *($13–$22;* ☎ *212-258-3826; www.supershuttle.com).* **New York Airport Service** express bus runs between Kennedy and LaGuardia airports and Grand Central Railroad Terminal *(free transfer to Midtown hotels),* and between Penn Station and Port Authority Bus Terminal daily *(from airports: 6am–midnight, to airports: 6am–10pm; JFK: $13, LGA: $10;* ☎ *718-875-8200; www.nyairportservice.com).* **Olympia Trails Airport Express Bus** *(daily 4am–midnight; every 10–15min; $12;* ☎ *212-964-6233; www.coachusa.com)* runs from Newark to Pennsylvania Railroad Station, Grand Central Terminal and Port Authority Bus Terminal. **Carey Limousine** *(reservations required;* ☎ *202-895-1200 or 800-336-0646; www.ecarey.com)* offers chauffeur-driven cars at fixed rates between Manhattan and Kennedy *($127–$160),* LaGuardia *($107–$140)* and Newark *($127–$160)* airports *(rates do not include tolls, parking or gratuity).* Other chauffeur-driven car services are available at the airport transportation counter via self-service telephones.

Rental Cars – Most major rental-car agencies run shuttle buses from the airport terminals to their lots.

Public Transportation – From Kennedy: **MTA** A train from Howard Beach station *(free shuttle service from airport).* From LaGuardia: **MTA** M60 bus.

TRAINS

The **Amtrak** rail network *(*☎ *800-872-7245—accessible in North America only, outside North America, contact your local travel agent; www.amtrak.com)* offers a relaxing alternative for the traveler with time to spare. Advance reservations are recommended to ensure reduced fares and availability of desired accommodations. Sleeping accommodations are available on overnight trains. Daily service to **Pennsylvania Railroad Station** *(Seventh Ave. & 32nd St.)* is provided on the *Adirondack* (from Montreal), the *Maple Leaf* (from Toronto), the *Silver Service* (from Miami), the *Lake Shore Limited* (from Chicago), and the *Crescent* (from New Orleans). The *Metroliner* high-speed, all-reserved rail shuttle connects Washington, DC and New York City in three hours. Travelers from Canada should inquire with their local travel agents about Amtrak/VIARail connections. **North America Rail Pass** permits unlimited travel in the US and Canada within 30 days. **USA RailPass** (not available to US or Canadian citizens or legal residents) offers unlimited travel within Amtrak-designated regions at discounted rates; 15- and 30-day passes are available.

Local rail service into **Grand Central Railroad Terminal** *(42nd St. & Park Ave.)* is provided by **Metro-North** *(*☎ *212-532-4900 or 800-638-7646; www.mta.nyc.ny.us/mnr),* which runs between Manhattan and New Haven, CT and Poughkeepsie, NY. Both the **Long Island Railroad** *(*☎ *718-217-5477; www.mta.nyc.ny.us/lirr)* and **New Jersey Transit** *(*☎ *973-762-5100 or 800-772-2222; www.njtransit.com)* operate out of Pennsylvania Railroad Station. **PATH** rail lines *(*☎ *800-234-7284; www.panynj.gov/path)* connect Manhattan with many cities in New Jersey.

BUSES

The **Port Authority Bus Terminal** *(42nd St. & Eighth Ave.;* ☎ *212-564-8484),* the city's main bus terminal, is used by long-distance and commuter services. From here buses to the area's three major airports leave regularly. Airline ticket counters are located on the main floor of the building. **Greyhound** *(advance reservations suggested;* ☎ *800-229-9424; www.greyhound.com)* provides access to New York City at a leisurely pace. Overall, fares are lower than other forms of public transportation. **Discovery Pass** allows unlimited travel for 4–60 days. Some travelers may find long-distance travel uncomfortable due to the lack of sleeping accommodations. **Peter Pan** *(*☎ *800-237-8747; www.peterpanbus.com)* offers service throughout the Northeastern portion of the US.

■ Why is New York called the Big Apple?

Originally used to describe the city as benefiting disproportionately from the nation's wealth, the term was most widely used in the 1930s and 40s by jazz musicians when they knew they were going to perform in New York. Making it here meant they had finally made it big.

International Visitors

PLANNING THE TRIP

Visitors from outside the US can obtain information from the multilingual staff at NYC & Company (☎ 212-484-1200; www.nycvisit.com), or from the US embassy in their country.

Foreign Consulates – In New York international visitors can contact the consulate of their country of residence.

Country	Address	Web site	☎
Australia	150 E. 42nd St.	www.australianyc.org	212-351-6500
Belgium	345 E. 46th St.	www.un.int/belgium	212-378-6300
Canada	1251 Ave. of the Americas	www.canada-ny.org	212-596-1628
China	520 12th Ave.	www.nyconsulate.prchina.org	212-868-2078
France	934 Fifth Ave.	www.consulfrance-newyork.org	212-606-3600
India	3 E. 64th St.	www.indiaserver.com/cginy. consulate.html	212-774-0600
Italy	690 Park Ave.	www.italconsulnyc.org	212-439-8600
Mexico	27 E. 39th St.	www.consulmexny.org	212-217-6400
Netherlands	1 Rockefeller Plaza	www.cgny.org	212-246-1429
Spain	150 E. 58th St.	www.spainconsul-ny.org	212-355-4080
Switzerland	633 Third Ave.	www.swissemb.org	212-599-5700
United Kingdom	845 Third Ave.	www.britainusa.com	212-745-0200

Entry Requirements – Starting October 1, 2003, travelers entering the United States under the Visa Waiver Program (VWP) must have a machine-readable passport. Any traveler without a machine-readable passport will be required to obtain a visa before entering the US. Visa Waiver Program requirements can be found on the official Visa Services Web site: http://travel.stat.gov/vwp.html.

Citizens of countries participating in the VWP are permitted to enter the US for general business or tourist purposes for a maximum of 90 days without needing a visa. For a list of countries participating in the VWP, contact the US consulate in your country of residence. Citizens of nonparticipating countries must have a visitor's visa. Upon entry, nonresident foreign visitors must present a valid passport and round-trip transportation ticket. Canadian citizens are not required to present a passport or visa to enter the US, although identification and proof of citizenship may be requested (a passport or Canadian birth certificate and photo identification are usually acceptable). Naturalized Canadian citizens should carry their citizenship papers. Inoculations are generally not required, but check with the US embassy or consulate before departing.

Health Insurance – The US does not have a national health program. Before departing, visitors from abroad should check with their health care insurance to determine if their medical insurance covers doctors' visits, medication and hospitalization in the US. Prescription drugs should be properly identified, and accompanied by a copy of the prescription.

US Customs – All articles brought into the US must be declared at the time of entry. **Exempt** from customs regulations: personal effects; one liter (33.8 fl oz) of alcoholic beverages (providing visitor is at least 21 years old); either 200 cigarettes, 50 cigars or 2 kilograms of smoking tobacco; and gifts (to persons in the US) that do not exceed $100 in value. **Prohibited items** include plant material; firearms and ammunition (if not intended for sporting purposes); meat or poultry products. For other prohibited items, exemptions and information, contact the US embassy or consulate before departing, or the US Customs Service (☎ 877-287-8667; www.customs.treas.gov).

BASIC INFORMATION

Driving in the US – Visitors bearing valid driver's licenses issued by their country of residence are not required to obtain an International Driver's License to drive in the US. Drivers must carry vehicle registration and/or rental contract, and proof of automobile insurance at all times. Rental cars in the US are usually equipped with automatic transmission, and rental rates tend to be less expensive than overseas. **Gasoline** is sold by the gallon (1 gallon = 3.8 liters) and is cheaper than in other countries. Most self-service gas stations do not offer car repair, although many sell standard maintenance items. Road regulations in the US require that vehicles be driven on the right side of the road. Distances are posted in miles (1 mile = 1.6 kilometers).

Electricity – Voltage in the US is 110 volts AC, 60 Hz. Foreign-made appliances may need AC adapters (available at specialty travel and electronics stores) and North American flat-blade plugs.

Emergencies – In all major US cities you can telephone the police, ambulance or fire service by dialing **911**. Another way to report an emergency is to dial **0** for the operator. See p 319 for important telephone numbers.

Mail – *See p 317.*

Telephone/Telegram – Instructions for using **public telephones** are listed on or near the telephone. Some public telephones accept credit cards, and all will accept long-distance calling cards. For **long-distance calls** in the US and Canada, dial 1 + area code + number. To place an **international call**, dial **011** + country code + area code + number. A list of country codes can be found in the front of the *Yellow Pages*. To place a collect call (person receiving call pays charges), dial **0** + area code + number and tell the operator you are calling collect. If it is an international call, ask for the overseas operator. The cost for a local call from a pay phone is generally 50¢ (any combination of nickels, dimes and quarters is accepted). Most telephone numbers in this guide that start with **800**, **877** or **888** are toll-free (no charge) in the US and may not be accessible outside of North America. Dial 1 before dialing a toll-free number. The charge for numbers preceded by **900** can range from 50¢ to $15 per minute. Most hotels add a surcharge for local and long-distance calls. For further information, dial **0** for operator assistance. You can send a **telegram** or money, or have money telegraphed to you, via the Western Union system (☎ *800-325-6000; www.westernunion.com*).

Money

The American dollar is divided into 100 cents. A penny = 1 cent; a nickel = 5 cents; a dime = 10 cents; a quarter = 25 cents.

Credit Cards and Traveler's Checks – *See also p 318.* Rental-car agencies and many hotels require credit cards. **American Express Travel Related Services** is located at 1120 Sixth Ave., 20th floor (☎ *212-640-2000*). Most banks will cash brand-name traveler's checks and give cash advances on major credit cards with proper identification: American Express, ☎ 800-528-4800; Visa, ☎ 800-336-8472; MasterCard/Eurocard, ☎ 800-307-7309; Diners Club, ☎ 800-234-6377.

Currency Exchange – Currency exchange offices can be found at Kennedy, LaGuardia and Newark Liberty airports. Chase Manhattan Bank (☎ *212-935-9935*) offers foreign currency exchange in all of their 500 New York City branches. Private companies that offer currency exchange include: **Thomas Cook Currency Services, Inc.** *(511 Madison Ave., ☎ 212-753-2595; 1590 Broadway, ☎ 212-265-6063; www.us.thomascook.com)* and **Ruesch International Inc.** *(460 Park Ave, 19th floor; ☎ 212-838-0500)*. Banks charge a small fee for this service; private companies generally charge higher fees.

Taxes and Tipping – *See also p 318.* Prices displayed or quoted in the US do not generally include **sales tax** (8.625% in New York City). Sales tax is added at the time of purchase and is not reimbursable as in other countries (it can sometimes be avoided if purchased items are shipped to another country by the seller). In New York City, clothing and footwear purchases under $110 are tax-free. In the US it is customary to give a **tip** (a small gift of money) for services received from waiters/waitresses, porters, hotel maids and taxi drivers.

Temperature and Measurement – In the US temperatures are measured in degrees Fahrenheit and measurements are expressed according to the US Customary System of weights and measures.

Equivalents

Degrees Fahrenheit	95°	86°	77°	68°	59°	50°	41°	32°	23°	14°
Degrees Celsius	35°	30°	25°	20°	15°	10°	5°	0°	-5°	-10°

1 inch = 2.54 centimeters	1 pound = 0.454 kilogram
1 foot = 30.48 centimeters	1 quart = 0.946 liter
1 mile = 1.609 kilometers	1 gallon = 3.785 liters

Time Zone – *See p 319.*

Getting Around

LAY OF THE LAND

Manhattan's streets are laid out in a grid pattern. Streets run east-west and avenues run north-south. Fifth Avenue is the dividing line between east and west addresses. Generally, even-numbered streets are eastbound; odd-numbered streets are westbound. In lower Manhattan (below 14th St.) most streets have names rather than numbers. To locate a particular address, consult the Manhattan Address Locator in the *Yellow Pages*. Downtown refers to the area south of 14th Street. Midtown stretches from 14th Street to 59th Street. Above 59th Street at Central Park is referred to as Uptown.

PUBLIC TRANSPORTATION

The **Metropolitan Transportation Authority** (MTA) oversees an extensive network of subway, buses and commuter trains throughout the area. MTA New York City Transit runs the city bus and subway lines. Contact the agencies listed on p 311 for route information and schedules to Long Island and upstate New York, New Jersey and Connecticut.

New York City Transit

The **Travel Information Center** (☎ 718-330-1234; *www.mta.nyc.ny.us*) provides route and fare information for subway and bus lines. System maps and timetables are available *(free)* on buses and at all subway stations, visitor information centers, and most hotels. In this guide, subway and bus stops are indicated with the MTA symbol.

Subway – *Map pp 14-17.* The subway is the most efficient way to navigate the city. Subway entrances are indicated on street level by a staircase descending to the station. Large globes also mark the stations: a green globe indicates that you can buy tokens or MetroCards; stations with a red globe have no token booths—you must have the fare available to enter. Virtually all lines run 24hrs/day every 2–5 minutes during rush hours, every 5–12 minutes during the day, and every 20 minutes between midnight and 5am. The cost is $2 per ride, no matter how far you're traveling. Purchasing a MetroCard saves you money on multiple rides *(see Fares, below)*. Platform signs indicate which trains stop at the station (Uptown trains are northbound; Downtown trains are southbound). Signs on the side of each train list the route number or letter. Local trains stop at every station; express trains do not. Conductors announce each stop. *When riding the subway late at night, avoid isolated areas ("off-peak waiting areas" are provided in stations), and ride in the car carrying the train's conductor (usually located in the middle of the train).*

Buses – New York City Transit buses generally operate daily 5:30am–2am. Some routes on major corridors run 24hrs/day. Weekend hours may be reduced on some lines. During weekdays, most buses run every 5-15min; frequency varies at other times. Pick-up points are recognizable by tall, round signs bearing the bus emblem and route number. Route maps are displayed at most bus stops and shelters. Stops are made at posted locations, two to three blocks apart. Stops may be made at other locations along regular routes upon request between 10pm and 5am. If you are unsure about the route, verify your desired stop with the driver. Route numbers are displayed on the front and sides (sometimes back) of each bus. Local bus routes are indicated by a letter prefix indicating the borough in which that line largely operates (for example M7):

M = Manhattan   B = Brooklyn   Bx = Bronx   Q = Queens   S = Staten Island

All buses are equipped with wheelchair lifts and kneeling features.

Fares – All system fares are $2 one way *(exact fare is required for buses; $1 bills, pennies and half dollars are not accepted)*, with the exception of express bus fare, which is $4. The **MetroCard** automated fare card can be used on both systems and includes a free transfer for each fare, between subway and bus or bus to bus within 2hrs of paying the initial fare. MetroCard may be used to pay for up to 4 persons at a time. Up to 3 children (under 44 inches tall) may ride free when accompanied by an adult. Tokens are also accepted by subway or buses.

MetroCard offers several **discount** passes: 1 day *(Fun Pass, $7)*, 7 days *($21)* and 30 days *($70)*. Reduced fares are available for senior citizens and persons with qualifying disabilities *(information: ☎ 718-596-8585)*.

MetroCards can be purchased (or value added) at subway stations and retail outlets. Discount passes are available only from authorized merchants, the Times Square Visitor Center, transit museum stores (Grand Central Terminal and downtown Brooklyn), and vending machines that are located in many stations.

Bus and subway travel information is available 24hrs (☎ 718-330-1234). Information can be obtained in 140 languages by calling ☎ 718-330-4847. Maps and schedules are also available online: *www.mta.nyc.ny.us*.

TAXIS

Only yellow taxi cabs with roof medallions showing the taxi number are authorized by the City of New York to pick up passengers on the street. All yellow medallion cabs are metered and share the same rate schedule (use other cabs at the risk of being overcharged): $2 for the first 1/3 mile, 30¢ each additional 1/5 mile, 20¢/minute is charged while the cab is stopped or in slow traffic; a 50¢ surcharge is added between 8pm and 6am. There are no extra fees for additional riders, although most taxis are only able to accept 4 passengers. In addition to the metered rates, passengers are responsible for any toll fees and drivers are usually tipped 15%. Taxis are easily hailed from the street in most areas in Manhattan; a taxi is available when its white rooftop number is lit. Taxi stands are located at most hotels, transportation terminals and entertainment centers (in other areas call for service). To report lost property, call ☏ 212-692-8294; be sure to give the taxi medallion number and driver's name and license number if possible.

New York Water Taxi *(☏ 212-742-1969; www.nywatertaxi.com)* is another way to get around while avoiding all of the city traffic. Water taxi pick-up and drop-off points are as follows: East 34th Street Pier; East 90th Street Pier; Pier 84 at West 44th Street; Pier 63 at Chelsea Piers; World Financial Center; Pier A at Battery Park; Pier 11 at South Street Seaport; Hunters Point Pier in Long Island City; Brooklyn Army Terminal and Brooklyn's Fulton Ferry Landing *(Mon–Fri 6:30am–8pm, Sat–Sun 10:30am–7pm; taxis run every 40min & every 20min during rush hours; hours may vary by landing).* A variety of options are available when purchasing water taxi **tickets**: One-way, one stop *($4)*; one-way, multiple stops *($8)*; all-day pass *($15; 24hr unlimited)*.

Taxis are a good way to get around New York City

DRIVING IN NEW YORK

Given the efficiency of the public transportation system and the ease with which many sights can be reached on foot, a car is not necessary to visit Manhattan. Keep in mind that roads are usually congested, public parking lots expensive and street parking extremely difficult to find. **Rush hours**, the peak transit times for business commuters, occur weekdays between 7am–9am and 4:30pm–6pm. Visitors are encouraged to avoid driving during these times. To ease congestion, single-occupancy passenger cars have been prohibited from entering Manhattan by any of the midtown or downtown bridges and tunnels weekdays from 6am–10am. At the Holland Tunnel, mandatory carpooling is in effect 24hrs a day. Also, there are significant restrictions to vehicular traffic below Canal Street; visitors to downtown neighborhoods are encouraged to use public transportation.

Road Regulations – The maximum **speed limit** on major expressways is 65mph in rural areas and 55mph in and around cities. Speed limits in the city range from 25mph in residential areas to 30mph on major streets. Use of **seat belts** is mandatory for driver and passengers in the front seat of the car, and children under 16 years old in the back seat. Child safety seats are required for children under 4 years (seats available from most rental-car agencies). In New York City, unless otherwise posted, drivers are *not* permitted to turn right on a red traffic light. The majority of streets in Manhattan are one-way (traffic flows in one direction only). In New York it is illegal to drive with a **mobile phone** in your hand; you must connect your phone to a hands-free device.

315

Parking – If you are successful in obtaining street parking, pay close attention to signs indicating restrictions. Parking is prohibited during posted street-cleaning times. Parking in some residential areas is by permit only (restricted to area residents). Vehicles are systematically towed for violations. If you believe your car has been towed, call the **Towed Cars Hotline** (☎ *212-869-2929*). The Manhattan **Tow Pound** is located at Pier 76 *(W. 38th St. at 12th Ave.; ☎ 212-971-0772; www.nyc.gov)*. For parking violations, call the city's **Parking Violation Hotline** (☎ *718-422-7800; www.nyc.gov/nypd*). Spaces identified with ♿ are reserved for people with disabilities only. Anyone parking in these spaces without proper identification is subject to a heavy fine. Privately operated parking garages are abundant throughout the city; rates range from $6–$15/hr.

Rental Cars – Major car-rental companies have offices in various parts of Manhattan, in the outer boroughs, and at the three New York City area airports. Most agencies will only rent to persons at least 25 years old, although some will rent to younger drivers for a daily surcharge. A major credit card and valid driver's license are required for rental (some agencies also require proof of insurance). Most rental companies offer seasonal discounts and accept membership privileges. The average daily weekday rate for a compact car, with unlimited mileage for 5–7 days, ranges from $75–$100. Note that rental cars are taxed 13.62% (not included in the advertised rate).

Alamo	☎ 800-327-9623	www.alamo.com
Avis	☎ 800-331-1212	www.avis.com
Budget	☎ 800-527-0700	www.budget.com
Dollar	☎ 800-800-4000	www.dollar.com
Enterprise	☎ 800-325-8007	www.enterprise.com
Hertz	☎ 800-654-3131	www.hertz.com
National	☎ 800-227-7368	www.nationalcar.com
Thrifty	☎ 800-331-4200	www.thrifty.com

Many limousine and executive car-service companies offer transport within the city and to the boroughs and will customize an itinerary for a day to suit any visitor's needs. For a specific listing of companies, consult the *Official NYC Guide (p 309).*

Toll Crossings *(for more information: www.mta.nyc.ny.us)*

Brooklyn Battery Tunnel $4	Cross Bay Memorial Bridge $2
George Washington Bridge* ..$6	Henry Hudson Bridge $2
Holland Tunnel*...................$6	Lincoln Tunnel*...........................$6
Marine Parkway Bridge.........$2	Queens-Midtown Tunnel $4
Throgs Neck Bridge $4	Triborough Bridge $4
Verrazano-Narrows Bridge.....$8	

managed by the Port Authority (www.panynj.gov)

Accommodations

New York City offers a wide range of accommodations, from elegant hotels *($300/day and up)* located in the vicinity of Fifth, Park and Madison avenues to lower priced hotels *($125-$300/day)* found in the Theater District. Budget hotels *(under $125/day)* can also be found scattered throughout Manhattan. Visitors who favor a less bustling neighborhood may prefer the Murray Hill and Gramercy Park or Central Park South areas. *For specific suggestions of hotels in New York City, see the Address Book at the beginning of this guide.*

Amenities usually include television, restaurant and smoking/nonsmoking rooms. Many hotels also offer a fitness facility, room service and valet parking. Most Manhattan hotels charge a daily fee for parking. Advance reservations are strongly suggested (especially during the summer months and Christmas season).

Hotels/Motels – Many hotels offer packages that include lodging, breakfast, sightseeing tours, and restaurant or theater tickets at significant savings. Major hotel chains with locations in New York City include:

Hotel/Motel	☎	Web Site
Best Western	800-528-1234	www.bestwestern.com
Comfort Inn	800-228-5150	www.comfortinn.com
Helmsley Hotels	800-221-4982	www.helmsleyhotels.com
Hilton	800-445-8667	www.hilton.com
Holiday Inn	800-465-4329	www.holiday-inn.com
Hyatt	800-233-1234	www.hyatt.com
Marriott	800-228-9290	www.marriott.com
Radisson	800-333-3333	www.radisson.com
W Hotels	888-848-5144	www.starwood.com
Westin	800-228-3000	www.westin.com

	☎	Web Site
Accommodations Express	800-444-7666	www.accommodationsexpress.com
Central Reservations	800-548-3311	www.reservation-services.com
Express Reservations	800-407-3351	www.express-res.com
New York City		
Vacation Packages	888-692-8701	www.nycvp.com
Quikbook	212-779-7666	www.quikbook.com
Utell		www.utell.com

Bed & Breakfasts and Apartments – Many B&Bs in New York are privately owned historic homes *($100-$250/day)*. A complimentary continental breakfast is usually provided at these properties. Private baths are not always available, and smoking indoors is usually not allowed. In many cases, small children are not welcome. Weekly and monthly rates may be available. At some properties, a minimum stay of two nights is required on weekends.

B&B Reservation Services	☎	Web Site
City Lights Bed & Breakfast	212-737-7049	www.citylightsbedandbreakfast.com
Manhattan Getaways	212-956-2010	www.manhattangetaways.com
New World Bed & Breakfast	800-443-3800	www.nycbestbb.com
Gamut Realty Group	800-437-8353	www.gamutnyc.com
The Inn Keeper	800-582-1643	www.theinnkeeper.com

Hostels and Budget Accommodations – A no-frills, economical alternative to high-priced Manhattan hotels, the following establishments average $15–$75/day. Amenities may include community living room, showers, laundry facilities, full-service kitchen and dining room, restaurant, dormitory-style and private rooms *(advance reservations recommended)*. The **YMCA** *(YMCA Guest Rooms; www.ymca.net)* offers accommodations in Midtown *(224 E. 47th St.;* ☎ 212-756-9600) and on the Upper West Side *(5 W. 63rd St.;* ☎ 212-875-4723).

For further information on hostels, check out the Web site: *www.hostels.com*.

Hostels	Address	☎
Midtown		
Chelsea International Youth Hostel	251 W. 20th St.	212-647-0010
Gershwin Hotel	7 E. 27th St.	212-545-8000
Chelsea Center – Youth Hostel	313 W. 29th St.	212-643-0214
Big Apple Hostel	119 W. 45th St.	212-302-2603
Uptown		
Jazz on the Park	36 W. 106th St.	212-932-1600
Hosteling International	891 Amsterdam Ave.	212-932-2300

Basic Information

Business Hours – Most businesses operate Monday to Friday 9am–5pm. Banking institutions are generally open 9am–3:30pm; some offer Saturday service (9am–noon). Most retail stores and specialty shops are open Monday to Saturday 10am–6pm (Thursday til 9pm), Sunday noon–6pm. Small, neighborhood convenience stores usually stay open past 10pm. Most stores on the Lower East Side and in the Diamond District *(47th St.)* close on Friday afternoon and all day Saturday for the Jewish Sabbath; stores keep normal hours on Sunday.

Fax Services – Many hotels, and businesses that offer copying or mailing services, will send or receive faxes for a per-page fee.

Liquor Law – The legal minimum age for purchase and consumption of alcoholic beverages is 21. Proof of age may be required. Most bars in New York City stay open until 4am. You can buy wine and liquor at liquor stores Monday to Saturday. Grocery and convenience stores sell beer anytime except Sunday 3am–noon.

Mail – The main post office *(441 Eighth Ave. at W. 33rd St.;* ☎ *212-330-3002)* is open 24hrs/day. Branch offices are located in all five boroughs; for location and phone numbers, check the blue pages of the phone directory under US Government.
Some sample rates for first-class mail: letter 37¢ (1oz), postcard 23¢; overseas letter 80¢ (1oz), postcard 70¢. Letters and small packages can be mailed from most hotels. Stamps and packing material may be purchased at many convenience stores, drugstores and post offices. Businesses offering postal and express shipping services are located throughout the city *(see Yellow Pages under Mailing Services)*. For additional information, contact the US Postal Customer Assistance Center ☎ *800-275-8777; www.usps.com*.

Major Holidays – Most banks and government offices in the New York City area are closed on the following legal holidays *(many retail stores and restaurants remain open on days indicated with *)*:

New Year's Day..............................January 1
Martin Luther King Jr.'s Birthday* ......3rd Monday in January
Presidents' Day* ....3rd Monday in February
Memorial Day* ....Last Monday in May
Independence Day* ....July 4
Labor Day* ....1st Monday in September
Columbus Day* ....2nd Monday in October
Veterans Day* ....November 11
Thanksgiving Day ....4th Thursday in November
Christmas Day ....December 25

Money – Most banks are members of the network of Automated Teller Machines (ATMs) allowing visitors from around the world to withdraw cash using bank cards and major credit cards. ATMs can usually be found in banks, airports, grocery stores and shopping malls. Networks (Cirrus, Honor, Plus) serviced by the ATM are indicated on the machine. To inquire about ATM service, locations and transaction fees, contact your local bank, Cirrus (☎ 800-424-7787) or Plus (☎ 800-843-7587). Traveler's checks are accepted in banks, most stores, restaurants and hotels. **American Express Travel Related Services** is located at 1120 Sixth Ave., 20th floor (☎ 212-640-2000). To report a lost or stolen credit card: American Express (☎ 800-528-4800); Diners Club (☎ 800-234-6377); MasterCard (☎ 800-307-7309 or the issuing bank); Visa (☎ 800-336-8472).

Newspapers and Magazines – The city's leading newspaper is *The New York Times* (www.nytimes.com). Check the Sunday Arts & Leisure and the Friday Weekend sections for entertainment information. Another daily paper is the *Daily News* (www.nydailynews.com). The *New York Post* (www.nypost.com) and the *Wall Street Journal* (www.wsj.com) are published Monday through Friday only. New York also supports numerous daily and weekly foreign-language papers, ranging from *El Diario* to *Sing Tao*.

Publications such as *New York Magazine* (www.newyorkmetro.com), the *New Yorker* (www.newyorker.com), *Time Out New York* (www.timeoutny.com) and the *Village Voice* (www.villagevoice.com) feature articles and reviews and provide informative listings of events in and around town. *City Guide*, *IN New York Magazine* (www.in-newyorkmag.com) and *Where New York* (available free at hotels and restaurants) are handy guides to shopping, restaurants, entertainment and nightlife. Alternative newspapers, including *Downtown* and *New York Press*, offer different perspectives of the city as well as diverse and comprehensive entertainment sections, while *Homo Xtra* and *Next* cater to the gay community. These free publications are available at downtown bars and music venues.

Safety Tips

■ The best way to explore New York City is on foot. Visitors are encouraged to use common sense, stay alert and avoid deserted streets and park areas after dark.

■ Avoid carrying large sums of money, and don't let strangers see how much money you are carrying.

■ Hold purses and knapsacks firmly, carry your wallet in your front pocket, and avoid wearing expensive jewelry.

■ Stay awake when riding on public transportation, and keep packages close to you. MTA vehicles *(p 314)* are equipped with devices that enable riders to notify personnel of emergencies. Exercise caution in the subway after 11pm. Ride in the conductor's car (usually in the middle of the train) if you are alone.

■ Always park your car in a well-lit area. Close windows, lock doors and place valuables in the trunk.

Taxes and Tipping – In New York City the sales tax is 8.625%. The city levies a 13.625% hotel occupancy tax per night for rooms costing $40 or more. Since hotel rates do not reflect taxes, travelers should be aware of these added charges. Clothing and footwear purchases under $110 are tax-free. Tax percentages in areas beyond the city limits may vary.

In restaurants it is customary to tip the server 15-20% of the bill (an easy way to calculate is to double the sales tax). Taxi drivers are generally tipped 15% of the fare, hotel bellhops $1 per bag ($2 in luxury hotels), hotel doormen $1 per taxi and hotel maids $2 per day.

Telephone – Local calls from pay phones cost 50¢ for unlimited use (calls from Manhattan to the outer boroughs and vice versa are local but require dialing 1 and the area code). For long-distance calls, it is best to purchase a pre-paid phone card, which is available in most newsstands or drugstores.

anhattan...212, 646, 917
onx, Brooklyn, Queens, Staten Island..347, 718, 917
dson River Valley 914
ng Island...516, 631

*te: The Manhattan region (calls to and from area codes 212, 646, 917, 347 and
18) has gone to a 10-digit dialing system, making it necessary to dial 1 + area code
the seven-digit number for a local call.*

nportant Numbers   ☎

mergency Police/Ambulance/Fire (24hrs).......................................911
lice *(non-emergency, Mon–Fri 9am–6pm)* 212-374-5000
octors *(24hrs):* ....Doctors on Call 718-238-2100
                              Hotel Docs 800-468-3537
ental Emergencies *(24hrs)* ......NYU College of Dentistry 212-443-1300
4hr Pharmacies......................CVS (4 locations in Manhattan) 800-746-7287
                              Duane Reade, 224 W. 57th St. 212-541-9708
                              Rite Aid (6 locations in Manhattan) 800-748-3243
oison Control Center *(24hrs)* 212-764-7667
ime 212-976-1616
eather 212-976-1212

elevision and Radio

Major TV Networks

| ABC | Channel 7 | CBS | Channel 2 | PBS | Channel 13 |
| NBC | Channel 4 | FOX | Channel 5 | WB | Channel 11 |

Major FM Radio Stations

	Classical	96.3	Jazz	101.9
	Country	107.1	Top 40	100.3
	Rock	102.7		

Major AM Radio Stations

| News/sports | 880 |
| News/talk | 820 and 1130 |

ime Zone – New York City is located in the Eastern Standard Time (EST) zone, which
s five hours behind Greenwich Mean Time. Daylight Saving Time is observed from the
irst Sunday in April *(clocks are advanced 1hr)* to the last Sunday in October.

Index

Chrysler Building........................Building, street or other point of interest

Sullivan, Louis...........................Person, historic event or term

Accommodations.......................Practical information

Place names outside Manhattan appear with the following abbreviations: the Bronx **B**, Brooklyn **BN**, Queens **QU**, Staten Island **SI**, Hudson River Valley **HRV**, Long Island **LI** an, New Jersey **NJ**.

Museums within New York City are grouped under the heading **Museums**. Numbered build ings appear under the name of the street (for 500 Park Avenue, look under Park Avenue) Hotels, Restaurants and Shopping are listed separately under those headings.

The following abbreviations may also appear:

NP National Park; **SP** State Park; **NHS** National Historic Site; **SHS** State Historic Site **NM** National Monument; **NMem** National Memorial; **NMP** National Military Park **NHP** National Historical Park.

Notes

Travel Publications

Michelin North America
One Parkway South, Greenville SC 29615, U.S.A.
☎ 1-800-423-0485
www.michelin-us.com
TheGreenGuide-us@us.michelin.com

Manufacture française des pneumatiques Michelin

Société en commandite par actions au capital de 304 000 000 EUR
Place des Carmes-Déchaux – 63 Clermont-Ferrand (France)
R.C.S. Clermont-Fd B 855 200 507

Typesetting : NORD COMPO, Villeneuve-d'Ascq
Printing and binding: I.M.E., Baumes-les-Dames

Cover design: Carré Noir, Paris 17ᵉ arr.